AF823756

LITIGATOR

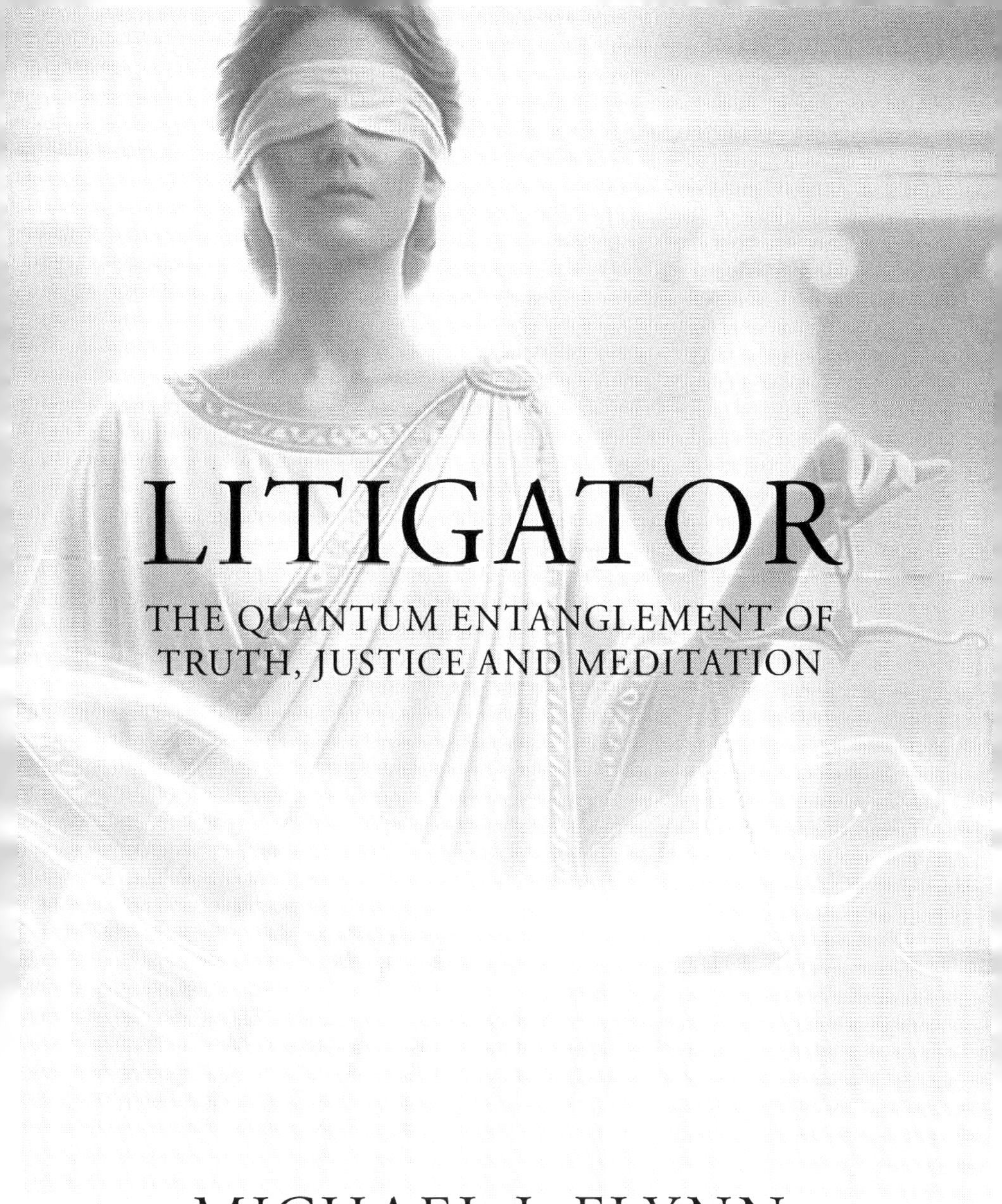

LITIGATOR

THE QUANTUM ENTANGLEMENT OF TRUTH, JUSTICE AND MEDITATION

MICHAEL J. FLYNN

Copyright © 2026 by Michael J. Flynn
Published by Michael J. Flynn

Cover design by Richard Bergin
For information, visit litigatorbook.com

All rights reserved

No portion of this book may be reproduced, stored in a retrieval system, or transmitted in any form by any means–electronic, mechanical, photocopy, recording, or other–except for brief quotations in printed reviews, without prior permission of the author.

Paperback ISBN: 9781971833002
Hardcover ISBN: 9781971833026
eBook ISBN: 9781971833019

Dedication

To Truth and Justice

ACKNOWLEDGEMENTS

Paramahansa Yogananda: My teacher who brought me home to God, Christ and "Self."

Maharishi Mahesh Yogi: His "Spiritual Regeneration Movement," aka "Transcendental Meditation," Awakened Me to Higher Levels of Consciousness

The "Mothers" who uphold dharma with love and compassion:

Daya Mata: President of SRF, my three decade guide and client

Mother Meera, my three decade guide and client

Amma, my three decade guide and client

In Memory Of:
George and Lucille Flynn, my parents: part of The Greatest Generation

Laima Flynn, my wife, a true human being of love and compassion.

My Children:
Michael James Jr., Rebecca Ann, Alison Kimberly.

This book, and the four following ones in the "Litigator Series" are the culmination of a lifetime of experiences in jury litigation and meditation. These books and the experiences contained in them would not have been possible without the countless individuals who have guided, challenged, and supported me throughout 81 years of life on this planet, and fifty-five years in American courtrooms. I owe immeasurable, eternal gratitude to my spiritual teachers, Paramahansa Yogananda and Maharishi Mahesh Yogi, and ultimately to the Grace of God and Christ, whose consciousness and love illuminated my path and brought me home to them.

I am also profoundly grateful to the spiritual mothers who have guided me in a path of dharma with love and compassion, notwithstanding my litigator ego; Daya Ma, President of Self Realization Fellowship, client, mentor and guiding force in two jury trials in which truth and justice prevailed over demonstrable evil and frauds. "Mother Meera," client, mentor and guiding force in a high profile, lengthy jury trial of a celebrity / meditator in which a jury rendered an unprecedented, historic verdict over evil and injustice. Amma, client, loving and guiding force in a case in which her divine consciousness exposed the depth of evil within the second highest court in America. That case continues in its second decade, illustrating the depth of evil and injustice that has swamped America's system of justice. Hence, the front and back covers of this first book.

These "Mothers" have sustained me throughout the hard journey between good and evil, between the greed of the "money changers" and their victims, in actual trials that are recounted in the Litigator Series. …

My deepest gratitude in the realized blessings of my life go to my family: my parents, George and Lucille Flynn, who were part of the Greatest Generation; my late wife, Laima, a true human being of love and compassion whose love and support enabled my litigation / meditation journey on this planet; my beautiful children, Michael Jr., Rebecca, and Alison, who have filled my life with meaning and the challenges of raising a family in present day America; and to my seven brothers and sisters, particularly my brother Kevin, whose financial support in this book project has endured throughout.

I must also acknowledge the clients, colleagues, and even my opponents in litigation who have shaped my journey. First, the sufferings I endured in two specific cases evolved into such profound blessings, and healing, I offer eternal gratitude to my client, SRF, and their Presidents, Daya Ma, Mrinalini Ma, and my dear friend Brother Chidananda, whose wisdom and integrity have been a constant inspiration for over three decades. My representation of SRF in the two jury trials triggered such a turning point in my litigation / meditation journey, words cannot express my profound gratitude to Paramahansa Yogananda for bringing me into SRF and the two specific jury trials that have shaped my journey in both litigation and meditation. These two cases are contained in Litigator 3, but are referenced herein.

My cases in the Litigator series involve numerous so-called "celebrities," whose public personas and private lives often revealed deeply conflicted contrasts between the world of illusion, wealth and fame with the deeper realities of elevated consciousness in God and Christ. In those cases, I experienced and learned the illusions of the world. Several so-called "famous" clients in specific cases reflect the foregoing reality.

Several individual clients have shown me real courage and endurance in the face of death and injustice. Wil Smyly, a true American hero in WW II, piloting his B-17 thru flak and German fighters while bombing German civilian populations on the orders of Roosevelt, Churchill and Stalin. In later life, Wil was redeemed by a terrible tragedy. Tim Blixseth, who defines courage in the face of overwhelming judicial and political corruption. Tim's case involving the Yellowstone Club, built on his courage, vision, and integrity was effectively stolen by the "money changers" by paying off a crooked judge and state Governor. Tim's case mirrors the horrific criminality by America's highest leaders over the past thirty years. Their "Deep Sate" crimes have turned our judicial system and Department of Justice into a swamp of "money changer" injustice.

I acknowledge my colleagues who fought exhaustive legal battles alongside me: Jay Curley in my earlier cases; Mike Tabb and Bill Sheridan in the 8 year "Scientology Wars" against L Ron Hubbard and his Scientology cult; Phil Stillman and Carla DiMare in later cases.

Even to my adversaries in the courtroom, from the brainwashed cult members and leaders of Scientology to the corrupt agents of the Deep State, who bribed judges and politicians to fulfill their greed, I offer a strange form of gratitude. In their opposition, they taught me the true meaning of forgiveness and strengthened my resolve to fight for truth and justice.

Richard Bergin: Editor and the creative force behind its visual identity. Richard took what was a lawyer's manuscript; linear, analytical, case-by-case, and transformed it into a narrative that reads the way a story should be told. Richard also designed our website and created the dramatic cover art that captures, in a single image, the corruption that is devouring our judiciary and the divine justice that we must restore. His media work on the Tim Blixseth / Yellowstone Club cases demonstrated a rare gift: the ability to convey in a few words and a single frame what thousands of pages of legal filings could not. Richard fuses the power of visual storytelling with literary narrative, and the result is something neither of us could have created alone.

Anjali Mahaldar: Anjali injected consciousness-awakening reality to the narrative with profound insights and contributions from her direct, personal, work with Maharishi and the Indian Saints she worked with for decades alongside Maharishi. Anjali is a knower of truth, immersed in deep love of the Divine; and a beacon of compassion throughout a lifetime of support for all who are blessed with her presence.

Richard Taylor: A monastic, former Marine and Naval Academy grad who has shared with me his penetrating intelligence and definitive insights into the divine timing of Paramahansa Yogananda's mission, which unfolded during two world wars and continues today, poised as we are on the brink of a third.

Finally, to you, the reader: thank you for joining me on this journey. This book is not about me; it is about the universal quest for truth, justice, and God that connects us all.

TABLE OF CONTENTS

INTRODUCTION

In the winter of 1987, I was a forty-three-year-old trial lawyer sitting in a silent meditation when I was suddenly thrown into the consciousness of a young Irish priest being brutally murdered by British soldiers in November, 1920. I did not know this priest, nor had I ever heard his story. I was a litigator, a man who dealt in facts, evidence, and the cold, hard realities of the courtroom. This experience was none of those things. It was impossible. And yet, it was more real than me telling you about it. It was one of the first clues in a lifetime of investigation into the true nature of reality.

This book is the story of that investigation. It is the culmination of fifty years spent in two seemingly opposing worlds: the combative, high-stakes "PIT" of trial law and the silent, transcendent realms of deep meditation. On the surface, these worlds are irreconcilable. One is built on conflict, evidence, and human injustices; the other on silence, consciousness, and divine truth. For decades I navigated them separately, a litigator by day and a meditator by night. But over time, the wall between these worlds began to dissolve. I started to see the patterns of quantum entanglement in the lives of my clients, the echoes of ancient yogic wisdom in the outcomes of jury trials, and the presence of a guiding, conscious force in the midst of unimaginable suffering and corruption.

From defending against the satanic cult of Scientology to exposing the crimes of the Clinton political machine, and from representing the victims of corporate, medical and Big Pharma greed to seeking justice for the families of dead children, I have been a witness to the best and worst of humanity. But through it all, my meditation practice and the teachings of the great masters like Paramahansa Yogananda provided a lifeline. They gave me the tools to survive the darkness and also to find the guiding light within.

This series of books, there are five in the "Litigator" series, are my final testament to the nature of reality gleaned from five decades of litigation and meditation. It is the evidence I have gathered, the testimony I have heard, and the conclusions I have reached. It is my argument that consciousness is not a byproduct of the brain but the very fabric of the universe; that we are not isolated beings but part of a quantum entangled web of existence; and that love, truth, and justice are not abstract ideals but the fundamental laws of our cosmos. I invite you, the reader, to sit as the jury. Read the evidence in these pages and decide for yourself. The verdict you reach may change not only how you see the world, but how you live in it.

CHAPTER 1

WAR BABY An Irish Catholic Childhood in the Shadow of Global Conflict

"I know not with what weapons World War III will be fought, but World War IV will be fought with sticks and stones." **Albert Einstein**

THE SHADOW BENEATH THE WAVES

Barely hidden beneath the choppy waves in the Pacific Ocean off the California coast, a 356-foot-long shadow lurked just beneath the surface. Japanese submarine I-17 moved with deadly silence, undetected toward its mission objective.

The late evening sky cast long shadows across the streets as people hurried home from work in Goleta, just south of Santa Barbara. An uneasiness hung in the air. Only two months before, the Japanese had attacked Pearl Harbor with devastating effect. Residents huddled with their families, gathering around radios to catch President Franklin Roosevelt's Fireside Chat at 7 p.m.

Roosevelt's calm and reassuring voice crackled through radio sets across the nation. In Wheeler's Inn, Goleta, Laurence Wheeler and his customers listened in tense silence to what FDR was saying about the fate of the nation, now entering World War II. Off the coast, tension also mounted as the crew of I-17 prepared to interrupt Roosevelt's speech.

Commander Kozo Nishino's voice cut through the humming of the engines as he commanded, "Senbōkyō o ageru!"—"Raise periscope!" Inside, a soft mechanical whir propelled the periscope above the choppy waves, transferring the view of their vital mission objective to the commander: it was the Ellwood oilfields of Goleta.

J.J. Hollister III, a boy of ten, pressed an ear to the large dark oak wooden cabinet that housed the valve-driven radio at his family home. The static filled the air as Roosevelt's words painted mental images of a world far different from the childhood his parents had envisioned for him. His innocent world, nestled amidst California's golden fields, was about to be changed forever.

"Mizu-agari-e"—"Prepare to surface," Nishino commanded. The sub surged upward and broke through the choppy waves, a dark silhouette barely visible from onshore. With characteristic Japanese efficiency, the deck crew rushed to their stations and readied their 5.5-inch main naval gun. Commander Nishino stood firm in the conning tower of the rocking submarine, binoculars scanning the oilfield as the gun fired its first shell, arching toward a Richfield aviation fuel tank just beyond the beach. It was 7:15 p.m., February 23, 1942.

Young Hollister was startled as FDR's speech was interrupted. "In a moment or two we heard a whistling noise and a thump as a shell hit near the house," Hollister excitedly stated later. He and his family members rushed out of their house in Winchester Canyon and saw the flashes and heard the eerie whine as shells hit the area of the oilfield. One round passed over Wheeler's Inn, next to the classic filling station that still stands today. The owner, Laurence Wheeler, called the Santa Barbara Sheriff's department. The deputy told Wheeler that warplanes would arrive shortly, but no planes came. A shell struck the Ellwood Pier, damaging it slightly. A derrick and pump house were destroyed, while a catwalk was damaged.

Hilda Wheeler described the scene: "We saw the shells tearing up the ground as they landed between us and the ocean front. We couldn't see the submarine because the sunset was very brilliant. We all thought at first it was target practice. And then we looked out back and saw the earth spurting up and we were scared to death. The third shot shook the building." Laurence Wheeler added, "The others whined overhead and dropped into the canyon across the highway. Their marksmanship was rotten."

Santa Barbara residents, and the oilfield in particular, were lucky the sea was choppy that day because it caused many of the shells to go off target. Rotten or not, the Japanese goal of frightening the population succeeded. Torpedo officer Nobukiyo Nambu climbed through the hatch to observe the situation through his binoculars and reported witnessing "a great deal of confusion" onshore. After twenty minutes, the Japanese crew had fired all seventeen available shells and the enormous submarine vanished beneath the waves.

The hysteria continued, and a day later reports of enemy aircraft led to the so-called "Battle of Los Angeles," in which American artillery was discharged over Los Angeles for several hours due to the mistaken belief that the Japanese were invading. The Navy responded by sending any usable ships it could deploy to patrol our west coast. My dad was a naval officer in one of the patrol ships.

A SOUL CHOOSES ITS MOMENT

I came into my body in this same area, only two years after the shelling incident on August 3, 1944. By the time I arrived, the world had turned into a documented bloodbath.

Just fifty-seven days before my birth, in the biggest military operation in the history of the world, the Allies landed at Normandy, suffering over 4,400 confirmed dead and 10,000 casualties just on the day of the landing alone. German dead are estimated at over 9,000 just on D-Day, June 6, 1944.

Before my birth, the Marine campaigns in the Pacific, in Guadalcanal, Saipan, Tinian, Guam, New Guinea, and others were raging with over twenty thousand American casualties, with 10,000 killed just in those campaigns. The Japanese had lost over 3 million, mostly dead, by August 1944. On the eastern front, the Battle of Stalingrad was over by February 1943 with over 1.5 million Russian casualties, with a total of 27 million for the whole war. Estimates of German civilian losses by August 1944, just in the bombing of its cities by Allied Bomber Command, were up to 600,000.

The American Eighth Air Force suffered over 26,000 dead alone in the bombing of Germany, more than all of the Marines killed in World War II.

The horrific inclinations and habits of humans killing humans are manifested throughout history. The two world wars may be its apex. By August 1944, the Nazi genocide of European Jews is estimated to have reached up to six million souls.

Yes, when I was born into it, the world was a documented bloodbath.

NAVAL SERVICE AND CONCEPTION: A FATHER'S WAR STORY

When war erupted on December 7, 1941, with Japanese planes screaming out of the sky over Pearl Harbor, my father had just graduated from Holy Cross College. He married my mother and entered the Naval War College in Newport, Rhode Island. Soon he was a twenty-two-year-old Navy officer patrolling the west coast in an aging minesweeper, along with outdated and decrepit naval vessels that could not have stopped anything, particularly the Imperial Japanese Navy. To prove that the civilian population was safe, in its inexorable wisdom, the Navy also sent the wives and families of the officers to the west coast.

My mom and my two siblings ages one and two, left Worcester Massachusetts and arrived in Santa Barbara in 1943. During that period, she said she was "a little fearful," but confident that our Navy would stop any invasion force. That's quite a joke, but that, folks, was the temperament of the time in America between 1942 and 1943.

The constant drone of aircraft engines and the endless scanning of dark horizons for enemy vessels became the backdrop of my dad's early married life. I was conceived during Christmas 1943. With no invasion imminent, my dad was then sent to the Aleutian Islands after the Japanese had been removed from the Aleutian chain island of Attu. The nearby island of Kiska was not defended by the Japanese who had already evacuated. This proved to be the only major Japanese attack on American soil following Pearl Harbor during World War II. During this period Dad volunteered for reconnaissance patrols on a PBY, an amphibious patrol bomber in which he learned to fly.

When I was born we had turned the tide of war in both Europe and the Pacific in our favor. Like now, however, even as of August 1944, the problem was "what to believe?" from our politicians and media. Was Pearl Harbor really a "surprise"? Our military must have known a major attack was imminent. How could Roosevelt get on the radio in early 1942, just months after Pearl Harbor, and say that there was no real threat to our west coast, when our Navy had been destroyed at Pearl Harbor in a surprise attack? Could it have just been bravado? Political finger-pointing, fear, and outrage permeated American consciousness. On D-Day, just two months before my birth, our soldiers, sailors, and airmen were dying by the thousands.

THE GREATEST GENERATION: PARENTS AS SPIRITUAL EXEMPLARS

My father himself was a "war baby," born in February 1918 during the First World War. Although we never discussed this specifically, given the history of his ancestors in the Young Ireland Revolt of 1848 (also known as the Famine Revolt) after which his great-grandfather fled Ireland as a young man and likely served in the Fighting 69th in the American Civil War. I believe my father's consciousness at birth was influenced by the Famine, the experiences of his ancestors in the Civil War, and a deep-seated resistance to British colonialism and oppression.

Like myself, my father had a strange connection to the 69th Irish regiment and an insightful perspective on British oppression of the Irish. His mother, Delia O'Callaghan Flynn, had fled Galway at the age of twelve in 1899, as the conflict between Irish patriots and British imperialists escalated, ultimately resulting in the 1916 rebellion and the 1920 Irish Civil War, where British imperialism crushed the spirit of a people already devastated by the Potato Famine.

My father was honorably discharged in late 1945 when the war ended, but the residue of his naval service remained in his consciousness. I've often wondered about the invisible scars in my father's consciousness and in the collective consciousness of that generation that may have shaped my own being at conception. The impact of the two world wars and my Irish heritage seems connected in some form I've never fully understood. Perhaps every child of the post-war generation carries this invisible inheritance.

I observed this as a child growing up. I'm one of eight children, third in line, raised in a traditional Irish/French Catholic family. (Curiously, DNA tests show I'm 87% Irish.) My father was a robust, hard-working, deeply loving third-generation Irishman who embraced his spiritual tradition and his family with tireless post-war energy, ensuring family cohesion and love for us children and our mother. He had a profound devotion to Mary, the Mother of Christ.

My mother was equally loving and deeply spiritual within her French Catholic tradition, a foundational pillar of our family whom we all adored and generally obeyed. My father adored her. They never had a conflict or argument in front of us. Mom possessed remarkable human skills, from self-discipline as a concert-level pianist to a profound spiritual practice made real in daily life, particularly when dealing with the mischief of the three boys in our family. Believe me, I was no bargain. "You were a born rebel," my mother would say with a mixture of exasperation and affection. When other kindergartners played contentedly in the sandbox, I insisted on the swings, and vice versa.

My parents truly embodied what we now call the Greatest Generation. The rosary, daily Mass, communion, and bi-weekly confession during Lent were hallmarks of our Catholic upbringing. Like it or not, these were their values. My mother raised three babies; ages one, two, and three (I'm number three) during the war, while my dad was basically gone for long periods. Her discipline, faith, and loyalty carried her. An amazing woman.

Although later, in my early twenties, I abandoned these early practices they taught us, I still view them as a solid spiritual foundation. In the 1950s, the religious institutions of my childhood did not appear to me as the corrupted entities they would later be revealed to be. I was only a naïve child who knew nothing about the world's complexities.

THE WORCESTER TORNADO: FIRST ENCOUNTER WITH COSMIC FORCES

The Flynn family of my youth was not spared life's shocks. In June 1953, when I was eight, the infamous Worcester Tornado tore through our newly built home in Shrewsbury, Massachusetts. The sky darkened to an unnatural green-black as the pressure dropped, making our ears pop painfully. Then came the sound...like a roaring freight train bearing down on us as we huddled in terror.

The tornado literally split our house in half while we crouched in the section that survived. Through the shattered windows, I watched in horror as the other half of our home was lifted like a child's toy and hurled into the woods behind our property. The screeching, raging sound and destruction remain vivid in my memory decades later. The storm killed a little girl in a nearby home, along with 124 others, making it one of the deadliest tornadoes in U.S. history. The National Guard camped on our front lawn in the ensuing weeks while we lived with our maternal grandmother.

How does one explain human suffering? Could it be that we experience natural disasters because of collective human failings? That's what Biblical interpreters claim. I have since learned, as most of us post-war adults have, particularly the baby boomer generation, that man's self-created terrors and horrific crimes against our fellow humans make the so-called natural disasters, denominated by us humans as Acts of God. It's an infinitely complex conundrum within our consciousness. One possible approach to this age-old paradox of human evils causing human suffering on a mass consciousness and reality scale, like the two world wars, is the application of cause and effect rather than attributing them to God's displeasure with His creation.

> "The sudden cataclysms that occur in nature ... are not 'acts of God.' Such disasters result from the thoughts and actions of man. ... When materiality predominates in

man's consciousness, there is an emission of subtle negative rays; their cumulative power disturbs the electrical balance of nature, and that is when earthquakes, floods, and other disasters happen." **Paramahansa Yogananda** (1893–1952)

SAINTS, PURITY, AND SEXUAL AWAKENING

"I find my earliest memories covering the anachronistic features of a previous incarnation. Clear recollections came to me of a distant life, a yogi amidst the Himalayan snows. These glimpses of the past, by some dimensionless link, also afforded me a glimpse of the future."

Paramahansa Yogananda

Unlike Yogananda, who remembered his early life from the womb onward, I have no conscious memories of almost anything between infancy and age seven. I do have disconnected feelings beginning around ages seven to eight, following my First Communion at age seven. It was coupled with the scrupulous training in the Baltimore Catechism imposed by my parents and local parish priests. later I opposed institutional corruption in the Catholic Church, which was purportedly acting as the mediator between God and man for salvation. I now consider my youthful spiritual education in the Catholic Church to be a blessing in awakening consciousness.

I began to have powerful devotional connectedness and mystical experiences of transcendental devotion to Jesus and to a boyhood saint, Dominic Savio, who exemplified devotion to Jesus from ages eight to fourteen. I prayed for the purity that characterized Savio's life and Jesus's forty days and nights resisting temptation. This prayerful intention paralleled my own awakening sexual urges toward girls and the female body. Savio's response to puberty and sexuality, like many saints, including Jesus himself, involved rigid purity in thought, word, and deed. Thus, I did have an early childhood immersion in spirituality completely associated with Jesus Christ. I refer to Christ here as the "Jesus" of my boyhood because I had no understanding of "Christ consciousness," but both "Jesus" and Saint Savio were very personal to me as a child.

An inter-family example of childhood innocence and death involved my mother's brother's daughter, sweet, beautiful Germaine. Everyone in the family said she was a saint. Like Dominic Savio, she died at sixteen of pneumonia. Some family members said she was in a spiritual reverie with Jesus. My mother, her brother and his wife, my grandparents...all were grief-stricken. It permeated our family. I was ten years old. At the time, I didn't really understand the spiritual basis for her death or absorb the grief, just that she had passed beyond this life, which she had prayed for.

To me at ages eight to fourteen, the Catholic Church indoctrination taught me that Jesus spent forty days and nights in the wilderness denying the temptations of sex! Sexual desire was the sin to be overcome. It was a Mortal Sin that, absent confession, would condemn me to hell. It was my Catholic duty to behave accordingly! As a child, I literally prayed for death before giving in to these "temptations of the flesh." Catholicism! Perhaps the well-known Catholic guilt complex arose in me from these boyhood aspirations and conflicts? I ultimately failed miserably in these aspirations, but Grace and consciousness eventually led me home. Thank God?

THE FIGHTING 69TH AND EARLY READING

In the metaphysical realm, as a war baby, I began to feel deep feelings of connectedness to events of both World Wars I and II, at least events in my mind. For example, the 1940 World War I film *The Fighting 69th* had a huge impact on me when I first saw it as a ten-year-old. I watched it repeatedly. With my newspaper route earnings, I bought a record of the music in the movie. I could feel and experience myself in the trenches as a soldier in the famed 69th Irish Regiment, particularly resonating with its well-known music that permeates the film. I read all the books I could find in the Shrewsbury Public Library on the 69th Irish Regiment and World War I, while also secretly reading sexual passages from the "sordid" book *Peyton Place*. Noble "warrior aspiration" coupled with sin! I read miscellaneous books glorifying the heroism of soldiers living and dying in the trenches like the Irish heroes in *The Fighting 69th* with "Fighting Father Duffy."

This same interest surprisingly also happened when I "happenstantially" heard some of the traditional German marching music on a record I purchased with money earned by delivering newspapers as a ten-year-old. It turns out that ten is a significant year in the development of human consciousness. The historical Germanic military music, later adopted by the National Socialists of Germany also resonated within my soul. But they were the enemy… or were they? Not to the Irish. The Brits were the enemy. It caused me to read numerous books on both world wars to determine why the Germans and the Japanese were the "bad guys" and we were the "good guys" as I had learned throughout primary school.

Growing up Catholic, the most fundamental principles I adhered to in the Bible are found in the Beatitudes and the two most basic commandments: "Love the divine above all else, and love your neighbor as yourself." It seemed clear to me that if we followed these fundamental rules of life, then we would live in a state of consciousness where these guidelines became our reality. In that consciousness, the kingdom of heaven would be realized within ourselves.

Remarkably, over the centuries, European powers individually and collectively considered themselves to be Christians while regarding their Christian neighbors as enemies. All these nations invoked divine assistance in killing their Christian enemies...a profound madness. The endless wars against and between the British, French, Germans, Spanish, Italians, Dutch, Irish, and others, while failing to follow the principles established in the Sermon on the Mount, demonstrated that the collective consciousness of these nations did not embody the spiritual ideals they claimed to uphold.

Looking back after five decades, I now understand that my birth during World War II was not merely a coincidence of timing, but part of a deeper pattern of consciousness that would shape my entire life's work. What I couldn't grasp as a young man was how the trauma and consciousness of that generation and those preceding would become encoded in my very being, influencing every case I would later fight and every method I would use to elevate my consciousness.

I have discovered a profound truth: consciousness transcends the boundaries of time and space, connecting us to both our personal histories and the collective experiences of humanity. My journey began in the shadow of global conflict, with my consciousness at birth becoming physically embodied and biologically connected on a cellular level to the collective trauma of war.

> "Out of war a few people make huge fortunes… How many of these war millionaires shouldered a rifle? How many of them dug a trench? How many of them knew what it meant to go hungry in a rat-infested dug-out?"
> **General Smedley Butler, War Is a Racket** (1935)

The trenches of World War I, where men huddled in mud and blood while artillery shells screamed overhead, are not merely historical events to me. On some hard-to-define feeling level in my brain cells, I am connected to those insane, reciprocal massacres where soldiers, many of Irish descent like myself were sacrificed by the thousands at the whim of aristocratic generals who never set foot on the battlefield. Even the American Civil War, where many Flynns fought in the Union Irish Brigades after fleeing starvation in Ireland, has left its imprint on my being.

These are not abstract historical events but living memories encoded in my cellular consciousness. My birth DNA and maturation as a human are intimately connected with these realities. The trauma of the Famine instilled an undercurrent of social consciousness in my life, shaping my views on oppression and injustice. This emotional resonance has fueled my fight for justice and understanding today. I abhor war because it is largely avoidable, yet the moneyed classes often create justifications for wars they profit from but do not fight in. Similarly, on a micro level, there are punitive wars on society's poor in the form of control and exploitation driven by the greed of these hidden moneyed classes.

FATHER'S PLANE CRASH AND MOTHER'S STRENGTH

When I was in the eighth grade, our family of eight children suffered our next big traumatic shock. My dad, a pilot flying his own plane on a business trip with three other men, crashed before it could reach the runway in a blizzard engulfing the Worcester, Massachusetts, airport. He ended up paralyzed from the waist down and endured two years of intermittent hospitalizations, some of it in a Stryker frame, compressed like a pancake to align his spine. When told he would never get out of a wheelchair, Dad said, "I will never get into one." He walked on Canadian crutches the rest of his life. Dad passed in June 1996 at the age of 78, never having gotten into that wheelchair, neither physically, emotionally, or spiritually. He lived as a true soul: true to himself, his family, his religion, and to God. A magnificent example of faith, hope, and love.

My mom emerged after the plane accident as a saint, a warrior, a healer, a protector, and a profound example of what I now consider to be a perfect merger of deep spirituality, faith, love, hope, courage, compassion, and the ideals that comprise the ultimate best in humans. She passed on March 27, 2019, at the age of 98, when I began writing the Litigator series. My parents were consummate human beings, exemplifying to us kids the ideals of what it means to be truly human, or at least to endeavor to live in God's love.

HIGH SCHOOL AT ST. JOHN'S PREP

I attended St. John's Prep, an all-male Catholic school with about 100 boys in my graduating class, one of the best sports high schools in Massachusetts. Still is. My academic inclinations alternated between mediocre and marginal, although miraculously I did graduate in the top 10% of my class. But that perhaps is more a reflection on the "jocks" at St. John's. My own sports ambitions were limited after my dad's airplane accident, by having to work during most of my high school years to help the family in my dad's construction business, although I did play a little football, basketball, and baseball.

I was not a stellar student but a reader. I devoured books on the two World Wars, on mystics, saints, Native American warriors, heroes, and villains. In high school, I particularly locked into books on legal heroes like Clarence Darrow, which intensified my desire to be a lawyer "fighting for justice for the little guy." I was overly idealistic and woefully ignorant of how our justice system really operates. Little did I know when I got on the Darrow "justice bandwagon" as a teenager that our legal system, particularly our Department of Justice and FBI, is not about justice. In fact, the opposite: they really serve "Deep State" money and create injustice.

As I came to realize in the world of litigation, it is about the manipulation of law by powerful, moneyed, vested interests, involving the majority of judges pandering to the money-driven politicians who appoint them. I thought I could make a difference. I wanted real, pragmatic change, not just phony baloney media lip service. In my second year of law school, I wrote an extensive Law Review article about racism and the "separate but equal doctrine's" innate evils, which got published in other journals. The article supported MLK. The CIA murdered him in April 1968, just after I received my draft notice. They followed this by the murder of Robert F. Kennedy. That is what America's Secret Government, the CIA, does, just as it did to JFK earlier, in 1963. Our CIA assassinates real political truth tellers.

I considered the Native American tribes to be the proverbial "little guys"...victims of naked oppression and greed exemplified in President Andrew Jackson's theft of Cherokee lands, sending them to die on the "Trail of Tears." Although inter-tribal warfare to protect their own territories was a Native American reality, it extended to their killing of the "whites" to preserve their tribal lands, so my experience with Native

American consciousness included a sacredness absent in the Euro culture that ultimately dominated them.

As a war baby, my consciousness always told me to be on the side of the little guy and fight for justice. It gets blurred, but I have tried my best, as recounted in these books. This is the consciousness-entangled reality that connects my birth as a war baby to my destiny as a litigator seeking justice in a corrupted system. The consciousness that chose to incarnate in 1944, amidst the bloodbath of World War II, was preparing for a lifetime of battles...not with bullets and bombs, but by seeking to transform the very nature of justice itself through elevated consciousness.

In the end, the greatest courtroom exists within our own consciousness. It is there that we must ultimately judge ourselves and choose which future we will create: one dominated by the same forces that have created war and injustice throughout human history, or one illuminated by higher awareness.

CONSIDERING THE PRIESTHOOD

I went through the almost typical Irish Catholic thinking about the priesthood, influenced by the Xaverian Brothers who founded and taught at St. John's Prep. They were good guys. My mother's religiosity also supported that thinking. My own immature, adolescent miasma, together with my pre-teen transcendental experiences idolizing the lives of Catholic saints like Dominic Savio, even before the testosterone kicked in, also pushed me in that direction. But thank God, cellular biology, or perhaps incarnation (see Chapter 13 on my "incarnation" of Father Griffin), and by some divine influences and Grace, I dropped those thought patterns in high school. Grace enabled me to avoid Catholic seminaries, priests, bishops, and priesthood.

Having said that, however, I must also emphasize that I have met and deeply admired many wonderful clerics, like Brother Andrew McManus at St. John's, who helped, inspired, and guided me to continue my education at Holy Cross College. At seventeen I was still deeply Catholic, and unaware where my Catholic heritage would take me.

Higher education for me, if it can be called that, involved more Catholicism. I attended the College of the Holy Cross, a relatively prestigious Jesuit institution and all-male at that time. It is a great academic school, currently ranked in the top ten of liberal arts colleges. In college, I had no grasp of what Jesuit history really involved. I do now. Like most Catholics more or less familiar with them, I thought the Jesuits were simply the "great intellectuals" of the Church and as such gained significant influence through these activities. However, they were often controversial because their close ties to royalty and political structures sometimes blurred the lines between religious, educational, and political influence.

My professors were good, but until my senior year, when I caught some semblance of an academic fire, I was a mediocre student majoring in political science and Middle Eastern history. I chose Middle Eastern history because as the Arab-Israeli conflicts raged in the Middle East, I thought I would learn more about its historical origins and the political empire-building of the British that seemed to be at the core of Middle Eastern conflicts, as elsewhere throughout the world.

Through my sophomore year, daily Mass and attendance at Holy Cross were mandatory. The liturgy expressed in the Mass and specific Catholic prayers presented wonderful spiritual principles and idealistic edicts as captured in the Sermon on the Mount. I was led to believe that the "Eucharist" represented the "Body of Christ," although I did begin to wonder why I was allowed to eat it!

I had also never understood and had resisted the Catholic teaching that "Christ died for our sins." I questioned how that could possibly apply to billions of souls over a period of 2,000 years who had lived, died, and "sinned" long after his crucifixion, to redeem us. Now I'm wondering if Christ's consciousness, a consciousness in which the Father lives in Him, He lives in the Father, and we live in the Spirit, explains "Christ died for our sins." If we accept this, does it wash away our "sins"? Paramahansa Yogananda says "there is no time and space in the presence of God." That aphorism may explain the reality of Christ's crucifixion as an event beyond time and space, that can be effective in guiding humanity away from "sinning" and toward realization in all ages and for all time. Unfortunately, washing away my "sins" is still a work in progress!

I went through a strange, paradoxical reaction to the Holy Cross College religious daily Mass structure. While rebelling against it, I felt an ill-defined and misunderstood need for it. This is hard to explain. I had sensed since childhood an elusive "something", an undefinable longing in my heart and mind, and have had it all my life. I rebelled against those religious controls over my life, but on a deeper level I wanted a relationship with God. I really didn't even understand what that meant, but I was drawn to my versions of prayer and an emotional feeling of spirituality. Many saints describe what I went through as "the natural tendency of the soul in every human to be drawn toward the Divine." It became the driving force behind both my litigation career and my spiritual practice. But at the time I was amidst the travails and miasma of early adult sexuality and confusions, and only in retrospect did I realize that daily Mass was a spiritual boon.

The corporate-type Church structures may have some legitimacy in leading us by the nose to God because intrinsically we want God, no matter how much we displace God with sex, drugs and rock and roll… or in my case with just plain old ego and pride. Interestingly, I abandoned the Roman Church and its Sacraments about three years after the birth of my son, November 22, 1968, at age 28. I was really drawn to the teachings of Jesus but couldn't fully grasp the deep meaning behind his teachings as espoused by the Catholic Church until many years later and after an ocean of learning that led me to finally discover the hidden esoteric meanings of his teachings. (See Chapter 14.)

MEETING MY FUTURE WIFE

In my junior year, I met the girl who would become my wife. I fell in love with her without really knowing what love was or the range of feelings that would erupt in me as the relationship progressed. It progressed from a cavalier attitude toward her and the relationship, to attachment, to overwhelming need as a sick, forlorn puppy, and then ended up in marriage.

The three biggest blessings in my life have been love for all things spiritual, my parents, and Laima and my three children. It has given me an understanding of the deep meaning of the stricture: "What God has joined together, let no man put asunder." However, the world grabbed me. Retrospectively, the Catholic gloss over deeper sexual energies and raw ambition could not keep up with the latter.

In high school and college I mostly worked for my dad after his plane accident, trying to help out our family of eight kids while attending classes, gambling with friends, engaging in stupid adolescent-type behavior, mostly a traditional college "sophomore slump", and getting involved more deeply with Laima.

I had always loved and done well in sports, although my participation on any significant level was frustrated by my dad's accident and our family situation. But I did play quarterback on our college intramural football team and on our basketball team. It did not involve a significant time commitment interfering with work. We went undefeated in both sports my senior year, and I won awards as the MVP in both. I later threw out the trophies I had received when I got on "the spiritual path." I considered my attachment to my minor athletic success as a hindrance.

VIETNAM AND LAW SCHOOL

When I was in college and law school during the Vietnam War, the Deep State was called the "military industrial complex." It sure was. It killed, wounded, and traumatized my classmates and close friends, while killing 58,000 Americans and causing the death of 3.8 million, half of whom were civilians.

I received my draft notice in April 1968, the same month Martin Luther King was assassinated. The Vietnam War was raging, and I faced the prospect of being sent to fight in a conflict I increasingly questioned. My wife Laima was pregnant with our first child, Michael Jr. She urged me to seek an academic deferment from the draft, the escape hatch for draft dodgers. I reluctantly applied. I received notice to report to a Hearings Board in July 1968 in Clinton, Massachusetts, to review my application. Meanwhile, I applied and tested successfully for Navy Flight training as an option to avoid the draft. I really wanted to fly F-4s, with the usual ignorance of what was really happening in Vietnam, particularly involving the "Hanoi Hilton" where captured Navy pilots shot down over North Vietnam were imprisoned. While my draft appeal was pending, the Navy pressured me to sign up.

In June, I received my law school grades and learned I was ranked first in my class, having achieved the highest first-year grade in the school's history with an 89 GPA. The next ten students were 84 and below. I attended the draft hearing before three grizzled, tough former and current military officials who looked like they wanted to draw and quarter any would-be draft dodgers. They sat behind a bare wooden desk in an almost-bare second floor of a partially abandoned government building in Clinton. The room smelled of dust and disapproval.

My heart pounding, I explained that my wife was pregnant, presented my exceptional law school grades and a letter from the Dean, and noted my family's military service: my father in World War II, my brother currently serving in Vietnam as a Navy officer, and my uncle who had been a Marine on Iwo Jima. I made it clear I wasn't a protester or draft dodger but was ready for Navy Flight school if they denied my deferment. After what seemed an eternity of stern looks and whispered consultations, they granted it. I was spared having to drop napalm on Vietnamese villages, and I now feel blessed to have avoided that service.

Just after getting my student deferment that summer, my son Michael was born on November 22, 1968, exactly five years after President Kennedy's assassination. Before his arrival, Laima worked as a teacher. We both worked part-time, she as a waitress and I as a busboy, pursuing the American dream while I attended law school. Michael was an amazing two-year-old, full of brightness and joy, but we had little choice but to send him to an East Boston daycare facility while I focused on Law Review and Laima worked. These were difficult choices...separating a young child from his mother, even if just for six hours a day to pursue a legal career.

Meanwhile, the civil rights movement was raging in the South and protests against the war were beginning. I felt aligned with African Americans who were seeking their long-deprived fundamental rights, exemplified in segregation and its evils. I admired Martin Luther King, but I was not a preachy type using a cause for my own hidden agendas, like some I perceived as hypocrites. My third year in law school, I was elected Editor-in-Chief of the Law Review, which consumed my life with sixteen-hour workdays. This left my wife and two-year-old son without much of a husband and father for an intensely difficult year. To maintain our income, Laima continued teaching while Michael attended daycare. Laima's eleven-year-old brother died of cancer that November 1969, making this period even more traumatic for our young family. No one is spared life's hardships. We make our plans, but larger forces determine outcomes.

JUDICIAL CLERKSHIP AND EARLY CAREER

I graduated magna cum laude, first in my class, and secured a prestigious clerkship with Associate Justice Paul Kirk of the Massachusetts Supreme Judicial Court. Judge Kirk was a battle-tested brigadier general with five medals from World War II combat campaigns. He embodied a magnificent combination of intelligence, insight, self-discipline, compassion, and love for humanity, family, and country. As a judge, he genuinely sought justice in his cases. Working for him was an honor and a blessing. Judge Kirk demonstrated such deep courage of conviction that he resigned halfway through my clerkship over disagreements with the court majority. Judges of his caliber are what our judicial system desperately needs, but too often, the system is controlled by those who serve power and wealth rather than justice. Judge Kirk exemplified true justice. Another blessing in my life and developing legal career.

During the course of my career I would soon see the dark side of litigation and injustice. On the negative side, my experiences range from the projected prejudices and influences of black-robed trial and appellate judges to outright corruption and bribery. Judge Kirk assigned me to Judge Spiegel when he resigned. Spiegel also had a real conscience. In the middle of my clerkship, the Supreme Judicial Court heard the DeChristoforo case. I worked on a dissenting opinion for Judge Spiegel in the first-degree murder conviction of Benjamin DeChristoforo, a very sad story of a young mobster raised in a family of "wise guys." I was also asked to stay on beyond the year of my clerkship to write the majority opinion in *Commonwealth v. Beneficial Finance*, the longest written decision in the Massachusetts Supreme Court annals. Looking back all these years later, I realize that these two cases and several other Supreme Court opinions, were proof of and set the stage for many consciousness connections in human thought, word, and deed even before my litigation career started. There are no accidents. The true meaning of "justice" is a vast subject, perhaps known only to God.

Next came a prestigious Boston law firm, Bingham, Dana & Gould. I didn't last very long in that big law firm. Instinctively, I disliked the culture: bill the clients, bill more, more hours, more billing… I felt "if this is practicing law, I'm walking away." I wanted to be a real litigator. I was naïve to the max, but I believe this impetuous reaction to a big law firm's practices was necessary to catapult me onto the next step in my litigation career.

CHAPTER 2

From Tax Memos to Mob Money: A Rookie's Rude Awakening

"The only source of knowledge is experience."
Albert Einstein

My very first case was a criminal case that ultimately served as a transformative experience in my understanding of justice. It taught me how light and darkness, law and crime, good and evil, mix together in American jurisprudence. It was a dance of light and shadow, a criminal case that blended stark contrasts of innocence and guilt, hope and despair. The integrity of all parties involved, including that of the judge, is the most critical ingredient in achieving "justice" in courtroom trials.

THE CALL TO BATTLE: A FRIEND'S FAITH

The phone rang, interrupting the quiet of my office at Bingham Dana. It was March 1972, and on the other end was Jay, a law school friend and classmate who commanded my respect. He was a former infantry officer in Vietnam who had nearly made it to the "Show" in Major League baseball. His voice carried an unusual urgency.

"I may need your help in a case I'm involved in," he said without preamble. "My father's on the Board of Directors at Wakefield Surety Bank & Trust. The Bank President, Dan, is under investigation. The place is crawling with state and federal regulators. Millions missing. Bad loans. Maybe embezzlement."

Jay's father wanted a lawyer to work with Jay to discuss the matter with Dan, someone who wouldn't be compromised by connections to other financial institutions. Jay trusted my legal abilities.

For the next three months, I became a nocturnal creature, driving almost nightly to Dan's mansion in Lynnfield, Massachusetts. There, surrounded by the trappings of wealth that now seemed precarious for a man being investigated for missing bank funds, Jay and I spent hours answering Dan's questions, researching legal issues ranging from extradition laws to potential charges and penalties, reviewing evidence, and assessing his chances of indictment and conviction.

I was a total and absolute novice. My senior supervising partner at Bingham Dana told me to turn the matter over to the senior litigators or withdraw from the case. Dan and Jay did not want a big law firm involved, knowing they represented one of America's largest banks, which potentially created a conflict of interest, and was exactly why he hired me rather than a major law firm with "associations."

Our first meeting was memorable for its brutal honesty, a poignant reminder of how my lack of experience loomed large in this critical moment. We met Dan in the impressive wood-paneled office at his mansion. He was at his polished mahogany desk but rose to shake our hands before some preliminary, rather impatient-sounding conversation from Dan. We could see he was under a lot of pressure, and by his nervous demeanor he didn't seem convinced this meeting was worth his time. He quickly got down to basics.

"Have you ever tried any criminal cases or represented any criminal clients?" he asked, his eyes sharp and evaluating.

Jay and I had not discussed how to handle Dan before this moment, we were winging it. I was a complete greenhorn, and naïve as to the best way to instill confidence and put my possible first legal client at ease.

"No. I've never tried any cases, civil or criminal. I've never even been in court or represented any clients, other than family. I just finished law school and a clerkship. I'm in the tax department at Bingham Dana & Gould, writing tax memos."

You could feel the tension rise as Dan looked down at the table for a moment, then looked up, his face darkened with disbelief. With a look of pained confusion he said to Jay, "Well, what the f... is he doing here?"

The room fell silent again. I could feel my career prospects evaporating in real time.

Jay leaned forward with an eagerness that was hardly warranted under the circumstances. "I think he will help you at least understand what you're up against before you hire F. Lee Bailey or some other big-name Boston criminal defense lawyer like Joe Balliro, the 'mob's lawyer.' Michael has had a great law school career, he's really good at research and can analyze anything and apply the right laws to your situation!"

Dan studied me for a long moment, weighing his limited options. Finally, he gave a resigned nod. "All right, let's see where this goes."

Thus began my baptism by fire into criminal defense, a clash of hard-fought ambitions and raw inexperience that would set the tone for my legal journey. Ultimately, the experiences stemming from this case helped shape my understanding and approach to litigation, leaving lasting impressions on my practice even up to this day. This case was over 50 years ago. My first dive into the deep end of the legal pool, with no swimming lessons and no flotation device except my ego and blind beginner's enthusiasm.

AN ANGEL BORN, A PROSECUTOR ASSIGNED: THE STAKES RISE

Amidst the tumult surrounding Dan's indictment, a profound new chapter in my life began. On May 13, 1972, my beautiful daughter Rebecca was born. Becky has the consciousness of an angel. Like her mom, she resides in goodness and love. Throughout her life, she has manifested love and compassion for anyone and everyone of all species...cats, dogs, horses, humans, anything that comes into her zone of love.

The same month that brought joy with the birth of my daughter Rebecca also saw Dan indicted on fifty counts of bank fraud and embezzlement. The Boston newspapers splashed his name across their front pages, the scandal feeding the public's appetite for tales of white-collar crime. The Boston U.S. Attorney assigned their top prosecutor to the case: George V. Higgins, the dominant Assistant U.S. Attorney (AUSA) in the organized crime section of the Boston U.S. Attorney's Office.

Higgins was no ordinary prosecutor. He specialized in "mob" cases, but he had another identity, that of a rising literary star who wrote suspiciously real-sounding mob fiction novels about Boston's criminal underworld that were filling his bank account and fueling his ambitions. The lines between his prosecutorial duties and his literary career were blurred in ways that would later prove significant.

I faced a momentous choice: remain at the prestigious blue-blood Boston law firm, enduring six months in each of their five departments before reaching my goal of joining their litigation section, or leave to open my own practice, beginning with the defense of a major felony indictment despite having zero experience in litigation.

On the day my daughter entered the world, I had to weigh the security of a potential partnership in a big firm against the chaotic unknown of my new path. After much internal conflict and discussions with Laima,

I chose to embrace the uncertain freedom of being my own boss...risking failure rather than enduring long months within the prestigious firm. I resigned from Bingham Dana. It felt like stepping off a cliff; my family and I were now charting unknown waters with a partner who was equally inexperienced, yet we were determined to forge our own path. My Irish heritage, steeped in tales of perseverance and defiance, urged me forward to embrace risks and challenges despite the vast uncertainties ahead. Rebecca was another of God's incomprehensible blessings, and I sought to ensure my professional ambitions did not overshadow my responsibilities as a father.

My family would now depend on my success in a field where I had no experience, and with a client facing decades in prison. The weight of this decision, fraught with uncertainty and responsibility, has haunted me throughout my life, casting long shadows over my professional choices and personal peace. The jury has been out all my life on that question. Maybe this book will help?

I now know that I was not the doer in that decision. It was only in hindsight, with the clarity of time, that I recognized my actions were not solely mine; they were driven by a deeper, almost predestined calling. Ego and my Irish DNA dictated my thinking when I left Bingham Dana & Gould and took on Dan's defense. The universe was prepping me. It preps all of us for our missions on this planet and in this incarnation; God has to work with us regardless of flaws, failures, and "sins." Perhaps life is ultimately about recognizing and fulfilling our unique missions, each step preparing us for the challenges ahead.

In the early 1970s, AUSA Higgins was immersed in multiple mob-type cases while simultaneously building his literary reputation. In 1970, he released *The Friends of Eddie Coyle*, republished in 1972 when he indicted Dan. Over the next few years, he released *The Digger's Game*, *Cogan's Trade*, and *A City on a Hill*...all Boston mob-related books that spanned the years Higgins was prosecuting Dan. Some of these novels, alongside works from various authors exploring this theme, became movies: *The Friends of Eddie Coyle* (1973 with Robert Mitchum) and *Killing Them Softly* (2012 with Brad Pitt).

George Higgins had potential "skin in the game" in the Surety Bank investigation, both as an AUSA and as a novelist fictionalizing real-life mobsters. This presented a potential ethical breach, depending on how and when he mixed his roles as a prosecutor and novelist. But at that moment, as I navigated the turbulent waters of a legal and ethical maelstrom, I began to understand my lessons from the intertwined lives of the prosecutor, the defendant, and myself. It would forge my career and also shape my own sense of justice and the complexities of truth that extend far beyond the courtroom.

Every individual and entity has their own perceptions and consciousness of reality, call it individualized truth. Regardless of whether it is an individual's truth that dictates their actions, conforms to law, societal norms, or the Ten Commandments, each of us has our own sense of "truth." I quickly learned that fact with the first, and subsequent panels of twelve individual jurors weighing their perceptions of evidence in every case.

Even the mobsters prosecuted by Higgins had their own sense of reality, however twisted or criminalized under legal standards it might be. His books and the movies made about them strongly convey the mobster's belief in his own truth justifying murder and chronic criminality. Hence the epithet "the underworld" to describe mob crime. Years later, I was to learn that our Government, the CIA beginning in the Dulles years, and other federal agencies manifested even more in the Clinton presidency, expanded further in the Bush, Obama, and Biden presidencies, is a bottomless pit of murder and corruption. The elected politicians have appointed judges who have systemically corrupted our judicial system. I saw it up front and personal in the trenches of litigation. (*Litigator 4* and *5*.)

A RETROSPECTIVE SIDE NOTE ON THE CRIMINAL CHARACTER OF OUR CIA AND THE CLINTONS

It took me decades of litigation to grasp the utter corruption that has swamped our political and judicial systems, but I jump ahead here to provide insights into several of the future cases in the Litigator series, so you, dear reader, may grasp how our political and judicial systems really work. The Higgins aggression against the mob as a prosecutor, while making money off his books and movies on those prosecutions is the extreme tip of a bottomless pit of governmental conflicts of interest and corruption that makes Higgins' profiteering a mere federal agency minor conflict of interest amidst federal agency murders and "weaponization" against political opponents and competing money interests.

Although our CIA and Secret Government, including Special Prosecutor Ken Starr (later Epstein's lawyer), covered it up, mobsters in the Arkansas "syndicate" murdered Vince Foster, Clinton's Deputy White House Counsel, on July 27, 1993; and then, sixty-six days later, on September 26, 1993, murdered his and Hillary's private detective, Jerry Parks. Foster and Parks knew everything about the Clintons' crimes and scandals contained in a box of documents in Foster's office when Foster was murdered. Whether these two murders were ordered by the Clinton CIA and Arkansas mob, based on what they deemed a necessary political "truth" for the Clinton presidency to survive amidst escalating scandals, is covered in *Litigator 5.*

For two months before his murder on July 27, 1993, Foster had been evaluating the "box" full of documented Clinton crimes and scandals submitted to him by a lawyer for the Church of Scientology seeking tax exemption. Monica Lewinsky's mentor, Linda Tripp, was Foster's "Executive Assistant" at the time. After Foster's murder, Ms. Tripp informed the FBI in a "302 interview" that on the night of the Foster murder, Hillary's aides cleaned out Foster's office and took the "Scientology box." In a desperate, utterly corrupt cover-up, Starr reported the Foster death as a suicide. (*Litigator 5.*)

The day after Parks was gunned down at a Little Rock red light in broad daylight, sixty-six days after "they" had murdered Foster, the FBI, CIA, and IRS Special Agents cleaned out all of the Foster/Parks communications from his home with no search warrant. That is how our CIA "mob" works. Crime is their truth. A week after the Parks murder, Clinton granted tax exemption to the Church of Scientology. The Government had rejected tax exemption for the prior forty years. The Supreme Court had rejected it in 1989. Just after the Foster/Parks murders, the "Scientology box" of Clinton scandals disappeared.

The Clinton grant of tax exemption to Scientology is only one of the most despicable, hideous perversions of justice, truth, law and morality, surpassing all of Clinton's depraved history as President. My hunch now: this will ultimately be the Clinton legacy.

Disclosure: More than three decades after the Dan Moore case in the Higgins prosecution, I represented Monica Lewinsky from 2001 to 2009. (*Litigator 4.*) Between 1979 and 1986, I represented numerous clients against the Church of Scientology. (*Litigator 2.*) In these and subsequent cases, I learned in the trenches the depth of political and judicial crimes, conflicts of interest, and corruption.

THE FUGITIVE CLIENT AND THE FEDERAL COURTHOUSE

In April 1972, Dan, without informing his legal "dream team", disappeared for a few weeks, evading the FBI who were on his trail. When Dan finally called me, likely on a phone tapped by the FBI...another legal violation they routinely committed in those wild-west days of Boston law enforcement. I told him to return immediately. He did, asking Jay and me to continue to represent him.

It was a tumultuous time dealing with the emotional uncertainty of supporting my family and questioning whether I had done the right thing in leaving a secure future partnership in a blue-blood law firm. My client being on the run added to my anguish and lack of sleep during this period. Higgins, Jay, and I maneuvered Dan's surrender, guiding him beneath the old federal courthouse in Boston to elude the media circus waiting above. As we entered the dimly lit building through the basement, it felt like I imagine a soldier would feel going into battle: relief that the wait was over, filled with adrenaline, observing all details and eventualities. As we strode forward, it seemed as if thick tension filled the air. Higgins greeted us at the door to the court with a cold, calculating gaze that pierced through us; he brimmed with a personal determination that transcended mere professional duty. He wasn't just prosecuting a case, he was hunting. Higgins was after the mobsters who had borrowed money from Dan's bank. Not an uncommon occurrence in the underworld of banking, as the Clintons knew in their involvement in the Whitewater and Madison Guaranty Savings and Loan scandals.

The old federal courthouse in Boston with its impressive columned façade had witnessed decades of legal drama. Inside Courtroom 3, the morning light filtered weakly through tall windows, beaten back by harsh strip lighting. The room had hosted its share of headline-grabbing cases: mob trials, political corruption scandals, and high-profile financial crimes that made the front pages of the Boston Globe.

Today, the gallery was surprisingly sparse for a major bank fraud case. A few reporters hunched over notepads in the back row, while a handful of curious attorneys and law students dotted the public seating area. The air was filled with the smell of furniture polish and anxiety. I straightened my tie for the fifth time, acutely aware of how my new suit, purchased hastily after resigning from Bingham Dana, couldn't disguise my inexperience. Beside me, Jay arranged our meticulously prepared briefs, his former military discipline evident in their precise alignment. Across the aisle, Assistant

U.S. Attorney Higgins reviewed his notes and threw a superior glance in our direction with the alarming confidence of a man who had never lost a case he truly wanted to win. In this case he had no doubts about winning against two rank amateurs like us.

Dan Moore sat between us, his expensive suit now seeming to hang a bit looser on his body after weeks of stress. Despite facing fifty counts of bank fraud and embezzlement, he seemed quite composed.

The side door opened, and the bailiff, a broad-shouldered man with a Boston accent thick as chowder, strode to the center of the courtroom.

> "All rise!" he commanded, his voice echoing off the wood-paneled walls. "The United States District Court for the District of Massachusetts is now in session, the Honorable Judge William Davis presiding."

The scrape of chairs and rustle of movement filled the room as everyone stood. Judge Davis emerged from chambers, his black robe flowing behind him. His deliberate pace to the bench suggested a man who never needed to hurry to command respect. As an African American judge in 1972 Boston, he had undoubtedly faced and overcome obstacles that made him impervious to courtroom theatrics.

"Be seated," he said, his deep voice resonating with authority as he settled into his high-backed chair.

The bailiff announced the case: "United States versus Daniel Moore, case number 72-CR-1493, arraignment and bail hearing."

Judge Davis surveyed the courtroom, his gaze finally settling on our table.

"I don't know either of you gentlemen," he said, studying Jay and me with undisguised skepticism. "Have you appeared before me previously?"

"No, Your Honor," we replied, my voice steadier than my nerves. My heartbeat pounded in my ears, but years of study and debates had taught me to project confidence I didn't feel.

"And your experience with sophisticated white-collar criminal cases?" The question stung like an accusation.

"I have no experience, Your Honor." The courtroom fell silent, the reporters' pens poised mid-air. "I've never tried a case, never represented anyone in a criminal matter, let alone a fifty-count bank embezzlement case. Until recently, I was writing tax memos at Bingham Dana." I couldn't tell whether Judge Davis smirked or smiled.

A patronizing sigh came from Higgins' table. I ignored it and continued, holding up my carefully prepared briefs, "But we've researched and studied the issues intensively and are ready to proceed with the arraignment and bail hearing."

Judge Davis leaned forward, the overhead lights accentuating the deep lines of experience on his face. He looked at me, Jay, and Dan as though we had collectively lost our minds. The courtroom was completely silent save for the occasional swishing sound coming from some courthouse system.

"Mr. Moore," he said, turning to Dan, "do you understand that you're facing serious charges that could result in decades of imprisonment? And you wish to proceed with these… gentlemen… as your counsel?"

Dan straightened his chair. "Yes, Your Honor," he replied without hesitation, his Boston Brahmin accent a stark contrast to our Boston Irish tones.

The judge removed his glasses and paused, as if pondering how to phrase his next words. When he looked back, his eyes had a look of deep concern. Years later, I wondered if Judge Davis' hesitation involved his unspoken concern that Dan would later claim inadequacy of counsel. It never happened.

"Are you familiar with the… zeal… of Mr. Higgins as a prosecutor?" he asked, with a slight emphasis that suggested "zeal" might be a polite substitute for something less complimentary.

"We're rapidly becoming acquainted with it, Your Honor," I replied, catching the first of many hints about what we were truly up against.

From the corner of my eye, I could see Higgins straighten slightly, taking the judge's comment as a compliment rather than the warning it was intended to be. The courthouse had seen many ambitious prosecutors come and go, but Higgins' reputation for pursuing mob cases and profiteering was already becoming legendary in Boston legal circles.

Judge Davis nodded slightly, a gesture that seemed to acknowledge both our spirited responses and the dangerous battle ahead of us.

THE BAIL BATTLE: DAVID VS. GOLIATH

Higgins rose to his feet, his tall frame emitting a confident, predatory determination across the wood-paneled courtroom. "Your Honor, the government requests that the defendant be held without bail. Millions of dollars are missing. The defendant disappeared for weeks and is clearly a flight risk." His voice dropped to a theatrical near-whisper. "Furthermore, there are 'bad loans' to some… questionable characters." He emphasized certain names ending in vowels, with a knowing look toward Judge Davis, a wink-wink suggestion meaning that the mob was involved and that there was more to this indictment than mere embezzlement.

To this day, I don't know what Judge Davis took from that "hint," but it has lingered in my consciousness ever since, just as Higgins' peculiar determination to "get Dan" mirrored the lengths some prosecutors would go to, driven not by justice, but by ambition and the allure of notoriety. Now, fifty years later, this perspective arises as an "aha" realization about prosecutors' motives and the systemic corruption within our justice system.

We should be aware that our "justice system" is mostly controlled by the personal ambitions, and often overly zealous misdeeds, of local prosecutors; and more egregiously by the conflicts of interest and moneyed greed of the judges. Coupled with this are the highest appointed DOJ officials with political agendas on the criminal side; and on the civil side of the DOJ by money-motivated political "ladder climbers" controlled by similarly motivated officials above them.

From my decades of courtroom experience, I have seen that some prosecutors can be worse than the criminals they pursue, using tactics like hiding, fabricating, and altering evidence for personal gain. Many prosecutors have salivated and feasted over high-publicity cases to enhance their careers, or used them as a bridge to private practice to make money. It's a bitter truth that when those sworn to uphold the law prioritize personal gain, the innocent bear the brunt. Our collective trust in the system is at stake, a reminder that every ambition has the power to skew justice. In some cases boatloads of money involving rampant violations of civil and criminal laws, regulations, and internal DOJ policies, have landed on my litigation plate.

Mr. Higgins used his position prosecuting Boston mobsters to write and sell books. Dan was no mobster, but he had loaned money to some of them. One of them was missing and presumed dead. His body was later found when we were in plea negotiations! And here I stood, no mob lawyer myself, entangled in a web of unsettling choices and haunting outcomes, the cries of justice obscured by money and ambition. As I navigated this uncertain path for my family and my client, I became aware of one salutary warning: in the relentless pursuit of ambition, the heart of humanity often gets lost.

After Higgins argued for "no bail," Judge Davis turned to us with a look that said everything: *What have you amateurs got to say for yourselves?*

With the courtroom's silence pressing in on Jay and me, it was a now-or-never moment as we both argued our points, mine legal based on my brief, Jay more on the facts. I gathered my resolve, stood up, and began: "Your Honor," I said, my voice finding strength in the research I'd done, "we respectfully request personal recognizance based on indisputable case precedent."

Silence.

The judge's eyebrows shot up at our request for no bail! For a case involving millions in missing funds, this was a huge "ask"!

I launched into a detailed explanation of bail precedent for white-collar defendants, emphasizing that Dan's voluntary presence in court contradicted the government's flight-risk argument. As Dan's attorneys, we both mentioned that he has five children and a wife, underscoring his commitment to fight these charges. "Despite the government's claims, he's here now, surrendering voluntarily even after the 'prevent departure' was ordered for his passport. He is gladly willing to surrender it for this purpose today!"

I then addressed the implicit assumptions underlying the government's argument that Dan posed a flight risk. "Mr. Higgins considers our client a flight risk based on missing money tied to questionable loans to individuals Mr. Higgins apparently knows well." Judge Davis raised his eyebrows. I gestured slightly toward the prosecutor, noting the flicker of surprise in his eyes. "If Mr. Higgins is correct that this case is not only about the alleged personal embezzlement of bank funds, but also about mob loans, then Mr. Moore does not possess the moneys claimed to be missing which would provide the motive and means for him to run. Indeed, Mr. Moore's appearance here today after Mr. Higgins claimed he had already attempted to flee prosecution, contradicts both of the government's positions. Under the briefed case law, Mr. Moore cannot be deemed a flight risk."

Judge Davis's gaze shifted between us and Higgins, whose face had hardened. I think he was expecting one of us to more easily buckle under pressure. The judge knew AUSA Higgins was an author profiting from his mob books, fueled by the same prosecutorial zeal now directed at Dan.

After thirty tense minutes in chambers reviewing our case citations, Judge Davis returned with his ruling: $25,000 bond. It would therefore cost Dan 10% or $2,500 to walk out, a total denial of what Higgins had demanded! We had the bondsman waiting. Dan also had a "friend" with cash waiting. As the transaction wrapped up, Dan's relief washed over him, a wave of gratitude that transformed his tense features into a look of newfound hope as he exhaled deeply. His trust in us rookies had been justified almost against common sense. We had survived the first battle against a prosecutor whose threats had loomed continuously over us for months with threats of no bail, missing records, and a potential sentence exceeding fifty years.

THE GRAND JURY WEAPON: DOCUMENTS, CONTEMPT, AND CONSTITUTIONAL RIGHTS

Going forward, Higgins was angry, frustrated, and dismissive of the two rookies. As perceived amateurs in a high-stakes criminal indictment, we had won the first round. His reputation on the line, his next move was immediate and calculated: a grand jury subpoena for the missing bank records. Corporate documents do not receive Fifth Amendment protection against grand jury subpoena; they are classified as corporate property rather than personal records. Dan refused to comply.

Federal Judge Garrity conducted a week-long contempt hearing that could put Dan in jail for the duration of the grand jury, about eighteen months, even before trial began. The government's proof that Dan had taken the records was strong but circumstantial, based on inferences rather than eyewitnesses. They presented detailed audits of the missing records, correlated with those they had, all pointing to Dan's involvement in specific transactions.

On Friday afternoon, after a grueling week of evidence, Judge Garrity ruled that Dan possessed the records and gave him until Monday noon to produce them or face the grim reality of prison on bad time for the next eighteen months.

Everyone with experience in the criminal justice system knows this is how the government "breaks" defendants, particularly white-collar ones unaccustomed to incarceration. And it's all "bad time," generally not counted toward sentencing. It's a powerful prosecutorial weapon, and Higgins was wielding it with singular determination, seemingly pursuing an agenda beyond what we could see.

I argued that although bank records traditionally had no Fifth Amendment protection, this case presented a unique statutory wrinkle. Since the 1929 Depression, federal law had specifically criminalized the theft of even mundane items like paper and staples from a bank. Since the government was throwing the book at Dan, he could be indicted for stealing the actual pieces of paper, regardless of their contents. While case precedent denied self-incrimination protection for document contents, there were no precedents regarding the theft of the physical paper itself.

Judge Garrity disagreed. Monday noon remained the deadline to produce the documents.

I worked through the weekend without sleep, fueled by desperation and coffee, preparing a petition for the First Circuit Court of Appeals. Monday morning, we filed for a stay. That afternoon, the court issued its ruling: the government had to grant Dan immunity for stealing the paper if it pursued the subpoena. After several legal battles, the government ultimately withdrew the subpoena, allowing us to shift our focus to negotiations. Higgins' fury intensified, but his focus shifted.

Negotiations began. The government seemed more interested in leveraging Dan's testimony against several mobsters involved in illicit loan activities, which could undercut the entire organized crime syndicate. As talks progressed, Higgins focused on documents related to ten or so specific loans to individuals with "connections"... Capiche?

We had some knowledge of the situation, but Dan remained tight-lipped even with us, his lawyers, regarding the importance of these particular documents to Higgins as an organized crime prosecutor. While we didn't fully understand their significance, Higgins' pursuit of sensational stories in his novels mirrored his ambition to capture powerful figures entangled in crime and corruption. Looking back fifty years later, the connections are astonishing. The dots have aligned in ways I couldn't have imagined back then.

Through decades of litigation experience in the trenches, I have witnessed firsthand how our justice system has been systematically dismantled. The corruption runs deep; judges, prosecutors, and government officials have become instruments of the moneyed elites, carrying out their agenda rather than serving justice. This institutional decay has accelerated since at least the Clinton presidency. The Department of Justice, FBI, CIA, and numerous federal agencies have been compromised at their core. Federal judges and politicians alike have fallen under the same corrupting influence. The pattern is clear: wealthy elites strategically place their chosen operatives in key positions throughout both state and federal government...individuals who have abandoned their duty to the public in favor of financial allegiance.

The Clintons exemplify this system—both products of and participants in a network where money determines loyalty, and public service becomes a vehicle for private gain.

For example, in *Litigator 4*, I present the hard evidence of massive judicial, DOJ, FBI, and IRS corruption, which included the bribery of the Montana Governor and the Montana bankruptcy judge. In January 2009, the Clintons installed their own lawyers; Eric Holder, Lanny Breuer, and Breuer's lackey Jack Smith, to control the DOJ.

At the same time in 2009–2011, these corrupted political appointments enabled the Obama DOJ to "weaponize" the DOJ, FBI, and IRS against my client Tim Blixseth and rip off Tim's wealth for billionaire Clinton donor Ron Burkle. The crooked, bribed bankruptcy judge and Montana Governor took millions of dollars of Burkle's and his co-conspirators' money to pull off the heist. The DOJ then weaponized the DOJ, FBI, ICE, IRS, and even Coast Guard to harass Tim Blixseth with baseless investigations, threats, false charges, and fraudulent tax assessments. Throughout all this we now know that Clinton, Burkle, and Epstein traveled the world in Burkle's 757 jet, "Air F..k One."

When President Trump was sworn in on January 20, 2025 with a grasp of the totality of government agency corruption, of which he had become a target, he immediately signed Executive Order 14147. This Order commissioned the Attorney General and DOJ to investigate, expose, and report the "weaponization" of federal agencies against American citizens. We have filed a complaint pursuant to this Executive Order and await the DOJ's response.

In their initial efforts to convict Dan Moore, Higgins focused on finding evidence of how much money Dan had personally embezzled, where it went, and how he spent it. His large home, potentially categorized as an "estate", suggested substantial spending, further complicating the narrative and revealing more about the intricate web we found ourselves entangled in as the case progressed. Internal FBI issues over the missing records intensified, and we realized we had significant bargaining chips. As we navigated the complexities of the case, what initially seemed like a bad-loan/embezzlement indictment began to reveal layers of deeper, more intricate issues.

One day over a hurried breakfast with Jay, the thought suddenly hit me like the Worcester tornado of my youth: in our extreme inexperience, we were missing the bigger picture. I really needed to know what the "money changers" really wanted. Jay saw my point and we shifted gears. I was on the way to finding out. They, the money changers, want control to secure money and power for themselves, while protecting themselves from criminal prosecution for the crimes they committed in the process. The realization hit me: it wasn't about justice; it was about control. The individual conviction of Dan wasn't the true objective, it was about who at the "money changer" level might be implicated and how to protect them.

Dan's involvement with, and loans to, several individuals under investigation became central to our negotiations with Higgins. Throughout the 1960s and early 1970s, when Higgins was pursuing Dan and writing his novels, Boston newspapers reported almost daily on gangland murders. His novels were hardly fiction, just thinly disguised accounts of the real "bad guys" that he and the FBI were investigating.

The manipulation of evidence by zealous prosecutors within our justice system highlighted a deeper corruption within layers of government power structuring. The Department of Justice (DOJ) has a decades-long history of protecting high-level Deep State, money-changer criminals using "fall guys" like Oswald in the JFK assassination to name but one high-profile "patsy," to shield the biggest criminals, in that case Allen Dulles, Director of the CIA. (*Litigator 4.*)

To this day, I believe that Higgins and certain FBI agents were protecting officials involved in higher-level crimes they feared might emerge in Dan's case. They needed to control all evidence. The word "cronies" to describe the FBI agents involved is a significant understatement. Several of these agents were deeply corrupt; some later went to prison in connection with an unrelated, infamous Boston mob murder.

In that case, corrupt FBI agents framed six "innocent" mobsters for a specific murder. I can imagine someone asking: so what, they are mobsters? But when the justice system twists and bends under the weight of many hidden transgressions, it breeds a malignant underlying corruption that permeates society, sowing distrust and despair among those who seek genuine justice. When the justice system is manipulated by those harboring even greater crimes, it creates a cancer that spreads throughout society, enabling greater corruption at higher levels. The Clintons expose this reality. For every innocent life caught in this machinery, countless others are forced to navigate a system that has abandoned its moral compass perpetuating cycles of poverty and crime.

As a young litigator, I thought the FBI stood for law, order, truth, and justice. NOPE. They became a tool of the Deep State under J. Edgar Hoover and his successors.

THE MISSING BODY AND THE MONEY CHANGERS' WEB

As negotiations intensified, one key mob witness, a "borrower" of bank money who served as intermediary between Dan and several top mob figures, had disappeared and was presumed murdered according to the FBI. A badly decomposed body was found in a New Hampshire lake and tentatively identified as one of the "borrowers." This "missing body" syndrome would reappear in similar contexts in several of my subsequent cases.

In retrospect, I can't help but feel that a higher power, whom I choose to call God (you might call it the universe or energy or fate), orchestrated my experiences, not as mere tests but as profound lessons about the justice system's complexities and the power dynamics at play. Each case taught me about resilience, morality, and the delicate line between justice and corruption that we all navigate.

In Boston, the Italian mob in the 1950s–60s was generally at war with the Irish mob, which in turn was fractured by internal conflicts, hence the 100-plus murders during this period. No one knows the exact number. Many bodies were never found, and many prosecutions dead-ended. "Tattle tales" weren't tolerated in that business. Murder and corpse concealment had reached pandemic levels in Boston and Springfield when I was a rookie litigator, and several civil cases put me before juries to determine whether "missing" individuals were dead or alive.

Thus, early in my career, death in my cases became a reality intertwined with legal issues. The missing go-between in Dan's case enabled Higgins to plea bargain with us. But we were blind to the vast web of influence lurking in the shadows.

PLEA BARGAIN AND THE PARADOX OF JUSTICE

Dan ultimately made a plea deal on June 26, 1973, receiving a seven-year sentence but with immediate parole for telling Higgins whatever he wanted to know. The truth was that Dan had been a target of the mob while trying to legitimately build his bank. They had outsmarted him with loan applications he believed were legitimate investments that would profit the bank. He made relatively little from their schemes; they had used him as a "pigeon", mob parlance for an easily fooled target, and never paid the loans. This was a forecast for the mob theft of hundreds of millions of dollars from the savings and loans industry in the 1980s. The massive criminality in the Savings & Loan industry was typified by the Clintons' scandalous participation in "Whitewater" and the Madison Guaranty Savings & Loan collapse, in which Madison and the FDIC lost over $60 million.

In Dan's case, some of the criminals at the top of the money chain, known to Higgins and his superiors, escaped prosecution. To my knowledge, the murderers involved in the dead body found in New Hampshire were never investigated or prosecuted. Those facts remained sealed in FBI files, classified by the same system that protects the highest-level wrongdoers.

For Jay and me, thoroughly novice litigators in our first major case, securing immediate parole for Dan with his five children seemed a just outcome. Looking back fifty years later, I see that the result was governed by forces beyond what I could have conceived then. The FBI and prosecution team were part of a system far more self-serving than we knew, their personal agendas, like Higgins' literary career, shaping the outcome. Thankfully, I now realize that I have never been the "doer" in any of my cases. My ego may have been involved. But God and His Grace surpassed my ego. Thank God and His Grace.

The reality of our justice system is that it embodies the ultimate human paradox: good versus evil, truth and justice versus fraud and corruption, all embedded in varying levels of human consciousness that transcend the legal definition. After all my years in the legal trenches, I've concluded that those tasked with upholding justice often operate at the same or even lower levels of consciousness than those they prosecute. Yet somehow, often mysteriously, God has intervened to achieve some semblance of truth and justice in my cases. Amid the shadowy machinations of both everyday deceit and larger corruption, the light of truth finds tenacious ways to pierce through, serving as a beacon of hope in our ongoing battle for justice against the encroaching darkness.

In this corrupt landscape, unscrupulous figures manipulated vulnerable bankers like Dan Moore, just as powerful politicians exploit the systems meant to protect public trust. It was a form of theft, but to prove the crime, the government must establish criminal intention *not* to repay the loan when it is taken out. This presents a formidable prosecutorial challenge..."proving the criminal mind," what the law calls *mens rea* (Latin for "a guilty mind"). This was a challenging task considering Dan was merely attempting to build his small bank, burdened by misplaced trust in the mob's hollow promises. He did not intend to steal its money; rather, his naivety left him vulnerable to being used as a pawn in their schemes. Banks exist to loan money and profit from interest rates. Hence, we secured immediate parole after defeating Higgins in both the bail hearing and the grand jury document subpoena appeal. Dan subsequently cooperated in revealing how and with whom the loans were made.

The shadows cast by Dan Moore's case stretched far beyond our small victory. His story was merely a microcosm of a much larger pattern of corruption that would metastasize throughout the American financial system. What began as local mob figures "pigeoning" a small-town banker would evolve into a pandemic of crime that engulfed the entire Savings & Loan industry in the 1980s; and later, in the 2007–2009 period, the total collapse of financial systems, losing over $16 trillion, was caused by massive frauds in mortgage-backed securities.

Unbeknownst to the average American citizen, the bundling of utterly fraudulent mortgages into tradable securities was sponsored by members of Congress, mostly liberal Democrats, and backed by federal insurance. When the entire Ponzi scheme collapsed, financiers like Fink at BlackRock engineered and manipulated the federal bailouts to resolve the crisis. Meanwhile, once again, the criminal perpetrators of the entire scheme walked away with billions. (*Litigator 4.*)

For a primer on this subject, see *The Greatest-ever Bank Robbery: The Collapse of the Savings and Loan Industry*. The criminality involved in the highest levels of the banking industry, as reported by Martin Mayer in the above book, in fact involves the depth of government, political, and financial corruption that, in turn, permeates every crime, every evil, every war and abomination embraced by our species, from mob murder to presidential assassination to the world wars. The coups d'état our CIA perpetrated abroad exemplify a systemic corruption often referred to as the "Deep State," the shadowy networks within government that operate independently of elected leadership. (*Litigator 4.*) Money, at least the desire for it, is "the root of all evil," says the Bible and other scriptures.

The Litigator series fundamentally explores the duality of quantum-entangled human consciousness: a struggle between the descent into corruption and the ascent to divine awareness and morality. Each case highlights this internal conflict, reflecting our society's battle against entrenched deceit. They are about good vs. evil, truth and justice vs. lies and injustice, material or money consciousness vs. spiritual or moral consciousness. By "money consciousness," I mean an obsessive pursuit of material wealth that often disregards ethical considerations, intertwining with the moral decay seen in systemic corruption. In contrast, "moral or spiritual consciousness" reflects the teachings of the Sermon on the Mount, urging us to nurture an inner kingdom of values as the foundation for a just society. By moral or spiritual consciousness, I reflect on lessons learned through trials faced in my journey, simultaneously echoing a struggle to discover the Kingdom of God within, rather than merely chasing after external material wealth that often leads us astray.

For humanity to endure, I believe we must transcend our fixation on external wealth and cultivate the Kingdom of God within. Recognizing and nurturing this inner richness can illuminate a path away from corruption toward a just and equitable society. In *The Kingdom of God Is Within You: Christianity Not as a Mystical Religion, But as a New Gospel of Life*, Tolstoy emphasizes the moral imperative to seek the divine within oneself rather than through wealth or social status, a theme critical to our understanding of conscious evolution.

After the 1980s Savings and Loan criminal schemes collapsed those financial institutions like stacked cards, the government paid out billions. In 1989, attempting to stem the tide of bank frauds by the biggest banks, Congress passed "FIRREA," which mandated "fair market value" appraisals of properties securing mortgages. The banksters immediately transformed this into a vast scheme of frauds by "bundling" the mortgages and selling them as "instruments" on global stock exchanges—rank greed. For a deeper understanding of how these frauds unfolded, one may refer to the documentary film *Inside Job*, which thoroughly chronicles the mechanisms of this financial deception. The Clintons exploited these schemes in their dealings with Madison Guaranty and their associates. As usual, the "liberal" politicians in Congress, like Barney Frank, fueled the government-subsidized giveaways both in the original mortgages for those who couldn't afford them and the ultimate bailouts. "OPM: Other people's money." The Deep State always steals our money and our labors. In the Clintons' Madison Guaranty frauds, they used the Federal Deposit Insurance Corporation to pay everybody off to reduce complaints and attendant FBI investigations. (*Litigator 4*.)

Greed permeated many levels of mortgage bundling fraud, from small local brokers to powerful bank CEOs, all driven by an ambition to profit at any cost. This widespread corruption laid essential groundwork for the eventual financial collapse that sent shock waves through the global economy. These expansive schemes of mortgage bundling and fraud infected every layer of lending, ultimately culminating in the 2008 collapse and the governmental bailouts that followed. International monster Swiss banks like UBS and Credit Suisse, with their secret numbered accounts, led the criminality.

The Clintons used these Swiss banks as part of their "pay-for-play" schemes. (*Litigator 4* and *5*.) To quote Yogi Berra, the 2008 collapse was "déjà vu all over again." The bank regulators who knew all along the massive scope of the frauds, also knew that our government would use us, the taxpayers, to bail them out. As taxpayers, we eventually bailed them out, despite having been kept in the dark about their fraudulent activities.

How was this chicanery perpetrated on us? In the wake of banking fraud orchestrated by major financial players, it became evident that the Deep State wields control over our government, elected officials, and their appointments to federal agency heads. The Deep State financial elites controlling our politicians murdered our President and reformers like JFK, RFK, and MLK. (*Litigator 4* and *5*.)

Banking fraud by the biggest banks has become a deadly global financial pandemic, the definition of quantum-entangled evil. The biggest money changers perpetrate a scope of evil reminiscent of the murder and crucifixion they orchestrated two millennia ago. When Jesus threw the money changers from the temple with a whip of cords, he provided humanity with the lesson, the prophecy, the example to seek the kingdom of God within, not in exchanging money or selling lambs for sacrificial slaughter. By becoming the lamb itself, the sacrifice, Jesus showed us what we must do to save ourselves and our species. He proved that although the innocent suffer most in the short term when opposing evil, they ultimately rise above it.

Fifty years ago, as a novice litigator involved in the Boston mob case surrounding "pigeoning" Dan, I caught only a glimpse of the banking fraud rampant in the system, while the top-tier offenders received lenience from the very Department of Justice that was supposed to safeguard the law. In turn, the DOJ was being controlled by the Fed, the CIA, and the global banksters. In fact, I was such a novice, naïve litigator in my first case that I had no concept of just how evil the Deep State money changers behave, or who they are. Over the decades, I discovered the true extent of the Deep State's machinations. I am watching this evil play out now. (*Litigator 4* and *5*.)

It is said that particles once connected remain forever entangled, regardless of the distance between them. We now call this quantum entanglement. Twenty years after defending Dan Moore in that Boston courtroom, I found myself suspended between earth and sky, riding a chairlift up the snow-covered slopes of Aspen Mountain. The January wind bit through my gloves as I recollected distant memories that I thought were long buried beneath the weight of countless other cases. I hadn't thought of Dan Moore in years, or so I told myself. Yet something about this day—with its razor-sharp clarity and infinite blue horizon, allowed my consciousness to soar back in time. The chairlift swayed slightly as it carried us higher, the ground beneath our dangling skis. My companion, a stranger, sat in contemplative silence beside me. Something about his profile caught my attention: the set of his jaw, perhaps, or the way he squinted against the glare of sun on snow.

"Beautiful day," I offered, my voice nearly lost in the mechanical groan of the lift cables. He nodded, his breath clouding in the thin mountain air. "Days like this make you believe in something bigger than yourself."

"Where are you from?" I asked, making conversation to fill the awkward space between strangers forced into temporary intimacy. "Lynnfield, Massachusetts," he replied, adjusting his goggles. The name struck me like an unexpected verdict. Lynnfield. The world tilted slightly on its axis. Memories crystallized like frost on a window. "I used to know some people from Lynnfield," I said carefully, studying his face with new curiosity. "A long time ago."

He turned toward me, his features emerging from the shadow of his ski cap. There was something hauntingly familiar in the lines around his eyes, his smile.

"Small world," he said, extending a gloved hand awkwardly in the confined space. "I'm Dan Moore."

Time collapsed. The steady rhythm of the chairlift, the creak and sway, seemed to falter. Moore. Not just any Moore from Lynnfield, but Dan Moore's son! The same boy who had sat silently at the kitchen table during our late-night strategy sessions, his ten-year-old eyes wide with confusion and some fear as we discussed his father's future. The child who had clutched his mother's hand in the courtroom corridor, too young to understand the full weight of fifty counts of bank fraud, but old enough to feel the shame that clung to his family name.

"You're Dan Moore's son?" I said incredulously, my voice barely audible above the wind that gusted between us, carrying ice crystals that stung my exposed cheeks. His eyes widened, then narrowed with sudden wariness. "You knew my father?"

The chairlift crested the ridge, preparing for our dismount. Below us stretched the vast white canvas of the mountain's back side, untouched and pristine. But I was seeing another landscape entirely: the wood-paneled walls of Dan's office, the Boston courthouse with its imposing columns, the headlines that had splashed across the morning papers.

"I was his attorney," I said as we raised the safety bar. "During the bank fraud case in '72."

We skied off the lift in silence, gliding to a stop at the edge of the run. "Are you Mike Flynn?" Around us, other skiers adjusted equipment and plotted their descents, oblivious to the cosmic convergence unfolding in their midst. Dan stared at me, the wind whipping loose snow around our boots. His face had drained of color beneath his tan. "You're kidding me. After all these years? Here?" I shook my head, as stunned as he was. "I don't believe in coincidences anymore," I said. "Not after thirty years of practicing law. The universe has patterns we're only beginning to understand."

We moved away from the lift, finding a quiet spot overlooking the valley. The vastness below us seemed to mirror the expanse of time that had passed, twenty years condensed into a single moment of recognition.

"How is he?" I asked, though I already suspected the answer from the shadow that crossed Dan's face.

No response.

I closed my eyes briefly, feeling the weight of the silence. The case had ended for me when we negotiated immediate parole, a victory of sorts extracted from Higgins' ambitious prosecution. But for Dan and his family, the case had never truly ended.

"He talked about you sometimes," Dan continued, surprising me. "Said you were green as grass but fought like hell for him. Said you succeeded in keeping him out of jail and believed him when he claimed he didn't know what those guys were really doing with the loans."

Something tightened in my chest...regret perhaps, or the belated recognition of how deeply our lives affect others in ways we can never fully comprehend. The thin mountain air suddenly seemed insufficient.

"I was green," I admitted. "First case after leaving Bingham Dana. I had no business defending a fifty-count federal indictment, but sometimes ignorance gives you the courage that experience would deny."

Dan nodded, a complex emotion crossing his features, the look of a man reassessing a lifetime of memories. "Those were hard years for our family. Mom never really recovered from the shame of it all."

The wind died momentarily, leaving us in a pocket of stillness. Below us, skiers carved elegant arcs down the mountain, their movements fluid and purposeful, their trajectories briefly intersecting before diverging again like our lives, touching momentarily before continuing on separate paths.

"And you?" I asked. "How did you..."

"Survive it?" He gave a short laugh that held more pain than humor. "One day at a time. Worked twice as hard to prove I wasn't my father's son, then worked even harder to accept that I was." He paused, adjusting his poles. "I saw then what I had missed before, the tension he carried in his shoulders, the vigilance in his eyes. The son who had chosen to guard the very gates his father had been accused of breaching."

"Your father was a pigeon," I said quietly. "Used by people who understood the system better than he did. He wasn't the mastermind they made him out to be in the papers."

Dan looked at me sharply, as if these were words he had waited decades to hear from someone who had been there… someone who knew. "He always said that," he replied, his voice rough with emotion. "But when you're a kid and everyone's whispering about your dad the criminal, it's hard to believe."

We stood there on the mountaintop, two men connected by invisible threads of circumstance and consequence, of actions taken and lives altered. The past was suddenly as present as the snow beneath our skis.

"I've often wondered," I said, "how many lives were shaped by that case. Not just your father's, or your family's, but everyone involved. Higgins went on to movies based on his books about Boston criminals. Some of the FBI agents involved later went to prison themselves for corruption in a separate case. The justice system is like quantum physics, everything affects everything else, often in ways we can't predict or control."

Dan nodded slowly, his gaze distant. "I used to be so angry," he said. "At him, at the system, at everyone. Took me years to understand that anger was just covering up the hurt."

The sun emerged from behind a cloud, creating two shadows momentarily aligned.

"I hope this meeting brings you some peace," I said, meaning it more deeply than I could express. "Your father was a decent man caught in an indecent system. He loved you very much, that was always clear, even during the worst of it."

Dan's expression softened, the release of a burden long carried. He extended his hand again, and this time when we shook, it felt like more than a greeting. It felt like closure.

"Thank you," he said simply. "For defending him then. And for this conversation now."

As we pushed off down the mountain, carving parallel turns through untouched powder, I felt a sense of completion I hadn't known I was missing.

Some cases never truly end; they merely pause, waiting for resolution in unexpected moments and unanticipated places. The universe, it seems, keeps its own counsel and its own calendar, sometimes allowing justice to arrive not in courtrooms but on mountainsides, delivered not by judges but by the mysterious workings of a cosmos where nothing, not even the briefest human connection, is ever truly lost.

"TIME AND SPACE ARE LINKED IN GOD."

Paramahansa Yogananda

Higgins' books. Money. Quantum entanglement. What did I learn from this case as a fledgling lawyer and the marginal success of getting a 'deal' done that was satisfactory to my client and his family? Actually, only a little, probably because that was all I could assimilate at the time in my incredibly naïve and narrow Irish Catholic upbringing. I learned much more later, as the universe doled out lessons and learnings over time as my litigation and meditation practice expanded.

The plea bargain was ultimately at least partially satisfactory to Higgins, if not to the rampantly obscene political 'ladder climbers' permeating the ranks of our Department of Justice, and the Boston U.S. Attorney's Office in the 1960's and 70's during the Kennedy/Johnson (Democrat), and Nixon/Bush (Republican) Administrations. Disgraceful political appointments plagued the DOJ landscape across party lines, suggesting a history of massive corrupt schemes involving various political figures and administrations. Events such as the assassinations of JFK, RFK, and MLK, the Watergate scandal, and other frauds like Madison Guaranty and the Clinton Foundation are examples of interconnected government and private sector corruption. As I learned, the system is mostly corrupted and controlled by federal agency appointments. The Clinton, Obama and Biden appointments are classic examples. A persistent Deep State has enabled severe corruption, from CIA Director Allen Dulles through the presidencies of Nixon, Johnson, Bush, Clinton, Obama, and Biden. Litigator 4 and 5.

Back in the Boston gangland murder scene in the 50's, 60's and 70's, the competing mobs strove for power by amassing, you guessed it, money. When conflicts arose over who controlled the sources of their money, drugs, sex, and even music - the music industry is notoriously corrupt, they just murdered their competitors.

Higgins was basically making the major prosecutorial decisions involving organized crime in the U.S. Attorney's office (Boston, MA) in the early 70's, while the appointed politicos played musical chairs as the U.S. Attorney. The rampant gangland murders mirrored the rampant political corruption in Boston and in the FBI and DOJ, so Higgins did whatever he wanted along with several FBI agents, like Connelly and Fitzgerald.

The loss of the Grand Jury subpoena effort to put Dan in jail before trial for 18 months really hurt Higgin's media-driven indictment and his agenda and ego. But it was instrumental in getting the plea bargain consummated for my client. So, no harm no foul? Higgins got what he wanted. He would have incarcerated Dan interminably to get what he wanted. We foiled that and accomplished a favorable plea deal. Or did we? Was justice done? You the readership are the jury.

Bank fraud embezzlement cases are document-intensive. And this was long before computers, the cloud, and alternative sources of evidence that existed within the bank documents at issue. The DOJ and Higgins never got the entire collection of documents that they subpoenaed and to my knowledge they have never surfaced. I never saw them! But it is likely irrelevant to what Higgins really wanted. I also don't know where all the loan money ended up.

Dan's personal use of bank funds may have been too insubstantial to convict Dan of anything more than the plea bargain achieved; bad loans to mobsters. Whether it would have led to kick-backs from the borrowers or a trail of money into accounts controlled by Dan or his agents remains an unknown to this day. I don't know because the only documents I saw related exactly to the bad loans that Higgins wanted, the 'loan applications'. In my experience, knowing how the FBI and DOJ really work, I have concluded that they wanted to know who needed to be protected so that those in the higher echelons would remain unscathed.

In truth, the Clintons and their cronies ripping off Madison Guaranty causing the loss of $60 million, made the losses at Dan Moore's bank insubstantial, and the attendant indictment, a grotesque example of government corruption. Dan got indicted. Clinton became president. Foster got murdered. Hillary created the billion-dollar Clinton Foundation fraud using her position as Secretary of State, and Bill Clinton's position as President, notwithstanding his sexual scandals.

Following Dan's case, similar Savings and Loan industry scams emerged, showcasing fraud; mobsters stealing money from the S&L's leading to their failure, then ultimately being bailed out by us the taxpayers. Same old story.

When the completely fraudulent bundled mortgage scams fell apart in 2007-08 leading to catastrophic bank failures, once again the taxpayers bailed them out. Once again, the money changers in control of our government, The Clintons, Bush, Obama, ripped us off.

Higgins's mind and motives, in my negotiations with him and several FBI agents, who seemed to form his personal detachment from the local and regional FBI offices, were predominantly fixated on mob participation in the bad loans, likely considering how to both include the scandal in a book, and how the FBI and DOJ could protect the higher-ups.

I am including this case in my book because it was my first foray into the very public litigation arena, and taught me a lifelong lesson; our government is often run by criminals worse than those they put in prison. The stark difference lies in the wealth and influence that the governing criminals wield over ordinary citizens, enabling them to manipulate the very systems meant to uphold justice.

The famous Greek sage, Aesop said it right 2500 years ago:

"We hang the petty thieves and appoint the great ones to public office."

In the Moore case, it became evident that some deceased members of the Boston mob were linked to FBI corruption and wrongful convictions, mirroring the Hillary/Comey/FBI frame-up of Trump and General Flynn years later. Higgins's aggressive tactics nearly pushed Dan into making admissions, but Dan ultimately avoided decades of wrongful imprisonment. These prosecutions often stem from personal or political motivations. Mueller's appointment as Special Counsel to target Trump illustrates this trend. Driven by ambition, prosecutors were eager to climb the ranks, while the politicians who appointed them took advantage of this ambition to gain votes and power.

The key takeaway from the Higgins/FBI prosecution is that Higgins used the FBI to gather material for one of his mob books, a strategy that failed spectacularly. Judge Davis and the First Circuit Court of Appeals stood firm, thwarting Higgins's aggressive scheme. Judge Davis was street smart and knew what Higgins was doing. The appeals court judges were intellectual heavyweights, who knew that immunity for the stolen pieces of paper was their only option. Later, in several cases, the First Circuit Court of Appeals also thwarted unjust prosecutions, emphasizing the importance of judicial integrity. Several of their decisions exhibiting fairness and integrity also played a crucial role in shaping my understanding of justice, leaving lasting implications that still resonate in my consciousness 50 years later.

On the negative side, the repercussions of recent events highlight a persistent cycle of corruption within our legal and political systems. As Jesus observed, "All that is hidden gets revealed," and a wise, albeit unknown author once noted, "The wheels of justice turn slowly but grind exceedingly fine." This serves as a reminder that truth, though often delayed, tends to surface in the realms of justice and morality. This idea is often attributed to Plutarch from the 1st Century AD, who referenced the common adage "The Mills of God" in his work *De sera numinis vindicta* (*On The Delays Of Divine Vengeance*). He critiqued the notion by stating: "Thus, I do not see what use there is in those mills of the gods said to grind so late as to render punishment hard to be recognized, and to make wickedness fearless." While I agree with Plutarch in real-time on this planet, consciousness ultimately catches up, as Christ suggested.

As a novice in litigation during my first case, I had little awareness of the power dynamics within the Department of Justice and the influence of politically appointed Federal judges. Throughout Dan's case, I was extremely idealistic to a fault, still believing that our Department of Justice and all its duly appointed U.S. Attorneys and their Assistants, like Higgins, were purely and pristinely motivated to achieve true justice. What a chump! Just look at what the Jack Smith and the Biden corruption machine have done to President Trump. I have learned personally and professionally just how corrupt Jack Smith is. *Litigator 4.*

Our U.S. Attorneys, who are politically appointed and generally change with each presidential administration, have over the last 50 years often been corruptly controlled by the 'money changers' who get our presidents elected. For the past 50 years, I've seen how judges are often controlled by the money behind the politicians who get elected and appoint the judges.

Intermittently over my 50-year career, despite repeated disillusionments, I have clung to fleeting moments of hope that perhaps, against all odds, the career prosecutors within the DOJ could exercise some ethical influence over the local U.S. Attorneys. They often seemed like mere puppets dancing to the tunes of their appointed agency heads who were controlled by their political masters, who in turn were controlled by deep state money. My hope has been to preserve a measure of justice amid the political control of U.S. Attorneys by the deep state.

Litigation and consciousness 'connectivity' became integral in my meditation practices. As an almost metaphysical connection to the FBI/DOJ prosecution of Dan, there are multiple events, like meeting Dan's son on the ski-lift, which started earlier and played out later, repeatedly in my litigation history, involving what can only be described as quantum entangled consciousness connections. I just have no other explanation. It may be that 'string theory' and 'super determinism' could explain the events in these books on a quantum level, but I'm content knowing the best I can report is the quantum entangled exploration of my litigated cases as my meditation practice progressed over 50 years.

CONSCIOUSNESS AND THE COURTROOM: WHERE MEDITATION MEETS LITIGATION

When we pause to reflect on our own awareness, we encounter a fascinating paradox: while we can observe and measure countless phenomena in the external world, the very consciousness through which we perceive everything remains elusive to scientific measurement. Our everyday experience of awareness, the foundation of all our thoughts, decisions, and actions, exists beyond the reach of our most sophisticated instruments. This doesn't mean consciousness is unknowable, only that it must be approached differently than physical phenomena requiring measurement. Through practices like meditation, we can directly experience different states of consciousness, even as we lack external tools to quantify them. Moreover, the nature of consciousness itself, the space in which our minds function, remains a deeply personal, subjective experience.

Just observe your own thoughts and ask: "Who is the observer of my thoughts?" Ultimately, after making this simple practice a routine, you will arrive at a state of awareness...you can call it the "soul," or if that term has too much religiosity around it, just call it a state of consciousness above or outside the mind. See where that takes you. After fifty years in the PIT while meditating, these books explain where that combination took me.

Many practitioners report experiencing moments of profound insight during meditation, what might be described as "quantum-entangled thoughts" that connect seemingly unrelated information in meaningful ways. These intuitive leaps often occur in heightened states of awareness, when the mind becomes still enough to perceive patterns and connections that normally escape our attention. While most of us experience these insights occasionally and sometimes partially, contemplative traditions suggest that with dedicated practice, this expanded awareness can become more consistent and comprehensive.

Throughout history, figures like Buddha, Jesus, and more recently Paramahansa Yogananda, Amma, and Mother Meera have been recognized for achieving extraordinary states of consciousness, either through their spiritual practices or merely by their apparent ability to connect with what can only be described as higher levels of consciousness. Over the millennia, mystics, sages, and saints have reported their connections to "God," "Christ," and advanced "beings." In my meditation practices, I gradually perceived these words to describe an undefinable, unmeasurable "state" of existence or "being" or "consciousness" more real than the physical world. The teachings derived from these advanced states—by humans connecting to God, Christ or Spirit, offer valuable guidance while reminding us that the path to deeper awareness is available to everyone, regardless of background or belief system.

Each person's journey toward expanded consciousness follows its own unique trajectory, with moments of clarity emerging through consistent practice. The Litigator series explores how these principles apply specifically to the practice of law and shaped the results in specific cases. Litigation demands both analytical precision and intuitive understanding, a combination that meditation naturally enhances. By developing greater awareness through contemplative practices, legal professionals can navigate the complex human dynamics of the courtroom more effectively, maintaining clarity under pressure and perceiving nuances that might otherwise be missed.

This exploration acknowledges the fascinating space we all occupy, balancing analytical thinking with intuitive insight, professional demands with personal development, and practical concerns with deeper questions of meaning and purpose. By bringing together the ancient wisdom of meditation with the modern practice of trying cases to juries who were absorbing not only the evidence I presented to them, but also the "state" of my own consciousness, I have discovered new possibilities for both personal growth and professional success.

THE DECHRISTOFORO TRAGEDY: CONNECTIONS TO INJUSTICE

Of the 100-plus gangland murders during the 1960s and 1970s involving the rival Irish and Italian mobs which Higgins feasted on both as a federal prosecutor with direct FBI connections and access to all of their files, and using them for his books, is the sad tale of Benjamin DeChristoforo. He was a young aspiring mobster and son of the infamous Boston "North End" "capo," Dante DeChristoforo. I have utterly strange quantum-entangled connections to them that compel some of the conclusions in this Litigator series. These connections guide me in recognizing the patterns of justice, corruption, and the intricate interplay of political and judicial power that defines our existence, urging me to continue my pursuit of truth in a world where the lines between right and wrong are often blurred.

In 1970–71, while working as a law clerk at the Massachusetts Supreme Judicial Court, my judge, Spiegel, asked me to analyze a pivotal dissenting opinion for the appeal of the young mobster Benjamin DeChristoforo, just two years before Dan's case. Following the resignation of Judge Kirk, I delved into the evidence and purported errors tied to DeChristoforo's conviction for the first-degree murder of another mobster, Joseph Lanzi, (360 Mass. 531, 1971), a landmark case that exposed systemic failures within our justice system. Benjamin's father, Dante DeChristoforo, was allegedly an "underboss" in the North End Angiulo/Patriarca mob family. Don't forget Dante's name… connecting the dots!

Ben's conviction swiftly sealed his fate under a "Life Without Parole" sentence, effectively imprisoning him for merely being present in the car during Lanzi's gangland murder. This highlights a recurring theme: much has been written about how "Life Without Parole" deprives individuals of all hope, with lifers asserting that losing hope can be far worse than death.

Talk about the "Three Stooges" of organized crime. The Lanzi murder was uncovered when the Medford police pulled the car over about 4 a.m. and Lanzi was dead in the front seat with a gunshot wound on the right side of his head, and three in his chest! Duh, shouldn't they have at least put him in the trunk!

Benjamin's case is a tragic example of overzealous prosecutors. My judge and the dissenting opinion I worked on sought to get DeChristoforo a new trial. It didn't happen. The trial involved egregious prosecutorial misconduct, fundamental unfairness, and related procedural errors. The majority opinion was authored by Supreme Court Associate Judge Reardon, with four others in the majority. Chief Judge Tauro, former U.S. Attorney, also dissented.

My comprehensive analysis revealed substantial prosecutorial misconduct and fundamental unfairness in the trial. We concluded that DeChristoforo's conviction for first-degree murder was neither legally justified nor fundamentally fair, as constitutionally required. Reflecting on the evidence and the contrasting plea deals, it became clear that DeChristoforo should only have been convicted of second-degree murder as an accomplice, thus rendering the first-degree conviction with no parole severely flawed. The case deeply troubled me, despite my non-liberal leanings at that time.

In stark contrast to Benjamin's harsh punishment, the two other charged defendants managed to broker deals for second-degree murder, which casts a pall of injustice over the legal proceedings and raises uncomfortable questions of equity. One of them, a mobster named Gagliardi (who also murdered the legendary "Boston Strangler," DeSalvo), was jointly tried with Benjamin. Gagliardi, a real mob hit man, pleaded guilty at the close of the government's case. Thus, the jury knew that Gagliardi had made a plea "deal", creating at least juror confusion and a probable inference that Benjamin was even more guilty than the actual shooter. Not fair. One minute Gagliardi is on trial in front of the jury for first-degree murder; the deal is made, and his participation is no longer being decided by the jury. When the defense began, the jury was instructed that Gagliardi had pleaded guilty! So the jury then knew that Gagliardi had agreed with the prosecution's evidence!

Benjamin was reportedly in the car seated behind the driver when Lanzi, seated in the front right seat, was murdered by either Gagliardi or another mobster who also entered into a similar second-degree murder plea deal. This issue was crucial on appeal, compounded by questionable statements from the prosecutor and the government's refusal to provide the defense with vital Grand Jury testimony that contradicted a cop's trial statements. What a surprise! Our justice system?

Furthermore, the government acknowledged that it was one of the other defendants who fired the gun that killed Lanzi...not DeChristoforo. However, since DeChristoforo refused a plea deal for second-degree murder as a witness or accomplice, the State of Massachusetts aimed to convict him as a "joint venturer" alongside the others. In other words, since he was present when the others killed Lanzi, he was deemed guilty of first-degree murder under a law that punishes association more than action, a conviction reflecting a grave miscarriage of justice.

The prosecutor, a state colleague of federal prosecutor Higgins in organized crime (and an alum of my college, but later... more dots, he worked with Kennedy lackey John Kerry, who ran against Bush in 2004), secured the conviction for first-degree murder, putting DeChristoforo in prison for life without hope... and he was not the shooter! Cogitate about that injustice. The actual shooter made a deal ratting out DeChristoforo, for which he was released in thirteen years. Upon conviction, Benjamin lost all hope for release from prison. He could have been executed. Fortunately, the jury recommended against the death penalty, but he was sentenced to life without parole.

I can still see Benjamin's face as the verdict was read...young, barely out of his teens, watching as his entire future collapsed before him. The shooter would walk free in thirteen years. I felt the weight of injustice as Benjamin faced eternity behind bars for simply being in the wrong car at the wrong time. He claimed that when he got in the car, he didn't know the others intended to kill Lanzi.

ENDING INJUSTICE

In an unexpected twist, my fellow law clerk Bill Weld, who had worked on the majority opinion for another judge affirming DeChristoforo's conviction before his one-year clerkship ended, played a significant role in Benjamin's future. Elected Governor in 1991, he reviewed all the facts and, in 1993, appropriately recommended parole for DeChristoforo, who had languished in prison for 25 years for merely being in the wrong place at the wrong time. DeChristoforo was saved from spending the rest of his life in prison for being in a mob car with a real mob hit man. Justice?

While working on the dissent, the judge's secretary, a very nice Italian woman named Connie who lived in the North End, informed me that she knew the DeChristoforo family; and that Ben, the son of Dante DeChristoforo, was really a "nice young kid" in the wrong place at the wrong time, and was not actually the shooter as the government had admitted.

Connie elaborated on the complexities surrounding the DeChristoforo family. "He was no angel," she murmured, cautious of the ears around us, "but he isn't what they make him out to be. He got caught up in something much larger than himself. But they're not sharing the whole story."

Her eyes darted around the empty office. "His father, Dante, now that's a different story. But Ben? He was just a kid trying to live up to his father's name. You know how it is in the North End."

I nodded, though I didn't really know. I was still too green, too sheltered in my Irish Catholic upbringing to fully comprehend the complex web of family, loyalty, and crime that defined life in Boston's Italian neighborhood.

The plea bargains of the other two occupants of the car raised serious issues about convicting Ben for first-degree murder under the law of "joint venture" while the other two, one the actual shooter, were entitled to parole within as little as ten years.

This is a big issue and a big weapon in a prosecutor's plea arsenal. My firsthand exposure to the justice system revealed a multitude of flaws, leading me to question the very pillars I had been raised to believe in. I worked hard on that dissent. Ultimately, my experiences with this case illustrated a troubling reality: it wasn't just about Benjamin, but a narrative echoing the vulnerabilities of justice itself. Each moment highlighted the biases woven into our legal framework, prodding us to seek fairness and integrity...the very principles essential for preserving hope. The prosecution's concealment of exculpatory evidence also served as a bitter reminder that the quest for conviction often eclipses the true essence of justice, prompting one to ponder the moral responsibilities we owe to one another in our judicial institution.

Following the extension of my clerkship after September 1971, I focused on the dissenting opinion in the DeChristoforo case while also drafting the "small loans" opinion, the longest published Supreme Judicial Court decision in the history of Massachusetts. Several judges then summoned me to the main conference room to ask me what my judge's secretary had said regarding the DeChristoforo case. How did they have any information on this issue? I explained that she had simply said that she knew the DeChristoforo family from the North End where she lived, and that the defendant was a "nice kid," and she wondered about his conviction. I defended her. The matter was apparently dropped because I never heard anything more.

However, I did know the DeChristoforo case was a huge, controversial "political/judicial football" being bounced around between the FBI, the prosecutors, the judges, and the North End mobsters. The Boston newspaper readers and the local politicians deemed themselves the power brokers in Boston. Now they are called "local Deep Staters." This begs the question: was justice ever truly served in the DeChristoforo case when Bill Weld approved his release? My response: absolutely not, as demonstrated by the glaring disparity in sentencing—thirteen years for the real killers versus 25 for DeChristoforo, who was merely an accessory, more likely just a "witness." To quote the Beach Boys' song: "God only knows."

The dissenting opinions of my Judge and Judge Tauro shined a light on an undeniable truth: Ben was unjustly ensnared in a web of legal misjudgment rather than deserving of a first-degree murder conviction with no parole. Plain and simple, it was unjust, based on the deals made with the two others in the car (one of whom killed Lanzi), along with all of the other errors in the trial; and there were many errors.

The First Circuit Court of Appeals, on the next level of appeal, agreed with our dissent and overturned the conviction. But the prosecutors later appealed to the Supreme Court, which reinstated it. Later, in 1976, the Massachusetts Supreme Judicial Court again reaffirmed it. What a lesson. DeChristoforo's life being mucked about by a bunch of old men in black robes, some of whom were more guilty of assorted crimes of corruption than young Benjamin was by merely being present when Lanzi was killed.

Make no mistake. I am no bleeding-heart liberal. For me, so-called liberal politicians are worse than hypocrites. They use the liberal ideology to garner votes and fatten their bank accounts: the Clintons, Pelosi, Obama, Biden, and many other politicians. While I advocate for justice, it's clear that the system routinely fell short, devastating the lives it was meant to protect. DeChristoforo deserved punishment, yet justice failed in his case—driven by the relentless zeal of a prosecution unwilling to acknowledge the truth. In DeChristoforo's case their threat was glaring: "If you refuse to comply, we have the power to ruin your existence; 'life without parole' is our game. Deal or no deal?"

POLITICAL EXECUTIONS AND PROSECUTORIAL AMBITION

The pursuit of justice within our legal system often reveals troubling patterns where political ambition and prosecutorial power intersect. The case of Billy Ray Rector in Arkansas provides a sobering example of how criminal justice can become entangled with political calculations. During the 1992 presidential campaign, then-Governor Bill Clinton returned to Arkansas specifically to sign a death warrant for Rector, an individual with an IQ of approximately 80 who many legal experts considered incompetent to stand trial. As noted in *Life Without Parole: A Reconsideration* (p. 8), this decision came in the political context following Michael Dukakis's 1988 presidential campaign, where being perceived as "soft on crime" had proven politically damaging. The utterly corrupt Clintons (including Hillary) had no compunction about sending a poor, imbecilic black man, Billy Ray Rector, to the electric chair, along with seventy other convicted criminals.

The Rector and DeChristoforo cases raise profound questions about how political pressures influence life-and-death decisions within our justice system. When electoral considerations appear to outweigh concerns about a defendant's mental capacity in a case where life and death hang in the balance, we must examine the ethical foundations of our legal processes. The execution of someone potentially unable to comprehend their punishment challenges our collective understanding of justice and mercy. In such instances, money and power outweigh life, death, mercy, compassion, and most of all… justice.

Similar concerns about man's ability to achieve justice against his fellow man later arose in my litigator life in 1978, where the intersection of politics and prosecution in the notorious "Motorgate" cases involving a witness to another murder by another infamous hit man. The witness was in a situation somewhat similar to DeChristoforo, but he walked scot-free. The zeal of the prosecutor to use the witness to get his "target" in order to enhance his own reputation resulted in a bizarre litigation scenario, causing an equally convoluted result, but exposed the utter corruption of the prosecutor, none other than 2004 Democratic presidential candidate and consummate phony John Kerry. Déjà vu all over again. In the four Motorgate cases, my client and I played a role to achieve justice—notwithstanding Kerry's ambitious, manipulative, media-hounding fakery. (Chapter 11.)

In the 1978 high-profile, highly publicized "Motorgate" cases, the newly appointed prosecutor John Kerry, using his Massachusetts and Kennedy family connections to get a job with the Middlesex County District Attorney, took credit for the work of career prosecutors. In 2004—like everything he had done since his Vietnam falsehoods, Kerry took false credit in the Motorgate cases; he used the New York Times Magazine's brazen Democratic bias to falsely promote his "prosecution career" while running against Bush II. When interviewed, I told the author of the NYT Kerry puff piece that Kerry's claims in the Motorgate cases were baseless. He published them anyway. (Chapter 11.)

DNC Clinton bootlicker Kerry became infamous for his false Vietnam claims, which were exposed in Jerry Corsi's book *Unfit for Command*.

These cases represent a pattern where prosecutorial corruption, a perverse by-product of our justice system, can be compromised by external political pressures to gain money and power, and fulfill the personal ambitions of the prosecutor. Thus, in working on the DeChristoforo dissent, and then representing Dan Moore—right out of my personal litigation gate, I became exposed to the corrupt motives of those wielding prosecutorial power. Even as a novice law clerk, I observed patterns of deceit and corruption in the judicial process that would later become clearer through my dual experiences in litigation and meditation.

What initially seemed like isolated instances of injustice gradually revealed themselves as connected phenomena, which I've come to understand through the lens of quantum entanglement with an evolving legal and meditative consciousness: human ego knows no bounds, but divine Grace eliminates it over time.

Through years of practicing both law and meditation, I've observed how certain systemic patterns in our justice system directly cause unjust outcomes. The influence of powerful financial interests, what some might call the "money changers" in our institutions, frequently works against individual rights and equality of justice. Successfully challenging these entrenched powers requires persistent effort and a willingness to pursue difficult cases despite significant obstacles.

My experiences in litigation have shown that justice, while possible, frequently demands extraordinary commitment against powerful opposition. The meditation practice that parallels my legal work has provided insights into how these challenges connect at deeper levels than conventional legal analysis typically recognizes. In future chapters, I'll explore how consciousness development through meditation has informed my approach to complex jury litigation—offering a perspective that bridges the practical demands of legal advocacy with the expanded awareness that contemplative practice can provide.

Throughout my years navigating the treacherous waters of litigation, I found unexpected wisdom in the teachings of Paramahansa Yogananda. His spiritual insights, which I regularly discovered during the most challenging moments of my legal battles—spoke directly to the moral complexities and systemic corruption I witnessed firsthand in our justice system.

The profound nature of Yogananda's understanding became crystallized for me in one particular exchange that has troubled my mind ever since. Once, when a seeker approached the great spiritual teacher with the age-old question "Is there really a Hell?" Yogananda's response was startling in its brevity: "Where do you think you are?" he replied.

Those six words contained a universe of meaning for me. In that moment, I understood that hell was not some distant realm of future punishment, but embodied in the very corruption, injustice, and moral decay I encountered daily in courtrooms across America. The hell Yogananda spoke of includes, but obviously is not limited to, the systematic perversion of justice by moneyed interests, the betrayal of public trust by those sworn to uphold it, and the suffering inflicted on innocent people by a system that had lost its moral compass.

At this point in my life, I am convinced there are no coincidences, no accidents; and our consciousness ultimately reveals all to us—but I have also learned that "I am not the doer." Now, fifty years into the litigation PIT, I navigate this struggle for justice against a tidal wave of governmental and judicial corruption as a common individual. The pressing question remains: how many lives shall be sacrificed before we recognize that our justice system is failing both innocent individuals like DeChristoforo and, by extension, society itself, as the moneyed elites control the politicians who appoint the judges, and appoint the heads of our federal agencies.

The crimes and lusts for money and power of the politicians, especially since the 1960s, have fueled utter judicial corruption, including appointed judges all the way to the Supreme Court. The jury is now out on President Trump. But if one can be judged by his "enemies," Trump is at war with America's Secret Government, the Deep State. "They" put a bullet through his ear, missing his brain by mere inches. They then used the legacy media to try to defeat his presidency, and used Jack Smith's corrupt justice department to convict him in a wave of phony "lawfare" prosecutions to destroy him.

As the narrative in these books unfolds, the revelations about Secret Government evil emerges in the form of the FBI's dirty secrets which are critical threads in my larger story of injustice. (*Litigator 4*.)

While in law school back in 1968, for a few days I attended the trial of six mobsters for the murder of Teddy Deegan—also a mobster. The evidence, if you can believe it, was based mostly on the testimony of Joseph "The Animal" Barboza, the notorious hitman from the Patriarca crime family. The result was a first-degree murder conviction. Three were originally sentenced to the electric chair, but fortunately for them the death penalty was abolished in Massachusetts before they were executed. They bore no responsibility for the murder of the other mobster, Teddy Deegan. The FBI and the money changers pulling the strings framed the six mobsters for a murder they did not commit—manipulating them into becoming scapegoats in a treacherous scheme.

With the perspective that only time and higher consciousness can provide, I now understand how our justice system truly operates. The "Force Fields" of higher consciousness have revealed to me the deep irony of my own position during those days when I clerked for the Massachusetts Supreme

Judicial Court. I was both innocent of the deeper corruption around me and ignorant of the very mechanisms I was helping to perpetuate.

Bill Weld was a fellow law clerk and also a "Yankee Brahmin," a member of the historically powerful, wealthy, Protestant, old-money elite of Boston and New England like his judge. Bill is married to Teddy Roosevelt's granddaughter and was also a *summa cum laude* graduate of Harvard as an undergrad. Bill was a law clerk to one of the judges in the majority who ultimately affirmed the conviction of DeChristoforo. Bill and I had lunch and drinks regularly, and I got the distinct impression he thought it was an unjust judgment; he must have realized at the time that DeChristoforo should only have been convicted of being an accessory. This was borne out later in 1991 when he became Governor of Massachusetts. One of his first acts was to commute Benjamin's sentence.

Of the six convicted, four of them still in prison, sought parole circa 1980–86: Tameleo, Limone, Greco, and Salvati. It was denied. Tameleo and Greco died in prison years later; Limone and Salvati were later exonerated. Robert Mueller, later FBI Director and special prosecutor against President Trump, a Bush political pawn, played a pivotal role in the parole hearings, effectively concealing critical FBI documents that revealed systemic corruption.

Between 1981 and 2000, Mueller systematically covered up crucial FBI records from the 1980 parole hearings. These documents conclusively proved that during the 1968 trial, the FBI knowingly allowed "the Animal" Barboza to commit perjury by manufacturing testimony to secure the convictions in Deegan's murder trial while suppressing evidence that would have exonerated the defendants. Through my journey, I have come to understand just how intricate the controls of our justice system are, revealing a compelling dynamic between those in power and moral accountability. It underscores that this narrative is not merely about one case, it is a powerful reminder that vigilant oversight is vital to safeguarding justice.

My judge as a law clerk, Paul Kirk, a bona fide jurist of integrity and compassion, resigned amid the political/judicial power brokering surrounding Benjamin DeChristoforo's case, and over another matter where we successfully fought to reduce the sentence of a poor, alcoholic army veteran who had been overcharged in the death of his son.

Did federal prosecutor George V. Higgins know that the Massachusetts Attorney General prosecution of the above mobsters was a frame-up? I don't know. Before working for the fed, he worked as a Massachusetts deputy assistant attorney general between 1967 and 1969, when the Deegan murder case was being prosecuted. I ask myself how could he not have known?

He worked directly with the crooked FBI agents. Just like I ask how could Bush senior not have known who assassinated Kennedy?

Had Mueller produced the FBI records as required during the parole hearings in 1980, the four defendants would have been freed during Mueller's watch. The consequences were devastating: two defendants died in prison, Limone endured twenty-one additional years of incarceration, and Salvati's sentence was only commuted in 1997 after the Boston Globe initiated its investigation and exposed the manifest corruption involved in their prosecution.

Without knowing it, my early experiences as a young law clerk established a "morphic pattern" as Dr. Rupert Sheldrake would describe it, within my experiences in jury trials, exposure to judicial corruption, and meditative insights into our justice system. Sheldrake's theory is "that all natural systems, from crystals to societies, inherit a collective memory from past similar systems through invisible morphic fields making future occurrences of patterns and behaviors easier." As I explain in this Litigator series, many of my experiences in later cases involved "morphic resonances" from past cases, which in fact did make my cases, particularly jury trials, "easier;" and more importantly the morphic resonance from my cases over time gave me greater insight into the inherent flaws in our justice system, primarily resulting from judges who ignore the law to attain their own personal agendas—generally involving money. Additionally, many of these "morphic resonance" experiences have led me to conclude that many of my litigation and meditation experiences manifest the confirmation in quantum physics of the reality of "quantum entanglement" as recounted in later chapters on specific cases. This is a vast topic which I develop throughout the Litigator series, as explained in Chapter 9. Stay tuned.

My later discoveries of grotesque DOJ/FBI and judicial misconduct (*Litigator 4*) were not random coincidences but manifestations of this morphic resonance where the original pattern of corruption that I encountered early in my career exposed later related instances of systemic deception in the judicial system, ultimately culminating in a billion-dollar "heist" perpetrated against my client when our opponents bribed a judge and governor in a completely corrupt bankruptcy case. Through meditation, my evolving consciousness has become increasingly attuned to this morphic field phenomenon, allowing me to perceive connections that exist beyond the linear cause-and-effect relationships that traditional legal analysis recognizes. These truths experienced in specific cases also involved specific instances of "quantum-entangled" experiences which cannot be explained within a normal/sensory/rational framework. Stay with me as we progress into these real-life realities.

These experiences have woven themselves into larger patterns of understanding about justice and its fragility when powerful institutions abandon their ethical obligations. The "morphic field" itself seems to carry the memory of each betrayal, each compromise, each moment when justice was subverted—creating a resonant pattern of connected dots that continue to reveal a deeper awareness of how corruption perpetuates itself across time.

Fourteen years after Mueller covered up the truth in the 1980 parole hearings, House Committee Report 108-414 (Feb. 3, 2004) exposed it:

"Beginning in the mid-1960s, the Federal Bureau of Investigation (FBI or 'Bureau') began a course of conduct in New England that must be considered one of the greatest failures in the history of federal law enforcement. This Committee report focuses on only a small segment of what happened. It discusses primarily the 1965 murder of Edward 'Teddy' Deegan, the subsequent prosecution of six defendants for that murder, and the actions of federal law enforcement officials to protect cooperating witness Joseph 'The Animal' Barboza and government informants Jimmy 'The Bear' Flemmi and Stephen 'The Rifleman' Flemmi.

In order to understand the FBI's misuse of informants in New England, it is essential to examine the Deegan murder prosecution. The story of this trial and subsequent events provides a foundation to assess what happened during the 1970s, 1980s, and 1990s, when Stephen Flemmi and James 'Whitey' Bulger allegedly murdered at least 19 individuals while serving as government informants. It is now clear that FBI Special Agent John Connolly developed an improper relationship with Whitey Bulger and others who served as government informants. Connolly now stands convicted of obstruction of justice for his role in helping Whitey Bulger escape by tipping him off to his impending indictment. Stephen Flemmi, as part of his plea agreement, has also implicated Connolly in providing information that resulted in the murder of others.

The results of the Committee's investigation make clear that the FBI must *improve management* of its informant programs to ensure that agents are not corrupted. The Committee will examine the current FBI's management, security, and discipline to prevent similar events in the future."

The italics supplied on the words "improve management" is intended to expose FBI hypocrisy. These House Committee members also concealed the truth on the scope of that corruption with their nonsense about "improve management." The committee members, made up of lawyers and former prosecutors, all knew that the FBI corruption is systemic.

The foregoing House Committee recital on the Deegan murder, my fellow Americans, is merely representative of the scope of DOJ and FBI corruption under Clinton, Obama, and Biden. (*Litigator 4.*)

CHAPTER 3

The Ferrari, the Blonde, and the Mob: A Young Lawyer's Education

"Truth is the soul's power of knowing God."
Paramahansa Yogananda

"It doesn't require many words to speak the truth."
Chief Joseph

"The truth is rarely pure and never simple."
Oscar Wilde

On the level of human truth and justice, after 81 years on this planet, and retrospectively examining my 55 years in the PIT of litigation, I submit that Yogananda's above quote nails down what truth really is. Chief Joseph's quote insightfully describes truth in human communication. Oscar Wilde's quote defines his state of consciousness within the bewildering miasma of the highly intellectual but undisciplined human mind.

Yogananda led a divine life. Chief Joseph led a loving, albeit suffering life for his tribe, the Nez Perce, the victims of horrific injustices. Wilde led a troubled life reflecting a high level of intellectual achievement and confused moral consciousness.

I preface this chapter to give you, dear reader, an insight into how to use your individual consciousness. Your verdict on the evidence in this chapter, without the collective consciousness of a jury of your peers, may awaken you to yourself.

With a striking blond woman in the passenger seat of a red Ferrari, Richard Sequeira drove out of the West Newton Chrysler Plymouth dealership on February 12, 1972. The roar of its engine was the last that was heard of Richard, and the good-looking blonde. No one watching the successful car dealer drive away could have imagined that this mundane Saturday morning would be the last time anyone would see either of them alive. He left behind questions and a mystery that has still not been solved to this day.

In the world of litigation, we often speak of evidence, facts, and legal standards. But sometimes a case emerges that challenges our understanding of justice itself; a case that dwells in what I've come to call "the PIT" of human justice, where certainty gives way to inference, and truth becomes a matter of perspective rather than absolute fact.

Before we get into the details of this case, I have a potential paradox for you dear reader, on what is justice—which you may resolve when you render your own verdict on this case. But be warned: don't let your inner projections and biases jump to unwarranted conclusions as you read through the evidence in this chapter. This case is yet a mystery to me, even after five decades. All is not as it may appear, and some of the facts reported in this chapter which never made it into evidence at the trial of this case, are subject to multiple interpretations and conclusions.

If you're quick to judgment on what really happened to Richard Sequeira, and who was really responsible for his disappearance, be warned: such an approach in this case might only reveal the tendencies, biases, and projections of your own mind, as well as your own level of consciousness. That realization is what happened to me, the fledgling litigator, with an extremely Irish Catholic, unsophisticated background—inexperienced in the ways of the world, and particularly of the 'Underworld'.

There was considerable publicity accompanying the Dan Moore v. George Higgins case. Jay and I formed a law partnership with an office in Wakefield, and the cases streamed in. Many of them involved a host of relatively minor criminal and civil jury and non-jury cases.

Despite our big bank case, I was very aware that I was still cutting my teeth. I began to get some jury experience in relatively minor, and some larger, cases. One case never got out of my office... for good reason. It involved, what shall we call him, how about "Pure Evil," 'PE' for short! His story, also on the front page of the Boston Globe, was that he owned a large 'ranch' in southern New Hampshire where the Feds had found several bodies. They were going to charge him with multiple murders and being a major New England heroin dealer. He had $200,000 in cash in a suitcase for a retainer when he walked into my office. He had read about Dan's case. We needed the money. We each had growing families. Dan had not paid the two 'amateurs' the going rates for top criminal lawyers. That was OK. We were neither experienced, nor possessed the experiential trial skills of the good criminal lawyers, but somehow Jay and I working together won a very difficult case. Grace.

After conferring with 'PE' for over an hour, I walked over to Jay's office, leaving 'PE' with his suitcase, and told Jay that if he wanted to see the essence of Pure Evil, come to my office. I told Jay we have little kids, and this monster is selling heroin to children. I'm out! I was never an 'everyone deserves a fair trial' lawyer. I refused representation with many subsequent clients, some famous, including Michael Jackson and others, even though it was long after I had abandoned Roman Catholicism. My decision came from a fundamental sense of justice, fairness, and decency.

I went back into my office and told 'PE' I was not the lawyer for him. I thought 'PE' was going to take out a gun and shoot me on the spot—he was apparently unable to handle rejection; likely a childhood issue. His eyes narrowed to slits, his face flushed crimson, and his hand twitched toward his jacket. He left my office almost ripping the doors off. Jay wondered why we didn't take some of his money, at least through arraignment to get more publicity and laugh all the way to the bank! I told him I refused to represent divorce clients, mobsters, drug dealers, or child molesters. And I never have. My emotional sensibilities and legal instincts, mixed with some higher-consciousness principles, dictated that thinking.

I believed that success would come not from shortcuts, but more from a sense of what I call "barnyard equity": hard work to get as close as possible to the 'truth'. From early in my career I possessed a strong, perhaps naïve perspective that my job as a litigator was to take cases which demanded justice.

Perhaps that explains the peculiar circumstances in which "Patty" (name changed) came to my office regarding the disappearance of her husband, Richard Sequeira. It was following Dan's case and in the midst of many smaller cases, both civil and criminal, that a lawyer friend of Patty's referred her to me. The lawyer-friend was a well-known, and very experienced criminal lawyer who had followed the Dan Moore case. He was extremely congratulatory and surprised by the result in that case, and seemed to have a deeper understanding of why the DOJ and Higgins entered into the plea bargain that resolved Dan's case… capiche?

Being a criminal lawyer, he knew how the Boston mobs operated, who the real bosses were, and he had a strong sense that Richard's disappearance was mob-related with underworld undertones and overtones… Oh no, more mobsters on my plate! Thus, unwittingly, I was thrown back into the 'wise guy' environment underlying this very strange case involving the disappearance of a well-known Boston car dealer. But, thank God, in representing the apparent widow of a successful, 'disappeared' car dealer, I was still on the periphery of any real knowledge, association, or connections to any mobsters.

Remember, Dan was a banker, not a mobster. He got 'pigeoned' by them. The money changers controlling the DOJ and FBI in Boston during Dan's case, along with major media like the Boston Globe, generally exercised powerful influence over Boston politics in the 1960s and 1970s as the gangland murders proliferated. Liberal corruption and decay are currently destroying Massachusetts, a once-great bastion of freedom where the American Revolution started. Morphic resonance theory applies to Boston in the most negative meaning possible. As political corruption expanded in Boston politics, the economic and moral integrity of the state has dissolved, making political and judicial corruption "easier." Read Howie Carr at the Boston Herald, and Breitbart. Massachusetts has become a political and societal swampland of liberal corruption, decay, and governmental tomfoolery.

In the 1970s as I began trying cases, young and naïve lawyers like Jay and I, along with the Boston citizenry, routinely read in the Herald and Globe the rapidly expanding 'body count' of gangland murders on which prosecutors like Higgins profited in varying ways and means. The DeChristoforo case is a good example of how the son of a mobster gets burned by the system, as the mobsters calling the shots at the top of the money chain evade prison while socializing with the politicians who controlled the state who appointed the judges.

An ounce of common sense should tell anyone that the top money changers—who were in cahoots with the top federal officials in Boston, could have stopped the 100-plus ongoing gangland murders. My judge, Spiegel, tried to inject applicable law, common sense, and decency in that case, but nope; it didn't happen. Putting a 19-year-old in prison for life with no hope of parole, who was in the wrong place at the wrong time and didn't want to rat out the mob, was not the answer. The answer was not making plea deals negotiated by the "Capos" who paid off the politicians. But that is too vast a topic for this book. Suggest reading Howie Carr as a primer, and *Litigator 4*.

On February 12, 1972, rich and successful Richard Sequeira, proud owner of a Chrysler Plymouth car dealership in West Newton, Massachusetts, disappeared. He was married to Patty with three kids. He walked out of his office and hopped into his red Ferrari accompanied by a young, very attractive blond. The blond, as we later found out, was apparently the girlfriend of a well-known North End mobster. Here we are dealing with mobsters again. Neither Richard nor the woman has ever been seen again. Just as I felt compassion and sorrow for the Moore family, particularly for his son, who was shattered by the publicity and indictment of his dad, I felt the same for Patty and her three kids.

Richard and Patty lived in a beautiful home in upscale Winchester, Mass., with their kids; the oldest was 10. Over time, as his success increased, Richard came home less and less. After his disappearance, Patty hired a well-known, high-profile lawyer called Francis Bellotti, who was subsequently Massachusetts Attorney General (1975–1987). "John," the minority shareholder of the car dealership, had seized control of the dealership and refused to pay any money to Patty to maintain her family. Bellotti brought an Absentee Petition in the Middlesex Probate Court to have Patty named as Administrator of Richard's Absentee Estate, including control over the car dealership. "John" did not hire a lawyer; he hired an access point. His chosen counsel was a well-known Boston attorney whose most valuable asset was not his legal acumen, but his personal friendship with the judge presiding over the case in Middlesex Probate Court.

This is a practice I have seen metastasize within the legal profession over the past fifty years—proving Sheldrake's "morphic resonance" theory. The hiring of counsel "connected" to the judge is a form of influence-peddling corruption of the system. It is a subtle but corrosive tactic that replaces the principle of a fair hearing with an impartial judge supplanted by the quiet leverage of personal connection. Because this ethical rot has now reached startling proportions, I have made it a central theme in my work to drag this metastasizing cancer from the shadows and into the light, particularly in *Litigator 3* and *4*.

Francis Bellotti, who represented Patty in the initial probate petition, was no lightweight. As the former Lieutenant Governor of Massachusetts, he had substantial political connections, particularly within Boston's Italian community. But even Bellotti's influence couldn't overcome the direct connection that "John's" lawyer had to the Middlesex Probate Court judge. They were both of the same ethnic background, not Italian. Bellotti lost the petition. When the case was referred to me by a lawyer friend of Patty, I was still green enough to be shocked by this. The lawyer who referred Patty to me understood exactly why Bellotti had lost… he knew how the system really worked. I was only beginning to learn that in the corridors of power, justice was often less about the law and more about who knew whom. It was a lesson that would be reinforced again and again throughout my career, but in 1972–74, I was still naïve enough to believe that the law, facts, and the better argument should win.

Although Bellotti informed me of the probate court issues and facts, and transferred his Sequeira file to me as new counsel coming into the case, I'm not sure even he understood the level of corruption in the Middlesex Probate Court. I was yet to learn the full extent of how the money changers operated in the judicial system. I was still a fledgling litigator with a strong sense of justice, but little understanding of how the system really worked.

Patty was a very attractive, intelligent woman with three young kids, who had been left high and dry by her husband's disappearance. She was desperate for financial support for herself and her children and she had no income. Richard had been the 75% majority shareholder of the car dealership which was worth millions, and "John" had seized control of the car dealership. So, without any financial support for herself and her children, Patty was desperate.

She told me that she suspected that Richard had been having an affair with a young blond woman, who, as we later were informed, was "connected" to a Boston mob...which mob, the "Winter Hill Gang" (Whitey Bulger), the Charlestown mob, or the North End mob, aka the Patriarca Crime Family, was unclear and never resolved. In the 1960s and 70s in Boston, gangland murders and disappearances were too common to beg notice, yet alone to resolve. In addition to the Higgins' books *The Friends of Eddie Coyle* and *The Digger's Game*, I recommend Howie Carr's two books: *Hitman: The Untold Story of Johnny Martorano* and *The Brothers Bulger: How They Terrorized and Corrupted Boston for a Quarter Century.*

In the Boston mob scene, mob "connections" were an amorphous, undefinable, and impossible thing to determine. Patty said that Richard had been acting strangely in the weeks before his disappearance, rarely coming home, and he seemed distracted and worried. She also told me that over the previous seven years, years before the two-year statutory period for insurance companies to challenge a policy, Richard had routinely purchased several large life insurance policies, naming her as the beneficiary.

After his disappearance, the insurance companies had refused to pay on the policies, claiming that Richard was merely missing, not dead. They required a death certificate or a court declaration of death—neither of which Patty had been able to obtain. The probate court had rejected her petition to be named administrator of Richard's "Absentee Estate," effectively leaving her without access to any of Richard's assets.

I decided to take a different approach. Instead of trying to have Patty named as administrator of Richard's estate, Jay and I filed a civil action in the Superior Court against the insurance companies, seeking a declaration that Richard was dead, and that Patty was entitled to the proceeds of his life insurance policies and his share of the car dealership. This would bypass the corrupted probate court and put the matter before a jury. By what I would now consider an act of fate or divine justice, now knowing how corrupted the case assignments in Boston Superior Courts can be, the case was assigned "on the wheel," meaning without the notoriously corrupting influence of clerks, to Judge Ruth Abrams, a brilliant jurist of impeccable integrity. She allowed the case to proceed to trial, despite the insurance companies' motions to dismiss.

There was no corpse. No evidence of felonious assault. No evidence of murder, or even a murderer. No death certificate either; the normal means of litigating post-death legal matters. No Richard, but lots of 'circumstantial evidence'. The trial therefore was a complex affair. Jay and I presented evidence that Richard's red Ferrari had been found abandoned with no sign of Richard or the blond woman. Patty testified that Richard would never have abandoned his family, especially his children, whom he loved dearly. In discovery, Jay and I learned that Richard had left behind $200,000 in American Express Travelers checks in his office safe, which he surely would have taken if he had planned to disappear voluntarily.

We also discovered more evidence through documents found in Richard's office suggesting that his business relationship with "John"—who owned 25% of the dealership, had become volatile and estranged. In their depositions, when John and several employees of the car dealership "took the 5th"...that is, invoked their 5th Amendment rights against self-incrimination, we got more clues just from their body language, the "feelings" they exuded.

I aggressively asked these folks a wide range of questions involving the car dealership, its goings-on, their knowledge of anyone who would kill Richard, who and what had been Richard's interactions with them and others in the period before his disappearance, and whether they knew of any individuals who frequented the dealership and hung around with Richard. Their wholesale invocation of 5th Amendment protection on every question also convinced us that Richard had been 'offed', and that John and one of his associates knew how and why. Their depositions standing alone, with no spoken facts or testimony, created an undefinable but powerful atmosphere suggesting murder. Strange how "feeling," by itself, perhaps because of the questions I asked and their "taking the 5th", resulted in some form of "morphic resonance," perhaps based on their prior conduct and interactions with Richard, and/or some things known only to them?

Their depositions established a probable certainty that Richard did not just take off. Their refusal to answer any question suggested their "quantum entangled" connection to Richard's disappearance, if not murder. Stay tuned on the nature and effects of quantum entanglement in later cases.

If they knew or suspected that Richard had taken off with his girlfriend, not an uncommon occurrence, why not just say it? After their depositions, Jay and I became all the more convinced of his murder. What did they have to hide? Taking the 5th created powerful inferences in a civil case—unlike a criminal case where no inferences can be drawn.

Why was there $200K in AMEX checks in the safe? Had cash been turned into those checks? Why? How? The bank statements indicated a purchase of the checks from one or more bank accounts, but not all? If Richard's plan had been to take off with those checks, why didn't he take them **IF** in fact he had run off with his blonde? Or did he just use the checks as a form of cash reserve for cash transactions outside IRS reporting requirements? Certainly, if he had been evading taxes, he would have taken the checks.

The employees' complete invocation of their constitutional rights on questions involving the AMEX checks, the cash that likely bought some of them in dealership transactions that they may have known about, the girlfriend, and even Richard's connections all seemed to be subjects that did not justify self-incrimination protection. Although there was no evidence proving homicide, it became increasingly likely that Richard had been killed for reasons unknown to us but known to them.

Maybe a 'North End' mobster didn't like his girlfriend cheating with Richard? Those kinds of jealous passions run deep. But so do those fueled by money, together with a myriad of other human motives and experiences.

After about six months of intense litigation while we had sued and were litigating against the Prudential Insurance Company, defended by the powerful Boston Brahmin law firm Hale and Dorr, with its powerful connections to many Harvard-connected judges—Jay and I decided to publicize a reward in the Boston Globe:

"Fifty Thousand Dollars for information concerning the death or disappearance of Richard Sequeira."

On May 27, 1974 'Mo' (last name excluded – it ends in a vowel, a 'soldier' in the North End Gang), then sitting in the Plymouth County jail awaiting trial for attempted murder, responded to our newspaper ad. He called our office one day and in a sinister voice he left the following grim message: "Put the $50K in my lawyer's client account and I will have Richard's teeth deposited on the steps of the Framingham police station." Progress at last.

The next day, I visited "Mo." He seemed to know how and why Richard had disappeared saying that Richard had crossed several ranking members of the 'outfit'. We agreed to deposit the money. The same day, we immediately contacted the head of the organized crime unit of the Massachusetts Attorney General's office (he was also a friend of George V. Higgins), who was working with the FBI, and informed them of our visit with Mo. We had been informing the organized crime unit of everything we discovered throughout our investigation into Richard's disappearance. They were of no help… an issue to this day, now knowing how the system works, suggested some complicity with some mobsters?

The very next day, May 28, 1974, Mo was found stabbed to death in his prison cell. Needless to say, we never deposited the reward money.

After speaking with Patty, consulting her former lawyer Frank Bellotti, sharing information with the organized crime unit, taking employee depositions, and confronting the shocking murder of Mo in his prison cell (how does that even happen?), I told Patty the investigation was over.

Whoever killed Richard are likely the ones that silenced Mo, and clearly they will do whatever they can to stop us from digging deeper. With 'that' in mind, it could get ugly, and would definitely be a protracted investigation, perhaps dangerous. I told Patty we would have to try the case with what we had.

There were three people, and three governmental agencies knowledgeable about our visit with Mo: me, my investigator, Patty and the organized crime units in the Suffolk County DA's office, the Mass AG's office, and the FBI. Importantly, none of those agencies ever did anything to resolve Siqueira's murder. Hmmmm. I infer that the organized crime units in the Suffolk County DA's office, and/or the Mass AG's office, and/or the FBI probably knew who murdered both Richard and Mo. But they were of no help. In retrospect, their failure to do anything to solve the Sequeira murder, convinces me that the local money changers were in control of the 'justice system' in Boston.

To this day, I'm not absolutely sure if Mo was killed because he responded to the reward, but because of the timing it seems highly likely… however, is it just inference? Remember that word. The 'dots' are most often inscrutable, and generally a mystery to our very limited human consciousness.

Trial Strategy: Inference, Evidence, and the Paradox of Proof

Jay and I went to trial in the fall of 1974. The trial lasted about 6 weeks. After a preliminary hearing with the judge, during voir dire, (a preliminary examination of a witness or a juror by a judge or counsel) she allowed 'John' and several of the employees to testify in front of the jury; but only with specific, very limited questions which she had allowed in voir dire. They all asserted their 5th Amendment right against self-incrimination in front of the jury on limited questions related to any knowledge of what had happened to Richard.

When a witness pleads 'the Fifth,' by definition, there are no hard evidentiary facts to be gleaned from a response. The plea is normally made in criminal cases, like Dan's case, where no inference whatsoever can be drawn against a criminal defendant. In civil cases, the law prescribes that only an inference can be made by the jury from the fact or facts embodied in the question. Thus, the court conducts a hearing outside the jury to determine what very limited questions can even be asked in front of the jury.

This was a controversial legal issue, but it became clear in voir dire with the broader range of questions we were permitted to ask, and subsequently, the limited number of questions the judge ultimately allowed to be heard by the jury, that the judge did the right thing. Fifth Amendment invocation against self-incrimination in a civil case is generally limited to inferences to be made from a defendant's testimony in the case, not witnesses.

The judge put Jay and I on a very tight rope in our questions to the employees. If I recall correctly, (I don't have the transcript), the questions were extremely limited and generic like "do you have any knowledge of how and why Richard has disappeared?" Period. Nothing else. Nothing that would specifically implicate any of them. Nothing about death, murder, mobsters, specific problems in the dealership, who may have been involved in the disappearance, or why? No names. No specific facts. Just do you have any knowledge?

Talk about the broad scope of amorphous generalizations! But the way the mind works, why would any of them take the Fifth? Maybe they were in on issues unrelated to the disappearance, but other illegal conduct? Judges give jury instructions against speculation and conjecture. The issue for the jury was: given all of the circumstantial evidence, was it more likely than not that Richard was dead? You know how sometimes a level of reality hovers over a situation. Morphic Resonance? Quantum Entanglement? That is what happened during the six-week trial. It gradually seemed to be a 'reality' that Richard was dead, almost apart from the evidence?

Did the employee 5th invocation help? After the verdict, the judge allowed us to talk to the jurors. A few were willing to respond. The ones who were willing to talk said the issue was hotly debated, but ultimately not necessarily a factor in the verdict because of disagreement. But did it create its own reality on Richard's demise? I suspect so, but I don't know, and I knew the evidence like the back and front of my hand. Did my internal conviction of his death, my state of mind, sway the jury? Morphic resonance? Perhaps. I definitely had that conviction, particularly after my meeting with Mo.

The left-behind travelers' checks, the reward, and other circumstantial and inferential evidence was heard by the jury. But, if I recall correctly, there was no evidence about Mo's demise except that he answered the reward, with no results. But we still had no body, no death certificate, no evidence of murder or a murderer, or a felonious assault.

Dear reader / juror: This is how consciousness often works. Some call it intuition. Human thought is energy. When facts are correlated to create a logical inference, lawyers call it inferential or circumstantial evidence. If it quacks like a duck, leaves tracks like a duck, leaves duck s...t , but no one sees the duck, a juror may still conclude based on all the evidence, that it was a duck.

In our Patty case, even such inferential evidence was thin. There was, indeed, no Richard, and no evidence of what happened to him, but the evidence of his lifestyle, his money consciousness, his ambition, his control of his beloved and very successful car dealership was the 'duck' the jury could not ignore.

The legal battleground became not only whether Richard was dead or vamoosed, but how Richard died, in order to trigger the life insurance policies for an "accidental death," allowed by the policy provisions. The insurer's defense lawyers argued that it was black letter evidentiary law prohibiting the jury from drawing an "inference from an inference." The jury first had to draw an inference from circumstantial evidence that Richard was dead. Then, since there was no other evidence of how that happened, they had to draw an inference from that inference, that he was dead by 'accident'.

The defense vigorously argued that no inference from an inference could be made by the jury based on the judge's instructions.

My partner and I argued that the totality of the evidence created one inference: 'dead by homicide'. Since there was no evidence of an accident, and no evidence that he had taken off and informed someone of his intentions, or made any plans to do so, the sole inferential evidence was death by homicide.

That issue was a two-edged sword, for and against us. But it did leave homicide as the only explanation for his disappearance. This impacted the language in the insurance policies by drawing an inference from an inference, but not necessarily resolving whether he was dead.

The judge ruled that homicide is an 'accident' to the victim, and accordingly instructed the jury.

VICTORY AND ITS AFTERMATH: INSURANCE MONEY AND ESTATE CONTROL

The jury deliberated for about four days. Verdict: DEAD. Patty and the kids were entitled to her deceased husband's insurance money. Hale and Dorr and Prudential first filed motions to set aside the verdict and for a new trial, in addition to the usual mountain of paper coming from big law firms representing big money interests. They lost those.

About a week after the verdict, the Hale & Dorr defense lawyer called me and said: "We have located Richard in Spain with his girlfriend." I said, "Good, then we can solve everything; let's go and convince him to come back, pick up his $200,000 in AMEX checks, he can sell his dealership for a profit, they get a divorce, and he and his wife Patty split the proceeds." A few days later the defense lawyer called and said: "False alarm, it wasn't Richard." They then forfeited appeal and paid the insurance proceeds and costs of suit.

Judge Ruth Abrams was a woman of integrity, very smart, and deserved her later appointment to the Mass Supreme Judicial Court. She was the kind of judge every trial lawyer hopes for and too rarely finds: a true jurist. The defense buried her in paper, filing motion after motion to have the case dismissed. They were hoping for a "Directed Verdict," to stop the case dead in its tracks; this is where a judge can declare the case over before the jury even gets to deliberate. But she was unmoved. She had listened to the evidence, she had applied common sense, and she had faith in the jury system. She denied their motion. In a world where judicial decisions are too often influenced by the power and prestige of the law firms involved, she was an island of integrity. She could not be bought, she could not be intimidated, and she could not be connected. Because of her, the case went to the jury, and because of her, Patty and her children finally received justice and the insurance proceeds they deserved.

For whatever reason, Richard was dead, and his family deserved the insurance money. At the time, that verdict fed my litigator ego, and our one-third contingent fee supported our families. My best explanation for the verdict is that the jury reacted strongly to the atmosphere in the courtroom of the family losing its father, husband, and provider by some very sinister means through no fault of the family or wife. I think somehow, deep within those jurors, their love and compassion transmuted the evidence into a just decision. Truth has a way of prevailing.

We then went back to the Middlesex County Probate Court, the county where Patty lived, and filed an estate petition for a deceased person with the verdict and judgment, as there was still no death certificate. We asked for a different judge than the judge on the previous Absentee Petition and had a favorable result. As Administratrix of Richard's now "death estate," Patty took full control of the car dealership, all other assets in the marriage, and we recovered the proceeds of a separate life insurance policy.

It was a stunning victory, and Patty was overjoyed. The insurance companies were ordered to pay out the policies, totaling over $600,000, and "John" was forced out. Patty and her children were financially secure. Jay and I received a contingency fee. Her next husband took over the management of the car dealership. She was riding high. I didn't notice a lot of mourning, however. Clearly, Richard had been cheating. Maybe it was done in private? As in Dan's case, the oldest son was very upset. When I engaged with him later, I explained that his dad was gone, but had left support for his family. That should have been where we left matters, but life has many surprises. This time it took the unlikely shape of a former Israeli paratrooper.

THE WEDDING CEREMONY: MEETING UNCLE DANTE

Several months after the verdict, Patty called to invite my wife Laima and me to dinner. She wanted us to meet her new fiancé, Moti, he was a former Israeli paratrooper with a commanding presence and charismatic smile, about half her age. They announced their engagement and invited us to their wedding, which was scheduled for later that year. He was no laggard. Romance was moving quickly; perhaps too quickly, as events would later reveal. But at the time, at 30 years old and with an Irish Catholic background I had no hint about what the Israeli Mossad or 'defense' forces were all about.

On the wedding day, the love birds had arranged a magnificent reception hall adorned with elaborate floral arrangements and crystal chandeliers that cast prismatic light across the gathered guests. In walked Laima and I, we were a bit unnerved and certainly in the dark about this specific wedding situation. The celebration was drenched in money, with plenty of 'family'—it spoke of wealth and influence, with no expense spared. The room hummed with conversation in various accents, some distinctly from Boston's North End. Here we go again Michael, were you really that naïve? Yup. What do you expect from an Irish Catholic kid?

Shortly after our arrival, Patty approached us with a smile that didn't quite reach her eyes if you know what I mean. "Michael and Laima," she said, taking my arm with a gentle pressure that suggested importance, "come, I want you to meet my Uncle Dante."

It was a scene right out of *The Godfather*. In the center of the ornate reception room stood the largest table, circular and seated with about ten people and surrounded by several males with ominous demeanor and bulging suit jackets. The two men with an attitude scanned us with suspicion as we approached. They had the focused intensity of predators assessing potential threats.

Uncle Dante stood up as Patty introduced us, his movements deliberate and controlled. The two men with bulging jackets moved closer, flanking him like the bodyguards they clearly were. In a voice characteristic of Don Corleone, deep and gravelly with a thick Boston accent...'Uncle Dante' thanked me for my work helping his 'niece' get her 'inheritance' as he phrased it. His handshake was firm, his gaze unwavering as he added, "We could use lawyers like you, Mr. Flynn. My lawyers will contact you next week." The men beside him watched me with the calculating stare of those accustomed to violence, their silent message clear: 'one false move, and bang!' I was getting the picture fast!

As we walked away, my somewhat naïve provincial Irish Catholic mind had to reset to Litigator mode as I went over the details of what I had just witnessed. My mind rapidly latched onto details. Patty had never mentioned an Uncle Dante before—why not? The dancing started so I chose this moment of distraction to quietly pull her aside.

Now reader, be fair to me. *The Godfather* movie had just come out. Not sure when I first saw it? I don't think it was until years later. I was only 30 years old with limited experience from a middle-class small town steeped in the Irish Catholic religion of my youth. My experience with the 'underworld' was limited to what I'd gleaned from Dan Moore's case and my brief meeting with Mo in prison. My understanding of how organized crime operated at that time was theoretical at best, so how was I to know what 'they' looked like or how 'they' operated? I had only met Mo in prison garb for about an hour; and yes, I did get a little flavor of 'outfit speak' and how they operated from Dan's case with Higgins, but I was still a naïve, young lawyer… honest!

More importantly, I had very limited consciousness to understand how the underworld operated. I simply did not know how to connect those kinds of dots at that time. Yes, I had represented Dan Moore and witnessed employees taking the Fifth Amendment. I had built our case around Richard's flat-out disappearance, arguing successfully to the jury that his profound attachment to money meant he would never have abandoned his successful dealership. The Fifth Amendment invocations had strengthened our position. But throughout Patty's testimony, she had never mentioned her family connections or relatives, and I possessed no definitive knowledge about what had actually happened to her husband. I was a young jury lawyer trying to convince a jury that Richard was dead, having left a widow and kids. My naivety was complete.

During Patty's wedding reception, the wheels in my mind started spinning like a race car at 150 mph. Patty had never mentioned "Uncle Dante" before. Michael: Are you stupid? Could he be... is it possible…? Remember what you learned in Dan's case? Remember that dissenting opinion you wrote for a guy named Benjamin DeChristoforo? I knew his father was connected to the North End mob. Both of your judges said there was something unjust in his first-degree murder conviction and life sentence with no parole. Wasn't Benjamin's father a mobster too? What was the father's name? Remember the inquiry on the judge's secretary from the "North End" by the majority Judges? Yet sometimes we are blinded, sometimes by our ego, focus or limitations, sometimes in the search for a just outcome by the blindfolded lady of justice, perhaps?

"Patty," I said, keeping my voice low, "I need to ask you something about your Uncle Dante." She looked at me with those seemingly innocent eyes that had convinced a jury her husband was dead. "What about him?" "What's his last name?" I asked, trying to sound casual. "Oh, didn't I tell you, Michael, my uncle's last name is DeChristoforo. Everybody knows who he is."

The dots landed where they should in my brain—'they' did it. It was an astonishing moment. Yup, this was none other than the daddy of that young man, Benjamin DeChristoforo, but actually meeting "Uncle Dante" in person was an entirely different experience. I had never encountered him before, never had any direct exposure to this level of organized crime hierarchy and certainly never imagined I would meet him! The reality was far more intimidating than any legal brief could convey.

How was it that I worked on the dissenting opinion for my judge, for Uncle Dante's son Benjamin; and then by chance represented Patty, the widow, in an apparent mob murder… followed then by this chance meeting with Uncle Dante who was sitting at this happy gathering not thirty feet from where we stood… a North End 'capo' at Patty's wedding to an Israeli paratrooper? What are the chances? Morphic resonance to the max. The connections suddenly aligned like stars forming a constellation. I should have seen this all along.

My naïve little Irish Catholic self began to get the picture. Within a short time following the reception, I believe it was the Monday after the reception, I called Patty, thanked her for the introduction to "Uncle Dante," but asked her to intervene, call her uncle, and remove me from his list of potential lawyers. She agreed without hesitation. As I later learned from experience in the PIT, it was not unusual for the bad guys to use lawyers who appear to either have certain skills or are just plain naïve of the 'underworld'.

That moniker fits on every level of consciousness. Just think of President Kennedy's assassination. Most informed, mature citizens of America now know the assassination was not the act of a lone gunman, Oswald; it was the result of JFK's collision with a shadow government that operates beyond the law, using the underworld. The criminal underworld is not 'under' at all; it is intertwined with the highest levels of power. The modern money changers are not just financial predators; they are the architects of a system where political influence, intelligence operations, and criminal enterprise converge.

Allen Dulles, the CIA Director implicated in Kennedy's murder, was the quintessential example, a man who served both the state we know of, and the shadow state we are only just getting familiar with. After fifty years of battling these forces in the courtroom and observing them in meditation, I have come to a stark conclusion: trying to distinguish between a high-level politician and a mob boss is often a fool's errand. They are two heads of the same hydra.

The plot thickened; I certainly had suspicions after meeting Uncle Dante, but still had not put 2 and 2 together. Still haven't, actually, beyond inferences. Patty was a great and believable witness at trial. When I was just starting out in my career, I thought all women were like my mom. Honest. But I was growing up rapidly in the world of legal inferences and inferences upon inferences, and yet I was still a little short on worldly consciousness, regardless of what came out of an individual's mouth. Still, certainly my clients, like Patty, would tell the truth, wouldn't they? She would have told me if she in fact had known how her husband had been killed and that it was Uncle Dante who confirmed it?

When the case was hanging in the balance, and she needed money to support herself and her children, I was sure she would have said something. She was as mystified as me about what happened to Richard, and her jury testimony came across that way. She was the one who said he would never have left his children, his dealership and the $200K in American Express Travelers checks. Never. I'm sure she was right. It all fit! Make no mistake, to this day I believe Patty and the jury did the right thing, and justice was truly served. Barnyard equity. Quantum entanglement on some undefinable level?

The most likely inference from all that subsequently came to light was that "Uncle Dante" was merely a source of information on Richard's disappearance. Nothing more. However, more inferences.

The Sequeira case was a stunning victory. But the story doesn't end there. After Patty's wedding reception, and my meet and greet with "Uncle Dante," subsequent events shed more circumstantial light on the Sequeira case. Fast forward about 6 months. A frantic phone call from Patty. Her voice was high-pitched, trembling with panic. "Moti is gone." She was nearly hyperventilating. "Cleaned out about $400,000 from one of our accounts." I told Patty I never did divorce work but could give her a referral. She said the matter could get complicated, but didn't explain. I still remained within my own little naïve world wondering what her statements were about. Nor did Laima, generally very perspicacious, see the implications of this strange chain of events.

That changed. Fast forward about another month. In my office, my secretary said that Patty's husband was on the phone. "This is Moti. You have no idea what or who you are dealing with Michael. Can't believe that you are that naïve." His voice was cold, controlled, with an accent I couldn't quite place. "They showed up at my parents' home in Israel. Give me your client account information. The balance of the money will be wired to your account." Click. Huh?? When I called Patty to relay this bizarre conversation, there was little reaction, she seemed unsurprised, and said simply; "I don't know, Michael, but I'm glad he's returning my money". She didn't elaborate any further.

My case of the disappearance of Richard Sequeira had received some publicity. But even then, I wondered if it was a good thing? To this day, I don't know any more than what I have written here. You, the reader can draw all sorts of inferences. Also, before you decide and reach unwarranted conclusions, please know that at some point several years later the dealership closed, amidst accusations that it was selling stolen cars and parts. Huh? Does the mob sell stolen cars and parts; and get upset when they are not fully paid? Does that explain cash turned into traveler's checks? Was one of the employees 'shorted' by Richard? Was the mob shorted? See reader, there you go, again, don't jump to inferential conclusions. Got ya! The bottom line was that Richard was dead; and his family deserved his life insurance policies and car dealership. The jury verdict was correct.

Who had the motive, opportunity and means, ("MOM" in detective-speak), to disappear Richard? It's a bit like the Jeffrey Epstein 'suicide' conundrum, when it appears very likely there are lots of candidates to have 'offed' a 'nice guy' like Jeffrey. But there is no hard evidence, just inferences. Conspiracy theories? Not in Epstein's case. Focus on the Israeli Mossad… Now, 50 years after the Sequeira case, I have a much deeper understanding of how the 'system' works, and how the money changers operate. I understand how the dark forces have corrupted our government and our justice system.

I still don't know exactly what happened to Richard Sequeira. I still don't know if Patty knew more than she told me. I still don't know if "Uncle Dante" was involved in Richard's disappearance. I still don't know if the Israeli paratrooper was part of a larger scheme. I still don't know if the money that was wired to my client account came from the Israeli paratrooper, the mob, from the Israeli government, or from some other source.

What I do know is that the jury did the right thing. They declared Richard dead, and they awarded his estate to Patty and her children. They did justice, even if they didn't know the whole truth. And perhaps that's the best we can hope for in this imperfect world.

Epilogue
THE INVISIBLE COURTROOM

Over fifty years later I can finally see the arc of my own journey, how the cases I tried and the meditations I practiced were not separate lives, but a single curriculum. Every soul is enrolled in one. Mine came by way of the PIT: harsh lessons from the school of hard knocks, followed, when I was quiet enough to notice, by moments of unmistakable grace.

To explain how the threads in my story seem to touch across decades, I use a plain, litigator's definition of what I call "Quantum Entanglement" (explored more fully in Chapter 9). It is an invisible interconnectedness within an unseen field, across time and space, in which the thoughts and thought-energies of one person can instantly affect the thoughts and thought-energies of another. Physicists observe something like this in particles separated by distance...a process so strange that Einstein called it "spooky." In life I've watched that same strangeness move through human hearts, courtrooms, and outcomes.

That is why the Sequeira case sits in my memory as more than a file number. The Moore case cracked the veneer of American justice. Sequeira shattered it. It was my first personal brush with the underworld, my first glimpse that there were no clean lines between law and lawlessness—between the courtrooms of Boston and the back alleys of the North End. Jay and I had won. Patty received the insurance money. A man had dissappeared, with no body as evidence and yet a jury, through inference, declared him dead. On paper, it was a victory. In my spirit, it was unfinished. We had a verdict, but not the full truth, and I was beginning to learn that justice and truth are not always the same thing.

The strangest part is what I couldn't fully name at the time. I had written a dissenting opinion in the case of nineteen-year-old Benjamin DeChristoforo, who refused the DA's cooperation and plea bargain, perhaps because it might have gotten him killed by his own 'family business'. And then, in the Sequeira case, I encountered "Uncle Dante," a man who was not an uncle by blood, only by association, and whose presence carried its own gravity. I didn't even ask who he really was. My ego was too busy counting the spoils of trial success, until a few bulging suit jackets quietly corrected my illusions. Only later did I understand the deeper chill—the past is never truly past. Threads can cross your path long before you recognize what's on the loom.

In those years I had no framework for what I was sensing, only the Catholic faith of my upbringing and the crude certainties of the courtroom. Evidence, testimony, documents, forensic analysis—this is the language of law. It is a necessary language, but it is not the whole language of truth. All of it is filtered through the consciousness of the people receiving it; jurors, judges, lawyers, witnesses—each carrying their own fears, ambitions, blind spots, and moral standing. When that consciousness is low, particularly when those with power are corrupt, truth and justice become unattainable. Individual vice metastasizes into institutional rot. The system meant to protect becomes an instrument of control. I saw this firsthand...how sexual and financial immorality in judges and the politicians who appointed them could decimate a justice system from the inside out.

And yet, in the same season of darkness, life placed a counterweight in my arms. Laima was pregnant with Alison as the Sequeira case unfolded. Alison arrived shortly after the jury verdict, and her presence felt like a mercy I hadn't earned, the epitome of purity and innocence in a landscape of moral ambiguity. I could not explain it then. I only felt that the same invisible hand that brought her into our lives had also guided a jury to its conclusion. Two events, one a verdict in an unsolved death mystery, the other the birth of new consciousness...seemed synchronous, in a way that defied my training. I lived the paradox: fighting in the muck of greed and violence by day, then holding pure new life by night.

Over the ensuing decades, as I stayed disciplined in meditation while litigating case after case, I began to see how my own thoughts and patterns were not private. In trial work, consciousness is contagious. A lawyer's mental state can shape the temperature of a courtroom, the attention of jurors, the resistance of an opponent. In meditation I learned to watch thought as energy, felt in a field, not merely held in a skull. Kriya yoga taught me that energy in the spine ascending toward the brain and Christ Center can lift consciousness into a higher register, sometimes into a palpable force field of love. Litigation, meanwhile, often pulled me downward—into ego, combat, and the intoxication of winning. For five decades it was a tug-of-war. Mostly I rose, sometimes I failed. The struggle itself was the lesson.

Looking back now, the Sequeira case was an early teacher. It taught me that sometimes the absence of evidence is its own kind of evidence—and that truth can be a luxury the justice system cannot always afford. It taught me to distrust the ego that wants to believe it is the doer. It taught me that we are instruments in a larger plan, and that our task is not to control the orchestra but to become a better instrument, guided by God-given intuition and by laws deeper than statute.

I didn't yet have language for any of this at the time, I only sensed that the story defied simple cause and effect. Later cases would supply more clues. Meditation would supply a different kind of courtroom—one not made of brick and stone, but of silence, attention, and the Grace that arrives when we stop pretending we are in charge. Now I have a simpler name for what I once called "spooky."

CHAPTER 4

The Science of Being Fuels The Art of Litigation

> "Transcendental Meditation opens the awareness to the infinite reservoir of energy, creativity, and intelligence that lies deep within everyone.
>
> Consciousness, fully awake to itself, is the Light of God."
>
> "Meditation makes the man Divine and brings the Divine to the world of man."
>
> **-Maharishi Mahesh Yogi**

A LITIGATOR'S RESTLESS MIND

The nights after the Sequeira verdict were fretful. The courtroom victory that should have brought satisfaction instead left me restless, my mind racing with unanswered questions. At 3 AM I stood at my kitchen window staring into the darkness, ice-cold water in hand. The ice had long since melted; my reflection in the glass looked tired, bloodshot eyes staring back. The jury had delivered justice for Patty and her children, at least the kind our system could provide—but something deeper was stirring inside me. I felt a change coming.

The red digital clock on the microwave blinked 3:05 AM as I replayed the case for the hundredth time: Richard Sequeira's disappearance, the blonde woman, the Ferrari never found, the $200,000 in traveler's checks left behind, the shadowy figures from the North End. And now the not-too-cryptic congratulatory call from Patty's lawyer-friend: "The North End mob knew that Richard was dead."

How did they know? What else did they know that never made it into evidence? What was the real truth behind the case Jay and I had just won? Three days of victory celebrations, congratulatory calls, and new client inquiries had begun to mount, but nothing quieted the relentless churning in my mind. I had been trained to dissect, analyze, and question everything; the very mind that had become my greatest asset in the courtroom was turning into my greatest liability outside it.

"You need to find a way to turn it off," Laima had said earlier that night, concern etched across her face as she watched me pace the living room. She stood in the doorway in her nightgown, hair tousled from sleep, eyes soft with worry. "You won, Michael. It's over. Come back to bed." But it wasn't over, not in my head, and I didn't return to bed until much later.

The Sequeira case had joined Dan Moore's in a growing constellation of interconnected dots I couldn't stop trying to connect: the corruption I was beginning to detect in the system, the money changers pulling strings behind the scenes, the thin veneer of justice covering something much darker. Outside my house, Boston slept, unaware of the quantum entanglements binding its citizens to forces they could not see or understand, forces I was beginning to glimpse through the cracks in our justice system.

I was building a reputation as a litigator, but at what cost? The cases were consuming me. Each victory brought more clients, more responsibility, more unanswered questions. My young family needed me present, not just physically but mentally, yet I often stayed up while everyone else slept. I was going over the day's events, especially those at work, because they were what brought the bread in, right? That's how I rationalized it.

I would replay the case: the moment Patty broke down on the stand, describing how Richard would never have left his children; the jury's faces as they absorbed her pain; the subtle shift in the courtroom when the employees asserted their Fifth Amendment rights; the almost imperceptible nod from Judge Abrams when I objected to opposing counsel's badgering. In court the pieces had come together perfectly. Now they were fragmenting, rearranging into patterns I couldn't quite discern but desperately needed to see.

A soft sound from the hallway made me turn. My daughter Rebecca stood there in her pajamas, teddy bear clutched to her chest. "Daddy? Why are you awake?" I forced a smile. "Just thinking, sweetheart. Go back to bed." "You're always thinking." Her small voice held no accusation, only a child's simple observation that cut deeper than any cross-examination. "I know, honey. I know." After tucking her back in, I decided something had to change.

AS I LITIGATED, MY BROTHER, CLASSMATES, AND FRIENDS FOUGHT IN VIETNAM

After the Sequeira verdict, in the fall of 1974, Vietnam was coming to an inglorious end for America. Saigon would fall in April 1975. My brother, my classmates, and my friends all nobly served in Vietnam on behalf of our country while I stayed home in law school. I was not there. I honor them here. Some died or suffered terrible wounds—physical, mental, and emotional.

My brother George Flynn served in the Navy on board the destroyer U.S.S. Noa and voluntarily patrolled up Vietnam's perilous rivers, patrols made more infamous by John Kerry's false claims about his own river service (see *Unfit for Command* by Jerome Corsi). My law partner Jay Curley had served in an Army combat unit in the early years of the war. My later law partner, Bill Sheridan, served as a Marine pilot and weapons officer, flying an A-6 Intruder at the height of the conflict in 1968–69. My good friend and fellow football/basketball teammate, Steve O'Neill, served in a Marine infantry unit that arrived at the horrific Battle of Khe Sanh just after the battle ended.

Many classmates and friends went from Holy Cross ROTC straight into Vietnam. Between 1962 and 1966, our years at Holy Cross, the Army, Marines, Navy, and Air Force offered Reserve Officers Training Corps programs that paid for college education but generally mandated four years of active service afterward. When my classmates signed up, most were oblivious to the horrors that awaited in Vietnam.

I borrowed money for my tuition at Holy Cross as a "day student." My tuition did not include room and board because I lived at home and worked to help support our large family while caring for my partially disabled father after his tragic airplane accident and partial paralysis when I was in eighth grade. This turned out to be a disguised blessing. I had to work, so no ROTC for me.

God works in mysterious ways. My deep dive into meditation has informed me that I was not spared in many prior historical wars. (See Chapter 13.)

Fulfilling their ROTC obligations, many Holy Cross men fought in Vietnam on behalf of our country—regardless of our retrospective judgments on that terrible war. Our soldiers were treated horrifically upon their return: spit upon, feces hurled at them. Outrage! The feces-throwing protesters should have hurled their garbage and human waste at the corrupt politicians and money changers who caused the war and financially benefited from it. *War is a Racket*, said Smedley Butler, the "fighting Quaker" and most decorated Marine in U.S. history.

American betrayers like Jane Fonda, who jeopardized the lives of American airmen imprisoned in the "Hanoi Hilton," should have been indicted.

I was no draft dodger, but my draft had been deferred even though I was gung-ho to fly F-4's. Unlike past wars, (I believe in reincarnation; see Chapter 13), I was focused on making good use of my 'stay of execution' with my 2-S law school deferment. I did, however, take notice of Vietnam-related events around me, such as the "Boston Massacre" at City Hall Plaza, where thousands of war protesters were brutally arrested. I could hear the protests from my office, so I went down twelve stories inside the Suffolk Courthouse where I was clerking for the Supreme Judicial Court, only to see bruised, maimed, and beaten Vietnam War protesters. It looked like a battlezone.

As the war intensified, thousands of black and white kids were drafted to "go kill the yellow man," as the song goes. Martin Luther King Jr.'s civil rights movement, which also protested the Vietnam War, had grown exponentially. So he was "coincidentally" murdered in April 1968 by some "rogue lone gunman." A few months later, in June 1968, another rogue gunman acting alone assassinated presidential candidate Robert Kennedy. Both men were killed at the height of the war while speaking out against the so-called military-industrial complex. Hmmm, JFK was also assassinated by a lone gunman 'acting alone'. Oswald. Somehow the New York Times–led mega-media, dominated by Rockefeller and deep-state money, convinced America that JFK, MLK, and RFK were all "coincidentally" murdered by rogue gunmen acting alone while they "coincidentally" challenged the deep-state military-industrial complex. If you believe that, I have some nice swamp land advertised as "beachfront" to sell you. Recommend *Litigator 4* and a deep dive into our CIA.

Between 1968 and 1974, while I was completing law school and thereafter wrestling with my all-consuming court cases, a revolution was unfolding on the world stage—one I was too preoccupied to notice. The ancient practice of meditation was making its dramatic entrance into the Western psyche, not through a well-funded PR campaign, but through the seemingly accidental, electrifying influence of rock and roll and the drug scene.

Throughout the 1960s, rock and roll bands like the Beatles, the Beach Boys, the Rolling Stones, and others had dominated the psyches of America's youth. As the Vietnam War raged and expanded in 1968, the rock and roll generation transformed into war protesters, the "flower children" or "hippies", who wanted to "give peace a chance," "make love not war," "smoke dope," and who created drug-addled communes advocating that America's youth "turn on, tune in, and drop out."

My cousin, a sophomore in college in 1968, bought into it and ended up "disappeared" in San Francisco's Haight-Ashbury at the height of the CIA's MKULTRA program targeting war-protesting "dopers" as they were labelled. My subsequent legal efforts to help his devastated family find "Jimmy" were fruitless. This was my first experience dealing with the most powerful, sinister, diabolical federal agency: the Central Intelligence Agency. The protesting flower children of America had become a cultural pandemic protesting the war, making them targets of MKULTRA.

Into this scene came Maharishi Mahesh Yogi and Transcendental Meditation (TM): how to get high without dope. Between 1898 and 1968, previous Eastern meditation teachers; gurus and saintly Indian mystics like Vivekananda and Yogananda, had arrived in America, teaching meditation and devotion to God and Christ.

But in February 1968, the merger of Maharishi and TM with the Beatles, the Beach Boys, and other rockers caught fire in pop culture. These bands made their now-legendary pilgrimage to Rishikesh, India, to sit and study at the feet of Maharishi, the founder of TM meditation using a mantra that allowed the mind to transcend. The global press corps followed, and suddenly this mystical Himalayan teaching was being discussed worldwide. Maharishi had already spoken at Harvard Law School in January 1968, but it took the "Fab Four" to transform his ancient wisdom into a cultural phenomenon.

In January 1968, I was oblivious, immersed in law school studies. I had no idea that the solution to the very turmoil that would consume me in my later cases was being offered to the world by Maharishi, promoted by the same two bands whose music was the soundtrack to my generation. Nor did I know that the second band, the Beach Boys, would become one of my most intriguing cases over twenty years later, unveiling the depth of rock-and-roll drug-addicted tragedy. The universe was sending a message, but I wasn't yet tuned to the right frequency.

As this phenomenon unfolded, still in law school in 1968, I was reading about the Tet Offensive in Vietnam, jeopardizing my friends and classmates. I had also received my draft notice to report the following September. It was a time of societal turmoil during the formative period of my legal career, one that kept me intensely focused to the exclusion of all else.

THE SEARCH FOR STILLNESS

"Within you, there is a stillness and a sanctuary to which you can retreat at any time and be yourself."
Hermann Hesse, Siddhartha

Despite early signs of positive progress in my career, it never seemed enough for me. I had sensed since childhood an elusive "something", an unspecified, undefinable longing arising in my heart and mind. Before I realized it, I was in the throes of trying cases, yet the longing remained. I wondered: was it litigation stress, or something deeper? As always, I did what I do: I researched and read.

It was Wednesday, November 14, 1974, sometime after my daughter and her teddy bear had interrupted my angst-laden, late-night cogitations. I went to the local public library near our home and looked up "Mind" to clear my brain of Dan Moore, Higgins, mobsters, and the befuddling Sequeira case. I was stressed with various other clients, their angst and pleas, and preparing for my next trial. No computers back then. I found the usual assortment of books on psychology and psychiatry. Somehow, remember..."I am not the doer", I discovered and glommed onto books on meditation. I remember it vividly because it was a huge pivot in my life.

One book I found was *The Science of Being and Art of Living*, authored by His Holiness Maharishi Mahesh Yogi. What is that? Who is that? I thought. A "Science of Being"? An "Art of Living"? Who is this "His Holiness Maharishi Mahesh Yogi"? A Hindu monk? I devoured the book. I still have it in my library. It is pure, unyielding, irrefutable truth.

In 1974, the only thing I knew about "meditation" per se was through the spiritual filter of my Catholic youth, education, and religiosity. I was in for a surprise. Maharishi and his TM program said it was based on "science." Reading the contents of Maharishi's book proved to be a sort of non-religious spiritual regeneration for the unwitting fabric of my mind and soul. Unwitting because I didn't yet realize I had become separated from God, and not only that, I had replaced the "God within me" with "Litigation." With this book and the subsequent techniques of Transcendental Meditation, I had unwittingly found a way out of the mind-and-soul traps I was building for myself.

AN INITIATION INTO TRANSCENDENCE

By coincidence, if there is such a thing, there was a newly opened TM instruction center in the little town of North Andover, near our home. I signed up for the five consecutive days of instruction.

I found myself sitting in a small, sparsely furnished room. The walls were cream-colored and bare except for a single framed photograph of a bearded man in white robes: Maharishi Mahesh Yogi of Beatles fame. Incidentally, just by their being around the Maharishi, and the international press corps being around them, yoga had taken off in the West. The air smelled faintly of sandalwood incense and herbal tea. A small fountain trickled in the corner, the only sound besides the occasional car passing on the street outside.

I was excited to see what they had to offer but still kept my skeptical wits about me. Meditation seemed like something for hippies and Hollywood stars, not for hard-nosed litigators. But desperation has a way of opening doors you'd normally walk past. So there I sat, uncomfortable in my suit and tie among the casual attire of about ten other attendees, waiting for my introduction to TM. My briefcase rested against my leg, filled with notes and pleadings that needed filing, a legal pad covered with notes for tomorrow's hearing, a deposition transcript marked with yellow highlighter.

The instructors were two young men in their late twenties with a serene air about them, spoke softly as they explained the basics. "Transcendental Meditation isn't about controlling your thoughts," one said, looking at me as if he could see the constant-motion machine inside my skull. "It's about transcending them, finding the quiet that exists beneath the noise."

I almost laughed. Quiet? My mind hadn't been quiet since law school, perhaps not even before that. The very idea seemed as foreign as practicing law without precedent. After I raised some questions, one of them said, "The legal mind may be particularly challenging," addressing me in particular. I felt a jolt of surprise at his insight. "Lawyers are trained to anticipate problems, to see every angle, to never stop questioning. These are valuable skills in a courtroom. But they can become a prison if you become too trapped in your mind." His words were beginning to make sense. "TM offers a way out," he said. "Not an escape from responsibility, but a door to a deeper level of consciousness where solutions arise naturally, where creativity flows, where the mind can refresh itself."

I liked the concept but didn't fully believe him. Still, I was desperate enough to try what they had to offer. The technique he taught me was deceptively simple: a mantra. Twenty minutes, twice a day. Eyes closed, sitting comfortably. No effort, no concentration, no control.

THE BLISS OF PURE SILENCE

The next step after five days of instruction was initiation: the giving of a 'mantra', a meaningless sound or word the mind could not glom onto. The mantra is bestowed in a Puja, a sacred initiation ceremony meant to anchor the experience. At the moment I received the mantra, I was immediately transcended into a state of pure silence and awareness I had never before experienced. It was an unexpected and surreal experience with ultimately vast horizons that I never could have predicted at the time. As the saying goes, I was blown away. What is this? Who am I? What is this state of consciousness I have transcended into?

The realization that I could practice the technique in my own home for the rest of my life, twenty minutes morning and evening, and each time experience the flow of joy and bliss I had just tasted was very exciting to me. I deemed it to be an immense blessing with profound potential. I was correct. But I was still naive.

The sense of quiet, the profound relaxation, the pure joy, and the literal timelessness of that experience set me free, at least on an incipient level. I was no longer trapped in the underlying angst I had felt almost my whole life; the search for something when I did not even know what I was searching for, the hole in my life indicating something was lacking but never quite pinpointed...this state of lifelong consciousness was gone in a few minutes. It was replaced by a sense of completeness I had always wished for but could never quite name.

Stumbling upon a simple meditation technique to counter the stress in my life was nothing short of a Godsend. Some might call it divine intervention. At the time I looked at it as a very therapeutic twenty minutes twice a day of relief, that is what Maharishi prescribed in TM. Little did I know that this simple technique would begin a process to reconnect my mind to my soul: real spiritual regeneration. Now I look back and see a much bigger picture. I see God quantum-entangling my life with a meditation foundation to rescue my soul.

To be fair, I also read Yogananda's *Autobiography of a Yogi* about the time I discovered Maharishi's book, but dismissed it as too fantastical... little did I know then that Kriya Yoga, and Yogananda, would later become the most important initiation of my life. But back as a young lawyer and family man, I was home with TM in a way that felt comforting and gently reassuring that all was well with me and my world. My search seemed over. I immediately told my wife, my son, my law partner, our staff, my friends, literally anyone who would listen. Many of them thought I had gone off the deep end. The truth was that I had. I was so enthused with having experienced this state of consciousness beyond my mind that I asked myself: "Who am I?"

It was a pertinent question, because something had changed inside me almost instantly. In truth, even in my altered state, my search, my path, was just beginning. Later, my wife, my nine-year-old son, and others decided to take up TM and meditate. As for me, there was still my karma to deal with. I was naive in my prophetic expectations after my spectacular experience of pure bliss in the initiation Puja. (In case you're wondering, the Puja is a small ceremony of gratitude performed by the teacher at the time of instruction, in honor of the teachers who came before. Karma is simply the sum of one's actions in this or prior incarnations.)

I diligently practiced TM regularly over the next fifteen years. I attended as many TM residence courses (retreats) as I could manage between family and cases. I used these to purge the accumulated stress from my days in the PIT. In 1987 I learned the advanced course for TM practitioners, the TM-Sidhis program which was designed to deepen the meditative experience of TM. More of that later in Chapter 13.

As I proceeded along my TM path, I found out that the famous Trappist monk Thomas Keating, Abbot of St. Joseph's Abbey, the Trappist Monastery in Spencer, Massachusetts not far from my home, had, during the same period circa 1974, introduced TM to the monks in the Abbey. He developed it into "Centering Prayer." Likewise, my spiritual sadhana has progressed over fifty years; an odd merger of my Catholic youth and meditation has converged. At times it has been an internal and external war zone, mixing litigation, Catholicism, and meditation.

BALANCING THE PIT AND HOME LIFE

More benefits emerged in my TM practice even as my days were immersed in the growing number of cases I was retained to handle. I was finding time to have some semblance of a family life: playing catch with my five-year-old son, tussling with my two-year-old daughter in the terrible twos, and awaiting the birth of Alison on the way. As my children grew, I treasured the regular and extended family dinners and outings, Mike Jr.'s Little League, Rebecca's ballet, Alison's riding, tennis, softball, touch football, innumerable activities with family and friends, wonderfully memorable (if limited) family vacations, and more. A treasure.

In contrast, jury litigation is extremely demanding. I don't wish it on the breadwinner of any family. It undercuts the opportunity to be more present with a less cluttered mind and the emotional stresses of litigation make it hard to fully enjoy the real pleasures of life with spouse and children, well, maybe not when they are teenagers! But I was doing my best to balance both.

Laima made our first small home a place of joy. After three years in law school with minimal income between us and no inheritance, no financial reserves, we borrowed $4,000 as a down payment on a $36,000 duplex from her Lithuanian immigrant parents, who had fled World War II as refugees. I'm one of eight kids with a partially disabled father, so no help there, actually the reverse; I worked throughout high school and college.

Early in my career, paying the bills was the typical challenge of a young family. After two years of litigation, we enjoyed a single-family home in Winchester, Massachusetts. Later, as I won more and larger jury verdicts, we had nicer cars and a more family-oriented home in North Andover and later Boxford, Massachusetts, but those early years were a financial struggle. Ironically, litigation success, family life, and our home should have been more than enough for my material, emotional, and spiritual needs. But a deeper need resonated within me.

We had departed Catholicism. My TM practice fulfilled that need as I litigated. Spirituality is needed at the heart of religion, and at the heart of religion is an infinitely greater need: to know God within oneself. In many ways, organized religion tends to obscure it. When Tolstoy wrote *The Kingdom of God Is Within You: Christianity Not as a Mystic Religion but as a New Theory of Life* in 1893 in the context of Jesus's Sermon on the Mount, he realized that man's quest for God and human brotherhood could only come from seeking God within, in a pragmatic way of living: nonviolence, turn the other cheek. Tolstoy wrote that classic ten years after *A Confession*. When he wrote *A Confession* in 1882 at age fifty, he was on the verge of suicide, devoid of any reason to live. He explained it in detail. In the next decade, he discovered what he says is the only "reason to live": to understand that in life we are in a form of school, where we are morally duty-bound to progress toward knowing God. We do that by realizing the Kingdom of God is within. Jesus taught it, and it saved Tolstoy from suicide, but it took him ten years to realize it. No worries. It took me about the same time, like most humans…

THE STRATEGY OF AN ADVERSARY

In trying cases to juries, I soon learned that if you could present your client's side through an adverse witness by challenging their credibility, the jury would swing to your side. If the jury didn't believe your opponent, or his lawyer, you were on the winning side right out of the gate. My key strategy in securing favorable verdicts for my clients soon became this: explain the basic facts in my Opening Statement to the jury, then call the opposing party and his or her key witnesses as my first witnesses before calling my own to the stand. My cross-examination strategies became the hallmark of my jury cases, the best skills I developed in trying cases. My direct examination skills have always been secondary and, in some cases, marginal.

In questioning the opposing party before they have undergone direct examination by their own lawyer, I generally needed the court to declare them "adverse." Opposing parties in our adversarial system are almost always "adverse" for purposes of examination in front of a jury, but not always. Allowing cross-examination rather than direct examination of your opponent generally involves a faster path to the truth if you can undercut their credibility. In cross-examination of an adverse witness, the lawyer can ask almost any question without the requirement of open-ended phrasing that direct examination demands. In direct examination of your own party or witness, the lawyer cannot ask leading questions that contain the answer. Direct questions must be open-ended, such as: "After the collision of the cars occurred, what did you do?" as opposed to: "After the defendant's car struck your car, did you jump out and tell him the accident was his fault?"

Thus the trial of cases to juries became for me a strategic and tactical venue of intellectual combat based on endless hours of preparation and cross-examining my opponents, generally based on their prior depositions before trial, and correlating documents to use against their deposition testimony. That became my litigation strategy… my bailiwick. Did it result in truth and justice?

SEEKING TRUTH AND JUSTICE

In our adversarial system of justice, cross-examination is the commonly held axiom for arriving at truth. You are now the jury: render a verdict on the cases and trials in this book. Read on. You, dear reader, can conjure up innumerable questions to cross-examine me on this book's contents. My experience has taught me that only a thoroughly corrupt judge can defeat this strategy in jury trials, as long as truth and justice are indeed on your side, and as long as the litigator chooses the right cases to litigate: those screaming for real justice!

The types of cases I chose in order to achieve justice were generally against the rich and powerful—and their rich and powerful law firms. They came with huge accompanying stressors.

In fact, in seeking justice, I soon learned that the profession of my choice was one of aggression, hostility, and confrontation, particularly in cross-examining my clients' opponents. There was no way around the systemic stress and conflict that our adversarial system entailed. Yet it was my profession by choice! Why? One might rightfully ask. I was merely strutting and fretting my hour upon the stage, to paraphrase Shakespeare, in my relentless pursuit of justice and something inside me. Hopefully this book answers these questions and mysteries about the inner conflicts between ego and truth.

Early in my career I lacked sufficient worldly experience to aid in my decisions. I generally approached my cases with the clarity of an *inquiring* intellect. That approach, in large part, has contributed to both success in my litigation life, the ensuing suffering that comes from worldly success, and the enemies I made along the way. Actually, my enemies are my ego-based badge of honor and the foundation for my forgiveness and transformation.

Early in my career I lacked sufficient worldly experience to temper my decisions, so I approached every case with the clarity of an *inquiring intellect.* It was that clarity, in large part that drove my success in litigation. It also brought the suffering that always follows worldly triumph, and it created the enemies I accumulated along the way. Those enemies became my ego-based badge of honor, proof I had been fully in the fight. More importantly, they became the foundation for my forgiveness and transformation.

There is, however, another component to my character that was the prime motivator in my having chosen litigation over all else. Here I need to be fair to myself. I've always sided with the underdog. I'm Irish. Over the centuries the Irish have been genetically prescribed to be oppressed by the rich and powerful aristocratic empire builders of the British Empire, which enslaved and exploited many in Ireland, India, and other developing countries in brutal fashion. The Cromwell invasion of Ireland in 1648 was a genocidal slaughter followed by centuries of oppression; enslavement, starvation, and the brutal suppression of rebellion (1798, 1916, 1920–21), resulting in the prolonged violence in Northern Ireland (1920–1998, "The Troubles").

The basis of my early decisions on which cases to take involved a strong sense of fairness and justice, permeated with an ill-defined and misunderstood ambition for material success that manifested as support for my family. I believed at the time that the laws of our country existed to provide justice and opportunity for each one of us; and what better way for me to uphold justice than to study and train in the law, and offer it my competitive best to ensure my contribution to a just and fair world? I was indeed competitive and idealistic to a fault, with an underlying ego ambition of which I was not fully aware early in my career. I learned the hard way that in trying cases to juries, I would have to navigate through the thorn bushes of excessive stress and the machinations of judges who were often governed by secret agendas closely identified with the rich and powerful—the money changers, as I came to call them. On the positive side, my sadhana in litigation and meditation became a lifelong lesson in humility, at times inch by bloody inch.

WHEN JUSTICE IS THWARTED:

In one case early in my career, circa 1974–75 (given only brief mention in this book), we caught a rich and powerful insurance company, its top executive underwriter, and their rich and powerful Boston law firm red-handed in blatant perjury. The key insurance company underwriter witness whom I called as my own witness to start the case was the foundation of their entire defense. During my cross-examination, his perjury was demonstrable. What did the Harvard Club, Brahmin-connected judge do after I exposed it? He declared a mistrial based on his personal "illness," so the defense could recover, avoid a negative verdict, and settle the case for less money. Big lesson for me.

The judge was a close buddy of a senior, well-known partner in this blue-blood law firm, all Harvard Club members. Who do you think you are, Michael? You and your misplaced idealism thinking you and a jury could get justice in my courtroom? These were my internal ruminations on the injustice this judge had just inflicted on me and my client, a widow. "Go back to Ireland"… I would, but I'm third generation, I internally opined.

That same defense lawyer, the same powerful senior partner in that Yankee, blue-blood, Brahmin law firm showed up a decade later in another case involving the death of a fifteen-year-old. In that case, there was no "Harvard Club" judge to protect him. Although the judge initially tried to force a settlement ostensibly in favor of the defense, the jury hammered the defense. We achieved an historic and unprecedented verdict, as you will read in Chapter 15.

THE KARMIC PARADOX OF MEDITATION

My introduction to TM in 1974 began the exposure of what I now call the "karmic paradox" of meditation. The more one meditates, the more one becomes aware of, or is confronted with, one's karma, or aspects of oneself that need resolution and/or reconciliation. This is a process of accelerated evolution: using the technique of meditation to dissolve karma. But too much bliss too fast may not allow the meditator to process his or her karma smoothly and completely. Make no mistake, TM is very powerful both in awakening transcendental consciousness and in bringing forth karmic tendencies that need to be more slowly processed.

Many TMers have suffered through this paradox: having sold themselves out in "bliss consciousness" while having extreme difficulty functioning in our crazy world of material consciousness. The contrast can become too great, creating a form of addiction to meditation. But is that really a bad thing? The world is dysfunctional. When asked if there really is a hell, Paramahansa Yogananda said, "Where do you think you are?" The real purpose and result of meditation is the soul "realizing" God within the Self. So, what is reality?

DYEING THE CLOTH IN A WORLD OF CONFLICT

Maharishi strongly and adamantly advocated a "dyeing the cloth" process to deal with reality. For every human who has ever lived, karma; past actions, good and bad, is a reality. Maharishi advised "dyeing the cloth": meditate for twenty minutes morning and evening, and absorb this dip into transcendental consciousness. Then pursue one's routine worldly duties and responsibilities in order to process higher levels of consciousness in the context of daily life.

One might understand it more specifically as everyday activity serving to infuse the experience of meditation into daily life until it becomes a permanent reality. As an analogy, imagine a cloth soaked in colorful dye. It's then laid under the sun to dry, and in the process the sun's rays make the color fade. You repeat the process until the cloth holds the dye. Similarly, after regular meditation, when one goes about everyday life, the experience of meditation might seem to last only a short time, but over a longer period it remains, even outside of meditation. Hence, "dyeing the cloth." The goal of this process is to incorporate into normal life the realizations one makes in meditation. This generally involves looking at oneself with less ego and more objectivity.

Importantly, as Maharishi instructed in *The Science of Being and Art of Living*, proper behavior is dependent on a state of mind and consciousness grounded in contentment, tolerance, joyfulness, and the warmth of meeting and giving love to our fellow man (pages 182–187).

He devotes a whole chapter (Ten) to right and wrong. For those not functioning in a state of pure being or pure consciousness, his instructions are simple: the intellect cannot by itself prescribe right or wrong actions when it is not guided by a pure state of consciousness. Thus, when acting in a lower state, you can help rectify the situation by obeying the scriptures and moral commandments, by meditating, and by grasping their usefulness.

Maharishi's foundational analysis of how the "monkey mind" functions is his basis for transcending it. He understood that the mind by itself cannot sufficiently concentrate to defeat the monkey mind's nonstop, unending stream of thought. Maharishi correctly analyzed that there is a gap between two thoughts within a steady stream of thought, and that gap is the state of pure being, or pure consciousness. If the body and nervous system are allowed to experience a state of restful alertness by living, breathing, eating, and living by natural law, Maharishi advocated that the mind will automatically seek to experience the gap of transcendental consciousness. In turn, that gap experience will automatically expand and eliminate the stream of thought (pp. 297–298).

As mentioned earlier, an essential part of overcoming the monkey mind while living in the world as a householder, as opposed to living as an ascetic or monastic, required adherence to natural law and a process that Maharishi analogized to dyeing the cloth. In his book on page 60, Maharishi explains this process as "constantly entering the realm of the Transcendent and returning to the field of relativity."

I followed this process for fifteen years through thick and thin. I might add some of it was very thick and very thin! Karma. (See *Litigator 2*.) As just mentioned, I did experience the cyclical states of mind and consciousness. However, back in the PIT of litigation, when I encountered stark evil as in the Scientology cases, I encountered extreme hostility, anger, confrontation, threats, and conflict: the essence of our adversarial system of justice. This became a conundrum throughout my litigation life; for me, my family, my clients, and most of all for my so-called opponents. Fortunately, as Yogananda says, it's all a dream. So does the song "Life Is But a Dream," written by the Harptones in 1955. Wonder if they were meditators?

QUANTUM ENTANGLEMENTS: THE BEACH BOYS CONNECTION

In 1972–74, as recounted herein, my two prior major cases involved bank fraud, mob mayhem, and murder but not meditation. My involvement in meditation later caught up with me when, twenty years later, I represented the Beach Boys and Mike Love in 1992–95 against fellow Beach Boy Brian Wilson, in which their 1968 joint experiences with Maharishi played an important role in the evidence. Mike Love is an ardent TMer. A short preview of Mike Love's case in the context of my TM experiences may illustrate the quantum entanglement of TM and my cases.

Since the early 60s, a crooked lawyer, along with Brian's father had been cheating Mike out of song authorship. Just after the Beach Boys returned from Rishikesh in 1968, the crook orchestrated the final blow: exploiting Brian to defraud Mike in the 1969 sale of their priceless "Sea of Tunes" catalog, containing many of the greatest hits co-authored by Mike and Brian.

Two decades later, after a lengthy jury trial, the jury returned an unprecedented twenty-five-page verdict in favor of Mike, restoring everything taken from him. The underlying fraud as found by the jury, once successfully uncovered, resulted in not only an historic judgment for Mike Love … it exposed the music industry as a corrupt cabal of money changers. The verdict has preserved history, notwithstanding the greedy music-mafia's controlled narrative to trash Mike and hype Brian. In truth, Mike Love was a dedicated TM meditator and was the good guy exposing the rock-and-roll industry, proving in documented, detailed evidence how its drug culture destroyed Brian Wilson and his brothers, and his father. According to Mike Love's autobiography *Good Vibrations: My Life as a Beach Boy*, notwithstanding the music mafia's effort to tar and feather him in the media, his book tells the truth inside the Love v. Wilson case. (*Litigator 3*.)

In 1974 when I learned TM, the Beatles' and Beach Boys' 1968 sojourn with Maharishi was merely old news to me. Decades later, I discovered the contrast: Mike Love stayed a serious TM meditator along with George Harrison, while Brian Wilson returned to fraud with his father, and drummer Dennis Wilson, Brian's younger brother—picked up two of Charles Manson's girls on Sunset Boulevard and then let Manson and seventeen of his harem live in Dennis' mansion for a year! Yes. Dope is for dopes. The Beach Boys story is shockingly toxic, I found to my great regret long after the unprecedented jury victory for Mike Love.

BLISS V. KARMA

Love v. Wilson was an extremely difficult case. However, after the verdict and settlement, Brian's legal guardian retained me to represent Brian in connection with a peripheral fraud perpetrated by his own crooked lawyer who was later disbarred in an unrelated matter. It is beyond coincidence that my litigation/meditation career has taken the trajectory it has. One theme that has stuck with me throughout my fifty years in the PIT, based upon my studies and meditation practices, is to "fight" my own delusions as well as the battles put on my litigation plate. The latter involve surrender to what "God", the Universe, or the cosmic field has entrusted me with.

The Bhagavad Gita adage to "fight" against both external evil as explained in that scripture in the real-world Battle of Kurukshetra, as well as the internal evils, delusions, and "sins" within *oneself,* is a core experience in my litigation/meditation life. Between 1979 and 1987 I confronted the satanic cult of L. Ron Hubbard and his so-called "Church" of Scientology. The scripture of "fight evil when it is put on your plate" ultimately saved me. But there are no words to describe the intensity, anguish, suffering, hostility, and threats I endured with my clients and family in those cases. (*Litigator 2.*) Through it all, I read Maharishi's *Bhagavad Gita*, which mandates to fight the forces of evil and delusion both inside and out:

"Surrendering all actions to me by maintaining your consciousness in the Self, freed from longing and the sense of mine, fight, delivered from the fever (of delusion)." Chapter III, Verse 30

Fight I did against the Church of Scientology. It cost me dearly, but it became part of my deliverance, part of my cloth dyeing. For better or worse, my sadhana as a fifty-year litigator was not to leave the world and retreat into solitary bliss, joy, and contentment. For me, some measure of solitude in prolonged retreat came decades later while I wrote this Litigator series. However, in doing so I resurrected past suffering and sorrows, which is itself very painful. I still have several cases in litigation. Lots of karma to get through.

In hindsight, after embracing Kriya Yoga in 1988, after fifteen years of TM, many TMers enthralled in the bliss of higher levels of transcendental consciousness have not sufficiently confronted nor worked through their karma, either in past lives or this one. Been there, done that in my practice of TM. Guilty. The post-Maharishi Beatles and Beach Boys experiences, particularly those of the Wilsons and John Lennon evidence this negative karmic cycle. The betrayal of Yogananda by "Swami" Kriyananda, his copyright violations, frauds, and sexual abuse of his devotees, for me, in my experience of having seen it all in the litigation trenches, cements this reality. In my opinion, they may have merely deferred the inevitable suffering of dealing with incarnational karma. But who am I to judge? To quote a Mike Love/Brian Wilson song: "God Only Knows."

As my TM practice deepened, observing the endless stream of thoughts and the "gaps" between them, occasionally transcending thought altogether, I began to realize who or what was watching: the "I am" behind the mind. Maharishi taught that the mind, when allowed, naturally wants to transcend into pure consciousness. The sages have called these states Cosmic, Christ, Unity, or God consciousness. They are correct. I have tasted them. Yet even in bliss and silence, karmic debt remains.

The paradox of Transcendental Meditation lies in the balance between allowance and intentionality. After tasting pure consciousness, the mind naturally craves return to it. But the will often intervenes, trying to force it—leading many TM practitioners to abandon willpower entirely in favor of *total allowance*, sometimes veering into mysticism. In the karmic scheme, the jury is still out on whether that's always wise. I'm not judging.

The total lack of focus in TM, allowing the mantra to enable transcendence, may explain why some long-term TMers on monastic "rounding courses" (Mother Divine for women, Purusha for men) struggle to re-enter the "normal" world. I've met Mother Divine and Purusha meditators at Mother Meera's in Germany who find our world almost impossible to navigate. Understandable. Our world is nuts. It is not real. Fortunately, Mother Meera is grounded in both the Divine and the earthly, offering a haven for those sold out on bliss.

Not me. I was dyeing the cloth in litigation and meditation. I stayed in the fight—family, cases, karma—while craving more bliss. It's like eating a little chocolate; you crave more. But digging and dumping the ego is mandatory to return to God. I didn't know that early on. TM gave glimpses; Kriya demanded confrontation.

When I later began Kriya Yoga, intentionality and concentration returned as the foundation. The focus is not on allowing the monkey mind's stream, but on using the will to direct energy up the spine, centering the mind on the chakras, the Sushumna flanked by Ida and Pingala, ascending from the coccyx through Sacral, Lumbar, Dorsal, Cervical, and Medulla to the Christ Center. That disciplined focus displaces thought, reconnects

God-energy in the spine to God in the Crown and Christ Center. It works like science.

This contrast, TM's gentle allowance vs. Kriya's disciplined willpower, has been the real classroom of my sadhana. Bliss alone can seduce; karma demands we stay in the ring.

THE PERILS OF BLISS WITHOUT MORALITY

Based on my personal experience, TM is so powerful and life-changing that it must be practiced with the strong strictures of baseline morality, the Ten Commandments, and disciplined behavior. The practice of Kriya Yoga proves this fundamental reality. The experience of advanced bliss can sometimes give one a sense of entitlement to behave as one desires, as if anything within range of the sphere of one's bliss is good and correct...even though it may cause harm to oneself or others. The "Swami" Kriyananda cases provide an example of this self-defeating syndrome. Particularly for those with deep karmic or character flaws it can create a pattern: to ignore or suppress them, thereby creating more karma through either overindulgence in desires or mood-making.

I am partially guilty of overindulgence while struggling against moods. In fairness to myself, I kept trying to "dye the cloth" by litigating and meditating. Thus I experienced intermittent periods of deep silent awareness while retreating in TM Residence Courses for three to seven days, particularly at the conclusion of an intensely litigated jury trial. This syndrome continued into my Kriya Yoga practice, into which I was initiated in July 1988. Kriya Yoga and the scripture-based Yamas and Niyamas, like the Ten Commandments, compelled me to confront my desires and attendant behaviors, sometimes in deeply painful and sorrowful Kriya Yoga retreats, again following intensely litigated jury cases.

In these retreats, I generally experienced cycles of suffering, release of karma, and deepening silent awareness. As I now perceive the world of sensory experience, it is an unreal and addictive immersion in the senses. If it is not cultured by deep meditation with which to gradually pull oneself out of the world's intrinsic delusion, it is a trap.

The meditation disciplines of Maharishi and Paramahansa Yogananda showed me a clear message: reject the world of materialism and follow the Commandments of God, enabled by the disciplines of meditation. Meditation connects one to God's Force Field. Maharishi lived in that

Force Field, which he called Universal Consciousness. In my personal experience, it is easy to get hooked on transcendental bliss and ignore his advice to obey scriptural mandated behaviors—recited in his book *The Science of Being and Art of Living*, particularly Chapter Six. Meditation mandates that one must behave according to the fundamental religious scriptures, natural law, and creative intelligence as embedded in the Ten Commandments and the Yamas and Niyamas.

A NOTE TO THE READER

You've just finished the first act of this story—my initial, rookie journey into the litigation trenches and the mental/emotional/spiritual necessity that brought me to TM meditation and ultimately, after years of Kriya Yoga, brought me to my knees confronting my desires. In Chapter 4, my life changed forever when I discovered the benefits of meditation...first Transcendental Meditation, then Kriya Yoga. The next two chapters you are about to read are different from the case narratives thus far. They are my retrospective reflections after fifty years of meditating and litigating, regarding future case experiences in this Litigator series. I diverge here to provide insights into the later cases in this book, *Litigator 1*, and my subsequent cases in later Litigator books.

The next two chapters are a deeper dive into the mental, emotional, psychological, spiritual, and philosophical framework of quantum entanglement, consciousness, and the nature of reality that has shaped my understanding of the cases you've been reading about and will read about going forward. These chapters are the "why" and "how" behind the "what" of my cases and meditation. If you are reading for the narrative, the courtroom drama, the human struggle, that is the heart of this memoir, I understand. It may be interrupted by these next two chapters.

Author and Daya Mata,
President of Self Realization Fellowship circa 2000

Author and Mother Meera circa 1994

Pramahansa Yogananda with tigerskin
circa 1920's. Photo courtesy of Self-
Realization Fellowship (SRF).

Author next to the tigerskin, given as a present by
SRF President Daya Mata. Photo Richard Bergin

CHAPTER 5

Meditation to Discern Between Human and Divine Truth and Justice

"Knowledge is structured in consciousness."

-Maharishi Mahesh Yogi

"I regard consciousness as fundamental. I regard matter as derivative from consciousness. We cannot get behind consciousness. Everything that we talk about, everything that we regard as existing, postulates consciousness."

-Max Planck

THE LITIGATOR AND THE "MONEY CHANGERS"

The jury is the last sanctuary of spiritual truth in a corrupted legal system. Twelve strangers, sworn to "speak the truth" (the original meaning of verdict), can override the machinations of corrupt judges, the wealth of powerful adversaries, the lies of paid witnesses. I have seen it happen. I have felt the collective consciousness of a jury rise to a level that transcends the individual biases each juror brought into the courtroom. It is, in its way, a form of knowing—the same inner knowing that Christ taught when he said the Kingdom of God is within you.

That teaching has always been dangerous. The Gnostics practiced it, and the Church declared them heretics and burned them alive. The Cathars inherited it, and were slaughtered by the tens of thousands in the Albigensian Crusade. The pattern was set at the Council of Nicaea in 325 AD, when Constantine and the Bishops struck a deal: political power for the Emperor, spiritual power for the Church, and centralized control for both. Together, they codified Roman Church dogma in the Canonical Gospels—not to liberate souls, but to control them. Anyone who taught that salvation could be found within, without the permission of priests or hierarchy, became a target. The same template that crucified Christ under color of Jewish and Roman law has repeated itself throughout history. Those who threaten the monopoly on truth must be destroyed.

As a litigator, I have faced the same enemy in a different form: judges who pervert the law, institutions that crush the individual, a system that serves money and power rather than justice. This chapter is about my place in that ancient war, as an Irish Rebel, a litigator, and one who has stared into the abyss of a corrupted legal system and resolved to fight back.

I am an Irish Rebel by nature, education, and, perhaps, by rebirth. My life has been a balancing act between two seemingly opposite pursuits: the inner stillness of meditation and the outer combat of the courtroom. Yet both are responses to the same ancient enemy. The Sanhedrin used Jewish law to murder Christ. The British Empire used starvation and murder to crush my ancestors. Today's Deep State uses corrupted judges and weaponized agencies to destroy anyone who threatens their power. The template never changes, only the uniforms. In Chapter 13, I will share an experience that convinced me this fight extends beyond a single lifetime: my encounter with the cellular memory of Father Michael Griffin, an Irish priest murdered by the British in 1920.

For over 15 years, I have been in the throes of fighting against massive judicial and political corruption by the Clintons, Obama, and Biden. My client Tim Blixseth and I have been fighting against the monstrous misuse of law by corrupt judges. In this Litigator Series, I am attempting to awaken America to the systemic corruption in our judicial system which has eroded the moral foundations of our Republic. The last two chapters on the Blixseth case close out this book, but jump ahead in my chronological case narratives to acquaint you, dear reader, with the current judicial corruption now confronting America. The details on the Blixseth case are in *Litigator 4*.

The crucifixion of Christ is the ultimate historical example of injustice and desecration of truth on the one hand and the evils of power and money on the other. Spirituality vs. materialism. God's laws vs. human laws. The Sanhedrin used Jewish law to condemn Christ, but divine law ordained His resurrection from death. Human law cannot conceive of such an abnormal event. If resurrection of murdered individuals occurred on a routine basis, all of our laws governing the multiple degrees of murder—First, Second, Voluntary, Involuntary, Manslaughter, the Felony Murder Rule...would have to be amended. The Richard Sequeira murder and the Benjamin DeChristoforo felony murder conviction would never have been litigated as recited in this book. Lawyers might become obsolete, a welcome event to most!

But resurrection is not routine, and the law remains what it has always been: a human system, fallible and corruptible. The ancient template of spiritual truth being crushed by corrupt human systems has repeated itself throughout history, from the Sanhedrin's murder of Christ to the courtrooms of modern America. Throughout my career I have faced my own version of it.

As a litigator, I've tread an often-tortuous path between defending the innocent and battling the pervasive shadow of corruption in courts where judges in black robes disguised their corruption and perverted the law, thereby destroying the foundation of all justice... truth. My journey has taught me that, in many cases, my clients were "more sinned against than sinning," to quote Shakespeare. Over many decades of trying cases, we've achieved many victories in difficult cases, like the Sequeira case, where the scales of justice weighed in favor of ultimate truth notwithstanding the difficulty in that case of no body, no death certificate, no evidence of felonious assault, and a jury rendering a verdict solely on circumstantial, inferential evidence.

In that case, we were blessed with a great judge, the truly Honorable Ruth Abrams, with an elevated consciousness, who allowed a jury to render a verdict reflecting a collective consciousness that transcended isolated facts. I am jumping ahead in this chapter and the next with retrospective perspectives to illustrate the corrupt power of judges immersed in money consciousness, who act without the protections of a jury, and how our system of justice can be utterly corrupted without jury protection.

My intention is to prep you, dear reader, for the case narratives in later cases and books; and establish how raising the collective consciousness of a jury can achieve justice. I hope it provides insights into the cases that follow in subsequent chapters in this book, which illustrate the power of meditation, the science of quantum entanglement, and the protections provided by a jury in our system of justice as it has degenerated into massive judicial and political corruption.

Back when I was in law school, 1967–70, based upon my readings in high school and college, I wanted to try jury cases. I had read throughout high school and college the lives and cases of many jury lawyers like Clarence Darrow, who convinced juries to promote justice to counter unjust laws and Deep State crimes and economic controls, particularly repressing the poor and disenfranchised. In the 1960s Civil Rights movement, the jury circumvention of unjust laws became known as "Jury Nullification." It worked. See *Jury Nullification: The Evolution of a Doctrine* by Conrad.

When the law was used to promote injustice, civil rights lawyers routinely used juries to nullify the effects of unjust laws as instructed by judges, to obtain acquittal verdicts. Jury lawyers "nullified" bad laws.

Currently, the problem is convincing juries to negate the instructions of either corrupt judges, and/or both the judges and the machinations of federal agencies—particularly the DOJ, FBI, and CIA, who routinely pervert otherwise "just" laws for the moneyed elite, now commonly called the Deep State. The current, hottest news scandal involving the Clintons, their billionaire donor Ron Burkle, and Mossad sex trafficker Jeffrey Epstein, flying the world in "Air F..k One," Burkle's Boeing 757, are front and center.

In June 2008, the DOJ, FBI, and CIA—doing the bidding of Israeli intelligence, entered into a monumentally corrupt "plea agreement" with Epstein. This illegal plea deal was authored by Epstein's lawyers: Reinhart, Dershowitz, and Starr. Starr was the infamous "Independent Counsel" involving his cover-up of the 1990s Clinton scandals and murder of Vince Foster. The illegal plea deal not only covered up Epstein's crimes, but also the sexual abuse of minors by Bill Clinton, Burkle, and 21 other "honey-trapped" Epstein targets. Reinhart was later made a federal judge who signed the search warrants on the FBI raid on President Trump's home at Mar-a-Lago on August 8, 2022. (*Litigator 4* and *5*.) See also *Perversion of Justice: The Jeffrey Epstein Story* by Julie K. Brown.

My law school years coincided with the government cover-ups of the assassinations of JFK, RFK, and MLK—three men murdered by money and power for daring to challenge the Deep State. I was no bleeding-heart liberal, but I recognized evil when I saw it: enforced segregation, unjust wars, and a legal system corrupted by those who controlled it. In 1969, I published a Law Review article advocating for desegregation through community control of public schools. But my real education came later, when I discovered that the key to justice in the courtroom was not just mastering the law, it was raising consciousness. When I began meditating in 1974, I realized a profound truth: by raising my own consciousness, I could raise the collective consciousness of a jury. That insight has guided every case I have tried since.

The article was published in several journals. But my consciousness on the depth of Deep State/CIA corruption of America and our political and judicial systems remained, in retrospect, very limited. However, in law school and thereafter, I studied and read extensively on how to try jury cases, particularly when and where injustices were then occurring right under my own, and America's collective noses. Although my grasp of jury consciousness as a collective reality in reaching a verdict, "to speak the truth", did not manifest until several years later when I tried the Sequeira and other jury cases, I began to realize that what I was really learning was how to raise the consciousness of the jury.

When I read Maharishi and Yogananda in 1974 about how to raise my own consciousness in meditation, I realized that in raising my own consciousness, I could raise the collective consciousness of a jury. This realization was and has been profound in trying cases to juries. It became the cornerstone of my trial strategy, but it also highlighted a terrifying vulnerability in the justice system: what happens when a case is shielded from the collective conscience of a jury and left to the whims of a single, fallible, corrupted judge? Been there, done that. (Chapters 22 and 23.)

In order to give you a glimpse of where litigation and meditation have taken me in my quest for justice over the past 5 decades, we must jump ahead 35 years after the Sequeira case. When I began meditating just after that case, I had no clue that litigation and meditation would take me into cases currently impacting pervasive judicial corruption in America. Currently, every American citizen can read on a daily basis in newspapers and online the efforts of the Trump Administration and DOJ to investigate and prosecute the massive corruption in multiple federal agencies: billions lost in USAID; health and child care frauds; sex trafficking of minors; Deep State money-changer control of Congress; Obama/Biden Administration corruption of the FBI, DHS, and CIA; drug cartel bribery of judges, politicians, federal agents; and perhaps most destructive to our Constitutional Republic, the massive systemic corruption in the judiciary. This widespread corruption is not an abstract concept; it has real-world consequences that can destroy lives and undermine the very foundations of justice.

The evil that crucified Christ continues today, 2000 years later. The Deep State, Secret Government uses corrupt politicians, federal agency heads, and judges, just like Caiphas and Annas—to spread their evil. The murders and cover-ups involving JFK, RFK, MLK, and the July 27, 1993 murder of Clinton's lawyer Vince Foster constitute inveterate evil by any legal or moral standard: "Thou Shalt Not Kill." Governmental or private sector framing of an innocent person for a crime he or she didn't commit is also inveterate evil. The Clinton/Comey FBI attempted to frame President Trump in "Russiagate." A cabal of three federal judges did the same to Tim Blixseth. (*Litigator 4*)

The Scientologists sued me 21 times and also tried to frame me, but it backfired. They paid one convicted, incarcerated murderer $50,000, another Italian criminal $50,000, and another career criminal $30,000 in their frame-up scheme; but the Boston U.S. Attorney indicted and convicted the $30,000 career criminal, while one recipient of $50,000 sat in an Italian prison, and the incarcerated murderer recipient of another $50,000 of "frame-up money" was in for life in the Massachusetts State Prison. (*Litigator 2*.) While my battles with Scientology were a direct confrontation with a cult, I would soon learn that the same corrupting influence of money and power operated with even greater impunity within the established pillars of the justice system itself.

On the day he was sworn in, January 20, 2025, President Trump signed Executive Order 14147, "Ending the Weaponization of the Federal Government." He signed related Executive Orders for the DOJ, FBI, and intelligence agencies to investigate high-level federal agency officials who had corrupted their agencies and corrupted the administration of justice. Within 60 days, President Trump instructed Attorney General Bondi to form "The Weaponization Working Group" headed by Ed Martin. Many Obama/Biden-appointed judges, like James Boasberg, and judges who had corrupted their offices, coupled with high-level federal agency officials, knew that Trump intended to clean out the Washington swamp. They knew the jig was up.

Similarly, Obama's CIA Director John Brennan had employed a computer hacker, Quarles Harris, during Hillary's primary run against Obama in 2007–2008. The Clintons first leaked to the media that Obama was not born in the U.S. and that his birth certificate had been altered. Harris hacked into the State Department Obama records and destroyed Obama records. A Grand Jury investigation pushed by Hillary ensued. Harris was subpoenaed. On April 17, 2008, he was shot execution-style on a Washington street. That murder has never been solved.

Before the Harris murder, during the Obama 2007 campaign against Hillary, Obama hired Brennan as his National Security Advisor. Hillary used her customary dirty tricks against Obama, leaking that Obama had a homosexual relationship with Donald Young, allegedly Obama's gay boyfriend and cocaine partner. On December 24, 2007, Young was shot in his apartment in the back of the head. That case was also never solved.

The Clinton/Democratic National Committee corruption has a long history. After Clinton was sworn in on January 20, 1993, the Clintons appointed their lawyer, Hillary's law partner and lover, Vince Foster to be

Deputy White House Counsel. While dealing with a "box" of Scientology documents given to Foster by a Scientology lawyer, Foster was murdered along with his investigator, Jerry Parks.

The Church of Scientology was an intelligence-collecting cult like the CIA. It also masqueraded as a religion. As soon as Clinton was sworn in, the cult immediately besieged the Clintons with a "box of Clinton crimes and scandals." The cult was seeking tax exemption, which had been denied for the previous 40 years, including a 1989 denial by the U.S. Supreme Court.

Hillary assigned Foster to deal with the Scientology "box" of crimes on the Clintons. Together they hired Arkansas private detective, former cop, Jerry Parks to work on the Scientology problem. Parks knew nothing about tax exemption, but he knew everything about the Clintons and a lot about the Scientology cult as a blackmailing intelligence operation. On July 27, 1993, while dealing with the Scientology "box," Foster was found shot in the head in a DC park near CIA headquarters. A car with Arkansas plates was seen at the park at the time of the murder.

Two months after the Foster murder, on September 26, 1993, Jerry Parks was shot to death at a red light in Little Rock. The next morning, the FBI, CIA, and IRS agents, with no warrant, raided the Parks home and cleaned out everything in his work for the Clintons and Foster.

A week later, on October 1, 1993, Clinton and IRS Commissioner Richardson gave tax exemption to Scientology—a multibillion-dollar gain for the "Church" of Scientology.

In April 1993, with the Scientology demand for tax exemption pending, Hillary had her friend Margaret Milner Richardson appointed to be Commissioner of the IRS. During this period, Foster's Executive Assistant was Linda Tripp, later made famous monitoring and tape-recording my client Monica Lewinsky. Linda worked on the Scientology box with her boss, Foster. Between 1994 and 1999, Ken Starr was appointed as Independent Counsel to investigate the shooting death of Vince Foster and multiple Clinton crimes and scandals.

In 1997, after Starr reported Foster's death as a suicide, Linda and Monica's mother, believing that Monica's life might be in danger, convinced Monica to turn over the infamous "Blue Dress" (stained with Clinton's semen) to Ken Starr. Talk about the fox guarding the hen house. Linda knew that her boss, Foster, had been murdered—not a suicide as reported by Starr. Linda knew that the Scientology box of Clinton crimes and scandals included Clinton's relationship with Jeffrey Epstein, which had begun as of at least 1989. Epstein and Harvey Weinstein, another sexual deviant, were frequent users of the "Lincoln Bedroom" at the White House soon after Clinton was sworn in.

In 2007, when Epstein was being investigated for a worldwide child sex trafficking ring by the West Palm police, who was his first lawyer? You guessed it: Ken Starr.

Amidst the alarming rise of political and judicial corruption in America today, what is the real value of morality, truth, justice, and righteousness? Does truth hold any weight when power and money, a deadly combination, seemingly destroys law, legal process, moral standards, and plain old truth? Jeffrey Epstein is the tip of an iceberg of immorality, greed, fraud, and political/judicial corruption. The legacy media is permeated with fiction, falsehood, and fraud protecting the Deep State moneyed elite. Many American courts are lock-step with the media, both governed by money. The quest for truth and justice can sometimes appear like a futile chase in a world layered with illusion, controlled by Deep State elite money.

Will the doctrine and implementation of "Jury Nullification" stop the judicial corruption? It's a real problem. We first need "Judge Nullification." In one case, we succeeded in getting around a corrupt judge with a reversal of his corrupt decisions on appeal, and thereafter getting the case heard by a jury after the judge was reversed. The corrupt judge remained on the case and tried to sway the jury—but we exposed the judge in front of the jury. We won. (*Litigator 3*.)

CAN AMERICA'S SYSTEM OF JUSTICE BE SAVED?

There is hope. Our jury system has not yet been destroyed. World spiritual leaders like Paramahansa Yogananda, Maharishi, Gandhi, the Dalai Lama, Martin Luther King, and many others have long pursued paths of truth and justice. Politicians like the Kennedys and others have attempted to resurrect America out of the grip of CIA crimes controlled by Deep State money. Sadly, like Christ, the Kennedys, MLK, Gandhi, and others have all been murdered. Trump is trying. Not coincidentally, 'they' have tried to assassinate him. The Butler, PA shooter, Crooks, was no lone gunman—the CIA favorite cover-up for political assassinations, like Oswald, is to use decoys. The Charlie Kirk murder will likely uncover the truth about the Deep State collective behind that murder.

Historically, even scientists like Isaac Newton supported the paths of Yogananda and Maharishi, proffering that truth resides in the silence of meditation. Newton famously said, "Truth is the offspring of silence and meditation." These elevated souls, steeped in divine consciousness / Christ consciousness, realized that meditation provides a conduit to higher levels of existence and divine understanding, creating a direct link to what we call 'God' and therefore divine truth and justice governing human truth and justice. Individuals in higher states of consciousness do not commit murder; they use that consciousness to raise the consciousness of those around them to expose evils like murder.

After 50 years in the PIT of litigation accompanied by the introspection and insights of meditation, I believe our species can advance from the caves of power, greed, and selfishness into the light and realization of God and the forces of goodness He gives to us. But we must act, pray, and meditate. In silence we gain footholds toward truth. Truth and justice must become the actual purpose and goal of our Department of Justice. It has gone off the rails. We must have legitimate judges, legitimate prosecutors, and legitimate litigators that will present the truth to a jury. We *must* have jurors who are God-centered, whose consciousness can be elevated, and who are not controlled by power and money.

In my role as a meditating litigator, I learned in the trenches that truth and justice can emerge in jury trials and their verdicts when the collective consciousness of the jury can be elevated, leading to their collective pursuit of truth. But isolated jury verdicts manifesting truth and justice have become isolated waves in the ocean of corruption that has taken control of American jurisprudence. Lawyers representing the Clintons during the Starr investigation of the Clinton scandals and Foster murder, were later installed by Hillary and Obama to control the DOJ. Political hack lawyers like Starr, and Jack Smith (whom the Clintons installed as Chief of the Public Integrity Section of the DOJ—an oxymoron if there ever was one, have not yet been investigated and brought to justice by the Trump DOJ – a manifest cover up. In the DOJ investigations into the Vince Foster murder, Ken Starr was really working for the Clintons, and currently, federal judge Bruce Reinhart, who not so coincidentally signed the Mar-a-Lago search warrant on Trump—was one of Epstein's lawyers back in 2008. No coincidence there.

There is much history to overcome. Allen Dulles, the CIA, the Clintons, Obama, and Biden have built a Deep State Secret Government that has destroyed 'due process of law' pursuing both their power and their greed. Nixon and the Bushes did nothing to stop a 60-year cycle of corruption of America, and in many ways contributed to it. Due process of law, as protected by the 5th and 14th Amendments, is rooted in procedural law and evidentiary rules, aimed at ensuring "fundamental fairness" in the adjudication of civil and criminal matters. Substantive due process encompasses fundamental rights such as life, liberty, and the pursuit of happiness without governmental interference. Procedural due process, along with equal protection, focuses on enforcing these rights through the judicial processes that guarantee them.

Obama's Administration was most notable in his recruitment of John Brennan in his run against Hillary in the 2008 Primary, a move that underscored his ambition to wield CIA influence to gain the White House. Brennan, an experienced, duplicitous CIA political hack, exemplifies the murderous CIA and its legacy of murder and corruption. With Obama, Brennan rose to the position of CIA Director, perpetuating Dulles' legacy in the shadows.

In my legal career I have observed, researched, and studied, often from the trenches of hardcore litigation, how the above presidents, their CIA and FBI Directors, and other federal agency appointees have destroyed "due process of law." A cabal of corrupt presidents and their appointees have used the DOJ, the FBI, the IRS, the CIA, and the legacy deep state media to corrupt and cover up massive corruption in America's political and judicial systems. The judges they have appointed have increasingly destroyed due process and equal protection guaranteed by the Constitution to such an extraordinary degree that corruption is now rampant in our judiciary. It has become obvious to anyone who cares to examine our justice system. I now know, having seen it in the trenches of litigation, up close and personal for five decades.

THE JURY AS A BULWARK AGAINST CORRUPTION

As the poor and disenfranchised discovered in medieval England, after Magna Carta in 1215, 400 years before Shakespeare displayed in his plays the horrors of royal government corruption (the old "Royal" Deep State), a jury of 'one's peers' is more likely to achieve human justice on a level that approaches divine justice than a judge. I discovered this truth while meditating on and litigating the realities of truth and justice over five decades. I came to the conclusion that juries are our last bulwark against judicial corruption. If the litigator is able to somehow circumvent the powers of a corrupt judge and get the case to a jury, truth and justice can emerge. But judges have extensive powers over juries. The solution is to raise the collective consciousness of the jury above and beyond the powers of a corrupt judge. It is a tricky problem. The judges instruct the jurors that it is their sworn duty to apply the law to the facts as he instructs them to adhere to what he says the law is. The doctrine of Jury Nullification arose out of this conundrum.

The Kriyananda copyright case (*Litigator 3*) illustrated the power a federal judge can wield to issue 'summary judgments', initially precluding the case from being heard by a jury. We obtained a reversal on appeal and remand for a jury trial, but the judge remained on the bench. After a month of trial, the jury saw through his machinations. My client, Yogananda's monastic organization, Self-Realization Fellowship, won an historic jury verdict, preserving Yogananda's copyrights.

There is an ironic reality to many of the cases that I have tried to juries and verdict. Humans are innately flawed when our thoughts, feelings, and actions are compared and weighed against the highest moral standards and moral laws underlying society—like the Ten Commandments. Whether we are all intrinsic 'sinners' or just individuals who have temporarily 'sinned,' it seems to me that we are all capable of raising our consciousness to rise above our 'sins.' Jurors are called to do precisely that in rendering verdicts. Even peanut farmer / President Jimmy Carter admitted to "lusting in his heart." Many presidents have pursued lustful encounters. Forgiveness may be needed as in the case of Clinton and Monica. But where a pattern of immorality is quantum entangled in serious criminality—including murder, i.e., Vince Foster, Clinton's White House Counsel, even our presidents must be held accountable.

Forgiveness is needed but so is accountability. Our accountability system has utterly failed. The Clintons, Obama, Biden and to a lesser degree, the Bushes have destroyed our DOJ. Bush hacks like Robert Mueller and William Barr were as bad as Comey, Garland, and Smith.

My clients have all made mistakes, as have I. But in the adversary system, my job was to show the jury that they were, as Shakespeare put it, "more sinned against than sinning." The Mike Love v. Brian Wilson case (*Litigator 3*) is a perfect example. Between 1989 and 1993, Brian Wilson first sued a crooked lawyer and music publisher who had defrauded Brian and his co-writer, Mike Love, out of their copyrights to their famous Beach Boys' songs. Mike did not join Brian's suit because Brian's lawyers had lied to Mike Love. During Brian's case against the crooked lawyer and the publisher, Brian's lawyers instructed Mike to lie in his deposition about several critical issues in that case. Thereafter, Mike sued both Brian and the crooked lawyer who had represented the publisher when the original fraud occurred.

Mike then sued Brian, the crooked lawyer, and the publisher. Brian's defense painted him as a womanizing rocker who had committed perjury in Brian's case. We hid nothing from the judge and jury, and admitted Mike's untruthful testimony. We admitted Mike's flaws and laid bare the bigger truth: Mike had been cheated and defrauded by Brian Wilson, Brian's father who controlled the Beach Boys, and by the corrupt lawyers and a crooked music publisher. Brian's lawyer, who had succeeded in getting a $10 million "settlement" from the publisher, was later disbarred on a different matter. Following Brian's settlement, Mike Love sued Brian, the crooked lawyer, and the publisher. We won. See Mike's book *Good Vibrations: My Life as a Beach Boy*.

The jury saw through the noise and delivered an unprecedented verdict for Mike Love. But it wasn't just legal strategy; it was consciousness. We were both meditators, and with the divine help of Mother Meera, whose presence permeated the trial, we raised the collective consciousness of the jury to a level where justice became inevitable.

The Sequeira case is also an example of raising the collective consciousness of the jury above the underlying realities of the problems in the Sequeira marriage and the shadowy issues in the car dealership which Richard Sequeira was involved in—as inferred in the minority shareholder asserting his 5th Amendment rights. All juries, of course, comprised of humans, know that all humans are flawed; but most jurors aspire to live a life in accordance with moral precepts, religious, and spiritual commandments. On that basis, the collective consciousness of the jurors can be elevated to do the right thing and render a just verdict on the collective weight of the evidence if it supports a higher truth than isolated facts that have come into evidence against your client.

The monumental example of the Kennedy assassination is an inverse example of how corrupt governmental interference, the Dulles/CIA driven conspiracy to kill JFK, thwarted truth and justice with no jury trial. The facts and indisputable evidence proving who, how, and why the CIA murdered JFK were never tried in court. It was decided by the money changers in the Warren Commission. Think about that. How did the Deep State avoid a trial? It was all prearranged. There was no trial because the CIA and Jack Ruby murdered Oswald, the "patsy" and presumed killer.

No killer to try, case closed, no need for a trial... and no jury... what a coincidence.

Had there been a trial, I feel confident that Oswald would have convincingly proved that he was a CIA 'cut out,' a "patsy," a decoy, part of the scheme used in the CIA operation to assassinate JFK in order to conceal the fact that the 'kill shot' came from a Corsican mob shooter on the Grassy Knoll. Two shooters equals a conspiracy as the House Select Committee on Assassinations concluded and reported in March 1979—46 years ago!

But the major media, including the New York Times which supported the Warren Commission, shut down opposition with its newly coined epithet—"CONSPIRACY THEORY." They were correct about one thing: they were 'in on' a conspiracy to conceal Deep State corruption as coconspirators. Recommend Sylvia Meagher's 1967 book *Accessories After The Fact: The Warren Commission, The Authorities and the Report on the JFK Assassination*. It is a masterpiece of journalistic excellence on the many books covering the assassination. America must wake up to the degenerate evil doers who have corrupted our system of justice.

The hiccup in the Dulles plan was that Oswald killed Officer Tippit, knowing that Tippit intended to kill him as part of the CIA operation to kill JFK. So the CIA then resorted to Jack Ruby to kill Oswald in front of every American on television. The public believed what the Warren Commission told them: that Oswald acted alone, that there was no conspiracy. Utter corruption. In *Litigator 4*, the JFK assassination is proven to be a CIA operation beyond reasonable doubt.

In the Kennedy murder, Dulles, the CIA, and the FBI all knew that real truth seekers, given a legitimate judge and the introduction of all of the forensic and eyewitness testimony available then and now—would convince a jury that the CIA Secret Government murdered Kennedy using a mob shooter from the Grassy Knoll. They used Oswald as a decoy, killed him, and used the phony baloney Warren Commission, controlled by Dulles, to thoroughly corrupt 'due process of law.' A legitimate trial before a jury would have exposed the corruption of the CIA, FBI, and DOJ, and the so-called Warren Commission. An abomination of justice that has corrupted the American soul would have been avoided with a jury trial.

For juries, the search for truth is not only a relevant and valid question—it is their constitutionally mandated, sworn, sacred duty. The 'sacred' part specifically raises their consciousness if the lawyer for at least one side emphasizes that sacredness. I always did in all my jury trials. The laws of our country within the aegis of our constitutional protections, particularly the most basic form of justice, due process of law, and equal protection of law, are a sacred obligation of our system of jurisprudence and the sacred responsibility of a jury. Without due process and equal protection we lose the foundation of justice forged in legitimate judicial/jury proceedings where facts based on truth are tried and tested. Our society, including due process and equal protection of laws, established in our Constitution and Bill of Rights and irretrievably and irredeemably break down if the judges controlling the laws are corrupted by the politically funded money elites who appoint the judges.

I have never ceased to be amazed at the many juries that I have addressed that have returned unprecedented verdicts achieving justice—sometimes against seemingly impossible odds when a corrupt judge attempted to thwart the truth. In such cases, juror consciousness has been raised. Almost universally in my experience, juries have ferreted through the machinations of both the litigators and, in some cases, the overt corruption of judges. In almost all my cases, my clients held virtually no power, or even a minuscule fraction of the financial resources, possessed by those we were up against. I have experienced how the collective consciousness of a jury can defeat corruption in the system, notwithstanding the power and money against us.

My faith in a jury of our peers to study, analyze, and weigh the evidence presented to them has remained unwavering and steadfast even though I have watched it break down in some cases. For example, the OJ Simpson acquittal may illustrate this principle: that human passions and desperation for lost love run deep in the human psyche. Simpson had a marital/love relationship with his victim, Nicole Brown. When he found her with another male, his attachment caused massive anger and horrific results. In his case, perhaps the jury understood that it was a crime of passion—not warranting the charge of first-degree murder with malice aforethought that the government aggressively pursued?

Perhaps their verdict was a form of Jury Nullification against the prosecutor for overcharging the case with premeditated murder versus a crime of passion? The government likely pushed too hard on the First-Degree Murder charge. The fact that the victims were both physically close together with Simpson when he stabbed them, as opposed to premeditated kill shots from a distance—suggested a crime of passion. The jury nullified premeditation in its acquittal. Truth? Justice? God only knows. OJ would have been better facing the music with a plea deal, likely rejected by a career, aggressive prosecutor.

Ironically, the OJ case allegedly holds the record for the longest sequestered jury trial, that is, where the jurors are 'locked up' so they don't get tainted by media coverage or opinions of spouses, relatives, friends, or onlookers. But, in fact, one of my cases may hold this record. (Chapter 11.)

CONSCIOUSNESS IN LAW, SCIENCE, AND QUANTUM ENTANGLEMENT

In retrospect, there are multiple factors that have helped me understand the contrasting phenomenon between man-made law vs. natural law, and divine law (a law of compassion, mercy, and forgiveness), and human justice vs. divine justice. The primary retrospective factor in my discernment over decades is meditation and accompanying prayer. In meditation, my mind has opened enough to displace my own ego-centered ideas, and allowed God to penetrate my mind enough to understand His laws. They are vastly superior to those of man.

"TRUTH IS THE OFFSPRING OF SILENCE AND MEDITATION."

Isaac Newton, 400 years ago, echoed the insights of the Rishis and Masters of Yoga when he said that truth is the offspring of silence and meditation. I have experienced this reality over 50 years of meditation. The ramifications of this science-based reality, directing our souls, minds, and hearts toward unifying natural law with divine law, might enable our species to avoid our own self-destruction.

Abortion is the ultimate example of human self-destruction. It eclipses wars, genocides, and holocausts in the human domain of intrinsic evil, arrogance, and stupidity.

JURY TRIALS AND THE FORCE FIELD OF CONSCIOUSNESS

In jury trials, the judge instructs the jury that they are the sole judges of the facts; and that their sworn duty is to decide on the facts based solely on the evidence presented to them. The judge instructs the jury on the laws to apply to the facts that they determine to be true. The judge instructs the jury to weigh the evidence presented to them in the context of witness credibility, the exhibits introduced into evidence, and to weigh all of the evidence in the pursuit of truth.

Based on these fundamental instructions, jurors generally start listening to the evidence in a case with their minds in "coherence" (a favorite Maharishi term), at least with regard to their singular purpose to find facts based on evidence that they deem to be true. In my experience, jurors take these instructions very seriously, and generally listen attentively to both sides in the presentation of facts by the lawyers admitted into evidence by the judge. Over the course of a trial, the evidence accumulates and correlates with related, relevant, admissible evidence in the jurors' minds. The longer the trial, the more evidence there is to weigh, evaluate, correlate, and determine what is true. My 50-year litigation history generally involved long, protracted trials, voluminous evidence and exhibits, and multiple experts to provide the jury 'expert testimony' on specific subjects beyond the ordinary knowledge of the jurors.

I have tried numerous 2–4 month trials, some contained in this Litigator series. I never considered jury verdicts notches on my belt so I never counted them...just as I have thrown out my few sports trophies. Non-attachment I consider a virtue. In the Motorgate case (Ch. 11), along with the locked-up jury, I endured what might be the longest sequestered jury trial on record, over six months, that's longer than the OJ Simpson trial! One recently married young male juror in that case, towards the end of the six months, was leaning over the jury rail salivating at his wife who was sitting in the front row of the spectators!

This isolated event tells a story in itself about jury trials, particularly locked-up juries performing their sacred, sworn, civil duty. The mind, body, and consciousness of a juror are saturated with extraneous thoughts and feelings, desires and worries, past life experiences, all of which are collected in and make up their consciousness; however they can still do the right thing and achieve a consciousness-raised verdict. Consciousness operates beyond mind as observed in meditation where the "observer" or soul observes the continuing chain of thoughts running through the 'monkey mind'.

We can distinguish ourselves from the Darwinian-evolved monkey minds through meditation, silence, and transcendence. Have you ever observed your pet cat or dog react instantaneously to whatever thoughts are triggered by external stimuli? We can escape that animal syndrome.

In long, high-profile trials, juror fatigue and mental and emotional aggression become potentially influencing factors in their verdict. From outside the jury room in some courthouses not sufficiently soundproofed from the courtroom, specifically in one long, difficult case, I heard the jurors loudly arguing, sometimes yelling at their fellow jurors. In that case, where their arguments became so intense that it filtered into the adjacent courtroom where I sat with my client and colleagues, I recall thinking that I might lose that case; and that those jurors should meditate a few minutes in silence before aggressively asserting their opinions on the evidence. Putting 12 souls together in a jury room to evaluate months of conflicting evidence in an important case requires gradually developing and ascending levels of consciousness within individual jurors to arrive at truth and justice. In that case, I think I was rescued by a good judge who forced the opposing party to settle the case while the jury was fighting. I'm not sure I succeeded in raising the consciousness of the jury.

Jurors learn from each other if they listen to opposing or similar, nuanced perspectives of their fellow jurors. The axiom of Isaac Newton becomes applicable: "Truth is the offspring of silence and meditation." Unfortunately, no such juror instruction exists—even though truth and justice are the ultimate goals most often achieved in silence and meditation. Corrupted judges who have sold out their consciousness to money are incapable of either practicing meditation in prolonged silence of even 30 minutes or grasping its importance in the administration of justice. Good judges seem to have an acquired skill to resolve cases more in conformity with Isaac Newton and Yogananda.

A jury is generally comprised of 12 souls with widely divergent life experiences and levels of consciousness. In most of my long trials, 4 alternates, or 16 jurors, were seated. The differing minds, hearts, and consciousness of a jury are critical to the understanding of how jurors ultimately decide a case. Most important is their consciousness—beyond mind, heart, feeling, emotions, and even the instructions on the law by the trial judge. Evil agendas with bribed jurors are rare, but the evils of individuals like George Soros using his money to influence judicial and political outcomes with prosecutors have been recently questioned in the bogus indictments of President Trump.

Our Constitution created a system of checks and balances designed to prevent the concentration of corrupt power. It also created the three separate branches of government; Executive, Judicial, and Legislative, with restricting powers so that one branch could not invade and corrupt the powers in a separate branch. That system has also been corrupted by the deep state money changers. Bankruptcy judges can avoid jury trials. In America, bankruptcy judges have reached a pinnacle of corruption where they can essentially do whatever they want and get away with it. See LoPucki: *Courting Failure: How Competition for Big Cases Is Corrupting the Bankruptcy Courts*. The Tim Blixseth cases (*Litigator 4*) showcase the reality of embedded bankruptcy court corruption.

The constitutional safeguards separating the three branches of government have died in America. The Deep State money control of our elected representatives in the Legislative Branch, which confirms judicial appointments selected by the President within his powers in the Executive Branch, have eroded the separation of powers and integrity of our judicial system. The First Amendment-protected major media, also controlled by Deep State money, have generally failed to expose the utter corruption. The "money changers" have destroyed our Constitutional system of jurisprudence, just as they crucified the purest form of truth and justice 2000 years ago. Nothing has changed.

In a jury trial, one of the most fundamental rights is the right to cross-examine the opposing party and witnesses. This right creates an adversarial, intellectual, factual confrontation to seek out the truth. Cross-examining the opposing party and the witnesses of an adversary, including his experts, and challenging his documentary exhibits during cross-examination, if the lawyer is thoroughly prepared, will generally result in the exposure of lies, falsehoods, and fraud.

This is fundamental to our justice system, as well as preserving transparency in both political and judicial systems. The jury absorbs the unfolding truth from the cross-examination, leading them to render a just verdict. Jurors unanimously tend to accept the truth when it hits their minds and hearts and elevates their consciousness. Truth and transparency are powerful elixirs combatting corruption in a field of consciousness. Perhaps in many cases, jurors use their hearts more than their minds, which seems to be closer to elevated states of consciousness. Our minds and hearts operate in a field of consciousness intersecting with each other. Many mystics, truth seekers, and 'saints' have reported their interconnected experience between their individual consciousness and a field of consciousness they call God.

What is consciousness as observed and understood within our limited human abilities and subject to our five senses, brain, biological chemistry, nervous system, imagination, and reasoning faculties? In essence, it is a state, a field, a filter, a means by which we function using all of the foregoing human attributes. The body, brain, mind, and emotions in our species exist in a state of consciousness. AI describes it as "the state of being aware of oneself and one's surroundings, encompassing subjective experiences like thoughts, feelings, sensations, and perceptions."

Yogananda says consciousness is the eternal fundamental reality of the soul, our true self—a fundamental, universal reality, the foundation of existence, a state of awareness not dependent on the brain, our actual state of knowing beyond sensory experience and ego identification. An example using Yogananda's definition would be defining myself as a litigating lawyer using my mind, intellect, and senses—essentially the ego. When my true existence is actually beyond all ego identification, I am capable of experiencing my true Self in a state of awareness where I am actually one with God. Self-Realization. When I do not grasp the latter reality of Self-realization, I am trapped in litigating lawsuits, making them my total reality. Ignorance. Meditation enables me to see beyond such self-limiting ignorance.

In the 12-soul, collective consciousness of a jury, with very divergent individual levels of consciousness seeking truth amidst an avalanche of evidence in a long, high-profile trial, I have observed a remarkable, synchronistic, what I now deem to be quantum-entangled, verdict within higher states of consciousness. When a jury that has argued over conflicting evidence achieves a unanimous verdict, in the context of their very disparate individual thinking and backgrounds (such as a bricklayer arguing with a college professor), but somehow concludes what is fundamentally true or even fair and just in their collective verdict, it is the result of a collective consciousness rising above their individual consciousness. Their collective consciousness almost miraculously transports them out of their individual biases, prejudices, ego identifications, and mindsets.

What is the 'field of consciousness' that enables this mystery to occur from 12 different minds and hearts? I have concluded, based upon Yogananda's Kriya Yoga meditation which takes one up the spine through one's brain to the Christ Center between the eyebrows, that the 'field of consciousness' is where God operates and quantum entanglement occurs. Maharishi called it "the Absolute," pure consciousness, pure 'Being,' pure awareness. Einstein said that he wanted to "know God's thoughts, the rest are details;" and called quantum entanglement "spooky" because it defied his special and general theories of relativity based on the speed of light.

Yogananda digested and synchronized all of the human sciences in his direct personal experiences of God in his most advanced states of consciousness, 'Samadhi'. He encapsulated these states of consciousness in the term "Self–Realization"; in a nutshell it is the experience that our souls are one with God. Once experienced, it is recognized as that elusive yet perpetually present attribute: the connectedness of the soul with God in a field of consciousness.

In my experience in meditation, we gain glimpses of our eternal connectedness to God. We can experience transcendence beyond the monkey mind flow of continuous thoughts. In my experience with juries, they ultimately render a verdict reflecting their highest level of collective consciousness—despite being repeatedly instructed by judges to focus solely on the evidence. Once deliberating and hearing the opinions of their fellow jurors, they are generally able to get out of their own mindsets to arrive at just and fair outcomes that transcend themselves and even the evidence presented. This "spooky" 'sacred' process tends to result in truth and justice. The Sequeira case may reflect that reality. Subsequent cases in the Litigator series definitely reflect that reality and the law of quantum entanglement beyond just matter and electrons. Stay tuned.

At bottom, jury cases, like life itself, involve paradoxes, conundrums, conflicts, 'sins', falsehoods, and ambiguities. Who among us lives in such a pure state, particularly within our system of justice, that we are not subject to all of the above? Not many, if anyone. Like every individual not operating on the level of God consciousness, we and our system of laws and justice are flawed. One man's truth may be another man's lie. Just look at the contrast between our political parties. The jury system, even immersed in injustice, can achieve a true and just verdict. Jury Nullification.

I consider myself a Libertarian. I don't trust either major political party, the politicians feeding off them, or government in general. I know from 50 years in the PIT that both parties, and the men in them, have been corrupted by the pursuit of money, and the money changers' control over America's political and judicial systems.

As the individual consciousness of jurors combines, conflicts, or meshes with that of counsel, parties, the judge, witnesses, documents, testimony, and court exhibits, a 'synthesis' generally occurs, resulting in a collective outcome: a verdict. It is a dynamic, sometimes mystical form of quantum entanglement in practical human affairs.

"What is truth?", Pontius Pilate asked Christ, knowing that the Chief Priests were trying to use Roman Laws against rebellion to crucify Jesus Christ. In truth, the Sanhedrin was using Pilate to murder Christ in order to preserve their power and Temple cash flows under Judaic law. The Chief Priests, Annas and Caiphas, had revved up a mob to coerce Pilate into doing their dirty work. Christ represented a threat to Sanhedrin power and cash flows when he threw the 'money changers' out of the Temple for turning the "House of God into a Den of Thieves." The pattern of using legal systems to destroy those who threaten entrenched power has not changed in two thousand years.

Trump should take some comfort in the "Durham Report," which established Hillary's frame-up of him in her "Russiagate conspiracy" to defraud the voting public, using the Comey FBI, and get herself elected president of our country. In a QE-related way, the Durham report also exposes the corruption within the FISA court controlled by none other than James Boasberg in allowing the Garland DOJ to illegally access data in at least 18,000 illegal intrusions into a database originally illegally acquired by Brennan computer hackers, one of which included my former client working for the CIA. I defended him when the FBI raided his home to retrieve evidence of CIA crimes. Strange how the quantum entangled dots in my cases have connected.

The word 'evil' is a loaded word meaning different things to different people, often depending on religious beliefs and membership in different churches, applying a variety of moral codes, laws, and 'Commandments'. Throughout the "Litigator" series, I use the word 'evil' in context, based on my legal experience over 50 years—to convey the most false, heinous, vicious, immoral, and wicked conduct that any reasonable fact finder, like a juror, would conclude and render a verdict on. Common sense tells us all that some conduct is so reprehensible, whether individually or collectively perpetrated, that the word evil applies, such as the money changer evil that crucified Christ and continues today, two thousand years later in forms both ancient and modern. I don't use the word evil in my books to convey my own personal beliefs.

The exchange and transmission of consciousness is fundamental to communication among all levels of our species. Research has established that less than ten percent of communication is verbal. Since more than ninety percent of communication is non-verbal, what is it that is being communicated? After so many years in litigation permeated with the mysteries of meditation, I believe that the what, when, how, and why of nonverbal communication involves force fields of quantum entangled realities.

The inherent sense of fairness in the collective consciousness of our jury system has prevailed, in my experience, and this has been reflected in their verdicts. In discussing their verdicts with them afterwards, I have often been amazed at how such different souls, minds, and hearts reached a collective result. In my opinion, it is a sacred event. Perhaps, on that basis, a field of force in collective consciousness has caused the result.

THE ADVOCATE'S DUTY AND THE READER'S VERDICT

When reflecting on the juries I have witnessed rendering their verdicts, I do not doubt for a moment that their verdicts also had to do in some way with the cosmic justice that was unfolding. Fighting the good fight for a good cause, beyond the obvious machinations of judges and their power brokers, seems to me to embody and embrace a greater truth than their power to corrupt it.

In pursuit of justice for clients, lawyers must adhere to rules governing attorney-client confidentiality. It involves necessary court disclosures, and full transparency with clients as part of their fiduciary duty. Throughout these chapters, I have strived to present the unvarnished truth while preserving client confidences. At this stage in the book, my biases, experiences, and perspectives, shaped by years in the justice system—should be evident. I have been forthright, calling a spade a spade, without fear of retribution. I have identified individuals and detailed their actions according to the laws of evidence and inference. I believe our country is deeply corrupted, aided by the major media's protection of Deep State criminals. Perhaps you will share this view?

The realities of litigation and meditation permeate these chapters. As a meditating litigator, I owed my clients "fiduciary duties," as well as the preservation of their confidences. I have fulfilled those duties. I know many truths based on many facts from clients that I have had to keep confidential. Such duties occasionally involve what is called full disclosure between myself and clients in the event I have conflicted or adversarial interests with clients. This type of issue is particularly illustrated in a situation where a powerful Washington 'Swamp' law firm represented both the Clintons and the Scientologists when Clinton's White House Counsel was murdered in 1993 at the time Clinton granted tax exemption to the Church of Scientology. (*Litigator 2*.)

In my own practice, I avoided conflicts of interest until one case came back to haunt me. A verdict I won twenty-five years ago became entangled in a client's marital dispute, forcing me to navigate loyalties I never anticipated. I mention this because I owe you, the reader, a disclosure: in this book, I am telling the truth about fifty years in the pit of litigation—the victories, the failures, and the enemies I made along the way. I will honor my duty to protect client confidences, but I will not sanitize the record. Some of the individuals exposed in these pages are powerful, and this candor may cost me. So be it.

There are exceptions to this rule of fiduciary duty when the client lies to the lawyer, and subsequent litigation develops between lawyer and client. This has happened in several cases. But in this Litigator series, I am continuing to maintain certain confidences even though I am legally entitled to disclose them, and they would greatly benefit me by disclosure. As an 'advocate' I make these disclosures to help you in your deliberations in the event you decide to act like a juror.

I have fully informed the jury in every case that I have tried as follows: "I am an advocate for my client in an adversarial system of justice. Your decision-making depends on your evaluation of the evidence, not mine. I will give you my evaluation of the evidence on behalf of my client to help and guide you. You may accept it or discard it as you decide, based on your own perception and evaluation of the truth. My opponent will give you his or hers. Your sworn and sacred duty is to render a verdict based on your collective understanding of the truth, not mine."

Disclosure: when I first represented any client, whether Dan or Patty in the cases you have read thus far, in accordance with my fiduciary duty to them, I accepted their version of the evidence which was admissible in court under the rules, as 'true'—unless contrary evidence, in my opinion at the time, made their testimony false, or gray, or so ill-defined as to be unknowable, or inconclusive. In the latter situation, I emphasized what I knew to be true.

Case in point: neither me, you, nor the jurors in Patty or Richard's case really knew from direct, percipient evidence how Richard died. There were no witnesses, no forensics, and no body. But we presented the evidence based on the inferences you have read about. The jury in that case rendered a verdict. You may render your own verdict, different from theirs...speculating that Richard ran off into the sunset with his blonde girlfriend, or that his murder was an inside job by the employees, or a myriad of other speculations? But I caution you to look inside yourself, discover your own biases, predilections, and deceptive or 'true' thought processes. To do that, you must know yourself. If you followed your conscience and consulted with 11 other souls on the Sequeira case, your own biases might get exposed and you might enter a field of collective consciousness to render a verdict in that case.

THE CONUNDRUM OF RESISTING EVIL: KNOWING OUR OWN 'SINS'

Now you know my role. I am an advocate in an adversarial system, not the doer. In truth, I now know retrospectively that God is the doer. If we obey His commandments and align our conscience with His guidance, we are duty-bound to accept and surrender to what He puts on our plate. Prayer and meditation are our God-given tools. If our egos defy His basic rules, we crash and burn. Been there, done that.

Proof of being the non-doer is most visible in cases where divine intervention was so tangible — like Sandra and Lester in Chapter 8 , that the result left me with no doubt. Other jury verdicts in this series confirm it. The cases I have selected support this truth. Following the Sequeira verdict and the ensuing events, I found myself compelled to delve deeper into my TM practices, asking questions about the nature of truth and justice. Can a jury truly understand the whole picture, independent of the skills and strategies of judges and lawyers? Collectively, does their unified consciousness result in true verdicts?

Ultimate truth and justice are known only to God. Human justice can only approach it. That cosmic reality is proven in several verdicts God obtained for my clients. Some verdicts, like Sequeira, demonstrate that if we surrender to God and Christ and obey His commandments, all things are possible—even against impossible odds. But we must align our will with His natural laws.

The Bhagavad Gita says "Stand up and fight." Christ's Sermon on the Mount says "resist not evil"... "turn the other cheek." Yet Christ made a whip of cords and drove the money changers out of the Temple, calling them thieves. Krishna told Arjuna to kill his adversary Karna even while trapped under a chariot, violating codes of honor, because dharma demanded it. I have studied both scriptures for decades. The lesson: elevate your consciousness in silence and meditation as deeply as possible—surrender, and do your duty. No matter what, stand up and fight the evil within yourself and the evil God puts on your plate. In litigation, these have been my guidelines.

Every trial lawyer faces an uncomfortable truth: your client may be flawed, even guilty of wrongs unrelated to the case. My goal has always been to show the jury that they were, as Shakespeare put it, "more sinned against than sinning." Mike Love v. Brian Wilson is a perfect example. Mike had flaws — he lied in a deposition under pressure from Brian's lawyers, but he had been cheated and defrauded for decades by Brian, Brian's father, and corrupt lawyers and publishers. We hid nothing from the jury. We admitted Mike's untruthful testimony. The bigger truth prevailed: Mike had been robbed. The jury saw through the noise and delivered an unprecedented verdict. Consciousness...not perfection, won the day.

I am no saint. I have overindulged, wrestled with ambition, and absorbed my own share of litigation ego into transcendental bliss. Guilty. But I kept trying to dye the cloth, litigating and meditating, because the fight never stops. TM gave me glimpses of stillness; Kriya demanded confrontation. The allowance of TM can lead to dysfunction; the willpower of Kriya means you stay in the ring, fighting the enemy within as much as the one without.

That is the conundrum I live with: resisting evil while knowing my own sins. Yet the cases in this series show that an imperfect human can still fight for truth and justice, not because he is pure, but because he is willing to keep showing up, keep meditating, keep surrendering, and keep fighting.

Fifty years in the pit of litigation has taught me that the battle for justice is not always fought in the courtroom. The conflicts I faced, against Scientology, corrupt judges, and against the crushing weight of the Deep State were merely modern expressions of an ancient war—that between spiritual truth and material power. To survive that war, let alone win it, required more than legal skill. It required a different kind of weapon.

Now do you, dear reader, understand why I needed meditation? It was not an escape, but a necessity. It was the only way to vent the anger and the sorrow, to find the stillness needed to see the truth behind the lies, and to prepare for the next battle. The deeper I went into the silence however, the more I realized that the conflicts of my own life were entangled with forces that stretched back through generations, and perhaps even through lifetimes. To truly understand the nature of this war, we must look deeper than the courtroom, into the very cells that carry the memory of ancient conflicts.

CHAPTER 6

The Biology, Metaphysics, and Entanglement of Cellular Consciousness

"Every cell in our body is conscious. It's like a little universe in itself... It is really composed of lifetrons of prana—there is prana in every single cell of our body".
Paramahansa Yogananda

"A total order is contained, in some implicit sense, in each region of space and time."**David Bohm**

Does a single cell have memory? Does it carry the echo of a war fought a century ago, or the trauma of a murder that happened in another lifetime? The question is no longer the domain of mystics alone. If everything else in nature recycles, it is the key to understanding my own life.

I was born a 'war baby' in 1944, into a world vibrating with the trauma of global conflict. I have always felt that the battles I fought in the courtroom were quantum-entangled with the wars that defined my parents' generation and the Irish rebellions that defined my ancestors. This chapter is an exploration of that connection, a journey into the biology of the soul, the metaphysics of memory, and the evidence that suggests our very cells carry the record of who we were, and who we are destined to become.

A jury trial taught me something I did not learn in law school: truth is not only argued, it is felt. Twelve strangers can enter a courtroom with twelve different lives, and leave it carrying one verdict. When that happens, it doesn't feel like mere opinion. It feels like contact with something higher. That is why the battle is not only 'out there' in institutions. It is also inside the human instrument that must perceive truth. Therefore we have to ask a more dangerous question: What exactly is the human being? If consciousness is real, and if it can rise in a jury, then we cannot keep pretending it begins and ends in the brain. In this respect, we must investigate cellular consciousness, memory, and the field where our wars, our karmas, and our choices keep reappearing.

Does our cellular consciousness at birth cast us into lives of past incarnational karmic reality, conflict and generational warfare... the very plague of humanity? Reflect on the First Law of Thermodynamics that states 'energy is neither created nor destroyed in an isolated system'? My meditation practice and litigation experiences have taught me that the human body is an isolated system within a quantum-entangled field of other humans also having consciousness. That consciousness is shared within the field.

The field is more than two or more minds thinking alike, sharing the same ideas and ideals, or even sharing the same faith, religious or political convictions. A unanimous jury verdict by individuals having very disparate observable brain functions, manifested in their intellectual and emotional responses to evidence, suggests that their shared perspective on what is true and just in a case with intense conflicts arises in higher states of consciousness that individually they would not normally experience. After 50 years of trying cases to juries, a unanimous verdict to 'speak the truth' supports a theory of quantum entangled minds and brains in a state of elevated consciousness. Within the biophysical system of a jury trial on conflicted facts, issues and even applied legal principles, the jury, judge and lawyers have accelerated both their learning capacity and their rapidly educated knowledge on the law and the evidence into a unified state of consciousness. In many cases it is almost supernatural.

A recent, exhaustive, peer-reviewed study in the *Computational and Structural Biotechnology Journal* titled "Evidence of quantum-entangled higher states of consciousness" provides a detailed analysis and statistical findings supporting this thesis. The article postulates: "What if quantum entanglement could accelerate learning by unlocking higher states of conscious experience? This study provides empirical and statistical evidence of how quantum entanglement influences consciousness at a *biophysical* level" (emphasis supplied).

The "biophysical level" referenced is us...our human bodies, brains, minds, feelings and consciousness. My 50 years in the PIT of litigation while meditating provides experiential evidence supporting the above article, its thesis, and the above quotes from AI and Yogananda. My past life reincarnation experience, as Father Michael Griffin, and the Sequeira case, coupled with transcendental insights while meditating, supports this thesis.

MY OWN CELLULAR CONSCIOUSNESS IN A FORCE FIELD OF TWO WORLD WARS

As a 1944 "war baby" born during the horrific aerial slaughters of WW II which were unlike any prior wars in human history where massive bombing campaigns destroyed entire cities and their civilian populations, the huge American and British bombers involved thousands of B-29's, B-17's, B-24's and British Lancasters in a single mission, each carrying 10,000 pounds or more of high explosives and incendiaries to create firestorms to completely destroy and burn down cities like Dresden and Tokyo in 1945. My own trial experience in 1985, more than 40 years after the bombings ended, involved a former B-17 pilot who participated in the horrific firestorming of Dresden, a city with no strategic military targets swollen with refugees fleeing from the Russian army 70 miles away.

At the Yalta Conference on February 4–11, 1945, Stalin, Churchill and Roosevelt approved the bombing of over one hundred thousand civilians just two days later, February 13–15, 1945. Dresden involved four separate aerial raids involving over 1200 bombers in each raid. It is one of the most obscene "war crimes" of WW II.

Fast forward 4 decades, I represented a former B-17 pilot whose 17-year-old daughter, Sisi, was killed by a drunk driver going the wrong way on a major Boston, limited-access freeway. The accident itself is surreal: a drunk going up the off ramp of Route 93 out of Boston, and immediately traversing three lanes against the oncoming traffic, cresting a hill and smashing into a car with 4 teenage girls who had recently graduated and were going home from a Boston Bruins game. Like several of my cases, the events in that case are almost surreal, supernatural, mystifying, and to me reflect the reality of quantum entangled fields of consciousness stretching across decades and arising out of tragic violence on both ends. The family of Sisi, who languished in a year-long coma then died, was devastated. Having represented several families involving child death, several of which are in this book, the unrelenting devastation is indescribable.

My client, Sisi's father, Wil Smyly, a magnificent human being, was the pilot of a B-17 who participated in the horrific, combined American and British annihilation of Dresden. Forty years later, the tragic death of Sisi somehow became quantum entangled with Wil's heroic duty in WW II. (Chapters 18, 19.)

Three weeks after Dresden, the three Yalta Conference killers sent 279 B-29 Superfortresses—each carrying 20,000 lbs of incendiaries and explosives, to firebomb Tokyo, killing over 100,000 civilians and wiping out

16 square miles of the city. In August 1945, America wiped out Nagasaki and Hiroshima with nuclear bombs. The massive technologically advanced aerial weapons of WW II followed just two decades after WWI, in which the world watched the obscene massacres in the trenches.

What is the common thread in all of the above death? Human consciousness limited to the limbic region of the brain? As man's consciousness ascends to Christ consciousness, is he capable of such barbarity? Once inside such a state, my meditation experiences, expanded over 5 decades in hardcore, very combative litigation, suggest that it is impossible.

My dad was born at the height of the WW I trench butchering insanity in February 1918. Did his cellular consciousness during and between these greatest wars in the history of our species impact my cellular consciousness? Common sense suggests how could it not? The above Biotechnology Journal study supports common sense. For two millennia, generations of Christians have professed allegiance to the Sermon on the Mount—love your enemies, turn the other cheek, judge not lest ye be judged, all while slaughtering each other in wars of unprecedented brutality. The two World Wars were fought largely between Christian nations. Christ offered humanity a strategy to avoid self-destruction, and our species has ignored it. Now, in the past hundred years, we have developed technologies that could either elevate our consciousness or extinguish our species entirely. The question is, will we evolve fast enough to survive what we have created? Ninety-nine percent of the organic species that have occupied this planet are extinct. Will homo sapiens be any different?

Christ and like sages provide insights into advanced states of consciousness, now buttressed with science and AI, which demand that we function in higher fields of God consciousness or become extinct... and AI may even hasten this. Our advanced technologies, including AI, must manifest the Sermon on the Mount. Maybe Elon Musk should program his AI algorithm with the Beatitudes? History and common sense, quantum entanglement, and the first law of thermodynamics scream yes, turn the other cheek, through millennia of genocidal madness. But no one other than Christ, and the apostles and martyrs actuated in Christ consciousness, when actually facing death are able to do it as history proves. The two world wars in part involved Christian nations against Christian nations.

The British Empire reliance on Christianity to colonize the world may be the greatest oxymoron in the last two millennia.

How does the foregoing insanity of two world wars impact generations born into it? Does an unyielding cycle of human conflict derive from our cellular connections in past lives? The modern evolutionary biologists analysis above suggests that the energy contained in our cells at birth, connected to prior incarnations, programs us. Christ, Tolstoy, Gandhi all laid out paths of non-violence based on the Beatitudes so that our species could avoid self-destruction, teaching us how to re-program our cellular consciousness in the Beatitudes. But in 2000 years, we have not conformed our consciousness to the Sermon on the Mount.

I now realize that over five decades, while seeking the peace of unity consciousness in meditation, I have been straddling an invisible, endless divide between meditation and spirituality on the one hand and the materialism and the intrinsic conflict of law in my cases on the other. What to do at 81 years old?

This chapter has set the stage for an exploration of the quantum entanglement between who I was born as, and who I appeared to be whilst litigating in courtrooms dense with alternating aggression and redemption; a journey of intellectual and courtroom conflict with my 'litigation enemies'. Is autobiography in itself a self-centered egotistical endeavor? I pray not. While writing, I mostly see my flaws. I hope my message in these books transcends my ego. Yogananda's *Autobiography of a Yogi* has given me enough perspective to act and write with enough reflection to understand my life's journey, including my own mistakes, errors and 'sins' to convey the message that the American system of justice is being destroyed in a swamp of greed, immorality, and massive judicial and political corruption. Although I miraculously and by God's Grace avoided the killing fields of Vietnam, my professional career has been hallmarked with protracted litigation wars to achieve justice.

My birth occurred in global conflict, and my legal battles echoed this strife, painted in shades of suffering and success. Suffering however held the keys to redemption, teaching me introspection through meditation. Success, with its heady allure, tempted egoism. Nonetheless, these elements intertwined, guiding me toward a semblance of grace, inching closer to the divine. Despite the myriad self-help volumes describing such journeys in abstract terms, I endeavor to ground this experience in the visceral 'mud blood and beer' terrain of my litigation odyssey.

"World War I produced an earth-chilling snowball of dread karma that swelled into World War II. Only the warmth of brotherhood can melt the present colossal snowball of sanguinary karma that may otherwise grow into World War III." Paramahansa Yogananda, *Autobiography of a Yogi*

Throughout my life beginning at age 7, the cellular consciousness in my brain and mind related on some ill-defined, murky, mystical levels with the insanities of the two world wars, and later, with Paramahansa Yogananda's above quote. I did not read *Autobiography of a Yogi* until 1974 during two very intense cases, to divert my mind from those case details, and to get my mind ready to try the next case. But I didn't really get it.

When I read it the second time in 1988, and thereafter read it again and again, and listened to the Ben Kingsley narrated audio book several times, the scope and breadth of the wisdom in *Autobiography of a Yogi*, including the time Paramahansa Yogananda spent with Gandhi, awakened within me new levels of consciousness. In truth, I am only beginning to appreciate its real significance as part of my higher Self.

Sure, the "make love, not war" cliché is an obvious solution to avoid our species wiping ourselves out with nuclear technology. But there is actually much greater wisdom and science in the above quote than simply expressed in the theme adopted by the Vietnam protesters, who surrounded me in Boston when I law clerked for the Mass Supreme Judicial Court.

The intrinsic nature of consciousness enables the human mind to rise above its primal instincts, transforming the Old Testament's "eye for an eye" mentality into the teachings of the New Testament Beatitudes. Human consciousness allows the brain to shift from habitual resistance against evil towards responses that absorb and transmute it into good. This understanding was shared and conveyed by Christ, Tolstoy, Martin Luther King, Gandhi, and sages throughout the millennia.

The energies described can be called 'Divine Love'; a love or energy in the cerebral cortex created by consciousness at levels outside of the brain far higher than the "eye for an eye" reaction of the brain stem's ganglia. Divine love energy ascends up the spine through the Medulla Oblongata, and enters the cerebral cortex to the Christ Center between the eyebrows. The ascent of this spinal energy through the "Chakras" is designed to replace the limbic brain's destructive impulses.

Maharishi explained this phenomenon in the context of coordinating hundreds or thousands of TM meditators together to create a resonance of divine energy and a field of consciousness radiating out into the surrounding environment. It works. The more powerful the vibrational consciousness of a divine being, the more powerful is the resonance and the longer it lasts. Getting a group of meditators together creates a higher field of consciousness. The radiance of Christ consciousness in billions of humans over two millennia might be evidence of this reality, notwithstanding Christian Nations killing other Christians. Maybe it would have been worse? Fields of divine consciousness may be the scientific / AI hope for continuing human existence. But divine consciousness appears to conflict with the materialistic world. Otherwise, why do Christians kill Christians? Some characterize it as the battle between Satan as a fallen angel and God.

My 8-year war in the trenches with Hubbard and Scientology, where Hubbard claimed to be the Beast 666... Satan in human form—proved to me the nature of evil on this planet conflicting with the reality of divine love. evil is an illusion in the sense that evil-doers grasp on to and exist within the illusory effect of power, greed, immorality, and the vices, abdicating their connection to their higher selves and God. It is a paradox of human existence where sensory and ego-minded addiction eclipses the divine reality of our higher consciousness. I know, I've been there.

My consciousness now weaves my childhood experiences into my journey of Self-Realization. However, I am far from following Christ's teachings of not resisting evil. My life in litigation has focused on resisting just that. In my early teens, drawn to books about the two World Wars, I discovered the story of a Naval pilot mortally wounded and in a damaged plane, he decided to take down the carrier and crashed his plane into the smokestack of a Japanese carrier during battle. On some deeper level, I identified with that pilot's mindset; destroy them before they destroy you. Was it childhood fantasy, or something deeper? Perhaps an absorption of their heroic drive, or perhaps the same military ego consciousness that drove them to vanquish the enemy. Likely both.

Our primal brains cast Japan as the villain of Pearl Harbor, but history is more complex. America's slaughter of half a million Filipinos and Roosevelt's aggressive policies pushed Japan toward militarization, a forgotten prelude to the world wars. In the melee of empire and ambition, "turn the other cheek" was absent from every leader's vocabulary.

War was in my Irish blood from birth, 400 years of empire-building encoded in my cells and I have always identified with the soldiers sent to die, never the generals who sent them.

I have long wrestled with a conundrum: why did Irishmen fight for the British Empire that was starving and murdering their own people? My father's grandfather fled the Irish famine, in which the British starved over a million of my forebears while shipping grain to England. A century later, Churchill did the same to India, starving four million Bengalis in 1943-44.

The answer, I believe, is grimly simple: when you starve the young men, they will enlist in the army of their oppressors just to feed their children. Clever insanity. The British Empire was built on this calculus of desperation, Irish regiments slaughtered in the trenches of the Somme, Indian Gurkhas fighting to save a homeland their masters had plundered. Everything the British aristocracy touched turned to death, war, and murder. I know this history in my bones. I experienced it. (See Caroline Elkins, *Legacy of Violence: A History of the British Empire*, 2022.)

Why did the Indians of the subcontinent, known as the "Jewel of the Empire," endure 200 years of British tyranny until Gandhi expelled them in 1947 without firing a bullet, through Ahimsa, non-violence, and Satyagraha, adhering to truth? This occurred even as Indian regiments, like the Gurkhas from nearby Nepal fought to preserve the British Empire in both world wars, much like the Irish experience. Perhaps the answer is that even in hard core litigation some "settlements" occur when the parties just give up the fight in order to survive. My clients did that in the Scientology 8 year war.

We humans generally seek to avoid conflict with compromise. I have had innumerable cases resolve by a compromised settlement before, during and after trial. My experiences have taught me that sometimes even manifest evil must be dealt with by ceasing resistance as Christ admonished, and turning the other cheek, giving away your shirt and coat, and surrendering to God. Although Christ whipped out the money changers, he didn't "win" until after they killed him, and he resurrected his body. THAT was the supreme victory.

The founders of our country in contrast violently rebelled in 1776 and fought back against British Imperialism declaring Independence on the premise that: "We hold these Truths to be self-evident, that all men are created equal, that they are endowed by their Creator with certain unalienable Rights, that among these are Life, Liberty and the pursuit of happiness…."

Some things are worth dying for. Our country was founded on the most basic belief, faith, and Truths, namely, that our creator gave us these rights and not the Brit King or any other human pretending to be God. America was born and became the 'home of the free and the brave' employing violence to throw off the yoke of tyranny, which enabled our Founders and later generations to free us from the evil of the 1776 'Deep State' in the form of the British King. God enabled our country to escape from evil by realizing that our 'rights' derive from our Creator. Notwithstanding the Sermon on the Mount, as Christians our founding fathers resorted to resistance and violence against the evil British Empire.

The Deep State adheres to the contrary principles. They enforce policies giving them, not God, control over us. As our Founders did, each generation must awake to the reality that we answer to God, not the 'Deep State Money Changers' that control our Treasury. It is time for America to stand up and fight the corruption within itself.

After our Declaration of Independence, our Founders gave us our Constitution and three branch government. This enabled the creation of the greatest country the planet earth has ever realized, formed by opposing the evils of the British Empire with war. The Founders dedicated our country to "One Nation Under God," later embodied in 1892 in our "Pledge of Allegiance." Globally, the period between the 1860's and the end of WW I represented a time and space cycle in the development of our species in which massive violence coalesced with massive gains in human spirituality.

The American Civil War, the Peasant Revolt in Russia, multiple European and Asian wars, culminated in the utter insanity of WW I, and were matched, and the species likely "saved", by vibrational energies raising human consciousness into spiritual realms. The period between 1860 and 1918 is a period of deep human transformation which occurred in the midst of massive violence, wars and genocides. The period is characterized by the lives and births of great 'saviors' like Abraham Lincoln in America, Gandhi in India, and great spiritualists on the consciousness scale.

Globally, these 'spiritualists' propelled our species forward on an evolutionary scale, while the Deep State of that period engaged in massive violence which contrasted with the non-violence of the Beatitudes of Christ, and writings of Tolstoy, ("The Kingdom of God Is Within You,") against the lower consciousness oppressors. These oppressors were British Royalty and the Monarchies of Europe, spreading imperialism and colonialism in their last dying gasps, culminating in WW II.

The vibrational energies permeating our little planet from 1900 and 2000 with the extermination of about 200 million humans by other humans in the aftermath of the horrors of two world wars, Korea, Vietnam, and lesser conflicts are a reality residing in human consciousness. Same with the fire bombings of Dresden and Tokyo, the nuking of Nagasaki and Hiroshima, and the "Holocaust." Throw in over 63 million abortions...and the scope of this tragedy unfolding in the hands of material consciousness is shocking.

In my perspective, the human realities take both physical and metaphysical form in our cellular biology and in our consciousness. We are programmed in our cellular energies and in our consciousness to fight evil, however we perceive it. Will it result in WW III? Like 99% of all species on this planet that have become extinct, will we nuke ourselves out of existence? OR will our consciousness employ the scientific principles enunciated in the Sermon on the Mount for instance, and save our species?

It's no accident that Tolstoy's *The Kingdom of God Is Within You* appeared in 1893, the same year Paramahansa Yogananda was born. That convergence feels like a quiet signal: a rising tide of collective consciousness gathering strength just as the 20th century prepared to unleash its unprecedented bloodshed. In America, the Transcendentalists—Emerson, Thoreau, Whitman, had already turned to the Bhagavad Gita and discovered that the Kingdom of God was not the exclusive property of any church. In Russia, Tolstoy reached the same conclusion, his book so threatening to imperial power that the Tsar banned it immediately. In India, in a remote corner of Banaras, Lahiri Mahasaya was quietly igniting a renaissance, teaching Kriya Yoga to devotee-bees from every part of the country. Across the Christian world, hymn writers like Fanny Crosby were pouring transcendental visions of Christ into music that still echoes today.

That 1893 moment marked a global spiritual counter-current—vibrational energies preparing humanity for the century of destruction and opportunity ahead. Maharishi would later describe *Being* as the fulcrum in the Art of Living, a silent field from which all action arises. Dr. Eben Alexander, the neurosurgeon whose coma journey in Chapter 17 would later challenge materialist dogma, would come to see consciousness not as a brain byproduct but as fundamental reality itself. My own Catholic upbringing framed this as a battle against sin, yet the Sermon on the Mount...love your enemies, turn the other cheek, judge not—offered the same roadmap Tolstoy and Gandhi embraced: non-violence as survival strategy for our species.

Yet the 20th century ignored it. The two world wars, the Holocaust, the firebombings of Dresden and Tokyo, the nuclear annihilation of Nagasaki and Hiroshima, the 200 million war dead, the 63 million abortions since Roe v. Wade—these were not accidents. They were the fruits of abominable material consciousness: limbic-brain dominance, ego-driven power, greed, and the illusion that separation justifies slaughter. The British Empire's reliance on Christianity to colonize and starve millions was perhaps the greatest oxymoron of the last two millennia. The CIA, the Secret Government, the Deep State money changers murdering JFK, fabricating Vietnam through the Gulf of Tonkin incident, all flowed from the same illusion.

Intelligent design scientists like Dr. Douglas Axe and Dr. Stephen Meyer now offer DNA-based evidence refuting Darwinian materialism, showing that life points to an Intelligent Designer. Yet the materialists persist, clinging to the dogma that consciousness arises from, is created by, and maintained in the cerebral cortex. They are the new religionists, stuck in a middle-age scientific creed. Meanwhile, the sages; Christ, Tolstoy, Gandhi, Yogananda, pointed to the Kingdom within, the transmutation of primal energies into divine love. My own path in litigation has been a lifelong wrestling with that divide: resisting evil in courtrooms while seeking the peace of unity in meditation. At 81, I see the stakes clearly. The choice is ours: elevate consciousness or risk extinction. The Sermon on the Mount is not poetry. It is strategy.

SISTER CLARE CROCKETT

Modern day 'saints' like Sister Clare Crockett are resurrecting the innocence of youthful realization of who Christ is; and making decisions to live 'in Christ' in their Sacramental practices. Sister Clare 'died daily' within the Sacraments of the Roman Church. These were her tools to elevate her consciousness in the profound humility of Catholic monastic 'perpetual vows' and the Church Sacraments.

It worked. Sister Clare plainly reached a level of Christ consciousness by her early death at age 33, in an Ecuador earthquake where she was serving Christ and as she put it lived "Alone with Christ Alone."

Her biography by Sister Kristen Gardner and the documentary on her life, both by the same title: *Alone with Christ Alone*, are truly inspiring. More specifically, Chapter 16 of Sister Gardner's work, "Betrothal with Christ Alone," recites from Clare's notebook, in Clare's own words, of her struggle to take her 'perpetual vows'. It reveals a profound truth in which the mind surrenders to the soul.

After 10 years of serving Christ as a Candidate and Novitiate, she experienced a profound spiritual crisis. It was just before taking her 'perpetual vows' betrothing her life to Christ for her entire lifetime. It's what John of the Cross describes as "The Dark Night of the Soul." The Gardner book reveals the critical issues in studying Sister Clare's remarkable life.

Surrender of the mind to the soul is in fact such a profound and spiritually cataclysmic event as Clare experienced, it requires a much fuller understanding. Some understanding and wisdom about how to achieve such surrender can be found in the realization of the meaning of Apostle Paul's Letter to the Corinthians. Although Clare found surrender in the Church Sacraments, as her biography reveals, it was the experiences of Edith Stein, and the description of those experiences just before Stein's death at Auschwitz after being ripped by the Nazis from the Carmelite Monastery in June, 1942, that put Clare over the threshold of doubt.

After reading and quoting the "in Christ" experiences in Stein's writing, before Stein was incinerated at Auschwitz, in the depth of her own crisis, Clare records:

"A group of Jews, after the holocaust of World War II, said to the Lord, 'We will continue to believe in you'...despite Your terrible silence. God, such humility, and perseverance move Your Heart. Keep me faithful in Your silence. Help me to hear Your silence. What does Your silence mean to me? Silence of God, Silence that wounds, Silence that listens, Silence that watches, Silence that speaks through actions, Silence that shouts in my interior, 'Look at Love!' Silence of the Lord, Silence that call me to Silence, Creative silence, redeeming silence, Silence that shouts in my interior, 'Look at Love.'" *Alone with Christ Alone* at p. 396; Fn. 261.

Sister Clare was 'there'. After writing the above, she again quoted from Edith Stein and knew that her doubts were relieved by the "Mother of God". Transparently, for ten years, Clare had lived in silence as a monastic Servant Sister. She knew 'Silence'. The silence of God. The silence that both the Christian mystics and Indian Swamis had lived and conveyed for two millennia.

That silence is truth as Isaac Newton affirmed. Real meditation provides it. That is what Thoreau and Emerson discovered in "The Bhagavad Gita." That is what St. Paul meant when he said: "I die daily." (Paul; 1 Corinthians 15:31.) So did Sister Clare. Kriya meditation is directly akin to the experience of St. Paul.

For a full exposition of the meaning of "I die daily," I recommend the explanation of Paramahansa Yogananda in *Autobiography of a Yogi* wherein he references to "going inside" in meditation in order to experience Christ. Paramahansa Yogananda explains:

"St. Paul knew Kriya Yoga, or a similar technique, by which he could switch life currents to and from the senses. He was therefore able to say: "I protest by our rejoicing which I have in Christ, I die daily." By a method of centering inwardly all bodily life force (which ordinarily is directed only outwardly, to the sensory world, thus lending it a seeming validity), St. Paul experienced daily a true yoga union with the "rejoicing" (bliss) of the Christ Consciousness. In that felicitous state he was conscious of being "dead" to or freed from sensory delusions, the world of maya. In the initial states of God-communion (savikalpa samadhi) the devotee's consciousness merges in the Cosmic Spirit; his life force is withdrawn from the body, which appears "dead," or motionless and rigid. The yogi is fully aware of his bodily condition of suspended animation. As he progresses to higher spiritual states (nirvikalpa samadhi), however, he communes with God without bodily fixation; and in his ordinary waking consciousness, even in the midst of exacting worldly duties." "Kriya Yoga is an instrument through which human evolution can be quickened. . . ." See also Paramahansa Yogananda's two-volume epic work on Christ and the New Testament, *The Second Coming of Christ* .

All spiritual paths, from the Bhagavad Gita to the teachings of Christ, agree that the Kingdom of God is within us. Beneath the dogma lies a universal principle recognized by saints and yogis alike: the path to higher consciousness requires transmuting our most powerful primal energies, mastering the 'temptations of the flesh.' That very conflict between the soul's longing for purity and the body's earthly pull, was a central preoccupation for 19th-century spiritual seekers who looked beyond their era's confines for answers. The Transcendentalists, in particular, wrestled with this tension, as Wordsworth so famously captured:

"ODE: INTIMATIONS OF IMMORTALITY"

Our birth is but a sleep and a forgetting.
The Soul that rises with us, our life's Star,
Hath had elsewhere its setting,
And cometh from afar:
Not in entire forgetfulness.
And not in utter nakedness,
But trailing clouds of glory do we come
From God, who is our home:
Heaven lies about us in our infancy!
Shades of the prison-house begin to close
Upon the growing Boy,
But he beholds the light, and whence it flows,

He sees it in his joy;
The Youth, who daily farther from the east
Must travel, still is Nature's Priest,
And by the vision splendid Is on his way attended;
At length the Man perceives it die away,
And fade into the light of common day.

THE WAR WITHIN: A WAR BABY'S CONFESSION

For better or worse, I now know I imbibed a war consciousness in my personal and professional litigation life. It made me an aggressive litigator. It opposed surrendering to anything, as Bruce Springsteen intoned in "No Surrender." It made me materially successful. I now see that attitude and approach as more ego-driven delusion, even in the pursuit of truth, which, as Kipling noted in his classic poem "IF," can be "twisted by knaves to set a trap for fools."

Separating the ego-mind from the Soul-Self is an incarnational task, and a very difficult one. Separating ego imagination from reality is also daunting if you pursue experiential, meditative truth. One generally perceives suffering and 'sins' on that path. But one also likes to conceive of himself or herself as a hero or heroine. The truth for all of us seems to be in between. The good, the bad, and the ugly.

The global consciousness and education I inherited at birth made me, unquestionably, one of the good guys fighting the equally obvious bad guys. Since we won, as victors writing the history books, Japan and Nazi Germany must have been the 'bad guys.' The Holocaust proves it. Yet the 1916 massacre of my Irish countrymen, the 1943 British starvation of 4 million Bengalis, the 1919 Amritsar massacre, the Dresden 1945 firebombing... it goes on and on, and yet all were left out of my history books. My childlike sensory realities and education validated the consciousness that the UK and America were in the right, fighting for a noble cause.

I have held that good-guy consciousness throughout my personal and professional life. I inherited the global consciousness of WW II, at least the American 'victor version' of it. But is it even true?

One of my more famous clients, Beach Boys singer Mike Love, says of me in his autobiography after we won an unprecedented jury verdict against his cousin Brian Wilson: "Mike Flynn is the ultimate Righteous Brother." See *Good Vibrations: My Life as a Beach Boy*, at p. 374. Aside from egocentric appreciation of such professional accolades, the issue of its accuracy remains. In some ways it is true, in other ways, not. I may not be the "ultimate Righteous Brother" at all times. There are few of those... Christ being one of them. Hopefully this book sorts out fact from fiction, truth from falsehood, and consciousness from ego-driven thought and emotion.

To accomplish this worthwhile endeavor together, we need to delve into the reality of consciousness. That can be uncomfortable, and obviously depends on our joint levels of consciousness... yours and mine.

I was six months old when we firestormed Dresden and Tokyo. I was a thriving, rebellious one-year-old when we wiped out Nagasaki and Hiroshima, so I am told. Hmm? I wonder if those events played any role in my metaphysical, if not cellular, consciousness? Are we really 'all one' as Jesus and the millennia sages teach? Do we absorb the consciousness of our parents, who absorb the consciousness of the world they live in? For at least four years, my parents lived in a war consciousness. I guess the answer is yes.

Nuclear weapons derive from quantum theory embedded directly in human consciousness. $E=MC^2$ illustrates Einstein's brilliant and evolved level of consciousness. He discovered it. Oppenheimer and our military used it. Does employing our consciousness to split atoms and create weapons of mass destruction, which we then use against each other, reflect the same level of awareness?

For most of my adult life, I thought the U.S. was justified in both using the nuclear bombs and firestorming the two cities in Germany and Japan, our so-called 'enemies.' My consciousness avoided grappling with massacring hundreds of thousands of civilians. Then came the Wil Smyly case and my beginning practice of Kriya Yoga. In retrospect I wasn't stupid to believe what we were told; now I know I was duped by clever propaganda. (Chapters 18–19.)

I have now observed how the billionaire power brokers, presently called the Deep State, or Global Elites, operate with thoroughly corrupt impunity, controlling America's Secret Government. They steal, kill, corrupt, and pervert justice on a scale unprecedented in American history. I now understand the 2000-year-old schemes of the money changers to murder the greatest 'good guy' of all, ostensibly under the law. As an experienced litigator, I know that the present propaganda spewed on us by the major money-driven media is dark propaganda, contrived to make more money for the Deep State. Our present politicians are their mealy-mouthed puppets. See Smedley Butler's 1935 book *War Is a Racket*. Butler is one of America's most decorated war heroes.

The global chaos we see today parallels the judicial and other manipulations I've battled in courtrooms all my life. These power struggles trace back through history, guided by the same ruthless pursuit of control. As technology advances, these age-old battles are merely laid out on a digital stage, but the underlying dance remains unchanged—a relentless grasp for dominion dressed up in modern veneers. In this ever-globalizing world, I stand firm against the tide of blind conformity, determined to illuminate the hidden puppet strings of the so-called Deep State. This legacy is part of my generational fabric, my Irish roots, a culture with stories of betrayal and loss that are calls to action, a push to acknowledge past grievances while learning to wield that history to fight against repeated tyranny.

As I navigate my journey, both personal and professional, I see the echoes of past conflicts in today's global tensions. Leaders teetering toward war must remember the lessons buried under battlegrounds. The ongoing turmoil in Ukraine and Gaza reveals a dangerous forgetfulness of history's heavy toll.

Now's the time to amplify the teachings of peacemakers. We need to arm our consciousness with compassion and understand that forgiveness does not erase accountability. It's the love entangling our decisions that will forge a path away from destruction. Our collective future, quite simply, depends on choosing unity over division.

Yet for all the wisdom of the saints and sages, for all the transcendental experiences available to us through meditation, the human mind remains perilously vulnerable to illusion. Addiction, whether to gambling, alcohol, sex, or even the thrill of winning jury cases—is the mind's surrender to material consciousness, the rejection of the Kingdom of God within in favor of the fleeting pleasures of the senses. In the next chapter, you will meet Tom Dwyer, a man who made that fatal choice. His story is a cautionary tale about what happens when ego triumphs over spirit, when we chase the mechanical rabbit of illusion instead of the eternal truth within. And in the strange, quantum-entangled events that followed his disappearance, you will see evidence that God's hand was guiding me, even when I was too absorbed in my own ego to notice.

For most of my life, I believed I was one of the good guys, fighting on the right side of history. I inherited the victor's consciousness from a world at war. But meditation and the strange, quantum-entangled nature of my own cases have taught me that the lines are never that clear. The same capacity for love and for slaughter exists in all of us, encoded in our very cells. The war is not out there. It is within. And the choice is ours to make, every single day.

CHAPTER 7

The Psychic and the Mob

"The intuitive mind is a sacred gift and the rational mind is a faithful servant. We have created a society that honors the servant and has forgotten the gift."
Albert Einstein

A DISAPPEARANCE IN THE SHADOWS

"Joan, you have to read this article about a missing person case," said Joan's friend excitedly. That was how Joan stumbled upon the widely covered Richard Sequeira case that had gained so much publicity, especially in the Boston area, where stories of mob disappearances were relatively commonplace... just not like this one that had so many fascinating, lurid and even mystical overtones.

After reading the articles Joan was convinced she was one step further in sorting out her husband's mysterious disappearance. She immediately contacted her lawyer who suggested he reach out to the lawyers who won the highly unusual court judgement in the Sequeira case. Joan's husband, Tom Dwyer, Vice President of an insurance company in Hartford, Connecticut, seemed to have vanished down a similar dark path. Was his disappearance the result of similar demons?

"When the spiritual malady is overcome, we straighten out mentally and physically... For we are now on a different basis; the basis of trusting and relying upon God."

The Big Book of Alcoholics Anonymous

If we accept the notion that our choices often lead us into a material consciousness, overshadowing any connection to a spiritual consciousness attuned to God, as described in the "Big Book" of AA, perhaps the answers to our questions align with the main theme of this book. Or perhaps they do not. Tom Dwyer was gone. Disappeared. AWOL. Like vapor in the air, his presence slipped away... More unpaid insurance claims. More questions swirling in the air. More frantic family members grappling with the vacuum left by a father now unaccounted for. And… lurking in the shadows, more 'wise guys', their presence a chill gust of danger in the case.

I incorporate this case in what is called in the East, God's 'Lila', the divine play or drama. It illustrates 'His' role in intertwining my litigation and meditation consciousness. There exists a profound, quantum-entangled connection between my thoughts and those of a celebrated "psychic" involved in this case. Remarkably, she unveiled her insights, sharing revelations without me divulging any specifics about Dwyer's predicament. The conclusions drawn by this psychic defy simple explanation. To me, they align with some mystical force of God, what many might call ESP. I would call it God's energy working to ensure justice using my willing hands as his tools. It was certainly not my doing alone.

THE DEVIL'S WORKSHOP

Had it not been for the psychic's uncanny insights, Joan's desperate pleas, and my wife Laima's heartfelt compassion for the family, I would not have engaged in this case. My past encounters with individuals like Richard, Patty, and "Uncle Dante" had already dulled my appetite for such tumult.

In an act of Divine Grace, the psychic altered the course of everything. We took on the case and initiated a lawsuit against the life insurance companies that had issued policies on Tom Dwyer but who were not paying Joan and her family. Our strategy mirrored that of Patty's case: prove Tom was dead, secure a resolution for his family, and ultimately deliver the financial support that life insurance was meant to provide. The evidence suggested he had vanished from a roadside bar in Springfield, Massachusetts. This was a location dripping with its own mobsters and mysteries. Decades later, in light of all my litigation and meditation experiences, this case and the psychic's insights stand as compelling evidence of quantum entanglement. I have no other explanation; all the critical facts and evidence point to this.

In the 1970s, Springfield was a small New England city, nestled just north of Hartford along Interstate 91. Steeped in history dating back to the 1600s, it was infamous for the "Springfield Rifle," its role in the Revolutionary War, and as the birthplace of basketball. Yet by the 1960s and beyond, the city had succumbed to decline, ravaged by organized crime, political corruption, and a highly suspect state superior court system marked by cronyism amongst the judiciary and the politicians who appointed the judges. Local lawyers openly corroborated this troubling situation to me.

"The devil was a murderer from the beginning, and abode not in the truth..." (**John 8:44**)

Tom had a severe gambling addiction, so it was the perfect backdrop for his weakness to spiral out of control, enabled by several 'players' from the Springfield mob. As they say, birds of a feather flock together. But Tom, like Richard Sequeira, was also a family man who tragically succumbed to his compulsive nature. With his position as Vice President of a Hartford insurance company, he squandered his salary on relentless sports betting. Over the years, I've learned that such addictions often cloak pathological narcissism, a reality spiraling beyond the confines of mere substance abuse. What happened to him weighed heavily on his family, and the evidence painted a bleak picture; he was betting on every game across every sport, and losing more often than not.

By this point, though still naively unaware, I had just enough experience, in my third year of litigating jury cases, to recognize how the 'wise guys' operated. So, we approached this case with more caution than Patty's, fully aware of Mo the jailed mobster's unfortunate fate. Fools rush in where angels fear to tread, after all. Thank God for Laima's common sense and sixth sense; her intuition was attuned to a remarkably high frequency.

Thanks to Transcendental Meditation, I could feel my intuition sharpening with each passing day. Getting involved in 'Vedic' knowledge as a TM practitioner felt like the best of both worlds. I combined hard-hitting courtroom evidence woven into a transcendental mindset, all bolstered by the support of thousands of other TM practitioners generating a collective coherence that guided me forward. Maharishi's 10% effect; where 10% of a society meditates, real change for the better takes place. It was a real experiment that worked, check it out.

I had already been meditating for over a year, convinced I was accelerating toward Enlightenment. That was what all the TM teachers, backed by Maharishi, assured me. Surely, I had become an expert in meditation, poised for transcendence; with my jury skills in tow. I thought I was unstoppable! With my rapid progress in Maharishi's "Science of Creative Intelligence" and my innate litigation abilities, the legal world better watch out! I imagined it would only be a matter of months until I reached my goal. I could just try a case, steep my mind in transcendental thoughts, and voilà, instant nirvana! And once I had won the case, I would simply empty my mind, retreat into 'Samadhi' (that ultimate state of transcendental consciousness), and shift on to the next case. Surely, any jury witnessing me, a dedicated meditator, would perceive only truth! It was a foolproof plan, right? Just another notch in my jury belt, and on to the next challenge.

But then, what was that pesky little thought nudging in my mind? EGO? No, I had it all covered! No 'ego' interference here... But exactly what is 'ego' anyway?

If you find any truth in these deluded musings I entertained during the mid-1970s, dear readers, keep reading. It's astounding how the mind can gravitate not only toward divinity like the teachings from Jesus, Paramahansa Yogananda, and Maharishi, but also toward more earthly desires such as sex, wine, pride, and the entrapment of ego.

THE ANATOMY OF EGO

Freud defines the ego as the 'mediator', the controlling psychological mechanism acting as an agent between the 'Id' and the 'Super Ego'. The 'Id' embodies uncontrolled, instinctual desires, the 'gotta have it' impulse. In contrast, the 'Super Ego' serves as the moralizing force, tempering these impulses with a 'better not have it' caution. In this light, the ego attempts to broker compromise: "let me just have one piece of chocolate cake". Freud articulated the ego as our sense of self, the aspect of the mind responsible for memory, intellect, and the synthesis of data from our five senses alongside illusory desires.

This leads us to ponder: where does this data originate? And how does God and religion fit into our minds' instinctual chase of illusory desires?

It's reminiscent of greyhounds racing at a dog track, tirelessly pursuing a mechanical rabbit, hopelessly chasing an illusion that they will never catch. The same can be said for gambling addicts banking on their next win. In Tom's case, his illusory desires ultimately paved the path to his downfall, an all-too-common tale in the human experience.

I too suffered under the illusion of wielding a phenomenal technique to transcend the mind and apply it to my litigation work. The hope for instant success was alluring, yet reality proved otherwise. Transcendence is a profound journey, and the world operates under rules that often elude our simplistic aspirations.

Freud never offered a concrete solution for the illusory desires stemming from sense perception, choosing instead to posit that humanity's need for religion arose from collective, unfulfilled, unconscious instincts deemed illusory in their own right. Thus, we chase after God in religion, much like the dogs in pursuit of the mechanical rabbit. Freud even labeled religion a "collective neurosis." If this sounds circular, circumventing the root of that neurosis or our entrapment therein, you're encountering the very conflict between material consciousness and spiritual or Christ consciousness.

Tom developed a dangerous delusion, the belief that he could beat the odds and maneuver through the world of wise guys without facing dire consequences. You might wonder what fuels such an illusion? What leads to an unchecked Freudian 'Id' with no guiding 'Super Ego'?

In my exploration of Tom's case and through my meditation practices, I initially dismissed his choices as mere stupidity and selfishness. However, as I delved deeper into more cases and engaged in meditation, I began to comprehend that he had turned away from the higher aspects of consciousness available to him. His 'Ego' had seized control of his self-identity, overriding his 'Self', the part of us that connects to the divine. Why would he choose such a path? Fear? A lack of love? A failing marriage or career? Emotional and psychological instability? The answers are elusive, but fear likely played a substantial role, as spiritual therapists like M. Scott Peck suggest.

At the same time this case was ongoing, a childhood friend of mine succumbed to alcoholism, literally drinking himself to death at just 33 years old. I had been the best man at his wedding, and the enormity of that loss weighed heavily on me. Why did he spiral down such a dark path? My meditation began to illuminate subtler layers of thought and feeling, intervening on my behalf before I reached for that one last beer or martini. I became more aware of how deeper emotional currents and mental streams could interfere with, and ultimately dictate, my decisions. Grace.

Through my TM practice, I gained greater discernment in sifting through facts and nuances in my cases, which became crucial in Tom's situation. In examining my friend's tragic decline, I identified a sense of uncontrolled fear that seemed to have taken the reins of his life, perhaps even echoing some distant, unresolved past. I cannot say for certain.

Some may view Freud as close-minded, trapped within the confines of material consciousness, that which he could perceive through the senses and his sense-engrossed mind. After 81 years on this planet, I find his close-mindedness valid. I have encountered the truth that meditation can elevate one beyond mere material existence, while I've also been deeply immersed in the realm of litigation. Carl Jung defines ego as a complex that embodies personal unconscious patterns of emotions, memories, perceptions, and desires; all centered around an individual's sense of power and status in relation to their environment.

Unlike Freud, Jung believed that God and religion emerge from the "collective unconscious" but do not constitute a neurosis. To Jung, they arise from consciousness itself, which he defined as "the function or activity that maintains the relation of psychic contents to the ego." While his insights are profound, both he and Freud seem somewhat trapped in their own definitions of consciousness. Nonetheless, Jung's experience and intellect far surpass mine, especially in the analysis of the human psyche, so I bow to their greater knowledge.

But isn't it circular reasoning to try and define consciousness while potentially being stuck within our own perspective? What if we could experience a part of ourselves that observes consciousness, some form of silent awareness where we can actually watch our own thoughts? This is what meditation has offered me: glimpses of a Self, existing apart from my mind, senses, and thoughts, pure awareness. This newfound awareness has profoundly influenced my work. Ironically, it even led me to consult a psychic in my drive to understand Tom better.

After over 50 years on this planet as a student of Christ, Paramahansa Yogananda and various other spiritual teachers, having traversed the dark night of the soul...experienced past lives, and tasted transcendental bliss—I discovered a crucial truth: surrendering our minds, freeing ourselves from their traps that include ego, is essential to accessing a higher level of consciousness and discovering its existence. I embarked on this journey through numerous experiences, wins, losses, highs, lows, suffering, redemption, transcendence and more.

As Christ, Tolstoy, Paramahansa Yogananda, and countless mystics have expressed, the Kingdom of God exists within us, a state of consciousness we typically overlook. This state is far more authentic than the experiences dictated by our sensory minds, free from the unending stream of ego-driven thoughts. If you begin to recognize the 'monkey mind', those incessant thought streams, you'll likely observe them in meditation and identify them for what they truly are: ego thoughts entrenched in material consciousness. By ego thoughts, I refer to the endless loop concerning events, people, and circumstances in our lives, where our sense of self, fueled by a form of subliminal narcissism, reacts.

Regardless of what Freud and Jung posited in their ideas, which some cynics dismiss as psychobabble, I aim to distill the essence of ego based on my life experiences in this book. To me, it means absorbing sensory experiences, good, bad, or ugly into the mind and allowing that data to dictate my actions on varying gradients in different situations. Do I indulge in another vodka martini with a twist, or do I abstain?

Herein lies the kicker: we often unconsciously habituate ourselves to choosing the extra martini instead of opting for higher levels of decision-making, as if guided by a "Kingdom of God within us" compass. Conversely, the latter choice might stem from addiction. Perhaps this duality seems overly simplistic, but it resonates with me after nearly five decades of meditation and litigation.

Reflecting on the 1970s, I recognized my own addiction to winning jury cases. It parallels Tom D's compulsive betting on every game in sight. Despite being a smart VP at a major insurance company, what drove Tom to his demise?

Where did his mind lead him astray, convinced he could outsmart the 'house' odds? Engaging directly with mobsters only compounded the danger. Is that the role of ego? Or do we fall victim to the "devil made me do it" mentality, which leads us away from turning to higher consciousness or God?

When I took on Tom D's case, was that my ego manifesting, or was it compassion for his wife and family? In retrospect, I would argue it was more egocentricity fostered by my wife Laima's compassionate guidance that dictated our collective decision. Back then, I was so engrossed in the pursuit of winning jury cases, while Laima and her connection to God were the true driving forces. Even the eventual outcome in that case wasn't solely mine of course; grace played the biggest role. However, I must acknowledge that I possessed genuine empathy for my clients, particularly those enduring profound loss. Being Irish, I have a tendency to downplay my accomplishments—perhaps centuries of British oppression linger in my DNA!

To be clear, I've never done drugs other than a few experimental puffs of weed after law school when I was around 27 or 28. As for sex and rock and roll, stay tuned. By rock and roll, I mean material consciousness. I enjoyed many cocktails with friends and clients, but I was never an alcoholic like many of my contemporaries in litigation. Meditation saved me from that addiction. Now, let's see how all this psychoanalysis and transcendental consciousness relates to the "hard" evidence in the Tom and Joan D case.

The factual evidence, as I understood it at that time, established that Tom was last seen in a mob-connected roadside bar just outside downtown Springfield. It was a distinctive place, resembling a 1920s bar split in two:

one side for the bar, the other a restaurant featuring old, vertical wooden booths that could seat four. This spot was a well-known hangout for gambling, whoring, and drug-pushing types—a gathering place for the 'lesser' bad guys mingling with the real criminals.

There's a hierarchy even in organized crime, after all. The bar was a smaller, rougher version of the one in the Buford Pusser movie, "Walking Tall." But I was TM'd enough to not walk so tall. In fact, after Mo, Uncle Dante, and Patty's paratrooper, and Laima's never-failing insights, I thought it best to be more of a walking small, low-profile, 'insurance type' inquisitor masquerading with my newly acquired, superior, intuitive tools.

Grateful for grace, thank you, God. It felt like my expanding ego from previous jury victories was mysteriously diminishing through meditation. I became more cautious. These 'bad guys' seemed more personal and closer to me than the Richard Sequeira and Uncle Dante types I had encountered. I was only 32, still green in real-world experience, yet my ego was inflated from several wins.

Tom had been seen in the restaurant half of the bar for hours, drinking in a booth with two men. They all left together inebriated. Before their departure, at least one anonymous individual hinted at hearing something about Tom's gambling debts to one of those men. I assured him I wouldn't tell anyone or call him as a witness. The police reports were vague, and the scant details from the few witnesses willing to speak were fuzzy at best. What a surprise? Springfield.

The bar was a notorious hangout for these types, known for never cooperating with law enforcement, which raised suspicions about their ties. Descriptions of the men Tom was with when he vanished were vague and inconclusive, another surprise. We entered the case about a year after Tom's disappearance, facing a complete dead end. The police had done nothing, a clue in itself about their relationships with Springfield's mobsters. This goes back to Chapter 3, where I suggest that between these cases and many subsequent events, the FBI, DOJ, and local law enforcement play a game of protecting the money changers. The more money involved, the more protection afforded. When you reach 'Billion dollars', there's absolute protection, with a toxic mix of judicial nepotism involving judges, FBI, DOJ, and the IRS. No one in law enforcement seemed to have a clue about Tom's disappearance. "Sorry, Mr. Fancy Pants Lawyer. There's the door." Hmmm? Why? Isn't it your job Mr. FBI agent, to ferret out criminals and secure indictments?

After Tom's disappearance, his car was discovered in the bar's parking lot. Joan explained that her husband had developed a penchant for drinking, heavy gambling, and accumulating debts. All she knew was that he had become entangled with 'gamblers' from Springfield. Our search revealed several phone records that connected to individuals in Springfield, including one known loan shark and bookmaker who was clearly a higher-up wise guy that no one dared cross. Having learned my lesson with Mo, we knew we needed to proceed cautiously. Now that I'm a dyed-in-the-wool meditator, close to being infallible, no worries... I'll make cautious inquiries about this loan shark.

I had already experienced some remarkable transcendental moments in TM. Several of these instances seemed to lead me to a place where vague knowledge and intuition, beyond hard evidence, were guiding me. Through several meditations while working on the case, the message was clear: avoid the wise guys, and you'll gather enough information to convince a jury. Spoiler alert: that didn't happen.

Having gained a bit of experience from the Richard S. case regarding how even the smallest corners of the larger 'outfit' operates, Springfield felt like the ideal environment for criminal activity to flourish. My inexperience with organized crime heightened my intuition about not digging too deep. The local cops confirmed my instincts, while the FBI showed little interest. Then came the psychic. She ultimately guided my decisions in many ways. How she knew what I'm about to share with you was, at the time, a mystery... a kind of ESP. When I reached out to her, I was doubtful, but some inner voice encouraged me to give it a try. Laima agreed: Grace.

I genuinely wanted to help Joan and her family navigate through this tragedy, but I had hit a wall, even with the Springfield police and FBI. The situation resonates closely with the current murkiness surrounding the Seth Rich murder and the Jeffrey Epstein 'suicide'. Seth Rich was a DNC computer staffer who leaked the Hillary Clinton / Podesta emails to WikiLeaks Julian Assange. He was shot in the back of the head after leaving a Washington DC restaurant. The Seth Rich murder, like many murders linked to the Clintons, Donald Young, Quarles Harris, Vince Foster, was never solved. (*Litigator 5*.)

THE KITCHEN TABLE SEANCE

People in the know in Springfield were well aware of who was connected to whom. My meditations indicated those connections typically involved outfit figures mingling with the ruling elite, just like the current 'swamp' in Washington. Nothing changes; it's like the other side of the same coin. Paired with my meditative practice, my intuition became increasingly reliable. It was then that Laima mentioned a 'psychic' from "Nutley," New Jersey – can you believe the name! The psychic, Dorothy Allison, a woman in her fifties, had allegedly helped the FBI identify the serial murderer of school children in Atlanta, Georgia. To reach her, I needed to go through the Police Chief in Nutley. He instructed me to bring a picture of Tom to our meeting. Some claimed she was legitimate, while others dismissed her as nonsense.

With my newfound status as a highly advanced 2-year meditator, teetering on the edge of enlightenment, I wondered what Dorothy could possibly know. Could she be the expert at discovering the fates of the deceased? One seasoned FBI agent assured me that she had indeed identified the black man who turned out to be the serial killer in Atlanta. She provided the FBI with critical details that led to the suspect's arrest and conviction.

Something deep inside urged me to give it a go. Laima encouraged me, so I hopped in my plane, flew to New Jersey, met the Chief, and was led to a small frame house where Dorothy, the 'psychic' awaited me in her kitchen. She asked me to place Tom's photo on her kitchen table face down. I provided no details, no backstory to taint her perceptions. I remained oblivious to what the Chief might have told her, though he reassured me that he hadn't shared anything. But doubt lingered in me; I was, after all, a doubting Thomas.

Dorothy placed her hand over Tom's photo and began to speak: "This man is seated in a wooden booth with two others. They are drinking heavily. This man is quite drunk, and an argument ensues over debts he owes to the others. After several hours, they leave the bar; he gets in the front passenger seat of a car, described perfectly by her. One man takes the back seat behind him, while the other drives. They head down an increasingly wooded road. In the back, the man pulls out a gun and shoots this man in the back of the head. They then drive to a quarry, weigh down his body with steel from the trunk, and dump him in." This is exactly as it happened, I kid you not!

Her description of the driver perfectly matched the person we had been investigating, the one to whom Tom owed money. My meditations had warned me: 'Watch out. Stay clear.' Dorothy's account of Tom's murder aligned disturbingly with the details of Lanzi's homicide in the Benjamin DeChristoforo case. Was this a mob 'Modus Operandi' for disposal? When I brought the information from the psychic to the Springfield police, even with the Chief from Nutley backing me, they did little more than offer lip service about looking into it. They never produced any evidence tying Tom's disappearance to our suspect. The quarry was deep and unsearchable. Nervous tension settled in. Even the cops suggested it might be best to steer clear of the 'wise guys' and mind my own business. I was a family man with three kids, and the suspect was a well-known figure in Springfield. His deposition seemed useless, more threatening than helpful. So, armed with my insights from meditation, I told Joan, Laima, and my colleagues that we would go to trial with the scant evidence we had.

I certainly didn't want another happenstantial 'Mo' to taint my young career. God, was I naïve! In a manner reminiscent of the Richard S. case following Mo's grim passing, I decided to proceed with the trial, albeit with flimsy evidence mostly involving gambling debts and unidentified bad guys, alongside the bar's unsavory reputation entering evidence almost sideways. I was fairly certain the unsequestered jury had read about its notoriety... something I was kind of banking on, despite jury instructions advising against such knowledge. Shhh, don't let on that I was pondering that!

VERDICT BY SETTLEMENT

The psychic's testimony was, of course, excluded. The trial dragged on for about five weeks. Our case appeared weaker than Richard Sequeira's, compounded by the looming "inference from an inference" jury instruction. As the jury deliberated, fighting like cats and dogs, the two lead attorneys for the insurance companies unexpectedly approached me with a settlement offer, ready to pay the full policy amounts! I was taken aback. We could hear the jury's animated debates from the courtroom. A favorable verdict now seemed a long shot. Joan, naturally, agreed to the settlement, but we would lack a death verdict to convert into a judgment. The judge strongly encouraged the insurance companies to settle.

After informing the jury about the settlement, the federal judge polled them. They revealed they were still arguing over the facts, with some leaning towards believing Tom had been murdered while others hotly contested that notion. They struggled with the jury instructions regarding inference and the language of the policy. It looked like they were headed toward a split. There goes my much-needed verdict, not just for my client but for my family, not to mention my ego.

But wait... saved by the bell? What bell were we talking about? The insurers chose to pay after two years of conflict, five weeks of trial, and a clearly divided jury grappling with core issues and facts. Their frustrations were palpable as they filed into the courtroom: some wore expressions of anger, others displayed sympathy for me and Joan, while a few shook their heads in displeasure. There was an undercurrent suggesting Tom was viewed as a useless, immoral 'waste' of a human. Why should the insurers pay? After all, it could inflate premiums for 'good' people. The overarching facts and the societal issues surrounding the case were collectively weighing on the jury's conscience.

So… why did the insurers ultimately decide to pay the full policy amounts? My hunch was that the judge and his connections in Springfield played a role, perhaps one of the lawyers? Who knows? My gut feeling, years later and with a bit more maturity, is that the judge was a decent guy who understood the ins and outs of Springfield. He likely heard about Tom's disappearance and sent a message to the defense lawyers to settle. I don't think he ever intended to give several specific jury instructions demanded by the defense, was sympathetic towards Joan and the kids, and possibly aimed to avoid a hung jury. Furthermore, the judge might have preferred not to extend his court time after a lengthy five-week trial. It's possible the players in Springfield wanted the case to disappear, perceiving me as an outsider in their local legal landscape, and the judge was well aware of it.

Okay, so it seems the influence of the judge might have played a significant role in helping me beyond the strict legal confines of the case and judicial ethics, but I had no idea about it, nor did I do anything to earn it? Quantum Entanglement? The consciousness of the judge, my opponents, and the jurors all somehow converged into a settlement? It was a collective consciousness result, not connected to raising the consciousness of individual jurors, but of all involved. It was a win for Joan, her family, and mine. However, it also inflated my ego, adding an unearned notch to my list of victories. At the time, I allowed myself to absorb this as a mark of my supposed expertise with juries beyond my actual skill level, when in truth, I probably would have lost.

But as always, God has a way of dealing with inflated egos. I should have remembered from sports, as soon as you get cocky, you can get your jock handed to you. Grace was my savior here. I was not the doer.

At one stage we could hear the jurors bickering and passionately debating in the jury room. At one point, they came out to ask a question about the jury instructions, exposing their sticking points. In retrospect, I doubt I would have won. GRACE. Yet, ego is persistent. Joan received the money, and my ego slightly swelled, though later reflection whispered, "Michael J. Flynn, you might have lost!"

You might wonder why I chose to include this case in my book. Answer: Quantum entanglement. How did Dorothy Allison possibly know and convey facts by putting her hand over an upside down picture of Tom D?? Though I knew nothing about quantum entanglement when this case unfolded, it fits retrospectively. Perhaps more so than any others. Ask yourself: what is ego, separate from Freudian and Jungian psychological jargon? To me, it's primarily a tool of the intellect allowing us to interact with others and events in our environment. It fuses sensory experiences and self-perception. Secondly, ego is part of our personality that can instill confidence if harnessed properly. That's the double-edged sword... If we wield it properly. Third, it must be acknowledged as a tool, a gift from God, meant to be utilized with humility in service to others. Plenty of reflection occurs on that point.

BUT, Dorothy Allison had no ego involvement? Or did she? She had gained a reputation as a psychic. But she had many naysayers. Although she may have been motivated to enhance her reputation, what if she had been wrong, and just made it all up? But I had been in that bar. She described it perfectly, even Tom's car. She even described the two men, which I conveyed to the Springfield police and FBI, who did nothing. One description fit a loan shark in Springfield. The details she recited with her hand over the upside down picture of Tom was surreal, beyond all normal discourse. Proof of quantum entanglement? Your verdict. None of her descriptions made it into evidence.

Easy for me to express this now. That's not the course my career took initially. My ego inflated, and not in the right way. The little humility I possessed got swallowed in litigation aggression, a familiar syndrome during the era I was biologically born into, marked by global conflicts. Fortunately, the nature of the human 'baptism' ritual, as illustrated in the biblical baptism of Christ by John, is a spiritual extraction potentially transcending biology. We are baptized in 'spirit' to elevate us beyond our human biological confines.

In *The Godfather II*, while Michael Corleone orchestrated murders, his baby was being baptized outside of the mob family, conveying a profound message.

Much like quantum entanglement, a baby, symbolizing new consciousness, becoming entangled with God consciousness in the baptism ritual, extricating the baby from DNA entanglements in Dad's mob? That's a deep one, it's a juxtaposition steeped in layers of meaning. I explained to several reporters the involvement of the psychic. They looked at me like I was delusional. But more cases flowed in. New clients, reading about my case in the Springfield Federal courts, had no inkling about the hung jury. It appeared I was a winner. Capiche?

BARNYARD EQUITY

Addressing the gap between the law and barnyard equity, I detail several later cases that hold moral lessons for me, perhaps for you, seemingly linked through Quantum Entanglement, this while I inhabited the PIT as a fledgling meditator on my litigation journey. Some cases pertained to what I came to understand as barnyard equity, yielding outcomes beyond my control, driving home the ever important point that I was never the doer. I realized that sometimes a substantial gap exists between the law and what I could gauge as true fairness and 'justice', independent of the influence of my adversarial lawyers, or the judge, or for that matter, in connection with the judge's own biases.

Lesson. When I interviewed several jurors after the settlement, their anger and biases emerged. Some did NOT want to award any money. Nope. Never raised the consciousness of the jury collectively in that case. I was spared a loss.

As you will read, the gap between these two forms of so-called 'justice', the law vs. fundamental fairness, often boils down to money. Sometimes, it's a lot of money. Jurors can easily get hung up awarding a lot of money to someone. The more money involved, the greater the opportunities for corruption within the litigation process and the perversion of so called 'justice'. Frankly, it was shocking to me, as my career progressed, how 'the law' could be warped to corrupt 'justice'. I was often a slow learner, trying to see the best in people, but eventually, as corruption has permeated our judiciary, I lost faith in our system of justice. As the Blixseth case proved, judges can be bought. In litigation, money translates to power on many levels.

The levels of corruption affecting justice include direct payouts to judges. Yes, that happens, along with more subtle forms of 'influence peddling'. This generally involves the wealthy hiring a prominent local firm with a senior partner who's connected to the judge, often someone who aided the judge's initial appointment. A common sight is a senior partner from a prestigious Boston Brahmin firm mingling at the Harvard Club alongside judges. You'll encounter a case or two related to this type of corruption.

Intriguingly, in my ignorance, the judge in Joan and Tom's case likely helped me quite a bit. Why? I'm unsure. Perhaps he was just a good guy pursuing barnyard equity in hopes of achieving a just outcome? Or maybe he was aware that the Springfield mob had 'offed' Tom and wanted to avoid further 'local repercussions'.

This stereotype of judges being connected to influential politicians and big firm partners is a prevalent mechanism of corruption across most cities and towns where courts operate. The large firms often cater to those with the biggest wallets, representing clients willing to pay a hefty sum to hire a lawyer known for their connections to the judge. Clients often go 'judge shopping' based on which lawyer is connected to a specific judge, thinking they can sway the scales in their favor. I encountered this throughout my career, like the Middlesex Probate judge who granted 'John', a minority shareholder, control over Richard S.'s dealership simply because John hired the judge's best buddy, 'George', as his lawyer. If you think that was mere happenstance, I have some swamp land in the Okefenokee to sell you... now better known as Washington, D.C.

In later cases like Tim Blixseth, you'll come across some shocking examples of judicial corruption. However, Patty losing her late husband's dealership stands as an early illustration of the challenges I faced early in my career with a prominent judge. Luckily, the jury in Patty's life insurance case was guided by a legitimate judge. I might add, Ruth Abrams was a great judge.

Regarding Uncle Dante, I withhold judgment. After all, I'm just the litigator. You are the jury... just don't let your biases cloud your judgment.

I've learned that juries are our only genuine protection. However, even they can be corrupted, and judges can obstruct access to a jury altogether. Ultimately, perhaps the Big Guy in the sky is the sole arbiter of justice for all parties. Who am I to judge? What is justice, anyway? In this book, by drawing connections or ascribing a moral to each case included, I seek to reflect what I learned along the way through meditation. If a case didn't possess a discernible metaphysical element of 'I am not the doer', then it's not part of this narrative in these books.

WHO LOVED THE OLD MAN?

Take, for example, a not-unusual case involving a lonely old gentleman, about 90 when he passed. He had some money and property but was estranged from his two kids; one a ne'er-do-well, the other recently distanced from him.

There was an estate battle between the children and the caretaker, who had cared for the old gentleman for about 20 years. The kids contested the last will, which awarded about 80% of the estate to the caretaker. Litigation erupted. The testator, the old man had explained his wish for the caretaker to receive such a substantial share, because he believed the caretaker was the only one who truly loved and cared for him in his later years. It had all the hallmarks of Shakespeare's King Lear! But herein lay the problem. Over two decades, the will changed numerous times, with the caretaker's portion gradually increasing, while the kids grew increasingly distant and resentful toward their dad.

In time, the caretaker assumed control of the old man's affairs, even managing the finances and writing most checks from their joint account. The kids alleged undue influence right from the start, escalating with the last will when the distribution shifted from 50/50 to 80/20 roughly eight months before death. During his final year, the testator was quite vulnerable, often unwell, and occasionally unaware of his surroundings and financial matters. What to do? Who wins? What does the law say? Justice?

The law and medical evidence suggested possible undue influence when the will's division changed dramatically in the last eight months. Evidence over the years hinted that some of the testator's money supported the caretaker. Barnyard equity argued that the caretaker sacrificed two decades for his friend, possibly motivated by monetary gain, given human nature. The old man was lonely and not quite alright. The caretaker, moving from age 21 to 40 during those two decades, never held another job. The kids didn't take care of their father during that time. Aware of the man's assets, the caretaker found comfort in being part of an 'odd couple'.

What say you, the jury? I won't disclose who I represented or the case's outcome. You must decide what's fair and just. This case was judge-decided. Neither party wanted to split the difference. I share this case because everyone involved was muddled in ego, pride, self-righteousness, anger, and greed, myself included. Looking back, I imagine the judge, feeling like King Solomon, contemplating splitting the 'baby' to discover genuine affection for the old man. Did anyone truly care for him?

My lesson in that case: My ego seeking a win probably trumped an honest quest for justice. Suffice it to say, my client(s), I'm not disclosing, were very happy with the outcome. The judge who had to work and had to render an opinion and judgement was unhappy with no settlement. What did justice even mean in that case? I just wanted a win for my client(s) while entangled in each party's utmost self-righteousness. My lesson now: Humans must love genuinely. Not the self-absorbed, agenda-laden version. Genuine Love. Not romantic nor preachy love.

The Christ and Yogananda kind demanding authentic sacrifice. The John Basilone machine gun style, saving his comrades on "Bloody Ridge" above Henderson Field in Guadalcanal, while mowing down hundreds of Japanese elite Sendai soldiers, as thousands charged into his machine guns. Sister Clare's dedication, trading a material life for education and guidance in a poor Ecuadorian village, these kinds of humans truly transcend the mind and body in selfless service.

Amma, the hugging saint, Mother Meera, Daya Ma and Brother Chidananda, all clients, are in the same category as Basilone and Sister Clare.

Christ would have resolved the old man, caretaker, and kids case by telling both sides to turn the other cheek, give away your coat and shirt if your opponent just wants your coat; and before prayer, go to your opponent and settle out of court. THAT is NOT litigation, but it is closer to meditation. Lawyers often dive in where "angels fear to tread". Trust me: I never was the doer. I lacked a lot of compassion for anyone involved in that case. But... it seemed the caretaker was the only person who genuinely cared for and took care of the old man. Barnyard equity? You can render your own verdict.

As for the original questions, my answers are consistent:

1. What caused the disappearance of Tom Dwyer? Tom did.
2. Who caused it? Tom did.
3. Why was he "disappeared"? Tom was deluded, living an "unreal" life of addiction and lies, believing he could pay off his gambling debts. His killers, caught in their own egos and delusions couldn't tolerate his deceit.
4. Would you have given the life insurance to the wife? Yes. That's what the insurance was for; his life.

When we choose addiction and unreality and face the consequences, do we choose Matter over Spirit? Yes. Our self-absorbed ego, selfish desires, and failure to love and obey God's rules can destroy us all. When such evil or maya permeates the consciousness of just one human like Tom Dwyer, it can spread through the collective consciousness of those he interacts with, turning them into killers. The collective consciousness of evil on this planet has historically spread like the firestorms that engulfed Dresden and Tokyo, according to the laws of quantum entanglement. Chapter 18. The world wars and their horrific atrocities serve as proof of this quantum entanglement of evil and maya.

In contrast, the lives of Christ, Paramahansa Yogananda, Maharishi, Amma, Meera, Daya Ma, Chidananda, and all the true 'Saints' of every religion, who have surrendered their egos and lives to God, demonstrate the quantum-entangled 'Good'. Stay tuned because there is a lot of bad coming in future cases.

CHAPTER 8

Sandra and Lester—God's Consciousness at Work

> "Suffer little children, and forbid them not, to come unto me: for of such is the kingdom of heaven. Verily, I say unto you, whosoever shall not receive the kingdom of God as a little child shall in no wise enter therein."
> **Matthew 19:14 (KJV)**

The above quote from Matthew has an interesting application to my early litigation career as my ego expanded with my successes. I was getting caught up in my wins, too self-absorbed as a young lawyer to realize that my success was not the causative result of my trial skills, level of consciousness, or intellectual prowess. I thought they were, but that was a delusion. I was disciplined in my preparation of all my jury cases, and that intense preparation was a factor in many of my early cases, but the truth is that in the cases I have included in this book, the wins were not the result of little me. They were a gift.

The jury consciousness was raised in the Sequeira case by a force field beyond the trial skills of Jay and I. The favorable Dan Moore plea deal when Jay and I were rank, know-nothing, inexperienced rookies proves this point. Yes, the First Circuit Court of Appeals reversed the incarceration order of Judge Garrity for not producing the bank documents based on my briefing, but the underlying reality of that case was that the overblown, author-ego of prosecutor Higgins likely motivated him to make the favorable plea deal to avoid a potential loss.

In the Dwyer case, I was profoundly encouraged by the incredible, quantum-entangled confirmation of the Dwyer murder by Dorothy Allison, the psychic. She played an almost mystical role in driving into my cellular consciousness the reality of Dwyer's murder. That underlying reality was conveyed to the jury on some quantum-entangled level, on actual evidence too thin to support a verdict, but at least caused deep conflict within the jurors to force the insurance companies to settle while being influenced by the trial judge. The clients in all three cases were all over the moon happy with the results, which only fed my ego.

I have included those cases, and others coming up in this book to prove several critical points. Make no mistake, God is the doer, even protecting with grace, love and compassion, an overly wrought, ego-driven lawyer. God uses us as instruments even when we don't pray to Him / Her. Early in my litigation career I had abandoned Catholicism, I was meditating, but not praying, and certainly not "worshiping" in any traditional sense. But His love, compassion and grace abounds. I had a deeply embedded desire to win so I worked my butt off in all my cases. But in reality, the truth is that every litigation and life success I have had, Laima, my kids, are directly attributable to God in a force field of higher consciousness that I was not even tuned into. I was meditating; but I was a rookie at that too.

Looking back, I attribute all my blessings to the gifts given to me as a child blessed with the remarkable love, faith, religious discipline and moral strictures of my parents, particularly my mother. Believe me, I was no bargain as a kid. My mother's faith, rooted in Christ within the theology and dogma of the Catholic Church permeated our family and my youth. Somehow, she transmuted her cellular consciousness to her children. Although I abandoned Catholicism as a young lawyer, Christ never abandoned me. My assessment looking back is that some mystical, ill-defined form of faith was instilled in me that I could prevail in my cases, even though both the cases and my work on them did NOT fully explain the positive results.

To me, looking back, the above quote from the Gospel of Matthew and the next case proves the foregoing points in spades: (1) the undeserved grace bestowed on me as a young lawyer; and (2) the mystical, quantum-entangled reality of how God and his force field of consciousness work. When Christ spoke the above admonition to his disciples telling them to allow the little children of Israel to come to him when they thought he was too busy in his ministry to deal with "little kids," he straightened them out by instructing them to bring the children to him because only those with the consciousness of a child can appear before God, and enter the Kingdom of Heaven. In other words, childlike innocence, detached from worldly ego, is the necessary level of consciousness to merge into the Christ level of consciousness.

When the next case appeared on my litigation plate, I was the overly "busy," ego-driven lawyer, the client did not have the money to pay me, and I initially refused the client begging for help. I was a bad disciple. Laima and God saved the day, and the lives of two young children. THIS case is proof in the pudding of a force field of quantum entangled consciousness beyond rational belief. You, dear reader, likely will not believe it. BUT every word in this chapter is precisely true. Believe it or not, your disbelief is on you.

I never set out to practice Family Law; in fact, this is the only child custody case I ever took on. Family court was the last place I imagined myself, and yet, somehow, I was swept up in the middle of its storm, pulled in despite every rational instinct telling me to stay away. What I didn't expect was just how much this case would challenge not only my understanding of the legal process but of consciousness itself. Yet here I was, amidst all its tumultuous heartache, taking on the custody case of Sandra and Lester for their distraught and loving father.

Can consciousness wield influence where the legal realm meets the unknown, where the principal actor, in this case me, is not even fully conscious of why he is asking a judge to make a specific ruling at the time he is asking for it, and where the judge does not want to make the ruling at the time of the request?

This case stands as a testament to the notion that God, not the self-sufficient litigant or meditator, orchestrates the play.

A FATHER'S PLEA

In 1974, Joe Hakey, who lived in Wakefield Massachusetts and worked for the Globe newspaper, called my office. He said he had read about the Moore case and the pending Richard Sequeira case. Joe's voice cracked with desperation. He had just lost custody of his young children, aged 8 and 10, to his ex-wife, an admitted alcoholic. "She's a fall-down drunk." "I need you to take my case," he implored. I said I had attended several divorce cases as a student in law school, swore to never do them, thinking it was the absolute "PIT" of human misery in a courtroom.

I was also diligently practicing transcendental meditation (TM) morning and evening, twenty minutes each session. By that time, I was really into it. I had gone on a 3-day TM 'residence course,' involving long meditations called "rounding" to vent my mind from the stress of my cases. The structure was simple yet profound: Twenty minutes of TM mantra meditation; twenty minutes of TM's hatha yoga postures, called 'asanas', and twenty minutes of rest...then do it again repeatedly, depending on the length of the particular course. Then afterwards, some insightful lectures.

During this immersive experience I was in fact having some transcendental experiences, shifting from the confines of my mind into a state of what the practitioners called "pure awareness". It was blissful, and a profound relief from my over-worked, over-agitated, legal, non-stop ruminations. The periods of bliss were intermittent, arrived unpredictably, unforced, yet I started to hunger for them. I could never 'make' them happen. I had to 'allow' the mantra to flow freely and automatically, without conscious intent or will on the more mindful level. This is a BIG topic in itself, to just somehow displace my stream of thought. Once I got into it, I realized my 'monkey mind' was a relentless torrent of mostly useless thoughts. In observing these 'useless' thoughts, however, I could slip into deeper levels of consciousness and become more aware of the tantalizing question of 'who' was truly observing my thoughts.

Maharishi, with scientific precision, taught that the mind naturally desires to settle into the tranquility of pure awareness. You just had to allow it to happen. Fourteen years later whilst doing Kriya Yoga I began to realize more deeply what meditation really is: self-realization of God within us once the monkey mind is gently put in its place, beyond thought, even beyond the treasured and sacred "silence" experienced in TM. Little did I know at that time but gradually learned, the 'who' is the soul wanting to return to God, the Divine energy. I see it as spiritual truth, and Maharishi, in this age of science wanted it marketed as such, not as religion.

Ultimately, after I had read everything Maharishi had written, including his very first book, *Love and God*, which the TM leadership really didn't promote in my opinion, I began to wonder about the perceived dichotomy between science and spirit. A few years later in my career I was dealing with this issue professionally, for TM.

Joe pleaded earnestly, begging me to at least "look into" the court records of his recent divorce. My wife Laima, with unwavering conviction, insisted I take the case.

After returning from a TM residence course, I was still undecided about Joe's case. Laima was strongly for it. 'I really think you should do this one,' she said. I wasn't sure; there was no real money involved, and it could become a protracted battle. Joe had just lost custody, even though children's welfare is always an open issue, how was I going to reopen the matter only 60 days later? I had other cases and more lucrative options. Laima became more strident: 'Take it.' She was always smarter than me.

Despite my hesitance and total inexperience in family law and my sworn vow in law school never to touch divorce or custody matters—I relented. It was in no small part due to the desperation radiating from Joe Hakey, but also from an intuitive feeling that I didn't fully comprehend at the time, yet recognize all too well now in my later years. Reluctance shadowed my acceptance. But an unspoken intuition that judicial misconduct (not uncommon in these cases) had played a role was important to my decision. I also felt connected mental rumblings filtering down from the Richard Sequeira case, which was also based in Middlesex Probate Court. Family court had always been a distasteful arena to me, yet against my wishes I found myself stepping into its grasp. This chapter emerges within a sea of countless "small cases," yet it stands out as the only child custody case I've ever undertaken; divorce law was territory I never intended to navigate.

I felt compassion for Joe. He clearly loved his children Sandra and Lester, and he was haunted by a chilling premonition—he 'sensed' that "something very bad is going to happen to them if they stay in that house." His words echoed a sense of foreboding that struck me from our very first meeting and persisted with each subsequent conversation. His cellular consciousness transmuted to me, his feelings of desperation stirred my intuition on a level I didn't fully grasp at the time. God was protecting him and his children.

At the time Joe reached out to me to take up the case of his children, I still clung to my idealism and constitutional convictions that the law achieved justice without much coaxing; and that judges were uniformly legitimate. A litigating force field was also educating me about how corrupt the judiciary can be.

BUILDING THE CASE

Sooo, "Alright, Joe. Let's proceed," I said, driven by a mix of curiosity and the persistent undercurrent of urgency in Joe's pleas and Laima's insistence. As I poured over the court records, an unsettling sense gnawed at me. Something was off. The connection between his ex-wife's attorney and the judge who granted her custody raised red flags and clearly played a role in the judge's decision to award custody to the obviously alcoholic ex-wife. This realization, coupled with a profound sense of injustice, intensified my resolve to proceed with the case for Sandra and Lester and their loving father.

Love is truly an extraordinary dimension of human activity, whether fully realized by the actors or not. A father's love like Joe's is like the mystical and sacred connection between God and his children. As I learned in a subsequent child death and coma case, a father's love does in fact transcend time and space (Chapters 18 and 19). A mother's love is similar but perhaps more firmly rooted in the earthly realm (Chapter 13).

> "The Power of influencing other's minds and the course of events is a Vibhuti (yogic power) mentioned in Patanjali's Yoga Sutras III-24, which explains it to be one of 'universal sympathy.'" **Paramahansa Yogananda,** *Autobiography of a Yogi*, p. 253 n.

Joe's profound love for his kids definitely exhibited that yogic power. I believe it shifted the outcome of their case, whether Joe realized it or not. I didn't realize it either, I didn't even want this case at the outset, but knowing what I now know, I certainly would've taken it again. I was not the 'doer,' even though I conducted the trial, and it ended in a somewhat humbling manner for me because I found myself pleading with the judge by the last day. Thank God I did! Wait until you read what happened next…

I asked Joe if he could afford a private investigator, but we both ended up footing that bill. We had him follow the ex-wife everywhere. Every bar, tavern, drinking hang-out she walked into...and crawled out of. We documented a tragic pattern of abject addiction. She was a very troubled and sorrow-filled soul. Everywhere she sought another drink. Every liquor store run. Every drunken 'fall down' and every drunken drive in her car. Every neglect of her children from a previous marriage, as well as Sandra and Lester. We did it for three weeks. She was out almost every night leaving her older kids, 15, and 17, and one of their friends at home with Sandra and Lester, Joe's kids. She was in fact a total, very sad, alcoholic. Enough.

Petition to change custody filed. Request to change judge filed. Request to have a judge from another county come in for the case. Rare. Unusual. Almost never, granted, but somehow done. The ex-wife and her 'connected' lawyer were enraged.

THE BATTLE FOR THE CHILDREN

The trial lasted five grueling days, brimming with documentation of negligence, habitual drunkenness, and a failure to take care of the older children by a prior marriage—including Lester and Sandra, who were also being potentially mistreated by the other teenage kids. The court appointed a "Guardian ad Litem," a court-appointed individual who acts as a neutral advocate for the children's best interests. He had been working diligently on his investigation with interviews and a detailed report to support our case. The ex-wife and her lawyer strongly resisted.

The trial was intense, filled with obstruction, lengthy objections, and combative cross-examinations, reaffirming my intense dislike for family law. I have never done it since. I poured all my skills and preparation into it. Sad. Traumatic. It deeply disturbed my meditations. The tragedy of 'motherhood' played out in an American courtroom. I found myself pleading for strength in the Irish Catholic manner of my upbringing: "Forgive me Father…." Even though I was no longer a Catholic.

These were five days of trying to be rational, lawyerly, and controlled, but something was 'growing' within me, like some kind of monstrous trepidation, all while trying to do my TM at nights. I was very agitated, not through fear of losing, which was always an issue with me—but more as a strange feeling that a tragedy was brewing. We were clearly winning, but the brought-in judge from Worcester County seemed ultra-cautious in the Middlesex County court. Looking back on it, his caution was appropriate. Judges do not like to step on other judges' toes. Our Petition to change custody was only two-plus months after the Middlesex judge's decision.

My 20-minute meditations were useless and getting worse as the week went on. Or so I thought. Meditation is supposed to develop intuition. It does, and sometimes we can't see the direct results of our meditative efforts, especially in a stressful situation like I was in. During the trial I felt no intuitions, and my meditations were seemingly so purposeless and agitated, I sometimes just gave up. Not good. The instruction was to stay with it no matter what. The agitated stream of thought brought in thoughts of prior transcendence, which then erupted in flat-out mental and emotional conflict. I was stuck in my mind replaying every nuance of every little detail in the trial. Oddly, those little conflicted nuances may have helped in the outcome, or at least connected me to a love... a 'universal sympathy' that I did not realize at the time; but was more real than my litigation skills.

At the time, I had no real comprehension or even grip on the magnitude of the events as they unfolded. I knew of course that taking custody from a mother of young children is an extremely contested issue in family law. I fully understood and presented the evidence and the law, yet, in hindsight, I did not even remotely understand the bigger picture of divine intervention taking place. God was intervening. Quantum entanglement was occurring. But I had no clue. Perhaps God intervened despite me and my role? God particularly loves his little children, whom he "suffers to come unto me."

MY DESPERATE PLEA

> "Ask, and it shall be given you; seek, and ye shall find; knock and it shall be opened unto you; For everyone that asketh receiveth; and he that seeketh findeth; and to him that knocketh, it shall be opened." Luke 11:9–10 (KJV)

Friday afternoon, late. Me, from my memory of what happened, not intended to be verbatim:

> "Judge, I submit, respectfully, in light of all such detailed and compelling evidence establishing Mrs. H's alcoholism beyond all applicable legal standards, and her total inability and gross failure to take care of any of her children—including Sandra and Lester, you must switch the existing custody and visitation rights now, today, and give custody of Sandra and Lester to Mr. H over the weekend. Mrs. H can visit on Sunday."

Judges do like the word "must." Lawyers use the word "ought" or "ought not" in requesting orders from a judge. I was begging, demanding. The judge did not like it. I don't know what got into me.

The Judge inquired of the other lawyer after my desperate plea. The opposing lawyer erupted in fiery protestations, fueled by anger and an eloquent flurry of lawyer-speak objections. It was a 'no way, blah blah, blah' rant.

Judge, frustrated: "Mr. Flynn I will have the GAL [Guardian ad Litem] report on Monday. I just checked with him. I think it prudent to wait, we will leave the existing custody and visitation orders in place and reconvene next week."

Me: "No Judge." I begged, laying out five detailed days of evidence, every nuance painstakingly reflected in my meditations...

The Judge, perplexed and getting angry at my persistence, retorted, "Mr. Flynn. Look, you have been seemingly rational all week, what is this about? Frankly, I really don't like it."

The Judge regarded me as if I had truly lost it, frustration etched on his face. Undaunted, I continued to plead my case vehemently, despite it appearing desperate to the court and confrontational to the Judge.

Judge: "That's it. I've heard enough. Orders switched. Mr. Hakey takes them for the weekend. Mrs. Hakey can see them Sunday for 2 hours." With that he stormed off the bench glaring at me. Massive relief flowed... never before or since had I felt so directed to so desperately plead for a case, against the odds, against logic and against normal court behavior or procedure.

"The things that we see are but a shadow of the things that we do not see." Martin Luther King, Jr.

Late that night, Sunday morning actually...it was three o'clock in the morning. Out of a deep sleep came a sharp, visceral alarm that pushed me into instant alert and wakefulness. I froze. The smell of acrid smoke hit my nose. I could literally smell my left hand near my mouth burning, literally as if it were on fire! TM had told us about a thing called "witnessing" that occurs whilst you are sleeping—sort of in between wakefulness and sleep with the mind or senses observing or experiencing, and receiving energies from a "quantum field."

It is the manifestation of energies in the higher Self from beyond normal sleep or wakefulness. At the time I was not aware of this nuance of reason. I bolted out of bed, yelled to Laima, "the house is on fire." Shocked and alarmed Laima joined me, not knowing why. "What's going on sweetheart? What's happening?" I didn't answer, I ran outside our room with the conviction of a madman to check the kids. All ok! Running downstairs, the house now in pandemonium... but nothing. Nothing. How could I have felt such alarm, smelled my hand burning? I staggered back to bed, confused. Laima hugged me, saying the obvious... "Mike it's just a bad dream." But it was 'real' to me. Still, I did sleep until the morning, albeit fitfully.

Saturday morning, last night's alarm out of mind, I made the coffee and got the Boston Globe from the front porch. I started reading casually until I got to the regional section. My hair stood up on the back of my head, tingling sensations ran down my spine right to my feet as I read "Three teenagers die in a Wakefield house fire." Alarmed, I called the Wakefield fire dept. They confirmed the address and that the fire had started at about 3 AM. The oldest kid was smoking in bed. No adult was in the house!

Incredibly tragic. The firefighters were crying uncontrollably while body after body was found.

I called Joe Hakey. Thank God!! Literally!! Incredibly, Sandra and Lester were not in the house. The two older kids and a friend all perished. The oldest was smoking in bed. The mother was not home. As I put the phone down my eyes welled up hot and painful as an emotional flood of tears from this event burst forth…. It was quite some time before I could bring forth the words I needed to explain to Laima what I had just read. It had profound implications, entrained as it was with quantum entanglement.

I knew the 'brought in judge' came in from Paxton, Mass, Worcester County. I managed to find his number and called. He had read it: "Don't know what got into you Michael. Or me. I didn't want to change those orders until Monday. I wanted the GAL report. The prior orders were only 2 months old. Frankly, you were pissing me off. But some little voice inside me toward the end of your rant said to do it based on several little points you made when you went off the rails."

"Little points"? I asked.

"There was no evidence about the potential harm, particularly to Sandra, from the three teenagers in the home, but when you alluded to it in your pleas about the teenage boys and the mother not being in the house, it hit me. Thank God that Sandra and Lester were not in that house! See you Monday."

Little points. Nuances. In my failed meditations, the *thought* arose repeatedly that the teenage boys could sexually abuse little Sandra. Just a thought. Agitated. No evidence. I was still a naive Catholic 'boy,' and this was long before the sexual abuse of children, as in the Roman Church, became such a public issue. I then had no exposure or experience relating to the magnitude of this problem. To this day, I do not know if any such abuse within that fractured family ever took place. But somehow it came up in my meditations, so I alluded to it with no evidence, with no specifics, with the judge looking at me like I was from outer space, a lawyer propagating facts that were not in the record!

Who *intervened* for Sandra and Lester? *Me?*...well, I had to be dragged in. Laima? Yes, she was definitely 'in tune'. I believe *Joe's fatherly love intervened* by being in the Force Field of 'universal sympathy.' Just plain old God's Grace—Sandra and Lester's soul karma? There are no accidents. The karmic consequences to the mother and the three dead children…maybe…?

Don't ask me tough questions about when and why God allows such tragedies. The sages have answers about suffering, karma, and God using suffering to have the souls return to him, a Catholic and Hindu perspective. We are in truth, all valuable little instruments, and God helps us to listen, which prompts us to act in grace. Unfortunately, much of the time we don't act because we don't trust our intuition until it becomes overwhelmingly obvious. The 'body count' on multiple levels goes up when we don't pay attention.

There are no accidents. Every facet of life on this planet connects intricately. It's woven within the quantum field of consciousness. Some physicists call it quantum entanglement, others 'Super determinism'.

Paramahansa says "time and space are linked in the presence of God."

That explains how one electron instantly identifies remotely with another. I now believe it. Call it quantum entanglement, ESP, a Force Field, or intuition. Linguistics fail to accurately describe it, but it is real. Perhaps more real than anything we see, taste, touch, hear, or smell. Call it what you will.

In the series of events between my Friday afternoon 'out of my mind' clash with the judge and "smelling my hand burning" at 3 AM, then waking up to read the Boston Globe deaths of the three older teenage kids, and all that occurred, I was in a state of very disturbed consciousness. What had just happened? Laima was mystified, incredulous, and knew I had woken up "smelling my burning hand," and checked the house for fire. She just said simply "it's God." I said "it was all based on your decision for me to take the case." She said "yes, I just knew you had to do it and I knew you didn't want to do it."

As time wore on, I thought it was *Laima's* intuition *stemming from Joe's fatherly love* for Sandra and Lester. Laima understood real love like few that I have ever met on this planet. She knew that love transcends matter. Spirit transcends the material universe. I know what fatherly love is. It controls all aspects of a father's relationship with his children. Laima understood it on an even deeper level, a God level. I now understand it more.

Now I realize to some degree how God interacts with us and saves us. Quantum entanglement is just a scientific explanation for God's love and Grace. That is what 'saved' Sandra and Lester. Why did the other three perish? I don't know. The Vedas and "Bhagavad Gita," provide an explanation of how karma works. Me, I'm a foot soldier trying to deal with my own issues. As a relatively inept, novice meditator, for years, I passed off the entire psychic episode as some mystical event involving forces with which I had no knowledge or experience. Somehow, I knew they functioned on levels above my poor litigating brain.

Now I think the power of Love is in fact the most powerful force in the universe. The fatherly love of Joe for his children must have given him access to higher intuition. That is what must have been the impetus for the urgency I observed when he was pleading, begging me to take the case. It dictated the outcome, with me serving as a litigator and relatively new meditator and conduit of sorts. I was in a field of quantum entanglement shared by Joe, his children, Laima and ultimately the judge. Whether or not we ascribe to a description such as quantum entanglement, the effect is that we are all connected far more than we imagine in a force field of love. Jesus may well have been talking in this manner when he said simply: "Love thy neighbor as thyself" and "suffer the little children, forbid them not, to come unto me." Neither myself, nor opposing counsel nor the judge could counteract the force of Christ consciousness captured in "forbid them not." Why the force field of love protected two children and allowed three others to perish, I know not.... We are all one.

Pray for those three teenagers who died. And for the alcoholic mother.

WHO OR WHAT SAVED SANDRA AND LESTER?

Joe's "victory," saving his children, was a profound relief, a rare moment of unambiguous light in the often-murky world of litigation. We won, and for the right reasons. The children were safe, and a father's love had been vindicated. The legal system had delivered a just result.

But the case left a deep, unsettling mark on me. The victory hinged on a moment of pure desperation—my last-minute, almost prayerful plea to the judge. It was not calculated legal strategy; it was my last-ditch attempt to sway the judge, an act of surrender because I had nothing more in my arsenal. I had knocked, and the door had been opened.

I knew taking custody from a mother of young children was an extremely contested issue in family law. I presented the evidence and the law fully. Yet in hindsight, I did not remotely understand the bigger picture of divine intervention taking place. God was intervening, but I had no clue. Call it intuition, consciousness beyond the five senses or quantum entanglement—that events separated by space and time can remain mysteriously connected. Whatever the name, it was real.

The question that haunts me still is this: Who or what saved Sandra and Lester? Was I simply a channel for something larger—a father's desperate love, a wife's intuition, or something beyond? I had resisted taking the case.

Laima insisted. Joe pleaded. And then, at the critical moment, I begged the judge to change custody immediately, against all logic and procedure, driven by a feeling I couldn't name.

This case stands as a testament to the notion that God, not the self-sufficient litigant or meditator, orchestrates the play. I have no doubt Joe's love for Sandra and Lester controlled the outcome. Joe's love was quantum entangled with the yogic power of "universal sympathy," whether he realized it or not. I certainly did not. I didn't even want the case, but given what happened, I sure would have taken it again. I ended up making a sort of fool of myself, begging the judge at the end of the last day of trial. Thank God I did!

How does consciousness work in moments like these? Does information seep into our hearts and minds in ways we don't consciously register, only to surface at pivotal moments when it's needed most? I believe it does. I believe consciousness can tap into a reality beyond what we can see, touch, or measure—a field of connection linking us to each other and to events we cannot predict. Why did Sandra and Lester's safety feel like a cosmic imperative rather than just another legal case? Most likely because they were innocent. Their consciousness was pure, unfiltered, unburdened by the ego and experiences that cloud adult perception.

When Christ said, "Suffer the little children, and forbid them not, to come unto me; for of such is the Kingdom of Heaven," was he instructing our entire species never to endanger, compromise, undermine, or "sin against" the innocence of children—which enables all of us to gain the Kingdom of Heaven? Their innocence, our innocence from worldly "sin," enables not only the children but all of us to live in higher levels of Christ consciousness. If we act in any way to "forbid them not," we create potentially catastrophic consequences, as played out in the death of the three other children. Maybe God was teaching all of us a lesson…

I wonder: Does a child's pure consciousness also perceive reality more clearly than an adult's? Not just metaphorically, but literally—does their uncorrupted awareness give them access to the field of consciousness that adults have lost? If so, perhaps Sandra and Lester weren't just passive victims waiting to be saved. Perhaps their pure consciousness was actively calling out across the quantum field. Joe's love, Laima's intuition, and my desperate plea were all responses to that call.

Our innocence is precious to God, and that is the likely explanation why a force field in the universe moved to save them, while their mother had submerged herself in addiction, violating Christ's admonition "forbid them not."

FOR OF SUCH IS THE KINGDOM OF HEAVEN

On this point I cannot help but introduce my decades-later representation of Monica Lewinsky, a 21-year-old White House intern who suffered through the sexual predations of William Jefferson Clinton. She was not a child, but compared to Clinton's obsessions, she still possessed a childlike innocence.

My litigator mind is similarly enraged by the demonic, pervasive exploitation of minors and teenagers. In June 2008, America's Department of Justice, FBI, and CIA covered up the Clinton/Epstein/Burkle statutory rapes of over 100 children (plus 21 other Epstein statutory rapists) by putting perpetrators on an illegal "Immunity List"...for who? The immunity list was engineered by none other than the same Bruce Reinhart, who on August 5, 2022, authorized the FBI Mar-A-Lago raid. During President Trump's first term, Epstein was arrested for sex trafficking; then Epstein was found dead in his prison cell, with sleeping guards and turned-off surveillance cameras. The immunity list is still under seal and inaccurately called the "Epstein Client List." Those granted immunity all violated Christ's edict. Who pulled the strings on the immunity list? Who would have the motive, opportunity, and means ("MOM" in homicide speak) to murder Epstein? For whom did Epstein and Ghislaine work, "honey trapping" world leaders, influencers, and billionaires like Burkle? The Mossad? The victims were just a few years older than Sandra Hakey. Now the truth is beginning to emerge. Maybe Clinton and his wife, and our entire DOJ, FBI, and CIA should read Matthew 19:14. See *Litigator 4* and *5*.

My later cases put the universal outrage against these sexual predators with their violations of Christ's "forbid them not" edict through massive sexual perversions and abuse of "little children" squarely on both my litigation and meditation plates.

Epilogue

This case created a growing sense of cognitive dissonance within me. I was living a double life. In the courtroom I was a rationalist, a master of facts and evidence, a player in a system that recognized only what could be seen and proven. But in my meditation, and in the quiet moments of my life, I was becoming increasingly aware of a reality that operated on entirely different principles—a world of consciousness, intuition, and unseen connections.

My TM practice was no longer just a stress-relief technique. It was becoming a doorway into that other world. It gave me the clarity to see the patterns in the case, the courage to hire the private investigator, and the stamina to endure the fight. But it also made the return to the courtroom feel increasingly jarring, like stepping from a world of color into a world of black and white.

In TM meditation, the mind dives deep, connecting to what Maharishi calls 'being,' or 'God,' or pure 'love.' As it traverses these finer layers of thought, it unlocks a profound understanding where thought, feeling, and energy become one. The subtlest thoughts link to that same pure being; when the mind experiences these increasingly refined levels, it grasps the finest connection points between thought, feeling, vibration, and energy. Energy itself links 'time and space,' exactly as Paramahansa Yogananda describes, and then thought, feeling, and energy all merge in transcendence. The being, the Self, ultimately experiences pure awareness, giving the mind a knowledge in which reality itself is known as God. This explains humanity's search for the divine over millennia.

I have experienced both the search and the realization. My father's near-death experience in 1958 in his airplane accident in a blizzard, for instance, awakened a depth of love that he shared with me and our family throughout his life. It marked the beginning of this journey for me. Writing this, I recall similar moments from the 90s, visiting Mother Meera. Between 1992–96, an agnostic journalist and I found common ground in Germany, where he sought to debunk Meera as a fraud. I was skeptical myself at first, but had witnessed and experienced so many instances of pure divinity through her that I warned him he might be surprised.

After attending Meera's "Darshan," the British journalist sent to debunk her was stunned. In both cases, our departed fathers came to us in altered states of consciousness, his father appearing in Mother Meera's presence, mine in a waking dream while writing this book, bringing love and answering long-held questions. These echoes of paternal love, whether during waking dreams or in Meera's presence, speak to a depth beyond our typical awareness. It's difficult for us to grasp; as we are just evolving.

There are no accidents; we are not in control. Free will is ours, but we are shepherded by forces beyond mere time and space. Love and compassion are more real and powerful than house fires, incinerated children, mobsters, death, disease, guns and bullets, wars and genocides. Through meditation, we access the enduring truths of love and compassion...forces more tangible than any earthly struggle.

Joe's children had been saved, but I was beginning to question if I could save myself. I was a litigator and a meditator, and I was no longer sure if those two identities could coexist in the same soul.

CHAPTER 9

Quantum Entanglement: Experiments In Measuring Consciousness

"Actually our human consciousness is Cosmic Consciousness, bottled up in a phial of flesh, corked with ignorance, and floating isolated in the ocean of Spirit." **Paramahansa Yogananda**, *God Talks With Arjuna: The Bhagavad Gita*

"The total number of minds in the universe is one. In fact, consciousness is a singularity phasing within all beings." **Erwin Schrödinger**

BEFORE WE BEGIN...

A word about this chapter: it's not like the others. Where previous chapters moved through chronological time and case narratives with meditative explanations, this one attempts to explain quantum entanglement in some depth. It's my attempt to grapple with the profound questions raised by the Sandra and Lester case, the psychic in the Dwyer case, and the befuddling "coincidences" in the Sequeira case when I met "Uncle Dante" after working on the murder conviction of his son while writing the dissenting opinion on that conviction. What is consciousness? How are we connected? What role does the divine play in our lives? I draw on quantum physics, yogic philosophy, Near-Death Experience research, and the wisdom of mystics and scientists alike. It's dense. It's demanding. And it's deeply personal.

I am not a physicist, and I make no claim to explain quantum mechanics in technical terms. What I offer here is personal testimony: experiences that felt, to me, like direct demonstrations of what Paramahansa Yogananda taught decades before these concepts entered popular discourse—namely, that 'time and space are linked in the presence of God.' The language of quantum entanglement simply became, for me, a modern metaphor that echoed an ancient truth I had already encountered in meditation and in the courtroom miracles I witnessed.

If you're here for the story, feel free to skip ahead to Chapter 10. The narrative continues without interruption. If you're here for the mystery, stay with me. This chapter is where I try to solve it, not with legal arguments, but with the tools of science and spirit. Your choice. Either way, I'm grateful you're reading.

AN UNEXPLAINABLE CASE

The Sandra and Lester case set the stage for my future as a litigator. It also pulled back the curtain for me on the sprawling, mysterious wilderness that is the human mind and soul. Here a legal battle, there a puzzle box of consciousness veiled in mental smoke. How to remove the smoke of maya? Maya is what the Hindus call mind delusion or illusion. For me, this fascination is both professional and personal. I've spent decades as both courtroom advocate and quiet observer on the meditation cushion, searching for what lies within each to further peace, truth and justice for clients who deserved both.

Back in 1974, I'd just picked up the basics of meditation. I was still prone to wandering focus at the time I handled the Sandra and Lester case under the extraordinary circumstances you just read about in the last chapter. My legal skills weren't much further along, truth be told. I use the word 'extraordinary' because if you took even a half-attentive observer and dropped them into the middle of that case's 'facts', they'd call it anything but normal. Now, with fifty years of litigation and silent sitting in meditation under my belt, I can tell you that the facts defied more than just ordinary explanation. They crashed right through the walls of what we expect from 'normal' everyday experiences and sensory perceptions.

The litigation basics are:

Reopening a child custody case less than sixty days after a judge had already awarded custody to the mother, whose severe alcoholism was no secret, just conveniently swept under the judicial rug by the court with a connected lawyer – not unlike attorney Bellotti's attempt to get approval for Patty in a Middlesex Probate Court for an "Absentee estate." None of it 'normal' or in accordance with correct legal procedure.

Removal of the Judge in Middlesex County who awarded custody to the alcoholic mother; and bringing in a judge 50 miles away from Worcester County. Not normal or in accordance with routine legal procedure.

The sheer weirdness of the proceedings with improbable timing: a five-day trial, ending with a nail-biting, last day, last-minute, Friday change to the temporary custody order. It was only set to expire when the full report from the 'Guardian ad Litem's' (GAL) report landed on Monday. Not normal. The record proves it.

The removal of Sandra and Lester from the mother's house that Friday night, and the subsequent burning to death of all three teenage occupants in their house at about 3 AM. But for the Court's last-minute, reluctant change in the Custody Order, Sandra and Lester would have likely died in the house fire. Not normal. The mother was again not home.

"Smelling my right hand burning," awakening me at 3 AM, reported to my wife, and checking my own home and my children. Not normal.

That Friday afternoon, now 47 years ago, the replacement judge was not going to change the custody orders on Sandra and Lester until at the very least, the following Monday. The drunken, never home, ex-wife, would have maintained custody over that weekend. Sandra and Lester would have burned to death like their two stepbrothers, along with a 15-year-old teenage girl hanging out unsupervised with the two boys—a frightening thought.

God works in mysterious ways. As for the karma of the three children who died and the sorrow that overwhelmed their alcoholic mother, I feel only compassion... no words or rational explanation suffice. I leave these questions to your judgment, mindful of the intuitive, non-evidentiary arguments I presented to the judge that Friday afternoon; arguments offered as if I were a lawyer possessed... unfettered by law, evidence, or the boundaries of time and space.

THE LIMITS OF MATERIALIST SCIENCE

Something in me was somehow transmitted to something in the judge beyond the hard evidence that had been proven in the week-long trial. I'm not so ego-driven that I think it was the evidence and my legal arguments, it wasn't. It was something beyond. The safe road for the judge, both in dealing with the case before him and in the Middlesex County courthouse politics involving the prior judge's ruling, was to await the GAL report on Monday. That report would have supported changing custody from the mother, despite the original orders being only two months old. But for some clearly mystical reason, he changed his mind right then.

I now call that causal link to the changed custody orders 'God's Grace'. Something in my consciousness somehow resonated in the judge's consciousness to cause him, almost in an instant, to reverse course before he left the bench, even though he didn't want to do it. It was beyond my paltry litigator efforts and had little or nothing to do with me. Generally, as litigators know well, once you start arguing with the judge it tends to become an ego clash, and it's usually never fruitful. But somehow the judge knew in this case it was not my ego. It was something else. Indefinable.

When final arguments were made that Friday afternoon, I was initially content to present my closing statement and wait for the GAL report to support the change in custody. But that, of course, was not what happened. I went off the lawyer-like rails.

Judges don't like getting mixed up in those kinds of hurried, last-minute arguments not based on previously admissible evidence, especially when they conflict with a colleague's prior ruling. It would have been far more 'normal' to wait for the independent GAL evidence on Monday, which would have supported the needed change despite the short time since the original orders were signed.

The idea to fight for the change in custody wasn't even on my mind when I began to present my arguments. Then some part of my brain, my consciousness, began pleading with him to change his mind and his orders before he left the bench. He became angry at me, looking to opposing counsel for relief. Opposing counsel started aggressively attacking me. I then became like an obsessive beggar, notwithstanding my usual ego-driven 'professional' demeanor. The whole sequence was stranger than fiction.

Somehow, that judge instantly changed his mind and changed his orders. How? Why? Anger? Frustration? No way! He became entangled with what I was entangled in...the "Just get those kids out of that house" divine intervention that was taking place. Going to a more logical hard-earth explanation, perhaps it was extra-sensory perception of a future event? But what is ESP? 'ESP' may be just another human word to explain a 'level' of divine grace. How can ESP alone conceivably entangle so many people in changing an event in the future?

What little thought particle in the judge's mind instantly connected with a remote thought particle elsewhere in the Universe? Is thought even a particle? Thoughts are energy. Dear reader, if you think it was just my random ramblings, I recommend you put this book down now—there's more to come!

Science rejects ESP as pseudoscience. There is no scientific, material evidence base to support it. Some of the reported historical cases of claimed ESP occurrence have been found to be flawed, twisted, and distorted. Some ESP evidence has been documented as objectively verified, but the mind component of an ESP event generally remains based on subjective reports of what the person experiencing it relates. This intersects with the subjective reports of near-death experiencers who report being in the 'tunnel of light' and in 'life reviews' with old, white-robed sages in 'heaven'. How do we even start to create a scientific framework to deal with this higher consciousness that seems so independent of laboratory test tubes, EEG scans, and peer-reviewed studies?

You might ask, where do those images and experiences even come from in the human mind? Unlike 'baby science', they are millennia old as reported in some of the oldest human writings, including the Bible. Are they just human projections of a species seeking higher answers? Perhaps. But how and why did the human mind correlate these images to God, or God-like creatures also clothed in 'white robes' in many instances?

A SEARCH FOR FRAMEWORKS: FROM SPOOKY PHYSICS TO YOGIC SCIENCE

The problem of observing thought in detail is that you end up explaining why thoughts are nearly impossible to study scientifically. It's the "Stream of Consciousness" problem in that human thought is constantly shifting. You see a table, and think 'table', then your eyes move to a chair, and now you're thinking 'table and chair'. Add input from all five senses over minutes, hours, or days, and you have an endless, unrepeatable stream of mental activity. Because thoughts are fleeting and subjective, they cannot be materially verified or replicated in controlled laboratory experiments. There's no way to capture and measure a single thought with precision because it's immediately replaced by the next thought in the stream. This makes subjective mental experiences like intuition, ESP, or mystical visions inherently resistant to scientific validation. Science demands repeatability and objective measurement, but the nature of thought makes that impossible.

If normal thoughts are so fleeting and unmeasurable, how do we explain NDEs? Unlike ordinary thought streams, NDEs are remarkably consistent across thousands of reported cases. They are highly detailed and memorable, not fleeting like ordinary thoughts. They are reported by people with no prior religious or spiritual framework to explain them and they are documented in medical literature by the tens of thousands of cases, plus books like Dr. Eben Alexander's *Proof of Heaven*. The challenge to materialist science is that if thoughts are just biochemical processes in the brain, why do NDEs, which occur when the brain is supposedly dying or dead, produce such vivid, coherent, and transformative experiences? Why aren't they just the random, chaotic firing of dying neurons producing chaotic streams of consciousness?

Materialist neuroscience says consciousness is produced by the brain, so when the brain dies, consciousness should cease or dissolve into non-existence, if that is even conceivable. How does the reality of knowing our existence, "I am," logically square with "I am not"? It's a paradox. The first law of thermodynamics says that energy is neither created nor destroyed so if the thought, "I am," is energy, then under the first law, there cannot logically at least, be a reality of "I am not." NDE evidence conforms to that law, suggesting that consciousness not only persists but becomes more vivid, coherent, and meaningful when the brain is clinically dead. This paradox supports the idea that consciousness exists in a field separate from the brain in what is called the quantum-entangled "Force Field" of God. NDEs are evidence that consciousness is not merely a product of brain chemistry but something that transcends the physical body and points toward a reality beyond materialism.

For many people experiencing NDEs, who had no religious, spiritual or educational data base on which to explain the thought processes that they experienced, they looked beyond the mind into a higher level of consciousness to find answers. "Utter nonsense", say many neuroscientists! However, one of their own, Dr. Alexander was an agnostic neuroscientist who at first thought NDE's were nonsense. He flipped on his colleagues and said 'been there, done that' I was biochemically dead for five days in coma, on a ventilator, with a certifiable EEG dead cerebral cortex, fully permeated with deadly meningitis and I experienced a vivid, life-changing NDE. Now what? Whoops. The neuroscientists, surgeons and neurologists have 'scientifically' postulated for decades that chemical changes in the brain at death explained the NDE experiences. They had no objective or subjective proof. They just engaged in these hypotheses on some bio-chemical basis of deductive reasoning in the form of: 'we see cells dying in the brain with no oxygen being pumped from a dead heart, so those bio-chemical changes must explain brain ideation or thoughts of white robed sages and tunnels of light. What else could it be?

Cycling back to the events of the Sandra and Lester case we can see that the events are objectively documented in the court record, death certificates, newspaper accounts, participant reports, including those from my wife and me and my own recollections.

True, my 'burning hand' testimony is subjective. Those thoughts in that time and space are not verifiable. They remain in my memory. So, you will have to trust me... a lawyer! I think that in the future, advances in quantum technology may allow such thoughts to be transmitted directly to an AI database, then perhaps read and expressed in full 'technicolor'.

Facts: The fire started at 3 AM Saturday morning. The mother's two teenagers by a prior marriage and their 15-year-old friend died in the fire. Sandra and Lester were removed from the house by court order only the prior day, the previous Friday afternoon. That Saturday early morning at 3 AM I informed Laima of my 'burning hand', and got up and searched our home. My hand was clearly not 'burning', but I smelled burning flesh! That evidence is subjective, but since my hand was not 'burning', it can only be relegated to the metaphysical world, assuming you believe this poor scribe? If not, I suggest the AY and some meditation.... and 50 years of litigation perhaps!

Outside of your formerly intrepid, now less than adventurous, current litigator, who else would believe this story unless you were party to it? I believe your intuition will give you the answer to that question by 'resonating' with it; that is receive the true vibrations of the event... entangle with it, and the facts in my report. All roads lead to QE despite the current recognized brains in quantum physics, like Leonard Susskind and David Bohm struggling to even figure out what quantum entanglement actually is. Even Einstein had to end up calling this phenomena "spooky".

QUANTUM ENTANGLEMENT, A RATIONAL EXPLANATION FOR THE UNEXPLAINABLE?

So what conclusion do we come to? Was it the way time, space, and events braided themselves together or were these mere coincidences? There are few 'rational' explanations available, but when we open up our options—calling it psychic phenomenon, extra-sensory perception, quantum entanglement, or divine intervention... then it begins to make sense to me, even logical perhaps.

Even as one of the key players involved in these time-space events, I had no so-called rational explanation at the time. What I do have, 50 years later on, is a working conclusion: what I would call divine intervention in God's Force Field. My current conclusion is supported by the psychic's remarkable findings in the death of Tom D, and by the facts, evidence and events recounted in prior and subsequent chapters in the books in this Litigator series.

If these books have one thread tying them together, it is that the human perceived correlations connecting time, space, and events such as the facts and evidence in litigated cases—although normally perceived within time and space by litigators and participants, can be perceived differently on higher levels of consciousness. Christ, Paramahansa Yogananda and other 'Yogis' possessing higher consciousness powers are able to perceive time, space and events within a consciousness level that removes time and space. At least I think so from my perspective, limited though it is in comparison to the Masters at least. 'To compare is to despair' as they say, so I will continue to share my experiences with you in these books.

If these books have one thread tying them together, it's the idea that connections between time, space, and events are not always what they seem. Lawyers, clients, seekers like me all perceive reality through the familiar grid of days and distances. Currently, there are theoretical physicists who confirm that time and space don't even exist! The universe is some sort of an illusion. Yogananda stated the same 100 years ago. He said this universe is the "dream world of God." In what appears to be an 'extra normal' event, the kids being saved, and my burning hand, may, in truth, not even be seen as unusual in higher levels of consciousness. Anyone reading Yogananda's *Autobiography of a Yogi* (the "AY"), for the first time, with no underlying yogic experience (the soul connecting to God), or meditative experience, would likely conclude that the events and individual experiences he describes in living detail are too extraordinary, too mystical, and too unbelievable to accept. However, concepts in his "AY" do explain the Sandra and Lester case.

For many years, 'my jury' was 'still out' on the more astounding feats described by the Yogis in the "AY". I was skeptical, holding fast to legal logic! After 50 plus years of meditating, and living through the events described in this Litigator series... no more. It is a miracle that I have survived but perhaps it is more easily explained by God helping out a poor pilgrim on his way. My whole life has been about God's Grace protecting me from my own flaws and failings.

I've come to recognize a particular kind of courage: the willingness to pursue truth even when it threatens your career, your reputation, and your place in the established order. I subscribe to the forward thinking of many such individuals, starting with the Saints and Avatars like Yogananda, whom I perceive to be authentic knowers of truth, one of those who have directly experienced the ultimate reality and returned to guide the rest of us.

But there is another tier of truth-seekers operating on a different level of consciousness: the scientists and researchers who are pushing the boundaries of their disciplines, often at great personal and professional cost. These are not the armchair theorists content to repeat the orthodoxies of their fields. They are explorers venturing into territory that makes their colleagues uncomfortable, asking questions that threaten the funding streams and power structures of institutional science.

Among this vanguard are the quantum physicists who have taken Einstein's "spooky action at a distance" seriously, refusing to dismiss quantum entanglement as a mere curiosity. Theorists like John Bell and David Bohm didn't just describe the phenomenon, they sought to understand what it meant for the nature of reality itself. Then there are the evolutionary biologists like Stephen Meyer and Douglas Axe, who have dared to challenge the Darwinian orthodoxy by exploring intelligent design, risking professional censure from the Neo-Darwinists who control the grant money and academic journals. And there are the medical pioneers, the science-based doctors who have broken ranks with Big Pharma's money-based medicine to explore natural healing modalities that actually address the root causes of disease rather than masking symptoms with pharmaceuticals.

Another such pioneer is Dr. Eben Alexander, the neurosurgeon who had the integrity to report what he experienced, even though it contradicted everything he'd been trained to believe about consciousness and the brain. Another is clinical psychologist Jordan Peterson, who has fearlessly explored the intersection of mythology, psychology, and spiritual truth in a secular age that dismisses such inquiries as unscientific.

These are the true science-based pioneers of our time. They are seeking to understand the mechanics of life, its meaning, and how we came to exist on this tiny planet and why the universe itself exists at all. They have looked beyond the now-discredited 1850s model of Darwin, which was based on his limited perception of evolution in the archaeological remains of animal species. Current advances in the microscopic and macroscopic archaeological record, evolutionary biology, genetics, and DNA analysis have left Darwinian theories of natural selection and survival of the fittest in the dustbin of history. Yet the Neo-Darwinists, financially supported by Big Pharma and trapped in their own ideological rigidity, continue to defend a paradigm that no longer fits the evidence.

The latest flagrant falsehoods fabricated by Dr. Anthony Fauci to gain Big Pharma money in the manufactured Covid pandemic also illustrates the arrogant, non-scientific postulations of the dust-binned orthodox, so-called "scientists."

In the actual experience of transcendence beyond the limits of the human brain, ego and intellect, Deepak has understood God as the ultimate level of human consciousness. As a medical doctor under the tutelage of Maharishi and innumerable Vedic scientists, in exploring Quantum Healing which is the title of one of his early best sellers, he writes about the foundational basis of healing. This is the healing entanglement of body, brain, mind and soul embracing man's highest state of consciousness to self-realize God within ourselves. Our 'wave resonance' matching that of God's. In that state all healing takes place. Yogananda postulated that in the consciousness of God there is no disease. How to become that consciousness? Meditate.

Consider our cave-dwelling ancestors. When they encountered lightning, a charging bison, or any phenomenon that threatened or awed them, they retreated to their caves and transferred their thoughts to painted murals. These images documented their experience of the natural world, but they didn't explain it. The paintings were symbols, not understanding.

Modern physicists may be engaged in the same activity. When confronted with quantum entanglement, the phenomenon where two particles instantaneously share the same state regardless of the distance between them, without anything traveling between them, Einstein and his colleagues were baffled. This violated their understanding of reality, including the "fixed" speed of light at 186,000 miles per second, which they believed was the cosmic speed limit.

Unable to explain it, Einstein called it "spooky action at a distance." He and his colleagues recorded it in a thought experiment (the famous 1935 EPR paper) and essentially left it at that. They documented the mystery. They created mathematical symbols to represent it. But they didn't understand it.

What then? Are they not just more recent cave dwellers? Instead of painting bison on cave walls, they paint equations on chalkboards. Instead of using ochre and charcoal, they use symbols and mathematics. But the fundamental activity is the same; transferring thoughts to symbols without penetrating the mystery.

The cave painters couldn't explain where the bison came from or why it existed. The physicists can't explain where consciousness comes from or why entanglement exists. Both groups mistake documentation for understanding. Both remain in the cave. The mystics, by contrast, have walked out into the light. They don't paint the mystery, they experience it directly. Famously, Einstein did say, in his ultimate rejection of a purely atheistic, matter-based cosmos (sorry Dawkins et al): "I want to know how God created this world. I'm not interested in this or that phenomenon, in the spectrum of this or that element. I want to know His thoughts. The rest are just details."

On the issues of "God's thoughts", suppose the transference of thought from one human to another without verbal, sensory, or written communication was called ESP, QE, or pick any other term. Paramahansa Yogananda says it is part of God's "natural world", but linked in God beyond time and space. According to the most advanced studies into QE, some of the most elite physicists agree with Paramahansa Yogananda. The AY describes the phenomenon of time and space not existing in the consciousness of God in remarkable detail, but admittedly circumscribed by human language.

How do you use language to describe what is beyond the human intellect? The above Einstein quote illustrates "The Hard Problem" of us humans trying to know God's thoughts, and putting them into language. It is a conundrum. Would a linguistic explanation even make it more scientifically approachable as worthy of scientific exploration? The leading chieftains in Einsteinian theoretical physics, and the leading brains in quantum biology are attempting to quantify consciousness. Seems like the ultimate paradox to me?

Einstein called quantum entanglement "spooky." Leonard Susskind calls it "freaky." In two 1935 papers written a few months apart on EPR, "Elemental Particle Reality," or the "Einstein, Podolsky Rosen" paradox, these three physicists attempted in a thought experiment to explain the entire physical universe in the framework of quantum entanglement. They concluded that they couldn't explain it. It was too "spooky"!

Paramahansa Yogananda: it looks to me like he was right back in 1935 stating that time and space are linked in the presence of God. THAT explains quantum entanglement on a physicist level with yogic speak – it essentially states what physicists are discovering decades later. If there is no time and space in God's presence, then two distant particles are instantly merged. If that doesn't make any sense to some of the classical physicists, it does to me on several levels. In transcendence, there is no time and space. I have experienced it.

On another more materialistic, crude, level, I know when I present a specific fact to a jury from which a juror can draw an inference about another fact, the two facts become entangled in the collective consciousness of the jury. The fact may get initially filtered through 12 different levels of individual juror consciousness; but when they end up with identical conclusions, what language can be used to describe that synthesis of their collective thought? Common sense? ESP? Rational logic? QE? Psychic phenomena? The jury gets their ultimate synthesis on a specific fact from my thoughts. That is how some force field prevailed in many of my jury cases, a few of which you have read about thus far. Some would call it common sense or just plain logic. I now call it quantum entanglement because I have no other explanation for Sandra and Lester, the psychic in the Dwyer case, and the verdict in Sequeira. After 50 years in the PIT while meditating, I confess to no other sensory observable conclusion but that we are all entangled in God's / Christ's consciousness.

It is also how I understand devotion and love for God. I'm no physicist, nor a spaced-out religionist, but since the physicists are scientifically adept at particle reductionism and refinement, which they call quantum mechanics, I will claim some level of non-scientific knowledge. For instance, juror reaction to facts which are mixed together to form 'inferences', which, in turn, cause a sequence of thoughts in the minds of judge, litigators and jurors such that they reach a Verdict. The Richard S. Dwyer, and Sandra and Lester cases are illustrative examples. There was no 'five senses' evidence of Richard's dead body, but 16 jurors 'thought' he was dead. Maybe he is still alive, living in Fiji, gone native, and the jury was dead wrong? Your verdict. My experience of smelling my hand burning was just mine. Maybe I was deluded, or my mind made the whole thing up, or I've created this falsehood to sell books? However, the thought, whether I created it or God planted it, caused a sequence of events that saved the lives of two young children.

Maybe the NDE'ers have all imagined or made up their experiences through a kind of unconscious thought transference, reading about the experiences of others and thereby creating a popular wave of 'tunnels of light' and 'life reviews' that gets repeated over and over. Perhaps it's just cultural contamination, not a real glimpse of the afterlife.

Obviously, I don't believe this. And here's why: Quantum entanglement is predicated on the scientific certainty that when one particle is measured, the partner particle will have the identical measurement, no matter how far apart they are. This isn't copying or influence, it's a fundamental connection at the deepest level of reality, currently acceptable to observable, repeatable experiment. If two particles can share the same state across the universe because they are entangled in a unified field, then why couldn't thousands of human consciousnesses report the same experiences when they approach death? They're not copying each other's stories. They're accessing the same underlying reality... the quantum-entangled Force Field of God.

The consistency of NDE reports isn't evidence of fabrication, it's evidence of a real, shared spiritual reality. This concept is the bridge between my litigation mind which demands evidence and my spiritual conviction which trusts in the reality of divine intervention, based on 50 years of meditation. Quantum entanglement is the rational framework that allows me to accept mystical truth without abandoning my commitment to logic and evidence.

My litigation life was based on a very simple concept: if I could prove an essential fact that the defense could not legitimately disprove, it would create an impenetrable wall in the jurors' minds, from which they could infer or deduce equally certain facts, call them 'partner facts', like 'partner particles' entangled with each other, on which to base a legitimate conclusion or verdict. Litigators like to call that 'Truth' and 'Justice". But so called 'truth' depends on one's level of consciousness. Therein lies the ultimate litigation conundrum. For example, in today's political climate, what is true to a Trump supporter on issues of abortion, gun control, and socialist economics for instance, is false to the anti-Trumpers. Same split on truth between the climate changers measuring carbon levels vs those measuring them with totally contrary interpretations. Unfortunately, there is currently no technologically acceptable instrument to measure the consciousness of potential jurors in a trial of very conflicted opponents.

In quantum entanglement, at the exact same moment that particle one's state becomes certain, the other particle's state also becomes certain. The reason that the physicists call it a paradox is that it apparently involves communication between the two particles at speeds greater than the speed of light, which is in conflict with Einstein's theory of relativity, fixing speed of light at a constant velocity of 186,000 miles per second.

Careful, you Einsteinian readers, our species is continually trapped in our measuring brains? Just how far down the evolutionary ladder are we? Just out of the caves on a time and space gradient? Who says time and space constitute the ultimate reality? Millennia of sages, mystics, yogis and 'saints' say "not so fast Sherlock."

Yogananda and Maharishi explain it. So does the Bhagavad Gita and Christ. On a transcendental level, that God supposedly works on, (I say "supposedly" because I don't live on that level), I'm drawing that inference from fifty years of experience evaluating evidence that there is total communication between everyone and everything in the "Kingdom of God within," and my intermittent, transcendental experiences. Time and space are "linked in God". Who, what is God, you may ask? Consciousness? A force field? Love?

Those questions may indeed be "spooky" and not capable of atomic particle reductionism, but billions of humans have experienced the question, the search. Many people over thousands of years claim to have experienced some form of God dating back to the cave-dwellers painting their image of 'God' in some form on their cave walls. Did those billions of souls create religion or spirituality, or simply fulfill their beliefs? I witnessed a tangible example of whatever this is in the Sandra and Lester case, a demonstrable, material event involving life and death. I know I didn't create it, so who did? Was it chance, the randomness of life, or fate? In my view, God saved Sandra and Lester. Their father's love transcended materialist reality.

The quantum entanglement paradox involved a debate between Einstein and Niels Bohr. There was likely some bit of professional ego involved. Einstein discovered relativity. Bohr took it further into quantum theory without the full acceptance of Einstein. His colleagues, Boris Podolsky and Nathan Rosen, developed the EPR (Elemental Particle Reality) paradox as a way of showing that the Bohr quantum theory was inconsistent with other known laws of physics. There were no methodologies to scientifically confirm the theories, so they all deemed it a "spooky" "thought experiment". Later physicists were able to conduct measurements of 'particle spin' which seemed to confirm entanglement.

Again, until a measurement is made, neither particle has a definite state. They are both in 'possible states', with an equal probability of having a positive or negative spin. After measurement, voila, identical states. How do the quantum theorists in all known physical phenomenon explain that?

Have you ever observed or experienced what love does when two people meet? While we are in the body, we are just a bundle of particles, right; a collection of atoms. But when my particles meet my lover's particles, kazam. That's the lover's version of quantum entanglement. There have been many humans who wished it wasn't so! The quantum physicists just explain it differently.

When they measure Particle A, its quantum spin gets set by the measurement. Mysteriously, particle B also instantly has the identical spin set. Einstein believed this was a clear violation of his theory of relativity. "Not quite so fast says Niels, but you are out to lunch on this "spooky" theory. I'm right. You're wrong." LOL. The conflict intensified. A later theoretical physicist, neuroscientist, David Bohm, partnered with Einstein and supported an alternative theory called the "hidden-variables theory." This postulated that quantum mechanics was simply incomplete. In other words, there must be more to be discovered. Something, some theory, some explanation was necessary to supplement the 'non-local effect' of two particles instantly becoming identical.

Bohm was a buddy of that yogi-philosopher and quasi-scientist, J. Krishnamurti. They thought they all knew how to solve "spooky" with hidden variables. Collectively, they all ended up postulating that the problem was not one of incomplete knowledge, but of an unknown reality. If you're confused, hang on, it gets worse.

Hey fellas: Albert, Niels, David, Lennie et al, can't we all be friends: how about supplementing or seeking reality with that force field we can call "God," the one only the mystics seem to understand? That's a reality beyond very limited human consciousness, 'n'est ce pas? Maybe God consciousness understands it all. Maybe you guys should also hook up with Dr. Meyer and the intelligent designers in evolutionary biology? They found something in the spine of the DNA which seems to explain the creation of our species. Just maybe, our little human minds trapped in atomic reductionism don't get it. Maybe measurement is just obsolete?

Dr. Eben Alexander, the neurosurgeon and NDE'er says he was dead and got entangled with heaven! Same with spinal surgeon, Dr. Mary Neal, and now thousands of others reporting subjectively what they experienced. Maybe subjective reporting can become a scientific reality. "Are you a Ph.D.?" "Yes, I'm a Doctor of Subjective Neuro Thought and Experience Quantology" It's a new field of science. Over the millennia, this was likely called "Faith." Oh no, don't hit me with that incomprehensible word....

Even further out, how about reading a little of Paramahansa Yogananda? Bohm's buddy Krishnamurti thought Paramahansa Yogananda was enlightened... entangled with God so to speak. Too far out? No worries, your collective consciousness I'm certain will get you there when you entangle your thought experiments with theirs. Like Einstein theorized, just because he couldn't see what God sees, might mean he was not in the same state of consciousness. Isn't that a scientific explanation?

Why keep reducing the atom and subatomic particles into more quanta? Enough of the Higgs Boson. Isn't quantum reductionism a one-way street? Isn't that why Albert and Niels got into a little tiff? The speed of light is fixed says Albert. Not quite says Niels. Albert and colleagues just ended up with "spooky." That's scientific materialism-speak for non-acceptance of a force greater than the four forces agreed upon by the classical physicists: the strong force, the weak force, the electromagnetic force, and the gravitational force.

These are measurable and recognized realities. "We don't want to add anything," says Richard Dawkins. "The earth really is flat," says Richard and Pope Paul V. Hang, draw, and quarter the so-called consciousness heretics, at least within the bounds of quantum mechanics, and according to the general and special theorists. More importantly, deny them government grants to pursue their theories; instead, let's channel public funding into pharmaceuticals.

CONVERGENCE: THE RISE OF NEUROQUANTOLOGY

I understand, as a nonscientist litigator, and apparently not a very smart one if you look at my adversaries that I got entangled with (*Litigator 2* and *4*), that the uncertainty in quantum mechanics involves a fundamental lack of what Einstein called definite 'reality'. To me, I take Einstein's statement about lack of a definite reality to be an admission that the higher 'reality' of God exists apart from wave-particle measurement. Not just a little lack of knowledge regardless of how that is supplemented with more experiments and theories, but a whole different reality. Until a measurement is made, particles are only in all possible states, not the one determined by a 'measurement'. Apparently, the theoretical physicists continue to play a game of dice with God with no definitive rules for what makes the universe what it is.

Bohr's view of quantum mechanics, which continued to be supported by the experimental evidence, is that the spin of Particle A and spin of Particle

B are not independent quantities within the quantum physics equations, but are the same. The moment that the measurement on Particle A is made, the wave function of both seemingly independent particles devolves into a single state. There's no remote communication taking place. They just instantly become one. Perhaps this explains a reality beyond time and space and beyond cause and effect?

Thus, Einstein's hidden-variables theory came to a dead end. Physicist John Bell postulated "Bell's Theorem." He developed experiments based on the non-entanglement of the two particles. In repeated experiments, Bell's experiments violated "independent quantities." This apparently confirmed quantum entanglement into a single state. To me, this seems to support a God theory, a force field of consciousness in which all matter has the potential to become one. A sort of instant convergence.

New theories of the mind, brain and consciousness seem to be approaching at least some form of convergence between science and, for lack of a better word, spirituality. Dirk Meijer, a Dutch neuroscientist and Professor, after decades in the lab and the classroom, posited in the September 2017 peer-reviewed Journal *Neuroquantology* that a field exists in a different dimension than the brain. This field interacts with our brains, or at least some of our more receptive brains, on a quantum level.

Neuroquantology is an academic journal that combines research from the fields of neuroscience and quantum physics. The more recent study in the January 2025 *Computational and Structural Biotechnology Journal* entitled "Evidence of quantum entangled higher states of consciousness" supports the previously labeled "mystics," and millennia sages like Christ, Yogananda and the Buddha to name a few. The real hard-core scientists like Stephen Meyer and Douglas Axe in the fields of evolutionary biology are being validated. Bye-bye Darwin and the neo-Darwinists like Hawkins and Harris.

Meijer posits that the mind is "a holographically structured field" that acts as a receptive mental workspace around the brain which is also able to access other fields outside of the brain. Hmmm. What might these other fields be? His and his colleagues' research and peer-reviewed papers, including that cited above, postulate that the other fields function in a fourth spatial dimension, a higher dimensional space than the one our brains are circumscribed in. Whoa, that is beginning to sound like a higher state of consciousness, where ESP and QE take place. Even more terrifying to the scientific materialists, Meijer's work seems to be approaching the "spooky" region of God consciousness.

Interdisciplinary entanglement with the mathematicians corroborates Meijer's theories proving that, in fact, the human brain intersects with these other fields in multiple dimensions. Meijer and friends have turned to quantum entanglement and "quantum tunneling" for answers to comprehend their multidimensional fields outside of the brain. As mentioned above, these states involve now observable and repeatable measurements that two particles instantaneously identify with each other, synching together despite being separated by immense distances.

Meijer et al now postulate that "Consciousness in the Universe is Tuned by a Musical Master Code." *Quantum Biosystems* | 2020 | Vol 11 | Issue 1 | Page 31-37

To my ungoverned spectrum of ignorant postulates, that sounds like the sound of 'OM' to me, which I have personally heard in my Kriya practice, and which Dr. Eben Alexander discovered when he 'died and went to heaven'.

The quantum physicists have also postulated that "quantum tunneling" can be observed when one particle maintains its motion and momentum after it strikes another particle which should have caused a rebound effect. But it doesn't. It keeps going with the same motion and momentum! What? How can that take place in a physical universe governed by the four forces, says I the litigator and meditator? No foolin?

The intrepid Meijer postulates that entanglement and tunneling illustrate how the fields outside the mind and brain convey data or information to both through 'quantum wave resonance' at instantaneous speeds. At quantum and sub-quantum levels, the fields outside the mind and brain transmit by 'wave resonance' to the neurons and particles in the brain through the mind. They interact instantaneously back and forth.

The quantum wave resonance postulate of brain and mind communication with an outside field also potentially solves what the quantum physicists call "the binding problem." This problem seems to arise in our brains when the speed of interaction in our brain neurons between different areas of the brain involving different brain functions, like vision, sound, cognitive and verbal responses work together at variable speeds individually, then are collectively processed. When we try to comprehend and digest different levels of reality, the neural activity in our brains seems to get stuck. Meijer and colleagues say that this problem is solved when we accept that the brain and mind are, in fact, functioning with synchronistic wave patterns transmitting information at the quantum level through 'resonance'.

This may be one giant leap for wave-particle physicists who support 'convergence' between physics and spirituality. But the religionist, dogmatic classical physicists stuck in four-dimensional 'force reality' may be the victims of a 'flat earth' consciousness. Material science, including the Neo-Darwinists may go the way of the Roman Church declaring Copernicus and Galileo heretics. Decades of reducing reality to the one-way quantum habit of identifying smaller and smaller particles with the CERN accelerator is beginning to look like an obsolete endeavor.

Now the rubber may be converging with the road. Just suppose that Paramahansa Yogananda, plus centuries of Vedic 'Yogis', steeped in Vedanta and Vedic scripture like the Gita or Upanishads for instance, exhibiting the profound powers that Paramahansa Yogananda explicitly explains in *The Autobiography of a Yogi*. Centuries of Christian 'mystic saints' also exhibited profound 'extra normal' powers such as levitation and 'resurrection' of the body, not to leave out Christ's resurrection, fully explained by Yogananda in *The Second Coming of Christ*. They are all scientifically understood and validated by 'the universal mind' of God.

THE YOGI'S PATH: CONSCIOUSNESS AS THE PRIMARY REALITY

Paramahansa Yogananda's fundamental postulate is: "we are not these bodies, or these minds. We are part of God." "Time and space are linked in God." Not the God of innumerable religious dogmas, beliefs, false starts, money-peddling prosperity religionists selling Jesus, nor Roman Church, papal pretenders in their strange garb. Rather, we are part of the fifth and universal force: "God."

Suppose there is a universal mind that we, as little humans, do not exclusively own or inhabit. Perhaps we are part of a vast, infinite consciousness field. One that, to our way of thinking, extends beyond time and space, through wave resonance in the mind, brain and external field that we can also connect with instantaneously across these boundaries based on the principles of quantum entanglement.

Suppose the yogis and mystics have been getting there for millennia through meditation, and prayer, where they experienced higher levels of consciousness connecting them to the force... God.

Suppose material science focused on consciousness as the primary area of exploration, by means used by the Yogis and mystics down through the millennia, distinct from splitting and accelerating particles in the limited confines of quantum mechanics? What if, instead of the material science perspective we've long followed, matter actually derives from consciousness rather than the other way around? Paramahansa Yogananda 1893–1952 had been preaching convergence for years, lived in God consciousness his entire life.

Meijer is a bit of a johnny-come-lately but his work is instructive. He says that the fourth dimensional field of mind is a torus shape. It is a non-local reality distributed throughout the universe. All fields are interconnected in wave resonance, entanglement and tunneling.

Dear Friends, if you've read this far, we probably share some common ground, a foundation for friendship and shared understanding. If all this talk of Quantum Entanglement has left you feeling a bit disoriented, don't worry; the complexities only deepen as we explore the more challenging aspects of human, so called "mystical" experience. (Just kidding!)

When we observe our lives, most of us will at some point marvel at how the 'dots have connected' on our life path. Is this a random occurrence? Our lives, each one with the other are intertwined in inexplicable ways whether we are acquainted with each other or not. That is why, even though we may not know a single person on a plane that crashed on the other side of the world, we feel instant angst when we hear of it. Most of us spontaneously send up a silent prayer for all those lost to us and the grieving families and friends left behind. Why? Because we are connected, and the silent force field that connects us is often referred to as consciousness for lack of a better term.

THE UNIFIED FIELD: EINSTEIN, RUMI, AND THE GREAT SPIRIT

Here's what Einstein says:

> "A human being is a part of the whole called by us 'the universe', a part limited in time and space. He experiences himself, his thoughts and feelings, as something separate from the rest, a kind of optical illusion of 'consciousness'."

Grasping the reality that this implies will enrich our lives on all levels. Einstein goes on further to elaborate:

> "This delusion is a kind of prison for us, restricting us to our personal desires and affection for a few persons nearest to us. Our task must be to free ourselves from this prison by widening the circle of understanding and compassion to embrace all living creatures and the whole of nature in its beauty."

How many of us have known this or felt it intangibly and how many have risen to the challenge and deeply changed our lives? The revered Sufi philosopher-poet, Rumi, speaks of this underlying reality of consciousness when he says:

> "Out beyond all ideas of right-doing and wrong-doing, there is a field. I'll meet you there." **Mevlana Jalal-ud-din Rumi**

When we close our eyes in prayer, meditation, or even in a moment of deep reflection, we are able to experience this field of consciousness that permeates not just our lives and all others, but all of nature, and all of creation.

The Native Americans have a name for it, the "Great Spirit":

"At the center of the universe dwells the Great Spirit and that center is really everywhere,

it is within each of us." Black Elk

The connectedness of all of our lives with the rest of creation comes from the interplay or quantum entanglement of this underlying area of life-consciousness. The Rig Veda, which forms an important part of the Vedic texts which are one of the oldest scriptures known, says the following:

"Truth is one: sages call it by various names. It is the one sun that reflects in all the ponds; It is the one water which slakes the thirst of all; It is the one air which sustains all life; It is the one fire which shines in all houses. Colors of the cows may be different, but milk is white; Flowers and bees may be different, but honey is the same; Systems of faiths may be different, but God is one. As the rain dropping from the sky wends its way towards the ocean, So, the prostrations offered in all faiths reach the One God, who is supreme." ~ Rig Veda

When we know consciousness in its pure state, it is akin to knowing God, because it is from this fundamental state that all of life emanates. Physics refers to this as the Unified Field from where all the forces of nature arise and are found in their unified state. More recently, one of the most elite, hard-core physicists in the world, Federico Faggin, inventor of the microprocessor, experienced a profound mystical experience of 'love' and afterwards weighed in on the physics of quantum entanglement as the fundamental model of reality in the article "Consciousness as The Ground of Being," published by Beshara Magazine:

"There are of course many models that try to explain reality. Many of them are philosophical or metaphysical, but they are not generally connected with physics. But I'm a physicist, and so whatever model I come up with, I think it must also accommodate what we know about physics. So that is the main difference."

THE CONSCIOUS UNIVERSE: FEDERICO FAGGIN, AND THE NATURE OF REALITY

Federico Faggin explained consciousness as well as anything that I have read from the perspective of a physicist, and which conforms to my level of consciousness and thought processing on the vast field of consciousness. I partially quote Federico and partially insert my thoughts into his thoughts below. But he has more persuasive power on this subject than me. He is a physicist, I am a lawyer. So I herewith borrow his thoughts and discourse at length on the vast field of consciousness from different times and places. My integration of his thoughts and mine are too extensive, so sorry Federico, I'm extolling your thoughts while putting them in my perspective:

"In the Big Bang cosmology, the universe has emerged from what physicists call 'the quantum vacuum', which is in itself deeply mysterious. The idea is that out of this vacuum come fluctuations which are unpredictable, and one of these unpredictable events created the universe. But in my model, everything emerged from a scintillating white energy which I saw so clearly in my first experience of meditation.

"That energy has three dimensions. It has an inner reality, the consciousness that knows and experiences. It has a conscious semantic reality, the level where meaning, purpose, and intelligence reside, where information is encoded (like the instructions in DNA or the laws of physics). And it has an outer symbolic reality, the material world of atoms, molecules, and physical forms that serve as symbols or expressions of the deeper conscious intelligence.

"Think of yourself: you have an inner awareness (you know you exist), a semantic dimension (you create meaning through language and thought), and an outer body (the physical form that others see). You are not just matter you are consciousness expressing itself through matter. The same is true, I believe, for all living organisms, from humans to trees to single cells. Each is a localized expression of the universal creative energy, embodying consciousness, meaning, and form.

"What is the essence of matter? Physicists are now pretty much agreed that it is information. We have found that essentially the particles, the atoms and molecules, that we thought constituted 'stuff' don't exist as objects at all. They exist only as states of fields, the fundamental quantum fields which interact with each other and then create everything else. The main point here is that these elementary particles are not separate from the quantum fields. We think we live in a world where there are objects, separate entities, which interact with each other in space and time. That has been the traditional worldview of science. But nowadays we have to think of objects as states of fields; they interact with each other, but at the same time they are not separate from the field. In the model I am proposing these quantum fields are conscious.

"To understand the nature of reality, start with this: everything, absolutely everything, is made of a single, undivided energy. This energy is not inert or unconscious. It has both the desire and the capacity to experience and know itself. I call this unified field 'One'.

"One exists 'before' the physical universe, though 'before' is misleading, since time itself is part of what One creates. What physicists call the 'physical universe', all the matter and energy we can measure is actually just the informational aspect of reality, the outer layer. The semantic aspect, the inner experience, the consciousness, the knowing of One, is what current physics refuses to recognize.

"Out of One emerge conscious entities: you, me, every living being. These entities are not separate from One, any more than a wave is separate from the ocean. Rather, each entity is a point of view, a unique perspective that One has about itself. Think of it this way: One is looking at itself from billions of different angles simultaneously, and each angle is a conscious being.

"Now, here's where it gets interesting. These conscious entities, these perspectives of One have the same desire that One has: to know and experience. But to know each other, they need to communicate. To communicate, they need symbols, just as we use words, gestures, and images to convey meaning to one another.

"In this model, each conscious entity is a quantum field. And the symbols they use to communicate are the states of that quantum field; what physicists call physical particles. In other words, matter itself is a language, a system of symbols that conscious fields use to interact.

"This is where the model diverges radically from contemporary physics. In standard quantum theory, fields are mathematical abstractions with no inner life. They're just equations that describe particle behavior. But in this model, these fields have consciousness. They have an inner semantic experience; they understand the meaning of the symbols they're exchanging.

"When two quantum fields interact, it's not just a mechanical collision of particles, it's a conversation between conscious beings, each one interpreting and responding to the symbols the other is sending. Just as you and I use words that carry meaning, words that we consciously understand and respond to, quantum fields use particles that carry meaning, understood by the conscious intelligence within each field.

"Yes, the fact that we have interiority is primary in our model. Consciousness and free will are foundational and exist from the beginning rather than emerging with the physical brain. In this model, it is the brain that emerges from the conscious fields as an informational-only structure. The meaning of the information exists in the conscious field which is what we really are. Matter is nothing more than the information that conscious entities use to communicate with each other to know themselves.

"So, I see this universe as playing the role of a kind of virtual reality, allowing us to know ourselves better when our consciousness is embodied into living organisms. The process is driven by the fact that this reality beyond space and time wants to know itself. And we have constructed this universe to better know ourselves by using a body that amplifies those traits that we wish to explore and comprehend.

"Think about the love that we may feel for a person. Can we ever express that love all the way? No, we cannot. We may try to do it in poetry, in music, or in painting. Whatever way we try, we will always come up short. No symbolic expression will ever capture the totality of what we are feeling. Our feelings give us the sense of who we are. They tell us what we still have to know about ourselves, which is the "unexpressed meaning we feel within; the urge that pushes us to know ourselves ever more. That urge manifests as curiosity, as courage, and as adventurousness, driving us toward the unknown.

"True. But it is important to also understand that we have to go beyond the quantum world described by physics if we are to understand where meaning comes from. Information in itself, whether we are talking about bits or qubits, has no meaning in physics; we give it meaning. A computer can learn to manipulate symbols, but it can never understand what their meaning is. So where is the meaning coming from?

"Similarly, we think of ourselves as conscious bodies. But we are only conscious because our bodies are connected with conscious entities that exist in a vaster reality of which space–time reality is just a projection. So what I am, the real 'me', lives in this vaster reality and it controls my body top-down. Our body is not conscious; it is made of electrons, protons, and so on, and it exists as information, as quantum-classical information. The simplest structure in the physical world that can host consciousness is a cell. Nothing less than a living cell can have its own consciousness in the sense that the physical structure can be controlled by a conscious entity.

"Yes, absolutely. We think that when the body dies, it is the end of our consciousness because we have been told that consciousness is produced by the brain. But as I said earlier, it is the other way around. It is the brain that is produced by consciousness. So, consciousness uses the body as a tool to know itself.

"Clearly our body is temporary, but we are not temporary because we exist outside space–time and we want to know ourselves. And we will continue to seek to know ourselves ever more, for, as I said earlier, the process will never end. Our identity may transform itself, but we never die. We are quantum entities, and a consequence of this model is the idea that we exist in what we might call 'eternity'."

THE FAGGIN POSTULATES ALIGN WITH YOGANANDA AND CHRIST

Federico Faggin's preceding summary encapsulates the Sermon on the Mount and clarifies the concept of the "Kingdom of God within us;" and asserts that space and time do not really exist in a state or field of pure love. His explanation of reality offers a foundation for understanding my ESP/QE experience in the Sandra and Lester case. The energies in that case transcended time and space, just like two remote particles instantly merging. Yogananda explains the Kingdom of God within as being a state in which we experience and maintain Christ consciousness, a state of pure awareness beyond time and space.

Meijer explains this phenomenon further. He postulates that quantum entanglement explains black holes, as 'event horizons'. Meijer postulates that consciousness has boundary characteristics akin to light or matter approaching a black hole. He says they don't disappear as thought, but "their information is projected on its boundary." That boundary is what separates the black hole from everything else.

The recent discovery by the Webb telescope that a huge "black hole exists at the outermost fringes of the universe proves that the 'Big Bang theory" is wrong.

Meijer compares black holes and their "event horizons" to consciousness resonating throughout the universe. Just as light moves through matter in the physical universe, he suggests that consciousness, as non-matter, resonates within an infinitely expanding and mysterious cosmos.

In sum, advanced yogis like Paramahansa Yogananda and Christ have a "quantum tuner" within themselves, beyond brain and even mind that resonates with a field called God, thereby allowing themselves to live in and with God. Heady stuff, don't you agree?

Faggin agrees with Paramahansa Yogananda's basic premise for all of life, that we are in a state of oneness with God, we just don't know it. Now that's entanglement! In *Autobiography of a Yogi*, he explains that certain physical qualities in human anatomy confirm what he describes as the link between humanity and God ...which sounds a lot like...quantum entanglement. He also shows us the path to get there. He wrote a chant "I am the bubble, make me the sea." That is quantum entanglement. The sea is God, we are a bubble, which is part of the sea, and also part of God. We just need to drop our mind set of existing separately from everything around us, including the perception of God as outside of us.

To us wee humans, the relationship between the mind and the brain is a mystery that is essential to our existence as an intelligent species of animal life. What is intelligence? Why is ours seemingly superior to other animal species. Is it because of our ability to adapt?

Traditional neurosurgeons believed against all contrary evidence that brain death terminated mind function. They had zero evidence to support this hypothesis except their own arrogance. "Not so!" say the NDE'ers, like Dr. Alexander and many of the yogis and mystics down through the millennia. The old school view that the mind is strictly a function of the brain; and that consciousness to whatever degree they accept it as a scientific reality, is solely the result of interactive neurons in the physical brain, is akin to calling the world flat. That is all changing, and rapidly.

Neuroquantology published a September 2017 review on current theories of consciousness based on the convergence of neuro and quantum sciences. The convergence of spirit and matter, religion and science, is becoming the holy grail of evolutionary biology, cosmology, medicine, physics and almost all 'technologies'. It's worth checking out.

One of my first questions after the Sandra and Lester trial when my investigation into ESP and so called "psychic phenomena" began in earnest, involved research on whether a fighter pilot's brain could automatically transmit thoughts to aircraft controls. This fascinated me personally, having narrowly missed flying F4 Phantoms in Vietnam due to my "Student 2S" status, though I later found joy piloting my own planes. The military has pursued this technology for decades, seeking the holy grail of aviation: thought becoming action for instantaneous reaction to threat without the delay of physical movement.

What began as curiosity about a military application opened a doorway to perhaps the most profound question humans can ask: Where does consciousness truly reside? Is it merely a product of our physical brain, a sophisticated but ultimately mechanical process, or does it extend beyond our neural circuitry into something more fundamental to the fabric of the universe itself? Plug in the rapidly expanding 'near death experience' research and reporting by doctors like Alexander and Neal, who have actually experienced it, and a clinical practitioner like Dr. Pim van Lommel, who regularly observes and reports it, and both quantum entanglement and the near-death experience rise closer to 'scientific' standards on understanding consciousness.

Van Lommel directly challenges the prevailing materialist paradigm:

"Most of the people who specialize in consciousness research, including neuroscientists, psychologists, psychiatrists, and philosophers, are still of the opinion that there is a materialist and reductionist explanation for consciousness. The well-known philosopher Daniel Dennett believes, and many with him, that consciousness is nothing other than matter and that our subjective experience of our consciousness as something purely personal and different from somebody else's consciousness is merely an illusion.11 According to these scientists, consciousness arises entirely from the matter that constitutes our brain. If this were true, then everything we experience in our consciousness would be nothing other than the expression of a machine controlled by classical physics and chemistry, and our behavior would be the inexorable outcome of nerve-cell activity in our brain. Of course, the notion that all subjective thoughts and feelings are produced by nothing other than the brain's activity also means that free will is an illusion. This viewpoint has enormous implications for concepts such as moral responsibility and personal freedom."

Of interest, over thirty years ago, I discussed this "field of consciousness hypothesis" in the context of experiments that several of my clients were conducting with a Belgian neuroendocrinologist, whose "guinea pigs" included a vast array of individuals ranging from advanced Yogis demonstrating extra normal yogic powers, which Paramahansa Yogananda explains in depth in the AY, which was written almost a century ago, to ordinary men and women with a wide range of IQ levels, personality types, and even down to individuals with severe intelligence deficits. The bottom line: advanced Yogis tapped into the 'field' at will. Others, not so much. That is exactly what the AY describes in 400 pages over 60 years ago!

According to Dr. Meijer, this field of consciousness outside of the brain, detects and receives information from multiple sources. On the quantum level, the human brain can entangle itself with the Earth's magnetic field and dark energy, as well as sources that are not physical. So, watch out. My later L. Ron Hubbard Scientology cases in *Litigator 2* dive into the details of Hubbard's satanic rituals to obtain money and power. And my resistance to this evil when one of his victims contacted me.

Like Meijer, other neuroscientists like Penrose and Hameroff believe "there is a connection between the brain's biomolecular processes and the basic structure of the universe." They have also called for a revolution in science. The flat earth view of consciousness is scientifically obsolete. Hameroff said in an interview: "Most scientists can't explain consciousness in the brain, so they can't say that consciousness out of the brain is impossible."

My perspective is that more and more neuroscientists are following this trend. I suggest shortcutting to Paramahansa Yogananda. You'll save decades. If you have a Sandra and Lester case experience like mine, you'll then understand the how it's happening, and why.

In "Lesson 9" published by Self-Realization Fellowship, Paramahansa Yogananda provides in the language of God and spirit, what the quantum entanglers describe in their language as a force field outside of the brain which controls the entire universe. Einstein resorted to the word "spooky" to describe this event of quantum entanglement, because he couldn't reduce that level of reality to any scientific theory, measurement, or atomic reductionism. The NDE'ers, intelligent designers and more advanced neuroscientists call this reality consciousness.

Here's how Paramahansa Yogananda describes this "non-local," "spooky," reality:

> "When you know all matter (including your physical body) to be made of immortal life energy; and when you know that energy is, in essence, vibrations of causal cosmic consciousness emanating from spirit and soul, you are then able to dwell in this world as intended by our creator."

So I ask you, dear reader: Are we truly the doers? When we align with higher consciousness, whether through meditation, prayer, or simply being fully present in service to truth and justice, are we acting alone, or are we channels for something greater?

My career of litigation suggests the latter. In my most effective moments as a litigator, when clarity and insight seemed to flow through me rather than from me, I was least identified with being the doer. In those moments of quantum entanglement with divine consciousness, love and compassion emerged as the dominant forces, not as abstract concepts but as tangible energies shaping outcomes in the courtroom and beyond.

THE LITIGATOR'S VERDICT: WE ARE NOT THE DOER

If Christ's Sermon on the Mount, the 'Beatitudes' provide the ultimate guidelines for life on this planet, and we align ourselves with them, we become conduits rather than originators. We occasionally channel God, love, and compassion. Hence, He or She is the doer when we quantum entangle ourselves with divine consciousness.

This is practical wisdom, not philosophical speculation and with profound implications for how we live and work. By recognizing that we are not separate from, but entangled with the field of consciousness that permeates all existence, we open ourselves to guidance, insight, and power beyond our individual limitations...exactly what I've witnessed throughout my career.

The verdict is clear: we are both less and more than we imagine; less as isolated individuals, yet infinitely more as expressions of universal consciousness. In that paradox lies our greatest potential and deepest truth. When we surrender the illusion of being the sole doer, we paradoxically gain access to a power and wisdom far greater than anything our individual ego's could generate.

This is the ultimate lesson of quantum entanglement for the litigator, the spiritual seeker, and indeed for all of us: we are never truly alone, never truly separate, and never truly limited to our individual capacities. We are nodes in a vast network of consciousness, capable of receiving and transmitting wisdom that transcends our personal boundaries, as long as we have the humility and awareness to recognize it.

Epilogue

Fifty years ago, I stood in a courtroom and watched a judge change his mind in an instant, saving two children from a fire that hadn't yet happened. I smelled my hand burning at 3 AM the next morning when three teenagers died in flames miles away. These events defied every framework I'd been trained to trust legal logic, scientific materialism, the boundaries of cause and effect.

This chapter has been my attempt to reason with science and logic in order to find a language for the inexplicable. Quantum entanglement. The unified field. God's force field. The "love" experience of Faggin. Yogananda's cosmic consciousness. Different words, perhaps, for the same truth: we are not separate. We are not alone. We are nodes in a vast network of consciousness that transcends time, space, and the illusion of individual existence.

You don't have to accept my framework. You don't have to believe in quantum entanglement or Yogananda's teachings or the existence of God. But if you've ever had a moment, in a courtroom, on a meditation cushion, or in the middle of an ordinary day when you felt connected to something greater than yourself, when insight arrived from nowhere, when grace intervened in ways you couldn't explain...then you already know what this chapter is about.

The field is real. It's been there all along. And it's waiting for us to recognize it.

Close your eyes. Listen. And as Rumi promised: "I'll meet you there."

CHAPTER 10

Transcendental Meditation and the Art of Allowance

"The Science of Being is a deep and practical philosophy of life. It is a systematic investigation into the true nature of ultimate reality. Although, like any other science, it is theoretical in its nature, its applied aspects, however, reach much further horizons of the supreme reality of life than those of abstract metaphysical speculations." **Maharishi Mahesh Yogi**, *Science of Being and Art of Living* at p. 20.

"You have a right to perform your prescribed duties, but you are not entitled to the fruits of your actions..." **Bhagavad Gita** 2:47

THE LITIGATOR'S PARADOX: QUANTUM CONSCIOUSNESS IN THE COURTROOM

"The paradox is the source of the thinker's passion..." Kierkegaard.

In the quantum field of consciousness that I explored in the previous chapter, there exists a profound paradox: the more deeply we understand the non-local nature of awareness, the more challenging it can be to access this understanding amidst the intense demands of daily life. Theory and practice, it seems, are themselves entangled in ways that both illuminate and obscure each other, like particles whose properties are defined by their relationship rather than their isolation.

Between 1974 and 1979, after the cases previously described and countless others of a more mundane nature, I found myself navigating this paradox with increasing frequency. Having glimpsed the expansive field of consciousness that transcends the individual brain, and experienced moments when I was clearly not the 'doer' but rather a channel for something greater, I now faced the practical challenge of maintaining this awareness while immersed in the trenches of litigation. When I relaxed and attempted to turn off concentrated trial preparation, my mind generally became a chatterbox of random thought streams about what I could have done better in any individual case.

The courtroom, with its demands for total presence and strategic thinking, became both my laboratory and my obstacle.

I moved from one Pit to another, each case offering its own lessons in the courtroom but presenting a consistent challenge to my meditation practice. These years became a testing ground for the very principles of quantum entanglement and non-local consciousness that had so captivated my understanding. Could these profound truths withstand the vicissitudes of a litigator's life, or would they dissolve under the pressure of depositions, motions, and trial preparations? The existential question.

What I discovered was that my mind, that sophisticated receiver of consciousness described by both quantum physicists and spiritual masters, became overwhelmed with signals during intense litigation. Thus, I sought a "Science of Being" to observe and discipline my random thought streams. Maharishi's book *Science of Being and Art of Living* resonated in my consciousness. Gradually, I observed that my thought streams arose both within my mind in some unknown or poorly understood pattern, combined with sensory data creating thoughts and feelings derived from, or caused by, my five senses? How to turn the resulting stream on and off?

The brain that could occasionally tune into the higher frequencies of universal awareness now found itself saturated with lower-frequency signals: case details, legal precedents, witness statements, and strategic calculations. I found that most trials hindered my meditations not because the principles were flawed, but because my receiver was overloaded, like a radio trying to capture a distant symphony while surrounded by the static of a thousand closer stations.

The experience was disorienting. In the courtroom, I could occasionally access that flow state where insights arrived unbidden, where I seemed to know exactly what question to ask without conscious calculation. Yet in meditation, where such transcendence should be more accessible, I found myself mired in the very thoughts I was trying to transcend. The irony wasn't lost on me: sometimes I was less 'doer' when most actively doing, and most trapped in 'doing' when attempting to simply be.

What I was experiencing, though I didn't fully recognize it then, was the quantum nature of thought itself. Just as particles become entangled across space and time, my thoughts about cases became entangled with deeper patterns of consciousness, creating what appeared to be random chatter but actually reflected the interconnected nature of mind and matter that quantum physics describes. My thoughts weren't simply mine, they were nodes in a vast network of consciousness, influenced by forces beyond my individual mind.

My mind became so highly concentrated on the details of law and fact that there was less allowance for transcendence in meditation. The very quality that made me effective as a litigator, intense focus and analytical precision, created resistance to the letting go required for deeper meditation. Here was the doer-observer paradox in its most practical form. How could I be simultaneously fully engaged in the battle while remaining detached from its outcome? How could I fight with total commitment while knowing, at a deeper level, that I was not the doer?

Thus, I sought a more disciplined approach to navigating this quantum field of thought. Maharishi's book *Science of Being and Art of Living* resonated in my consciousness not just as spiritual guidance but as a practical methodology for applying the theoretical understanding I was developing. If consciousness truly was a field that extended beyond the brain, then there must be reliable techniques for accessing it even amid the storm of litigation. There had to be a way to be both fully present in the courtroom battle and simultaneously connected to the transcendent field of awareness.

Gradually, I observed that my thought streams arose both within my mind in some unknown or poorly understood pattern, combined with sensory data creating thoughts and feelings derived from, or caused by, my five senses. The question became not just philosophical but practical... how to tune this receiver? How to turn the resulting stream on and off at will? How to be in the world but not entirely of it?

I tried to make my TM meditations more disciplined by at least sitting down for the mandatory twenty minutes twice a day to allow the mantra to come into my mind. That is the instruction, 'allow'. Don't force, don't concentrate, in contrast to other meditation techniques... allow the mind to dive deeper into silence where the mantra takes over as a matter of natural law. That is the science of Transcendental Meditation.

This principle of allowing rather than forcing, paralleled what quantum physicists were discovering about observation itself, that the very act of concentrated observation affects the outcome of experiments. Perhaps meditation worked on a similar principle: the harder one tried to force transcendence, the more elusive it became. The key was learning to be simultaneously active and passive, engaged and detached... a quantum state of consciousness that transcended simple dualities.

The challenge I faced was not unique to me but reflects a fundamental question for anyone seeking to integrate spiritual awareness with worldly engagement: How do we maintain connection to the infinite while immersed in the finite? How do we access the field of pure consciousness while navigating the dense forest of thoughts, emotions, and sensory experiences that constitute daily life?

What would unfold over the coming years was not just a series of cases but an evolving understanding of how to navigate the quantum field of consciousness while fully engaged in the demanding world of litigation. The journey would challenge everything I thought I knew about both meditation and the practice of law, ultimately revealing that the two were not separate paths but different expressions of the same fundamental reality, a reality in which the question 'Are we the doers?' would continue to unfold in unexpected ways.

WHAT IS TM? THE SCIENCE OF CREATIVE INTELLIGENCE

According to Maharishi, creative intelligence is the essential fabric of the mind and 'Being'. It is the basis of nature and natural law. Creative intelligence is innate to every living thing. I gradually discovered that Maharishi was using the term "the Science of Creative Intelligence" for the purpose of making mantra meditation into a science. His intention was to shift the intellect from thinking in the language of religion and God, to experiencing the certitude that the mind and soul experiences when the mind naturally transcends. Thus, it is a science.

Maharishi's foundational premise is that the mind's natural desire, instinct and composition, is in reality, controlled by the soul. The soul's nature is to dive into silence where God is found, which is in fact, the single most fundamental scientific reality. When the soul experiences the silence of God, it experiences itself, transcends the mind, and experiences higher levels of consciousness: Christ Consciousness, God Consciousness, Unity Consciousness... The Bliss of God.

I have realized those levels of consciousness described in subsequent chapters. Kriya yoga taught me to utilize TM to integrate gradients of such consciousness into my earthbound activity.

Maharishi may be correct on this fundamental natural law. What the world did not readily know, and likely would not understand, is that the mantras that the TM teachers were distributing are in fact what are called beej or seed mantras. These are very small, simple sounds without a meaning attached to them. They come from ancient Vedic texts and are considered to be so potent, that over time they began to be associated with the names of the Gods of the Hindu tradition, since the Vedic texts form the bedrock of that tradition. It is precisely the sound element that makes them effective in the TM practice, because the sound value allows the mind free rein to settle down to its own silent state. Is that beginning to sound like Dirk Meijer's "musical master code" studies, and the experience of Dr. Alexander when he went to heaven? More to the point, is this sound, precisely what Paramahansa Yogananda describes in the AY in connection with the OM vibration, and the mathematical nature of musical sound one and the same?

Had a meaning been attached to these sounds, regardless of the ability of varying intellects to understand its meaning, by its very nature, the mind would be caught up in the contemplation of it, not allowing it to settle down, but rather just stay lost on the surface level of thinking.

The effectiveness of the TM technique comes from its ability to allow the mind, through the use of the mantra to experience quieter states of thought, ultimately leading to its quietest state and thereby allow the nervous system of a human being to experience very deep levels of rest while remaining in a state of heightened awareness, which is characteristic of the state of transcendence. Numerous studies conducted worldwide have supported this result, and I have experienced it many times.

TM AND THE LAW: RELIGION OR SCIENCE?

Like me, each individual receives at initiation his or her own mantra. Some media have distorted or misrepresented these mantras. This purported misrepresentation of the beej mantras became a legal issue for the TM organization's plan to put TM meditation into the New Jersey public schools. Its opponents claimed that the mantras were the names of Hindu Gods, thus making TM into a religion in violation of the "Establishment Clause" of the First Amendment. That clause in our Constitution's Bill of Rights prohibits state sponsored religion.

In truth and in law, the above arguments were based entirely in ignorance. But our jurisprudence is decades, possibly centuries, away from understanding the true nature of sound, and its role in the human physiology, mind, nervous system, and even an understanding of what soul is, in a quantum entangled universe created by God. After all, we are just out of the very dark ages in the cycle of yugas (an age of time as mentioned in the ancient Vedic literature) in which, in the western world, the most advanced human being was able to be crucified for no valid legal reason.

I played a legal role for the TM organization, advising that it would likely lose the legal case. I wrote a memo explaining that our legal system was still in the dark ages, and that almost any court in America would be unable to accept or even possibly discern the true scientific nature of TM and its 'meaningless sound mantra'. I advised that TM had become embroiled in New Jersey jurisprudence; significant because it is not that far in distance or space from the New England witch burnings in the 1600's. Based on the very crude legal case precedents interpreting the First Amendment "Establishment Clause," it was highly unlikely that TM would withstand a constitutional challenge. It didn't. It lost on summary judgment. *Malnak v. Yogi*, 592 F.2d 197.

Several years later, I was consulted again both by the TM folk and by Dr. Deepak Chopra to defend them against very contrived fraud claims, wherein a group of 'Ex TMers' filed a lawsuit in the Washington DC federal court, based on the allegations that TM held itself out as a science when it was a religion. Ipso facto; fraud. We used the New Jersey case precedent in our defense arguing that if TM was a religion as held in the *Malnak v. Yogi* case, then under The Free Exercise Clause of the First Amendment, the federal court was barred from even inquiring into the nature of its religious practices. We used the TM EX claimants' positions to dismiss their own case. We won.

Both the TM people and Dr. Chopra were of course, very grateful, and relieved to not have to defend that litigation.

My years of meditation practice has shown me that natural law, God, is experienced in very intimate, and very sacred silence. Sounds like religion, yes? Meditation may expose you to the truth of both religion and science. As a scientist of the stature of Isaac Newton realized experiencing such silence is a profound truth in itself, regardless of how human minds categorize it. That, dear reader is a fundamental reality, once experienced. The TM mantra indeed takes you to that experience. That is quantum entanglement with the soul's connection to God on the deepest level. The obstacle is the active mind and its endless streams of thought on what might be called lower frequencies. In silence, there are no frequencies. At least a transcendent mind in bliss doesn't seem to experience them.

THE PRACTICE: ALLOWANCE, CONCENTRATION, AND THE PATH TO SILENCE

Since the TM technique is based on the fundamental principle of allowing the mind to drop into silence by means of the mantra, the paradox becomes one of disassociating intentionality from allowance. According to Maharishi, any effort to use the mind to concentrate on the mantra becomes self-defeating and against natural law. By natural law he meant God. He advocated the path to God through the natural surrender of the mind to the mantra.

But one can ask: how can that be a science? The answer is that the essence of science is to continually explore, investigate, experiment and analyze the material world until it reaches a repeatable, measurable conclusion. For humans, such scientific endeavors into materiality can only end in God. They are all founded in the consciousness of humans to even pursue or conduct such experiments and analysis.

Maharishi sought to avoid using the mind to concentrate on the mantra while immersed in its normal swirl of thoughts. On at least one level of consciousness, Maharishi is logically correct. The silence of God once experienced is the end result of all human quests. You will know this truth in the experience itself.

In contrast, when concentrated meditation becomes lost, or experienced in endless thought streams, the mind tends to turn to religious ritual and dogma. If you analyze how established religions really use ritual and dogma to define themselves (and, among other things, obtain tax exemption as in the case of The Church Of Scientology), the logical conclusion seems to be that ritual and dogma in themselves to seek and find God, both oppose science and contradict true religion. (*Litigator 2.*)

The word religion derives from the Latin, "to bind back." That has the same meaning as Yoga, which is also to bind back, or merge the soul with God. Such may be the infinite and eternal result for humans in the material world. Hence convergence of religion and science.

KARMA, THE NERVOUS SYSTEM, AND THE ADVERSARIAL MIND

Maharishi recognized that a meditator using concentration resulted in the practitioner getting stuck in the mind of random thoughts, and that this was generally caused by their karmic patterns. The reality in the material world is on the level of karma, duality, cause and effect, in which the mind becomes attached to sensory data coming in through the five senses. That is also a reality which seems to swamp higher levels of consciousness. So, the Bhagavad Gita battleground becomes the state of allowing the mind to transcend thought and experience silence. That is quite a battle, and requires a very rested nervous system. Karma is a collection of past experiences, memories, good and bad actions, stuck in man's being.

The Buddha seems to agree with Maharishi. He said that: "Meditation is not to control your thoughts, but to prevent your thoughts from controlling you."

How does one do that? The Buddha advocated mindfulness. Buddhist monks like Thich Nhat Hanh, the author of many books on the practice of mindfulness in its most elemental form, teaches simple awareness of breath. Observe the breath naturally. Allow it to just flow in and out. As it does, allow the mind to observe it. Regular practice of this simple exercise gradually takes the mind into silence.

In the mad mad world of litigation, the human nervous system becomes a major factor in the ability to meditate. How do you settle both the mind and the nervous system while embroiled in intellectual, emotional and mind conflict in an intrinsically adversarial system on which our judicial system is founded? One party presents his or her facts and arguments within the law as the lawyer, as litigator understands it, acting as an advocate for his client. The other party presents theirs. Generally, they are pretty much at polar opposites. The judge applies the law. The jury decides what is 'truth' in order to arrive at a just 'verdict'.

Beginning in high school, I was fascinated by adversarial justice, and also both world war I and II. The world seemed to be a place of good guys and bad guys, truth and falsehood. Where did this proclivity come from? Past life? Cellular DNA? Quantum Entanglement?

As a TMer, I found that I had to go on residence courses after a trial to bring myself back down from a hyper nervous system, and an overly active and reactive mind, in order to allow my mind to sufficiently experience the mantra to enable transcendence. Once the mantra dominated my mind, obscuring streams of thought, I generally sunk into silence, often experienced transcendence, and occasionally experienced profound realizations.

As I learned with more and longer meditations, calming the nervous system is vital to transcendence. TM intrinsically enables that calming process. But for me, in the intellectually and physically demanding world of intensely combative litigation, as recounted in the Sandra and Lester case, more techniques were needed. This must have been the same for mostly everybody practicing TM based on my observations of people on Maharishi's Residence Courses.

FLYING AND MEDITATION: THE "ILS" ANALOGY

Maharishi structured what TM called 'Rounding', a meditation practice combining TM, yoga postures, and rest. This practice was typically structured in 3 – 7 day Residence Courses. These were basically retreats participated in by anywhere from twenty to 100 or more individuals in a group setting. Rounding consisted of a cycle of 20 minutes of TM, 20 minutes of yoga postures called 'asanas', and 20 minutes of rest practiced individually in private. Then the group would meet for instruction or training, mostly founded in the "Science of Creative Intelligence" in which the physiology of meditation to calm the nervous system would be explained, along with Question and Answer sessions and shared experiences.

These courses evolved into much longer courses of anywhere from a month to a year in locations such as Seelisberg, Switzerland, and thereafter into the TM Sidhi' Program; and thereafter into Ayurveda 'panchakarma' treatments based on millennia old Vedic medical prescriptions. I also experienced many of these treatments, generally for week-long clinical sessions. The longest residence course I attended was 7 days in which I had my 'no death' experience. I also participated in the two week TM Siddhis' Program in July, 1987, and thereafter numerous 'flying' or Sidhi sessions at the Dome in Fairfield, Iowa. Sidhi's are powers one can gain, one of them is the ability to levitate somewhat...hence 'flying'.

One of my celebrity clients was Mike Love, lead singer of the Beach Boys. Mike is a TM'er who did the six-month course in Switzerland in 1971, after being personally trained as a teacher by Maharishi in 1968, along with his fellow Beach Boys and the Beatles. In the 1960s, Mike had been cheated out of his co-authorship to at least 35 of the Beach Boys' biggest hits with Brian Wilson. Between 1992 and 1995, we engaged in a 4-year litigation battle to recover his musical legacy. We won in an unprecedented 25-page jury verdict; and then traveled to India where Mike gave 'propitiations to the Gods' in two weeks of purification rituals.

In light of the Beach Boys' wild history, purification in every form of Hindu rituals, TM programs, Rounding and Residence Courses, were imperative to be able to calm their nervous systems. The Beach Boys have a particularly toxic history, which only Mike Love transcended out of with his disciplined TM practices. Instead of drugs, the bane of so many rockers, Mike turned to TM.

For me, between 1974 and 1986, the residence courses, and study of meditation increased as my litigation schedule intensified. Between 1979 and 1987, I was immersed in the 8-year "Scientology wars." (*Litigator 2*.)

As of 1979, I had read all of Maharishi's books: *Science of Being and Art of Living*; *The Bhagavad Gita. A new Translation and Commentary*; *Love and God*; and more books by other authors about TM and meditation. In 1974, I had read the *Autobiography Of A Yogi*, but in retrospect, was not ready to embrace the incredible depth of Paramahansa Yogananda's life and teachings.

Maharishi's commentary on the Gita and 'Love and God' I found compelling. So, is this what TM is really about? Loving God? The answer is a resounding yes! Maharishi just adjusted this theme as he left the Himalayas and started "The Spiritual Regeneration Movement" in India. He tried to amalgamate what became TM into a science...language alters the mind.

Is the science approach that TM sells in "The Science of Creative Intelligence," ("SCI"), and the 5-day course leading up to initiation into TM, just a bait to fool egotists; or is it to attract true seekers? In retrospect, back in 1974, I was a mix. I later wondered whether the science approach in Science of Creative Intelligence by Maharishi was a sort of bait and switch to bring those enamored of science and opposed to religion, like me, stuck in their minds, back to God. Moi? No, I was way too smart to be fooled by an Indian monk selling transcendence as a science. Stay tuned. After practicing litigation and the science of meditation, I don't believe, in truth, that there is any difference. It's all God.

The New Jersey school case, and my minor role was in the past. But my actual litigation involvement in the Washington DC federal fraud case that "TM Ex," a group of allegedly fooled ex devotees of TM, brought against Maharishi and TM, was instructive to me. Using the legal weapon the opponents of TM in New Jersey had used, The First Amendment, I used it against the frivolous case other opponents of TM filed in Washington.

I began to study Gandhi, and his principles of non-violence, Satyagraha, and Ahimsa. I read Gandhi's Gita, autobiography and just about every biography on him. I particularly enjoyed *God Makes the Rivers to Flow* by Eknath Easwaran. Check it out.

Meditation also began to extricate me from both Catholic guilt, mostly about sex and pride, and other Catholic dogmas, rituals and doctrines that I could not justify in my evolving worldly experience. These included the Virgin Birth of Christ, the Resurrection of Christ, the divinity of Christ as the Son of God, the infallibility of the Popes, and the absolute correctness of all Catholic thinking and writing. The latter having to be approved by the doctrines of 'Imprimatur' (declaration of approval) and 'Nihil Obstat' (literally 'nothing hinders'); once approved by 'Nihil Obstat', there was 'nothing in the way' of the document being disseminated.

Please don't misunderstand me. I accept the divinity of Christ, his resurrection, and the son of God words to describe his sojourn on planet earth. I just became less of a believer, and more of an intuitive knower. I became a Gnostic, like the early Christians who were banned, persecuted and burned as heretics as of at least the Council of Nicaea in 325 AD.

What happened is that as I got deeper into the levels of my mind in the context of transcending, transcendence became an experience more real than my thoughts. I, the observer in me, call it soul, perceived my thoughts in a more transitory or unreal state. My thoughts did not grip me. This helped me enormously dealing with my testosterone driven sex drive. I saw, my observer saw, where my mind was stuck or fixated. Transcendence enabled me to naturally, without emotional conflict, or blockage, shed dogma and or doctrine, because the latter existed on levels of mind, more involved in belief than experience.

The experience of transcendence was gradually taking over my life. Inch by inch. I began to understand who I am in the context of Christ's dictum, "The Kingdom of God is Within." That realization became real. My consciousness shifted.

That's the good news. The bad news is that TM, at least on the level I practiced it, did not make me, or most other TMers I know, really deal with our karmic issues...our sins. I tended to ignore them. My past violations of the Yamas and Niyamas, do's and dont's, became less central to my previously very Catholic outlook. It took another Master, Paramahansa Yogananda to take on that beast within me. But to be fair, TM for me was likely the bridge to deal with my karma.

There was no doubt that my practice of TM was positively affecting my life in a number of ways. It definitely alleviated the burden of stress I carried largely due to my court cases. It also allowed me to function more efficiently as the technique is the only one that enables the use and experience of the entire range of the mind - otherwise, according to prevailing expert thought, we use only about 10% of our mental potential simply because we have no way to tap into the rest of our minds. We have the ability to view things in deeper and greater detail, as research on practitioners of the TM technique demonstrates that there is greater brainwave coherence as we practice the TM technique. This makes for organized, clear thinking which allows for greater success in our actions.

The deep rest that I experienced during 20 minutes of practicing TM is almost twice as much as one might get in six to eight hours of deep sleep. It is this deep rest experienced during the practice that spontaneously neutralizes the deep-rooted stress we accumulate daily. This stress is responsible for more than 90% of today's illnesses, often considered psychosomatic. My own experiences confirmed these research findings.

I had also read the extraordinary book *Autobiography of a Yogi* by Paramahansa Yogananda. It was the second book I had found at the local library when I began exploring meditation. Like most who have read it, I was overwhelmed by its sheer magnitude and his vast achievements that I had previously considered as unattainable by me. Importantly he taught that 'anyone can be a Yogananda'. It made a lasting impression on my mind, one that would prove to be a major blessing in my life later on.

In my fifteen years of TM practice, the scientific research as promoted in support of the TM technique had my rapt attention. After every major successful sojourn in the courtroom, I would attend the next TM retreat that would be offered and it always proved to unburden me of the stress I had picked up in the 'Pit'. In 1987, I enrolled in the TM Sidhi advanced program and began to include it unfailingly in my daily routine.

Maharishi Mahesh Yogi's book, *Science of Being and Art of Living* warrants exceptional attention. It is no coincidence that the group led by Sri Sri Ravi Shankar, not to be confused with Ravi Shankar the sitar player and long term friend of George Harrison, is called 'The Art of Living'. This name was picked by Sri Sri Ravi Shankar as a direct result of his having been apprenticed to Maharishi Mahesh Yogi.

THE BHAGAVAD GITA AND THE BATTLE OF KURUKSHETRA

Maharishi's commentary on the first six chapters of the Bhagavad Gita was one I referred to constantly. The Bhagavad Gita is part of the Vedic texts of India, one of the oldest civilizations of the world. These Vedic texts are replete with wisdom that is both spiritual and practical and the Bhagavad Gita is looked at as its essence. The treatise comprises eighteen chapters in the form of a dialogue between Arjuna, considered to be the most valiant warrior of all time, and his charioteer, Sri Krishna on the battleground of Kurukshetra. Krishna is the embodiment of wisdom stemming from complete enlightenment. What makes this book alluring is that it applies to everyday situations and can provide meaningful solutions to them.

The dialogue is an exchange that discusses karma, applicable to our everyday actions that must be based on 'Dharma' or righteousness, in order to be effective on all levels. My own battle of Kurukshetra was raging in the courtroom and was slowly finding its way into my personal life as well. The area where our battles are waged is referred to in Vedic texts as 'Karma Bhumi' and mine certainly seemed to be the proverbial 'Pit'.

While the TM technique was a major positive influence in my life, I found myself looking for answers on how and why to perform my own actions (karma) so they always support righteousness or 'Dharma'. Maharishi's approach was that as we continue our practice of TM, all our actions will spontaneously be in accord with that which is right because when we meditate, we allow our minds to settle down beyond even the finest impulse of thought, i.e., we transcend or go beyond all thought. This place is the fountainhead of peace, joy and all knowledge. Also referred to in Vedic texts as Sat-chit-ananda or truth, consciousness, bliss.

It is from here that Nature functions in our lives and it is also the same field that permeates all of existence and therefore is characterized by power. As we continue to meditate, this powers our every thought and therefore our every action as we become familiar with it on a daily basis. It sounded good, made sense to me, and I experienced it in both my litigation and meditation life.

For it to be a reality, the stress from our nervous system must be cleared. The purer our nervous system, the more it will allow for perfection in our lives. During the Scientology wars, (*Litigator 2*), the intensity of that litigation was impeding this possibility. I needed to find a way around it. While I did not feel the nagging void anymore, the stress of my profession was taking its toll. My wife was in great physical pain with severe rheumatoid arthritis. The constant stress from my work, especially the intense pressure caused by the Scientology attacks and operations against me, affected my entire family. My children were growing up under this enormous strain, and my wife needed much-needed peace to recover.

Throughout my legal career, I often found myself fighting other people's battles, compelled by the fiduciary duties that come with being a lawyer. During the 'Scientology wars' as I call them, the need for spiritual support, for both myself and my family, became a pressing reality. I maintained my TM practice during these turbulent years, but as the conflict ended, I recognized a deeper need for guidance on how to act and behave. Facing new challenges, I realized my responses had to be grounded in wisdom, a wisdom that had felt unreachable in the chaos of opposing Hubbard and Scientology. After eight difficult years, I found that embracing Christ's message from the Sermon on the Mount offered a higher sense of reality.

Later, after the Scio wars, in 1988, as I was driving in Southern California where my family and I had relocated, I came across a big sign that indicated it was a place founded on the teachings of Paramahansa Yogananda. The name immediately rang a bell and triggered a memory of that spell-binding book I had read years ago. I decided to take a look. Fate was playing its role yet again. From TM, and the blessings of TM and Maharishi, I discovered my life teacher, Paramahansa Yogananda.

But first I had to get slapped around in the PIT. Back to 1977-79, and pre-Scientology. Among other things, my TM meditation studies and practice at least showed me that my professional PIT practice was enabling my successes in front of juries. Truth and meditation are a karmic mix, for me often worked out in the quantum soup of litigation and vice versa.

Meditation enhances truth in the mind of the litigator. Hopefully, that truth is transferred and entangled in the minds of the jurors. Truth and fact presented to juries in our adversarial justice system are a karmic mix. Litigation and meditation are also a karmic mix. That needs explanation. Unfortunately, a singular explanation is not so simple. For me it has been a journey, and I'm sorry, dear readers, if interested, you will have to keep reading.

Unfortunately, TM meditation for me, per se, did not fix the problem of the karmic mix. Like nearly everyone, I had to work through my karma, repay its debts, and commit to deeper meditation in order to evolve toward greater truth and justice, both personally and professionally. It was not easy.

My mind was naturally aggressive, particularly in cross-examining my opponents. So, I began to just choose cases where fairness and justice at least 'appeared' to be squarely in my corner. Was it self-justification or ego-driven full attack mode to obtain my perceptions of truth and justice? There is always an inverse reaction to everything. So, then I perceived myself as fighting on the side of only good against only evil.

Over time, this litigation approach gradually evolved into a hazardous 'I'm always right' mindset, especially problematic when Satyagraha, or 'affirming only truth,' clashes with both the specifics of your client's case and your method of presenting it. This tension is central to the book and will be explored in greater detail later.

There are no sinless clients. So casting stones as a lawyer for the ones you think are 'without sin' becomes a study in Satyagraha. It is no accident Gandhi gave up practicing law but succeeded in throwing out the Brits without firing a shot.

I wish the IRA and Sinn Fein had employed Ahimsa in 1798 and 1916. I might not have been killed...but that's a reincarnation issue that I'll explain in Chapter 13. The Brits might have been tossed out of Ireland sooner, and the 'Troubles' avoided, Northern Ireland not made a Brit stronghold, and all Irish Counties united...But, alas, sectarianism and the money changers always seem to win; at least in the illusory human construct of time.

Family life with Laima and the kids was wonderful whenever work in the PIT didn't take over. We enjoyed family skiing, tennis, pickup basketball, and stayed active with some running and swimming. I loved attending the kids' activities, little league games, dance and ballet performances, horseback riding, and more. My son Michael excelled as an athlete, eventually becoming a three-sport captain at Phillips Exeter Academy. Rebecca truly embodied the child ballerina, performing in productions like Boston Ballet's "The Nutcracker." Alison was California's top hunter-jumper rider, earning so many Blue Ribbons that they filled two large trunks. Good years. The Lord giveth and the Lord taketh away. Or is it just plain old pride and EGO that he taketh away? God just watches, and likely cries when our pride exceeds our humility.

FLYING AND MEDITATION

In 1975, I began taking flying lessons and flying my own plane, so the "Instrument Landing System" that guides a pilot into an airport was very important. I became IFR (instrument flight rules) qualified, which enabled me to fly in all weather conditions, which I did. I accumulated thousands of hours over the next 30 years, including hundreds of actual IFR flights. That training saved my life on one or more occasion. As any IFR experienced pilot can affirm, when the weather is bad and at the "minimums" for finding an airport and landing, flying can become nasty. On a couple of occasions, including 3 engine failures, I actually came closer than I would have liked to in fulfilling the old maxim, 'there are old pilots and there are bold pilots, but there are no old, bold pilots'. I was a mix thankfully.

Pilots just limited to VFR 'visual flight' rules are particularly vulnerable to accidents when weather conditions deteriorate. There are countless tragic examples of this flying maxim. The real danger for such pilots is disorientation. VFR pilots, when they cannot see a visual horizon, in contrast to being in a car, which moves primarily in two dimensions, are prone to disorientation. This tendency can often lead to deadly consequences. The recent Kobe Bryant tragedy likely evidences the pilot disorientation problem.

I've landed many, many times, perhaps a hundred, using the Martha's Vineyard and Nantucket ILS (instrument landing system) landing approaches. Many times the haze and fog were at 'minimums' with only 200 feet visibility in some areas. Minimums is the standard which requires a pilot to have the airport environment in sight as you come down the glide path. As you reach 200 feet above ground level, you can then decide whether to break off or land.

Without visibility, you are searching for the runway, counting on the ILS receiver in your plane to keep you lined up with the runway and keep precisely vertical on the glide path. If you don't visually have the airport at 200 feet, the FAA law, airport rules and common sense mandate that you break off the approach. The airport fire department doesn't like picking up the pieces.

Unless you use your auto pilot, only usable under certain restrictions, and other variables, the pilot on an ILS approach manually controls the plane, with rudder, ailerons, flaps and power controls, keeping the needles on his cockpit ILS receiver centered where they are supposed to be in accordance with the guiding signals sent out from the transmitter at the end of the approaching runway. The needles show you the position of your plane in relationship to runway and glide path, both of which the pilot can review in advance as shown on an "approach plate".

In the last 200 feet, the pilot must decide to land or abort the approach dependent on having the runway environment in sight after descending through fog, rain, snow, or cloud. Focus, concentration, and rapid decision-making through the senses, and the training registered in the intellect is required, and the practice of meditation helps enormously. No room for squishy mind ruminations, only total awareness, of the kind central to practicing TM. The clearer and the more silent the mind is, the 'slower' everything seems in your environmental awareness, and thus the more precisely you can concentrate on keeping the ILS needles centered and in conformity with the plane's required location. If this is done the aircraft should be precisely aligned to the approach of the runway.

In other words, although TM initiates practice 'allowing the mind to transcend', what is then experienced is a clarity, an awareness, an ability to concentrate with more precision than experienced in the normal waking state. Athletes experience this as being in the 'zone' or having the game 'slowdown' to such a degree that they remain in perfect control of their performance.

A TM'er, as distinguished from many other types of meditation practices, such as Kriya Yoga, which I practice now, follows an auto pilot path, regardless of all conditions, emotional states, anxieties, inner conflicts and, a biggie... restlessness. The TMer is taught to 'allow' the mind to transcend itself and take you to pure awareness, or bliss. No intention, no will, no forced thinking about the mantra.

In TM, the instructions are designed to take subtle, mindful intentionality...as distinguished from true will which you learn about in Kriya Yoga practice, out of the normal stream of thought processing in the waking state. The concept is to allow the mind to settle down by itself, using the mantra as a sort of tool to allow the mind to experience its quieter states of thought, when it goes beyond, or transcends all thought. With continued meditation, this silence is then experienced even outside of meditation as the gap between thoughts.

It's in the awareness of that gap that the mind realizes he or she is an observer of the mind. Then the question arises who is the observer of the mind; the stream of thought, the mantra, or even the transcending silence. The answer is the soul. Maharishi refers to this as the field of 'Being'.

It's all about evolving awareness and evolving mindfulness of the power of the mantra, the power of silence, and awareness of the Self in the awareness of God. These are levels of consciousness that can be experienced in meditation. One reaches a state where one can 'hear' silence. It is delicious, indescribable! And you get 'out of your mind' a huge plus for litigators, not so for pilots in an IFR environment. Their minds must focus more precisely with heightened awareness.

THE TRAGEDY OF JFK JR.

John F. Kennedy Jr. is another tragic example of VFR pilot disorientation, one that would have a profound personal impact on me for reasons I'll explore.

Reportedly, he had failed his IFR training several times according to aviation reports at the time. He departed from a New Jersey airport around 8 p.m. in July and flew into the well-known Nantucket haze near Martha's Vineyard. Having trained at the Falmouth and Martha's Vineyard airports, I was very familiar with the disorienting haze that challenges VFR pilots. JFK Jr., however, was determined to reach his destination, an attitude that can prove deadly for VFR pilots. The radar signature of his plane, a new Piper Saratoga equipped with an excellent autopilot, indicated severe disorientation. Had he recognized his disorientation in time, he might have engaged the autopilot to level the wings and survived.

But sometimes you literally cannot tell whether you are going up or going down in low or non-visibility conditions without scanning your instruments, such as your artificial horizon, altimeter and vertical speed indicator. Success in IFR conditions depends on thoroughly scanning all required instruments, along with mandatory training and qualification. He took off in marginal weather, possibly unaware that the "Nantucket haze" can be even more disorienting than flying in a cloud. In total zero-visibility, such as in a cloud, he could have relied on autopilot if he felt uneasy and monitored only the basic instruments, making it possible to simply reverse course if needed.

I mention JFK Jr. for several somewhat tangential, but potentially interconnected reasons that may interest some of you. For many reasons his manner of death was a significant jolt. I've experienced disorientation while flying myself. Once I flew from Boston to New Jersey in a blizzard to try another lawyer's case; as fatigue set in, only constant scanning and using my autopilot kept me safe. I had to make it for court...just had to. Pilots refer to this as 'get-home-itis', a mindset that can become dangerously fatal. It's not something to take lightly.

My read on the tragedy of JFK Jr. is that he flew that night not only without IFR qualifications, but without sufficient training in actual IFR conditions to control his airplane using his instruments, even the basic ones, in order to maintain sufficient three-dimensional, disciplined monitoring of his basic flight controls. At some point he became disoriented, lacked sufficient environmental awareness to properly control the plane by adjustments to the flight controls based on what his instruments were telling him, and lost control. There is a crucial difference between a mind that can concentrate with clarity, filtering out useless thoughts to focus precisely on the task at hand, and a mind that cannot concentrate at all because it remains trapped in urgent, chaotic, undifferentiated streams of thought.

Mental discipline is necessary in meditation to allow the mind to experience, or at least, observe, the differentiation between thought streams and the mantra, and subsequently what Maharishi calls pure awareness. There needs to be an understanding of not only the observable differentiation itself, but of the process to accomplish it. That comes with practice. The more one practices real meditation, the ability to concentrate and focus increases. The result is found in disciplined commitment to the practice.

I have seen TMers unable to function after the "Mother Divine" and "Purusha" courses for women and men respectively. They meditate sixteen hours a day immersed in bliss. Even after week-long residence courses, I have observed individuals unable to fully adjust to the world afterwards. Been there. Done that. I have observed clients, one in particular, a famous TMer, be so 'allowing' in their thought patterns, that common sense, morality and practicality, at least in the short term, seemingly disappeared. This individual had written books and was a psychiatrist to the stars.

I don't know specifically what happened in JFK Jr.'s mind that caused his plane to crash, but the radar signature of the accident suggests the type of disorientation I have experienced in IFR training under the hood. In that training you realize that you cannot differentiate between up and down, the 3-dimensional configuration of the plane, until your instructor tells you to lift the hood revealing your instruments. Then you learn from the instruments the exact configuration of the plane regardless of what your mind and body are feeling or thinking.

There is yet another minor dot connection to JFK Jr. He was killed in that plane crash. I don't subscribe to the conspiracy theory about his death. But I do believe based on all existing evidence, as discussed in *Litigator 4*, that the CIA, Allen Dulles killed his father; and that the CIA killed his uncle, Robert F. Kennedy, MLK and Thomas Merton, all the latter murders in 1968 relating to their opposition to the Vietnam war. I believe those vicious, horrific, truly unjust murders by true evil-doers, have impacted our planet. And it has all been suppressed by our Secret Government. Suppression of truth under any circumstances is bad for humans. It has been very bad for the Kennedy family. JFK Jr. as the victim of his father's tragic murder, and the suppressed truth of who did it, may be the sequelae of that tragedy. I believe that the way quantum entanglement works, somehow these tragic events are connected, but not in any way to suggest that JFK Jr. was also murdered.

Could it have impacted JFK Jr.'s thinking and life style? Only God knows. Death wish? The violent death of his father, the subject of a massive conspiracy by the money changers, is a metaphysical issue to me, particularly because I have represented clients opposing the CIA, and / or the secret deep state government. I trained extensively in the Martha's Vineyard disorientating haze where JFK Jr. died. My familiarity with those flying conditions and my investigation into his father's assassination are deeply embedded in my mind and heart. *Litigator 4.*

I also believe that the CIA and the military industrial complex hated the Kennedys to such murderous depths, that they created an 'environment of death' for the Kennedy family, including the assassination of Robert Kennedy. How that has played out in hard core factual terms, history may be able to decipher, but let's remember that there is no death in the conventional sense. Consciousness, like energy in physics, cannot be created or destroyed, it only changes form. The patterns of our life experiences likely continues to influence the quantum field long after our physical form has dissolved. This is a realization that doesn't diminish the tragedy of violence or the reality of death or suffering, but it gradually raises your consciousness to understand these realities of life on this planet. Instead, it places these experiences in a larger context that then offers the possibility of healing and transcendence.

But make no mistake, Allen Dulles, head of the CIA in 1963, orchestrated the murder of President Kennedy. Those vibrations don't go away. *Litigator 4.* They live in our cellular structure. The closer one is to an organically similar structure, like father like son, the more quantum entangled the cellular structures.

Additionally, evil propagates evil. It enables real evil doers, like Dulles, Hubbard, Epstein, and the money changers to thrive. The dark energy of quantum entanglement is a reality. It gets 'synched' between and among the evil doers. Hitler, Stalin, and their countries are some of the most heinous examples. The more the evil doers get away with their insanities, the more evil proliferates, and the 'body count' goes up with real dead humans. Such evil is accompanied generally with societal, and moral decay. Ultimately, the evil doers either self-destruct, or societal dharma exercised by those duty-bound to stop the spread of evil, intervene with the Grace of God. The Bhagavad Gita explains these realities.

The mental, emotional, spiritual impact on JFK Jr. of his father's murder, knowing who did it and why, may have made him vulnerable to mental and emotional states, which perhaps could have been relieved by meditation. There are no accidents. I know what it takes to manually control a plane in nasty weather. And I was a TMer for 15 years. I know what it does to focus and concentration. JFK Jr was emotionally damaged at age 3. I speculate that he then grew into an adult knowing on some level who killed his father and his uncle. This is my opinion knowing how some of the players operate, and having represented Ted Kennedy's ex-wife. A remote, hazy, and indeterminate dot, yes, but a significant one.

Quantum entanglement is real.

I have experienced similar dots, in my cases. You have already read several. It is no accident I smelled my left hand burning the night Sandra and Lester were saved, and the other three were not. I could even make an argument that the CIA killing of Jr's father, and that residue in his energy body, mixed with the spirit body of his father, made him vulnerable to a premature death. When I worked on *Litigator 4*, I could feel President Kennedy's presence. On some level, those energies are analogous to my burning hand.

Given the convoluted, CIA/Dulles controlled Warren Report on his father's death, I understand why Jr. may have been emotionally and energetically entangled in that horror. We may just need a bigger vision to encompass these ideas.

There is no death. We are not the doers. We need compassion for all of our fellow deluded humans as we are from seeing truth by the mayic veil of illusion that both conceals and reveals ultimate reality. The Sanskrit term 'Maya' refers not merely to deception but to the creative power that manifests the universe while simultaneously obscuring its true nature. As we continue on our journey, the quantum entanglement of consciousness reveals itself in ever more profound ways, urging us to look beyond the veil of maya to the underlying unity that connects us all. It is through this lens that we'll examine the extraordinary case that awaits us in the next Chapter.

We move from the theoretical understanding of quantum entanglement to its direct experience in one of the most challenging cases of my career. The principles we've explored throughout this chapter; the persistence of energy patterns, the entanglement of consciousness across time and space, and the illusion of separation will manifest in ways that both clarify and complicate our understanding of reality.

CHAPTER 11

Assassin in the Courtroom: The Motorgate Cases

> "The castle of Macduff I will surprise; seize upon Fife, give edge to the sword his wife, his babes, and all unfortunate souls that trace him in his line." **Shakespeare,** *Macbeth Act 4 Scene 2*

For six grueling months, I tried a case before what the legal system euphemistically calls a "sequestered jury"—where twelve individuals are effectively cut off from the world, their families, and normal life while they deliberated on matters of justice. These poor souls, isolated in their hotel rooms each night and shuttled to and from the courthouse each day, experienced a peculiar form of what Eastern tradition calls 'maya'—the cosmic illusion or delusion that obscures our perception of reality. This case, perhaps more than any other in my career, demonstrated maya operating at multiple levels of human consciousness, all entangled with various manifestations of what we might call 'evil'.

The sequestration itself was the first layer of maya: the illusion that isolating jurors from external information would somehow lead them closer to truth, when in fact it created its own form of distortion. Cut off from the wholeness of life, these jurors were asked to make judgments based on carefully filtered information presented in the artificial environment of a courtroom.

Before I get into the case proper, I feel it may be helpful for me to preface it with a few thoughts to set the stage for understanding the events on a deeper level.

THE METAPHYSICAL FOUNDATION: YOGANANDA AND THE IRISH PRIEST

As we explored in the previous chapter, quantum entanglement reveals how consciousness extends beyond the boundaries of individual minds. To understand the deeper significance of what transpired in that courtroom, we must first consider a remarkable account from Paramahansa Yogananda. In his classic best-seller book, *Autobiography of a Yogi* (which I've been referring to as the "AY"), Yogananda describes a metaphysical experience that transcends conventional understanding of consciousness. He teaches that "Meditation is the science of reuniting the soul with Spirit" and that in Spirit, all is possible. Once, while meditating in his room in India, Yogananda suddenly found himself experiencing death through the captain of a British battleship during the Battle of Gallipoli in World War I.

The Captain's death in Gallipoli occurred contemporaneously with Yogananda's meditation in India, so it was not a reincarnation experience. He was experiencing reality through the captain's body-senses at the exact moment the man was shot and killed. Yogananda felt the impact of the bullet, experienced the Captain's final thoughts, and witnessed the transition of his consciousness as it separated from the physical body. This experience is better understood as the instantaneous exchange of energy as explained in the field of quantum entanglement. I offer it here as real-life experiential proof of that law of quantum physics outside of the laboratory of measuring electrons. Yogananda's description of the experience is as reliable as thousands of descriptions of experiencers of NDEs and of the altered states of consciousness described in over 13,000 experiences of Edgar Cayce.

I strongly recommend a study of Cayce's work. It is pure quantum entanglement that Cayce realized in a force field of God's power to heal Cayce's "patients," who came to him over 40 years to heal every form of disease suffered by our species.

At some point, the reporting of subjective experiences of these altered states becomes so voluminous, detailed and irrefutable, the evidentiary reality of them, notwithstanding the lack of measurable data, becomes scientifically undeniable.

Yogananda's dead Captain experience wasn't a dream or vision in the conventional sense. It was a direct experience of consciousness transcending the boundaries of individual identity, time, and space. Yogananda's account provides extraordinary insight into what he calls the "delusion of death," the mistaken perception that consciousness is confined to and terminates with the physical body. According to Yogananda, what we perceive as death is merely a transition of consciousness from one state to another. The apparent individuality of our consciousness is in itself a form of maya, a necessary illusion for the purposes of physical existence; the learning of vital lessons for the progress of our souls. Remarkably, he teaches that our true nature is unbounded awareness that cannot be destroyed even when the physical body ceases to function.

This explanation in *Autobiography of a Yogi* took on profound personal significance for me in July 1987, when I participated in a two-week Transcendental Meditation "Sidhi" course. The TM-Sidhi program, developed by Maharishi Mahesh Yogi as an advanced extension of the basic TM technique, is designed to develop higher states of consciousness. This is what traditional yoga texts describe as "siddhis" or 'yogic' powers... expanded capabilities of human awareness that typically remain dormant.

During one particularly deep meditation session in this course, I had an experience that paralleled Yogananda's in remarkably similar ways. Suddenly, without warning or transition, I found myself experiencing reality through the body of an Irish priest in 1920, during the Irish War of Independence against British occupation. (Chapter 13.)

Let me be clear, I wasn't just visualizing this priest; for the duration of the experience, I was him. I felt the rough texture of his clerical collar against my neck, smelled the damp stone of the church where he stood, and experienced the complex mixture of courage and fear as he confronted a group of British "Black and Tans", the notoriously brutal paramilitary force sent to suppress the Irish independence movement.

Most vividly, I experienced the exact moment when these soldiers murdered him. I felt the impact of bullets entering his body, the shock and pain that followed, and most significantly, the transition of consciousness as it separated from his physical form. There was fear, then surprise, then an extraordinary expansion of awareness as his consciousness (my consciousness in that moment) transcended the limitations of the dying body.

This experience resonates in me to this day, 36 years later, with a reality more vivid and immediate than the words I'm writing to describe it. It wasn't a dream, a fantasy, or even a vision in the conventional sense. It was exactly the same phenomenon that Yogananda described from his own experience.

This perspective offers a profound reframing of what we call personal identity. If consciousness can extend beyond the boundaries of individual experience to encompass other lives across time and space, then who we are extends far beyond our current biographical details. Death is a delusion, "The Kingdom of God within" survives the death of the body; instead, we might visualize ourselves as nodes of a vast network of consciousness, which I call the 'dots', receiving and transmitting patterns of awareness that transcend conventional understanding of selfhood.

These philosophical reflections on maya, consciousness, and the nature of evil are not abstract speculation. They are the lens through which I now understand what I experienced in 1977 when I sat next to a real-life assassin for six grueling months. At the time, I saw George Edgerly as simply a criminal, evil incarnate. Now, decades later and informed by Yogananda's teachings and my own mystical experiences, I see him differently. Not as less evil, but as a man trapped in the deepest delusion of maya, quantum-entangled with forces he neither understood nor controlled. This is his story, and of course mine.

ENTER GEORGE EDGERLY: A MODERN MACBETH

This chapter takes us inside the pure evil, and utter stupidity, of a real-life assassin. He sat right next to me for six sequestered jury months, all the time conveying a subliminal reality that he intended to kill me and my client. I got his message throughout the six-month trial, I ignored it and ultimately, my client and I helped put him in prison for life. In a bizarre event after his incarceration, the 'Church Of Scientology' followers visited him in prison in an effort to frame me in one of their fabricated schemes to undermine my client's cases against them. (*Litigator 2.*)

Knowing that Edgerly hated me, one can often be known by his enemies as well as his friends, Hubbard and the Scientologists paid Edgerly $50,000 to fabricate an utterly false, and laughably stupid scheme against me. George took their money of course, but their efforts did not succeed. (*Litigator 2.*) If there really is no death, and you believe, as Christ said, 'that all is revealed, and all paths are made straight', maybe George will have to reincarnate, along with Hubbard, and both of them, along with Miscavige and their deluded followers apologize to me, my family, my clients and all the many thousands of people who were duped into taking the indoctrination's they call 'Operating Thetan ("OT") courses'. Stay tuned.

In "OT VIII," Hubbard claimed to be Satan himself! Is it a coincidence that for millennia our species has deemed Satan to be the essence of evil?

THE NATURE OF EVIL: MACBETH, MAYA, AND MURDER

In his Tragedy *Macbeth*, Shakespeare plays out the multiple murders of King Duncan, his supporters, and thereafter, the Macduff family based on the illusion and delusion of greed and power vested in him by three witches. To sustain his illusion, Macbeth murders Macduff's innocent wife and children. Although Macduff escapes, he ultimately kills Macbeth in battle. The tragedy, however, begins in Macbeth's own mind, his thoughts fueled by the witches, who are in essence manifestations of his own dark desires within his entangled consciousness.

In Vedic scripture, evil is described as maya, an illusion or delusion that makes the unreal appear real. It is seen as a mental construct, a thought arising from wrongful desires, simply more thoughts. As both history and personal experience show, evil exists, perpetuates itself, and becomes entangled with good.

The point of these vignettes is to illuminate the quantum entanglement of human thought, word, and deed in the commission of evil, particularly the paradox of 'righteous evil', where good men do terrible things while believing themselves justified.

The Bible warns, "There is a way that seems right to a man, but its end is the way to death" (Proverbs 14:12). This is the tragedy of righteous evil: the bomber who believes he is serving his country, the pope and his papal inquisitors burning the Cathars at the stake, who believes they are serving God, the soldier who believes he is defending freedom, all convinced their hearts are pure, even as their actions bring death and suffering.

Shakespeare understood this in *Macbeth*. When one's heart is transparently malevolent, motivated by greed, power, avarice or wrath, the evil is obvious and undeniable. But the more insidious evil is the one that hides behind righteousness, duty, and obedience. It is the evil that quantum-entangles entire societies in atrocity, because no one questions whether the 'right' cause might lead to a terrible end. It is the evil of a paid off judge who utterly corrupts the judicial process for money.

Using the above as a foundation for analyzing good versus evil, let's examine the widely publicized and infamous Motorgate case. George Edgerly, whose deeply disturbed mind led him to murder his wife, a General Motors' auditor called Frank Smith, and others, also believed in his own, deluded justifications. This will give you a snapshot into hard-core evil begetting more evil, an analogous lesson in itself of Newton's Third Law, whereby evil forces are set in motion, which then cause an equal and opposite reaction of the same forces. I now label these as the dark side of quantum entanglement.

In this particular litigation, murder itself caused more attempted murder, rape, theft, larceny, fraud and conspiracy...don't forget that crime! It was a pattern of criminal activity reminiscent of Shakespearean Tragedies, that would make Satan himself grin in satisfaction. One man's illusions, delusions and thoughts, conspired with others to cause massive suffering for many, including this poor pilgrim litigating his brains out. 'Motorgate' became a hard-core, quantum-entangled reality in my litigation life, separating me from my wife and family for approximately six months of sequestered jury litigation.

Oh, the indictments in the four "Motorgate" cases all involved "conspiracy" charges. Notwithstanding the deep state's use of the epithet "conspiracy theories," be advised that the criminal indictment for a "conspiracy" is simply two or more individuals agreeing together to commit a crime. Does that sound like the Washington swamp? Does that raise the issue of two shooters killing JFK, one, allegedly Oswald, shooting from the sixth floor book depository and the other from the grassy knoll, while the Warren Commission led by CIA Director, Allen Dulles, fabricated the "lone gunman" nonsense. The deep state criminals commonly use "conspiracy theory" in the legacy media to cover up their crimes.

A "sequestered jury" as seen in the O.J. Simpson case is a jury that is locked away from spouses, families, friends and work, because of the highly volatile publicity in a high-profile case. In the Simpson case, the jury was reportedly sequestered for 265 days, or 10 days less than nine months. The theory and goal is to prevent the jurors from thinking, considering, evaluating anything impacting their verdict outside the courtroom evidence. Thus, even their reading materials, newspapers, magazines, TV, radio etc. are monitored and removed from them, if they involve anything to do with the case.

The Simpson case is reported as the 'longest sequestered jury case' in U. S. history. The Motorgate case was also one of the longest sequestered jury cases in the annals of American jurisprudence. It was certainly pure misery for the jurors, and for me separated from my wife Laima and family. Even worse, unwittingly and uncognized at the time, further separation from God....

After months of preliminary motions and court battles sixteen jurors were empaneled and 'locked up' first in Brockton, MA, then after a juror was caught reading about the case, that trial was "mistried" and we started all over again in Clinton, MA, the venue having been changed from where the corpus of the crimes took place in Lowell, MA.

This involved judicial and prosecutorial gamesmanship in itself, because the case was being reported in the Boston Globe, sold throughout Massachusetts, and other newspapers, some nationally and a few internationally. The chances of my client getting a so-called fair trial, as you will read in the overall context of massive criminality, was a jurisprudential impossibility. But human justice as our government ordains, supposedly under the ordinance of our Constitution, must prevail? As you will read in subsequent chapters, that has degenerated into myth at the hands of the money changers.

My memory is that the sequestered trial began in Brockton, MA circa March, 1977 and proceeded for about eight plus weeks (needs to be checked), or about 60 sequestered days, when the judge declared a mistrial. Apparently after being 'tattled' on by another juror, one juror admitted to reading, or being exposed to a comprehensive newspaper article about the case involving far more than just the conspiracy crimes for which the Brockton jury had been sworn in. In fact, there were four Motorgate cases involving murder, attempted murder, rape, plus the longest conspiracy case all being tried separately. The judge concluded that the jury was tainted, and aborted the first trial.

He then ordered the conspiracy case transferred to Clinton MA, another justiciable ruse, where supposedly, the jury pool from which sixteen jurors would be sworn in, would be an impartial jury. Theoretically, the pool would not include potential jurors from that hotbed of criminal activity, Lowell, MA, just about 50 miles away from Clinton, where the Chevrolet Dealership, the center of the criminal conspiracy was located.... Yeah right.... but it does bring jurisprudential philosophy into the limelight.

After reading this book, you may ask, is there such a thing in man-made systems of justice as a 'fair trial'?

The sequestered jury trial at the Clinton, MA venue lasted about seven months, from June to Christmas Eve, 1977, totaling approximately 210 sequestered days, give or take twenty. This brought the interrupted total to around 260 sequestered jury days, which is close to the O.J. trial and the 'Guinness' record, according to the Public Law Institute.

The media labeled this litigation the "Motorgate" cases, which I litigated in 1976 -77, just five years into my career. Motorgate involved these four cases exemplifying a Shakespearean Tragedy of far lesser mortals than in the kingly realms of Shakespeare. But the conspiratorial scheming involved fraud, murder, attempted murder, even the John Kerry fabricated (later Dem Presidential candidate), phony rape case. The substantive crimes of murder, attempted murder, frauds, etc, were all wrapped up in a massive conspiracy, multi-count indictment to steal millions of dollars by 44 indicted employees of Butler Chevrolet who, according to the prosecution, were "all in on it".

My client, the President of Butler Chevrolet, Ted Kemos, was assuredly not in on George Edgerly's campaign of criminality. Ted and Edgerly hated each other. Edgerly was the Service Manager of the dealership. But the case gets complicated.

These four interconnected cases all spun around a modern-day 'Macbeth', George Edgerly a man with blood and fraud on both his hands. Edgerly had already murdered his own wife and also a General Motors' auditor intent on exposing his crooked kingdom. He then tried to kill the only witness to his earlier crime.

But the story's cast swelled. Decades before his presidential aspirations, John Kerry inserted himself into the mix, angling to pad his résumé by orchestrating a phony rape indictment, one more innocent dragged into legal quicksand for someone else's ambition. The list of prosecutors leveraging human wreckage for their careers is long. Remember poor Benjamin De Christoforo and the sharks that circled him? John Kerry wasn't alone; Bill Clinton, in his presidential dash, made his own infamous stop in Arkansas to greenlight an execution of a man with the mental acuity of a child (see Chapter 3). Jerry Corsi's book "Unfit for Command" has great information on John Kerry... a quintessential Presidential sidekick. There are layers within layers here. Quantum entanglement indeed.

Motorgate, as the name implies, all occurred within the 'Castles' of the automotive industry. These four cases exposed me to the malevolent dark side of QE. How could just a single, murderous thought of a modern day, very ambitious Macbeth type character, operating in his own 'Castle' in a Chevrolet Dealership, set in motion such massive human suffering, death, and tragedies!

We have all witnessed this to varying degrees in our own lives and seen it reported in the news, especially in cases often labeled as "crimes of passion", such as the highly publicized O.J. Simpson trial, where he was accused of reacting violently to his ex-wife's relationship with Ron Goldman and ultimately acquitted. According to scriptures, crimes of passion, and the desires that drive them, frequently spiral into even greater evils. These acts are fueled by the troubling thoughts or demons that reside in the human mind. In reality, these demons or thoughts are illusions or delusions, as they rarely yield the desired outcomes of happiness or freedom from suffering. They are seldom rooted in any form of truth. Instead, they tend to result in much deeper suffering.

In the Motorgate cases, 'Macbeth' is the murderer named George Edgerly, who, like Macbeth, had murdered a wife, but in his case, his own wife. Sort of like O.J, allegedly, also murdered his former wife. But O.J. was acquitted, and strangely, George was also acquitted for murdering his wife. He convinced a jury that he didn't do it. He cut up his wife, Betty Edgerly's body into so many pieces that only her torso was found. No arms, legs, head, fingers for fingerprints, jaw for dental identification etc.

There is a certain kind of evil in George's acquittal for the murder of his wife which I have seen throughout my litigation career. Evil begets evil. The evil then expands in the consciousness of the evildoers to the extent that they believe that they can 'get away with anything'. And they do, in the short term. Take O.J. Simpson, he was arrested and convicted of armed robbery in 2008, thirteen years after his acquittal of murder in 1995. In the case of the JFK murder, the term of concealed evil has lasted over 60 years. When a judge starts down the path of evil... bribery, or just false rulings, the evil rapidly perpetuates into bigger evils culminating in total injustice. The Blixseth cases in *Litigator 4*, proves this principle.

The Motorgate cases, specifically starting with Edgerly's knowledge and experience that he could get away with anything after he murdered his wife, illustrates to the max the foregoing principle.

Eminent, and deeply thoughtful, and clinically trained psychologist, Dr. Jordan Peterson, a real clinical, in the trenches, truth teller, explains how the thoughts, translate into the fears of his patients and control their lives when not confronted. Such therapeutically unconfronted thoughts and fears can get worse, exponentially worse. He explains how transferred thoughts can lead to the actions of serial killers, creating a causal link of evil that extends to modern-day school killers. These killers study the numbers of victims' of other crimes and even compete to outdo them; demons driven by malevolent evil, as Dr. Peterson describes.

M. Scott Peck in "People of the Lie" explain the foregoing syndrome as the foundation of mental illness. The life of L Ron Hubbard and his sequential, expanded evils, originated in his malicious narcissism, and expanded to his insane delusion that his mission in this incarnation, was to destroy Christianity!

Although Edgerly had previously murdered his wife, many might say like OJ Simpson did, and had escaped conviction, his consciousness became even more evil. Edgerly evolved into a killer demon in his own mind, without remorse and without consequences. Hmmm does that sound a little like OJ? Exactly how does QE work in these types of situations? Thought transference? Demons invading the consciousness of others?... as Christ taught and demonstrated by 'casting them out'. L. Ron Hubbard proliferated evil, some use the term Satanic, in a cult causing untold hardship and suffering in society which continues to this day under the management of their new leader David Miscavige. *Litigator 2*.

What happened next with George, the 'innocent' wife killer, does it get worse? Don't tell me it does... oh, it definitely does. It seems that, for George, as the saying goes, "for as he thinketh in his heart, so is he" So he does it again and perhaps many times over.

George was engaged in fierce competition with my client, the dealership's president. They were each striving to out-earn the other in their respective areas of work, Edgerly in the back end of the business, where profits are made, versus Ted's front end car sales. When Ted and the Chevrolet Moor Division attempted to intervene, George's response was nothing short of murderous, a rampage fueled by greed and a desperate need for dominance.

Like Macbeth, Edgerly spiraled into pure evil. Ted Kemos was powerless to control or halt him. Amidst the chaos of a seven-plus-two-month conspiracy trial, I sat next to Edgerly and my client, and the feeling of the demons was so intense I could see his threats forming, mouthing them silently...I could actually sense his murderous intent, an almost tangible malevolence that filled the courtroom air. The government arranged the seating to force Ted to plead guilty. We refused.

My client and I played a role in terminating Edgerly's reign of terror. Eventually, Ted's role was more like MacDuff, who was the antagonist to murderous Macbeth and who eventually restored the rightful King, Malcolm, to the throne. In this analogy, we could say Ted restored justice. We aided in Edgerly's subsequent first-degree murder conviction. Later still, in 1984 -85, George retaliated by assisting the Miscavige attempted frame up of me. While still in prison, Edgerly took money from the Scientologists and signed an absurd affidavit to try to frame me, false on its face. I am happy to report that he failed on every level. Grace and God won. Bill Weld even played a role as the Boston U. S. Attorney. Bill indicted another mobster who was also taking money from the Scientologists. *Litigator 2*.

MOTORGATE: THE CASE THAT CHANGED EVERYTHING

In the 1970s, my client, Ted, was the President of "Butler Chevrolet", a substantially profitable car dealership in Lowell, Mass. Defending Ted,

I became thrust into the highly publicized, "Motorgate" cases and the attendant evils exemplified by Edgerly.

In this case, the application of our constitutional laws, administered by an impartial judiciary, was undermined by the prosecution's efforts to convict my client, Ted Kemos, alongside George Edgerly in what amounted to a conspiracy to create injustice. Fortunately under the circumstances, we achieved just outcomes in different instances. As in O.J. Simpson's trial, the justice system largely failed, though we managed partial success.

The system faltered because John Kerry, acting in his political interests, was responsible for overcharging in the conspiracy indictment, while Edgerly managed to outmaneuver him on the attempted murder charge. The overlapping murder indictment against Edgerly for the murder of GM auditor, Smith, including conspiracy charges relating to the 40 plus employees of the car dealership, including Ted Kemos, in the main conspiracy multi count indictment charging conspiracy to commit larceny became a nightmare of conflicted evidence.

In his separate first degree murder case, Edgerly attempted to piggy back on the main conspiracy indictment falsely concocting theories that Gordon Butler, the owner, and Ted Kemos conspired to murder Smith using a hit man. It was total nonsense, but Edgerly almost convinced a jury in the separate murder trial. But for Ted and me, he might have succeeded, had it not been for Ted and me. Ted Kemos and George Edgerly were as different as night and day, yet both were charged together in the main conspiracy case, so I endured about nine months with Edgerly sitting next to me at the defense, conjoining tables. Our partial success came from the jury, who, after seven months of deliberation in the retried case, recognized that the charges against Ted were excessive and that Edgerly was the offender.

As I will explain, but with no ego or back-slapping for me and my client, we ultimately helped put Edgerly in prison for life, but Ted paid a heavy price! The quantum entanglement factors I've spent my career studying, how consciousness, intention, and energy interact in a courtroom, played a decisive role in the Motorgate outcomes. QE influenced the jury's partial acquittal of my client Ted Kemos, shaped the eventual murder conviction of George Edgerly, and even manifested years later when the Scientologists, still quantum-entangled with Edgerly's malevolence, attempted to frame me.

In terms of publicity, murder, mayhem and misfits, the 1977 Motorgate case not only mirrored the Shakespearean evil recounted in Macbeth, it was actually a larger version of the Simpson case of its day, involving far more lives, and infinitely more quantum entangled issues, evil thoughts and misdeeds. In terms of complexity, it dwarfed the Simpson case. The Motorgate scandal actually involved four separate criminal cases and multiple civil cases, all of which became intertwined on multiple levels, shared defendants, overlapping evidence, interconnected timelines, and common witnesses. The criminal rules governing justice required that each jury pool in all four cases remain untainted by publicity or prejudicial information.

Yet in the conspiracy case, John Kerry's prosecution team deliberately violated this principle, attempting to contaminate the jury pool to secure a conviction.

The Motorgate cases quickly devolved into a chaotic tangle of evidence: who did what, who killed whom, who attempted murder, who committed rape, who conspired to kill, and who stole millions through fraudulent warranty claims. Just a few years into the litigation, I was almost naively idealistic and believed I could secure justice for my client. In some ways I did and in some ways, we both did. Looking back, I realize now that God and Grace were preparing me for a hard truth, that there is no reliance on human justice in this world.

Somehow, I have had an evolving perspective on how God and Grace work and how God's justice is achieved. Bottom line: love, mercy, forgiveness, compassion, The Sermon on the Mount quintessential quantum entanglement.

THE MEDIA CIRCUS AND JOHN KERRY'S AMBITIONS

The media's portrayal of the Motorgate case added another layer to the complex legal drama unfolding in the courtroom. Having established their pattern of selective narrative construction in other high-profile cases, the mainstream media quickly recognized the sensational potential of these interconnected crimes. In 1976, they dubbed the four crimes "Motorgate" because they involved a broad range of offenses from murder to attempted murder, to the massive $33 million warranty fraud scheme to defraud General Motors by fabricating false warranty claims paid for by GM. Edgerly was the architect of the warranty frauds

But the 'gate' suffix wasn't applied randomly. The connection to Watergate came through James St. Clair, the attorney who represented the owner of the Chevrolet dealership at the center of our case. St. Clair hailed from the Boston Brahmin firm Ropes and Gray, a prestigious establishment

I had tussled with on several occasions in previous litigation. What made St. Clair's involvement particularly noteworthy was that he had recently defended President Nixon during the Watergate scandal that had captivated the nation. Nixon, like Shakespeare's Macbeth, had been a leader whose ambition led to his downfall, a wannabe king who suffered the tragic loss of his crown through the Watergate investigations and subsequent resignation.

This connection through St. Clair created an irresistible parallel for the media, who deemed the Motorgate cases worthy of the Watergate epithet. The '-gate' suffix would later become standard media shorthand for any scandal, but at that time, the comparison carried particular weight and suggested a similar level of significance. The media coverage, however, often simplified the complex legal issues at stake and focused disproportionately on the sensational aspects rather than the painstaking legal work required to bring the perpetrators to justice.

The Motorgate cases had everything a litigator could hope for in terms of professional challenge and public significance. They also attracted political opportunists, most notably John Kerry, who served as a prosecutor in the phony baloney rape case, but he didn't do any of the trial work in the three main cases. But he framed up a rape charge against Edgerly who had a relationship with a local prostitute. Typical Kerry ambition hunting. Kerry, who had positioned himself as a Vietnam veteran turned prosecutor, would later become the 2004 Democratic presidential candidate against George W. Bush. During the Motorgate proceedings, Kerry spent considerable time taking credit and garnering publicity while the substantive legal work was being performed by other prosecutors who received far less recognition.

Kerry's approach to the Motorgate prosecution reflected his political ambitions and understanding of how to leverage his position for career advancement. His Kennedy connections proved invaluable in Massachusetts politics, where such associations have historically carried significant weight. He effectively used these connections to advance his politically appointed ambitions, first as a prosecutor and later in his broader political career. The pattern of behavior that began during Motorgate would continue throughout Kerry's career, later scrutinized in Jerry Corsi's book, "Unfit for Command," which raised questions about Kerry's conduct in Vietnam and his subsequent political opportunism.

The media's framing of Motorgate exemplifies a broader pattern in how information about significant cases is filtered and presented to the public. Just as they have supported the false narrative that Oswald acted alone in the Kennedy assassination for 60 years; and similarly maintained the official story about the Vince Foster murder being a suicide for over three decades. Media organizations create frameworks that shape public understanding in ways that often diverge from the more nuanced reality. This tendency to establish and maintain particular narratives, regardless of conflicting evidence, represents another manifestation of maya, the veil of illusion that obscures deeper truths.

As the Motorgate trial progressed through its six months of testimony and evidence, these layers of media framing and political posturing created additional challenges for those of us committed to pursuing justice based on facts rather than narratives. The courtroom became not just a venue for legal arguments but a stage where broader social, political, and media dynamics played out in ways that both illuminated and obscured the truth of what had actually occurred.

While I represented Ted Kemos the President of the dealership, St. Clair represented Gordon Butler, the owner. Forty-four persons were indicted in the fraud and conspiracy case. All plead guilty except Kemos and Butler. We went to trial, for nine, long, hard, locked-up, interrupted months. It was brutal. A recently married juror, after a few months of gazing at his new wife across the courtroom and having no visitation rights, looked like a drooling, forlorn puppy. I could strongly identify with him.

I myself felt like a more complex version of him, a forlorn litigator imprisoned in a courtroom alongside the sequestered jury without my wife Laima and the kids, sitting next to the murderer George Edgerly for nine months! Edgerly, already infamous for being acquitted of wife-killing, was awaiting trial on another murder indictment, this time for the killing of a General Motors corporation auditor. The scene was further complicated by a politically driven Middlesex District Attorney, who had twice lost to Edgerly, and an inexperienced publicity-hungry figure named Kerry. Coupled with a relentless media barrage eager to convict someone of anything, all these factors defined the turbulent Motorgate cases.

John Kerry was yet another complication to the case. He had made a name for himself as a Vietnam war protester, after serving there as a "Swift Boat" officer. He then betrayed his comrades by coming back and promoting himself with stories about the alleged misconduct of our military. It was at the height of the growing war protest movement in this country which Kerry latched onto like a carpetbagger after the civil war. Same with Motorgate. Kerry leveraged his Kennedy connections to secure an appointment to the Middlesex DA's office just as Motorgate garnered media attention. Some suggest he had never previously tried a case, implying his primary goal was to attract media coverage. I know. I watched his pathetic, publicity-grabbing, media-hounding schemes for a year. A disgrace.

The Butler family who owned the dealership was wealthy and politically connected on both sides of the aisle. Gordon's brother, George Butler, had raised millions for John F. Kennedy's presidential bid in 1960. Gordon Butler was purportedly dating a Hollywood starlet at the time.

THE MURDER OF FRANK SMITH AND THE CONSPIRACY UNRAVELS

The Chevrolet Motor Division auditor, Frank Smith, assigned to reduce the warranty frauds being perpetrated by Edgerly, was murdered during his auditing of the car dealership warranty records. Notorious assassin, service department director, George Edgerly, was charged with first degree murder. So, the case had everything any media hound could want.

Of interest, Kerry's focus was on Ted Kemos, and on Edgerly in a separate, phony rape case, not on the Butler family and their Kennedy connections. The intertwined facts in all four cases however created a problem for any protection Kerry could give to the Butlers. The real prosecutors who actually did the work were after everybody, including my client. They wanted Ted to plead and testify against Gordon Butler. He refused.

The Motorgate cases initially erupted in the media after the February, discovery of Frank Smith's body, the General Motors auditor who had been investigating Butler Chevrolet. Smith was found floating in the Danvers River, shot in the head execution-style. While auditing Butler Chevrolet's service department, Smith uncovered grossly fraudulent warranty claims, which had soared under service manager Edgerly. He sat beside Smith during the audit, and the two became drinking companions. Eventually, Edgerly, Smith, and a Vice President of Chevrolet Motor Division agreed to conspire to reduce the inflated warranty claims to a more "manageable level." However, Edgerly did not agree on the figures involved.

James Dolson, one of Edgerly's subordinates in the service department, had good reason to fear his boss. Edgerly's reputation as a notorious killer fostered an atmosphere of fear throughout the dealership. Dolson believed that Edgerly had murdered several people including his own wife, Betty Edgerly. The case, famously defended by F. Lee Bailey in his first trial and detailed in the first chapter of Bailey's book as "the Torso Murder case," began when Betty disappeared. Only her torso, headless, legless, and armless, was discovered. Who could commit such a gruesome crime? Was it the work of demons?

George Edgerly was a pathological, yet cunning liar. After Betty vanished, he took several polygraph tests, yielding mixed results. Although the police suspected Edgerly, the absence of a fully identifiable body hampered their investigation. Months later, Betty's dismembered torso was finally found in a brook in Dracut, Massachusetts, and George Edgerly was indicted for her murder. Despite a 17-day trial, Edgerly was acquitted, an outcome reminiscent of O.J. Simpson's acquittal years later. The Middlesex County District Attorney was enraged with the verdict.

Disposing of bodies in rivers and streams was apparently Edgerly's modus operandi. When Smith's body was found in the Danvers River in February,1974, the Middlesex homicide detectives focused on Edgerly. This time the DA had an eyewitness, one James Dolson. Dolson had seen Edgerly shoot the Chevrolet auditor, Frank Smith. They were in the process of making a deal with Dolson to testify against Edgerly, which Edgerly found out about, so he tried to eliminate Dolson before Dolson squealed.

It was Motorgate Case No. 1, Commonwealth v Edgerly for the attempted murder of Dolson. While the investigation was pending and Dolson was secretly talking to the cops, or so he thought, Edgerly, a hooker, a thug named Shanahan, and Dolson all drove to a shack in the woods to party. Dolson didn't know that Edgerly was on to his secret dealings with the D.A. for the Smith murder which Dolson had witnessed. So, Edgerly (or if you believed Edgerly's story, Shanahan), planned to kill Dolson. Edgerly had the motive, opportunity and means, "MOM" in detective parlance, to kill Dolson because Dolson witnessed the Smith murder, not Shanahan.

So here's the crux: It was either Edgerly, or, Shanahan who plotted to kill Dolson. If you buy Edgerly's version, it was Shanahan who plotted to kill Dolson. Edgerly however ticked every box in the detective's "MOM" checklist: motive, opportunity, and means to kill Dolson because Dolson witnessed the Smith murder, not Shanahan. Quite simple really isn't it? In your position as a jurist, dear reader, I'm sure you have already decided the verdict...but read on.

According to Dolson, they arrived at the shack after a heavy night of drinking. Edgerly went out to the car and came back in with a knife and proceeded to stab Dolson multiple times in the chest and gut. They carried Dolson out and put him in the trunk leaving the lid open. They went back in to tidy up the shack. Dolson crawled out of the trunk with his guts hanging out and crawled about a mile to a house. He hid from his would-be killers and survived. They drove the bloody car into a pond. The three stooges, Edgerly, Shanahan and the hooker, believed they'd cleverly and covertly attempted a murder no one would ever discover.

At the trial, Edgerly testified that he didn't do the stabbing. Shanahan did it. Shanahan had made a deal to testify so the jury was confronted with Dolson and Shanahan saying Edgerly did the stabbing, and Edgerly saying, "moi?" no way, how does Shanahan know all those stabbing details? The Assistant D.A. said Edgerly's motive to kill Dolson was obvious, Dolson's eyewitness testimony in the Smith murder.

Now here's the incredible bit. Edgerly, being a pathological and convincing liar, got on the witness stand, and was acquitted! Now the Middlesex DA was really upset. The case was beset with evidentiary commingling of the Smith murder, the warranty fraud evidence, the Dolson-Edgerly work connections, hooker issues, questionable jury instructions, and overreaching prosecutorial zeal. Edgerly was incredibly clever and he used that to his advantage.

My client, Kemos, intensely disliked, in fact hated, and had almost nothing to do with Edgerly's control over the Service Department of the dealership. Kemos had opposed Edgerly's employment by the Butler family. Kemos and I were hoping and planning on Edgerly's conviction for the attempted murder of Dolson. Incredibly, Edgerly took the witness stand and planted at least enough doubt resulting in his acquittal in that case.

Motorgate Case No. 4. Commonwealth v Edgerly 4. The Middlesex D.A. later framed Edgerly on a phony rape case involving another prostitute. Edgerly was convicted when he was likely innocent in a case of consensual hooker alleged rape. Irony!

In the main conspiracy case, the nine month trials, career prosecutors did all the work in and out of court. Kerry just showed up on the courthouse steps at the end of most trial days to get photographed, talk to the media and take credit. He later took credit for the rape conviction.

Motorgate case no. 4, was not really about the Motorgate crimes, it was an unconnected rape case, but since it involved Edgerly, Kerry piggybacked on the main Motorgate cases to garner the publicity he craved, and some believe that he used the massive publicity about just how bad Edgerly was to gain the conviction. A media hound using the media to get a conviction aside from the hard evidence in the case. The 'rape' of a hooker... justice? Karma? The media was busy making Edgerly into a really bad guy, so the focus on the Butler, Kennedy connections would be diverted. A disgrace. A repeat of his character as described in "Unfit for Command". Not surprisingly, Kerry's politics have always been aligned with the Deep State. He is just one of their minions.

At the heart of the Motorgate scandal was Case No. 2: Commonwealth v. Butler, Kemos, Edgerly and 44 Butler Chevrolet employees. This prosecution represented the central and most extensive legal action in the Motorgate affair, encompassing not only the dealership's management and staff but also reaching into the corporate hierarchy of General Motors itself. Among the defendants was a Chevrolet Motor Division Vice President who had allegedly accepted bribes from Gordon Butler, the dealership's owner, to facilitate and conceal the fraudulent warranty scheme.

This case constituted what could truly be called the 'main Motorgate' prosecution. It involved the sequestered jury trial that stretched over nine months, with significant interruptions that complicated both the proceedings and the jurors' lives. These interruptions stemmed from various legal challenges, evidentiary disputes, and procedural complications that repeatedly halted the trial's momentum. Throughout these proceedings, evidence related to the other Motorgate cases frequently surfaced in court, despite vigorous objections from myself and St. Clair who argued that the District Attorney's office was improperly using the combined conspiracy charges to prejudice the jury against our clients.

The government's case centered on an elaborate warranty fraud scheme that allegedly defrauded General Motors of millions of dollars. According to prosecutors, the 44 indicted individuals had participated in a systematic operation to file false warranty claims, charging for repairs that were never performed or deliberately misrepresenting the nature of actual repairs to increase reimbursement amounts. The scheme's sophistication and scale suggested coordination at multiple levels within the dealership's operations.

The case extended beyond state jurisdiction when federal authorities launched their own parallel investigation. The Federal government subsequently indicted the same group of defendants for conducting a similar warranty fraud operation at a companion Toyota dealership also owned by Butler. This dual prosecution at both state and federal levels underscored the scope and seriousness of the alleged criminal enterprise, which had apparently expanded beyond a single automotive brand to target multiple manufacturers' warranty systems.

The government's evidence over the lengthy trial, was quite damning. The D.A. had plenty of false warranty claims. For example; a customer could bring his car in to have the windshield wiper motor repaired and

Edgerly would submit a warranty claim for a new engine! This fraud was a pandemic in the industry during the 60's and 70's.

The car manufacturers knew it was happening, couldn't really contain it, and for over a decade, considered it just part of the cost of doing business. Edgerly took it to a whole new level. The standing joke, if you will, at Butler Chevrolet was that "George had everything handled." Chevrolet was afraid he would blow the whistle on an industry-wide practice, the cost of which was ultimately footed by the consumer on the pricing of a car.

Chevrolet and Smith over a period of years had been telling Edgerly to just "get warranty down in a manageable range less than $30K per month." Edgerly had pushed it to over a $100,000 per month in brazen opposition to Kemos. Edgerly received 4% of all warranty claims. As the President of the dealership, Ted Kemos benefited from the service department's back-end revenues. The front end sales department, Kemos' specialty, was hugely successful, mostly because of Ted's business acumen in the industry.

Edgerly was envious of Kemos for many reasons, including the front-end's success. Kemos was a legitimate car industry guy. Edgerly was never legitimate even in his back-end domain, which he controlled to the exclusion of Kemos, reporting directly to Butler.

Kemos hated Edgerly and inherited him as the service manager when he became the President and General Manager of Butler Chevrolet. When Kemos arrived the entire back-end of the dealership, the service department, was under the dictatorship of Edgerly's criminal schemes and everybody knew it. Kemos tried to bring warranty claims into a manageable range as dictated and admitted by Chevrolet. Kemos knew nothing about the bribery of the Vice President.

All the service department employees at Butler Chevrolet were allegedly in on it. The mechanics were paid for their warranty work, the service writers, the secretaries typing up the claims, the accountants and bookkeepers, all allegedly knew that phony warranty claims had become a tidal wave of fraud for many years.

Kemos was a sales-oriented person focused on selling cars, not fixing them. He convinced me he had a story to tell to gain an acquittal. Kemos, like the others, were indicted on many counts of fraud and conspiracy. I don't recall the exact number. Conviction would have put him in prison for many years. I don't recall the sentencing guidelines at that time, but the D.A. had over- plead the case. Conspiracy convictions are the easiest for a prosecutor to obtain. Two or more people talking about, and doing any affirmative act to commit a crime is a conspiracy. It is the go-to crime for a prosecutor in a complex case. Kemos benefited from the warranty submissions, which became our biggest problem. He fought with Butler to get rid of Edgerly and was told that it was not doable.

Everybody pled guilty or entered into some type of deal except Kemos and Butler.

The interrupted part of the case was started in June 1977 and the judge was trying to finish the case by Christmas.

The judge also hammered the defense. St. Clair and myself and my colleagues suffered the most. In early October, just as the government wrapped up, and the defense began, the judge announced he wanted to finish the case by Christmas. So, he ruled over our objections, that the trial would start with 10-hour days going forward, then go to 12-hour days, then if not concluded by the end of November trial would go to 14-hour days. Madness. Trying to defend such a complex criminal fraud case under those conditions was just brutal.

The jury returned its verdicts on Christmas Eve. Gordon Butler was convicted on several counts of conspiracy and fraud. Ted Kemos was convicted on two conspiracy counts but acquitted on the vast majority of the charges. He received two years in the House of Corrections with lenient parole.

To call Ted's conviction a hiccup in the justice system would be an understatement. The conspiracy charges were so broad and vague that they could have ensnared anyone remotely connected to the dealership. Ted's "crime" was association—he worked in the same dealership as George Edgerly, spoke to him, and failed to immediately report his suspicions to authorities. But notwithstanding his opposition to Edgerly's fraud schemes, as the President of the dealership, he benefited on the bottom-line financial statements. Under the government's theory of conspiracy, that was enough. The sentence may have been light, but the verdict destroyed Ted's future in the automotive industry. A slap on the wrist that ended a career. Ted, a real trooper, offered no evidence on Gordon Butler in an offered plea deal.

Now for the more interesting part of the whole matter. What goes around, comes around.

MOTORGATE CASE NO. 4: THE MURDER TRIAL THAT EXPOSED A PATHOLOGICAL LIAR

Motorgate Case No. 4 represented the darkest chapter in the scandal: *Commonwealth v. Edgerly* for the first-degree murder of Smith. While the other Motorgate cases involved financial crimes and attempted murder, this case dealt with the deliberate taking of a human life. The prosecution centered on Edgerly, already implicated in the warranty fraud scheme, who now stood accused of executing Smith in cold blood. This murder case was inextricably linked to the broader Motorgate scandal, as the killing appeared to be connected to silencing a potential witness to the warranty fraud operations.

The prosecution's key witness was Dolson, who provided damning testimony against Edgerly. Dolson described a harrowing sequence of events: a drinking marathon involving Edgerly, Smith, and himself; Edgerly waving a gun while intoxicated; discussions about the warranty schemes and frauds, and finally, Edgerly taking the heavily intoxicated Smith to a secluded location and shooting him in the head. The prosecution presented this as a calculated murder to silence someone who knew too much about the warranty fraud operations.

Despite the seemingly straightforward evidence, the case took an unexpected turn during the government's presentation. Incredibly, Edgerly and his defense team were making progress with a narrative that, to those of us familiar with the facts, was sheer nonsense. Yet somehow, it appeared to be gaining traction.

THE 'NO SENSE' DEFENSE

This wasn't the first time Edgerly had constructed an elaborate false defense. In the previous case involving his attempted murder of Dolson, another Motorgate-related crime, Edgerly had contrived a defense claiming that Shanahan had stabbed Dolson, not him. Now, facing a murder charge, Edgerly was preparing to deploy the same playbook: deny responsibility and shift blame to others.

As the trial progressed, Edgerly and his lawyer developed an alternative narrative: that the mob had killed Smith at the behest of Butler (the dealership owner) over a drug deal, and that Dolson had actually committed the murder for Butler. Their presentation to the jury even intimated that Ted Kemos (my client) was somehow involved. This defense strategy mirrored his previous tactics, that is, to create confusion, spread blame widely, and hope reasonable doubt would emerge from the chaos.

THE PROSECUTION'S DILEMMA

The defense strategy, though built on fabrications, was proving surprisingly effective. The District Attorney, growing nervous about potentially losing another case to Edgerly, made a troubling decision. The prosecution offered Edgerly a plea deal: an involuntary manslaughter conviction with a sentence that would run parallel to his warranty case and rape case sentences. Under this arrangement, Edgerly would have been released from prison in less than 10 years; a remarkably lenient outcome for someone who had committed first-degree murder.

The case reached a critical juncture when Edgerly announced his intention to call both Butler and my client, Kemos, as defense witnesses. Edgerly's strategy was transparent: he expected both men to invoke their Fifth Amendment privilege against self-incrimination, which the jury might interpret as supporting his narrative that they were the real culprits behind Smith's murder.

THE STRATEGIC COUNTERMOVE

The judge conducted what is known as a "voir dire", a hearing outside the jury's presence to determine what Butler and Kemos intended to do if called as witnesses. St. Clair, Butler's attorney, instructed his client to assert the Fifth Amendment, which Butler did.

I had a different conversation with my client, Ted Kemos. Ted harbored a deep hatred for Edgerly, and we both recognized an opportunity to ensure justice was served. I explained a strategy that might finally give Edgerly what he deserved, though it carried significant risks. The easy and conventional path would have been for Ted to simply invoke the Fifth Amendment, as almost any criminal lawyer would have advised. Instead, we made a bold decision: during the voir dire Ted testified that if called on rebuttal by the government, he would testify telling the truth and exposing Edgerly's defense for the fabrication it was.

I approached the District Attorney with our plan. I explained that Edgerly was not just a liar but a pathological one, and that previous prosecutors had failed in their cross-examinations by being too aggressive and too brief. We agreed on a counter-intuitive approach: if Edgerly took the witness stand (as he had in his previous cases), the prosecution would inform the court that they intended to call Kemos as a rebuttal witness. This would force Edgerly to testify, knowing his lies would be contradicted.

The key insight I shared with the DA was to keep Edgerly on the stand as long as possible, even if it initially appeared he was winning the exchange. Given enough time and questions, a pathological liar will inevitably begin contradicting himself. The strategy required patience and restraint, qualities previous prosecutors had lacked when facing Edgerly.

JUSTICE SERVED

The strategy worked exactly as planned. Given enough time on the witness stand, Edgerly began contradicting himself, his carefully constructed narrative unraveling under the weight of its own inconsistencies. The jury returned with the verdict that justice demanded: guilty of first-degree murder.

Edgerly died in prison in September 2007, having served decades for his crimes. Before his death, however, he participated in one final act of deception. The Church of Scientology, L. Ron Hubbard's organization which I would later confront in court, used both Edgerly and Shanahan to fabricate an operation against me, a story I detail in *Litigator 2*. The quantum entanglement of these cases, spanning decades and connecting seemingly disparate events, continues to reveal itself in remarkable ways that I will refer to in subsequent writings. (*Litigator 2*)

Years later, in 2004, when Kerry was running against Bush, I got a call from the bow-tied New York Magazine journalist, Jeffrey Toobin. He was puffing Kerry up for the Democrats and wanted to discuss how the young, brilliant prosecutor, John Kerry, had supposedly put that infamous assassin, George Edgerly, away for life. He asked if I was the Michael Flynn who had defended Kemos in the Motorgate case. He said he was doing an article on Kerry, set to publish just before the election, about Kerry's outstanding legal career.

I asked Toobin if he was joking. I explained how, in fact, Edgerly was ultimately convicted for Smith's murder because of me and my client, and that Kerry was just an opportunist and "face job" seeking publicity. The career prosecutors had handled the warranty case, with Kerry showing up just for his media appearances. And he had nothing to do with the Smith murder conviction; in fact, he was offering Edgerly an involuntary manslaughter plea.

And what about the article on Kerry? Toobin, despite all that I had told him, complete with evidence, still wrote the article as a puff piece, misquoting and misrepresenting our conversation. What a surprise! The liberal media at its best. But Kerry lost anyway, so perhaps there is justice after all?

QUANTUM ENTANGLEMENT AND MEDITATION WHILE CONFRONTING EVIL

I counted the end result in Ted's case as a quasi-win, professionally speaking. He was mostly acquitted. He admitted that he knew what Edgerly was doing and couldn't stop him. It was true.

My meditations throughout the Motorgate case disintegrated into mere fragmentary attempts at inner peace. In the final month, the courtroom consumed fourteen hours of each day, with another four to six hours of preparation following. Sleep became a luxury measured in short hours, my dreams harried by legal arguments and witness testimonies and the fluorescent lights of the courtroom still burned behind my eyelids even in the darkness of fitful sleep.

My body remained in the physical world while my soul, the part of me that had once soared in meditation, felt trapped in legal complexity and human deceptions.

My previous jury successes had created a reputation that led Ted Kemos to seek my representation in this highly complex, highly publicized case. Though I'd been litigating for only four years when Motorgate began, several of my cases had already attracted significant media attention that I had neither sought nor welcomed. I instinctively shied away from publicity, having a distrust of media that would eventually deepen into disgust as my career progressed. The mainstream media, I would come to realize, served the interests of Deep State money, if not completely owned by it, while alternative sources at least attempted to pierce the veil of illusion surrounding us.

NINE MONTHS IN HELL: THE SEQUESTERED JURY TRIAL

The truth was painfully simple: after discovering Transcendental Meditation, all I truly wanted was to meditate, to explore the vast inner silence that had revealed itself to me. But reality demanded otherwise. With a wife and three children depending on me, I had responsibilities that couldn't be abandoned for spiritual pursuits. Between my marriage in 1967 and the Motorgate trial in 1977, I had gradually become more entangled in worldly affairs. I loved my family deeply, but with each courtroom victory, my litigation ego expanded, a development my deeper self recognized as a spiritual stumbling block. Worse still, the demands of litigation increasingly interfered with my meditation practice until, during the nine-month Motorgate ordeal, it virtually ceased to exist, except for brief, exhausted attempts on weekends when I drove home to my waiting family.

My distraught wife and children received only the remnants of my energy and attention in those days. The courtroom became a quantum battlefield where invisible energies collided as surely as the visible legal arguments. For nine months, I sat just two seats to the left away from George Edgerly, a murdering, lying psychopath whose dark presence seemed to create its own gravitational field. The entire case was immersed in fraud, murder, deception, and corruption. It created a force-field of negative energy that permeated the entire gruesome proceedings.

At the time, I possessed only a vague conceptual framework for quantum entanglement, but my meditation practice and intuitive understanding had taught me that our inner state profoundly impacts our environment and everyone around us. I had witnessed how meditation energy could transform a room, shifting its energetic frequency toward peace. I also learned that the dark energies destroy the light energies of meditation where the soul really lives. Now I was experiencing this reverse phenomenon sitting next to George Edgerly, his dark energy a constant presence.

I believe that Ted's conspiracy conviction and minimum sentence were somehow connected to my previous considerable efforts at meditation, even though those efforts had crumbled under the weight of the trial. On the downside, my client Ted's promising career in the automotive industry lay in ruins; he had once been headed toward owning his own dealership. No more. Gordon Butler was financially and reputationally destroyed. The Butler family, who had helped elect John Fitzgerald Kennedy to the Senate and White House, found their legacy severely tarnished. The 'King' they had helped create was long dead, and now their own empire had fallen.

I hated the case. It was so desperately dark. In contrast, when the case finally ended on Christmas Eve, lightness seeped back into my life as I was united again with my family for the Christmas holidays. I was acutely aware of the effect such darkness had on my psyche, and consequently told Laima that in order to survive, I had to go on a week-long meditation retreat to regain my mental and emotional health. My words came from a place of desperate spiritual hunger, a recognition that something essential to my being had been compromised. Physically, I had endured. But my meditation discipline had evaporated and my soul hungered for the inner silence that I had discovered in the previous 4 years.

GRACE IN THE DARKNESS: REFLECTIONS ON MOTORGATE

What I couldn't articulate to my family then and what I barely understood myself was that throughout those grueling months, an unseen hand had been guiding and protecting me. Only in retrospect did I recognize that God's grace had preserved my sanity during that litigation nightmare. What I could never have anticipated was that just two weeks after the case ended, I would experience something so profound, so utterly transformative, that it would alter the trajectory of my spiritual journey forever.

The nature of this life-changing event exceeded my capacity to comprehend it at the time. I knew only that it confirmed the power of TM meditation in ways I couldn't have imagined. Now, forty some years later, and after practicing Kriya yoga for many years, I understand its significance with a clarity that was impossible then. The quantum physics I've studied since has provided a scientific framework for what I experienced intuitively, that consciousness itself is non-local, that we exist in multiple dimensions simultaneously, that what appears as separation is actually profound connection.

Through this understanding gained experientially, scientifically, and mystically, I have come to know what Love truly is. Not the limited human emotion we typically associate with the word, but the fundamental force that binds the universe together. God is this Love, and we exist within a quantum soup of this divine essence, even amidst what our limited perception interprets as suffering. The darkness of the Motorgate trial, viewed through this expanded awareness, was not separate from the light of consciousness but part of its infinite expression.

After Motorgate concluded, I felt a kinship with the Buddha's experience when he first encountered death, disease, and evil beyond the palace walls. His sheltered existence shattered by reality, he began the spiritual quest that would lead to enlightenment. Similarly, my encounter with the darkness of human nature during Motorgate was merely a prelude of more darkness to overcome. One of these experiences, which I will recount in the next chapter, revealed the ultimate truth of 'no death'; a reality I would encounter again in chapter fifteen through my inexplicable connection to a young Irish Catholic priest murdered by British "Crown Forces" during the Irish War of Independence around 1920.

I feel the quantum threads that connect these seemingly disparate events; the Motorgate trial, the spiritual breakthrough that followed, and the transcendent experiences that confirmed the illusory nature of death itself. For the grace that has guided me through this journey, and continues to this day, I offer my eternal gratitude to Maharishi and his devotees. Their light has illuminated even the darkest passages of my experience, revealing that what appears as separation is actually connection, ending is actually beginning, what we perceive as death is merely transformation, and that nothing is truly lost, not even in our darkest hours.

Epilogue

REFLECTIONS ON JUSTICE, EVIL, AND GRACE

The Motorgate trial ended on Christmas Eve of 1977, but the reverberations of its darkness continued for years. My client, Ted Kemos, though spared the worst of the charges, saw his promising career in the automotive industry destroyed. Gordon Butler, the dealership owner, was financially and reputationally ruined; the Butler family, who had once helped elect a president, found their own empire tarnished. Of the forty-four people indicted in the conspiracy, all but Ted and Gordon had pleaded guilty, their lives forever marked by their association with George Edgerly.

And what of Edgerly, our modern Macbeth? His conviction for the murder of Frank Smith was eventually secured, and he was sentenced to life in prison. Yet even from behind bars, his malevolence continued to ripple outward. In the mid-1980s, he accepted money from the Church of Scientology to sign a fabricated, laughably false affidavit against me in their coordinated attempt to frame me, a final, impotent act of malice that ultimately failed. George Edgerly died in prison, a man consumed by the very darkness he had so eagerly cultivated.

THE TRANSFORMATIVE EVENT

Two weeks after the trial concluded, exhausted and spiritually depleted, I attended a week-long meditation retreat. I knew I needed to reconnect with the silence I had lost, but I could never have anticipated what was to come. During one meditation, I experienced a spiritual event so profound, so utterly transformative, that it re-calibrated my entire understanding of reality. It was a direct, experiential confirmation of everything I had intellectually grasped from Yogananda's teachings, a glimpse into the boundless nature of consciousness that I will explore in the next chapter.

At the time, I had no words for it. I knew only that it was real, and that it was a manifestation of the same grace that had protected me, unseen, through the nine-month ordeal of the trial. It was the light that proved the darkness was not absolute.

THE PARADOX OF RIGHTEOUS EVIL

My encounter with the pure, unadulterated evil of George Edgerly forced me to confront 'righteous evil', and in this context I think of my client, Wil Smyly, a truly good and courageous man. On February 13-15, 1945, following orders from his superiors, he piloted his B-17 over Dresden, Germany, and dropped tons of incendiary explosives, contributing to a firestorm that killed tens of thousands. Wil harbored no hatred or fear; he was a 21-year-old pilot "doing his job," and he believed his heart was pure. Yet the death and devastation were undeniable, an unacknowledged war crime born of strategic calculation by his 'superiors'.

This is the terrible mystery of human action. What happens when a good heart is an instrument for a devastating act? What is the karmic weight of a bomb dropped with a pure conscience? Unlike Edgerly, who acted from a place of greed and malice, men like Wil Smyly force us to look beyond simple dualities of good and evil and into the quantum-entangled web of cause, effect, and intention.

ON THE ILLUSION OF HUMAN JUSTICE

Motorgate shattered my remaining idealism about the legal system. After witnessing the political maneuvering of John Kerry, the media's hunger for a simple narrative, and the immense pressure placed on a sequestered jury, I was left with a question that has haunted me ever since: Is there such a thing as a 'fair trial' in a man-made system of justice? Socrates, condemned by the courts of Athens, might have had an answer. My own experience has taught me that what we call 'justice' is often just another form of maya, a set of rituals we perform to convince ourselves that we can contain the chaos of human behavior.

As you will read in subsequent chapters, this myth of impartial justice would be further dismantled at the hands of the 'money changers,' the powerful forces who corrupt the system from behind the scenes. In the later billion-dollar Blixseth case, I would come face-to-face with a judge who was so obviously corrupted, having been bribed, that the very idea of a fair trial became a grim joke. The true search for justice, I realized, could not be found in a courtroom.

Looking back, I now see the Motorgate courtroom as a quantum battlefield. The intense, negative energy was palpable. This was the dark side of quantum entanglement, proof that just as consciousness can be a conduit for grace and light, it can also be a vessel for malevolence that infects everyone it touches.

I believe my own meditation practice, however fractured it became, created a kind of spiritual shield that protected me and my client. But the cost was immense. The experience taught me that evil is not an illusion in its effect; it is a tangible force, a distortion in the field of consciousness that can be measured in ruined lives and shattered souls.

GRATITUDE AND GRACE

And yet, grace persists. The deaths of Richard Sequeira and Tom Dwyer, their bodies never found, now seem to me a profound metaphor for the unreality of death itself. Where are they? Not in a grave, but somewhere in the boundless field of consciousness that Yogananda described in his 1915 vision and the mystics have expounded upon; the same field I touched in my own small way in my 1987 experience of the dead priest.

For the grace that has guided me through this journey, and continues to this day, I offer my eternal gratitude. To Maharishi, for giving me the tools to navigate the darkness. To my family, who paid their own price during those long months of my absence. And even, in a strange way, to George Edgerly, for showing me the absolute reality of evil, and in doing so, forcing me to seek the absolute reality of God.

In the end, I have come to see that nothing is truly lost. Even in our darkest hours, we are held in a quantum soup of divine Love, and what appears as an ending is merely the prelude to a new beginning.

CHAPTER 12

The Reality of 'Unity' Consciousness: We Don't Die

"The Self is one. Unmoving, it moves faster than the mind. The senses lag, but Self runs ahead. Unmoving, it outruns pursuit. Out of Self comes the breath that is the life of all things." **Katha Upanishad**

"At the center of our being is a point of nothingness which is untouched by sin and by illusion, a point of pure truth, a point or spark which belongs entirely to God." **Thomas Merton**

After Motorgate: The Need for Reset. You would think from studying the true mystics and their millennia-based wisdom I would have learned my lesson in the nine-month courtroom brutality of the Motorgate case getting beaten up by the big, bad world. But no. My ego, ambition, and the challenge of taking on bigger bad guys drove me to seek fundamental fairness, a righteous pursuit of justice you might say...for the little guy. This of course meant that more litigation wars were my destiny.

My nervous system however, after six months of merciless litigation, demanded a reset. The great sages nailed it on the nature of thoughts and actions creating your destiny.

"Watch your thoughts, they become your words..." **Lao Tzu**

Litigation thoughts, words, actions, and character had become my destiny. It became a chain of cause and effect in the force field around me, making me the living, breathing, acting embodiment of a very much quantum-entangled, and not liberated Litigator. More is the pity because my confrontation with evil characters with all the attendant suffering for me and my family, was increasing.

Perhaps my litigation immersion in Motorgate, sitting a few yards away from the evil presence of Edgerly for nine months put me in a quantum entangled force field of such evil it prepped me for exponentially greater evil to litigate against? It makes sense to me, and I was certain of one truth as I went through Motorgate, that God was merciful and I was allowed to see the lifelong blessings and protection through many trials of life, both in courtrooms and in my personal life.

Like Sigmund Freud, getting stuck in my head is easy for me. I had to get out of my litigation brain. How do I do that after nine months of litigation madness next to maniac 'Macbeth' Edgerly. Some type of mind surrender must be needed, so I decided to go on a 7-day intensive TM residence course. My inquiry into 'who am I' 'what am I doing' and 'am I wasting my life fighting useless court battles' needed it. Those battles mostly turned-on money and how the more powerful money changers use the justice system to get what they wanted regardless of truth. This became an expedient, second only to supporting my family.

THE UNITY CONSCIOUSNESS EXPERIENCE: JANUARY 1978

The Unity experience I had in the TM course in January 1978 following the Motorgate trial was more real than anything I had ever experienced in my life. It had a limited similarity to a few experiences I had in childhood that could be described as spiritual or 'religious fervor' from my Catholic upbringing, but not with the same dimension of reality. Not even close. I had experienced other events during transcendence but even those were not in the same dimension to what I had experienced for about an hour and a half on that TM Residence Course where there was no time and space, no beginning or end. No birth, no death. I know what imagination is and it doesn't compare to this experience.

Years later, as I studied the writings of Yogananda, I identified the Unity experience with his very explicit explanations in the AY, and his home study Lessons on the varying levels of consciousness. He definitively states that "time and space are linked instantly in the presence of God." This is quantum entanglement. He also explains in discourses on the laws of foundational physics, that are in accordance with Einstein's conservation of mass energy, ($E=mc^2$), that energy is neither created nor destroyed.

His proof of these physical laws are explained in his personal experiences, and those of other yogis, both in the reality of Christ's resurrection and the resurrection of his Guru, Swami Sri Yukteswar. He describes the event in stunning detail in *Autobiography of a Yogi*, Chapter 43, and in *The Second Coming of Christ*, Chapter 75.

"Before my open and astonished eyes, the whole room was transformed into a strange world, the sunlight transmuted into supernal splendour. Waves of rapture engulfed me as I beheld the flesh and blood form of Sri Yukteswar!"

This resurrection quote is at the beginning of chapter 43 when Sri Yukteswar appears to Paramahansa Yogananda in his Bombay hotel room on June 19, 1936, three months after Sri Yukteswar's physical death.

ROUNDING: THE PRACTICE THAT OPENED THE DOOR

January 1978, Litchfield, Connecticut. I was on a seven-day TM residence course at the TM 'farm'. Seven days of bliss. The course was based on a TM program called Rounding. Rounding consisted of three 20-minute processes. The first, 20 minutes were of asanas. These are generally understood to be hatha yoga positions, of which TM had developed its own set to practice for 20 minutes. If you know nothing about yoga, think of the asanas as configurations of the body in which you observe your breath and your life force while in a particular posture.

After the asanas, the program called for 20 minutes of the mantra-based meditation in which you allowed your mind to effortlessly return to the mantra from the normal thoughts streaming through your mind. The teaching and theory is that if permitted the mind will automatically return to the mantra, because it is more blissful, and awakens higher levels of consciousness than the normal thought stream if practiced correctly.

Volumes have been written on different meditation techniques to observe one's thoughts or breath. They mostly conclude with the question 'who' is watching my thoughts?

The simplest way of discovering this is by just observing the breath. Somehow the mind, when observing, takes the practitioner into the body and into higher states of consciousness without a mantra in the mind.

The third phase of rounding involved just lying down on your bed for 20 minutes, allowing the physiology to drop into a deeper state of rest naturally resulting from the TM meditation practice. It works.

BEYOND TIME AND SPACE: THE EXPERIENCE ITSELF

On the third day into my rounding program, during my first round of the morning, with my nervous system more rested from sleep and prior rounds of the days before, I began to meditate following the asanas. Suddenly, with no effort I dropped into a state of consciousness which I will now attempt to describe. The truth and reality is that it is indescribable because it is beyond words, thoughts, and language. There are no words. Words come from thoughts. This state was beyond thought and consequently I can only use language to attempt to describe it; words to describe something that cannot be described with words.

During the TM meditation, my mind dropped deeper into greater levels of silence as the mantra began to disappear in my mind. There were no other thoughts replacing the mantra, and I became aware of infinite silence within myself. I was experiencing or observing my mind in the act of realizing this silence.

I had no thoughts in that field of pure awareness, but I was watching my mind blissfully aware of the silence and aware of no thought, just silence. I was not even breathing. You might say, 'aah-ha', that was your thought, aware of the silence, aware of not breathing. No, wrong. There was experience, awareness, but no thought interrupting the silence and awareness. My mind could still generate thoughts, but they were like distant clouds on the horizon, present, but not obscuring the vast sky of awareness. They were suspended in the periphery, outside the absolute awareness that I was experiencing.

Suddenly, 'I' was watching my mind have the experience. Then, but not aware of when 'then' occurred, I was aware of 'me' as eternal, never having had a beginning or end, but this experience came from pure awareness, not thought, just the direct knowing of no beginning no end. At the same time, I was aware of my mind watching the awareness of the experience. You might call that a thought but it wasn't like ordinary thinking. I was in a state of pure, transcendental bliss, what I later came to call 'cosmic consciousness', 'unity consciousness' or 'God consciousness'... whatever way you want to describe it. There was only experience which seemed to be 'I' as well. No distinction between the experience and the experiencer. Just unity. Oneness. Perfect ease.

My mind thought...or I thought, I'm not sure which, as I write over 40 years later, "OK, the twenty minutes are up, time to lie down". The pure awareness of no beginning and no end, pure bliss, pure experience of indescribable perfect 'being', continued for another 20 minutes as I lay down. I was aware of time but not existing in it. I was aware that my mind could think and observe, like, "Ok, when do I get up to do the asanas?" This is the most perfect experience I have ever had, and I began to wonder when it would end. It didn't. I got up and did the asanas. The experience continued unabated. I did notice that as long as I kept surrendering what I was observing so my mind was not attaching to the experience, it continued with greater, expanding bliss.

After the round of asanas, I sat down to do the next 20-minute meditation. Thinking about it now, I surrendered within myself to places of consciousness I had never experienced. At the time, the pure bliss, pure awareness, pure experience continued unabated through the whole meditation. I knew I was never born and would never die. I lay down again.

The experience continued and after 20 minutes of laying down, my mind thought it was time to go down for breakfast; and I thought oh no, this experience will now end. I went down to the kitchen area of this farmhouse and started eating some cold cereal. I then became aware of my mind 'layering in' over the experience. My mind thought, OK just surrender, just let go and it will continue. I tried. It didn't work. The experience ended and has never recurred. I have transcended, BUT never again experienced what I have just described. Truth is that this description doesn't come close. The best way I can describe it is through Tagore's words, as follows:

> "When I go from hence, let this be my parting word, that what I have seen is unsurpassable. I have tasted of the hidden honey of this lotus that expands on the ocean of light, and thus I am blessed let this be my parting word. In this playhouse of infinite forms I have had my play and here have I caught sight of him who is formless. My whole body and my limbs have thrilled with his touch who is beyond touch; and if the end comes here, let it come - let this be my parting word." —**Rabindranath Tagore in 'Gitanjali'**

Paramahansa, Tolstoy, Bonhoeffer and thousands of mystics, saints and yogis have written about it for millennia, without the fancy language of either theoretical physics or religious dogma.

THE TM NEW JERSEY EXPERIMENT AND THE COURTS

About a year after the rounding experience, some upper-level TMers in the TM Movement, including one of their lawyers contacted me asking me to write an opinion memo on their chances of introducing TM into the New Jersey public school system. Maharishi, and the Movement leaders were gung-ho to have public school students initiated into TM. I was now a gung-ho TMer.

Their New Jersey lawyers had advised Maharishi and the leaders that if challenged, they would win the legal battle. The concern was that fundamentalist Christian parents would look into the essence of TM, and The Science of Creative Intelligence, and find this strange practice of meditation was religious, not scientific. When I got involved, the legal skirmishing had already begun. So, they sought my opinion which they didn't like.

I told them they would lose and wrote a lengthy memo. I explained that TM, the initiation process, and the mantra itself, seemed like a prayerful invocation, from what I had been told, to Hindu Gods. (Later, I learned that was my misunderstanding.) The initiation was clearly at least for me, a spiritual experience. I told them that a case could be made against them, that such a spiritual experience, if garbed in any traditional religious form of ritual, American courts would rule that it violated the "Establishment Clause" of the First Amendment. This would prohibit the State from pursuing actions and policies that tended to establish any particular religion.

I explained that the essence of religion derived from the Latin verb 'religare' meaning to 'bind back' the soul to God. I opined that TM constituted yoga, to unite the soul with God; and that the 'puja' itself in the initiation was an ancient, traditional Vedic procedure to allow the mind to experience God.

In my Unity experience, my soul was bound back to God. I experienced God.

TM argued correctly that all education is designed to acquaint the mind with higher levels of intelligence, higher levels of thinking, higher levels of consciousness. True. TM said their meditation practice was purely scientific. It was based on the scientific reality of how the mind really works; it naturally wants to go deeper into higher levels of consciousness and that TM merely provided a scientific technique, the mantra, to do it. All science, all religion, all education is supposed to do that. And TM achieves it. I agreed with TM, but I explained that American jurisprudence and

Christian culture was not ready for TM in the public schools. My opinion was that its origins appeared to be in the Hindu religion, and that TM's origins, initiation, and mantra would scare away any U.S. court, regardless of the truth!

In that time period American jurisprudence was not ready for Advaita Vedanta spirituality in our educational system. Instead, it has sunk deeper into secular materialism, emerging wokeism, transgenderism, and moral degeneracy. TM disregarded my advice, spent millions in legal fees and lost. My advice did not ingratiate me with them. *Malnak v. Yogi* is the case name. But years later they hired me to defend them. The truth is that Maharishi is correct. TM is a science which through formal, repeatable procedures, axiomatically produces the "kingdom of God within" as a science, not as religion. It is a convergence of science and spirituality if the latter, by natural law, produces transcendence. That folks, is the truth.

The founding fathers sought to prohibit any state sponsored religion. This was an outgrowth of centuries, since ancient Greek and Roman times, of governments murdering religionists who had beliefs contrary to those of governments. Classic examples include Romans feeding Christians to the lions, Constantine banning the Gnostics and Arians, and making Roman Catholicism the state-sponsored religion so that they united and fought under the banner of the Christian Cross to help Constantine win his war against Maxentius at the Battle of the Milvian Bridge.

So, we must separate church and state said the founding fathers to themselves and to a receptive public of mostly persecuted Protestants who had fled Europe: Amish, Mennonites, and Lutherans, to mention but a few.

Feeding one's non-conformist Christians to the lions was the strategy of choice in the Roman Empire. The New England villages' practice of burning witches, pre-Constitution, is another example closer to home. As the Roman Church expanded down through the centuries, killing its "heretics," like the Gnostic Cathars by burning them at the stake in the Albigensian Crusade, 1209–1229, became the strategy of choice to prove papal dominance and land control. Generally, within religious dogma each religion kills the members of the opposing religion, but labeling the other religion as the enemy is a convenient way of stealing property, lands and countries. Ireland is a good example of a Protestant Christian crusade led by Cromwell in the name of God to massacre the Irish Catholics, 1648–50, who were also Christians. The Elizabethan era (1558–1603), generally heralded as the Golden Age of English Monarchy and Shakespearean literature, followed by Cromwell's massacres, is especially illustrative in the annals of British so-called "Christianity," when genocidal massacres and individual murders became the weapon of choice for the "Crown." Even members of Shakespeare's maternal family were killed by Elizabethan Protestants. Cause and effect. As European Christian nations, especially England and France, warred throughout the Middle Ages, followed by both world wars, Christians genociding Christians became the norm—not exactly a "Christian" thing to do, n'est-ce pas?

Reality is that the so-called Christian European, Empire building nations had all become the Sanhedrin money changers, controlled by the centralized Jewish banking empires like the Rothschilds.

Paradoxically as science and the dynamism of human consciousness gradually merge together, where quantum physicists strive to uncover a unified field, explore the boundaries of quantum entanglement and super determinism, isolate the Higgs Boson, or decipher the God Equation in string theory—methods like Transcendental Meditation (TM) are poised to deepen our grasp of consciousness in a way that transcends religious frameworks, including even Advaita Vedanta. Maybe meditation will replace war??

If science endorsed meditation as a technique to understand and evolve human consciousness, when the legal issues arise again, cases like *Malnak v. Yogi* could reach a different result. Humans are evolving, and the acceleration of that process does appear to be greatly enhanced with meditation.

The next closest experience in my life after transcendence, but in an entirely different dimension of reality to me, would be falling in love with my wife Laima, and having children. That involves human love on this planet, which is not remotely close to the unity experience, but an experience of what real human love is.

First, the Unity experience far surpassed any typical human emotion, including the divine aspect of loving Laima...the mental, emotional, and feeling components of that love. As we all know, human love is transient and frequently depends on external factors, changing environments, fluctuating emotions, and even stray thoughts leading to the inevitable ebb and flow of falling in and out of love. Even when that love embodies the most divine qualities ("what God has joined together, let no man put asunder"), it remains vulnerable to the highs and lows, joys and sorrows, loss and renewal that characterize the human journey. It's a universal experience.

Unity Consciousness, however, transcends duality. It does not depend on an object. It does not fluctuate. It is not subject to time or circumstance.

It is the ground of being itself, everlasting, unchanging. So, what is 'it', this Unity experience of no death? Here is the paradox: the very fact that I can speak of 'it' as something I experienced reveals that I am no longer in that state. The separation between the experiencer and the experience has returned. Language itself requires duality, a subject describing an object.

And yet, I did experience it. In that hour and a half in January 1978, 'I' dissolved into 'it', and there was no separation. The litigator, the meditator, the husband, the father, all gone. Only pure awareness remained, aware of itself, infinite and eternal.

I speak from direct experience. Whether you believe me or not, I can only report what I know to be true.

Much of my adult life and the impetus for this book centers on my clients' experiences within the context of my legal work, especially as these stories unfolded into courtroom dramas. In previous chapters, I briefly recounted the events surrounding the children rescued from the Wakefield fire, as well as the psychic elements involved in the disappearance and murder cases of Richard S. and Tom D. My perception of these cases, and the facts and events within them, became real for me only through the lens of my own consciousness. What I learned from the Unity experience is that the I exists in a state of consciousness distinct from the mind. In that experience, I observed my own thoughts from a heightened awareness more vivid than anything I had previously known. This wasn't due to any unusual quality on my part. "I'm nothing special", as ABBA sang, just a "bit of a bore." But I could try cases like Agnetha can sing.

But who is the 'I' that experienced Unity? Does the "I" exist if the brain and body are "dead." What is death? Does consciousness survive "death"? In my so called "Unity Consciousness" experience, "I KNOW," "I" had no beginning nor end. How to explain this phenomena? How to explain Sandra and Lester? How to explain how the "dots" have connected in many of my cases like the DeChristoforo father and son?

I turn to comparisons and analogies drawn from my own most significant adult experiences, particularly, my legal cases. Over decades, they have helped me gradually differentiate between my mind used in the intellectual challenges of litigation, and my being, whose deeper nature yearned for a return to "God," aka, a state of "consciousness" that exists in the mind and body, but survives both after death. Can levels of consciousness be detected in brain dead cases in the deepest level of "coma," and / or where people have been declared dead, as in the case of NDE's like

Dr. Alexander, then "returned to life"? What follows are three of my cases involving my early involvement in "consciousness" issues.

The later case of Sisi Smyly is covered at length in chapters 18 and 19; and thereafter in an NDE analysis. To get started, lets try three early cases.

SEVERAL CASES WITH QE CONSCIOUSNESS COMPONENTS

1: FRED – CONSCIOUSNESS IN COMA

Let's start with Fred. Fred was the manager of a K Mart. One night after work, his 16-year-old son on a driver's learning permit picked up Fred at work about 8 PM, drove about a mile, and drove into a tree. An accident. Fred had four broken ribs, but no other injuries. No neurological injury. His chest, not his head, absorbed the impact of the car hitting the tree. The problem was that two of the ribs were in front of his chest, and the other two were in the back, called anterior and posterior rib fractures, causing what is called 'flail chest'. This is a term the docs use to describe the instability of the chest wall; and the potential danger to lung puncture and the difficulty in the healing process of joining the fractured rib components together while trying to breathe normally.

Before ventilators were available, doctors would literally hang patients from hooks to prevent the chest wall from collapsing and puncturing the lung, allowing the ribs to heal. With the advent of respirators and ventilators, treatment changed; patients were sedated with muscle paralyzers like curare, which was originally used on the tips of poisonous arrows by indigenous people, and ventilators were used to regulate breathing. The CIA and KGB notoriously used curare on its targets. In the infamous case of one doctor who allegedly murdered his wealthy wife, he allegedly used curare, which can be undetectable in the blood. In the medical context for treatment of posterior and anterior rib fracture, it was used to prevent movement and patients were then placed on a respirator with a set tidal volume of air delivered through an endotracheal tube.

In Fred's case, they put him on a ventilator and gave him an intravenous muscle paralyzer to let the ventilator control his breath and chest movements. They dialed in what they thought the ventilator should deliver to Fred in each breath, which was 800 milliliters of air. As the night wore on, however, the resident on duty and the nurses noticed that Fred was having a difficult time and 'fighting' the ventilator. The types of machines used in this hospital were state-of-the-art and had alarms that would go off under different sets of circumstances if the patient was having breathing difficulties.

The problem was that the alarms were routinely sounding so the nurses commonly turned them off and relied on visual observation of the patients. Fred's alarms got turned off. It was unknown when the alarm was turned off. It was not in the nurses' notes or the respiratory therapist's notes. Of course this sounds suspicious, but perhaps the nurses were just covering themselves for turning off the alarms.

As the night wore on, Fred struggled so violently against the ventilator that the young resident on duty attributed his distress to anxiety and pain. In response, the resident prescribed increasingly larger doses of Pavulon, a synthetic curare, which the nurses administered through Fred's IV.

Ultimately, the resident gave Fred enough dope to paralyze a horse. The times and amounts of the Pavulon doses were in the nurses notes; BUT, neither the respiratory therapist nor nurses notes recorded anything about anyone manually checking the delivered tidal volume of air coming thru Fred's endotracheal tube.

Tragically, Fred was unable to breathe and went into a full scale respiratory incident, followed by cardiac arrest. A cardiologist responded to the Code 99, ordered the ventilator to be disconnected and checked, and began extreme measures to bring Fred back, but his brain had been deprived of oxygen for at least 5-7 recorded minutes from the supposed time of the onset of the respiratory arrest...likely longer. Fred was then in a Level 1 coma, some original twitching, but completely unresponsive to any external stimuli. He was seemingly devoid of cognitive function, or as the docs would claim at that time in the late 70's, 'lacking all responsive consciousness to external stimuli'...we'll come back to that shortly.

When the cardiologist ordered the ventilator disconnected and checked, problem solved: The disposable tube from the Puritan Bennet ventilator, which was functioning properly, to the trachea was leaking approximately 80% of the dialed in 800 ML tidal volume of air. BUT, there was no record given to the family about the leak, nor any record of any diagnosis of what caused Fred to go into respiratory and cardiac arrest?? HMMM...There was nothing in the medical records about the cause of his coma? There was no disclosure in the respiratory therapist's or nurses notes about the leak. The family was in the dark, the critical records were all concealed. Hmmm.

When Fred went into arrest with an oxygen deprived brain. Fred's wife and children were in shock the next morning but with no explanation. As his coma dragged on, the more questions they asked, but the less answers they received. The family gradually contacted their local lawyer and friend, who called my office. We ordered the records. Where is "the Incident Report" routinely made in coded incidents? Where is the medical explanation for Fred's condition? No explanation. No reference to severe hypoxia. No disclosure of the requisite, fully prescribed 800 ML of air, while Fred was getting less than 100 ML of air. No complete record of exactly how much Pavulon Fred had received? Suspicion mounted on the undiagnosed cause of Fred's coma?

How did this happen to Fred and his family? He was basically Ok after the accident, fully conscious, neurologically sound. He was in pain due to the broken ribs, but fully communicative with his wife and kids. Fully conscious! When the family saw Fred the morning after, he was in a diagnosed Level 1 coma, completely unresponsive to external stimuli, absent signs of any consciousness, with minimal EEG brain wave recording, but no disclosure of the leaking tube!

For the next 6 months their beloved husband and father was on a ventilator, feeding tubes, with minimal brain wave activity characteristic of the deepest level of coma and lack of consciousness – at least as the medical profession in the 1970's understood consciousness as solely a brain function. As the months wore on with no change in Fred's condition or diagnosis, the family was deciding whether the ventilator and feeding tubes should be disconnected to allow Fred to "die!

Check out Neurosurgeon, Dr. Eben Alexander's book: *Proof of Heaven*. It was a somewhat similar problem, but only 7 days in coma suffering from cerebral meningitis. There was no dysfunctional ventilator involved nor medical "mistakes." But Dr. Alexander was in a Level 1 coma with a "dead brain" – minimal brain waves on an EEG – decision needed by the family to let him "die." The ventilator was turned off, feeding and IV tubes disconnected. Eben 'wakes up' and says "hello everybody, I've been in "heaven.") (Chapter 21).

The doctors first hypothesized that Fred had 'stroked' from a previously undiagnosed, undocumented, unrecorded, undetected, brain injury immediately following the accident. Unmitigated rubbish. The family initially accepted as true whatever the docs and hospital told them, which is not unusual in the circumstances.

After some time of getting confusing even contradictory answers, they contacted the local family lawyer to request the medical records. This was mostly for the family to make decisions about continuing Fred on life support rather than them wanting to investigate. Their lawyer gradually became suspicious and contacted yours truly. I began reviewing the medical records, and noticed what I knew from experience in prior medical cases; there were gaps in the nurses' notes, gaps in the doctors' notes and no notes or reports from any staff member ordinarily charged with operating the ventilator. Per medical record protocols, these notes should have been in the medical records. There should have been an "Incident Report" on the Code 99. I followed up by requesting additional records. That's when everything truly began to unravel.

Somewhere in those initial inquiries, I learned there had been a "Code 99", a cardiac arrest, and an incident report on the whole sequence of events that night that was not contained in the medical records. Enter defense lawyers when I began to call the medical personnel on duty. Still no filed lawsuit. 'No, you cannot have the incident report." I instructed the family not to make any decision on Fred's life support yet as further investigation was needed. When I called the cardiologist, and called the Resident on duty who had moved to Arizona – no disclosure. They said the defense lawyers had instructed them not to speak with me.

I was stone-walled by the defense lawyers. It was becoming increasingly clear that the entire on-duty staff was concealing what really happened that night. The cardiologist was a legit guy, but when I directly contacted him and subsequently contacted several other staff, including the Resident in Arizona, and the very nervous respiratory therapist, all of whom had been shut up by the defense lawyer, who I knew from other cases, triggered the alarm bells in my consciousness, that it was time to play hard ball.

Meanwhile, Fred' life was hanging in the balance with no diagnosis and a family decision needed to let him die. I filed a lawsuit in Superior Court, Massachusetts. The litigation battle raged. Defense fought tooth and nail to prevent the incident report being seen, even though Fred lingered in an undiagnosed Level 1 coma. Amidst a confusing and contradictory landscape of case precedent, where some cases required disclosure of incident reports prepared in "anticipation of litigation" and others did not, the Court ruled that they must produce it. I explained that Fred' s life was hanging in the balance, decisions shutting off life support were needed to be made with no diagnosed cause of his Level 1 coma. The speculated brain injury / stroke made no sense and was not supported in the existing records. If there was anything in the undisclosed 'Incident Report" that would explain Fred's coma, and / or result in a specific diagnosis, it must be produced. The cases on medical records prepared in anticipation of litigation had no relevance because if the Report was made when the "incident" occurred, which the court made the defense admit, then no lawyers had been consulted, and the cited defense cases were not relevant.

To me, Fred's case in that time and place, resurrected the memory in my litigator consciousness, that my argument to the judge demanding the "Incident Report," while the defense fought to conceal it, reminded me of the previous Sandra and Lester case, but without the desperate emotional overtones. "I" saw that fight with the defense as a matter impacting Fred's life and death. It did. Once we discovered the cause of Fred's Level 1 coma as a result of the leaking ventilator tube causing an unknown period of severe hypoxia, after further neurological consultation continuing to reveal no discernible, specific brain trauma, the family decided to keep Fred alive!

When we soon uncovered the hypoxia and overdosed Pavulon causing Fred's arrest and subsequent coma, it led us to depose everyone involved under oath. To do this, I flew my Cessna 206 to Arizona, accompanied by Laima, who had been working on the case with me. During our trip, we even flew between the Grand Canyon walls, a thrilling experience which the FAA has now forbidden, but which makes the memory that much more unforgettable. The resident physician on duty that night at Fred's hospital bed had since relocated to Arizona but I needed to depose him. I felt compassion for him. He hadn't realized that the ventilator tube was leaking, causing 80% of the delivered tidal volume to escape. He mistook Fred's struggle against the ventilator for pain and anxiety and increased the intravenous dosage of Pavulon, the muscle paralyzer, while Fred became increasingly hypoxic fighting for his breath and life. Since the heart and lungs are muscles, this caused them to shut down, leading to Fred's cardiac arrest. Needless to say, he was devastated.

The whole sorry, tragic, saga of cover up was exposed. There was no detectable brain injury from the accident. Fred's heart was in good shape. The cardiac arrest deprived his brain of oxygen and resulted in a coma from too much Pavulon and too little tidal volume of oxygen. The underlying problem was that Fred couldn't breathe.

Quantum Entangled Note: In TM meditation, which was my disciplined meditation practice at that time, during Fred's case, the breath, the observation of the breath in the mind, the allowance of the mind and body to permit the mind and body to transcend the breath and ascend into a "breathless state" is a physical goal of meditation. Same with Kriya Yoga. As explained by Maharishi and Yogananda, in the breathless state, the mind, and body transcend into Samadhi where the union of the soul with God takes place. Yogananda explains in specific cases that the nature of consciousness is such that in Samadhi the body can be sustained in a breathless state for long periods of time – without external life support – without an external breathing apparatus, like a ventilator! Quantum entangled consciousness energy comes into the brain from an external field of consciousness.

"I," your humble scribe, have experienced the breathless state – infrequently - the longest for an estimated 10 – 20 minutes; and generally after a long period of meditation, and "rounding." According to Yogananda, "prana" can sustain the body through the medulla oblongata at the base of the skull. The Unity Consciousness experience that "I" had lasted for about an hour and a half, during which "I" was not aware of my breathing. I might have been breathing but "I" do not recall being conscious of it? I now believe that the Unity experience, very simply, is the soul uniting with God.

Fred had been in an hypoxic induced coma without sufficient air while overdosed with Pavulon. His lungs, a huge muscle, ceased to function resulting in cardiac arrest. It is universally accepted in medicine that oxygen deprivation for 5 – 7 minutes causes cardiac arrest and death. After his "incident", Fred was in coma for six months. I explained to the family my TM meditation practice, and that somehow, the breathless state, experienced by Yogi's for long periods of time, seemed to defy conventional hypoxic induced brain death. In Fred's case, once his hypoxic episode was disclosed, further neurologic evaluation, and testing took place. The Doctors still thought Fred was "brain dead" with minimal EEG resonance.

Decisions were needed to be made on Fred's continuing coma, life support, and his oxygen deprived episode for some unknown amount of time. But he was getting at least 100 ML of air when he arrested. Over the 6 months that this tragedy unfolded with the truth, Fred had begun to show some neurological responses, but no "cognitive motor function" where the brain processes cause observable physical response. The family and I began to talk to him and explain in his ear what was happening. More responses. More progress and some movement.

At some point, the doctors had previously approved the termination of ventilator support but the family said no. During that same period we had obtained the court order to get the incident report which uncovered the truth of what had actually happened. After this, strange events occurred in sequence. It was as if Fred had been hanging on until we uncovered the truth of what had happened to him.

Once we obtained the incident report, Fred gradually began to emerge from coma. How does one explain that specific correlation of events? I see it now as a QE experience.

After his coma, Fred did not report the experiences of the normal NDEers like the tunnel of light, life review, sage old men in white robes and beards, Heaven, and choices of returning to life or not, as now almost universally reported by those who have gone through near-death experiences. But I wonder now in light of subsequent cases and events whether Fred just didn't tell us? Many NDEers, including my dad, after his plane accident in which he experienced an NDE, had deep and enduring reluctance to inform others. See Brinkley, *Saved By The Light*. I met him for dinner, and he told me he was also fearful people would think he was nuts. Dr. Alexander and others have expressed similar feelings.

As for Fred, I don't know. My memory of discussions with him suggest now that he didn't want to tell us whether or not he wanted to stay where he was, in coma, or return to his family. He did report awareness in the coma, he had consciousness of intermittent nightmares. He said that some part of him was watching and experiencing the nightmares which were involving fear, and concern for his wife and family. Fred was conscious in a Level 1 coma. Dr. Eben Alexander remarks that nightmares in NDE cases are actually incomplete NDEs.

The case settled. The manufacturer of the leaking endotracheal tube was a primary part of the settlement. The family was paid a large amount of money. Fred got better and better, gradually restoring partial use of his limbs.

The consciousness lesson for me: Fred in a Level 1 coma was conscious.

This evidence prompted me to dig deeper, leading to further research and, years later, discussions with clients, scientists and meditator / physicists about the force field said to surround us as humans. One of them described collaborations with a Belgian neuroendocrinologist, focusing on meditating yogis who could access this field during meditation. At the time, it struck me as similar to the advanced stages of Transcendental Meditation. I propose that this force field is, in fact, consciousness itself, the stage where quantum entanglement takes place. It was this field that kept Fred alive in his coma, and God, present within it, that brought him back to his family. Today, thousands of near-death experiencers recount similarly transformative encounters.

Fred's case objectively highlights the divide between my I...the litigating mind I use to navigate the world, and my deeper being, the essence that seeks departure from the physical realm and a return to spirit. In his coma, I now see him as being in both dimensions, offering a profound reminder of this duality within us all.

CASE 2: ANN M: CONSCIOUSNESS WITH BRAIN STROKE

In the case of Ann M v Dr. Neurosurgeon X, different facts involving different "medical mistakes" occurred involving the brain. Ann M suffered from an "acoustic neuroma", a non-malignant, rapidly growing tumor in the 8th cranial nerve which is the ear canal into the brain. She was a mid-forties, vibrant woman, who began to experience headaches and other clinical symptoms. Ultimately, Ann was referred to Dr. X, a highly credentialed neurosurgeon from one of Massachusetts's most highly regarded hospitals. Dr. X scheduled surgery for a Friday morning. That same afternoon he was scheduled to depart on his large sailing yacht to participate in the famous Newport to Bermuda sailing race.

Surgery was uneventful. The tumor was removed. In this type of surgery, the medical protocols at that time dictated the need to drill a hole through the bony skull into the sac in the middle of the brain and insert a "ventricular peritoneal shunt". The purpose of this procedure was proactive to relieve intracranial pressure as the invaded tissues from the surgery tended to inflame, give off fluids, and increase pressure within the brain that could cause stroke. The sac in the brain, given the confines of the bony skull surrounding the brain, is designed to accept and relieve pressure before the brain 'strokes'. The shunt is designed to drain off excess fluid and prevent increased intracranial pressure.

Dr. X drilled the hole through the skull, inserted the shunt, and took off on his sailing trip. Before leaving, he ordered a CT scan of the brain area he worked on. He left a resident in charge of Ann and before the CT scan results were reported by the radiologist. The shunt never made it into the ventricle sac. This failure was recorded but not reported on the CT scan until the next day. Too late. That night, Ann's brain blew up from rapidly increasing intracranial pressure. Ann stroked and was mostly vegetative with limited cognitive motor function and confined to a wheelchair.

The family sued. The defense first concealed, then fought over the production of the CT scan – ring a bell on the Fred "Incident Report." Doctor X refused to settle notwithstanding the ultimately produced CT scan. He and his lawyer, whom I had also tangled with in several cases – a very good trial lawyer - aggressively fought over the production of the scan and report. The litigation alone to obtain it, suggested more medical concealment that showed that the shunt never got into the ventricle sac. The case went to the jury after six weeks of intense trial. The defense relied in part on the technical defenses of waivers. Ann had signed pre-surgery waivers of any liability for malpractice by the doctors or the hospital. The doctor was intransigent, essentially testifying that liability for such mistakes were assumed and waived by the patient. It was brain surgery after all.

The jury did not like his arrogance, nor his leaving Ann for his yacht race before seeing the CT results. The jury did not know that the defense had first concealed the CT scan; and it took a prolonged legal battle, like Fred's incident report, to get it. The scan and report were shown to the jury and explained to them by our medical doctor expert witness. I called the arrogant Doctor defendant to the witness stand in the plaintiff's case, and placed the scan in front of him and on the overhead projector so the jury could clearly see that the shunt never made it into the ventricle sac. We physically passed the CT scan report among the jurors with Dr. X on the witness stand. He bobbed and weaved, waffled, evaded the questions, was instructed to answer, but refused to admit what the jury could see. The shunt never made it into the ventricle. His defense – brain surgery – anything can happen

During jury deliberations after weeks of trial, the defense insurance carrier kept increasing its settlement offers. Doctor X had previously refused permission to have them settle. Pre-trial, there were no offers. The defense was seemingly unmoved with Ann lingering in her semi-cognitive, wheelchair bound condition. As the trial progressed, increasing settlement offers were made. During deliberations, they shot up into the millions, but a long way from what I thought the jury would award. Ann had to be taken care of for life.

The family pressured me during jury deliberations to take the highest offer, which was far less than what I thought the jury would award. My partners also pressured me. I spoke to Ann throughout, trying to discern her ability to make a decision. The level of her conscious decision-making was at issue. She had a childlike trust in me. Ouch, responsibility for the client's decision shifted to me. Throughout the years of pretrial discovery, the retention of expert medical witnesses, and throughout the trial, Ann deferred to my judgment, trusting like a child does with his or her parents. As the jury deliberated, I spent hours with Ann trying to decide what to do, and her conscious ability to make a decision apart from me or her family. She always deferred to me. It was heart wrenching.

My consciousness was impacted by the intractable ego - driven consciousness of Dr. X; and the deeply embedded conflict within me involving my ego and "soul consciousness." Between Ann, Doctor X, the jurors, the judge, the defense lawyers, myself and my partners, I could not discern a "collective consciousness" on the right thing to do as the defense increased their offers? Part of me said that a jury verdict would vastly exceed the offers.

The amount of any jury verdict would have a huge impact on Ann's life, future medical care, support, and lifestyle. The financial recovery was critical to any decision on acceptance of a settlement amount, pre-verdict. This is why our jurisprudence provides for civil damages. Where else does the money come from to rectify the wrong? The amount of the recovery was patently a major issue to Ann, her family's support, and to my entire firm who had worked so hard for years on her case on a contingent fee basis. But Ann was like a child. I was conflicted. Unlike the Dwyer and Sequeira cases where the full insurance was recovered, even with a conflicted jury in Dwyer, I wanted a verdict.

The family and my partners prevailed. "I" caved in and we settled without a verdict. The case settled during jury deliberations. The judge was honorable throughout, and then at the end did a very unusual thing. She asked both us and the defense if we would agree to bring the jury into her conference room and to poll them as to where they were in their deliberations. All sides agreed. I think she knew that we settled too low.

The polling showed: 16 jurors (there were 4 alternates empaneled) were in the process in deliberations of awarding a minimum of $30 million up to about $40 million. There was one juror, a young man, an alternate, who was determined to vote defense. When questioned by the judge, he said: "I don't think people should be suing their doctors". In pre-trial voir dire questions, I had asked if he could sit on a jury in which a patient was suing their doctor, and if the evidence established negligence, could he vote for an award to the patient. He had said that he could do it. Now he said he had changed his mind after studying malpractice case histories during the case, which he had been specifically instructed not to do!

Ann's case, against my inclinations, settled for a fraction of where the jury was going. But still, to a lesser degree, she was taken care of financially for life. Justice?

At the time I thought I had won the case through skill—through preparation, strategy, expert witnesses, and the work of my partners, and persuasive argument. My ego was fully engaged. I believed I was the doer, the architect of victory. That may be why I settled before the verdict: I wanted to lock in the win, to control the outcome, to avoid the risk of losing at trial.

But I was wrong. My judgment failed me. I should have waited for the verdict.

As the trial lawyer, I was not the doer. The case wasn't won by my skill, nor by sympathy, nor the great work of my partners, particularly Bill Sheridan and Mike Tabb. Juries are explicitly instructed to disregard sympathy, but it is like telling them to disregard a blizzard while walking in it. The settlement, viewed as a victory during jury deliberations wasn't even won by the strength of our medical evidence, though our experts testified that the CT scan clearly showed the shunt had failed to reach the ventricle sac.

Maybe a large jury award would have decimated Dr. X's ego, and blown up mine? Maybe my blown up ego would have been very displeasing to a God demanding humility in his children. The collective consciousness of the jury deciding to render a huge verdict was probably correct; and my failure to grasp that collective consciousness was incorrect. Bad judgment. In later cases with large verdicts, several in this book, my consciousness became quantum entangled with jury collective consciousness, and we held out for a verdict

The defense mounted formidable counter-arguments: Ann had signed multiple waivers. They argued causation – the norm in medical cases – that she would have suffered the stroke regardless of proper shunt placement, that the misplacement was not the proximate cause of her condition – a common causation defense in medical cases. They emphasized the inherent risks of neurosurgery, suggesting that bad outcomes don't equal malpractice. These were legitimate defenses. Many juries would have ruled for the doctor.

So what tipped the scales? The Doctor's intractable ego consciousness? Taking off on his yacht? Sympathy for Ann sitting in that wheel chair with decreased cognitive motor function? I concluded that the most dominating factor in that case was an unknown intangible, which to this day, I don't fully grasp. I include it in this book because in my meditative efforts to find truth and justice in my cases, I KNOW that truth was achieved in Ann's case but it was diminished justice. A large dollar verdict would have represented collective consciousness jury justice. Neither the arguments of myself or defense counsel, nor even the medical evidence on the misplaced shunt, explains why we settled without a verdict. Maybe it was the consciousness of Ann herself, resonating within the consciousness of her family who strongly advocated settlement. A loss would have meant their care for Ann without financial resources.

As a man thinketh in his heart, so is he. Jury verdicts illustrate that collective truth. The fears, desires, egos, ambitions, etc of a litigator can enhance jury consciousness or interrupt it.

Ann had the consciousness of an innocent child: no anger, no resentment, no agenda for money, just pure innocence and a surrendered soul. Although her cognitive faculties were measurably impaired, this left her consciousness unsullied by ego or calculation, what the yogis call "mind stuff." Her consciousness functioned fully, perhaps even more clearly, outside of her impaired cognitive faculties.

She touched the hearts of fifteen of the sixteen jurors. They didn't just understand her damages, they felt them through quantum entanglement. Her essence communicated directly with theirs, and they responded with justice. The jury understood it, felt it, knew it, and related to her on that level. It was a lesson I missed at the time attributing that her condition would win sympathy with the jury, notwithstanding the judge's instruction not to do that.

When we questioned them in the judge's conference room post settlement, they said their deliberations were not based on sympathy. They had properly evaluated the evidence, the doctor and Ann. Their consciousness on those factors guided their deliberations. Most of them said that they didn't buy into the defense causation positions, but that they just knew something had gone terribly wrong, and the catastrophe should never have happened

It was similar to Fred's case in several critical respects. A major medical mistake, first covered up in the concealment of the CT scan, then truth emerging like a gift from God.

My litigation experience in almost every type of case from those medical cases, to the previously reported cases, including Sandra and Lesters, Sequeira, Dwyer, and subsequent cases in these books is that a litigator must fight very, very hard for the truth, often against all sorts of devilish, defense tactics. In the cult cases reported in *Litigator 2* and in the Blixseth cases covered in *Litigator 4*, defense tactics range from concealment of evidence, paying off the judge and even criminal operations designed to destroy one's opponent including the lawyer.

Ann's consciousness, far greater than her diminished cognitive motor function, coupled with the doctor's self-righteous mind projecting arrogance, devoid of the type of consciousness we as humans intrinsically relate to, is likely what won the jury. Ann and enough jurors functioned on the same wavelength of consciousness. Emotion takes place in consciousness, but consciousness is infinitely more powerful in jury cases than emotion.

I can't describe consciousness, except to describe my own experiences and to compare cases and use analogies, comparisons, and experiences. One thing is for sure, it's bigger than our mind's ability to grasp. Much bigger.

I consider the synthesized or collective consciousness of the jury, to be a sacred event.

At the time of that trial, my 'I' comprised my litigator ego. Now 'I' see the entire case as Ann's surrender to her 'being' in her return to God. That was the higher level of reality in that case.

CASE 3: THE AIR FORCE COLONEL AND HIS WIFE – A MOTHER'S CONSCIOUSNESS

This is the story of a 'religious' Air Force Colonel and his even more religious wife. Embedded in the wife's religion was a mother's consciousness to protect the baby in her womb. Her consciousness enveloped in a mother's love – perhaps the highest form of consciousness in our species – screams against abortion.

The Colonel called me one day "Hi Mike, my name is Colonel …., a mutual friend, Phil, also a colonel in the Air Force, referred me to you. My wife's case has been with the F Lee Bailey firm there in Boston for some time, but nothing seems to be happening. Will you look at it?"

I tentatively agreed and then had a face to face meeting with the Colonel and his still grieving wife. It was about two years after the case arose. She had a history of Spina Bifida in her family so during her pregnancy, she was closely monitored and tested for it at the Wilford Hall Medical Center in Texas where he was stationed. Four months into her pregnancy the purported test came back positive for Spina Bifida. If I remember correctly, at least two tests were conducted between the 16th and 20th weeks of her pregnancy: a blood test; and an amniocentesis. There may also have been a sonogram, but I don't recall.

The doctors recommended an abortion. She was strongly, and religiously opposed to the suggestion. She cried, grieved, consulted her Pastor, sought psychiatric counseling, and prayed. Every instinct in her consciousness said 'no, I will not abort my baby'. The doctors, her husband, and at least one of her counselors strongly advised her to have an abortion "for the sake of the child." She did it.

A male fetus came out, which she observed to be normal at the time of the abortion. Her observation was not necessarily conclusive, although she emphatically and very emotionally said her baby was normal. She questioned the doctors who said and put in her medical records that the fetus had Spina Bifida.

In the depths of her consciousness, she didn't believe it. She also stated that at certain times her baby was communicating with her, telling her that he was normal! Her husband began to worry that her unrelenting grief would affect her mental stability so he consulted Bailey's office to seek a resolution for her. He requested her medical records and agreed to investigate further, but despite this initial interest, the matter remained unresolved and stagnant for nearly two years.

When they came to me, the grief-stricken mother broke down several times, sobbing as she described her conviction that her baby was communicating with her. The husband appeared somewhat apologetic, yet quietly protective of his wife. I set about collecting all the hard evidence available, including her detailed observations regarding the aborted fetus and any relevant medical records they could provide.

Initially, I hesitated to get involved, a response much like my initial reaction to the Sandra and Lester case. Another law firm was already involved. In my experience very distraught clients can sometimes obscure the clinical picture, making it more difficult to discern the hard evidence. That was my honest, professional reaction at the time. I sensed that the mother's emotional upheaval was compounded by her having an abortion that violated her religious beliefs, while the husband, for his part, was simply doing his best to support her under impossible circumstances.

The grief of the mother for her aborted child dominated the entire matter, even more than any objective evidence that the Spina Bifida tests were incorrect, and that the baby was in fact, normal. The couple had no record of any autopsy on the fetus but had a pathology report suggesting that visual observation of the fetus confirmed the original test results. This contradicted the wife's visual observation. The pathology report appeared to be dated some considerable time after the date of the abortion. I thought that was odd and asked the wife about it. She said that she had asked the doctor treating her during her pregnancy for a report several days after the abortion because she believed the baby was normal and that he had later obtained it from the pathologist who signed it. The amniocentesis and blood tests appeared conclusive when I checked with my expert.

Laima's reaction mirrored her response in the 'burning hand' case involving the three teenagers deaths, indicating she wanted me to take on the case and delve into the matter. Her goal was to at least soothe the couple's anguish and bring some resolution to the mother's grief by reaching the definitive conclusion that the baby indeed did have Spina Bifida, the very issue that the Bailey firm seemed to be probing. Like the previous case, initially I believed I was wasting my time heading down a rabbit hole with little chance of clinical success, and much less chance of establishing legitimate legal claims. Nonetheless, I again trusted Laima's intuition and had the couple sign releases and waivers to access all pertinent medical records.

I called the doctor who signed the pathology report. He said he didn't remember the matter and may have routinely prepared it based on the records. He had never in fact seen the fetus and suggested I should contact the treating physician who may have more information. He became evasive and then refused to discuss the matter further. Hmmm. That got me interested.

We took the case and began taking depositions of all involved. It became clear that there was a cover-up, that in fact the aborted baby was normal, that somehow the pathology report was fabricated outside normal medical record-keeping protocols, and that the Colonel and his wife were in fact given the test results of another couple!

In tracking down the other couple, we found out that the mother had given birth to a Spina Bifida baby and been given my clients' test results which were normal! The whole matter had such serious and unequivocal consequences for all involved. The Air Force doctors had covered it all up and had been caught doing so.

Circa 1979, the case settled. A strange event occurred. Remarkably, I received a phone call from the then army colonel / brigadier general, Colin Powell. He was then in the office of the Secretary of Defense, not a military lawyer? He said, and I quote: "It looks like there have been some shenanigans in this matter and I would like to settle it between us right now on this phone call." We did.

The discussion focused on the "shenanigans;" and the "monetary" value of the unborn, three-month fetus at issue, as repeatedly occurred in my later cases, some explained in this book - like some mystical instruction by an outer force field against abortion? Also at issue with colonel / general

Powell was the value of the family loss? The value of the mother's grief, pain sorrow and loss of companionship with her baby then in the first trimester? Tough questions in an environment of routine abortions after *Roe v Wade*, 1973.

I don't know if my client, an Air Force colonel, discussed the matter with his superiors??

The consciousness lesson: The basic reality in this particular case was not the visual observation of the mother immediately after the baby was aborted, because in a Spina Bifida birth, visual observation of the aborted fetus may be useless and inconclusive. It was the mother's consciousness that dictated the end result. On some level of consciousness...she knew that she should not have aborted her baby! And the case involved yet another medical cover-up of evidence.

Many of the world's scriptures, including the Bible and the Bhagavad Gita, state that truth always ultimately prevails over falsehood, and good over evil. That has been my experience, but mostly, only after severe stress, griefs, and trials, and a body count. But the battle must be endured, no matter the consequences and / or the result. THAT is the essence of the Gita, the Battle of Kurukshetra, Krishna's advice to Arjuna, and the crucifixion of Christ. We must endure human injustices and suffering to return home to God.

Somehow, in the face of two positive clinical test results and overriding pressure to abort the baby, the mother knew her baby was normal, and that she had gone against her conscience and her consciousness. It resulted in inconsolable grief and a shocking result not only for her, but for the other couple who had actually given birth to a Spina Bifida baby. They learned that their intense misfortune had been manipulated into causing intense grief in another couple's life.

It seemed clear to me that my clients, the Colonel and I were operating mostly on an ego level, applying logic, training, and a desire for control. His wife, by contrast, moved from a place entirely different; a deeply emotional, intuitive space where her consciousness sought to connect to her baby as a 'knower' in her maternal being. Whether or not the baby was truly communicating with her is something that of course can't be proven scientifically one way or the other. My experiences in consciousness tell me it is likely. The wife was a smart, compelling, but very emotional witness. In many other cases, I have seen grief like this particularly in child death cases. It is a grief deeply lodged within human consciousness, especially in the maternal instincts of a parent, and beyond the reaches of normal comprehension.

This case, along with others throughout my career, has profoundly shaped my consciousness, stirring in me a deep awareness of life's inherent sacredness. I recognize that abortion is an extraordinarily difficult and morally complex choice; one of the most challenging dilemmas humans face, weighing profound loss against difficult circumstances. I personally see it as a monumental evil at the extreme end of human atrocities, and contrast this with the way the 'service' of abortion is supplied in the sterilized manner of pulling a tooth. I also believe that our consciousness, if we trust and remain attentive, can serve as a guiding light, helping us navigate these morally challenging areas with compassion and discernment.

Above all the foregoing considerations, getting closer to the "evil" scale on abortions, is the pharmaceutical industry paying for late term abortions to extract the heart and brains of a fetus. Although characterized by the pharmaceutical industry as a "conspiracy theory," RFK Jr. interviewed a doctor working for a pharmaceutical company that paid premiums to extract the hearts and brains of "babies" in late term abortions. The interview as posted on You Tube and later banned. Recommend research into the final years of David Rockefeller who died at 101 in 2017.

DR. RICHARD B.: A CASE STUDY IN CONSCIOUSNESS AND EVIL

Next up on the consciousness lessons: Dr. Richard B was a highly acclaimed Harvard Medical school and Mass General Hospital (McLean) psychiatrist. He was also a fall-down drunk married to Mary (name change). There were three cases involving his life and death. First, his premature death at age 41. Richard was suffering from severe alcohol withdrawal and delirium tremens. He was admitted to BHF, an alcohol rehab facility. After several days there, during the night he fell out of his hospital bed, fractured his skull and sustained a subdural hematoma, which is a bleed within the brain generally resulting from a traumatic blow to the head which was undiagnosed after the fall. He was simply placed back in his bed.

That same night, he died from the hematoma. Medical protocols call for close monitoring, immediate diagnosis and drilling into the skull at the site of the hematoma to drain off the bleeding and relieve the rapidly increasing intracranial pressure.

The medical staff at BHF did nothing to Richard after he fell and struck his head, just put him back into bed. Same old story. Altered and concealed medical records, cover-up by the nursing staff and intense investigation by my firm, exposing the whole cover-up and failure to diagnose, treat and care for Richard. The case was filed in federal court, settled within a year after intense investigation and discovery. Mary received millions of dollars for her deceased husband.

Justice? You are the jury. Richard, a full-fledged "western trained" medical doctor exclusively using drugs to treat his alcohol and drug addicted patients, while decrying "spiritual" based modalities like AA, became a victim of his own drug treatment plans for his patients. Some might say that Richard's addiction, along with his self-prescribed drug treatment for himself, was self-caused so why should his widow profit from it? But alcohol rehab facilities, where Richard died from their negligent care and altered records to conceal their negligence, make millions of dollars on treating and purportedly rehabbing their "patients" with more drugs when the best "medicine" might be AA, which Richard opposed?

Modern jurisprudence prescribes "tort" remedies for negligence by an entity or individual who owe a "duty of care" to their victim. Where there is a wrong, there is a remedy. A duty of care arises when laws prohibit certain misconduct – like running a red light; or where an entity like an alcohol / drug rehab facility holds itself out as offering a certain quality of care to make money off the addiction.

Like rehab facilities for addiction, senior living facilities have sprouted up around the world making fortunes off their elderly "patients," while plaintiffs' lawyers sue them for negligent care when their patients are injured or killed as a result of violations of the "duty of care" owed to their victims.

Right? Wrong? What else to do? How to regulate the misconduct of a profit motivated entity, often masquerading as a non-profit? Government regulation is susceptible to bureaucratic incompetence and / or pay off spawning more lawsuits against the government who claim immunity so no "justice" is ever achieved? What is justice for an individual who causes his own deep-seated misbehavior arising from an addictive lifestyle. There are laws for "contributory negligence" by individuals who cause their own damages, injury or death, like an individual who runs a yellow light, who could have stopped, but is hit by a drunk driver who accelerates as the light turns green.

Is the game of law and justice purely monetary? How does money compensate for loss of a loved one who created an addictive lifestyle when negligently killed by someone or something else? In truth it cannot. But if legal and societal standards are violated in a case, what else is there?

Should there be some recognition of the violations? Some recompense for it? Since the loved one is dead, there is no monetary need for them. But for a surviving spouse and family dependent on the decedent's income, of course, money becomes a major factor in a jury award.

THE CONSCIOUSNESS LESSON:

The reason this case is in this book is that Richard was a highly educated, successful and practicing clinical psychiatrist, one of the "Outstanding Young Men of America" in 1968, who subscribed to a materialistic drug consciousness, in the diagnosis and treatment of his patients based on drug therapies. He did not subscribe either personally or professionally to a spiritual consciousness for either a clinical diagnosis or treatment modalities for his patients outside of drug therapies. His professional success was followed by severe alcohol addiction. Sound familiar?

The law measured Richard's value in his death estate case brought by his widow based on his income production, which was substantial as a highly acclaimed doctor of psychiatry. His alcoholism served as a factor in diminishing his future projected income, but his past income was the primary foundation for the future projection of his lost income as a highly successful 41-year-old medical doctor. His alcoholism led to his BHF admission, which led to his death. People go to the hospital or in this case an alcohol rehab facility to get healed, not get killed.

Once again, this case presented a significant question of causation. Some might argue, "Richard was a confirmed alcoholic; he would have died eventually." This perspective not only challenges the causation of his actual death, but also the perceived value of his life. I have often contemplated the difference between human and divine justice. Human justice recognizes a 'duty of care' owed by everyone to everyone else, especially by corporations, and of course including treatment facilities for severe alcoholism. For example, the duty of care is applied to every driver of every car on the road to follow the laws of the road. In the realm of divine justice, perhaps we never definitively know...only God knows what is true and just, but I think I have some inkling of when God has intervened in human affairs to obtain some form of justice.

Dr. Richard B's trained, clinical mind had all the educational tools for professional success according to modern precepts of psychiatry. His psychiatric assessments of his patients were entirely based on a scientific analysis of how the mind functioned from observable data. He made his clinical assessments and treatment with drugs entirely devoid of any recognition of God, or higher powers, spirituality, or the personal responsibility of his patients. Like many clinical psychiatrists of that era, he did not accept spiritual consciousness as a diagnostic factor in his drug related therapies. That, coupled with raw ambition, in my opinion, is what led to his addiction. Richard's medical training stated that alcoholism is a disease, suggesting that the individual is not responsible for his or her condition, but I think that is nonsense.

The "Twelve Step" program of Alcoholics Anonymous is spiritually based, founded on the essence of consciousness, recognition of a higher power beyond the mind, and the absolute necessity of taking personal responsibility for one's addiction, in order to escape one's own addiction - responsibility and accountability to one's own conscience and consciousness. All these factors increase the consciousness needed to deal with the addiction.

Richard's clinical assessments of his patients and himself did not involve any of the fundamental elements of consciousness such as awareness that the mind is controlled by consciousness, which by nature, must acknowledge and adhere to the precepts of a higher power governing human existence. Failure to understand this leads to addiction and unnatural lifestyles. We see it all around us now in the 'woke'/ homosexual / transgender culture. Richard's addiction to manmade therapies – drugs, coupled with rejection of a higher consciousness, caused Richard's addiction which killed him.

In Richard's case, like many of such cases, the medical profession lied, cheated, and covered up their mistakes. True, conscious recognition by Richard of his own mistakes, failings, flaws and "sins" would probably have prevented a sequence of them in the first place. True conscious realization by Richard on the "cause" of his addiction might have led to his healing of it. Self-reflection is a powerful antidote to one's own mistakes.

Failure to self-reflect for one's own accountability may be the lowest level of human behavior that the medical profession in our society makes vast amounts of money on? Take these drugs, here's my bill, and if something bad happens, call 911. Richard would have been better served seeking psychiatric treatment himself and adhering to the experiences and teachings of another clinical psychiatrist: M. Scott Peck. In 1978, Dr. Peck published his ten-year work in progress of treating patients with clinically observable mental disorders: *The Road Less Traveled: A New Psychology of Love, Traditional Values and Spiritual Growth.*

Although the Peck book was first published during the period of Richard's BHF treatment, the psychiatric profession had been wrestling with The Twelve Step Program, which for decades mandated reliance on God and personal responsibility. Richard was aware that Dr. Peck's assessments and treatments of mental disorders founded in spirituality and traditional values were gaining increasing traction, but little acceptance in psychiatric journals.

Such healing modalities involved exactly what Dr. Peck's title later conveyed. Any legitimate clinical psychiatrist, throughout the 60's and 70's, unless they lived under a rock, and never actually saw patients, knew that the Twelve Step program was founded on using a higher power to treat addiction as opposed to the 'oh it's a disease, prescribe drugs' diagnostic approach.

Big Pharma has a business model that is inherently evil, driven by profit not a desire to heal, and often acts unethically. Richard, a cog in this wheel, overlooked the role of consciousness in healing mental illness, including his own. He remained attached to disease-centered approaches that relied almost solely on medication.

In 1983, Dr. Peck wrote *People of the Lie: The Hope for Healing Human Evil.* I'm sure you'll agree that is a pretty incredible title for a book by a clinical psychiatrist in the 1970-2000 period of psychiatric miasma led by Big Pharma! The profession at the time did not like the term evil, with all it's spiritual connotations. But stay tuned, in later books, you, dear reader, will encounter Hubbard and his "Church of Scientology," "The Beach Boys" case, the Kriyananda / Ananda case, the Tim Blixseth case. These are all clinical courtroom studies in human 'evil'.

Several of the later cases in this book analyze underlying causation to understand human law and justice when measured against divine law and justice. It is likely that obedience to the Ten Commandments prescribes a cure for human misconduct degenerating into evil. In my representation of many clients like Monica Lewinsky in grasping the inveterate evil of the Clintons, or representing Tim Blixseth in grasping the evil of bribed judges, the ultimate analysis is simple - overt violations of the law and degenerate violations of the Ten Commandments by individuals like the Clintons, Jeffrey Epstein, L. Ron Hubbard. "Swami Kriyananda" and many of my opponents, etc constitute the cause of societal decay which we currently observe.

If you have any lingering doubt, I strongly recommend Dr. Jordan Peterson, his books and podcasts, on the subject of psychological evil, along with the works of M. Scott Peck. They expose and explain the psychological factors that "People of the Lie" suffer from, that makes them transmit their evil to those around them through transmitted wrong doing and degenerate behavior. In the context of my cases it equates to quantum entanglement on a negative scale.

DR. B'S INSURANCE FRAUD CASE

Richard's death was also linked to a second case involving judicial corruption. His life insurance carrier refused to pay out, arguing that Richard had overtly lied on his application by concealing his struggle with alcoholism. This was within two years before his death, the statutory termination period for the carrier.

The application contained standard questions regarding alcohol use, substance abuse history, prior medical treatment, and hospitalizations. Richard provided false answers to all material questions, and actively attempted to conceal medical records documenting prior treatments, including a prior hospitalization for delirium tremens—the potentially fatal withdrawal syndrome characteristic of severe alcohol dependence.

The policy application was jointly prepared by Richard and the insurance company's commission-based agent. The new policy was issued approximately one year before Richard's death. The critical fact: this new policy replaced three prior policies that had already achieved "incontestable" status. Under the standard incontestability clause required by insurance law in most states, after a life insurance policy has been in force for two years, the insurer cannot void the policy or deny claims based on misrepresentations in the application, even if those misrepresentations constitute fraud. Richard's three prior policies had all passed this two-year threshold. They were legally bulletproof.

Yet the agent induced Richard to surrender these three incontestable policies and replace them with a single new policy thereby restarting the two-year contestability period and, crucially, generating a substantial new commission for the agent. This practice is known in the insurance industry as "Twisting": the unethical or illegal practice of inducing a policyholder to lapse, forfeit, or surrender an existing insurance policy for the purpose of taking out a new policy, primarily to benefit the agent through commissions rather than to benefit the insured. This, dear reader, is a huge factor in insurance industry profits.

When Richard died approximately one year after the new policy was issued, well within the two-year contestability period the insurance company conducted a routine investigation, discovered Richard's material misrepresentations and concealment, and denied the claim based on fraud. But the story and case do not end there. Had Richard retained his three original incontestable policies, the death benefit would have been paid regardless of the misrepresentations. The agent's commission-driven misconduct, combined with Richard's desperate fraud, destroyed the very financial protection Richard had sought to provide for his widow.

So for me the case became what did the insurance company know about Richard's alcoholism, when did it know it; and did it know that their policy had been "twisted" by its own agent? If the insurance company knew that its agent had "twisted" the later policy, as to the widow, who should bear the loss? What say you dear reader? What is the purpose of life insurance that companies make billions of dollars on selling based on mortality tables and risk based on medical conditions? How often do they "look the other way" to fuel their bottom lines?

The case went to trial before a jury of the widow's peers. I had discovered that the insurance underwriter in charge of Richards policy had a secret habit of concealing his knowledge of a patient's actual medical history, as well as replacement of existing policies in order to get a policy issued for the commission-based agents. This deceit would protect the company in the underwriting process if a claim was made. He had a practice of writing the truth in a somewhat cryptic manner by handwriting within his large, stamped date markings on the underwriting documents.

Incredibly, the information he wrote inside his date stamped evaluation of the medical history and risk assessment on Richard's life insurance application, contained what he knew about both Richard's medical condition, and whether the policy was "twisted".

Fortunately for my client, I discovered this 'dirty little secret' of the senior underwriter of the life insurance company...and it was a very large policy. When I put the underwriter on the stand in front of the jury, he swore up and down, five days from Sunday, that he had absolutely no knowledge of Richard's alcoholism, nor of the agent's "twisting" of the policy. But then I produced his own handwritten note, tucked away inside that overlarge date stamp he carried, and displayed it, magnified, before the jury: "DT [delirium tremens] MGH records. Case of twisting."

The jury was visibly aghast at the perjury. Judicial corruption: a few days after the perjured testimony of the underwriter, the judge, who happened to be from an old Brahmin law firm and a "Harvard Club" buddy of defense counsel, suddenly declared himself sick and called a mistrial. The company quickly caved and paid Mary, but the jury never got the chance to render a verdict on how these insurance industry scams actually work.

The mistrial, in my view, was nothing short of overt judicial corruption.

Justice? Consciousness? One after another: hospital staff lying and concealing, an underwriter executive perjuring himself and hiding evidence, a judge clearly influenced, most likely corrupt. Weaving through both cases, a drunk atheistic psychiatrist charged with treating addiction patients while struggling with his own severe issues, prescribing away with even more drugs. His own addiction, lies and concealment ultimately led to his own death and leaving a bereaved widow. In the end, everything, every heartbreak, every so-called resolution was sorted out not by ethics or truth, but by money.

Where does consciousness fit in? All the truth got exposed in both cases, but where is justice to be found in such circumstances?

Did Richard get what he deserved? He paid for his addiction with his life. And the widow? She had lived on Richard's salary and there were no kids. Me, another notch in my litigation belt, but where was my conscience and consciousness? Truth came out, but was justice done? Human justice said yes. When you consider quantum entanglement as part of reincarnation cycles for instance, the cosmic permutations of Divine justice can be a hard matter to understand for us mere mortals.

Richard was a drunk. BHF, the medical provider, cut corners to fatten its bottom line, shrinking nursing staff, maximizing bed occupancy, bending (and often breaking) its own and AMA-regulated protocols. Lying and record-altering as a consequence became routine, and all of it contributed to Richard's death. Meanwhile, the insurance company ran its own game, gladly taking premiums from a well-known alcoholic doctor who could alter his own records right at the source, during the application process.

Looking back on litigating Dr. Richard B's case, I can clearly see that I was stuck in my own ego but why God, or the Universe, or the quantum field of interconnectedness placed these monumental challenges squarely on my litigation plate, I now attribute to God's Grace to teach me lessons and move me toward humility and love.

When I first learned to meditate, in my very first sitting, even before I was actually meditating, during the process of instruction itself when a small expression of thanksgiving to the source of the knowledge is performed, I was immersed into what I later learned to be transcendental consciousness. Because this field is beyond all boundaries, it is necessarily boundless. So, there are many facets of it that permeate experience.

However, once someone has truly encountered the sheer magnitude of unboundedness, where heightened awareness blends seamlessly with profound rest, they are never quite the same. The lion of the relative world, having tasted the 'blood' of the Absolute, cannot return to its former state. What emerges is a subtle, intuitive knowledge, not the shifting truths we chase in daily life, but an unchanging Truth at the foundation of everything. This knowledge coexists with a deep sense of well-being held within an unbounded expanse of awareness. In the Vedic literature of ancient India, this is known as sat-chit-ananda: existence, consciousness, and bliss.

This experience helped steady my mind through the many struggles that necessarily were part and parcel of my life, both personal and professional. Increasingly, I was becoming aware that there was little joy in the victories of my professional life. Whilst I was very grateful for the material comforts that were made possible for me and my family, I was becoming increasingly aware that these comforts could not quell the anguish in my soul nor could they shield me from the agonies created through my work.

In the subsequent Scientology war, *Litigator 2* of my series, the constant impending threats - implicit and explicit, both to my person as well as to my family's well-being, the attempted assassination of my character in a fabricated "frame up", the incessant looking-over-my-shoulder, and the resultant stress taking valuable quality time away from my family and my life outside the courtroom, were all taking a toll.

Litigating numerous complex cases involving consciousness, with a diverse range of clients all with their intricate problems, some like the Scientology litigation became like a quagmire, descending into nightmarish depths. As I look back now after many more such battles especially in the Scio cases, I know with absolute certainty it was God and Grace that kept me afloat. Looking through a different lens, it was a test that pushed the frontiers of my abilities and faith, molding me into a stronger, more discerning Litigator and human being.

"Yet, Oh Lord, you are our Father, we are the clay. You are the Potter; we are all the work of your hand." Isaiah 64:8 The analogy is that of the Divine Potter kneading and beating upon his creation of clay relentlessly from the outside with one hand, until it acquires the desired shape. Yet, all the while, the potter ensures that his creation of clay neither breaks nor cracks, for he simultaneously holds it tenderly with his other hand, supporting it from the inside. We are that clay. God is the Divine Potter.

Throughout my journey, deep inside, as I continually read the "Gita," meditated, and litigated my cases, I held no doubt that God and Grace were the Divine Potter, kneading the clay of my life. I knew, with an unshakeable inner conviction, that I was on the road to finding my way back home, to God. And now, the path plunges. The nightmarish descent into hell, to confront Satan himself begins. A confrontation that, in its ultimate unfolding, would merge my consciousness into God and Christ through His messengers in meditation. But in between that dawning and this present moment lay a mountain of suffering, an abyss of darkness that had to be traversed.

Understanding how and why this Consciousness experience and others occurred, the philosophical and scientific frameworks that explain it requires a deeper dive into consciousness, quantum entanglement, and the nature of reality itself. For those who want to explore these questions further, I've provided an Epilogue to this chapter alone, that examines the relationship between science and spirituality, the quantum mechanics of consciousness, and the path from TM to Kriya Yoga.

If you're reading primarily for the story, the legal battles, the cases and the human drama, you can skip directly to the next chapter.

Choose your own path. There is no wrong way to read this book.

Epilogue

CONSCIOUSNESS, SCIENCE, AND THE PATH TO GOD

THE SCIENCE VS. RELIGION PARADOX

I've decided to share some deeply personal experiences with you, even though we've never met. I do this because I suspect many of you face the same subtle dilemmas I've faced, not the everyday ups and downs of life, but the fundamental questions that shape everything we do.

Through meditation I've learned something that changed my life: beneath the surface of all the shifting, changing aspects of existence—the thoughts, emotions, sensations, and circumstances that dominate our attention, there is a deeper reality. A substratum. A field of pure consciousness that is untouched by change, pristine and silent.

Different traditions call it by different names. Christians call it the Kingdom of God within. Muslims call it Allah residing in the silent state of the mind. Others call it Nature, or simply God. The name doesn't matter. What matters is the experience of a direct encounter with the source of all life, the foundation that upholds and nourishes everything, like the unseen sap sustaining every part of a plant.

Most of us live our entire lives on the surface, unaware that this deeper dimension exists. We're like fish swimming in one kind of water, never realizing there's another kind we could adapt to. To my great good fortune, I learned to adapt through meditation. And that has made all the difference.

The Unity Consciousness experience in January 1978 was a turning point. It gave me direct, experiential proof that death is not real, that consciousness transcends the body, and that the "I" who experienced that infinite silence is not the same "I" who argues in courtrooms.

The lesson from TM meditation is simple: consciousness functions beyond and regardless of human science and religion. Science is still groping in the dark, trapped in atomic reductionism—breaking matter into smaller and smaller pieces (molecules, atoms, quarks, bosons, and the Higgs "God particle") and believing that if we can just find the smallest piece, we'll understand the whole.

But here's the problem: science relies on consciousness to function. Every measurement, every equation, every experiment requires a conscious mind to observe, interpret, and understand the results. Yet science cannot measure consciousness itself. It can only measure the material effects of consciousness—brain waves, neural activity, chemical reactions.

This creates the ultimate paradox: we are using consciousness to try to measure consciousness. It's like trying to see your own eyes without a mirror, and if we program artificial intelligence to do it for us, we've only deepened the conundrum; now we're using programmed consciousness to measure the consciousness that programmed it.

Religion, in effect mindful devotion and worship of an external object, whether God, Christ, Krishna, Paramahansa Yogananda, or even Einstein, does the same thing. It externalizes consciousness. While it is true that attention on any specific thing tends to quiet the endless mind chatter, true meditation involves an empty mind. No attention on anything external, but complete awareness of both the external and the internal. A paradox. But a blissful one. It is in truth, in experience, a state of consciousness that has no equal, nor any way to describe it with mental word/intellectual concepts.

Anything beyond such analysis, according to the present-day Neo-Darwinists attempting to explain creation, is religious, faith-based speculation. Thus, to them, bad! But they are wrong. They are locked into their own intellectual consciousness without experiencing a scientific alternative: God consciousness. Richard Dawkins' book, *The God Delusion* reflects not only his Oxford-based intellectual arrogance, likely motivated by money, it proves his own trapped consciousness, particularly in his overt misrepresentation of historical facts surrounding biblical literature. I'm no bible thumper, but Dawkins needs to be exposed for literary misrepresentations. In *Litigator 3*, I take on the delusional content of his book.

The sages throughout history have understood what modern science refuses to accept: consciousness is not a product of matter but the ground of all experience. Every scientific observation, every measurement, every equation passes through the lens of consciousness. As the ancient wisdom teaches, "As a man thinketh, so is he." Einstein himself acknowledged this truth.

Science has not yet evolved to the point where it can understand consciousness, and perhaps it never will. Why? Because consciousness is immeasurable by definition. It cannot be quantified, weighed, or reduced to mathematical formulas. It is the measurer, not the measured. Any attempt to capture it with material tools is fundamentally misguided, like trying to use a ruler to measure love.

To most scientists, quantum entanglement remains "spooky," a phenomenon that violates their materialist assumptions. But the mystics have always known that reality is not what it appears to be. Consider the word religion itself, derived from the Latin "religare:" to bind back. This raises the ultimate question: What are we binding back to?

The litigator in me wants to interrogate this question: Who is binding back? What part of me seeks to return? Is it my consciousness, my brain, my mind? Who am "I"?

But here's the paradox: the litigator asking these questions is not the true "me." The true me, the consciousness that exists prior to thought, prior to intellect, is already engaged in the process of binding back to God. The questions are just the mind's attempt to understand what the soul already knows.

Maharishi calls it "Being." Man, himself, seems like the inescapable measurer with his mind, of repeatable scientific testing and results. This raises the rabbit hole of whether man's mind can even function without consciousness. Dead men tell no tales. Science concludes that once dead, no more consciousness. Religion, faith, and consciousness itself, however, when experienced as separate from mind, says the opposite.

In my Unity experience, I experienced the opposite—mind being observed by my consciousness, as more real than mind, body, or existence through the senses. Nine years later, after 8 years of litigation hell, I experienced an even more inexplicable experience. The 'dead priest'. (Chapter 13).

With this acceptance of consciousness as the one inescapable "tool" to engage in any science, miracles or matters of so-called faith, such a tool should not be instantly relegated to the scientific trash heap. Seems like we must keep looking. Although, history does tell us that unscrupulous humans have routinely used religion, faith, dogma, miracles etc. to foist unspeakable horrors on our fellow humans, including fleecing the gullible of their money, the work of real money changers. The Neo-Darwinists, like Richard Dawkins, financed by the money changers are now pushing with a religious fervor, global attacks on the intelligent designers reminiscent of the Pope's and the Roman Church's persecution through the centuries of any and all non-believers of their manufactured nonsense. Most of the Neo-Darwinist researchers appear to be getting money from Big Pharma.

Indeed, techniques such as meditation should be used to garner a greater understanding of consciousness itself, without mandated attribution to any religiosity. This played a substantial role in the judgment against TM in *Malnak v. Yogi* within the current parameters of First Amendment precedent and law in our constitutional framework prohibiting state sponsored religious practices. In my view as a 50-year student of our underlying constitutional principles, including the First Amendment, I view TM's loss in New Jersey as temporary.

The future will prove that Maharishi was way ahead of his time. Same with Paramahansa Yogananda. A more enlightened period is coming for our species, hopefully more resonant with the Sermon on the Mount. It must, or God will destroy us.... Higher consciousness to save us is the salvation of Christ, a higher consciousness within that saves us all...in my not so humble, but experienced, litigation opinion.

The history of Advaita Vedanta, the real source of TM, in its practices of mantra meditation is all designed to realize God as part of the Self. The Constitution worked against TM. So, TM peddled its meditation techniques as science, claiming it was just a technique, not a religious belief. In truth, TM is correct. It is a science of higher consciousness, but in New Jersey, that case was like casting pearls before swine. Oddly, TM chose this path believing its techniques were more marketable as such. In doing so, it seemed that it attempted to conceal or circumvent its history-based Advaita Vedanta origins.

QUANTUM ENTANGLEMENT AND THE UNITY EXPERIENCE

There were about 60 people, if I remember correctly, on that weeklong retreat, where we were practicing rounding meditation. Maharishi expounded on this phenomenon of having 10% of a group, or a community practice TM, which he said would cause positive changes in the entire group. TM called it the Maharishi effect. Volumes have been written on it, TM, alpha brain waves and consciousness by TM teachers, physicists, MDs, Ph.Ds. and plain old practitioners. I suppose this is becoming another one.

In that January 1978 residence course, everyone, every teacher, attendee, retreatant was rounding. I became entangled on a quantum level synching my wave resonance with theirs. Voila, the Maharishi effect x 60. It put my brain, mind, intellect, body, spirit, soul, call it what you want, into a field of pure consciousness which some other attendees were also experiencing. Simple. Right?

THE PATH FROM TM TO KRIYA YOGA

Now, I believe that Maharishi's thought to leave his cave and help the species is itself proof of quantum entanglement. He had a thought particle in his Himalayan cave after meditating there for a decade that instantly identified with God's thought particle within the unified field all around him. When he explained his singular "thought" to leave his cave, and go back into "the world," to a nearby cave meditator, the latter told him: "don't go down into the world, it is all mud." Maharishi ignored his nearby cave dweller and pursued his "thought." Hence, he then came out into our physical field of mud; and brought us his field of consciousness to help us. We poor souls mired in the mud of material life were exposed to Maharishi's consciousness through the practice of TM.

Quintessential Quantum Entanglement for all those who experience TM meditation supports Maharishi's 10% affect. My mind immediately grasped the mud reference in a TM tape...the mud! Of course, that's what I was stuck in. No wonder that my litigator successes were overshadowed with the unease brought on by added stress and the feeling that there was something more and different that life must offer. It cannot be simply about acquiring more wealth, more fancy cars, boats, planes even a loving vibrant family. It was this mud that made me feel like progress on the material level was so difficult.

Maharishi explained that the stresses of daily life both past and present can be and do get neutralized through deep rest. The deeper the rest, the more deep-rooted stresses can be cleared out of the nervous system. In Transcendental Meditation the level of deep rest is greater and more profound than simply relaxing on a beach, listening to music, or even greater than the rest gained through six to eight hours of deep sleep.

Maharishi advocated TM for twenty minutes twice a day, interspersed by activity during the day. The repeated process of TM followed by activity, like the dying of cloth, allows the quality of Being or Transcendental consciousness which is experienced during the TM practice in the state of deep rest, to be infused into daily activity making for a more effective life. Maharishi calls this process activity for the infusion of Being. So, when we do TM, all our daily activity serves this purpose of infusing more effectiveness into our lives.

This made sense and my practical life experiences validated the theory. Up to a point. The cloth I was dyeing involved an awakening realization that my nervous system needed first to be clean before it could be dyed and infused with Being. My professional life was not conducive to keeping a nervous system free of stress and the growing feeling that I needed to get out of the mud clung to me relentlessly. I continued to follow my TM practice and the advanced programs, yet I needed some specific guidelines on the right conduct during my activity that would give me the extra push I needed to get out of the sinking sands of my life without abandoning my responsibilities to my work, my clients, the fight for justice and above all, to my family.

Grace led me to the path through one of the greatest spiritual giants of our time, Paramahansa Yogananda. It was he who taught me to face the challenges of my own battle of Kurukshetra, and do it in a noble way to ensure that my activities support my own spiritual growth as well as promote wellness all around me. He introduced me to the 'Yamas and Niyamas' as outlined by a renowned Vedic philosopher Patanjali in his Yogasutras, a renowned and respected ancient Vedic text.

In short, I was now learning how to behave in the outside world to complement the growth of my inner life through meditation. For the first time I realized my unease was from my lack of complete knowledge and the extent of my ignorance was only now dawning on me. That in and of itself is a huge realization, which gave me a calm reassurance that the way was clearing for me and in place of despair, I was now waking to a boundless hope of the infinite possibilities that could and would open up to me, to bring me face to face with the Grace and presence of God as I had hoped throughout my life but from which I had slowly but surely turned away. My life's compass was reset, and for the first time I saw the power within my reach, the strength that could finally pull me out of this 'mud' once and for all.

DEATH, RESURRECTION, AND REINCARNATION

In connection with death, resurrection, and reincarnation, it's appropriate here to mention a remarkable experience that I had 9 years later, in July 1987 on another TM course, which is covered in Chapter 13 of this book. That too was more energetically real on some level of consciousness than any of my normal life experiences. But it was the opposite of the Unity experience. It was a past life reincarnation experience of death that I relived. Again, it was beyond normal reality, and it was shockingly traumatic, the opposite to the experience of pure joy and bliss experienced in the Unity experience. It also evidenced a form of resurrection, but in the context of a reincarnation experience.

After over 35 years of Kriya meditation and studying the teachings of Paramahansa Yogananda I now know that my prior death experience was a transformation of incarnational energy in a previous death into a form of release into higher consciousness energy. It was enabled by the quantum entanglement of physical energies in my spine to the consciousness in my 'Christ Center' between the eyebrows. It was a form of resurrection from a prior incarnation and release of energy.

At the time, whilst taking part in the TM Sidhi Course (an advanced course for TM practitioners) I did not fully understand the physical and spiritual laws of spinal energy transformation which is the essence of both the TM Sidhi Program and Kriya Yoga meditation, both based on Patanjali's Yoga Sutras, both involve the ascendancy of spinal energies. The intellectual connections remained unclear to me for several more years. It wasn't until I began practicing Kriya in 1988, that I started to understand the relationship between the physical and spiritual experiences. Only 30 years later, as I wrote this book, has the full picture emerged. What can I say, I'm Irish; educated in the school of hard knocks! A slow learner.

Paramahansa Yogananda states:

> "By ascent of the consciousness through the subtle centers of life and spiritual awakening in the spine, the yogi learns the inner science of changing the consciousness of gross matter into the consciousness of its primordial principles." Paramahansa Yogananda "Lesson No. 9." (Copyright, 2019 Self-Realization Fellowship)

I now get it. The 1987 traumatic transcendental death experience followed an 8-year litigation war against Scientology, a deadly cult. *Litigator 2.* Thereafter, it took years of spinal energy Kriya practice for this knowledge to hit home enough to write about it in this book.

I received some comfort in reading Paramahansa Yogananda's final realization of his knowledge of resurrection upon meeting Sri Yukteswar in the flesh, 3 months after Sri Yukteswar's physical death on March 8, 1936. During that 1936 "meeting" between Yogananda and his "Guru," as described in Yogananda's book, Sri Yukteswar demonstrated the reality of his resurrection and delivered a comprehensive discourse to Paramahansa Yogananda on death, consciousness, and resurrection. He explained these concepts within the framework of the physical, astral, and causal worlds that make up reality.

After his visit from Sri Yukteswar, Paramahansa Yogananda exclaims:

"Never from song or story had I ever received such inspiring knowledge. Though the Hindu scriptures refer to the causal and astral worlds and to man's three bodies, how remote and meaningless those pages compared with the warm authenticity of my resurrected Master."

Autobiography Of A Yogi P. 414

Whether or not you believe Yogananda's writings and teachings, I certainly do, because I have been blessed with experiences that, though not identical, reflect the essence of his truth.

> "Our limited minds cannot grasp the mysterious force that sways the constellations." **Albert Einstein**

The courtroom dramas of the highly publicized Motorgate trial, which for over nine months involved intense, testosterone-driven intellectual combat, stood in stark contrast to the later, grace-bestowed Unity experience. The former entailed genuine suffering, while the latter was an incredible state of bliss. Nothing I had ever experienced before or since remotely approached the transcendental reality of that moment...during which I knew there is no death. A blessed experience. The later death experience provided supplemental proof to me of QE consciousness and basic physics. Energy is neither created nor destroyed. This includes our own energy. It is just transformed in and out of death. In Kriya meditation, it is transformed in the spine. Coincidentally or not, QE or not, both experiences followed intense involvement in extremely dark energy cases in which 'Macbeth Edgerly' emitted the energy of the satanic force.

Similarly, often after a period of deep Kriya meditation, which is practiced in order to shed karma, I have had suffering experiences where past stressful or even 'sinful' karmic events came into my awareness. Thereafter, I have observed a gradual release from the grip of those events. That is the blessing of Kriya meditation. As this book relates, my experience of that gradual release from past karma differed between TM meditation and Kriya meditation. The former gave me a place to hide from my karma, and the latter compelled me to confront it. The difference is difficult to quantify in a few condensed sentences or paragraphs. It is also an unfolding journey, perhaps too personal to convey. Despite everyone's differences, the common theme for everyone on a spiritual path...and aren't we all, seems to be the 'binding back' of the human soul to God. I attempt to convey mine in the mix of meditation and litigation; stories of suffering, sorrow, and redemption.

COMPARING THE INCOMPARABLE

The next closest experience in my life after transcendence, but in an entirely different dimension of reality to me, would be falling in love with Laima, and having children. That involves human love on this planet, which is not remotely close to the unity experience, but an experience of what real human love is.

First, the Unity experience far surpassed any typical human emotion, including the divine aspect of loving Laima...the mental, emotional, and feeling components of that love. As we all know, human love is transient and frequently depends on external factors, changing environments, fluctuating emotions, and even stray thoughts leading to the inevitable ebb and flow of falling in and out of love. Even when that love embodies the most divine qualities ("what God has joined together, let no man put asunder"), it remains vulnerable to the highs and lows, joys and sorrows, loss and renewal that characterize the human journey. It's a universal experience.

Perhaps there are those out there who have always lived in pure love with no suffering and no change in their human love relationships. I have met and observed the life and consciousness of a few such people: Mother Meera, Amma and Daya Mata; and perhaps Mrinalini Mata and Brother Chidananda. Interesting the foregoing are celibate 'saints'. That's not my path. I place Paramahansa Yogananda, together with Amma and Meera in a category very close to Christ even though I never met them, except in a few mystical experiences and those also don't come close to the Unity experience.

A LITIGATOR'S REFLECTION: GRACE IN THE MUD

Looking back, I can see how a reader might find this chapter jarring. How can an experience of timeless, boundless unity coexist with the brutal realities of the courtroom reality of lies, corruption and suffering? How does one reconcile the bliss of pure consciousness with the mud of litigation warfare?

I don't have a simple answer. For more than forty years, I've lived with that paradox. The Unity experience didn't lift me out of the mud forever. Far from it. In the years that followed, I was dragged into even deeper, darker pits, confronting evils that made the Motorgate case look tame. The experience however, gave me something unshakable: a frame of reference. A North Star. It was a direct, experiential knowing that the mud is not all there is. It proved to me, in a way no book or scripture ever could, that consciousness is primary, that grace is real, and that the universe is fundamentally benevolent, even when it appears hostile.

That knowledge didn't make the legal battles any easier. It didn't stop the attacks from the Scientologists, or prevent corrupt judges from obstructing justice. But it gave me an anchor. When I was drowning in the details of a case, surrounded by deception and malevolence, I could close my eyes and remember the silence. I could remember that the person they were attacking, the litigator, the husband, the father, was not the real me. The real me was untouched, untouchable, eternally at peace.

I believe that is what grace is. It's not the absence of suffering. It's the presence of a deeper reality that sustains you through the suffering. It's the quantum field of God, silently operating beneath the chaos of the material world, protecting you even when you don't feel protected. I didn't earn that Unity experience. It was a gift. And it has been the gift that has kept on giving, sustaining me through every trial, every threat, every dark night of the soul. Without it, I have no doubt that the mud would have swallowed me whole long ago.

CHAPTER 13

The TM Sidhis Program and Fighting Father Griffin

"The soul is never born and never dies. It is unborn, eternal, ever-existing, undying and primeval." **Bhagavad Gita (2:20)**

SALVATION THROUGH SUFFERING

It was December 1986. The legal war with the 'church' of Scientology had finally ended. Hubbard was dead. His wife imprisoned for executing church policies that violated every principle of human decency. The Church, now under David Miscavige's control, was being dragged, kicking, screaming and biting to seek a settlement with us; not from anything approaching moral awakening, but from strategic necessity. The litigation had been a trinity of experiences: the good, the bad, and the unspeakably ugly.

The good: We had exposed the cult across multimedia platforms. After the eight-year slugging match concluded, we had secured court judgments confirming both the organization's malevolent policies and Hubbard's severe, lifelong mental illness.

The bad: The devastation left in its wake. My wife Laima, my children, myself, and clients like Gerry Armstrong all carried wounds that transcended physical, emotional, and spiritual boundaries; the human fabric can only withstand so much stretching before it tears in places invisible to the eye. That is how destructive the Scientologists' behavior was.

The ugly: The settlement itself was formed through contortion under extreme duress, a compromise that partially suppressed the truth we had fought so hard to reveal. Miscavige leveraged our silence, and used the settlement to secretly lie about our cases in a scheme to obtain tax exemption. Unfortunately, the settlement didn't stop their campaign of greed or their attacks on their perceived enemies; it had merely changed their battlefield.

I refuse to call myself a victim, though the clinical term 'PTSD casualties' applies to me, my family, the partners in my law firm, and our clients all in varying degrees. The residual trauma clings to us even now, the unwanted inheritance from years spent battling Hubbard's satanic 'church' policies. And yet, curiously, this is where my story of salvation begins—not in victory, but in the smoldering aftermath of a war where even the winners emerged broken. The ruin I found there became a threshold. My journey through litigation hell had unexpectedly opened a door to spiritual awakening...proof that salvation often wears the disguise of suffering.

Desperate for sanity after eight years of courtroom battles with the 'Scios,' I turned to meditation, reaching for solid ground in the seemingly uncertain space where the veil between worlds thins. To my delight, with each meditative breath my spiritual steps became "anchored in that which is changeless" to quote Krishna in the Bhagavad Gita.

What began as survival gradually became something transcendent. The return of God to my life arrived in stages; first through Maharishi's TM Sidhis Program, then Paramahansa Yogananda's Lessons and Kriya Yoga Meditation Teachings. These practices not only healed me, they saved me from complete dissolution. Through them, I encountered phenomena beyond rational explanation...glimpses of reincarnation, observation of others experiencing levels of levitation, and moments of resurrection from past lives. None of it was metaphor or soothing psychology. These were encounters more real than the chair beneath me as I write, more vivid than the courtroom memories that had consumed nearly two decades of my life. This is the story of how I died in one life and was reborn in another, without ever leaving my body.

However, the trauma actually still continues today in some subliminal form within us and within the tens of thousands of Scientology victims. Most researchers into Scientology realize that the Scio Church's inveterate, unchangeable frauds, and nazified policies, remain unabated. Worse, in October 1993, after 40 years of government rejection, the so-called "Church" was granted tax exemption as a "religious non-profit" by one of our most corrupt presidents—Clinton. He granted tax exemption in the context of the murder of his White House counsel, Vince Foster, Hillary's boyfriend; and the murder of their private detective, Jerry Parks. Here is the timeline:

1979–1988: Myself and my law firm litigate against the "Church" of Scientology after eleven of its leaders, including Hubbard's wife were convicted of multiple felonies.

January 20, 1993: Clinton was sworn in. He and Hillary appointed his lawyer for 20 years, Vince Foster, a partner at the Rose Law Firm in Little Rock, Arkansas, where Hillary was also a partner, as Deputy White House Counsel.

February 1993: A Scientology lawyer, a partner at Williams and Connally in D.C., where Clinton's law school friend and lawyer was also a partner, gave a "box" of documents containing 20 years of Clinton crimes and scandals to Foster while demanding tax exemption for the Church of Scientology.

May 1993: Clinton appointed Hillary's friend, Margaret Milner Richardson, as Commissioner of the IRS. The IRS had denied tax exemption to Scientology since 1958. The Supreme Court denied it in 1989.

July 27, 1993: While dealing with the "box" of Clinton crimes, Foster was shot in the head.

July 27, 1993: The night after Foster's murder, Hillary's "aides" remove the "box" of Clinton crimes and scandals from Foster's office.

September 26, 1993: Jerry Parks, Foster's and Hillary's private detective, working on the tax exemption problem, was shot and killed at a stop light in Little Rock. The next morning, IRS, FBI and CIA agents raided the home of Parks, with no search warrant, and cleaned out all of the Foster / Parks communications and documents on their work on the tax exemption; and relating to the crimes and scandals in the "box" of documents sitting in Foster's office.

October 1, 1993: Clinton and Richardson granted tax exemption to Scientology—a billion dollar benefit to Scientology, and loss to American tax payers.

1994–1997: Foster's Executive Assistant, Linda Tripp, the mentor of Monica Lewinsky, in multiple interviews, informed the FBI and Starr Independent Counsel Commission that Hillary's aides took the "box" of documents from Foster's office.

After my 8-year war exposing the cult and its crimes, including its "operations" against me and my clients, particularly Jerry Armstrong, we were shocked by Clinton's submission to the notorious, well documented "blackmail" policies and operations, brazenly admitted to by the leaders of the cult! Myself, Armstrong, and other clients were shocked by the Clinton approved tax exemption. In the following years, when I represented Ms. Lewinsky, and knowing what I knew from our 8-year war against Scientology as a diabolical evil, I knew that our country had descended into levels of political and judicial corruption, and rank immorality by our highest leaders, from which it might never recover.

THE COST OF RIGHTEOUSNESS

The litigator in me personally hated to admit my own PTSD from the Scientology wars. Toughened by decades of legal conflicts against the metastasizing evils that became systemic in the Clinton presidency, as demonstrated by the Scientology tax exemption, and Clinton's brazen immorality, including his alliance with Jeffrey Epstein, I had created an internal wall against the suffering that Laima and my family had endured. Guilt became my personal residue from the Scientology wars. My wife Laima's suffering, and terrible rheumatoid arthritis, was so much, much worse than my own, particularly as her arthritis kept getting worse through the whole eight years. No medical modalities had worked. Being married to me, a litigator, was a terrible burden for her, and she had been a saint through it all. She stood by me through thick and thin and needed a separation just to physically survive.

My son, Michael was 18, graduating from Exeter and on his way to the University of St. Andrews in Scotland. He had been a three-sport Captain and star athlete at Exeter, but having to watch the family and his mother go through the ordeal of Scientology for 8 long years was tough for him. It began when he was a 10-year-old child, and lasted through her devastating illness which was too much to ask any child, even a rapidly maturing one. It was a blow to his security, belief in the integrity of our family, and the underpinnings of love that every child wants to experience in his parents' marriage. I felt that I had failed as a husband and father. I live with it to this day. I had chosen to litigate against Hubbard as the evil doer who embodied the anti-Christ.

Hubbard admitted that he conceived himself as Satan, The Beast 666. Notwithstanding my personal commitment to slaying this "evil dragon," wrapping myself in a self-righteous nobility to rid society of his evils, I am left with the nagging question of how much of it was ego? Christ and the sages have said: "Resist not Evil." I did when it was put on my litigation plate. After it ended, it was very hard for me to justify the devastation in my marriage against the rationale for litigating against Hubbard and his cult. My Catholic upbringing and innate belief in Christ served as a rationale to have fought the war. The Gita said: "Stand up and Fight." I can rationalize the suffering within myself with an intuitive understanding that resistance to evil inside and outside of ourselves is a life-long reality. But the loss of love and my family's suffering remains.

The mind can justify anything...was I like the early crusaders who just wanted to get out of the rainy castle and find adventure? Had I become an adrenalin junkie, bent on winning more and bigger cases? It's something I argue with myself a lot these days but back then I piously read Gandhi's and Maharishi's Bhagavad Gita every day, believing I was an honorable crusader...but even at the time I sensed I was following my own storyline and not being quite authentic with myself or others. The jury is still out on this.

Over the years, however, I have come to realize both through my own personal growth as well as direct wisdom from spiritual luminaries like Mother Meera, Amma, and Daya Ma, that ultimately what each one of us goes through in life is a matter of our own debts that we are required to settle for our own holistic growth. That is why I understand that it has never been me as the doer, but God who is directing the show of our lives including my clients, my children, my beloved Laima, and mine too.

The Bhagavad Gita extols the absolute duty to fight against unrighteousness, and I found resonance in those words during my years in the trenches. Hubbard's deranged policies were designed to destroy perceived enemies and extract obscene sums from the vulnerable, charging over $100,000 for OT III (Operating Thetan Level III). This occasionally left some payees schizophrenic as a combined result of the bizarre nature of the course and perhaps the inner conflict at having to justify such high costs. The harrowing flood of stories in my office, from more than four hundred victims, including the suicides we later chronicled in *Litigator 2*, became impossible to ignore and came to define the battleground. This ongoing avalanche of suffering fueled my resolve to press forward and gave me all the justification I needed to continue through eight years of litigation warfare.

After it all ended, none of this was sufficient justification. At the time, when all was said and done, I felt that my family had paid a horrific price. I was beset with grief and guilt. Laima wanted to separate and move to California. I sought comfort in more meditation so I started preparing for the TM Sidhis Program. I gave her most everything we had in the way of money and assets.

Rebecca was 14 years old. She was a developing ballerina with enormous potential, having danced in the Boston Symphony's Nutcracker at age 11. She had been accepted as a resident student at St. Paul's School which had an exceptional ballet program. That meant separation from the family, but amidst all the Scientology chaos over the prior years, she tried, but was not emotionally capable of watching her parents' split and her mom move to California. On top of that pain, our beloved family dog died in her arms as she was getting ready to leave. She joined her mom in California after one year at St. Paul's. She then became an A+ student at Torrey Pines in Del Mar, California in college level courses. She then went on to Colgate where she majored in Philosophy with equal brilliance.

Alison was 12 years old in early 1987 when the Scio war ended. Since age 4 she had lived through eight years of absorbing her mom's traumas and illness, and my desperation to litigate the Scio war to a just conclusion. I will never forget the scene of her mom just having been diagnosed with rheumatoid arthritis, yet trying to give Ali a birthday party away from the madness of the litigation. The look on Ali's little face, seeing her seated at the dining room table for her seventh birthday party with all of her little friends is still searingly fresh in my memory. Mea Culpa.

I tried to mend my marriage. It wasn't working. Laima needed a separation for physical, psychological, spiritual and emotional healing. We had become too emotionally estranged. She had more insight and wisdom than me. I was too overworked and drained mentally, emotionally and spiritually to see what was really needed so I resisted separation believing we could heal...which was the wrong approach.

Looking back, I think I was clinging to the marriage mostly out of Catholic guilt and fear, even though I had long ago abandoned the so-called Roman Catholic Church. Deep inside, there was the fear of loss of love and resultant loneliness. "what God has joined together, let no man put asunder" resonated throughout my being. But I did not recognize who I had become and what was really needed. I was 43-year-old with a beautiful soul mate for a wife, father of three beautiful children, and I believed that I had sacrificed it to litigate on the side of righteousness in a version of the hero's journey that had me dead center. Was it ego, ignorance, or an honorable desire to help that got me entwined in something that I couldn't let go of? It's all of the above; as humans we are so full of contradictions that it is hard to be definitive.

In fairness to myself, my dedicated attempt at providing my family with all the comforts that I wanted for them was part of my motivation. To that end, I succeeded, Laima had an upscale lifestyle, my children were not just well provided for throughout their lives, they went to the best schools of their choosing. In material terms, my professional successes ensured they lacked for nothing. But perhaps the spiritual aspects of our lives suffered? My choice as I considered it at the time was to lead an average, mundane life and be more available for my family or to work hard on litigation for just causes in order to ensure that my family was always very well provided for. I made my choices like all flawed human beings, with predominantly selfless intentions.

Had ambition taken over my soul? Neither of us trusted or believed in the Catholic Church. No relationship is a success or failure because of any one of the parties involved but perhaps Laima's inclination and insight were correct. Maybe I had wandered too far from my real self.

I turned to more spirituality, thinking it would heal me, but not the church kind. Meditation is different. I had been doing TM for 14 years. I had experienced transcendence; and I had experienced "Unity" consciousness, in the TM residence course after the Motorgate case. Here I knew that I had no beginning and no end. I knew meditation worked and opens up consciousness horizons not normally experienced. I had dived deeper into the foundational elements of meditation, called Advaita Vedanta – Vedic scripture to eliminate duality in thought, word, and action through meditation.

TM was serving this purpose along with studying the Gita. But duality permeated my being. I had become the opposite of what I was striving for. In writing this book 36 years later, I know I was 'venting', sifting through past karma to properly learn life's lessons. Only then could I progress.

THE TM SIDHIS PROGRAM: SPINAL ENERGY

For several years before 1987, TM and Maharishi had been offering the "TM Sidhis Program". I listened to TMers I knew, including my clients, Anjali and Sushil Mahaldar, administrators of Maharishi's international programs. They described the Sidhis Program as based on the meditation techniques of Patanjali, an ancient Hindu sage, said to have lived between the second century BCE and 4th century AD. He had compiled the 'Yoga Sutras'. One of them, the TMers called the 'Flying Sutra'. A sutra means an aphorism designed to stitch together the body with the soul in the practice of yoga...uniting the soul with God. It sounded exactly like what I needed.

At that point I was defending TM and its leaders in Washington DC in a federal lawsuit brought against him and Maharishi and the TM corporate entity by a group called "TM Ex". These folks were claiming that the TM "Science of Creative Intelligence" courses, philosophy and practices, along with Maharishi's Ayurvedic medicine practices were a fraud. The essence of their lawsuit was that TM was marketed as a science, when it was actually a religion.

Anjali and Sushil had previously taken the Sidhis course in 1984, experiencing energies in the spine, which led them to accept its authenticity. The Mahaldars explained Maharishi's brilliant research, and I learned from both their teaching and my own experience that practicing the program allows one to act from the level of transcendence experienced during meditation. This familiar state ensures effectiveness in one's activities and helps to culture and stabilize similar experiences in everyday life.

My 14 years of TM practice had acquainted me with the reality of transcendence from the mind and had also experienced an out of body type of altered consciousness. I wondered hopefully if I could transcend to such a degree that I could actually do what the "TM flyers" were doing as shown on video? They weren't actually flying through the air but were clearly in a transcended state whilst spontaneously hopping about like leaping frogs! It's all recorded! I had studied Patanjali's Yoga Sutras and understood the theories underlying the practice. A year later, in 1988, I reread Paramahansa Yogananda's *Autobiography of a Yogi*, where he confirmed:

"A yogi's body loses its grossness after use of certain pranayamas. Then it will levitate or hop about like a leaping frog. Even saints who do not practice a formal yoga have been known to levitate during a state of intense devotion to God."

Talking to Deepak and other TM'ers that I knew, they explained that they were experiencing an ascending flow of energy in their spine up through the crown chakra that caused them, at least the flyers among them to spontaneously hop, as though governed by some powerful internal force!

Good news: in July 1987 I took the two week Sidhis Course.

Bad news: I didn't lift, hop, or fly.

I could, however feel the energy in my spine flowing toward the top of my head, the 'crown chakra', seemingly trying to lift me up. No flying, or even leaping like a frog for me! Nope. But importantly I could feel the powerful energies ascending in my spine.

More good news: what was that spinal energy doing in me, even if I was not levitating or even hopping? The best way I can describe the process involved in the flying sutra, is that my consciousness was expanding. In the first few days of the course, there was an accelerated reality, at least in my mind and body, of the ascending energies in my spine, which expanded my consciousness beyond normal thinking, feeling and everyday awareness. I became aware of my own being, similar to transcendence, but with an added quality of experiencing the energies in my spine.

I had learned to watch my mind in my TM meditations over the prior 14 years, had experienced transcendence on many occasions, and had the Unity experience in 1978. Patanjali's flying sutra that I first practiced in Maharishi's Sidhis course integrated the transcendence in my TM practice with the energies in my body ascending from the root chakra up through all of the spinal chakras to what is known as the Christ Center, then on to the Crown Chakra at the top of my head. I felt these energies trying to lift up my body. No luck there either. The energies were as physically real as all five of my senses experiencing taste, touch, hearing, seeing and smelling.

St. Francis of Assisi, St. Joseph of Cupertino, and many other saints have been seen levitating and many written accounts were made of these extraordinary feats as part of their elevation to sainthood. Yogananda wrote about "The Levitating Saint" Bhaduri Mahasaya, whom he physically met. You can read the account in chapter 7 of his book *Autobiography of a Yogi*. He vouched for this pranayama technique, often called a vibhuti or supernatural power with which you could levitate. It was first explained in Vedic scripture by Patanjali, as quoted above. Maharishi created his Sidhis Program based upon the ancient Vedic texts modeling Patanjali's Yoga Sutras.

Possible bad news pour Moi...was I a spiritual slug? I never even hopped? Perhaps this is not the way to look at it, after all, visual verification of one's spiritual progress is an oxymoron isn't it?

Deepak is a board-certified endocrinologist who, inspired by Maharishi, walked away from the Big Pharma drug prescriptions for all disease madness and became the foremost, world-famous advocate of alternative medical modalities. (*Litigator 3*.)

When he and the Mahaldars suggested that I try the two-week in-residence Sidhis Course scheduled for July 1987 in Washington, I thought, why not? My wife and family are in dire need of healing, along with my very troubled and maxed out nervous system. Laima was indifferent, even though we had all lived through 8 years of Scio hell and likely been saved by the agency of meditation, Ayurveda and panchakarma, God and his Grace. Laima however was suffering from severe rheumatoid arthritis and meditation had not healed her. She had become a skeptic and she wanted a separation. I fully understood and agreed, although it was breaking my heart.

I was looking for options. I had completed numerous Ayurvedic programs at the Maharishi Ayurveda Health Center in Lancaster, Mass. It was headed by Deepak and run by the Mahaldars for Maharishi and

TM. I knew its effectiveness. Laima had been to one week-long Ayurvedic panchakarma treatment modality but was advised against further treatments by her Rheumatoid Arthritis doctor.

I was not happy with her doctor's advice. Enough said on that point. I however had 14 years of TM practice and signed up for the Program. Laima had already scheduled the sale of our home north of Boston and had purchased a condo in Rancho Santa Fe, CA. The die was cast. I went to the Sidhis course a forlorn and troubled soul, while Laima prepared to move to Rancho Santa Fe. I gave her almost everything we had.

The first few days of the course was mostly comprised of learning the aphorisms, or if you wish, the mantras of the flying sutra, which we were instructed to practice while sitting on thick foam mattresses in a large room where all the males practiced in one room and the women in another. The routine involved first doing the regular TM mantra meditation and rounding in our hotel rooms, then going down for the flying sutra. There were people hopping around me, lifting up in the full lotus position. Me...I never moved, but the energy in my spine was real, activated, I experienced it, and it was undeniable.

Unlike the reports about St. Francis of Assisi, and other Catholic saints, I never observed any one fully levitated. I never even hopped, but the energy in the room was otherworldly. I knew there was a major energy shift occurring both in my body and consciousness, and in those around me. I could feel it energetically and physically in my spine. I could feel it with moments of transcendental joy and bliss in my mind, heart and consciousness.

THE "EXECUTED" PRIEST: FATHER MICHAEL GRIFFIN

About three days into the two-week course, I was sitting in my hotel room in the morning doing the regular TM practice of 20 minutes of mantra meditation, 20 minutes of Asanas (basically hatha yoga postures), and 20 minutes of rest or rounding. Like that past experience of unity consciousness in Chapter 12, while rounding, what happened next is literally indescribable...and this time far more complex and real, and hard to believe.

I was fully alert, more than normal waking consciousness, hyper-alert you might say; in a way that only true meditation can induce. I then began to actually experience...it wasn't remembering...it was reliving this extraordinary experience which wasn't a vision. Suddenly I was in an earthen type room with a heavy wooden door. Somehow I knew I was an Irish Catholic priest, locked in this cell. Incredibly, I heard two men talking outside the door saying words to the effect that they had orders to execute me. One questioned whether they should kill a priest. The other man replied flatly "he knows too much". The voices sounded British.

My "being" in that moment was reliving the experience of me in a prior incarnation as a young Irish priest being killed by British "Black and Tans"; the thugs and murderers the British Crown forces had assembled, including those let loose from English prisons, to terrorize the population of Ireland. That is what my consciousness experienced in real time, not a component of memory...only the present reality of stark fear. In that moment, I was that young priest, reliving the last moments of a past life in those troubled times. No component of memory diluted the stark fear; it was visceral, immediate, and all encompassing.

The cell door opened, and I felt the shocking fear of impending death. The two soldiers entered the room quickly. One of them raised his rifle and shot me point blank in the right side of my chest. It devastated my body and the roar of the gun was deafening in that empty, echoing room, now filled with a cloud of cordite from the bullet's explosion. Blood spurted from the wound in my chest as the other soldier stepped over my now prone body and used a pistol to shoot me in the head execution style. Curiously I didn't feel pain, and was immediately floating above my body in the cell, watching myself die and leave my body. Then the experience ended.

Quantum entanglement. No time, no space, just reality. My current particles entangled with the priest's? My trapped QE energy still resonant in my being, somehow resurrected in me, then being released in a Washington DC hotel room over 60 years after the original death? Past karma released? The 'resurrection' of the priest in me, the litigating meditator, or meditating litigator (it was sometimes hard to distinguish which was my priority). Was I being freed from that traumatic death, or was I still trapped in it? I don't know, other than knowing without a shadow of a doubt that "I" was that priest when he was killed.

My body was gripped by a state of near-shock as I returned to conscious awareness in that Washington DC hotel room. Was I back to July 1987 or still in 1920? The line between past and present had been blurred, leaving me to grapple with the profound implications of what I had just relived. You be the judge and jury. That is precisely what I experienced, and it still remains more real, more vivid than actually being in the present here and now.

Yogananda had a somewhat similar, but different, contemporaneous experience in 1915, as he recounts in *Autobiography of a Yogi*:

> "As I closed my eyes in meditation, my consciousness was suddenly transferred to the body of a captain in command of a battleship ... But alas! a stray bullet ... ended its furious flight in my chest. ... 'At last, the mysterious footstep of Death has caught up with me,' I thought ... then lo! I found myself seated in the lotus posture ... A soft rumbling vibration formed itself into words: 'What has life or death to do with Light? ... The relativities of life and death belong to the cosmic dream. Behold your dreamless being! Awake, My child, awake!'"

As a 22-year-old Swami at the time of the Churchill Gallipoli disaster, Paramahansa was meditating at home in his fourth floor room when his consciousness was transported into the body of that British battleship Captain who was shot in the chest after he swam ashore from his sunken ship. AY p.315. That vision taught him that there is no death, and that the reality we live in is made up of God's light. Physical reality as we experience it in the senses, is actually a grosser dimension of a higher, more refined, non-physical reality in our consciousness. The more refined our consciousness, the more we realize that our true Self, our soul, is actually one with God. See also: St. Therese of Avila's "Prayer of the Quiet."

Paramahansa Yogananda experienced multiple resurrection experiences, including one with Christ, and one with his Master, Sri Yukteswar. AY chapter 43. Paramahansa Yogananda was in his Bombay hotel room when the resurrected Sri Yukteswar, still alive in a resurrected flesh and blood body, 'visited' him.

In contrast, whilst I was in that Washington DC hotel room, did I somehow resurrect the experience of that young Irish priest from his past life, or was I formerly the dead priest killed by the British forces in a prior incarnation? The question that has to be asked is; could it have been all my imagination? That is doubtful bearing in mind the spontaneous nature of, the high level of details and the visceral reality that the experience came with.

The energy and the reality of that experience lasted about 30 minutes, then dissipated and dissolved, leaving me in a state of utter bewilderment. When my mind was back in my body at the time, I was stunned at what had just taken place and I began to question what had just happened to me.

Had I been a young Irish priest in Ireland in the 1916-23 period in the Irish war for independence and been executed by British Black and Tan soldiers? The relived experience was so real, it said I had. I concluded that it had to have been a prior incarnation because there was no stimulus whatsoever at the time to even hint of a scene like this, and whilst I could have invented the visual and auditory stimulus of the scene for some reason, I could not have concocted the physiological chemicals necessary to put me into a state of paralyzing fear that imminent execution would have done. No, I couldn't have made that up.

There was a re-occurrence of the experience nine years later. I had not thought much about it during the interim, and I came to realize that it was actually a 'real' re-incarnational memory. The Black and Tan's had killed me once and I was somehow quantum entangled with the event to such a degree that I could access that event under certain circumstances.

The relived experience of the execution of that Irish priest reoccurred in September 1995, after 5 days of taking the deposition of Kriyananda as recounted in *Litigator 3*.

My mind had placed the experience around 1916-23 in Ireland during the "Easter Rising", but that arose in my mind afterwards. During the original experience, in the mind and being of the priest, I knew I was an Irish priest, a supporter of the local IRA (Irish Republican Army) commonly known as "Republicans" fighting for a free Ireland from the British. They were being hunted and killed by the local Black and Tans and knew that I was a supporter. That was my understanding during the experience.

My consciousness during the experience was more of an experiential observer. While my being relived the trauma. "I" watched myself being shot and killed, then hovered above that body. I previously had no other connection whatsoever to that priest other than what I have described. I have had other transcendental meditation experiences that support the validity of my being observing my mind but at the time of the event I had no other correlating facts to the killing of the priest except what I discovered 36 years after the event!

It was an amazing experience that I took very seriously, exhaustively going over the details to establish if there was any element of my imagination involved in constructing the experience. I concluded there wasn't. It was a genuine reliving of an event that I was somehow in quantum entanglement with.

My mind has resonated with the energy of the experience in that context. But I don't know and cannot convey from the experience itself anything other than what I have described. Since that date I have studied with some degree of diligence the nature of consciousness, quantum entanglement, super determinism, the laws governing the "conservation of energy," mind-body energy, reincarnation, near death experiences, resurrection and what many call altered states of consciousness. No explanation satisfied my quest to understand the event, and if asked, I can only convey what I have described here. Like the Unity experience of 1978, it remains one of the most intensely real moments of my life, an indelible truth that defies easy categorization or comprehension.

FATHER MICHAEL GRIFFIN

Disclaimer: Being a lawyer, the following sections do not support a "Fair Inference" in the law of evidence admissible in American jurisprudence.

Dear Reader: Given my career as a litigator, it may come as no surprise that I am, by nature and necessity, a cerebral person. In my professional life, success hinged on my ability to construct a harmonious sequence of carefully analyzed thoughts, presented in a logical, coherent flow, to "raise the consciousness", as I understood it, of a jury. This meticulous approach was essential for securing just jury verdicts based on fair, unbiased, and irrefutable facts. Over time, with 50 years of relentless litigating, this left-brain logic permeated every aspect of my life, extending far beyond the courtroom.

Around 1990, my right brain meditative introspection encountered the work of Dr. Brian Weiss, a Columbia and Yale-trained psychiatrist of the Jewish faith. It's crucial to note that Dr. Weiss had no cultural leanings towards esoteric thought; in fact he was a skeptic, which fits with his academic training. His practice as a psychotherapist however, brought him face-to-face with a startling reality. During a recorded session, one of his patients began to recount experiences from a previous lifetime and even periods between lifetimes. Needless to say this was startling to him and led to more research and finally his trail-blazing book, a runaway NY Times bestseller, *Many Lives, Many Masters.*

The book reminded me of the work of Edgar Cayce, who during "trance states" experienced profound, insightful, reincarnational, healing events for his patients. A deep dive into Cayce's work is recommended. In over 13,000 "sessions" with patients, Cayce reported metaphysical, quantum entangled, experiences that enabled his patients to heal, while also reporting deep insights into the lives and teachings of Christ.

The Weiss book records astounding revelations that emerged during the regression sessions with his patients and even included those of his own dead son. The original patient who exhibited this apparent past life regression knew nothing about him previously and had up until then had many health issues that seemed to be unresponsive to various medical treatments. However, through her past-life experiences, many of these issues came to be correlated and understood in a broader perspective, gradually freeing her of her ailments as the sessions progressed. Needless to say, after this Dr. Weiss wasn't a skeptic anymore and millions of people worldwide were intrigued by his findings.

I mention this because both as a litigator born and raised in the Irish Catholic faith, the subject of past lives and reincarnation was not within my scope of reasoned understanding, yet, when personal experience flies in the face of rational comprehension one needs to look deeper to come to an explanation. With this in mind, the following narrative is my attempt at bridging the chasm between my personal experiences and my effort to comprehend them. It's my hope that I can add to our collective thinking to enable each one of us to lead fuller lives on the basis of a greater understanding that ultimately our lives are far greater than merely the few parts that are immediately obvious to us.

"Realize that life is more than meets the eye. Life goes beyond our five senses. Be receptive to new knowledge and to new experiences." Brian Weiss, MD in *Many Lives, Many Masters*

If you recall in Chapter 3 on the disappearance of Richard Sequeira, I explained the law of drawing inferences governing evidence admissible in a court of law, and the supporting arguments that can be made for and against inferential evidence. The supposition that the milkman delivered milk because you saw the tracks in the snow just after a snowfall, even though you don't actually see the milkman leaving them, allows the inference that the milkman delivered the milk. As explained and ruled upon in that case by the court, drawing inferences from inferences is not permissible in the law of evidence. But drawing collective inferences leading to one logical conclusion is permissible. Admittedly, the mind can easily get lost in these distinctions.

In that case, the court ruled that the evidence supported an inference that Richard was dead, but there was no evidence as to how he died, or the circumstances surrounding his death. Thus, the defense argued that if he was dead by homicide, it required the jury to draw an inference from an inference, that is, an inference of death, and then an inference of dead by homicide. We argued to the jury that the inference of his death in the context of all of the evidence conjointly supported death by murder, and that the insurance policy did not exclude death by homicide as accidental death under the provisions in the policy. The Court adopted our position and allowed the jury to decide.

Also consider the story from Chapter 7 involving the murder of Tom D. Even there, all so-called 'psychic evidence' was excluded, despite the testimony of the N.J. police chief and its corroboration by tangible details, like the roadside bar where Tom's car was found. None of what follows would be admissible as evidence to prove the ultimate fact of my relived reincarnation, if that's even what occurred. These are quantum entangled questions raised by me, your scribe; perplexing facts that linger outside the realm of courtroom certainties.

LAIMA'S HEALING AND RECONCILIATION

I had completed the two-week Sidhis course without having achieved the slightest levitation, but I had tasted profound states of bliss, a prize I definitely would not exchange for a hop or a levitation. An ascendancy of energy was coursing through my spine. It was a sensation both novel and ancient, as though my cells were awakening to some long-forgotten truth.

Returning home, however I was deeply grateful for my new-found bliss because the life I had labored to build for Laima and my family was on the brink of dissolution. The house which was once a symbol of security was now in the process of being sold. Two weeks later, escrow completed, I helped Laima move to California. No one was rejoicing, and my own spirit was adrift in the space between material loss and the deep security of meditation.

> "Be anchored Oh Arjuna in that which is changeless."
>
> **extols the Bhagavad Gita**

In those days, I clung to the Sidhis Program and daily practices. I was a scientific meditator, still tethered to the rational, the empirical. I had not yet learned devotion, and to embrace the humility of prayer, nor had I yet recognized the arrogance inherent in my intellectual approach to the divine. It was ignorance pure and simple; a stubborn, unconscious refusal to surrender to the deeper mysteries of the soul that contained the tender salve I was at that time unaware of.

Raised Catholic, I should have remembered the power of prayer. If I knew it as a child, that knowledge had been shelved or outright abandoned somewhere along the path, replaced with the persona of a litigating meditator. Now that gap in my spiritual arsenal was beginning to show. Call it a wake-up call, or just the slow realization that old truths were resurfacing.

Professionally, I kept up appearances, showing up to the office every day, working cases with my partners and staff. We were defending Deepak in Washington, I was deep in the Wil Smyly/Sisi case (details that unfold in coming chapters), and the firm's litigation calendar was as relentless as ever. But with my home sold, Laima and the kids gone to California, and little left of my former life but an apartment within walking distance to my downtown Boston office. I deeply felt the absence of family life and needed something more than the routine of practicing law.

HANTA YO

So what does a man do when he is forlorn? Me, I bought a big boat to live on. Not a super yacht...only a 54 ft Hatteras motor yacht with two diesel engines in a walk around engine room, 3 staterooms, 3 heads, Captain's quarters, three levels, and a Bridge about 15 feet above the water. It cost me a bunch. My mind was awash in materialism. I hired a Captain and a cook. I took the yacht from its berth in Boston...well, it was not actually me at the helm...it was my newly hired "Captain Bart", former Coast Guard, who was at the helm as we sailed for Nantucket.

As I look back, the deep loneliness besieging me was nearly catastrophic. I had always considered Laima my soul mate since early in our relationship. I was meditating my brains out and bicycling and swimming all over Nantucket for the next 4 weeks. Boating was a panacea, but a short lived one. Thank you God.

It was a sad time as I separated from Laima and my son Michael. I flew him to London, then on to St. Andrews in Scotland, the birth place of golf. It was also time for him to start a new page in his life and begin college. Leaving Michael in rainy Scotland added to the sadness of this period. As I think back now, the sadness returns and almost overwhelms me.

On parting I gave him my own copy of Maharishi's Bhagavad Gita. In the front I wrote:

"To my beloved son, Michael: In this book you will find the answer to all human suffering and unhappiness…. You will learn that in your life you can fulfill all of your goals and aspirations. You can live a life of complete happiness and fulfillment. You can become fully alive and aware of your own consciousness. I love you. Dad."

I flew back to Boston, then sailed, or 'stink potted' as the real, sailboat sailors commonly called it, a derisory term for diesel boats, down the east coast all the way to south Florida and around the tip to the Bahamas and Keys. I was saddened beyond the ability of my mind during this period, and even meditation didn't seem to deal with this vast emotional upheaval I was going through. Even now I couldn't begin to describe the darkness I had sunk into at the time. My soul was starved for my mate Laima, and I didn't realize it at the time, but I was also starved for God.

Where does consciousness and karma fit into my little story? I had named the boat, *Hanta Yo*, Oglala Lakota Sioux for "Clear the Way, in a Sacred Manner I Come." Not exactly a nautical name! In February 1988, as I sought solace and recovery from the Scio wars, I found myself aboard *Hanta Yo* in the Florida Keys, diligently practicing the TM Sidhis Program and TM meditations but without much success. The boat, a sanctuary of sorts, was meant to be a place of healing and reflection. Yet one morning, in the quiet aftermath of meditation, a sudden and profound realization struck me with the force of a tidal wave. "This boat is a mistake," my intuition whispered urgently. "This boat is not my spirit. My lifestyle is misaligned with the name and spirit of this vessel. I must leave this boat. Now."

The clarity of the message was undeniable, a call to action that demanded an immediate response. It was as though, in the stillness of the meditation I had tapped into a deeper truth, one that would set me on my soul's true path. I was still wrangling with the after effects of my experience of that murdered priest, and why I had reincarnated as him. Why did I even have that experience? What is he telling me? What was his mission on earth? These feelings at the time radiated from my core and made me feel an urgency of some as yet undefined shape. It galvanized me into action. I immediately bought a plane ticket for San Diego to see Laima and Alison; she was my only child at home then.

We tried to resurrect our marriage. It did not help Laima's health. I was then back and forth between Boston and San Diego on my cases. *Hanta Yo* sat in Florida.

MY 'REINCARNATION' WITH SRF AND PARAMAHANSA YOGANANDA

One day in 1988, March 7 to be precise, how could I forget it? I was driving down Route U.S. 101 through Encinitas, California, a town adjacent to Rancho Santa Fe. We had just bought Laima a big new luxurious house. I was still deluded and in the throes of material attachment, thinking this would help. As I approached Encinitas, I saw the large lotus-flower-designed towers that are so prominent beside the 101. It was Paramahansa Yogananda's hermitage on the ocean in Encinitas. I thought: "Hey, I read his book back in 1974 when I took up TM," so I went into the retreat office looking to buy *Autobiography of a Yogi* and read it once more. The receptionist said: "The bookstore is down the street in the Temple."

I went to the Temple, saw the little book room at the entrance, bought *Autobiography of a Yogi* and went in and meditated for about an hour. No bells and whistles. As I was leaving, there was a little open-faced rack on the wall with schedules. I took one and saw that there was some type of event scheduled that night in honor of Paramahansa Yogananda's "Mahasamadhi," his transition out of this world into the astral on March 7, 1952, 38 years before.

I decided to attend the ceremony that night. It was a God-inspired move. I was transcended throughout both the entire pre-ceremony meditation and during the hour-long main ceremony, a length of about two hours. On some level I had known that I needed much more than just TM and its flying sutra. After this bliss-drenched experience it was clear that Paramahansa Yogananda's path would help me. The next day or so, I subscribed to the Self-Realization Fellowship Lessons. My life was about to change. God, Paramahansa Yogananda and Grace were telling me there was a large void between my true Spirit-Self and my litigator self.

I re-read the AY, discovering again Yogananda's explanation of reincarnation, levitation, the physics of cellular transformation from death to life, and the reality of no death. I read about his explanation of Christ's and his Guru's resurrection. I thought "everything Paramahansa Yogananda is conveying is truth!"...and answered all the questions I had about my 'Priest' experience.

I read that Paramahansa Yogananda's fundamental prescription for every human, the goal of life on this planet, is to seek and find God. I was beginning to get the message in this incarnation: the world is full of dark energies. The dead priest had encountered them. They had killed him, but he was not dead. He was still searching for God just like me.

The darkest of dark energies on this planet lives in us all as humans, but they are redeemed by the energies of God. The battle between good and evil exists in us all and we have been fighting Satan in the form of our sins. This is mostly our tendency to ego-size our every thought, word and deed into some form of self-absorption, which the religionists call pride.

Following the Sidhis course, and Laima's departure to California, I was split between the dark and light energies in my mind, heart and soul. In my litigator mode, I was as far from the spirit of the dead priest as those who killed him. I was as far from the spirit of Ahbleza in *Hanta Yo*, as Custer was from the reality of his insane charge into the Indian encampment at Little Big Horn. I have dots of entanglement to the Second Wounded Knee, a century later when my client, Russell Means, and the American Indian Movement ("AIM") protested the 1890 massacre, and performed their tribal ritual "Ghost dance" at second "Wounded Knee" in 1973.

I dived into studying Paramahansa Yogananda's meditation techniques in the lessons. They resonated in me as truth. His extensive explanations of reincarnation and resurrection in the AY, his writings and Lessons helped me reconcile my recent extraordinary experiences. At the same time I re-read parts of *Hanta Yo* and meditated on the meaning of the dead priest. I began practicing the Self-Realization meditation techniques. First, SRF's version of Yoga asanas, called the energization exercises, then Hong Sau - breath observation, then OM, sound awakening within the mind and brain.

Amidst recurring cycles of sorrow, karmic patterns, joy, and awakening heart feelings and more sorrow, I prepared for the Kriya Yoga initiation at the 1988 SRF world convocation. My litigator self however also held me in a vice grip as I fluctuated between God and the heavily karmic world of litigation.

I was also feeling the painful physical absence of Laima. I needed love, and I needed a woman badly.

CONVOCATION, 1988

I attended the last Kriya Yoga initiation to be held at the SRF world headquarters, called 'The Mother Center', at Mt. Washington in LA. The initiates rode on a bus to and from the downtown Hotel Bonaventure, where the convocation took place and where I stayed. During the three-hour ceremony, I was transcended completely. On the bus ride back, I remained in another dimension...all was pure awareness, pure bliss. God and Yogananda were giving me a glimpse, a renewed taste of reality. I had transcended in TM, as described; but now I had new work to do.

The SRF teachings, unlike TM, are not just founded on meditation techniques to achieve transcendence. Paramahansa Yogananda is a trainer, a taskmaster, a disciplinarian, who teaches in his lessons that we have options. By applying his teachings diligently we will ascend the path back to God realization. Meanwhile he intuitively monitors his devotees, every step, every meditation along the way. We just need to learn to behave and apply the teachings. For me that mandated self-confrontation, humility, honesty, integrity, my full and immediate acknowledgment of flaws, failings and 'sins'. It was the beginning of dealing with what I had become, through the illusions and delusions I had fallen into that had created a gulf between my spirit and my litigator mind and persona. Mea Culpa.

TM fell away as Kriya practice required my doing the meditation techniques: Hong Sau, Om and Kriya. Also in my case, rigid adherence to the Yamas and Niyamas, the ethical rules, the do's and don'ts of true living. The five Yamas: non-violence, non-stealing, truthfulness, moderation (mostly in sex) and non-greed. The five Niyamas: self-discipline; self-reflection; contentment; cleanliness; surrender.

I went through years of success and failure. I made daily diary entries about my past failures in the developing consciousness arising from my then daily meditation practices, and numerous retreats at the Encinitas Hermitage and Hidden Valley retreat farm. After about 5 years, I realized they were needlessly negative and yet another attachment, so burned them all. The details of my sins I am not confessing. Hey, even St. Augustine in his "Confessions" did not report the details of his "sins." So neither am I. They're not that bad....

THE BAD CARDINAL

In one seven-day retreat at Paramahansa Yogananda's hermitage in Encinitas California, circa 1991, I had another mystical experience. I had been doing my Kriya practice for about three years but I was still in my mind. The experience did not rise to the level of the 1987 dead priest experience, or the 1978 Unity experience but was significant nonetheless.

I was standing, in reflection, by one of the Palm trees at the SRF hermitage next to the area where the Temple had been which was lost to cliff erosion. There is an empty swimming pool there now. The dead priest had been with me in my meditations now for about 4 years. From the deep mud of my past I suddenly felt in my mind that the dead priest for some reason had redeemed the life of a bad Cardinal of the Roman Catholic Church who had lived as in the Napoleonic era. I had a misty awareness that the Cardinal had illegitimate kids, mistresses, and had engaged in improper financial transactions for the Vatican. But I had no other identification with him. Just that he was a bad guy. This hazy awareness included the detail that the Cardinal had reincarnated later in the 1800s to redeem his mis-guided life with the good deeds of the dead Irish priest.

As that awareness dissipated, it left me with extremely intense desires for sexual intimacy and love for a woman. Intense does not adequately describe the state of my being. Overwhelming desperation is closer to the mark. Through this confusion of energy came the intuition that I had met Yogananda when I was a very young adult or late teenager in the 1940 period. I had accepted him and his teachings, yet then abandoned both to join the Army Air Force after the attack on Pearl Harbor, and was killed in an F4U Corsair engagement with a Japanese carrier. I got the message that the Guru saved me from a similar result in Vietnam given my flying propensities.

LITIGATION VS MEDITATION IN A TROUBLED SOUL

I was back and forth in my mind, heart, body and law practice. To and from San Diego and Boston accumulating hundreds of thousands of travel miles. I was immersed in awakening sorrows and channels to get out of them. At times, the loneliness and need for love was relentless. The marriage was over. The duty to take care of Laima and my family remained. The torturous path between spirit and gripping desires for love, sex and worldly wants was unforgiving. I attended many, many SRF retreats in Encinitas at the

Hermitage; and at SRF's male monastic, Hidden Valley Ashram and farm in Escondido, California. I bought land and built a little house at Hidden Valley next to the Ashram with an easement into the land given to me by Daya Ma, my client, friend and President of SRF. This is where I have been writing these books for the past four years, living more or less like a monk.

I was caught between meditation, prayer and all-consuming sexual desire for a woman. I found one and suffered beyond my ability to either explain it to you or confess it. Thank you for your guidance Yogananda. I now see it as his and God's grace to beat me up with such intense suffering that I got back on track. Lessons: sex and love must be integrated in a meaningful relationship, preferably marriage, and procreation with the endorsement of God. The suffering showed me my real "I" from the depths of my real Self. A tale of overwhelming pain too much to dump on you dear reader.

I believe I now know the answer to all that suffering: finding a teacher, Paramahansa Yogananda in my case, who showed me how to reach God and saved my soul.

> "The Garden of Eden story is a metaphor for the energies in the spine ascending up the spine from the genitals to the Crown Chakra. When you do Kriya meditation you transform those energies." **Paramahansa Yogananda, *Autobiography of a Yogi***

The deeper I ventured into Kriya meditation, the more I recognized its profound connection to quantum physics. Science has begun to grasp what ancient yogis understood millennia ago...that quantum entanglement offers a mathematical glimpse in the spin of an electron analogous to what Kriya practitioners experience as lived reality. However, even the most elegant equations barely capture the essence of what unfolds when consciousness turns inward during deep meditation. As they say 'The map is not the terrain' and so the mathematics may describe the phenomenon, but the experience transcends description.

I now see the seemingly random birth and British murder of Father Griffin, living just 16 miles from my paternal Grandmother, Delia o'Callaghan in Galway, Ireland, born 4 years before Father Griffin, as quantum entangled energies. Delia's family, active in the Irish Republican Brotherhood, opposing British occupation, put her on a boat at 12 years old in 1899 for America to spare her the coming resistance and violence.

Father Griffin was then 8 years old. In my life now, I no longer see anything as coincidental.

Everything to me now are manifestations of divine grace, cosmic threads woven by unseen hands to guide me back to God. The synchronicities that once appeared as mere curiosities now reveal themselves as a meticulously orchestrated return journey. I have finally understood what saints and mystics have always known: I am not the doer. God and Christ live within me, expressing through this temporary form I call myself. Everything else, litigation battles, professional achievements, even personal traumas are merely details in a much grander narrative.

Yet unresolved questions linger at the edges of my consciousness. How has my dual identity as both litigator and meditator shaped my soul's journey? To what extent have my past lives, particularly that of a passionately rebellious Irish priest who died fighting British oppression influenced my present consciousness? The boundaries between incarnations now seem increasingly permeable as my meditations deepened.

After fifty plus years in what I can only describe as the PIT, and over eighty years in this particular incarnation, the scope of consciousness and its transmuted energies has become evident to me in ways I could never have imagined when I first entered a courtroom or sat on a meditation cushion. The litigation wars that once consumed me now seem like necessary crucibles...painful but essential transformations on the path to awakening.

Epilogue

HISTORICAL VERIFICATION

The experience of reliving the shocking murder of Father Michael Griffin was not a dream or a psychological drama; it was a direct, experiential knowing, more real than most of my waking life. For years, it remained a sacred, private memory. But the litigator in me, the part that always seeks evidence and corroboration, could not let it rest entirely. As I edited this chapter on April 15, 2023, thirty-six years after that night in the Washington D.C. hotel room when I relived the murder of the Irish priest, I felt a compulsion to investigate.

After a two-hour meditation, I began to search online for any connection between the British Black and Tans and the execution of an Irish priest during that tumultuous period. After only a few clicks I landed on a

Wikipedia article that sent a shock wave through my system. The details matched my experience with chilling precision.

"On the night of 14 November 1920, during the Irish War for Independence, Griffin, a known Irish republican sympathizer, left his home at 2 Montpellier Terrace but never returned. 'After being lured by British forces to leave the house, it's thought he was taken to Lenaboy Castle, on Taylor's Hill, where Auxiliary forces were stationed. There, he was questioned and ultimately killed.' On 20 November, his body was found in an unmarked grave in a bog at Cloghscoltia near Barna; he had been shot through the head. The day after Griffin's body was discovered, the Bloody Sunday massacre occurred in Dublin. On 23 November, after Griffin's funeral mass at St Joseph's Church, the funeral cortege processed through the streets of Galway. Three bishops, 150 priests and in excess of 12,000 mourners participated. The priest was buried in the grounds of Loughrea Cathedral.

"Griffin was most likely killed by the Auxiliary Division of the Royal Irish Constabulary (RIC). Due to his known Irish republican sympathies, he would have been a target for reprisal killing by Crown forces, who had already committed several such killings in Galway in the preceding months. He had given the last rites to IRA volunteer Seamus Quirke, who was shot and killed by the RIC on 9 September 1920, and took part in the funeral mass for Sinn Féin councilor and local businessman Michael Walsh, who was killed by a group of armed men 'with English accents' who claimed to be 'English secret service men.'"

I felt compelled to investigate further. Assuming energy is neither created nor destroyed as the physicists claim, the 'wave resonance' of that prior incarnation from another field or dimension may have instantly enveloped my being and my mind 60 years later in 1987 in the 'presence of God', or in meditation as I would describe it during the Sidhis program. It certainly seems like time and space don't exist in meditation, but this cannot be proved in a science lab. I will however vouch for the experience itself; it was undeniable to me.

After finding the Wikipedia article on Griffin, I read all of the references at the end of the article. I learned that during the Irish War for Independence, 1920–22, Griffin was an active and known supporter of Sinn Féin and the IRB activists who opposed the Treaty with the British. There were others in his parish who supported the Treaty, including an alleged traitor named Patrick Joyce, who had been abducted and killed just weeks before the Griffin murder by the IRB. Some articles suggest that Griffin was murdered by the Black and Tans as a reprisal for the killing of Joyce.

In the Wikipedia article, supported by other references, there is a statement by the Chief Secretary of Ireland to the British House of Commons that Griffin was "an extreme Sinn Feiner". Allegedly, shortly before his murder, Father Griffin told his congregation "that some among you were as bad as the Black and Tans". The clear inference from that alleged statement and the reported articles and known facts at the time of the murder is that Father Griffin, because of his position as a priest who was hearing confessions from those in his parish, knew who the spies and traitors were for the Black and Tans, as stated to the House of Commons.

It was an extremely violent period during the War for Independence at that time, especially in western Galway and Clare. It's also possible that RIC auxiliaries also took part in Griffin's murder. They had initially denied their role in the murder, but six months later, their former commander admitted that they had some "involvement" in it.

"HE KNOWS TOO MUCH"

Thirty-six years later when editing this chapter, after reading that Griffin had told his congregation "that some among you were as bad as the Black and Tans", I immediately connected that statement to what I heard outside the cell door during my relived experience. One of the killers said: "He knows too much." In other words, Father Griffin knew who the Black and Tan spies were in his own congregation. I heard that voice outside 'my' cell door.

During my editing process for this chapter, I obtained Leeson's book on Kindle, *The Black and Tans*, which is referenced in the Wikipedia article, in which the Griffin murder is historically contextualized. Leeson concludes that crown forces murdered Griffin. He didn't however distinguish between the RIC Auxiliaries stationed at Lenaboy Castle, and the Black and Tans. He documents and footnotes his sources including period official records and news articles.

Leeson recounts this period of British terror in Galway and Clare with specific facts and details including the general fear engendered by crown forces, whether the RIC or the Black and Tans, among the Catholic Priests and Bishops supporting Sinn Féin and the IRB. He quotes one letter threatening the local Bishop:

> "If any members of His Majesty's forces are interfered with in Galway, you will meet with Father Griffin's fate—Beware."

Source: D. M. Leeson. *The Black and Tans: British Police and Auxiliaries in the Irish War of Independence, 1920-1* (Kindle Location 2328). Kindle Edition, quoting Connacht Tribune, 18 September 1920, 5-6.

This is an important subject to me regardless of any provable and verifiable connection I have to Father Griffin for several consciousness reasons which I have experienced since childhood. First, I was raised in a very Irish Catholic home with aspirations as a child and teenager to be a Catholic priest. Second, in my extensive reading as a child and teenager about the world wars I have idolized the Irish fighting for independence; blamed the British for both world wars, including the utter insanity of stalemated trench warfare, and the bombing of civilian populations. I blamed the British Crown for its arrogant oppression and atrocities in Ireland including the Irish 1840's famine. I also have an instinctive hostility to British Empire Building and colonization; and a "zealous" nature to restore justice. It's in my DNA.

I have also checked my family lineage and confirmed the following facts. My Dad's mother, my paternal grandmother, Delia Theresa o'Callaghan, was born in 1888, in Ballyvaughan, County Clare, Ireland, on Galway Bay. The Griffin family lived in the nearby village of Gort about 16 miles away. Griffin's father was an activist in the Irish struggle for independence. He was jailed by the Brits in the 1880's in the 'Land War' for inciting non-payment of rent. In the late 1800's, West Galway and West Clare were very sparsely populated. It was generally known that almost everyone knew everyone else in the surrounding towns. Father Michael Griffin was born in 1892.

Delia's father, brothers and cousins, like almost everyone in Ireland, particularly in Cork and Galway, were also active Irish Republicans opposing British rule and supporting Independence. In the period between the late 1800's and early 1900's, about 20 to 40 years after the famine, the entire area around Galway in both counties, Clare and Galway, like most of Ireland in that period, was engulfed in "Irish Republican" resistance to British occupation and oppression.

According to the Flynn family tree, the Flynns on my father's side are from the rebel county Cork. The Cork Flynns were activist Irish republicans many of whom had fled the 1840's famine, or had resisted the Brits. Many of them fled to America and several of them joined the Union Army in the Irish Brigades.

Like the Griffin family, I understand, but have not completely confirmed, that Delia's family, the o'Callaghans, were well known Irish Republican activists in both counties Clare and Galway, as well as in Cork. Many were members of the "Irish Republican Brotherhood," the precursor to the IRA, later formed in 1919.

My paternal grandfather, George Flynn married Delia o'Callaghan in 1913 in Haverhill, Massachusetts. He supported Sinn Fein and the IRB in the War for Independence. My father, George Henry Flynn Jr. was born 5 years later in February,1918 at the height of the trench warfare stalemate.

According to numerous articles and publications, including Wikipedia, Father Michael Griffin was murdered at age 28 on November 14, 1920 in the midst of that Civil War. The precise circumstances of exactly where he was murdered, whether he was kept in an "earthen cell," and exactly who murdered him, are unknown. The murder has never been officially solved, but the British police were then in control of all official inquiries and investigations.

BLOOD AND REBELLION

While writing this book, I traveled to Ireland and visited Father Griffin's grave at Loughrea Cathedral. While there, by pure chance I met the son of one of the pallbearers at Father Griffin's funeral. He took me to the local library where I later bought the book "A Zealous Priest; The Murder of Fr. Michael Griffin 1920." I contacted the author, Pat O'Looney, who confirmed that back in the 1920's there were several sheds on the premises of Lenaboy Castle, including an "earthen" type shed! The O'Looney book confirms that an examination of Griffin's body, but no formal autopsy, reported that he was shot in the head execution style, but nothing about a bullet wound in his right chest? This detail may seem obsessive, but my personality has always been "zealous" and as those who know me would attest, particularly my clients, this quality has been helpful in heavily litigated matters.

Several period publications reported that Griffin was taken to Lenaboy Castle, occupied by Crown Forces where cells were used to imprison IRA prisoners; and that he was shot in the head, execution style, and buried in an unmarked grave. The facts reported in multiple period news articles stated that he was murdered for his involvement in IRA opposition to any treaty with England other than total independence.

Griffin was shot execution style in the head as was reported. The reports did not mention him being shot in the chest as well. Could this have happened and not been mentioned? In my relived experience I was also shot in the right side of my chest, and I watched myself die hovering above my body after they shot me in the head. Your verdict.

FATHER JAMES O'CALLAGHAN

Delia's cousin from County Cork was an Irish Catholic priest named James O'Callaghan, (capital "O" for the Cork O'Callaghans vs small "o" for the Galway o'Callaghans). He was a friend of Michael Griffin's. Both were Irish Republican Brotherhood activists and collaborators. Father O'Callaghan is pictured on a post card with Griffin, as one of the three priests killed by the Black and Tans in the Irish War for Independence.

Fr. Michael Griffin (Athair Ó Gríofa) in IRB uniform circa 1920 Photo courtesy of Galway Diocesan Archives

Author at Fr. Griffin memorial, Loughrea Cathedral grave, County Galway, Ireland 2025 Picture taken by the son of Griffiin's pallbearer after a chance encounter

Grandma Delia fled Ireland with another female family member, named Bridget, in 1899 at age 12, as the male members of the family stayed behind to resist and rebel against the British. Irish Republican resistance culminated in the 1916 Easter Rising and the later War for Independence generally dated between January 1919 and July, 1921.

Father James O'Callaghan was also murdered by Crown Forces on May 15, 1921. However, Father O'Callaghan was shot to death in a safe house in front of his housekeeper and her mother in County Cork. He was not killed in a cell.

Thus, I have potential QE connections to both these priests; Father O'Callaghan by blood lines to my grandmother, and to Father Griffin by the physical location of the Griffin and o'Callaghan families in West Galway, and their involvement in Irish Republican opposition to British rule between the 1880's and 1920's.

The actual relived death of an Irish priest that I experienced while being executed by the black and tans in a cell is of course, entirely subjective. There is no objective evidence, except my testimony of what happened to me as I recount it. Remember that I knew nothing of the priest at the time and only researched into his existence 36 years after I had the clear experience of his death.

The mind of the priest in the experience I relived, at the moment that the door of his cell was opened, confirmed to me that his killers were two British soldiers wearing black and tan uniforms. From what I have read, the murder of a Catholic priest in 1920's Ireland was a significant issue to the Catholic Church, and to the local population, notwithstanding the pervasive violence rocking Ireland at the time.

Many believed in Ireland during the Irish war of Independence that the murder of a priest would have only been done by the Black and Tans, and not the Royal Irish Constabulary, who may have had some involvement, but would not actually pull the trigger.

I know from my background that if the matter was being litigated in some judicial process at the present time, for example, to determine lineage in some probate matter—any correlation between myself and Griffin based on my relived experience would of course be excluded from any admissible evidence. My testimony, like that of the psychic in the Dwyer case in chapter 7, is plainly too subjective, too speculative, and not capable of objective substantiation. If Griffin's body was exhumed, it would be interesting to me to see if he had actually been shot in the chest as well as the head...but this will not happen. Maybe only his energy was transmitted to me...a voice from the grave, like Yogananda's battleship captain experience?

THE TRANSMISSION OF ENERGY

My present-day consciousness and its connections to Father Griffin, my anti-Empire sentiments, recollections of youthful pride in the Fighting 69th, and a persistent hostility toward British generals for their reckless command over Irish troops at Passchendaele and Gallipoli, all feel quantum entangled with a web of other metaphysical inquiries. Take the trilogies *Letters from a Living Dead Man*, for example. These books illuminate the energies linking the so-called dead to the living, and offer—along with Brian Weiss's work, Edgar Cayce's work, and much of Paramahansa Yogananda's teachings, thoughtful explanations for the continuity between life, death, reincarnation, resurrection, and those curious communications across the divide. Each points credibly toward a single, resounding idea: that there is no death, only the transmission of energy.

In the fall of 1988, just months after my initiation into Kriya Yoga, during which time I was mostly in a state of transcendence—I found myself on a retreat at the Self-Realization Fellowship Ashram in Hidden Valley, California.

Nestled in the hills above Escondido, Hidden Valley ashram is a place where the ordinary and the ethereal seem to coexist seamlessly. You might come in as a "normal" person, but on leaving, change is always apparent. The landscape outside the ashram includes winding paths through high desert wilderness, with gardens and tranquil meditation spaces inside the ashram grounds. It is deeply entangled with my life's story and has been my writing sanctuary for the past four years as I've written the Litigator series. During that retreat, I confided in a monk friend about my dead priest experience. In response, he provided me with printed pages from the trilogy *Letters from a Living Dead Man*.

The books were first published just after WW I and are considered rare manuscripts. They contain letters written by the author and psychic Elsa Barker during WW I, based on quoted communications she received directly from a deceased Judge Hatch. He was living in the astral world, describing to Elsa what he observed on earth.

The third book, *War Letters from a Living Dead Man*, contains graphic, detailed, horrific descriptions of the WW I battlefields and the confused and tormented souls of recently killed soldiers hovering above the battlefield. The souls of the soldiers are being pursued by demons that lie in wait above the battlefield. The book is more descriptive than *Dante's Inferno* in describing the living hell of the battlefields and its aftermath for the dead before the love of Christ saves them. Here are a few excerpts:

"Those who hang over the battlefields where they met their fate are still thrilled or horrified by the noise of the battle horns, they can still hear the shriek of shells and feel the shattering force of the explosions. Day in, day out these unfortunate earthbound ones live over and over again the emotions of war, night after night they dread the morning when the sounds will begin again. They cannot get away. They are not free merely because their bodies are buried under a few feet of earth, or worse still left unburied. I advise you to avoid for some years at least the actual scenes of these battles.

"I hear every day the shrieks of those who are making the vicarious atonement for the race. When they lie mangled on the battlefield, the arms of the cross are being driven through their quivering flesh, and the petals of the rose are unfolding in their hearts. They are dying for love at the hands of hate, for love and hate are opposite and omnipresent. Their love for their country is their call to the atonement, their at-one-ment with the God who established the law of the East and the West, the Height and the Depth, the opposing forces of Love and Hate. They have accepted the sacrifice. For them shall be the resurrection and the life, after their sojourn among the dead, their sojourn in hell. They shall appear to the Magdalen at the door of the sepulchre, the one whose sins were forgiven because she loved much, and who shall call the disciples to give them the tidings of great joy. The soul of the world is the risen Christ, and the disciples rejoice at the tidings."

In 1995, during one of my 4-day weekend 'Darshans', or meetings with Mother Meera in Thalheim, Germany, an inner voice suggested that I visit the WW I battlefield in Verdun, France. I had read about the Battle of Verdun in high school. The sheer horror of it had never left me. During the three days between the weekend Darshans, I drove to Verdun. There, I walked the battlefield and discovered the Douaumont Ossuary. It contained the skeletal remains of approximately 130,000 French and German soldiers. I meditated and prayed for the soldiers in the large room above the Ossuary.

I cannot describe that experience. I could feel the horrors of their collective deaths during the battle, and tears welled up in me. I knew and understood the redemption of their souls by an inner presence of Christ's love for them all. This experience followed about 9 months after the unprecedented, miraculous 25-page jury Verdict in the Mike Love case. In that experience in that Ossuary, I knew that Mother Meera, not me, had restored justice for Mike Love. *Litigator 3.*

BIRTH CONSCIOUSNESS AND QUANTUM ENTANGLEMENT

Throughout my teenage years in a Catholic prep school, I was contemplating becoming a priest. Now, in light of the corruption in the Roman Church, I have lost respect for them as a collective category controlled by the Vatican, but not in the individual priests that I know. I believe I now know the resonance I feel to the Irish revolutionary priest, Father Griffin, and why I sympathize with, and admire the many Indian friends that I have, including the Mahaldars, SRF monks, and devotees. I know now why I admire Gandhi and his heroic, brilliant and saintly method to get rid of the British without firing a shot.

There are many reports of past life experiences from a prior life in the *Autobiography Of A Yogi* at p. 254 ff. One involves the reincarnation of Kashi, one of Paramahansa Yogananda's students at Ranchi ashram and the resurrections of Sri Yukteswar and Lahiri Mahasaya, chapters 43 and 35. Paramahansa Yogananda explains reincarnation in the AY as "cellular energy transformation".

He said:

> "Every gram of flesh has within it enough energy to light the city of Chicago for two days."

And:

> "Thought is the primary energy and vibration that emanated from God and is thus the creator of life, electrons, atoms and all forms of energy. Thought itself is the finest vibratory energy, the speediest power among all powers."

Does the "speediest" reference by Paramahansa Yogananda sound like the current physicists attempting to explain the instantaneous identification of two remote particles that Einstein called Spooky?

There are many different schools of thought describing what reincarnation actually is. In my case, if I was in fact Michael Griffin, I still had his traumatic energy trapped within my 'transmuted', reincarnated Michael Flynn human body both in July 1987 and again in September

1995. (*Litigator 3*). This of course is speculation within the laws of evidence, but not within the laws of metaphysics.

Later, I reported the reincarnation experience in detail to a doctor of Jungian Psychology and Psychic. She confirmed that Father Griffin was a relived past life experience and the second relived experience was a trapped energy release. I have reported it to many friends and family; Laima, kids, colleagues, fellow meditators, the SRF monk who recommended "Letters From A Living Dead Man," over the past thirty years. It was an issue in my friendship with Wil Smyly in the mid 1980s when I litigated his case. Chapters 18-19.

Thought is energy and at death our bodies are transformed energy. That energy is neither created nor destroyed, it is just transformed: For me, the Michael Griffin death is proof of some type of energy transmutation, if not possible reincarnation.

ON KARMA, CONSCIOUSNESS, AND THE MECHANICS OF GRACE

The historical records on Father Griffin validated the core of my experience, transforming it from a subjective event into a verifiable intersection of personal consciousness and objective history. Was this proof of reincarnation? For me, it was proof that consciousness is not confined to a single life or a single body. It is a continuum, and the debts and dramas of one life can, and do, echo into another.

This raises a critical question: What is the relationship between the suffering I endured during and after the Scio war, the spontaneous eruption of a past life trauma, and the subsequent form of healing that unfolded for both Laima and me? I have come to see them not as separate events, but as a single, interconnected process governed by the laws of karma and grace.

The eight years of litigation were a crucible. They burned away my professional arrogance, shattered my family, and brought me to a place of profound surrender. It was only from this state of brokenness that a deeper spiritual process could begin. The TM Sidhis program and my initiation into Kriya Yoga were not escapes from my suffering; they were the tools I was given to process on a much deeper level. The spinal energies awakened during these practices were, I believe, the mechanism through which deep-seated karmic knots, like the trauma of Father Griffin's murder, could be brought to the surface and released.

The yogic scriptures teach that the spine is the highway of enlightenment, but it is also the storehouse of our karma (called samskaras in Sanskrit). The intense energy that was created in me during the Sidhis program was, in essence, a profound purification. I believe it was life force or Prana that dislodged my deeply embedded traumas, not just from this life, but from lives past. The murder of the priest was a violent, unhealed wound in my soul's history. It had to be relived to be released. My suffering in this life, fighting a righteous war against a corrupt power, was the catalyst that brought that ancient trauma to the surface.

And what of Laima's illness? Her suffering was inextricably linked to mine. As I began to clear my own karmic slate, the field of consciousness that we shared as husband and wife began to clear as well and enabled her to visit Mother Meera and receive a healing. Her decision to learn meditation was her own, but it was also made possible by a shift in the subtle environment of our relationship. Grace, it seems, is not a solo performance. When one person in a family system begins to heal, they create a space for others to do the same. Her healing was the external manifestation of an internal, shared spiritual process. It was the ultimate proof that the unseen world of consciousness has a direct and measurable impact on the physical world.

This chapter has involved spiritual powers and phenomenal experiences but at the end of the day it is about the mechanics of grace. It is about how suffering, when met with sincere spiritual practice, can become the very fuel for our liberation. The trauma of the Scio wars, the pain of my family's dissolution, and the violent death of a priest in a past life were not random tragedies. They were the precise ingredients needed to force me out of the courtroom of the ego and into the cathedral of the soul.

CHAPTER 14

The Warrior's Path: Russell Means, Crazy Horse, and the Spirit of Resistance

"He who conquers himself is the mightiest warrior."
Confucius

HANTA YO: 'CLEAR THE WAY'

Father Griffin receded into the quantum field. But the questions he left behind remained as I transferred my gaze to the physical world once again. The experience of the priest's murder and my entanglement with him left me with the question of 'how can we carry the weight of multiple consciousnesses?' I thought I already knew the answer was 'we can't' and that is the reason when we reincarnate that we forget our past lives. My experience was an aberration, a tear in the matrix that allowed me, for whatever reason, that brief glimpse of my former life. Coming out of this experience I also questioned how one reconciles the sacred with the mundane? I sought answers not in further stillness, but in motion...I decided that this ancient dialogue had to be between myself and the vast ocean.

BETWEEN SKY AND SEA

In mid-September 1987, with Laima newly relocated to California and the legal settlement with the Scios cemented, I found myself aboard *Hanta Yo*, sailing through Nantucket Sound. The vessel cut through waters past Newport, R.I., through Long Island Sound, past the towers of New York, and down the east coast. We navigated in and out of the inland waterway stretching from New York to Florida, a liquid highway carrying me away from courtrooms and meditation cushions alike.

When we reached Cape Hatteras, something in me, perhaps the warrior spirit I'd come to recognize, craved the tumult of its legendary weather and waves. "I want to experience it," I told Bart and the cook. They looked nervously at each other, obviously questioning my sanity but obliged. It wasn't long before my madness was confirmed; the weather deteriorated, dark clouds and roiling sea rose up to meet us as we hit the awesome power of mother nature head-on; huge waves crashed over the entire boat, drenching us and throwing the boat about like a matchstick in the storm. Perhaps they were right...and maybe it was selfish of me to include them in my emotional wrangling, for in my madness I believe I was seeking release from the emotional storm within.

TWO VOICES: WARRIOR AND PRIEST

The name *Hanta Yo* was no sailor's choice. Neither was "Crazy Horse," the name I'd given to the Boston Whaler we used as a tender. But I was no conventional mariner, just as I was not fully a litigator. I always knew from childhood that somewhere 'in my spirit' I owned 'two voices'. As I matured physically, emotionally and spiritually into an adult, and became immersed in the so-called legal profession, the two voices became very distinct. I possessed one voice as a litigator, and a second voice in my spirit as a meditator.

I had done some 'sailing' in real sail boats, but mostly 'stink potted' as the sailors jokingly refer to motorboats, but seamanship wasn't my calling. The name of my boat came from Ruth Beebe Hill's book *Hanta Yo*, Oglala Sioux for "Clear the way, I come in a sacred manner." Fantastic book on native American spirituality—the native American fictionalized history of the Oglala Sioux up through the Crazy Horse period. The book is sort of a fictionalized version of American "Indian" spiritual culture, akin to Yogananda's *Autobiography of a Yogi* in its exploration of Oglala spirituality. The name *Hanta Yo* resonated with something ancient in me, something that had awakened during my meditations, so it was emblazoned on my 54' Hatteras, causing inquirers to ask if it was a nautical term? I recommended the book to them.

I had always admired Crazy Horse, the warrior who fought the oppressors of his people, just as the Irish had fought theirs. The connection wasn't coincidental, not after my experiences with Father Griffin. It took Ms. Hill twenty-five years to write the book, fifteen in original Sioux, ten to translate. It was published in 1979, just as my own spiritual journey, and war with Scientology began intensifying.

I identified with one character in the book in particular, Ahbleza, a warrior leader of his tribe, akin to the historical Crazy Horse of the Oglala Lakota Sioux. Ahbleza understood what it meant to live with divided consciousness. He said in the book:

"But now I hear only my familiar voice, my spirit's voice."

A year after the Scientology litigation ended, on March 7, 1988, when Self Realization Fellowship celebrated Yogananda's "Mahasamadhi," I was sufficiently awakened to understand my own two voices and the call of "my spirit's voice." The voice of the litigator in intellectual combat within the 'PIT' and the silent voice of transcendence in meditation. Unlike Ahbleza I hadn't succeeded in unifying my voices—the goal of self realization. The white-pipe ceremony in Lakota culture was comparable to the transcendent experiences that I had in TM meditation and Self-Realization practices and their attendant experiences of transcendence. It's power was similar to the power of the 'Vibhutis', yogic powers that Patanjali advanced, and Maharishi taught in the TM Sidhis course, although I don't believe the Lakota ever hopped! Crazy Horse was believed to have mystical powers where enemy arrows or bullets could not touch him.

Throughout Scientology as I suffered, I didn't accept that their horrific operations, threats and frame ups could not "touch me." See *Litigator 2.*

The white pipe ceremony was essential to communicate with 'the Great Spirit' as they call it in Native American Indian Lakota culture. The Yogic powers of Patanjali were millennia old traditions in the religion of India. The former could be experienced just once in the life of a Lakota warrior. The latter in Vedantic tradition could be made a part of everyday life.

Hill's book, together with Maharishi's *Bhagavad Gita* and "Science of Being" all resonated within me with new clarity after my 'Father Griffin death experience' during the TM Sidhis Program. Together with the 'Unity Consciousness' experience of 1978 they had revealed to me the power of spirit...the realization that life and death form a continuing conjunction of existence itself. In childhood I had always suspected that somewhere 'in my spirit', I possessed two voices.

As the boat pitched and rolled beneath me, I contemplated Ahbleza's words:

> "For certainly I never truly own the power for the white-pipe ceremony, perhaps only once man will own this power."

Just as Ahbleza felt he hadn't owned his power, in a similar manner I have not experienced Unity Consciousness again since that first experience in January 1978. I wish I could experience the second voice 24/7, but I don't. Here, however, between sky and roiling sea, for a short while at least, I felt the boundaries between my two voices, litigator and meditator, warrior and priest, begin to blur.

RUSSELL MEANS AND THE AMERICAN INDIAN MOVEMENT

About a year after the upheavals of the Scientology wars in July 1987, and in the wake of my Father Griffin experience I was immersed in the *Hanta Yo* book when, as fate would have it, and there are no accidents, I crossed paths with Russell Means, the legendary leader and activist of the American Indian Movement. A genuine soul, beyond labels, beyond politics. He became not just a client but a true friend, forging a bond rooted in shared cultural history, authenticity and respect.

When the movie "Dances with Wolves" came out in 1990, I identified with Costner's character for many reasons. To me, Russell was "Kicking Bird," a Lakota medicine man. He told me once "maybe I am". I said "you should have played the role rather than Graham Greene." Russell had played "Chingachgook" in the 1992 film "Last of the Mohicans," as well as many roles in TV shows and other movies.

Russell was a "true human being" to quote Kicking Bird. There seemed to be a deep connection between myself, Russell, my reincarnation experience involving the murdered young Irish Catholic priest, and the movies of that period mentioned above. The common thread between us involved oppression of his people, the Lakota, and mine, the Irish, at the hands of the colonizing British Empire builders. We exchanged ideas on these issues of his work in the American Indian Movement and in the context of "Second Wounded Knee"; the killing of his friends, and the killing of the two FBI agents.

DANCING WITH WOLVES AND SHARKS

I had spent my professional career 'dancing with wolves', more commonly known in the legal business as sharks. Thankfully I had a parallel path to balance this in the form of my spiritual path of meditation, so I fully resonated with Kicking Bird's advice to Dances with Wolves, once he was accepted into their community: "You are now on the path of a true human being."

The movie portrayed the white man as a post-civil war, brutish barbarian invading native American lands and in my life, the murdered, reincarnated priest resonated in my soul as a victim of British oppression. I was sick of all oppressors, in all forms and masquerades. I was sick of L. Ron Hubbard, and his so-called "Church" with him at it's head as a self-described Antichrist mocking Jesus Christ, the greatest example of unconditional love that our planet has ever experienced. I was also sick of the money changers I had litigated against...but there was more to come. It was like playing 'Whack a mole', but nowhere near as fun. For me personally, Hubbard and his satanic crew were the worst in this lifetime. My office was flooded with his victims, 1979–1987. *Litigator 2*.

When I met with Russell Means, we were instantly on the same wavelength. Now I know it was a quantum entangled encounter. He had come to my office to discuss the possibility of demanding a retrial for Leonard Peltier, which I then agreed to look into. We consequently had many talks on the first and second Wounded Knee incidents. The sacred native Indian Ghost dance had played a big role in the two Wounded Knee massacres by our government. The 1890 massacre being the mass murder of approximately 300 Lakota men, women and children. The 1973 Second Wounded Knee protests involved our government's military response to the Lakota resurrection of its true "spirit voices" in the form of the Ghost dance.

In 1973, the Bureau of Indian Affairs could not tolerate the audacity of the Lakota being Lakota in their tribal rituals, because they realized a higher plane of consciousness than that which was embedded in the Bureau of Indian Affairs, which, in turn, was controlled by the low-lifes in Washington who tried to stop it without worldwide protest.

Russell Means and I shared a deep sense of awareness regarding the profound injustices his people suffered during the white man's invasion and theft of Lakota lands in the 1800s—European progress without real Christ Beatitudes.

The 1973 AIM Second Wounded Knee protest resurrected the injustice of that period. The AIM sought to do it with traditional Lakota rituals like the Ghost Dance. The Bureau of Indian Affairs officials, sensing a loss of control, brought in U.S. Marshals who were armed to the teeth. Nothing changes. 'Control the savages'. The dead Irish priest, murdered by the Black and Tans, confirmed to me that the Deep State money changers always murder their perceived enemies who live in spirit vs living in materialism.

Ms. Hill's imagery is extraordinary: with the enemy tribe advancing on his people, Ahbleza leads them away:

"Ahbleza climbed the ridge. Looking back, he saw that Tonweya (his spirit brother from youth), riding beyond the reach of the enemy. And so, his eyes shining, he gave breath to a great feeling. 'Hanta Yo, hanta yo,' he cried, his voice sent to sky and earth and four directions. 'Clear the way, in a sacred manner I come.'" ...."A remarkable surge of power carried horse and rider to the summit."...."I am man, Ahbleza heard himself saying, but I, also own two voices. But now I hear only my familiar voice, my spirit's voice."...."For certainly I never truly own the power for the white-pipe ceremony, [The sacred Lakota ceremony connecting man in vision to pipe Ska Win, the sacred female teacher], perhaps only once man will own this power."...."Two Pani arrows, straight and swift, had pierced the Shirtman's [Ahbleza] breast, one point entering his heart."

[Pp 803-804. Italics supplied to show the meaning of this passage. The "I" is consciousness realized and "owned", "only once" at death, by man owning his breath/spirit and offering it back to God.]

In Yoga, the yogi offers his breath to God to achieve Self-Realization. Ms. Hill got it all correct. Does this imagery remind you, dear reader, of anything? Perhaps Christ on the cross, with his breast pierced by a Roman lance dying for us, his people? And after asking the Father if he has been abandoned in his sacrifice, he gives up the Ghost, offering his last breath to God. This is how Christ lived and died. This is how the Lakota sought to live...for one another. A truly communal people.

This is how Father Griffin lived and died, like Ahbleza, for his people, my Irish forbears, including my own Grandmother, in their war of independence against the British oppressors. It is history repeating itself, again and again.

Since high school, I had been an ardent reader of books on Native Americans, its leaders, and the almost universal experience of different tribe's Trail of Tears, at the hands of the European influx. Not just the Cherokee from which that term derives, but all tribes from New England to the southwest, suffering death, disease and dislodgement from their homelands.

At some point in my youth, I believe the 8th grade, I had read *Black Elk Speaks*, a 1932 book that was then republished. Black Elk was a Lakota Sioux medicine man who had survived the 1890 Wounded Knee massacre. It captured me and my childhood imaginings and at times I could feel the sacred bond of a Native American community which brought up feelings of sacredness within me. In the consciousness of my youth, I had fancied myself a mystical warrior in the Oglala and Lakota Sioux traditions.

When Hill's book was published in 1979, I devoured it, exclaiming to all to read it. There was no other book like it. At that time, I also undertook the Scientology litigation which was appropriate because I hate oppression but didn't realize where those feelings came from.

In my readings on the subject I inevitably came across the great Indian warriors: Crazy Horse, Sitting Bull, Chief Joseph of the Nez Perce, and others like Red Cloud. They were my heroes fighting against oppression just as the Irish had since at least Cromwell in 1648. Crazy Horse was so named because when he galloped into battle, he charged headlong into the enemy astride his horse like no bullet or arrow could touch him; and they didn't. The plains Indians were fearsome warriors capable of firing several arrows with remarkable accuracy whilst bareback riding into battle. According to oral legend, with some historical context, he led the charge at the Little Big Horn against Custer and the 7th cavalry.

As my knowledge in the law grew, and I studied how the law was manipulated and corrupted against Native Americans and other minorities, including African Americans, I became increasingly enraged at their treatment and plight. In my DNA, it was Ireland's fight for independence.

As I investigated Leonard Peltier's case, Russell Means became a friend and client. It was not a coincidence. I had already read *Hanta Yo* and we discussed it in detail. He, Dennis Banks and Leonard Peltier had been charged in connection with the 1973 AIM protests at the Second Wounded Knee. We discussed the first Wounded Knee and agreed that the government showed it could not tolerate any form of independence to their rule...even in the form of Indian spirituality. When they massacred mostly old men, women and children at the Pine Ridge reservation in South Dakota it became one of the most outrageous crimes in American history.

Leonard Peltier was indicted for the killing of the two FBI agents at Second Wounded Knee on the same Pine Ridge Reservation. He always denied his involvement. The government initially indicted Banks and Russell Means to squeeze them to give evidence against Peltier, but the charges were later dismissed. I met Russell years later.

Peltier was in prison for first degree murder. I investigated the matter for Russell who was trying to help Peltier. I ultimately decided it was a lost cause. I had my own deeply held convictions on the original 1890 massacre, the 1973 occupation and the goals of AIM. I liked Russell. He gave me a picture of Red Cloud, knowing the esteem in which I held him, and particularly Chief Joseph who famously said when he finally surrendered after a 1,200 mile fighting retreat:

> "From where the sun now stands I will fight no more forever."

FROM WHERE THE SUN NOW STANDS

When the Scio wars ended in 1987, I identified with Chief Joseph's above statement and my future in litigation. I sent it to my children. In Red Cloud's speech following the 1890 massacre at First Wounded Knee he highlighted the U.S. government's repeated violations of treaties, particularly the 1868 Treaty of Fort Laramie, which promised support but instead led to more land loss and more suffering. In a later speech at Cooper Union he said:

"The Good Spirit made us both. He gave us lands and He gave you lands;

He gave us these lands. You came here and we received you as brothers."

These speeches should be read by every American student in junior high school. The Second Wounded Knee occupation on the Pine Ridge Reservation in South Dakota in 1973 resulted in the unfortunate deaths of the two FBI agents. I felt grief for their families. I also sympathized with Russell and the protesters for their overall cause. The Bureau of Indian Affairs, managed by our government, are both notoriously corrupt.

Russell explained that the conviction of Peltier for the killing of the FBI agents had much greater meaning to the Lakota than the hard facts of the case. It involved overriding historical rage, mixed with Native American, Lakota, spiritual metaphysical meaning. There is much debate and conflicting facts as to what ignited the original 1890 massacre.

The army under Colonel Forsyth had mandated that the Lakota at Pine Ridge, Wounded Knee creek, move on to specific reservation land; and not engage in their Ghost dance, which the army believed was a mystical call to war against the whites for killing tribal ancestors and taking tribal lands.

To the Lakota at Wounded Knee, Forsyth's military force, his orders and menacing display of weapons, including Hotchkiss Mountain guns, and three hundred troopers, represented their oppression. They had been forcibly removed from their tribal land that they had been promised and never received as a result of the broken treaties of the past 40 years. The Lakota had been lied to by the government for decades and had only experienced broken promises, broken treaties, starvation, threats of military force, and loss of their freedom. Additionally, the administration of their so-called reservations was incredibly corrupt.

My Irish genes identified with the Lakota as I studied the British starvation of my ancestors. It was coming from the same playbook.

The Lakota were controlled and enforced by a corrupt but exceedingly powerful white man's government and army. This was made even worse by the inability of the Sioux to fight back in any meaningful way within the scope of the white man's laws. In fact, if you drill down into the treatment of the Sioux, under American judges and laws, it is a disgrace. On that, Russell and I agreed...in spades.

Traditional tribal customs and dances representing Lakota sacred rites invoked the Great Spirit's aid necessary to their survival and their resistance to oppression, and loss of freedom. It was a call to their version of Divine Mother, the feminine force in nature.

When Russell and the 1973 AIM protesters occupied Wounded Knee, using the mystical power of their dances and tribal customs, they also displayed some small arms and rifles. The Government responded with armored personnel carriers, machine guns, and a large enough army of Marshals to begin a civil war. To the Lakota, they were invoking their sacred rites to resist government oppression. To the mad militarists making decisions for the government it was 1890 Wounded Knee all over again.

It was similar to what Janet Reno did under Clintons' watch in Waco to David Koresh and his cult, The Branch Davidians—a massacre of 76 men, women and children. Amongst them were twenty-five children and two pregnant women. Monstrous. I'm an anti-cultist having litigated against Scientology, Ananda and other cults that use lies, deceit, and financial crimes to make money, the characteristics of a cult, as opposed to self-liberation. Indeed, the difference between a cult and a true "religion"...binding back the soul to God, is precisely this distinction. Does the group follow the "voice" of materialism? Or the true "spirit's voice"?

The former murdered Christ when he interrupted Temple cash flows. The current "prosperity religionists" like Osteen, Copeland, Creflo Dollar, Hinn, the pioneer, Pat Robertson, and proliferating TV evangelists, all sell Jesus to make money—"send a check and you will be saved, praise Jesus." These parasites now permeate our culture. Hubbard built a billion dollar fortune, he labeled as a "Church" to get tax exemption based on science fiction pseudo psychotherapy sold by an intelligence/CIA type organization specializing in frame ups, defamation and blackmail.

True religion is characterized by teachings like the Sermon on the Mount that represent authentic "Self-Realization," not dependent on clerical structure, lies, deceit, financial manipulation, and doctrinal, dogmatic, nonsense.

In the 1973 Wounded Knee occupation, the AIM protesters were remembering the murder of their ancestors, and like in 1890, they were defenseless to resist the full force of the government weaponry. It was the murderous Hotchkiss guns all over again. They were defeated by a far superior military force and so the occupation was really over before the protest started.

They had intended to display the power of their spirit. The Lakota believe that ultimately the Great Spirit will achieve justice for their people. Second Wounded Knee was a step in that direction, but like the First Wounded Knee, the government would not tolerate such freedom and independence from a bunch of savages.

Russell was not a racist. He was a realist and activist for his people, and he was right. In his now famous 1989 speech to the U.S. Senate, he said:

> "The major factors presenting American Indian people were the existing rights to self-determination. American Indians suffer under a system of dual citizenship, that is U.S. citizenship and Tribal citizenship, maintained by the BIA. Only Hitler did that. The dual citizenship is a major obstacle in the free exercise of individual and tribal sovereignty. The continuing loss and attrition of existing lands to various federal, state, and local laws and/or regulations is a hindrance, the abridgment of sovereign rights to remaining lands and the arbitrary monetary policies of settlement of these rights whenever they are recognized."

My feelings were evolving in the late 1980s, and early 1990s when Russell became a client. These feelings aligned with my developing disgust for the Deep State and its control over our institutions and our way of life. Back then it was still called the military industrial complex. As always, it was about money, greed and power. The Native American tribes just got in the way beginning in the 1600s and continuing to the present. Same for the Irish opposing British empire building.

Russell's views and the justness of his native American cause comported with mine. We discussed the reality that Ms. Hill's, Ahbleza, and her entire book, were a metaphor for Native American oppression by the U.S. government. It depicted the end of real native culture and the advancement of European culture.

Russell felt that Peltier's conviction was just an extension of the oppression. But two FBI agents were dead. Their innocence, or lack thereof in the context of fast-moving events, is not documented in the available evidence. Did they trigger the ensuing firefight? The government was and is in control of those facts. One fact was clear, the two FBI agents intruded into the fire zone within range of the AIM protesters by driving their car within range of the AIM building, knowing that they possessed high powered rifles which could reach the location of the agents. Provocation?

Our Government is doing the same today by sending our aircraft carriers to the Middle East, and also weaponizing the war lord Zelensky in the Ukraine. There, they are spending billions and billions of dollars to weaken Russia, and also preserve Ukrainian assets for the money changers masquerading as western bankers.

The two Wounded Knee tragedies, and the government-caused deaths of the Cherokee on the Trail of Tears was a manipulation for land and money by the then newly formed Democratic Party in the 1830s. The pursuit and decimation of Chief Joseph and the Nez Perce is the typical Deep State response to anything that challenges its power. It is covered in more depth in *Litigator 4*.

For my purposes in this book, the Second Wounded Knee issues and facts, having drilled down into them personally with Russell, essentially involve the disparity and conflict between Lakota native American consciousness in its tribal rituals, and the consciousness of a violent military force to oppress it. Like First Wounded Knee, the government, lacking such consciousness, even as late as 1973, could not abide the Lakota practicing the Ghost dance in it's heavily militarised face.

To this day, Peltier claims he was not the actual shooter. The evidence tends towards ambivalence. He was present with a rifle together with two other AIM activists when the agents were shot. The most troubling part of the whole sorry saga to me, was that the government prepared autopsy reports of the two agents, stated that they were ultimately killed at close range, execution style...But that's the governments' story. It has substantial gaps.

I know that the JFK autopsy results were altered. *Litigator 4*. I know that the Vince Foster autopsy results were altered. *Litigator 5*. I know that the Deep State Secret Government murdered them both and covered up their murders. The Irish priest was killed execution style. It was barbarous by any measure. The British deep state in the form of the Black and Tans literally got away with murder of Father Griffin. I feel the connecting dots in my soul.

And like the Secret Service, FBI, and CIA involvement in the plainly corrupted autopsy on President Kennedy, the FBI autopsy on the two dead agents raises suspicions to me of whether our government falsified them to obtain convictions against Peltier. I know how they fabricate and alter evidence. Chapters 22 and 23.

Russell explained to me the depth of the hatred in some of the AIM activists at Pine Ridge in their remembered spirit of their ancestors. But my conscience could not abide the execution-style killing of the agents, assuming it to be true. Nor can it abide the corruption within the Bureau of Indian Affairs, and its big brother, now called the deep state. My involvement was only limited to an investigation for my now deceased friend Russell Means, one of the good guys on this planet.

I did not take up Peltier's cause. I am left with abiding ambiguities in my own consciousness to this day. The execution-style killing of the agents in 1973 appears to be what the U.S. army did in 1890 at First Wounded Knee to the Lakota Indians, slaughtering and executing men, women and children with rifles, Hotchkiss guns and random murders, chasing and killing women and children as they fled. Pay back for Custer? If you care to play with the idea of quantum entanglement, did the particles exhibiting the same wave resonance from 1890 reappear in 1973? Can we then posit from this that the Black and Tans, barbarous instruments of the British crown, murdered my prior incarnation in 1920, and that a fragment of that QE reappeared somehow in my Father Michael Griffin episode of 1987 in my Washington hotel room 67 years later?

In 1890, the 7th Cavalry Commander, James Forsyth, later claimed in a military inquiry, basically a cover-up, that the Lakota fired first. His superior, General Miles disputed Forsyth's version of what happened. Forsyth controlled the body count. The Lakota disputed it. It was murder, pure and simple. Three hundred troopers with enough weaponry to destroy the confederates in Pickett's charge, against 300 plus mostly starving, freezing, women and children and old men. One hundred and thirty five years later, despite the massively larger body count and modern high tech weaponry, doesn't this sound a lot like the genocide in Gaza? When will we learn? This is injustice on a scale that raises my non-meditative homicidal instincts.

THE .303 ENFIELD

There was a remarkably similar massacre just 3 decades after Wounded Knee, at Amritsar in India in 1919, in which another white government, the British again, slaughtered hundreds of local "Indians," between 379 and 1000 according to different reports and with hundreds more wounded. The casualty figures are disputed. The British controlled the body count. About two thousand Indians were protesting peacefully for Indian Independence in a closed arena in violation of British General Reginald Dyer's orders. Same as Colonel Forsyth's prohibiting the meeting of Lakota for their Ghost Dance.

The protesters defied Dyer and assembled at Amritsar. His imperialistic consciousness, like Forsyth, could not abide such a flagrant protest to British Power as it arrogantly occupied Indian land. He arrived with fifty troopers and two armoured cars, again reminiscent of First Wounded Knee, and proceeded to open fire directly on hundreds of men, women, and children peacefully protesting British imperialism and occupation of their country. Thankfully, the armoured cars couldn't fit down the narrow lane to Jallianwala Bagh, the enclosed garden where the protestors had gathered. Had they reached them, the body count would have been exponentially higher—instead the troopers were armed with.303 Lee Enfield rifles. White imperialism slaughtering Indians! On their own home turf!

General Dyer said at a later so called military "Inquest" as the international fury erupted and demanded it: The army came with two armoured cars equipped with machine guns but couldn't get them through the narrow gates, '"otherwise we would have used them." Instead, they 'just' used riflemen firing 303 Lee Enfield rifles. The 50 troopers fired 1650 rounds directly into the crowd for 10 straight minutes. There was no cover, nowhere to go. Many jumped into a well to escape the merciless fire of General Reginald Dyer. Most of those drowned. During the absurd, British style inquest into the massacre, at least one military member of the inquest team inquired into the measures that were taken to treat the wounded. The arrogant, piece of horse dung, General Reginald Dyer, who ordered the massacre, replied that:

"aid was available to those who asked for it."

The sympathetic Amritsar inquisitor then asked:

"How does a child shot through with a .303 Enfield request aid?"

This was eerily reminiscent of the consciousness of Colonel Forsyth in 1890 at Wounded Knee, who left the untreated wounded to die, and their bloodied, freezing bodies left in the snow for picture taking...perhaps thinking 'Let that be a warning to yah.'

For the murderous Black and Tans in Ireland between January 1919 and September 1921, the .303 Enfield was the weapon of choice to kill my Irish forbears. Oh, it must be justified I hear the English say! Just ask Winston Churchill, First Lord of the Admiralty. The 'First Lord' moniker is an oxymoron if ever there was. He starved 3 million Bengalis in 1943 and later on other titled 'Royals' firebombed Dresden leaving over 100,000 civilians incinerated in a firestorm. My consciousness has always resonated with the karmic consequences of these massacres. That evil is hard to stomach.

THE CONNECTING DOTS

Russell and I saw eye to eye on the parallels. The British first hunted down then executed Irish men suspected of IRA affiliations, then, following the "Easter Rising," they enforced their laws that lacked any semblance of fairness or due process and executed the surviving IRA leaders. Today, those executed are hailed as Irish heroes. To me, there are similarities to the later AIM protesters of 1973, martyrs in their own right.

The convergence of these experiences, revealed the shocking reality of self-imposed human suffering. My encounters with Russell Means shortly afterwards, the quantum-entangled memories of World War II events and the realities of both Wounded Knees, shook me to my core. It must be no accident that just before this event I had concluded the punishing eight year Scientology wars. There were undeniable parallels with their policy of "make money, make more money, make others make more money" that had left a trail of victims at my office door, and opened a window of realisation for my awareness of man's inhumanity to his fellow beings.

Whether these experiences represent past life reincarnation, I cannot say with certainty. I have had no direct reincarnation experiences with Native American cultures. Yet somehow, every nuance of injustice inflicted on Native Americans, which seemed to pour out of Russell Means like Niagara Falls, resonated with the deepest wounds within me, quantum-entangled with British oppression of the Irish, and their colonization of India.

My consciousness, shaped by fervent study of Gandhi and support for his independence movement, my representation of TM, and Maharishi Mahesh Yogi, and the life-transforming impact of Paramahansa Yogananda, had led me towards India's spiritual heritage. All of these influences created quantum entanglements with issues of justice and oppression that transcended individual cases.

The profound spiritual insights gained through decades of meditation practice and quantum entangled experiences had given me tools to understand many of life's mysteries. Yet as I would soon discover, some tragedies, particularly those involving the innocent, would challenge even my deepest spiritual understanding and force me to grapple with questions that meditation alone could not fully answer.

BRIDGING TRADITIONS: FROM LAKOTA WISDOM TO YOGIC MEDITATION

The dead priest experience of 1987, together with Ms. Hill's book *Hanta Yo*, prepared me for a re-reading of *Autobiography of a Yogi*, an introduction to the Self-Realization Fellowship Lessons, and the Kriya Yoga ceremony and meditation disciplines—all of which I pursued a year later beginning on March 7, 1988. The Kriya Yoga initiation is a once-in-a-lifetime ceremony. Perhaps that is what Ahbleza meant in the "white pipe ceremony." I was transcended throughout my own Kriya Yoga initiation ceremony.

In the AY, Yogananda describes the reality of higher states of consciousness in and through the lives of yogis in this state, and the impact on his own consciousness as he encountered these super-conscious yogis. Some of these yogis were also highly educated academically speaking but their consciousness transcended the difficulties that their narrower educational levels might have created. He recounts that in his search for God realization, he met many yogis, but that it was his Guru, Swami Sri Yukteswar, who directly bestowed on him the experience of cosmic consciousness.

This syndrome of one realized Master bestowing on his disciple their own self-realization is a critical component of Vedanta philosophy and theology. It has similarities with the 'wave resonance field' of quantum physics, where synchronization between them is attained through a shared vibrational state or 'resonance'.

Yogananda gives a detailed account of Sri Yukteswar not only giving him a very specific, direct experience of God, but also training him on how to realize and repeat the experience of God within himself. The SRF Lessons explain in precise detail how to do it. Before he died and entered Mahasamadhi, Yogananda also stated that "only love will take my place."

This profound remark serves as a prophetic insight into the state of quantum entanglement and actually reveals the channel that we can use to enter it; it's love that governs our species within the force fields of God.

Whether God consciousness was either imparted to, or awakened within Yogananda by his Guru is a significant question, yet here's what strikes me as most profound: on a transcendental level, both approaches arrive at the same truth. Whether consciousness is awakened or imparted becomes less significant than the undeniable reality of the experience itself. Once someone has touched that divine awareness, the mechanism becomes secondary to the fact that it happened. This transcends Einstein's concern about "incomplete knowledge" and "hidden variables." At this level of experience, there are no hidden variables because the reality simply is.

Whether mystical experiences represent reincarnation or energy transformation, the experience itself carries its own authority. It needs no external validation or theoretical framework to justify its existence. In the realm of direct spiritual experience, the reality simply is beyond all our attempts to capture it in concepts or explanations.

THE WARRIOR AND THE PRIEST BECOME ONE

Yogananda explains this seeming paradox of automatic awakening of higher states of consciousness based on prior incarnations vs the imparting of Christ consciousness from a true Guru. In the guru-disciple relationship of Jesus and John the Baptist alternating lifetimes as Elisha and Elijah, Yogananda describes the transmutation of bodily flesh into energy in the reincarnation process. This is the combination of Elisha and Elijah of the Old Testament reincarnating as John the Baptist and Jesus in the New Testament fulfillment of Scripture. *The Second Coming of Christ* at pp. 887-890.

Yogananda explores the nature of human existence and reality in Chapter 35 of *Autobiography of a Yogi*, focusing on the life and passing of Lahiri Mahasaya, a Christ-like prophet:

"It is the Infinite, the Ocean of Power, that lies behind all phenomenal manifestations. Our eagerness for worldly activity kills in us the sense of spiritual awe... In science, our relation with Nature is like that between an arrogant man and his servant... We cross-examine her, challenge her, and minutely weigh her evidence in human scales that cannot measure her hidden values."

Wow. The litigator in me who has cross-examined many a captive in the witness box felt like I had been struck with a thunderbolt when I read this. Guilty as charged. How do I escape this self-made prison? In that realization, I knew that Ahbleza had correctly explained the white pipe ceremony. The ceremony itself, the initiation into Spirit, provides the realization, "perhaps only once..." In other words, once awakened, that's it. There is no going back into ignorance.

At this level, there is no meaningful difference between 'realizing the Self' and 'experiencing God directly.' They are two descriptions of the same instantaneous contact with ultimate reality. This would explain Christ and his dictum that 'the Kingdom of God' is within us. In reality, we are one with God, as Yogananda says, all we have to do is increase our knowing to the point of self realization...union with God. It strikes me that if space and time are eliminated in God consciousness, as Yogananda stated, the quantum physicists are getting closer to explaining the reality of Christ, Paramahansa Yogananda, and all the Self-realized mystics and yogis throughout earth-bound time.

The connection between Sri Yukteswar and Paramahansa Yogananda, and the receptivity of disciple to Guru's God consciousness, may be what modern day quantum physicists, like John Bell appear to be calling super determinism; that all matter is connected in string theory, or Dr. Meijer confirms as quantum entanglement. Are they flip sides of the same coin; humans as part matter and part spirit? Are these the "two voices" of Ahbleza?

In the AY, Yogananda describes such connectivity among the yogis he encountered almost a century before quantum theory had arrived at a similar conclusion. He explained it in terms of needing a Guru to achieve Self-Realization. One particle needs to identify with the other. Meijer's studies seem to confirm it as quantum entanglement, just as in the Bible, the Guru and disciple advance through cycles of reincarnation as Elijah, Elisha, and John the Baptist and Jesus did maintaining their entangled state throughout multiple incarnations.

THE DISPELLER OF DARKNESS

When I learned Transcendental Meditation, a whole new world had opened up to me. My mind, which had been disturbed by the relentless stress of my courtroom battles, was experiencing a very welcome silence. It filled me with hope and introduced me to the ancient culture of India. Maharishi himself had spent 13 years under the tutelage of his teacher, Guru Dev, who was part of a spiritual lineage dating back thousands of years. This is the Vedic tradition of India.

A teacher is referred to as 'Guru' in Sanskrit. Literally, the term means 'dispeller of darkness.' This refers to the light of knowledge that the teacher imparts to his or her students to dispel the darkness of ignorance. In Vedic culture, teachers are highly revered and respected. They offer profound solutions that lead to a smoother, more contented, and successful existence. Without a Guru, it would be near impossible for the individual to achieve this stature without arduous spiritual dedication and practice that goes to creating a genuinely effective spiritual teacher...the Guru.

My original glimpses into the depth of this culture occurred when I began working with Maharishi's brilliant assistant, Anjali Mahaldar; and others in the TM leadership, including one who would rise to become the current head of TM – Dr. Tony Nader, a neuroscientist. Tony became a friend and I gave him an office in my Boston office when he was a student at MIT. Tony's books on TM are recommended: *Consciousness Is All There Is*; and *One Unbounded Ocean of Consciousness: Simple Answers to the Big Questions in Life.*

Similarly, the remarkable consciousness of Anjali Mahaldar, a teacher of Maharishi's TM, and practitioner of TM Sidhi Yoga, is illustrated in her description of personally meeting a saintly Guru, describing the subtle levels of consciousness that are possible in the Guru-disciple relationship.

"There was the thrill of anticipation... the reigning Shankaracharya of Jyotirmath, a direct disciple of Guru Dev was going to be in our midst... The Shankaracharya, Swami Shantananda Saraswatiji arrived with His entourage amidst Vedic chanting. The whole atmosphere was charged and through it there was the unmistakable effulgent presence of a tall, luminous saint standing almost apart from everyone, radiant to the point of being dazzling... What happened next is something surreal in nature... the Dandi Swami looking in my direction... Without a second thought and spontaneously I reached to where He was sitting, kept a distance and with palms together, fell to my knees in front of Him. I wanted to say the words 'Jai Guru Dev' but found I couldn't find my voice... The Dandi sanyasi said in very warm Hindi, using the familiar second person pronoun 'You are Anju?' You are with Maharishi? I bent down as is the custom of my tradition to touch His feet but He gently stopped me saying that it was not for the Divine Mother to do that... If it were possible to drop the body, that would have been my choice, the exhilaration of being in His attention... This Divine being went on to say that I was doing very good work and some very kind things which I have treasured every day of my life since that sublime moment... I would learn later that this great saint was His Holiness Swami Vishnudevanandji, a direct disciple of Guru Dev who would soon assume the title of Jagadguru Shankaracharya of Jyotirmath."

The concept of utmost reverence for the teacher is hardly unique to the Vedic culture. Another example is the Sufi tradition, which derives its roots from Islam, and also honors this bond, as evidenced in the following from Farid-ud-din Attar's 'The Conference of the Birds.'

THE COMMON GROUND OF CONSCIOUSNESS

The full impact of such an association did not dawn on me until destiny led me several years later to find my teacher, Paramahansa Yogananda. Through my own experience I learned how very rare and precious the connection with one's spiritual teacher, the Guru is. The gifts of this association are limitless to me, and brings forth a sense of gratitude so deep that one knows it can never be repaid, nor is it required. In fact, the evidence of real-life quantum entanglement is compelling within and beyond rational, logical thought and experience, and thankfully we are gradually moving towards the instruments that the materialistic, modern scientists demand in order to measure it.

Federico Faggin, Tony Nader, Steven Meyer, Douglas Axe, Dr. Alexander and many other neuroscientists, whether by formal education or experiential knowledge gained in meditation and clinical experience, are getting closer to describing and defining consciousness, if that is even possible? Like Einstein, if these seekers of ultimate truth continue describing consciousness in materialist language will they end up with the word "spooky"? Or will they get branded as "scientific heretics," by western trained materialist "scientists?"

BURNED AT THE STAKE OF PSEUDO-SCIENCE

Atheists and pseudo scientists like Richard Dawkins, making millions on his books, while not actually teaching real biology at Oxford, only teaching the history of evolutionary, Darwinism, along with his fellow atheists, Hitchens and Harris, have attacked the intelligent designers, sages and mystics, and others as "heretics" to "real science." Talk about the pot calling the kettle black. They sound like the medieval popes burning the scientists of their age at the stake, but currently using "the stake" of modern media false propaganda to sell their books.

The Roman Church historically labeled "scientists" who opposed Church dogma as "heretics." They burned them at the stake and / or persecuted them. Like the Sanhedrin, they were the consummate medieval materialists. The Roman Church had a long list of burned / persecuted "scientists" and philosophers, eg, Servetus, (burned); Galileo; (spared by renouncing heliocentrism); Bruno (burned); Copernicus (spared), Bacon (imprisoned and died in a Franciscan monastery) etc etc.

The reality seems to be that the current consciousness explorers are being burned at the stake of pseudo-science propaganda. Our species has faced the paradox of science and religion in the context of consciousness for millennia. The scientists have never accepted miracles, and those who have experienced miracles have never capitulated to science because experience can be an undeniable truth. The dead priest did that for me.

The bottom line and end result of the exercise of living in the higher states of consciousness described by these yogis, on three planes of reality: the physical, the astral, and the causal, is the same as Christ taught: "The Kingdom of God is within you." Love God with all your being; and love your neighbor as yourself. Why should we do this? Because the Love force is not what one might think it is. It is far beyond human notions of love and romance. It is foundational to one particle identifying instantly with another...they become identical...hence love your neighbor because you and they are one.

Yogis living in higher states of consciousness lived their lives under the almost identical prescriptions of the Christian Sermon on the Mount and the Hindu Bhagavad Gita. It is true that Ms. Hill's book, *Hanta Yo*, is historical, mystical, and spiritual fiction, but it vividly portrays the authentic experience of Lakota life, highlighting how it surpasses the religiosity of European proselytizing. The deeply ingrained oral, tribal traditions, vision quests, ghost dances and white pipe ceremonies passed down through the centuries of the Lakota native American experience hold a profound reality in both the natural and the Spirit realms unlike the enforced religious doctrines, dogmas and rituals of their oppressors.

If you deem the American Indian cultures to be as savage as represented by the so called Christian purveyors of history, I strongly recommend a study of the two world wars between our 'sophisticated' European Christian countries. Chapter 18 in this book on the bombing of Dresden should put those misperceptions to rest.

Hanta Yo's primary example and exponent of such love and sacrifice, following the prescription of his Vision Quest, and resulting in Self-realization, is Ahbleza. He is killed by an opposing tribe while saving his people by leading the enemy away from his tribe towards himself. Reminiscent of Christ? The final scene in the movie "Dances with Wolves" from Blake's 1988 book is said to come from Hill's book when Costner and his wife leave the tribe to save it from the scourge of the attacking U.S. army.

Ms. Hill provides an incredible description of Self-realization in the context of sacrificial death within the realization, or vision within the Lakota White pipe ceremony. That ceremony essentially involved a vision of White Buffalo Calf Woman aka the divine feminine, appearing and bringing truth or Divine consciousness represented by the Sacred Pipe. To the Lakota, it was the most powerful earthly power of connection to the Great Spirit. In Advaita Vedanta, it would be Divine Mother. In Catholicism, it would be, Mary, "The Mother of God," with Christ her son.

Paramahansa Yogananda would likely call the pipe ceremony, the appearance of or manifestation of Divine Mother. She appeared to him and guided his life on many occasions as described in the AY, just like the pipe ceremony guided the Lakota. That was their Self-realization. It was a sacred trust from the Great Spirit.

My encounters with Russell Means, the quantum-entangled memories of Wounded Knee, and the echoes of Irish rebellion in my past life experience, revealed a pattern of human suffering so vast and so brutal that it seemed to mock the stillness I found in meditation. The warrior in me raged against the injustice, demanding action, while the priest sought solace in the silent, eternal laws of karma and consciousness.

I came to realize that these two voices are not necessarily in conflict. They were two sides of the same sacred duty. The warrior's righteous anger is the engine for change in the material world, the force that confronts the money changers and defends the innocent. But that anger, if left untempered, consumes itself. The priest's path, the path of meditation and surrender to the Great Spirit is what gives the warrior his true power. It is the source of the vision that guides his hand, the wellspring of love that prevents his heart from turning to stone, and the quiet certainty that even in the face of unspeakable tragedy, a higher justice prevails.

The Lakota knew this. The Yogis of India knew this. The warrior and the priest must become one.

Epilogue

LAKOTA SPIRITUALITY AND THE RESISTANCE TRADITION

The story of my encounter with Russell Means and the naming of my boat, *Hanta Yo*, is incomplete without a deeper understanding of the spiritual and historical tradition he represented, and I have consolidated the essential context here. This epilogue explores the profound spiritual practices of the Lakota people, their history of resistance against a shared 'Empire Consciousness,' and the legacy of a man who embodied the warrior's spirit.

My immersion in Ruth Beebe Hill's book, *Hanta Yo*, was the gateway to understanding the Lakota world. It is a mystical story based on oral tradition, mixed with spiritualized fiction involving the treatment of the Oglala Sioux from the early 1700s through the mid 1800s. For me, it described the plains Indians' experience of the Lakota and its leaders from their origins before European contamination. More importantly, it described a native American spirituality based on the natural connection of all things: man to earth, man to animals, man to man, and man to the Great Spirit. It is the Lakota version of quantum entanglement.

The book captures just how nourishing to the body, mind and spirit that type of human community was. Though a quasi-fictional biography based on oral traditions, it received mixed reviews. Its facts, at least as known and recorded by the white man, convey a strong sense of actual history within Lakota tribal culture. To me, it is the native American version of *Autobiography of a Yogi*. Though very different books from different cultures, they share a similar metaphysical and spiritual message about the nature of reality. They both transcend time and space.

At the heart of this tradition are the Seven Sacred Rites, including the sweat lodge, Sun Dance, Ghost Dance, vision quest, and spirit keeping. These are not mere rituals, but technologies of consciousness. The Sioux Native Americans experienced the same spiritual powers in their Vision Quests and Ghost Dances that the followers of Christ accept and believe were present in the resurrection of Christ. The legendary Chief, Crazy Horse, apparently possessed such powers on a regular basis. He was able to ride into battle with no fear of death, possessing a realization that enemy weapons could not touch him.

In everyday practice, the Lakota called this Spirit keeping or Lakol Wicohan. They followed the Sermon on the Mount, not in a biblical sense, but within their communal structure: 'live and treat life, and all those in their ambit of communal life and love, as if given as a gift to them by the Great Spirit'. Everything was sacred, made of the Great Spirit, and living in this spirit would merge them at death within that Great Spirit. This is virtually the same sentiment as the Christian realization of the Kingdom of God Within.

WOUNDED KNEE: THE TWO MASSACRES

This spiritual tradition was met with brutal force. In America, in 1890, government troops massacred over 300 people, mostly old men, women and children, at Wounded Knee. This was the greatest mass shooting in American history and committed as the Lakota practiced the Ghost Dance, a spiritual ceremony to invoke the protection of the Great Spirit. As the defenseless Indians worshiped, the army gunned them down, even as they fled. They also used Hotchkiss Mountain guns that fired 1.65" shells. That, dear reader, is what the money changers do to the innocent when they get in the way of 'progress'...read 'profits'.

Eighty-three years later, in 1973, at that same sacred ground, Russell Means, as the leader of the American Indian Movement, attempted to resurrect Indian spirituality. He organized a protest against the history of broken treaties by the government and against the thoroughly corrupt "Bureau of Indian Affairs". Russell resurrected the Ghost Dance in the Oglala Lakota tradition to prove that native spirituality was more powerful than U.S. Marshal and FBI guns. He lost. The government responded with enough military presence to destroy the protest. Ultimately, as seen in his 1989 speech to the U.S. Senate, it might be argued that in the long term, at least morally and specifically as 'truth spoken to power', Russell won.

EMPIRE CONSCIOUSNESS: A SHARED HISTORY OF OPPRESSION

The oppression of the Lakota was not an isolated event; it was part of a global 'Empire Consciousness' that my own Irish ancestors knew intimately. In his book, *The Famine Plot: England's Role in Ireland's Greatest Tragedy*,

Tim Pat Coogan describes the horrors of British imperialism. He quotes an American philanthropist, Asenath Nicholson, who visited Ireland in 1851 and observed the wretched condition of the Irish:

> "I could scarcely believe that these creatures were my fellow-beings. Never have I seen slaves so degraded; and here I learnt that there are many pages in the volume of slavery, and that every branch of it proceeds from one and the same root, though it assumes different shapes. These poor creatures are in as virtual bondage to their landlords and superiors as is possible for mind or body to be. They cannot work unless they bid them; they cannot eat unless they feed them; and they cannot get away unless they help them."

In India and Ireland during the 1700s to 1900s, the British starved and oppressed millions of 'natives' to build their Empire. In their original conquest of America, they did the same to American Indians. The "Trail of Tears" between 1830 and 1850 involved the ethnic cleansing and deaths of thousands of Indians by our government.

In the light of such oppression, many turned to forms of spirituality to deal with their oppressors. In India, Gandhi responded with non-violent spirituality in his Ahimsa and Satyagraha movements. The British responded with mass murders at Amritsar in 1919 and the starvation of 3 million Bengalis in 1943. Ultimately, Gandhi's spirituality won when his actions forced the British out in 1947.

THE LEGACY OF RUSSELL MEANS

Russell Means educated me in vivid detail how the same thing was done to his Oglala Sioux ancestors. In his 1989 speech to the U.S. Senate, he declared:

> "In these United States of America, this great country of ours, we American Indians, we can be anything we want to be except American Indians; and that is created by the laws of this nation and condoned by its subsidiaries, the so-called Tribal Government, and designed for the Indian to fail, to be expendable, to be eliminated."

Russell championed many American Indian Chiefs from different tribes including Red Cloud, Sitting Bull, Crazy Horse, and Chief Joseph of the Nez Perce. He saw in them a wisdom derived from a state of consciousness beyond mere educated intellect. As Sitting Bull said:

> "I am a red man. If the Great Spirit had desired me to be a white man, he would have made me so in the first place… He put in your heart certain wishes and plans, in my heart he put other and different desires… Each man is good in his sight. It is not necessary for Eagles to be Crows."

This history of oppression and spiritual resistance is the deep context behind the name *Hanta Yo*. It is also the backdrop for the 'two voices' we have discussed and which I have carried within me; the litigator fighting against the modern money changers and their Empire Consciousness, and the meditator seeking the silent voice of the Great Spirit. They are a sacred resistance, fought with spiritual integrity, against a world that seeks to eliminate all that is sacred.

CHAPTER 15

The McCuish Tragedy: Justice Triumphs over Greed

> "Children don't start wars and they have no power to end wars but they are the ones who suffer the most." **Catherine Russell**

—∾—

There are presently, by reported accounts, over 20,000 dead children in Gaza, along with approximately 200,000 other Palestinians, killed by the Israeli Defense Force. It's a number growing by the minute, as bombed-out buildings are excavated. The consciousness here is not much different to the levels of human atrocity and genocide in 1890 Wounded Knee, 1919 Amritsar, 1943 Churchill / Bengali starvation, 1848 Irish famine starvation (about a million), and the 1945 firebombing of Dresden (over 100,000 revenge killing of civilians by Churchill, Stalin and Roosevelt—Chapter 18). Only the body count varies. Are the dead Gaza children, who didn't start or have the power to stop the war, the result of Israeli greed for land, or Israeli survival as recounted in the historic battles in the Old Testament, continuing through the centuries of the rise of Islam and Zionism?

The Nazi war machine holocausted about 6 million jews, with now over $86 Billion in German reparations to Jewish families based on Israeli claims. The British Empire genocided over 200 million, 1700–1950. Stalin murdered about 40 million. Communist China about 76 Million, 1949–1987. Estimates currently are that humans killing their babies, abortion, since Roe v Wade, exceeded 600,000 annually just in the U.S. How do we as a society stop genocide and atrocity?

Does it make any difference to innocent children, or infants in the womb with a consciousness seeking life, who or what caused their deaths? Is there any accountability?

Jesus said:

> "Suffer the little children, and forbid them not, to come unto me, for such is the Kingdom of Heaven." **Mathew 19:14.**

How many ways do humans "forbid" little children to come unto God? Was abortion one of the accepted human mechanisms of death for the unborn decreed by humans or God? The Supreme Court has recently overturned Roe v Wade, the previous "legal standard" regulating who dies and who lives in the womb. It's a human contrivance, now called "legally incorrect", after 50 years of infant death for the past 5 decades...at least 32 Million dead babies. In good conscience, does 32 million dead kids make the 20,000 dead kids in Gaza seem a small number?

On the minimalist quotients, in the last decades, Jeffrey Epstein and his traffickers, sexually abused and corrupted over 250 teenage children in order to "honey trap" perverts like Clinton, and other influencers and individuals with power, a small number against 32 million! But the sheer perversity of it shocks the conscience of all law abiding and goodness seeking souls. On the macro scale, the above human history of atrocity, genocide, abortion and death cannot be really understood by a consciousness believing that "love" is the most powerful force on this planet of death—or can it? You are the jury on this verdict. Do you have a consciousness of love or an eye for an eye, a tooth for a tooth?

One must ask what was the cause of all this death at the hands of humans killing other humans, inside or outside of the womb? War is clear: humans do it mostly for territorial conquest, power, money and partially for political, religious or cultural control. Without actual war, in a supposed civilized environment and society, why do humans kill other humans, whether intentionally, unintentionally, negligently, or by "accident"?

One thing I have learned in 50 years in the PIT, there are no accidents. We are all quantum entangled. I have seen it in the litigation trenches; and experienced it in meditative transcendence. In several small, so called "accidental death" cases, I grappled with not only the causal connections involving how humans kill each other, I measured the consciousness of the participants in the collective consciousness of juries, judges and the devastating grief of parents. The three cases of McCuish, O'Brian and Smyly follow. They have a specific resonance and connectedness in my consciousness, so they are in this first volume of the five-volume Litigator series.

Three very different cases with one common theme, death of young humans before they experience life. When measured against the above cited human atrocities and genocides, these three cases are seemingly of little consequence. When experienced through the lens of parental grief, these cases explain the reality of life and consciousness. I imagine the grief of the parents, probably also dead, of the 5300 dead Gaza children.

All three of these child death cases continue to have a huge impact on my consciousness. I grieve for the parents of every child who has been "forbidden" by human evil to come unto God, inside or outside of the womb. I grieve for the children whose lives intersected with mine who may or may not have entered the Kingdom of God when they died. The Smyly case where I whispered into the ear of supposedly comatose, 17 year old, previously "non-responsive," Sisi, still resonates within me as proof of consciousness over death; and proof of redemption for my client. Chapter 19.

The spiritual preparation I had received through years of meditation practice were about to be tested in ways I could never have anticipated. The most challenging cases for me have always involved child deaths. We have already read in Chapter 8 about the 'burning hand' case and the harrowing experience of Sandra and Lester, Joe Hakey's 8 and 10-year-old children, who were miraculously saved from being burned to death in a house fire. It was a quantum entangled emotional roller coaster that tragically involved the deaths of their two step-brothers. It is hard to quantify, or even attempt to describe the abject, soul-wrenching grief of parents losing their children in the harsh reality of inexplicable loss....and for me, it shifted both my professional and personal consciousness into uncharted territories that I had hoped I would never enter again, yet here I was once more.

A GRIEF BEYOND MEASURE

In 1980, Gail and Don McCuish came to my office carrying a grief so profound it seemed to alter the very atmosphere of the room. Their fifteen-year-old daughter Karen had been instantly killed in what appeared to be a minor traffic incident; a Volkswagen bus rolling over in a low-speed intersection collision with a Toyota sedan on a twenty-mile-per-hour city street. No speeding. No red light or stop sign violations. It was a simple case of obstructed vision when the Toyota driver failed to see the Volkswagen, when his view was blocked by a tree at the intersection.

The cruel mathematics of the tragedy defied comprehension: two people in the Toyota walked away unhurt. Five other teenagers in the Volkswagen, including the sixteen-year-old driver, emerged without injury. Only Karen, sitting on the middle bench seat died instantly when the top of her head was sheared off in the rollover.

Even four decades later, this tragedy still lives within me, visceral and unresolved across different levels of my consciousness.

From the perspective of history and biology, death is ordinary. Over the centuries, humans have killed each other by the hundreds of millions... and eight billion of us now populate the earth. Every physical body dies. This is the surface reality, but the 1978 TM Unity meditation experience revealed a deeper truth to me: consciousness is eternal. Our spirits have no beginning and no end. Death, in this sense, is an illusion. These two realities, the undeniable fact of physical death and the eternal nature of consciousness created a profound conflict within me. When I confronted child deaths in my litigation practice, specifically Karen's nearly inexplicable tragedy, the emotional anguish became an enormous karmic burden. I knew on one level that her consciousness was eternal, but I was also witnessing the devastating finality of her physical death and the resulting unbearable grief of her parents.

Their anguish poured over me in waves of incomprehension and not a little anger at God's ways. "How could God take our baby in an accident where seven others are untouched? How could he allow my little girl to die in such a way? How could God do this to us?" This became a recurring theme in my cases.

Their plea to me was raw and desperate: "Michael, will you investigate, do whatever research you can so we can find out what really happened because this makes no sense to us! We cannot afford extensive legal fees, but can you still help us? Will you take this on contingency, if not, how much do we need to pay you? "

Because of my natural reluctance to get involved with family related cases and the highly charged emotional aspect surrounding them, my initial assessment was perhaps too pragmatic, even clinical given their pain: "This is tragic, shockingly tragic, but this appears to be one of those unfortunate accidents with no clear legal liability, no assignable blame. The city should have cut that tree down, certainly, but under traditional tort causation law, it would be hard to actually prove the presence of a tree actually caused Karen's death? I'm sure the Toyota insurance carrier will offer their coverage limits".

I recall it being around ten or twenty thousand dollars, "and the Volkswagen insurance carrier will offer their maximum coverage as well. You don't need me for that kind of settlement."

But Gail and Don's response revealed the deeper dimension of their quest: "No. No way. No settlement with anyone or any company. We want to know why our little girl is dead. There must be a reason."

Something in their certainty that answers could be found, that Karen's death was not merely random tragedy but contained meaning that could be uncovered, resonated with my own growing understanding of consciousness and causation. "Okay," I told them. "I will investigate, and I will also take it on contingency. No settlement until we have all the answers."

Now, four decades later, I think of Karen's death against the dead Holocaust children, the dead Gaza children, the starved Irish children, the dead Ukrainian children, the dead aborted children, etc etc, and ask God...WHY?

What followed in 1980 was four years of intensive investigation, research, depositions, motions, and court proceedings, the full machinery of litigation grinding toward what we hoped would be truth. The case would ultimately go to jury trial, but the real trial for me was the one taking place within my own consciousness as I grappled with questions that transcended legal causation and entered the realm of cosmic justice.

The causes of fifteen-year-old Karen McCuish's death, although eventually presented to a jury on legally cognizable grounds, remain in the larger context of life and death a virtual mystery to me. The death of the Irish priest, which I would experience three years after this case was tried, I understood. In experiencing his death itself, I knew from his consciousness that he was fighting injustice and the oppression of the British Crown. When I tried the McCuish case in 1984, I did not yet have that experiential compass to guide me and make sense of this horrific tragedy. I would gain it three years later after the 1987 TM Siddhis course, but I still grapple with the fundamental question: Why did God allow this particular tragedy to happen?

Four years later, after intensive investigation, research, depositions, motions, court proceedings ad nauseam...this is what the litigation business is all about...we took it to jury trial.

THE VALUE OF A LIFE

First day in chambers before the assigned Massachusetts Superior Court Judge: Volkswagen's lawyers from one of the biggest law firms in Boston:

"Judge, the largest verdict in the Commonwealth for the instant death of a "minor," (that's "Karen" as denominated by the defense throughout the trial) is $100,000. In fact, there are no larger verdicts in any state involving the instant death of a minor with no pain and suffering and with no history of earnings. We have not found any case over that amount. It is indeed a tragic accident that she was killed instantly with no others even hurt, but we will never offer any more money." The law supports our position.

Judge: "Mr. Flynn is this true? $100,000 is the maximum recovery in this type of case by verdict or settlement?"

Me: "Yes Judge." "Then how on God's earth can you demand more and what are we doing here in my courtroom?"

Me: "Judge, my clients want a trial. We have all the evidence you have seen in the four years of pleadings. But we have even more reserved for cross examination of the Volkswagen experts. The mother and father of Karen are prepared to go forward today. We know that the circumstances of this tragedy and the value of Karen's life as a vibrant 15-year-old teenager with life ahead of her far exceeds $100,000."

The judge getting madder by the minute, not liking my answers:

> "Mr. Flynn, you go out into that court room and tell the parents that I want this case settled. The offer is $100,000, a fair amount. I want it settled. Don't come back in here until we have a settlement. Tell them I grieve with them, but all my courtroom can get them is money, we cannot get Karen back".

This is the collective consciousness in courts across the country, intrinsic to civil tort and death cases. It's only about money. Or is it? Is the consciousness of those involved in a tragedy of this magnitude; the consciousness of our judges, the consciousness of the defendants responsible, and our societal collective consciousness underlying our justice system...is it just about money?

Is the real issue consciousness itself, truth itself, or how civil law determines responsibility for tragedies? Consider the nature and value of life through the consciousness of a 15 year old on the verge of discovering her identity, purpose, dreams, and desires. And for those left behind it is the profound loss of a growing daughter, whose consciousness held limitless, unknown potential. As individuals and as a society, our collective consciousness forms the foundation upon which our court system exists. In cases of wrongful death, especially involving a 15 year old, is the focus on financial compensation, or is it about confronting the societal issues and facts that led to such a tragedy? Our team approached the case guided by the latter principles that seem essential to the very fabric of life.

Money obviously plays a role in death cases. There is no other compensation. The size of the verdict is based on the collective consciousness of the jury in assessing not only the value of life but what life really is, and what caused death. A verdict in a monetary amount provides some measurement about how our society values life. A jury is the voice of the community. If a 'wrong' causes the loss of life, the community must respond. If a grievous and callous wrong has occurred because profit took precedence over life, particularly where a conscious decision was made on the side of profit, then society has vested in juries the responsibility to correct the wrong.

Compare the 20,000 child deaths in Gaza. No courts. No juries. Nothing. Even the families of the Holocaust victims received compensation as of 2018—over $86.8 billion, based upon Israeli claims. See the reports and records of the "Holocaust Claims Processing Office." Will Israel ever compensate the Gaza families? The world must demand it. Who is making those claims? Is there any international court with any enforcement authority to make the claims independent of Israeli influence? Is the world of international justice based upon monetary influence by the deep state billionaires like the Rothschilds?

Remember, in 1917, in the "Balfour Declaration" from Lord Balfour to Lord Mayer Rothschild, the Rothschild's bailed out the United Kingdom from their devastating war debt and depleted treasury with loans by the Rothschild banks and related American banks in exchange for British promises to the Zionists to give Palestine to Israel. As the war progressed, these banks became concerned about repayment if the allies lost. These banks induced President Wilson to bring America into WW I to insure an Allied victory so the loans would be repaid to the banks. See *War is a Racket* by Smedley Butler. Its all about the "Money Changers."

In 1984, Karen's case was tried to a 16-member jury for over two months. Of course, our team knew about the Volkswagen company, and its Nazi origins. The Volkswagen company originated during the Third Reich in an attempt to create an affordable car for the German people. Volkswagen used both Jewish and non-Jewish forced labor, primarily from eastern Europe. The company operated four concentration camps and eight forced-labor camps on its property. But that really didn't play any part in my consciousness at that time in presenting the evidence. Although armed with a deeper understanding of how quantum entanglement interacts with consciousness, I still find myself wondering about the many possible connections.

After being yelled at by the judge, I went out to the courtroom to talk to Gail and Don while my partner and the defense lawyers chatted with the judge in chambers. I was gone for about 40 minutes; it went like this:

Me: "The judge is hammering us to settle and take their $100 K."

Don: "No way. Not happening. We now know what happened and why Karen died, so does VW. Let's prove it to him and the jury. We both know that this minor collision didn't kill Karen."

Gail: "Mike, it's been four years. You have the evidence to win, don't you? Do you still believe in Karen's case? If so, the judge, jury and Volkswagen need to know that Karen died to help others on these issues; and the bigger issues of how these companies make safety decisions solely on money, profit and price competition with other companies. If VW had just complied with the basic regulations governing these accidents, Karen would not have died. We've gone this far, I know in my heart that going forward and not settling is the right thing to do".

Don: 'Mike: Do you still believe we should let the jury decide and not this judge? Do you still believe the evidence proves our case?"

Me: "Yes. We have the evidence on what I have explained as liability... that their conduct, and their product caused Karen's death. The judge may beat us up on some pre-trial issues but I think we can even get around that. The real problem, as we have discussed, is what the law allows for damages for the death of Karen, a minor, who had no so-called earnings history."

Don: "I don't care about their $100,000 as long as we prove that if they had obeyed all these safety regulations, Karen would still be alive. I know you and your firm has spent four years on the case, a huge amount of attorney time and over a hundred thousand dollars in costs but will you take the risk?"

Me: "Yes. I told you from the beginning I try cases to verdict. Settlement is not my option. It is yours. My partners are a little nervous. But full speed ahead. (Into the valley of death rides the six hundred). If the judge locks me up, will you bail me out? Just kidding!"

Back in chambers, the Judge was staring at me with barely concealed fury. The tension was thick.

Judge: "Well, we have a settlement, don't we Mr. Flynn?"

Me: "Judge, if I can explain..."

"Explain?" His voice exploded. "I don't want an explanation, Mr. Flynn! Is that even your name? How long have you been practicing law?" His face was flushed red now. "I want a yes answer to my question! Do we have a settlement or not?"

I could feel the defense attorneys watching, waiting. This was the moment. Karen's parents had been clear; 'no settlement without answers... without establishing what really happened to their daughter'.

I blurted out "Judge, my clients want a trial. They want to establish causation and prove that Karen's life has an incalculable value, more than money, and certainly more than $100,000, if that's what this comes down to."

The judge glared at me for a long moment. I could see him weighing whether to hold me in contempt right there... Finally, he turned to his court officer.

"Call the jury down. We are empaneling."

Just like that, we were going to trial. No settlement. No easy way out.

Defense counsel: "Both sides have many motions in limine that need to be decided before we empanel."

Judge: "Ok: in the courtroom...now."

THE TRIAL BEGINS

Motions in limine are pre-trial motions generally involving evidentiary issues: evidence that the defense does not want the jury to hear; and evidence it does not want to be admitted into evidence and put on record. From the Plaintiff's side, same thing, evidence to be admitted and objections to the defendants' effort to exclude it. Karen's case involved numerous pre-trial motions that didn't even involve evidence issues.

The judge hammered us relentlessly. Motion after motion he sided with the defense. Our requests for discovery? Denied. Their motions to limit evidence? Granted. Their attempts to exclude our expert witnesses? Granted. I watched our case being systematically dismantled piece by piece. Each ruling felt like another nail in our coffin. The defense attorneys were barely able to conceal their smirks. They knew what I knew; we were getting destroyed before we even reached the jury.

The message was crystal clear, settle this case or watch it die in front of twelve jurors.

But something remarkable happened once we got in front of the jury. By the third day of testimony, I could see it; the judge's entire demeanor had shifted. He was listening differently, ruling differently. The same man who had been ready to eviscerate me in chambers was now leaning forward, engaged, even protective of our right to present our case. The defense attorneys noticed it too. Their confidence began to crack. How did we turn him around in Karen's case? How did we transform a hostile judge into an ally?

Every litigator knows that cross-examination is one of the most potent weapons in the courtroom arsenal. The law provides wide latitude in questioning hostile witnesses, making it very difficult for even an adverse judge to shut it down.

More importantly, juries understand the unique value of cross examination. They know from common sense and from the judge's instructions that testimony elicited on cross-examination is fundamentally different from direct testimony. It hasn't been rehearsed, doctored, or scripted by the lawyer for the witness to say whatever the lawyer wants him or her to say. In fact, quite the opposite: adverse witnesses actively resist agreeing with the opposing counsel questioning them, and they have had no advance warning of the questions. This makes any admission they do make far more credible to the jury.

At the last minute we changed our strategy and the sequence of our evidence. Under civil litigation rules, a corporation designates a representative to act and testify on behalf of the company. Volkswagen designated an extremely intelligent, well spoken, well dressed German engineer who was fully knowledgeable on all the issues in the case. We had taken his deposition under oath during the discovery phase of the case over the prior years, and thus we knew his position and sworn testimony on critical issues and facts. On one key issue, the engineer was irrevocably stuck with his sworn deposition testimony.

We had intended to call the German engineer as our witness later in the case. As Plaintiff's this is generally not done in this portion of the case. He was their key witness appearing as the face of Volkswagen, and he was an excellent witness. Generally, the plaintiff wants the jury to get a good feel for the lawyer and at least several witnesses favorable to his case. In Karen's case, it was critical to put at least one parent, and a sequence of our witnesses at the beginning of the evidence where the jury would understand up front how the accident happened, and get a solid feeling for the character of the people seeking a verdict from them. Going after an adverse witness 'hammer and tongs' out of the gate can be effective but also risky. If the witness wins the cross, it is unlikely you will win the case. We went ahead anyway.

THE GERMAN PATENT

During the 'openings' in which each side explained their case, they explained their version of the expected evidence to the jury. For our part, I decided to take a significant risk to see if I could swing the judge before he destroyed me, and also Karen's case. I explained the accident to the jury and why Karen was dead because of the fault and violation of safety regulations by Volkswagen. I explained the three key issues in the case that would prove liability:

(1) the failure of the VW bus windows to withstand the required amount of resistance when struck by an occupant in an accident, a National Highway Traffic Safety Administration, ("NHTSA") regulation.

(2) The failure of the windows to even stay in place when the vehicle 'torqued' during an accident, another NHTSA regulation.

(3) The infamous 'roll over tendency' of a VW bus to roll over even in minor collisions, which then caused all the windows to pop out so they could not even meet the resistance requirements.

In my opening I asked the jury to pay very close attention to the testimony of our first witness, the German engineer who would testify on the history of the three above issues, and VW's knowledge of the problems, and history of fixing it.

The violation of the regulations caused Karen to die instantly. She was in the right center passenger seat; and when the bus rolled to its left, she was catapulted across the seat through the opening where the windows had previously popped out. The top of her head was sheared off by the roof rail. A gruesome detail for parents and a jury to hear was that there was no glass under Karen's sheared head. An important point is that the judge is required to instruct the jury that they cannot indulge in sympathy in their deliberations or verdict. They have to deal with facts alone, not emotion.

In his opening, Volkswagen's lawyer asserted that there were no violations; and that Volkswagen complied with all safety requirements and had no knowledge of any problem with the window retention parameters of their bus. He told the jury that they would call Herr VW as their witness as he was knowledgeable about VW safety policies. He added that they would also call three 'causation' experts on how the accident happened to show that our version of events was wrong. When he told the jury what Herr VW would say about VW's knowledge of the window problem, I decided then and there to call him in our case as one of, if not my first witnesses.

I had previously taken his deposition. We called Herr VW as our first witness; what is called a 'hostile' witness. The defense objected. After I cautiously described, without giving away the farm, why I was calling him, the judge got interested. Like the defense, the judge sensed something significant was about to happen. It did.

In that cross examination, I repeatedly used the VW Engineer's deposition testimony to make him repeatedly testify in front of the jury that VW had never considered the window retention issue to be a significant problem that would impact the safety of the occupants in any way, and VW had never attempted to design an alternative window system, or recall and fix the problem with any alternative design. Herr VW did not know that we had gone to the German Patent Office, and had translated a patent from German to English on that precise issue! We displayed that patent in front of the jury in the form of a 4'x6' photo enlargement. For added drama we had the photo covered with a sheet and then at just the right moment revealed it.

As I went through the details of what this patent revealed, the judge visibly shifted, he leaned forward, then after my statements and the German engineer's response, he leaned back in his chair with his hands folded in anticipation. The jurors rolled their eyes. The mother cried. Defense counsel called for a side bar claiming unfair lack of disclosure. The judge shot them down. He made a colloquial remark like "that horse is long gone from that barn".

We then presented four more weeks of testimony with reconstruction experts and witnesses as to exactly how the accident happened. We presented experts on the federal regulations governing window retention, grommeting, shatter proof glass, and rollover issues. We called Karen's parents, teachers, friends and siblings to present a solid case of just how outstanding a 15-year-old she was. Some children as we all know, are just exceptional from birth, gifted with a consciousness of God and love for everything around them. That consciousness radiated from Karen. She was such a teenager.

They seem to die young, however; like my cousin Germaine at 16. God's ways are inexplicable. Karen was a unique, beautiful, soulful, 15-year-old. Her unique qualities magnified the parents' grief. But back in 1984, Massachusetts law allowing for parental grief was a mess. The defense claimed that it did not. We claimed that loss of companionship for the death of a child intrinsically incorporated grief. The issue came down to the language in the jury instructions and what we could argue to the jury. The judge favored ours. That issue alone was argued on appeal for the next three years after the verdict.

If you can figure the emotional distinction between grief and loss of companionship, aside from sophistic platitudes, please write and let me know. Karen's death, the intense grief experienced by her parents, and the unusual, almost surreal circumstances of the accident, where no one else was harmed, mirrored the mysterious and mystical events surrounding the coma and eventual death of 17 year old Sisi several years later. Both cases involve God 'taking' a child whose consciousness was elevated above us normal humans, imho.

The defense spent a small fortune defending with every form of expert imaginable on liability, damages, causation and just how wonderful a company VW is. If I remember correctly, they had a total of six expert witnesses. Incidentally, the VW started life with the concept name of the KdF-Wagen (Kraft durch Freude-Wagen, meaning "Strength Through Joy car") and when they were first made in the 1930's they changed it to VolksWagen "The People's Car"(Volks=People, Wagon=Car) during Herr Hitler' reign.

A VERDICT FOR KAREN

The jury deliberated for over a week; a very long deliberation. Verdict: Three million U.S. Dollars!

VW then exhausted every appeal, all the way to the Supreme Court of the U.S claiming the damage award was unprecedented and had to be overturned under existing law governing the deaths of minors with no pain and suffering. VW argued that there was no other verdict amount like it in the entire country. It was to no avail, the verdict was affirmed. We had won against all odds!

Even then, VW still wouldn't pay. We had to start foreclosing on its dealership franchises. Five years after the verdict, eight years after the case began in 1980 Don and Gail finally received payment in 1988. With legal interest, the total came to $5.6 million. Karen, watching from heaven, had finally been valued by our legal system at what her life was 'worth'. That is how our society chose to measure it. I felt that the verdict as a whole was an indicator from the jury that Karen's case should be made an example of. In truth, that money was merely a yardstick of this society for the value of Karen's life, her consciousness, and regardless of the hard evidence, the consciousness of all sixteen of the jurors, their minds and hearts, connected with Karen's consciousness in that courtroom.

Karen was definitely in that courtroom and lived on in that case to diminish the suffering of her parents, siblings and to guard others in the future. That is what the trial really accomplished! The judge agreed. He denied all defense post trial motions. Same in the next two chapters. God, in his way of linking consciousness in time and space, rendered that verdict to alleviate further suffering. Another example of redemption delivered by God's love and Grace?

Did that amount of money prove how our society should value the life and consciousness of a 15-year-old child? I submit that what happened in that court room is that Karen's consciousness permeated the consciousness of the jury. That is what explains the verdict and why we prevailed all the way through three levels of appeal, against all odds. I know. I was there. I personally conducted every aspect of that case; all the witnesses, all the cross examinations, all the direct examinations, all the arguments, and all the appeals. My colleagues in my firm, Mike Tabb, Bill Sheridan and Tom Greene worked on motions, pleadings and appellate briefs among others. But guess what, it wasn't "I". Yes, it was my body, intellect and mind, but the consciousness that won that case was bigger than little old me. I was just a messenger on a quantum level. I was not the doer. Unmistakably, God was.

> "See that you do not despise one of these little ones. For I tell you that their angels in heaven always see the face of my Father in heaven." **Matthew 18:10**

I pray that the Gaza children and their families, just like the Holocaust families, receive Israeli compensation. Human and divine justice.

PHILOSOPHICAL THOUGHTS ON CHILD DEATH

The toughest cases for me have involved child deaths. In specific ways, certainly in experiencing the abject soul- and heart-wrenching grief of parents, the deaths of their children shifted my professional and personal consciousness into the most sensitive area of my heart where almost inexplicably, the emotional angst became an enormous karmic burden. That is why I tried to avoid heart-wrenching cases... but in this respect I wasn't very successful.

I was quite capable of presenting the causes of 15-year-old Karen McCuish's death to the jury on a legally cognizable basis. However, in the big picture of life, death and reincarnation, the complete understanding still remains a virtual mystery to me. The death of the Irish priest, which I experienced three years after this case, I did understand. In my experience of his death, I knew from his mind that he was fighting injustice, and the oppression of the British Crown. When I tried Karen's case in 1984, I did not have that experiential compass to guide me and make sense of the horrific tragedy. Three years later after that 1987 TM Sidhis course I did, but it's still a difficult subject.

The McCuish tragedy involved a precedent-setting legal case, and is often cited in later cases for many reasons. For me, the case was then, and is now about the mystery of death, and compassion for the grieving parents. Since the mid-90s, I have been unable to take child death cases... or even read about them. I also can't even watch the ads involving child cancer patients.

Some of my intrinsic consciousness on the death of children was undoubtedly transferred to the juries involved in the cases in this, and the following two chapters. During those cases I had no conscious intention on my part to avoid taking them. I was troubled on some level, but took them anyway. In all three cases, some inner conviction guided me. It is with difficulty that I include them in this book. There is a reason. It is founded upon the above quoted teaching of Christ; and why God allows children to die prematurely despite natural law prescribing longer human life spans to grow our consciousness. Human and divine causation, like human vs divine justice are very tough issues.

If there is a merciful and loving God, why did babies routinely die in childbirth in the past, and why did many children never survive past childhood? These are tough questions, especially given the innocence and helplessness of children, both in the womb and during childhood. If children in our species come directly from the Kingdom of Heaven, as Christ taught, then why does God, nature, or humans as a species kill children prematurely?

In several instances, I struggled with God. My consciousness hardened, anger and frustration disrupted my meditations, and what little faith I had in religion faded away. We think of children as being taken 'early', but time is a human concept. Is it possible that from a higher level of consciousness there is ultimately no death, so repeated karmic evolution through all and every experience actually benefits the soul? Despite my hardened litigator mind, even the explanation that suffering helps us to move back to God does not comfort me.

Dear Jurors: Better not think about this paradox of utterly tragic human existence unless you feel that your consciousness will grow in some framework of love. For me, I had no choice. I had to become a believer in a higher power, higher levels of consciousness, to deal with the anger and at times rage that swelled up in me. As a litigating meditator, or vice versa, I had to surrender all vestiges of my egoic need to understand.... and I'm still trying.

Karen's case in this chapter involved a consciousness level within me no different than the hard realities of Sandra and Lester's case, or other death and abortion cases. As in those cases, I did not know how the QE level of consciousness worked when I litigated her case. The only explanation for my burning hand experience is the same one I have now for Karen's shocking death. Years of litigation, suffering and meditation have only left me with quantum entanglement and God's love. In my heart and consciousness, they have become the same. Time and space must be linked in God, not in lower human consciousness. This way we can fully participate in his plan. I don't see any other frame of reference.

By the Grace of God, Sandra and Lester lived; and thankfully I was on their side as a litigator. But their step-brothers and a fifteen-year-old friend died horribly. If it was God, or some energy of consciousness that enabled Sandra and Lester to survive, is it equally true that God or that lack of energy of consciousness connectivity allowed the others to die in that fire? Is it possible for us to know the answers to these questions? On a litigating level of consciousness it is not. From a meditation perspective which takes us to a higher level, it may be. I have no other practical answer within the realm of human understanding.

As a litigator and meditator, I now realize that my consciousness absorbed these facts and tragedies that I wasn't able to grasp at the time. I was immersed in the litigation and trial of these cases, focused on the immediate legal challenges rather than their deeper implications. In Karen's trial, both the value and the cause of death of a fifteen-year-old were at issue. The legal questions were complex, but the human questions were far more profound. What is a life worth? When does consciousness begin, and when does it end? Our legal system struggles to address fundamental questions about the nature of human existence. In the midst of battle, whether in litigation or in life itself, our immediate demands often push aside the more profound levels of consciousness available to us.

My recent identification of Father Michael Griffin has changed my perspective on this entire story. The connection between his death fighting injustice and these cases involving questions of life's value seems to operate on a level that transcends ordinary causation.

Each shifted my consciousness, opening to deeper realities, and each caused a deep sorrow within myself, sorrow that I now recognize was transmitted to me from their parents, both then and now.

Karen, Derek, Sisi, and Father Griffin, all dead in the conventional sense, but in a higher sense are they? In each litigated case, and incidentally in Father Griffin's death I was thankfully advocating for the recognition of life's inherent, immeasurable value.

The mystery remains: in a universe where consciousness appears to be quantum-entangled across time and space, where the dead priest's experience can become part of my own awareness, what does death really mean? And if death is not the end, what does that tell us about the beginning? These cases taught me that life, under all circumstances, carries a sacredness that transcends legal definitions and monetary valuations. The next case would test these emerging understandings in ways that would challenge everything I thought I knew about life, death, and the nature of consciousness itself.

Epilogue

THE CURRENCY OF CONSCIOUSNESS

The $5.6 million ultimate judgment in Karen McCuish's case was a legal victory. But to see it merely as a monetary award is to miss the profound spiritual transaction that occurred in that courtroom. The jury, in its collective wisdom was not just assigning a dollar value to a life; it was making a statement about the nature of life itself. It was a verdict rendered not just on the facts, but from a deeper level of shared consciousness.

This brings us to the fundamental conflict between how our society values life. In criminal law, we recognize that taking a life is the gravest offense. Yet in civil law, we are forced to translate that immeasurable loss into a currency of compensation. This contradiction is perhaps most stark in the legal frameworks surrounding the beginning and end of life. The 1973 Roe v. Wade decision, for example, created a legal framework that attempted to define when life becomes legally protected, but it left many philosophical and moral questions unresolved. A nine-month-old baby who dies tragically generates universal sympathy and substantial legal damages. Yet the same child, moments before birth, might have different legal protections depending on circumstances and jurisdiction. The spina bifida case I handled, where a child's potential for life was debated and ultimately extinguished, illustrated these heartbreaking complexities.

These inconsistencies troubled me not from a political standpoint, but from a consciousness perspective. If my meditation experiences were teaching me that consciousness transcends physical death, what did that mean for how we should understand the beginning of life? And how do we reconcile the sacredness of life with a legal and economic system that often reduces it to a line item on a balance sheet?

The Indian sage Sri Aurobindo offers a profound perspective on this. He wrote that money is a "universal force" that, in its origin, "belongs to the Divine." However, it has been "usurped for the uses of the ego" and "perverted" by demonic or negative influences. He argues that we must not shrink from this power, but "reconquer it for the Divine" and use it for a divine life. He writes:

"All wealth belongs to the Divine and those who hold it are trustees, not possessors. It is with them today. Tomorrow it may be elsewhere. All depends on the way they discharge their trust; while it is with them, in what spirit, with what consciousness in their use of it, to what purpose." Sri Aurobindo: *The Mother*

I first read *The Mother* by Aurobindo circa 1992, after the Motorgate case, the Scio wars, and Karen's case. I found it in Mother Meera's home library when I stayed there with her devotees and assistants. I was four years into Kriya yoga at the time. I had a substantial amount of litigation experience, and enough scriptural study of the world's religions to know how the money changers displace the sacred aspects of life with materialistic greed. I became a believer in Aurobindo's dictum to return to work to return the monetary force to Divine Mother. I pray that force works for the Gaza children.

The cases that follow, including the baby O'Brian trial and the Smyly tragedy would continue to illuminate these profound questions about life's inherent value. In our society, we recognize in criminal law that taking a human life is the gravest offense, often punishable by death itself. Yet in civil law, we attempt to assign monetary values to lives lost. And in other areas of law, we grapple with when life begins and what protections it merits.

The 1973 Roe v. Wade decision created a legal framework that attempted to define when life becomes legally protected, but it left many philosophical and moral questions unresolved. The cases I litigated involving children from nine months to seventeen years old revealed the arbitrary nature of some of these legal distinctions. A nine-month-old baby who dies tragically generates universal sympathy and substantial legal damages. Yet the same child, moments before birth, might have different legal protections depending on circumstances and jurisdiction.

These inconsistencies in how our legal system values life at different stages troubled me deeply. Not from a political standpoint, but from a consciousness perspective. If my meditation experiences were teaching me that consciousness transcends physical death, what did that mean for how we should understand the beginning of life? The spina bifida case that wasn't, illustrated some of these complexities; the intersection of medical technology, legal precedent, and fundamental questions about human worth.

The Air Force colonel's wife in a prior chapter aborted her 3-month intra-uterine baby believing in her heart that he was normal despite the doctors saying he was not; then realizing after the abortion, that he was in fact normal. Her heart was correct. Her doctors were wrong. She paid a price of unrelenting grief and guilt I have rarely experienced with any client in any of my many tragic cases.

An interesting component of that settlement with General Powell was that the aborted child had no entitlement to damages. He obviously had no earnings history to measure damages, and under the law of Roe v Wade, which in my opinion was a monstrous abomination based on legal trickery, it could not be recognized as a live human whose damages included loss of his life caused by others, however well intentioned they were.

This is similar to what happened in the McCuish case, however, in addition, the jury, acting as the conscience of the community attained justice from a corporation that had misused its duty and abused the trust of the public. The Jury declared that the life of a child, the consciousness of a vibrant fifteen-year-old girl, was worth more than the cost of a safer design. The jury used the only tool the law gave them; money to make a spiritual statement.

The mystery remains: in a universe where consciousness appears to be quantum-entangled across time and space, where the dead priest's experience can become part of my own awareness, what does death really mean? Karen, Derek, Sisi, and Father Griffin are all gone in the conventional sense. But are they? Their stories, their consciousness, now live inside me, and through this book, I hope they live inside you too. They taught me that life, under all circumstances, carries a sacredness that can never be measured, only honored.

CHAPTER 16

The Value of a 9 Month Old: The Paradox of Human Worth

"If anyone causes one of these little ones – those who believe in me – to stumble, it would be better for them to have a large millstone hung around their neck and to be drowned in the depths of the sea." **Matthew 18:6**

DEREK'S JURY TRIAL AND VERDICT

There is a profound paradox involving abortion death and infant death before 1 year of birth age. In the case in this chapter, the paradox involves valuation, causation, "viability," "SIDS" (Sudden Infant Death Syndrome); and a sneaky defense strategy to link the value of a baby born alive, to the value of an unborn child in the aftermath of Roe v Wade. After Roe, in general, depending on causation, an aborted, "viable" baby, even at full term, had no value.

By 1990, abortion in American society was as commonplace and legally acceptable as throwing out the trash. Medically, a SIDS baby death could not be linked to any cognizable harm in the law or obstetrics. Linking the two together, even if the SIDS defense causation failed in front of the jury, depending on multiple evidentiary, and medical expert witness factors, an 11-month old infant had minimal, monetary value – the defense generically labeled such cases as having "nuisance value" – $5000 to $10,000.

My firm decided to test the above factors and issues in front of a jury. I was opposed to abortion. To the parents of Derek O, and to me, his death was not a "nuisance." The defense strategy to link the value of an aborted, Roe v Wade baby death, which permeated American culture in 1990, to Derek's death, backfired on the defense $3 Million times over.

Derek's case proved that notwithstanding a defense strategy linking causation and damages, to the prevailing societal, "abortion norm" on valuing either the unborn or the just born as having de minimis value, an American jury could send a message that all life, in or out of the womb, had intrinsic value. The defense in Derek's case in a two month jury trial utilized a strategy to throw everything at the jury: causation based on fabricated, expert witness SIDS testimony, 27 years of abortion law jurisprudence and cases permeating state laws on the death of infants, all based on a masqueraded, societal acceptance of abortion.

In 1990, after 27 years of Roe, the colossal money chain of pay for play abortion death was trending toward its most insidious peak of 1.6 Million per annum. Everyone in the chain could make money: the doctor; the abortion clinic, a pharmaceutical company, and in some cases, even the mother.

By 1990, the case of Derek O. vs a baby walker manufacturer involved a defense strategy based on assessing the value of babies, in and out of the womb, as worthless. Abortion law involving fetal injury, pre or post birth, based on Roe v Wade "viability" had generated an encyclopedia of case law, medical and legal publications, medical technology, and diagnostic criteria for the cause of infant death before 1 year.

What's the value of a nine-month-old, fully developed, unborn baby compared to an 11-month-old infant who suffers a traumatic death in a defective "baby walker"? Should a defense strategy based on mixing abortion law with wrongful death law to diminish any damage verdict, impact a jury? Under the previous, now reversed, "abortion law" founded in Roe v Wade, the unborn, full-term, aborted baby had no rights and no value. In Derek's case, a jury decided that all life at all stages of gestation before and after birth had sacred value. The jury rendered a THREE MILLION DOLLAR VERDICT.

By 1990, during the peak of the legally approved "abortion killing" of the unborn in the aftermath of Roe, American society had degenerated into utter moral and legal chaos on abortion. The killing of babies at any time in any trimester, and the "sale" of fetal tissue, had become rampant.

THE DEFENSE STRATEGY: A BABY IS WORTH NOTHING

Defense strategies to diminish the value of infants in civil wrongful death cases mirrored the degradation of American culture. The full force of abortion law, generated by Roe and its sequelae, across the legal spectrum in criminal cases, and in civil wrongful death cases, assessing the medical "viability" of the unborn, in part based on advances in obstetrics technology, had reached a level of legal pandemic.

In this context, a jury rendered a verdict of $3 million for Derek and his parents after he died in a defective "baby walker," when his seat collapsed and he choked against the tray.

What was the difference between valuing abortion death and infant death in Derek's case? He was born alive. Derek and his parents were protected by the full force of the law. The 9-month full term, aborted baby, had no rights. Anatomically, there was almost no difference between Derek in utero, and Derek 11 months after birth.

Derek's jury sent a powerful message to the abortionists who had taken over America: we recognize and value human life in or out of the womb. Society put no value on life in the womb, and the Supreme Court had sanctioned it's destruction. The law put little value on an eleven- month-old infant, and the defense built its entire strategy on that devaluation. They were banking on a legal and cultural environment in which the rampant killing of the unborn had been approved in many states; may put no value on life in the womb when it can be intentionally aborted, and the law may put little value on an 11 month old infant. But the jury said: here is our message in the face of the defense strategy to convey Derek's lack of value in a legal and cultural environment of the rampaging killing of the unborn, which had in many states, legally approved abortion of the unborn, right up to full term gestational limits. Twelve citizens examined the details and answered with a three million dollar verdict!

This chapter will analyze the value of human life in money, morality, law and developing science. The tragic case of Derek O vs a Chinese baby walker manufacturer illustrates how the law and our society over the past 50 years, 1973–2022, approved the murder of the unborn, but protected post-natal childbirth... a paradox so profoundly irrational, abhorrent, and contrary to our constitutional protections, the Supreme Court reversed and rejected Roe v Wade on June 24, 2022. It was long overdue. In the interim, the figures vary, but the estimated "abortions" in America were over 63 million.

It is time for a scientific, moral, societal and cultural wakeup call in America: even after the Supreme Court reversed Roe v Wade on June 24, 2022, currently, a 9-month full term, unborn baby, can still be "aborted" in a Colorado abortion clinic. The heart and brains of the baby can be gashed out and sold to a pharmaceutical company. The more advanced the baby's organs are, the more money to be made by Big Pharma. This chapter will present the "law of abortion" for what it actually is: the ghastly violation of the most fundamental protections afforded by the law of human life: "Thou shall not kill," either intentionally or negligently.

For 5 decades under Roe v Wade, 1973–2022, the unborn baby was not protected, had no rights, and his heart and brain could be sold to a pharmaceutical company. The difference between Derek in utero, and Derek sitting in his baby walker, was measured by a jury in mere days and weeks, yet their assigned values in a society, which for 50 years under Roe, had legally approved killing the unborn, diverge dramatically. The jury sent a message:

> "If anyone causes one of these little ones… to stumble…
> better for them…to be drowned in the depths of the sea."

The day after his birth, Derek, could have been murdered, and those responsible held accountable for the crime of murder; or in Derek's "baby walker" case, in civil tort law, a jury held the manufacturer of the defective "baby walker" accountable for negligently causing his death in order to protect their bottom line manufacturing cost. The collective consciousness of that jury told society that our babies must be protected. The day before Derek's birth, the parents, a doctor, an abortion clinic, could have made money selling his brains, heart, kidneys, etc to the pharmaceutical industry. What's the difference in how we measure "Life"? What law did the Supreme Court invent in Roe v Wade to fabricate such an irrational, nonsensical, inhuman result allowing the killing of "life" in the unborn?

THE AFTERMATH OF ROE V WADE: EVIL BEGETS EVIL

For 50 years, a fully developed nine-month in utero baby was not only denied protection, indeed, the law of Roe v Wade approved his/her murder under circumstances decided by a doctor, and/or abortion clinic. Under this manifestly irrational Supreme Court decision, the in-utero baby was deemed to have little or no value, except to Big Pharma, and those in a pay for play death chain to make money. Cases where repeated pregnancies occurred to "sell" the unborn to Big Pharma became increasingly frequent. See "Deliberations of the Human Fetal Tissue Transplantation Research Panel."

As Roe v Wade abortions exploded in American society, the gestational "life" of the unborn became measurable not by "first trimester viability"

– an unscientific oxymoron, but by money. Evil begets evil. According to the Supreme Court in 1973, "viability" was measured in trimesters – when the baby could survive outside the womb. However, it was soon common knowledge that abortion became subject to the decision-making of paid for doctors and paid for clinics. Go to the right abortion clinic, get the right doctor, Big Pharma, and everyone in the chain of death made money off the brains, hearts and organs of dead babies.

Congressional research efforts in 1993, (not coincidentally as investigations into Clinton crimes and scandals expanded), attempted to curb the exploding abortion industry. It was like shoveling sand against a rising tide. Notwithstanding federal laws prohibiting fetal tissue sales, Congress endeavored to expose the monstrous evils involved in selling the "tissue" of the murdered unborn children of America.

Typical of the frauds and crimes currently besieging modern America, as our society became increasingly immoral, particularly after the Clintons and his association with Jeffrey Epstein and Harvey Weinstein, if money was to be made, abortion laws were ignored. The abortion industry became a billion-dollar ponzi scheme for Big Pharma. Everyone in the chain of illegality, in some cases, even the mother, to the doctors and clinics to Big Pharma, abortion became a source of profit. See the 1993 congressional investigation: "Fetal Tissue: Is It Being Sold In Violation of Federal Law"? See "Blood Money: Getting Rich Off a Woman's Right to Choose." (Everett). America was "shocked" to find out the truth of this rapidly metalizing criminal epidemic. But little has changed even after the reversal of Roe. The Supreme Court had opened a floodgate of abortions. Now, closing it is akin to repairing the Hoover dam amidst a flood.

Measuring the life or death of the unborn by a money motivated, ill-defined parameter of "viability" based on the mother's physical, emotional and mental health became a billion dollar industry. In essence the scheme enabled pay for play murder – pay the right amount to the right doctor, or abortion clinic, regardless of "gestational age," and human life was ended – a dead baby to sell to Big Pharma – the later the gestational death, the more money to be made on the more developed "tissue" in the hearts and brains of the baby. Late term abortions became a profit center.

Legally, gestation is defined as the period from conception to birth. Yogananda states unequivocally that "life" begins at conception, when the soul chooses rebirth. The modern science of quantum entanglement provides an atomic structure validating an instantaneous cellular "life," and cellular consciousness exchange between the mother and her baby. The cells of the unborn baby becomes instantly "alive" with the cells of the mother.

Modern obstetrics establish maternal-fetal exchange between the cellular "life" in the mother and her baby resulting in life-long cellular "memory." See "Fetal maternal microchimerism: the surprising bond between mom and baby." (Anderson). This should come as no surprise as science moves toward the interconnectedness of all life in a force-field of consciousness beyond particle/wave theories. The obvious difference in the development of the fetal cellular structure of the baby and that of the mother, does not diminish the "life" in any specific fetal cell. So the law, society, the conscience and consciousness in all humans must ask: in an abortion, are we killing "life"? I submit that in law, logic and common sense, the answer is clear and unambiguous.

THE SCIENCE OF QUANTUM ENTANGLEMENT AND LAW OF ABORTION

For example, in a force field of elevated interconnected consciousness, a human being begins life at conception when the soul enters the mother's womb and her egg is fertilized. I accept the science of quantum entangled life between a mother and her baby; and the current, scientific, obstetrics research on the "mom/baby" cellular connectedness. Current science is catching up with Yogananda's physiology, anatomy, obstetrics, and theology on this issue.

On June 24, 2022, the Supreme Court rejected the irrational, fabricated foundation of Roe v Wade, holding that there is no "federal right" to abortion; and rejecting the utterly specious legal underpinnings of Roe – that the Fourteenth Amendment governing due process and equal protection of law, as applied to the states, conferred a "federal right" to a woman to abort her first trimester baby. In *Dobbs v Jackson Women's Health Org.*, Justice Alito delivered the 5-4 majority decision that "abortion is not deeply in the Nation's history and traditions."

Indeed, in *Dobbs*, the Supreme Court stated the obvious: before Roe v Wade, abortion was a crime, not a constitutionally conferred right. Think of the consequences and common-sense reversal of Roe: humans do not have the right to murder human babies in the womb; and fascist "money changers," masquerading as liberals promoting a fictional, fabricated "woman's right" to terminate her baby is against Constitutional, natural, manmade, and "God's laws." In current, scientific, understanding of "natural law," the connected cellular consciousness of mother and baby is fundamental to the preservation and continuation of the human species. Abortion is not only contrary to any man made "federal right," it violates any societal standard in the history of all human culture and civilization. Thus, it is a "crime."

Moreover, as proven since Roe, for the past fifty years, abortion has created and promoted an "abortion money chain pandemic," in which everyone from mother, to abortion doctor, (an oxymoron), to abortion clinics, to Big Pharma cannot legally, morally, constitutionally, make money off murdering other humans. Although humans operating on lower levels of human consciousness have historically murdered each other in wars, genocides, serial killings, Empire building, etc etc to obtain power and land, and make money, the natural evolution of consciousness as prescribed by Christ in the Sermon on the Mount, constitutes a higher evolutionary consciousness for our species.

This truth is also scientific. The Roe v Wade artificial construct of three trimesters, in which the killing of the unborn could lawfully occur in the first trimester of purported "non-viability," defies law, reason, logic, medical obstetrics, and fundamental due process for the baby alive in the womb. It now defies science. The leftist agenda pushing "women's rights" to abort/kill their babies violates not only natural law, it retards the evolution of consciousness, which is almost universally supported by societal, manmade law, to regulate human civilization.

The crime of abortion can also now be analyzed and concluded to be a violation of not only modern obstetrics and natural law, but also evidence that the killing of a fetus at any stage of development is proven to be the killing of "life" as demonstrated in the scientific law of quantum entanglement.

The Supreme Court has gradually accepted the biological reality, reversing the demonstrative and biological irrationality of Roe v Wade, that killing a fetus in utero is the killing of human life, notwithstanding the machinations and agendas of the money changers making billions off the abortion industry. Natural law, ie, God's laws against the murder of the unborn may be evident in the evolving scientific proof of quantum entanglement. (Chapter 9). The cellular structure of an infant in the mother's womb is completely connected on a quantum level, meaning an atomic level, meaning that every atom and molecule in the infant is connected to the atoms and molecules in the mother, instantaneously making up the cellular structure of both the infant and mother as the infant grows and evolves within the cellular structure of the mother.

The denial that life exists at the quantum level at any time from conception through the 9 months in-utero, defies not only natural law and advances in scientific, biological obstetrics, it violates the scientific law of quantum entanglement founded on the instantaneous and contemporaneous vibrational state of atoms, molecules and particles in the bodies of both infant and mother.

There is nothing more essential to the continuation of our species than the living, molecular "connectedness" of mother and infant in the womb, establishing biological living cells in the embryo at the moment of conception. The currently established scientific evidence in quantum physics, beyond theory, supports quantum entanglement of particles in a vibrating force-field all around us, beyond the four forces that science has recognized for over a hundred years. This vibrating force field may be the sought-after 'unified field' that physicists have theorized about as quantum physics moves into the realm of consciousness as a foundational force field; and/or the most critical factor in understanding all of the cosmos. In other words, the field of consciousness itself is becoming a scientific, albeit unmeasurable reality, consistent with what advanced spiritual Masters like Yogananda have opined on for centuries.

On June 24, 2022, the Supreme Court moved our species toward a higher level of consciousness, trending away from limbic brain function, and bridging the chasm between primitive survival and higher levels of thought and consciousness in the cerebral cortex. When the Supreme Court overturned Roe v Wade in *Dobbs v Jackson Women's Health Organization*, the Court not only stopped a pandemic of fetal homicide, it established a higher level of consciousness in setting the legal standards for killing the unborn. When the Court recognized the blatant falsehood established in Roe v Wade, that the purported constitutional, "federal right" to an abortion is a mythical chimera, it also effectively, and logically, although not stating it, reestablished Fourteenth Amendment protection for the unborn, which applies federal due process and equal protection to the states, ultimately creating or conferring a federal constitutional right to life in the unborn. The future will prove this reality.

Unfortunately, currently, the Court has restricted its decision based on "state's rights" to enact its own abortion laws. Each state can enact laws either protecting the rights of the unborn, or make laws governing the mother's "rights" to choose: abort vs her baby's right to "life". This has enabled the individual states to make laws approving gestational killing limits on superannuated, fictionalized theories on "viability." In other words, state laws governing abortion turn on "viability" – a modern day life or death chimera for the unborn.

The day before Dobbs, for the prior 50 years after Roe v Wade, our society had trended toward murdering the unborn at any gestational stage. America had made life and death in the womb legalized sport, subject to profit making by the mother, the abortion clinics and the pharmaceutical companies, all the way up to just before full term birth. The day after Dobbs, societal conscience and consciousness is being partially restored – but states like Colorado legalize 9 month, full term murder of a baby while North Dakota prohibits all abortion. A casual observer of this life and death issue, could conclude based on the current political ideologies drowning our constitutional Republic, that in general, blue states are trending toward the legal validation of gestational murder, while red states are trending toward either a total prohibition, or the preservation of life based on viability.

In North Dakota a mother can be charged with murder. In Colorado, a mother can profit selling her fully developed baby to Big Pharma. If a mother traveled to Colorado, no gestational limit, OK to kill before birth. In California and Massachusetts, although setting different gestational periods on viability, both facilitate murdering the unborn. Using fetal "viability" to measure murder when every cell in an unborn baby is alive with connected cellular consciousness and "memory" to the mother, is akin to approving murder of anyone who is asleep – the ultimate oxymoron governing life and death. The viability standard is a legal, obstetrical and cellular consciousness fiction. Many courts have ruled that it is. At this stage of human and embryonic development it is cave man obstetrics, medieval "science," and Marxist, nazified law.

An example of the contradictory, confused, body of case precedent from state to state was stated in the 1973 case of *Wolfe v Isbell* by the Alabama Supreme Court during the same period Roe v Wade denied viability of the unborn in the first trimester: "M]edical authority has recognized long since that the child is in existence from the moment of conception, and for many purposes its existence is recognized by the law."

Compare also the 400 year old "wisdom" in English jurisprudence of the rights of the unborn based on "viability" enunciated by Sir Edward Coke:

"if a woman be quick with childe and by potion or otherwise killeth it in her wombe, or if a man beat her, whereby the child dieth in her body, and she is delivered of a dead childe, this is great misprison, and no murder:

but if the childe be born alive, and dieth of the potion, battery, or other cause, this is murder; for in law it is accounted a reasonable creature, in rerum natura, when it is born alive."

Query: has human consciousness evolved since Shakespearean England? In the 17th century, "misprison" was a serious offense against the Crown falling short of a capital offence/murder, based on legal concepts of concealing criminal conduct from the Crown, based on its right to know whether an abortion had taken place. In other words, abortion in secret was a crime, but did not rise to murder unless the baby was born alive, then died as a result of the woman aborting or being beaten, or "other cause".

Before Roe, abortion in America was mostly a concealed, criminal offense, in most states targeting the abortionist, not the woman, and based on whether the fetus had "quickened" when it was aborted.

I submit that American jurisprudence on abortion must conform to reality, science and moral standards governing the preservation of human life. Viability is irrelevant to the core issue of when "life" begins, not when it is sustainable outside the womb. In America, liberalism has become a masquerade for "wokism," transgenderism, anal homosexuality, Marxism, communism fascism, and state sponsored degradation of not only moral standards, but also the evolving, scientific understanding of the interconnectedness of life and consciousness in and out of the womb.

THE FORBIDDEN FRUIT

State created and controlled collective consciousness founded on drugs, sex, and the murder of the unborn is abhorrent in a civilized society. State allowed abortion of full term babies, as in Colorado, is only slightly different from the KKK murdering individuals with a different skin color; and the Nazis murdering the jews.

In the pharmaceutical research industries, fetal heart and brain tissue from late-term abortions has enabled monstrous profits for nominal costs. The drugs developed from the gashed out, living, brain and heart cellular tissues of late term aborted unborn babies, can sell for tens of thousands of dollars per dose. Notwithstanding Big Pharma's controlled media schemes to ban discussion on drugs like Adrenochrome, using their favorite epithet, "conspiracy theory," one courageous doctor previously working for a pharmaceutical company, appeared on an RFK Jr. podcast describing her horrific "gashing out" of living brains and hearts from unborn babies, just weeks before birth, to get the "living cells" delivered to her employer! The company paid a premium if the cells were still alive! The podcast has been banned on You Tube. Hmmm. Who owns You Tube? Who made that decision?

The above stark economic disparity standing alone, aside from the legal and moral issues of killing late term unborn babies, reveals how Big Pharm profits influence not only societal valuation of human life at its earliest stages, but also how money displaces baseline morality – The First Commandment: "You shall have no other Gods before me," aka: God consciousness before money consciousness. The Fifth Commandment: "Thou shall not kill" – particularly for money.

Meanwhile, in my little world of litigating jury cases, and meditating on truth and justice, in Derek's case, I watched the collective, societal, consciousness on abortion play out in contrived medical evidence on SIDS – Derek would have died with or without the baby walker; the cross examination of the distraught mother on contrived questions, planting seeds in the minds of the jurors about difficulties in Derek's pregnancy; the parents' intentions to have another child; and requested defense jury instructions on the valuation of life pre and post birth connected to SIDS "viability." The defense involved a mirage of horse manure. Needless to say, it backfired; but the company and its legal team risked a defense strategy believing the judge, as in the McCuish case, would overturn any verdict above $5000–$10,000. Defense counsel literally told me any verdict over $10,000 would be reversed!

In the routine 'wrongful death' valuation of a minor case, or in this instance, the value of an 11 month old infant, legal settlements typically involve what the defense has promoted as "nuisance value."

The defense in Derek's case not only attempted to blame SIDS as the legal causation of his death, notwithstanding no creditable evidence to support this theory based on paying off an expert, who was shredded on cross examination, It cross examined the mother on whether she had ever had an abortion, whether she was pursuing another pregnancy, whether her loss of Derek's companionship could be replaced with another baby! The judge allowed the questions, while the news was filled with late term abortion cases and controversies arising out of the peak Roe v Wade decision. Not a good time to try a baby death case, or was it? The jury answered.

This raises many questions about consistency in how we value human life and the laws our politicians enact to enable these outcomes. It also exposes the very dark underbelly of the evil abortion beast if we analyze the value of life just before and after birth. Before: money for Big Pharma. After: money for the victims of families losing their babies caused by bad behavior and bad, greed driven, bottom line obsession with profit – but generally not enough money to warrant the costs in a lengthy jury trial.

Baby Derek was 11 months old when he choked against the tray of his baby walker as the seat collapsed in the living room when his mom was only feet away in the kitchen. Horrific parental grief, more investigative work, legal analysis and costs for the lawyers with medical experts, accident reconstruction, and potentially minimal money, whilst navigating the legal and emotional consequences of being immersed in their suffering. It created unanswerable questions for me about a loving God that was supposed to be protecting us all.

The baby Derek jurors had no knowledge of the nature of Karen's death in the Volkswagen case; nor of that jury verdict of $3 million, just six years before. Somehow, the dots connected between these cases on some strange, quantum entangled identical valuation of human life? Somehow the Derek jury rendered a verdict for the identical amount in an infant's death with no loss of earnings and no pain and suffering, as the jury did in Karen's death involving a 15 year old vibrant teenager. Quantum entanglement? There were obviously no "minors" on either jury – no "jury of their peers" as ordained by our Constitution – but rather a jury of their parents' peers representing American laws, culture and commitment to the value of human life, notwithstanding Roe v Wade, decades before Dobbs.

Derek's jury plainly could not relate directly to Derek's experience; but it could relate to the suffering and loss of Derek's parents. Derek's jury, like Karen's jury, included parents who loved their children, as well as jurors who had no children. How did the backdrop of abortion in America in the late 1980s play out in Derek's case? If you were defense counsel, in a Roe v Wade how would you attempt to bring in an abortion related psychological and valuation defense involving an 11 month old infant to reduce a potential verdict: "oh, they can have another baby and many parents these days wish they never had a child."

The judge, getting ready for another long trial, empaneled a jury comprised of 16 adults (including 4 alternates). These were real people including mothers and fathers who had once been babies themselves and were children of parents they loved. Like most members of our species, these jurors understood what love is and measured it the only way available to them within our legal system, which is through a monetary verdict.

How do we reconcile a society that can simultaneously place such different values on human life based on circumstance rather than inherent worth? And what does this reveal about our collective moral compass? Both verdicts in both Karen's and Derek's case reflected the conscience and consciousness of the community, offering a stark contrast to how our legal system sometimes values life in other contexts. The Karen and baby Derek jury verdicts demonstrate how ordinary citizens measure the value of children's lives when given the opportunity to do so. The jury of the parents' peers' returned a verdict of Three million dollars in both cases!

As you have read, this identical verdict in Karen's case for a 15-year-old, beautiful, teenage girl, to me, represented some form of collective, raised jury consciousness even though I did not know what quantum entanglement was in the 1980s when both cases were tried? I did oppose abortion on instinctive right to life, rather than moral grounds. In both cases, there was no evidence of earning capacity or lost earnings. The death of a 'minor' case rarely has such large damage awards. If there is instant death with no evidence of pain and suffering, as in Karen's case, or no evidence of such as in baby Derek's case, the damage awards are generally very low. (Chapter 15 explains the legal issues involved). The jury in Derek's case seemed to grasp intuitively what our legal and economic systems sometimes fail to recognize; that the worth of a child's life transcends conventional economic metrics.

As I stood in that courtroom watching the jury deliver their verdict for baby Derek, I couldn't help but reflect on the arbitrary distinctions our society makes. The primary difference between a nine-month fetus and a 11-month-old infant is location and legal status, not biological development or human potential.

A PATTERN OF GRIEF

I tried the baby Derek case six years after Karen's trial, three years after Sisi's life support ended, and about nine years after representing the Air Force Colonel and his guilt-stricken wife in their 'wrongful abortion' case. Fifteen years had passed since my only child custody case, the 'burning hand' trial, in which two children were "saved." It was the only such case I took in five decades of litigation because I found them to be so emotionally abhorrent – two people who had once "loved" each other, and created life, fighting over custody! I'm not litigating that kind of case! I took the baby Derek case because the defense refused to recognize the right to, and valuation of life.

Along the way, Wil Smyly, in the litigation trenches, along with my own parents, along with my love for my own children, showed me how parental love connects directly to God, beyond time and space. Before I took on baby Derek's case; and three years after the "reincarnation" experience with the dead Irish priest, I had a deep grasp of the magnitude of suffering involved in how parental love and loss in child death impacts us as humans.

Query: if we reincarnate, death is not that big of a deal? Right? Death is just a stepping stone to raise our consciousness to return to God? Right? We are born. We suffer. We learn how not to suffer. We experience higher levels of consciousness as we evolve through lifetimes, ipso facto, there is no death. We die to progress on the scale of consciousness – just like Darwinian evolution?

At that time in 1988–90, after the Father Griffin experience, reading the AY, and practicing Kriya Yog, I started to understand the energy conservation and transference involved in reincarnation; and in what I currently consider to be its logical framework for life...the law of conservation of mass; 'matter is infinitely transferable'. With this information and all my experiences and research I am inclined to believe baby Derek has already returned to our earthly classroom – maybe even staying out of baby walkers. Live and learn. Right?

These two 'death cases' were both tried to verdict. Others, like the Air Force colonel and his devastated wife, involving a real but "mistaken" abortion – if there is such a thing – were litigated with monetary results. Sandra and Lester's case, involving child death of their siblings, represented an entirely different legal/consciousness experience for me and for their father. Life was saved while life died. But if there is no death, maybe it is all just a lesson? Sort of an illusion: "Life is but a dream…"

There was no money or valuation involved in the Hakey custody case, except cessation of child support payments to the alcoholic wife.

The common denominator between these cases and the reason for their inclusion in this book, separated from too many others to count, is that they illustrate how consciousness and QE worked in litigation for me, your not-so-humble, ego-driven, meditation-evolving, litigating author. The selected cases in this book and sequential Litigator series are my best efforts to show the value of meditation and prayer in the evolution of my consciousness by the Grace of God.

What is the difference in the baby Derek case compared to the others, or more specifically what is the difference between a nine-month-old, unborn baby and an 11 month-old baby on a consciousness level...there is none. On the other hand, in values measured by the money changers, aka Big Pharma, and the abortion industry... the value of human life is measured in money! These jury verdicts are measured in money, BUT are they? I can't tell you dear reader, how many judges have said to me – "its all about money – just settle the case" while I retort – "no your Honor, its about reality, truth and justice." They look at me like I am from outer space. Maybe I am? I explain that human beings evolving in consciousness, regardless of the stage they're on, don't measure life in the same way as Big Pharma and those in favor of the convenience of abortion measure it.

Candidly, I submit that the difference between life and love vs death and profit is illustrated in these verdicts. A jury knows how to raise its collective consciousness and do the right thing....

The essential qualities of consciousness, love, grief, compassion, responsibility, morals, and maternal protection built in by Mother Nature together with the instructions that guide these qualities; "The Ten Commandments" or of whatever religion you adhere to, allow us to call ourselves 'human beings'. Without these qualities and strictures that bind us together into an orderly society, we would collectively be in-cohesive and chaotic, especially in the US where our culture is a new experiment unlike Europe or China for instance, with its many binding social norms that survive apart from a transitory governmental system.

The biggest stricture that is common to all 'ten commandment' type religious teachings such as the Bible, the Hindu Yama Niyama's ('do's and dont's') from the Bhagavad Gita, to the Koran and others, all talk about 'Thou Shalt Not Kill'. If you're a real human, you measure life by real human values. If you're a money changer from Big Pharma or an abortionist, you measure life by drug development, convenience, and money. But even most of the less evolved 'animals' have enough of the innate protections Mother Nature builds to protect their young. Most humans, Yes. Abortionists, No. The Garden of Eden metaphor applies. The forbidden fruit that Genesis expounds about, is sex divorced from the moral responsibility to take care of our progeny. Procreation and preservation of our children in or out of the womb is governed by Natural Law. Deviation from this law represents the fall of man. There is no greater fall than killing the product of sex, which is our children.

We humans possess enough of the innate protections Mother Nature build in us that we instinctively protect our young. The issue that muddies this automatic response...even for those of us who are logical and have moral clarity is the persuasive nature of the dark forces that create seductive reasoning for abandoning ones cherished inner guidance system.

The clearest example of this in recent history is the change in the law after the infamous case of Roe v Wade, with its ludicrous contradictions. It was man-made and approved. It made it lawful to carry out the murder of children we deem to be too inconvenient for modern society. Create life then change your mind? No problem, we have doctors who will undo it for you...all you have to do is deal with your conscience...now that is far easier said than done. There is a price to pay.

Ask anyone with a conscience that has had an abortion. Like all the murderous things humans are capable of, take Dresden, Tokyo, the Holocaust, Gaza, the Somme, Passchendaele, Wounded Knee, Amritsar... they all seem logical at the time, have a very convincing, carefully framed argument that smoothly persuades the perpetrators that what they are about to do is completely normal and logical. In practice however, as soon as the deed is done, that formerly pervasive argument that supported our actions is nowhere to be seen...we are immediately dropped out of the seductively convenient propaganda bubble and left to justify our actions to the innate, tender instinct to protect life that we all possess.

THE ULTRASOUND THEY WON'T LET YOU SEE

Inevitably the phrase 'What did I just do?' repeats through our bewildered conscience. What just happened was sleight of hand. If you are facing cancer, the doctors show you where the cancerous tumor has grown and how the surgeon will cut it out. There's no emotion for the tumor because it clearly, logically needs to be cut out and destroyed. Not so with abortion; the procedure differs dramatically. The Mother is carefully steered away from looking at the ultrasound because it will unlock the natural protective maternal emotions present in all females that will react in horror at the thought of harming their child. It's clearly not a tumor; it has fingers and toes and a heartbeat, just like us. Whenever there is an attempt to persuade and influence our actions we have to look carefully away from the argument and check in with our natural tendencies.

Thankfully, Roe v. Wade has now been overturned, but before we analyze how the flawed legal reasoning in Roe contrasts with the recently overturned Roe decision in Dobbs, frankly, the illogical insanity of abortion makes my stomach churn.

THE COLLAPSE OF THE SEAT

The facts of the case were ultimately simple. Derek, a very healthy, 11 month-old infant, no diagnostic criteria supporting SIDS, was in his baby walker manufactured by a Taiwanese company, one of the biggest baby walker makers in the world. With his mom in the kitchen, Derek was in the living room vigorously peddling the walker around the room. After not hearing any sounds coming from the living room for about 10 minutes, mom went into the living room and saw Derek's walker pushed up against a wall. The seat in the walker had collapsed. Derek was trapped with his arms under the tray, his body sitting on his haunches, and his throat trapped with the weight of his body against the tray. He had choked to death.

Another shocking real-life tragedy confronting parents who loved their little baby beyond themselves. And a case on my plate with very demonstrable causation on the legal level, but inexplicable causation when looking through the divine lens of God supposedly loving little Derek, his parents, and the rest of us. From my later point of view I could understand the drama through the lens of reincarnation, but at the time this case was tried, it was after the Scio wars when my wife and I had separated, and my life was a mess. This made dealing with the case extra hard. Somehow, I got through it, and my emotional state may even have contributed to the success of the case.

You cannot begin to understand the hysteria, the trauma, the grief, the agony, the loss, that this tragedy inflicted on this family. They treasured their baby, and for me it was like a dark version of groundhog day; a repeat of previous cases; Karen, Sisi, the distraught Colonel's wife all over again, and again and again. Derek's parents treasured the love and affection they shared with him even though he was 'just an infant'. It's called human love. They treasured the value of his life, not in money, but in the inexhaustible well spring of the human heart. They saw in his life the value and love intrinsic to all infant life.

They were also angry at the baby walker manufacturer and they grew angrier as the callous defense counsel offered, if I remember correctly, about $30,000, before the verdict came in. The parents knew that the defense was convinced that the jury would never offer more, and if the jury awarded more, the court would take it away. It was Karen's case all over again, but they had only enjoyed 11 months of life with their baby, however their feelings were the same for the 9 months he had been in utero. Most expectant mothers and fathers know this; that the anticipation gets greater, and the intensity of their love grows as birth approaches.

Those who advocate for ending life with an arbitrary line drawn at the moment of birth, for whatever reason, ignore the fundamental instincts and emotions of human parents, arguing blindly that it is just a fetus immediately before birth. This legal fiction of instant person-hood at birth stands in stark contrast to centuries of societal understanding of the undeniable human instinct to protect life. It reveals an agenda directly at odds with the love of life itself.

From 1988 to 1990, as Derek's case unfolded, his parents and the jury lived in the undeniable reality of human love, while the world lived in the undeniable reality of killing babies in an ascending arc of evil. Like the families in my previous cases, Derek's parents were consumed by the need to understand how and why their baby had died. The very idea of aborting a child was beyond their comprehension, notwithstanding outrageous defense questions, planting the seeds of society reality. Disturbingly, every move by the defense seemed calculated to devalue baby Derek's worth, using his short 11 months of life as justification for a low monetary verdict by suggesting that as he was just above the threshold of being aborted, his life worth could only be measured as slightly above nothing...the value of an abortion.

Just like Karen's parents, Derek's mom and dad demanded a verdict, a decision that always escalates the burden on litigators. Securing a positive verdict in death cases required years of grueling preparation, immense stress, prohibitive costs, and months spent in trial. For me, it often meant subsisting on barely four hours of sleep a night.

As a litigator, the Derek case was deja vu all over again, and again, and again, to quote Yogi Berra. I can tell you, 'Transference' is real, I absorbed the depth of the feelings of my clients. I was able to maintain a clinical, professional detachment to a degree in order to try the case...but when it was over I fled to meditation to vent my own depth of transferred grief and loss of love experienced by the parents in children's death cases. Ultimately, meditation is how I avoided the pandemic of our profession; alcohol in abundance...which I confess I did consume my share of...but not the raft of other vices that my mostly wealthy but unhappy colleagues were cursed with consuming to cope with the stress of their legal careers.

Derek's case was tried under the ominous shadow of comparing an 11 month-old infant to the value of a fetus. They were essentially putting a value on his life. In 1990, the societal climate was that the fetus had no 'societal value' in the womb. Abortion was an abiding, acceptable, societal, cultural, legal and economic reality. A fetus in the womb was an 'it'. A baby outside the womb was a 'person'.

In this case, both sides had to be extremely cautious, working in the shadows of just the weeks between the demarcation point of what constitutes life in the womb and life outside of it. Does a mother experience the living reality of her baby in or out of the womb? Clearly both.

On our side, as the Plaintiffs, we had to circumvent the law of 'no recovery for parental grief' when ironically, grief permeated every day of Derek's trial. On the defense side, they had to avoid appearing cynical while taking advantage of the 'no grief' jury instruction, and designed damages/valuation/defense. The defense essentially posited that there was little difference between Derek at 11 months old and a nine-month-old, "worthless" fetus in the womb...a point they presented with remarkable cleverness, however, in the end, their case collapsed under the weight of its own cold-blooded argument.

SCIENCE VERSUS SOPHISTRY

Our valuation of Derek's life, from the family's perspective, was built upon the unshakable foundations of logic, common sense, sound medical science, and inherent human values. We knew the defense's strategy, which hinged on the prevailing and often controversial parameters of infant valuation influenced by the abortion debate would ultimately collapse. This was particularly true given the monumental strides made by molecular embryologists in the late 1980s and early 1990s, nearly twenty years after Roe. Their work had fundamentally transformed our understanding of life; precisely what it is, when it commences, and its intricate developmental stages.

The legal foundation of Roe v. Wade, specifically the concept of fetal viability which underpinned the trimester framework for constitutional privacy, was fundamentally flawed. For those with a strong stomach and who have the moral courage to read about the barbaric process of aborting a fetus, one cannot fail to agree that it sounds like a cruel and heartless medieval practice of torture.

Roe v Wade's callous, legalistic, embryological viability arguments fueled our medical positions in Derek's case. Modern legal analysis currently exposes Roe as constitutional nonsense. Even the constitutional abortionists working to protect abortion rights through state constitutions admit it. Another aspect of the case lurking in the shadows of the law was the product liability for the Taiwanese baby walker manufacturing company, which involved the ever-present considerations of corporate economics and profit margins. Product liability law provides recovery for defective manufacture and design, and the old stand-by of 'failure to warn' of defects that could injure or kill. There are also laws governing strict liability for inherently dangerous products. All of these factors were mired in the evidence of valuation in Derek's case. It was not based on the value of Derek's life, but on the factors involved in designing, manufacturing and use of a baby walker at a particular price point.

THE DEFENSE'S CYNICAL STRATEGY

The defense was exceptionally cunning. A favored tactic for plaintiffs' lawyers in product liability cases, including my own practice, is to expose whether a company made a cold calculation that it was more economically viable to release a defective product and absorb the costs of subsequent injuries or deaths, rather than invest in genuine safety. This direct confrontation of money and profit against the sanctity of human life is always compelling to a jury. The cynical undercurrent of the defense's position was unmistakable. In a society obsessed with wealth, babies are deemed to have minimal worth. The very existence of abortion, even for fully developed fetuses, was implicitly presented as proof of this devaluation. Why then, would they expect significant financial penalties? The internal logic was brutal: 'Babies have little value! Perfect, no jury will ever hit us for more than $10-20K!' This was simply factored into their business model.

The defense's approach was admittedly cunning but faulted. They sought to manipulate the jury's perception subtly, through innuendo and inference, linking the value of baby Derek to that of an aborted fetus, without ever making the comparison overt. In addition, their experts spent weeks testifying on industry product safety standards, pricing, and manufacturing, but the insidious undercurrent of their testimony was clear:

it was by the parents selecting that particular baby walker at its specific price point, in the defense's view, implicitly set the value of their child's life. The implication was that had they chosen a pricier baby walker the death could have been avoided. According to the defense, the purchase price was the ultimate measure of Derek's worth. Does this method of valuation strike you as inherently evil?

The extended inference was that our society that supplies free abortions does not put much value on infants. Neither did the parents in their selection of baby walkers. The defense: "They claim that our product was defective, yet they could have bought a better one and the parents also knew it was made in China." Their experts and their lawyer cleverly slipped in the innuendo of 'infant valuation' throughout the trial without supporting their SIDS argument with actual medical evidence. Expert witness games?

The baby walker in Derek's case was in the middle price range of such products and was the most widely sold. The defense tried to make a subtle case that even if the seat failed from defective design and defective manufacture, or that the company failed to warn of the dangers of seat failure, the parents bought it because it was at the price point it was and they weren't willing to buy a more expensive one because they didn't value their child more highly. It was a cleverly developed argument but callous and crass and the jury saw through it.

It aligned with what their well-known, highly successful defense lawyer told me before the trial began.

"Your chances of winning are slim. We'll go the distance. The walker met industry standards. The parents bought that walker on its price point. That's how the parents valued their infant. That's how our society values infants since abortion mania. Even if you get a verdict, you'll never get more than $10-20K, $50 K max. The cost of doing business. I'm looking forward to this one. Check out my track record with juries. Take it or leave it - $30 K".

In trial he even hinted to the jury, and I'm paraphrasing: 'what's the big deal. You can even make another one anytime'! It was a bad move considering the death and parental grief my clients were going through... and of course it backfired.

The defense's valuation analysis permeated every aspect of Derek's trial, relentlessly pushing the narrative that 'you'll never get more than $50K.' This legal proceeding took place against a backdrop of intense public discourse, with the U.S. media constantly highlighting abortion cases and the often-volatile clashes between pro-life and pro-choice advocates.

Crucially, the jury remained uninformed, because they were never presented with evidence that the legal foundation of abortion, as established by Roe v. Wade, was rooted in a profound constitutional fallacy.

They were also not made aware of the powerful forces at play; the immense greed and profit motives of major pharmaceutical companies, often cloaked by the term 'stem cell research'. Our jury never grasped that the significant hedge fund investments in these pharmaceutical entities were underpinned by billions in taxpayer-funded government grants that generated exorbitant, 'easy-money' profits for those I call the 'money changers'. While the staggering financial scale of the 'abortion industry' was not a direct point of contention in the trial, it undeniably shaped the prevailing societal perception of a fetus or infant's value in 1990.

THE JURY SPEAKS

Thank God though, the verdict was governed by a jury of the parents' peers, as our Constitution provides. The alternative would have been bleak; a judgment sought through seven old curmudgeons appointed to the Supreme Court through political cronyism by catering to politicians. They move up the judicial ladder through graft until they are virtual prostitutes sold out to the money changers. Their reward is that they get the appointments, and the biggest sell-out leads to the biggest appointments. They achieve high status but they are at the beck and call of what the monied interests tell them to do.

We had genuine 'humans' on our jury; individuals who, in their wisdom disregarded the prevailing abortion climate and its associated justifications. Their verdict was a resounding repudiation of the defense's valuation strategy and their three-million-dollar award hammered home the true worth of a child's life. Derek's case however, was tried under the pervasive shadow of Roe v. Wade, a climate the defense heavily relied upon. At that time, Roe's fundamental legal premise, that 'viability' only emerged after the first trimester, was considered the settled law of the land. Yet any lawyer with a solid grasp of Constitutional law, a basic understanding of molecular medicine, and plain common sense now recognizes that Roe v. Wade was anatomically, legally, and fundamentally flawed. Even the law clerks and legitimate justices on the Supreme Court in 1973 understood the legal basis and reasoning for Roe to be utter nonsense.

The abortion lobby remains powerful and supported by huge moneyed/pharmaceutical/deep state, profit motivated influence over the courts and FDA. Even the Dobbs case, although a step forward, still allows states like Colorado to murder the unborn at full term.

As I always remind myself so my litigator's ego doesn't get ahead of me; I am not the doer. However, prior to my involvement, baby Derek's parents were advised by other lawyers to take the low monetary offer of the defense because "that is what the case is worth". It took me years of work and preparation to try Derek's case; and after a lengthy trial obtained a just verdict. I didn't do this solely to represent my clients, the grieving parents, I also wanted to prove the value of human life for my own personal reasons which were inspired by what you might call meditation-inspired intuition...hence not being the doer!

In preparation for the case I had advised the parents that we were up against centuries of precedent on human life valuation of minors. They were familiar with the McCuish case which had received substantial publicity, and was widely cited in legal publications and subsequent cases. But Karen was 15 years old at death, and Derek was 11 months, really just out of the womb. The case was fraught with paradox and unfavorable legal precedent, making it risky to take to trial at that time due to prevailing societal views on abortion and the rights and value ascribed to late-term pregnancies. The rights of a 11 month-old infant were hardly recognized in the predominant legal/societal trends going against us.

Maybe Dobbs, and consciousness emerging in the recognized, scientific, force fields of consciousness; and "intelligent design" established in the spine of the DNA molecule, will gradually force low-level human behavior into higher levels of consciousness and attendant correct conduct? I pray that baby Derek's case, as explained in this book in the context of the quantum entanglement between mother and child, will help in shifting public opinion? It worked with 12 jurors 35 years ago.

When I tried Derek's case, I believed in my heart and mind that life is so precious, it really doesn't begin or end. The 1978 Unity experience, coupled with the dead priest experience, confirmed for me that the death of a 11month-old Derek had to be measured by our jury as more precious than dollars. I explained to the jury in Derek's case that his defenseless little voice, when reflected in its verdict, had to inform our society of the value of life whether 11 months, in the womb, or 90 years.

Epilogue

BEYOND DEREK: SCIENCE, SOUL, AND SOCIETY

The moral paradox at the heart of Derek's case extends far beyond the courtroom, touching upon foundational questions of human responsibility and Natural Law. The Garden of Eden metaphor applies here with profound clarity. I believe that the 'forbidden fruit' that Genesis expounds about is sex divorced from the moral responsibility to take care of our progeny. Procreation and preservation of our children in or out of the womb is governed by Natural Law. Deviation from this law represents the 'fall of man.' There is no greater 'fall' than killing the product of sex: our children.

The scale of abortion after Roe v. Wade represents a tragedy of staggering proportions. It has been estimated that over 200 million human lives have been terminated worldwide since 1973, 63 Million in the U.S. To place this in historical perspective: the Holocaust claimed approximately six million lives; Stalin's purges killed an estimated 30 million; Communist China: 40 million; Pol Pot's regime murdered nearly two million; and the combined civilian deaths from the fire bombings of Dresden, and Tokyo: hundreds of thousands; Gaza: 20,000 children, 200,000 Palestinians. The worldwide abortion toll collectively dwarfs them all. This is not to diminish those other atrocities, but to confront an uncomfortable truth: the quiet, clinical, legally sanctioned destruction of life in the womb has exceeded, in sheer numbers, the most notorious acts of mass killing in human history.

It is a sobering testament to our species' capacity for self-deception when ideology and convenience are permitted to override our most fundamental moral obligations.

Derek's final jury verdict demonstrated that the legal foundation of Roe v. Wade, specifically the concept of fetal viability which underpinned the trimester framework for constitutional privacy, was fundamentally flawed. The archaic anatomical models of viability traditionally used in obstetrics, which were the legal and medical underpinnings of Roe, were changing faster than the weather. The advances in molecular embryology from at least the early 1980s, along with the massive advances in DNA research from that period, were conclusively proving that a human being is the immediate, and scientifically distinguishable product of fertilization, during which 'the sperm and the oocyte cease to exist as such and a new human being is produced.'

The medical and DNA literature from at least the early 1980s, just a few years after Roe, was trending toward major discoveries in molecular embryology, ultimately concluding with an indisputable scientific understanding of human life: it begins at fertilization, connecting the soul's entrance into the mother's body, just as Yogananda said in 1939. Modern science provided a clear and indisputable answer to the question of when a unique human life begins. As documented in extensive medical literature, a new, genetically distinct human being is created at the moment of fertilization – a new organism, with its own unique DNA, is formed.

Nine years after Derek's case was tried, although the literature beginning in the early 1980s supported our medical models at the time, science began to separate fact from myth. For a comprehensive science-based article on this subject, see "When Do Human Beings Begin? Scientific Myths And Scientific Facts."

Our medical positions during Derek's case were in the early stages compared to current medical science; but for purposes of rebutting the shadowy defense innuendos about an 11 month-old being valued the same as an aborted fetus, both science and human love, are reflected in the jury verdict.

The Dobbs overturning of Roe v. Wade has not ended this debate but rather returned it to the democratic process, where it continues to be fought in state legislatures and courtrooms across the nation. Derek's case, tried decades earlier, was a harbinger of this shift. It demonstrated that a jury of ordinary citizens, when presented with the profound reality of a life lost, could instinctively grasp a truth that the highest court in the land had obscured: that the value of a human life cannot be measured by its location, its stage of development, or its perceived convenience. The three million dollar verdict was not just compensation; it was a moral declaration.

THE CONSTITUTIONAL ALCHEMIST

I deem it helpful to the debate, 53 years later, to expose the absurd history and reasoning of Roe v Wade. The author of that opinion, Associate Justice Harry A. Blackmun, stretched his purported intellectual prowess to obscene limits, conjuring up a hitherto non-existent 'privacy right' as the constitutional foundation for his decision. Since then, countless legal scholars have provided a plethora of reasons denouncing Roe, even if, paradoxically, they personally support abortion.

Blackmun himself received his aggrandized power appointment to the Supreme Court by Richard 'Tricky Dick' Nixon. The country was coming out of the Vietnam War, sexual liberation, societal upheaval, drugs, and moral breakdown were the norm. With liberated women, a permissive society, and 'make love not war' attitudes, came exponentially increasing pregnancies. Uh, oh, we can't indict all these people under the 50 individual state criminal statutes making abortion a crime! We would have to put all the 'free lovers' in jail, and our jails can't hold them all! Society will have to adjust.

Our society had just gone through the murders of JFK, RFK, MLK, racial violence, and the Warren Commission's nonsensical findings which the majority of intelligent citizens refused to accept. See *Litigator 4*.

America was enslaved in the reality of 58,000 dead American soldiers in Vietnam, massive violent protests, and internal conflict not seen since the Revolutionary war.

Nixon had appointed Blackmun in 1970 in the middle of it all. The Watergate scandal erupted between 1972 and 1974 when the Roe case came to the Supreme Court. The media justifiably crucified Tricky Dick; he was, after all just another crooked politician. Blackmun's appointment was inextricably linked to Nixon. In his effort to separate himself from Nixon, Blackmun turned left of Karl Marx; and degenerated into a legal schizoid, despite being cognizant that our cities were burning, and our country was in revolutionary fervor.

The Roe decision fashioned by Blackmun at the height of this governmental crisis exhibits the thinking of a neurotic, constitutional alchemist. His decision magically reversed constitutional gold on which our country was founded, and turned it into base metal. The Roe decision, rendered in 1973, was inextricably linked to the escalating Watergate scandal, a period when the liberal media ruthlessly targeted and discredited anyone associated with the Nixon administration. In this crucible of public opinion, Justice Blackmun's actions suggest a profound, almost willful ignorance of the larger moral implications, drawing a chilling parallel to a segment of the German populace who claimed unawareness of the Holocaust's horrors.

One might infer Blackmun's internal rationalization: 'My association with Nixon is purely coincidental. Despite our shared conservative background and his role in my appointment, I am fundamentally different. My landmark Roe decision serves as irrefutable proof of my independence; I am no mere Nixonite.' This perceived need to forge a distinct identity, to shed the political baggage of his patron, appears to have profoundly influenced his judicial philosophy.

REASONS ROE WAS NONSENSE

Here are the legal reasons why I believe Blackmun's majority opinion not only lacks constitutional merit, it doesn't pass the smell tests for the federal right to an abortion:

There is no "Privacy Right" in the text or history of the Constitution. The majority just made it up in utter disregard of our three branch constitutional system of government, where the Legislature makes law – not judges. What do you call a fabricated, manufactured law by the Supreme Court? Fraud? Evil? Seven judges in our Supreme Court made it 'The law of the land'.

The Supreme Court has been very discriminating and ultra-judicious in two centuries of rulings on what makes a right 'fundamental'. The Blackmun Court grossly violated centuries of legal reasoning and precedents transforming abortion from being a crime to a "fundamental right" under the chimera of 'privacy'. There are almost no constitutional scholars who support this legal chicanery other than those being paid by Big Pharma to obtain fetuses for drug development and sales. It is frankly absurd. The bottom line to the entire analysis lies in Blackmun's mental health. Candor is warranted. He was an egomaniac running away from conservative Nixonian politics as our cities were burning and the abortionists catering to our pregnant citizens were seeking to escape indictment.

Blackmun's analysis and conclusions on making viability the point where the fetus has the "capability of meaningful life outside the mother's womb" at the end of the first trimester, was an "artificial construct," unsupported by medical evidence as decided in a confused batch of contradictory pre and post Roe cases. The 'constitutional test' for when a woman's fundamental "right of privacy" begins and ends based on "viability," is so fundamentally flawed, it defies logic, 200 years of our constitutional precedents, 600 years of English common law, the then criminal statutes of all 50 states and ultimately the rapidly developing advances in evolutionary biology with DNA research and development that were trending in 1973.

As a three Branch Constitutional Republic: Executive, Judicial, Legislative, the Legislature (Congress) makes law. The Judicial, the Supreme Court, interprets laws made by Congress. The Executive signs off on the laws, mostly as a constitutional safeguard or check against Congressional overreach. The Supreme Court stands as the final constitutional bulwark against Legislative and Executive violations of our Constitution. It's jurists are sworn to interpret the Constitution based on centuries of precedent, and its plain language and common sense meaning, as a safeguard and check on man's tendency to corrupt government and when exercising 'absolute power, to corrupt absolutely'. Blackmun and his colleagues circumvented all of these checks and balances foundational to our system of governance; and turned the Supreme Court into a congressional law-making group of 9 old senile misfits. He and his fellow malefactors literally took the law into their own hands, exercised absolute power, and violated the very essence of our constitutional safeguards. His collaborating constitutional misfits in the majority on Roe manufactured out of whole cloth the entire new "law of abortion" based on a nonexistent constitutional right of privacy. All 50 State legislatures had laws opposing abortion supported by centuries of precedent, research and sound reasoning. Blackmun and the others just ignored them.

The Court's other majority opiners and their clerks must have been asleep at the wheel when they analyzed existing state criminal statutes. Perhaps it was their nap time when they caucused and voted. Somehow, they twisted and distorted the purpose and legal weight of state criminal abortion statutes to protect the rights of the unborn and the health of the mother into no rights for the unborn and applying a little graphic hyperbole: "let's allow mommy to kill her baby to protect her health!" Now that one makes a lot of sense. It will apparently be healthier on a physical, emotional, mental and psychological level for Mommy to kill her baby! These are the factors they cited! If you believe that psychological claptrap, I recommend that serial killers take over in writing the "Diagnostic and Statistical Manual of Mental Disorders". I submit that Blackmun and his colleagues would fit right into their diagnoses....

The Court utterly misrepresented in its reasoning the history of abortion. Blackmun went off on a fanciful excursion into its history that was not only blatantly inaccurate, he couldn't even get his reference to Hippocrates right. The most applicable adjective to his neurotic, historical imaginings is: 'Fabricated'.

The opinion utterly mischaracterizes the "common law" of the British Commonwealth, which for centuries in English jurisprudence, made abortion a crime. English "common law" is what American jurisprudence is founded on. Our "common law" criminalizing abortion became embodied in all State statutory frameworks following the mandated Legislative research, committee hearings, investigation, societal standards, balancing of the rights of the unborn etc. This fundamental process is the bedrock of our law-making, yet Blackmun and the majority utterly destroyed it. He engaged in an obscene reversal of established criminal, legislative history in the states' history, transforming his concept of 'quickening', a first-trimester analysis of embryonic life, into a ridiculously unscientific and unhistorical fiction. This fiction, moreover, has since been unequivocally proven by scientific advancements to be utter nonsense.

The Court's three-trimester analysis was not only completely unsupported by the science of human embryology, more critically, it constituted a profound act of judicial overreach, seizing fictionalized obstetrics to bastardize, (pun intended), the fundamental legislative power to create law. This power is properly exercised through Congressional Committee investigation, research, and analysis, a meticulous process capable of establishing a sound scientific, and legal basis for enacting any law. Instead, Blackmun and his constitutional co-conspirators simply imposed their aberrant will, thereby severely violating precedential constitutional law. Such an act was monstrous.

The Roe majority narrowly construed the traditionally expansive 14th Amendment, an amendment broadly applied to protect civil rights impinged by state law. In a move devoid of comparable precedent, they concluded, based on the narrowest interpretation imaginable, that unborn children are not 'persons.' This created a historic and blatant contradiction within the Court's own traditionally broad construction of the 14th Amendment. To incorporate its fabricated 'privacy right', a concept nowhere referenced in the Constitution, into the 14th Amendment, and to establish a constitutional foundation for when a fetus becomes 'viable' to impose on the States, the Court arbitrarily created a new classification for 'persons.' This classification defied logic, medical science, common law, statutory and legislatively adopted law, and plain common sense. Consider the absurdity: according to these justices, a fetus anywhere in the world, one day after the first trimester, suddenly becomes 'quickened' and 'viable,' yet is still not a 'person' capable of independent life. I suggest, among other things, that current members of the Court visit modern obstetrics wards, consult with legitimate embryologists uncompromised by pharmaceutical interests, and perhaps even speak with my grandson Freddy, born at a mere 30 weeks. Human gestation, for context, is generally considered 40 weeks or 280 days from the last menstrual period.

The Roe case actually involved two cases on which the Court accepted Certiorari (a writ or order by which a higher court reviews a decision of a lower court.) on abortion issues. The famous one, Roe, is effectively contradicted in law, reasoning and common sense by the other one, Doe. In Doe, the Court's ruling that the factors governing the health of the mother, cited above, physical, mental, emotional, etc. effectively undercut its reasoning in Roe. Duh! Who were these so-called jurists?

There are many, many, more legalistic, let alone human, natural law-based reasons the Roe case was unfounded on its face, but oddly, the decisions of later courts attempting to fit the square peg of Roe into the round hole of legal legitimacy and logic has exposed it for what it is: Legal nonsense encouraging violations of related laws in a web of quantum entangled lawlessness. The legal framework established by Roe v. Wade has evolved in illegal, illicit, violations of multiple laws, such as non-enforcement of fetal tissue sales that permitted and financially incentivized increasing late-term abortions across state jurisdictions, ultimately resulting in some states legally supporting full term abortion, ie murder. The practice of fetal tissue research, while ostensibly regulated, has created troubling economic incentives within the abortion industry. The clinical procedures involved in these late-term murders of the unborn, and subsequent tissue harvesting are, when examined honestly, deeply disturbing to anyone who values human life.

The hundreds of cases decided in Roe's wake have produced a legal landscape marked by contradiction, confusion, and moral ambiguity. Each judicial attempt to shore up the constitutional foundation of abortion rights has inadvertently expanded the scope of legally sanctioned killing of human life, creating precedents that would have been unimaginable when Roe was first decided. What began as a narrow constitutional holding has metastasized into a legal and moral abyss.

The Roe sequelae cases make constitutionally protected fundamental right to life in the unborn obvious. Six hundred years of Common Law provides a rock-solid foundation to overturn Roe in all its inhumanity. When a species starts murdering its progeny, it not only violates the fundamental right to life, it creates a system for its own extinction.

I've been studying the Constitution, and using it in my litigation practice since law school in a myriad of 'Con law' (Constitutional Law) cases ranging from the First, Second, Fourth, Fifth, Sixth, and Fourteenth Amendments, in heavily litigated court room cases. I haven't found that 'privacy right' yet. My cases have not been the academic high-brow type that con law professors theorize about. No, they were real cases like Derek's, involving real people, real due process and real equal protection rights. I believe that an unborn fetus, or an 11 month-old baby, like Derek should have the same equal protection and due process rights as all of us. So did Derek's jury.

Modern allopathic medicine invests billions of dollars to preserve the lives of prenatal babies, reflecting our belief in the sanctity of life. At the same time, when the law punishes those responsible for negligently or intentionally killing a baby after birth, it reaffirms our commitment to protecting the foundational rights of life, liberty, and the pursuit of happiness. As a society however, we reveal our contradictions by permitting abortion and allowing the sale of fetal tissue to pharmaceutical companies who profit from this practice. These contradictions challenge our values, exposing the conflict between upholding life as sacred and succumbing to materialism.

Based on both my legal Aristotelian, logic-based education, which finds the Supreme Court's legal reasoning to be nonsensical, and my spiritual analysis, I believe killing unborn babies is murder. My perspective is heavily influenced by working with countless grief-stricken parents who would give anything to save their children. One of my grandchildren was born 6 weeks premature. His medical care to preserve his life was inspiring to the family, and indicative of the advances in preterm medicine. He is now a beautiful, joyful, soul-filled, healthy child whom the entire family just adores.

Based on both my legal training and spiritual convictions, I believe abortion is the taking of human life. This conclusion is rooted in decades of experience representing parents who never doubted their children's right to life, regardless of age or development. It is reinforced by my education in law and logic, which exposes the fundamental incoherence of the Supreme Court's reasoning in Roe v. Wade, a decision built on arbitrary distinctions rather than constitutional principles.

The 10 week premature birth of my grandson illuminated for me a simple truth: his worth as a human being did not begin at birth. It was inherent from the moment of his existence because the family could see his value and loved him. I thank God for the system that also valued his life so highly and fought so hard to give him the opportunity of life.

CHAPTER 17

Death As A Doorway: Evidence For Consciousness Beyond The Body

"My experience showed me that the death of the body and the brain are not the end of consciousness, that human experience continues beyond the grave. More important, it continues under the gaze of a God who loves and cares about each one of us..." *Proof of Heaven*, **Dr. Eben Alexander (Neurosurgeon)**

"The soul is not born; it does not die; it was not produced from anyone. Unborn, eternal, it is not slain, though the body is slain." **Bhagavad Gita 2:20**

For over fifty years, I have lived in the world of evidence. As a trial lawyer, my professional life was dedicated to the rigorous examination of facts, the cross-examination of testimonial witnesses, and the construction of arguments that could withstand the most intense scrutiny. I learned to distinguish between credible evidence and mere speculation, between corroborated testimony and unsubstantiated claims. My mind was trained to be skeptical, analytical, and grounded in the material world.

And yet, as this autobiography has detailed, I have also been a lifelong practitioner of meditation and a student of yogic philosophy. I have had my own profound, inexplicable experiences: the living experience of Father Griffin's murder, the experience of Unity consciousness that defied the neat categories of my legal training. These were not abstract philosophical concepts; rather they were personal, visceral encounters with a reality that seemed to operate outside the known laws of time and space.

For years, I held these two worlds in parallel. The courtroom was for evidence; the meditation cushion was for honing my intuition and offsetting the stress of litigation. But as I delved deeper into both, I began to realize that this was a false dichotomy. What if my mystical experiences were not just subjective feelings but a form of evidence of consciousness itself?

This chapter is a short inquiry into the survival of consciousness beyond physical death. I will present the testimony of credible witnesses:

an Indian Yogi, a Harvard-trained neurosurgeon, a respected orthopedic surgeon, a decorated Spitfire pilot, and others who have journeyed beyond the veil and returned with remarkably consistent accounts. I will treat their near-death experiences not as anecdotes but as eyewitness testimony and we will consider the scientific and philosophical implications of their testimony. This is not a departure from my life as a litigator; it is the ultimate application of it and I am not asking you to believe; I am asking you to weigh the evidence. Let us proceed as if we are in a courtroom of cosmic proportions, and the question before us is the most fundamental of all: what is the nature of reality, and what is our place within it?

THE INCORRUPTIBLE BODY: YOGANANDA'S FINAL TEACHING

Paramahansa Yogananda explains that death is only a temporary respite, "not final escape from life," where we go to an astral world to obtain "finer perceptions and more sensitive responses" to the beauty of life; and then reincarnate until we obtain "final freedom from the rounds of physical reincarnation".

When Paramahansa Yogananda's 'Mahasamadhi', or conscious exit from his body occurred on March 7, 1952, his body did not undergo the decay of death. Here is what the Mortuary Director wrote twenty days after Yogananda's passing:

"The absence of any visual signs of decay in the dead body of Paramahansa Yogananda offers the most extraordinary case in our experience.... No physical disintegration was visible in his body even twenty days after death.... No indication of mold was visible on his skin, and no visible desiccation (drying up) took place in the bodily tissues. This state of perfect preservation of a body is, so far as we know from mortuary annals, an unparalleled one." Letter from the Mortuary Director; Paramahansa Yogananda, *Autobiography of a Yogi* (Self-Realization Fellowship) (p. 548). Kindle Edition.

The mortuary director of the Los Angeles Mortuary reported this unique phenomenon, the description of which is eerily similar to reports of the bodies of many saints that have been deemed incorruptible. Joan Cruz' book on the subject is a serious research study:

"The more carefully we consider the preservation of the incorruptible's, the more baffling does the subject become, for their conservation seems to be dependent neither on the manner of burial nor on the temperature or place of interment. Nor were they adversely affected by extended delays between the time of death and their burials, by moisture in the tombs, by rough handling, by frequent transference's, by covering with quicklime or by their proximity to decaying corpses. The greater majority were never embalmed or treated in any manner, yet most were found lifelike, flexible and sweetly scented many years after death, in sharp contrast to the specimens of the other two classifications above, who without exception were found stiff, discolored and skeletal." *The Incorruptibles: A Study of the Incorruptible Nature of Various Catholic Saints* (Joan Carroll Cruz, TAN Books, January 1, 1977)

Based on my five decades of research into cellular consciousness and documented observations, it came as no surprise to me that Yogananda's body did not begin decomposing when he left the body on March 7, 1952. His case, no matter what your exposure to esoteric or medical literature, presents an intriguing case study. The first law of thermodynamics states that energy cannot be created or destroyed. This may provide a theoretical framework for understanding cellular energy and how a body could potentially be preserved under extraordinary physiological conditions. The hypothesis suggests that the documented high levels of neurological coherence and metabolic regulation exhibited by the subject during life may have influenced his state of cellular preservation after death. The duration of such 'cellular maintenance' remains an open question requiring further investigation.

PERSONAL CRISIS AND SPIRITUAL SEARCHING

The aftermath of the Scientology litigation wars, together with many of my litigated cases, such as Sandra & Lester, the shocking instant deaths of Karen, and baby Derek, and prolonged coma and death of Sisi Smyly (next chapters) coupled with my two personal meditation experiences of no death, caused me to go within to search and study the realities and mysteries of death. In 1988, I was suffering intensely as my marriage dissolved, which was made far worse with the onslaught of the psychic events caused in the context of the Scientology schemes to destroy me. Given my cases working with clients who were experiencing such profound trauma and grief initially led me to focus more on the concrete realities of life and death and later the abstract mysteries surrounding these cases.

My dear wife Laima during the Scio wars, 1979–1987, began to suffer from severe rheumatoid arthritis as a direct result of the stress we were under as a family. My children also suffered from the Hubbard insanity. Despite the freedoms they experienced from the financial rewards of my success as a litigator I still haven't shaken off the nagging doubt that perhaps I was at fault for dragging them into this quagmire of fear, illness and sadness that permeated our family at the time.

During the Scio wars I had poured my litigation experience and knowledge, psychological health, substantial money, and the resources of my law firm into fighting that litigation war. My almost daily reading of both Maharishi's and Gandhi's Bhagavad Gita motivated me into believing that I was fighting a modern day 'Battle of Kurukshetra' for truth, righteousness and justice, against Hubbard's pure evil. I don't use the term "evil" lightly – even Hubbard's own son testified that Hubbard believed himself to be Satan whose mission was to destroy Christianity! Hubbard's mental illness / malicious narcissism, has been confirmed in irrefutable documentary evidence. *Litigator 2.*

During this period of intense searching and suffering and particularly while processing the traumatic experience of reliving the Irish priest's murder, I began expanding my studies into the deeper questions of human existence from many different angles. I re-read *Autobiography of a Yogi*, subscribed to the Self-Realization Fellowship lessons, and devoured every book I could find on Gandhi's concepts of ahimsa and satyagraha. I began to understand that nonviolence was not just withholding action, but included a very disciplined, peaceful state of mind.

I also delved into quantum mechanics, trying to understand whether consciousness might exist on levels beyond the physical brain that we could somehow access. This in turn led me to explore writings on psychic phenomena, including Edgar Cayce and other individuals claiming psychic abilities. My interest in psychics had been sparked after I had a first hand experience in the Dwyer case when I visited a renowned psychic to find out what happened to her missing husband. Amazingly, the psychic simply placed her hand on a face-down photograph of Dwyer and then described his murder in a scene so vivid with details that it was just as if she had been there herself at the exact roadside bar and restaurant where Dwyer had been with his killers. It was an extraordinary event to witness.

In December, 1991, the Mahaldars invited me to have dinner at Maharishi's Ayurveda clinic with Beach Boys' lead singer, Mike Love, Shakespearean theatre Director and actor, Andrey Gregory, George Gaynes, movie producer and actor, and their wives. One of the wives had a serious health condition and described how she had been healed by a young Indian mystic in Germany, Mother Meera. Mike Love was looking for a lawyer to sue Brian Wilson. I was looking for healing from the Scientology wars. After hearing about Mother Meera, I immediately booked a flight to Germany and underwent 3 weeks of life-changing healing just by being in her "Darshans."

In April 1995, after returning from India with Mike Love, celebrating his unprecedented jury verdict in his lawsuit against his bandmate, Brian Wilson – mostly attributable to Meera's divine intervention (*Litigator 3*), the President of Self-Realization Fellowship, Daya Mata, summoned me to discuss SRF's ongoing copyright case against Kriyananda and his Ananda organization, (1990–2002). Before and after our meeting, while represented by another law firm, the judge in that case issued thoroughly improper, highly suspicious "Summary Judgments" against SRF, which my firm later appealed in 1997–98, and reversed.

Our meeting in April, 1995 occurred before my law firm and I had committed to representing SRF in its copyright case against Kriyananda / Ananda; and before taking on Kriyananda's sexual misconduct case. *Litigator 3*.

After much thought, and Daya Ma's "suggestion," I decided to consult with a Buddhist psychologist, who had Jungian training, who came highly recommended, about taking on the sexual abuse case against Kriyananda / Donald Walters. I was told that the psychologist possessed extraordinary psychic abilities. It turned out she did. *Litigator 3*.

During our lengthy meeting in June, 1995, the Jungian psychic strongly warned me not to take the sexual abuse case, describing Kriyananda's malevolent, vampiric powers that she believed stemmed from his past lives; powers that he would surely direct against me and could well lead to my "death"! Whoa! Her predictions proved partially accurate, though I managed to survive the ordeal. My girlfriend at the time, a fellow lawyer, echoed similar, less specific, intuitive type concerns, as did several friends and colleagues who all had deeply unsettling feelings about the case. *Litigator 3*.

The Jungian Doctor's "psychic" warnings in June, 1995, later experienced in hard core traumatic events, September, 1995–March 1998, confirmed the reality of force fields of consciousness that I had experienced over years of previous "quantum entangled" / psychic events, which had taken place in my litigated cases; and with the dead Irish priest. My discussions with Russell Means about Native American spirituality; and innumerable discussions with clients, scientists and friends, confirmed my grasp that reality involves levels of consciousness far greater than our sensory reality trapped in the 5 senses.

SAVED BY THE LIGHT: DANNION BRINKLEY'S TRANSFORMATION

In 1991, after the baby Derek case, I read Dannion Brinkley's book, *Saved by The Light*. It makes for mystical, other-worldly, reading. Brinkley writes that he was essentially one of the 'bad guys'—a military sniper during the Vietnamese war, sent to Cambodia and Laos to assassinate enemy officers and politicians. One day in 1975 whilst back on leave during a storm, a bolt of lightning struck him through his telephone, sending thousands of volts through his body. After failing to resuscitate him the doctors transferred his body to the hospital morgue where he lay clinically dead before inexplicably returning to life. What happened during those minutes of clinical death transformed him completely and helped my understanding of consciousness.

Brinkley came back with an extraordinary account: a journey through a tunnel into a radiant crystal city, where he encountered a "cathedral of knowledge." There, thirteen angelic beings shared with him 117 specific revelations about the future...95 of which have since come to pass. Even more remarkably, he returned with psychic abilities, including the power to read minds. Despite these gifts, few believed his story of spiritual transformation, except those who had similarly experienced an NDE or 'near death experience,' as they are known.

A second near-death experience later reunited Brinkley with his angelic instructors, who revealed his life's purpose, which was to use his newly acquired psychic gifts to comfort and assist the dying. True to this calling, he dedicated himself to serving the sick and elderly, while sharing his remarkable journey through public speaking engagements and seminars worldwide.

After my January, 1992 emotional, spiritual, physical healing with Mother Meera, I convinced Laima to go see Mother Meera for a healing of her severe arthritis. It worked. She went into remission. Later, after frequent visits to Germany to receive Mother Meera's Darshan, after staying at her home with other devotees, and having worked with her on the construction of a new Darshan hall, and having helped her with a minor legal issue, I had a profound Kriya Yoga experience in her private presence; and learned very physically how she "works in the spine" to accomplish healing. My experience with Meera confirmed the incredible power of the Kriya Yoga techniques working in the spine at the "Chakras;" and the almost "supernatural" flow of energy in the spine from the coccyx to the Christ center. I also realized in that experience that my nervous system was too unrefined, too low on the consciousness scale, to sustain the shocking amount of energy flowing in the spine.

During a 1995 visit to Mother I had another strange, quantum entangled, type experience when I met the journalist son of a WW II Spitfire pilot. The son, a reporter for a large London newspaper had come to see Meera with the intention of writing a negative article on her for his London editors. Chapter 19 describes the incident. After the father and son incident in Germany, I sensed a connection to Brinkley's near death experiences, so I contacted him directly and met him for dinner. Brinkley confirmed every detail of the fathers "release" with unwavering conviction. He also confirmed the psychic's recital of the facts involving the death of Dwyer. I also explained my "Sandra and Lester "burning hand" experience. Brinkley said that such experiences are routine within specific levels of consciousness in which the gross material world of matter is experienced as existing in a "far greater spiritual world – for lack of a better term."

More astonishing still, I asked him to demonstrate his ability to know what I was thinking as he described in his book, in which he stated that after his near death experience – his body dead in the morgue, while he was in "heaven," – he had acquired psychic abilities to know what people were thinking! Brinkley proceeded to tell me exactly what I was thinking in specific, detailed thought experiments. His accuracy was chilling.

"Whoa!" I remember thinking, "What is this?" The boundary between the physical and spiritual realms seemed to dissolve in that meeting.

His book, *Saved by the Light*, chronicled his journey in detail, and I found myself recommending it to others who, like me, were grappling with experiences that defied conventional explanation. Brinkley's account resonated with my experiences; inexplicable moments that had punctuated my career and spiritual practice. The burning sensation in my hand during the Sandra and Lester case; the psychic's precise vision of Tom D's murder scene; Sisi's impossible tear as I whispered in her ear; my 1987 TM Siddhis experience reliving the Irish priest's death; and my 1978 unity consciousness experience. Together, these formed what Einstein might have called a "spooky" reality, a level of consciousness beyond time and space that I, as both litigator and meditator, could no longer deny.

MY FATHER'S SECRET: A NEAR-DEATH EXPERIENCE REVEALED

Shortly after meeting Brinkley, I had dinner with my parents. The conversation turned to Brinkley's experience which they hadn't heard of, such as the tunnel of light, the life review and the choice to return to finish some aspect of his incarnation. As I described these elements and Brinkley's initial reluctance to share his story for fear of ridicule, something shifted in my father's demeanor. This man, typically reserved and far removed from anything esoteric, suddenly became animated in a way I'd never witnessed.

"I need to tell you something," he said, his voice uncharacteristically quiet. What followed stunned me into silence. My father, the quintessentially pragmatic, stoic, 'man of few words', began to describe his own near-death experience during his 1958 airplane crash. For nearly four decades, he had carried this secret alone, fearing ridicule and that people would think he had 'lost it'. Brinkley's story and his own fear of ridicule before talking about it had somehow allowed him to finally release his own astonishing experience.

His memory was as sharp as a tack as he related the details. Flying back from Long Island on a business trip, his V-Tail Bonanza was caught in a blizzard approaching the Worcester Airport. He was wrestling with a plane that was being buffeted like a toy by the gale force winds, and he was blinded by blizzarding snow as he made a desperate attempt to land on the Massachusetts Turnpike near a toll booth. Providence had placed him there. If the crash had occurred elsewhere, no one would have witnessed it, no one would have rushed to his aid as a small engine fire began to spread.

As rescuers pulled him from the twisted metal, my father went into respiratory and cardiac arrest, and he reported being surrounded by a "heavenly light," that seemed to block the excruciating pain from the initial impact. The medical records documented cardiac arrest, but they couldn't possibly capture what he experienced in those moments outside of his physical structure. He described floating above his body, watching the frantic efforts to revive him. Then came the tunnel of brilliant light, drawing him forward into a realm of indescribable peace.

"I saw my entire life events rush before my eyes," he told me, as his eyes seemed to focus back to the event. "It wasn't just the events that I saw, but their meaning became clear...the impact of every choice, every word spoken in anger or kindness." Then he said the life review came to an end and there was a moment of decision for him. Amidst the bright light came the offer; to remain in that place of perfect peace or return to a broken body and years of pain. The decision, he said, was immediate and clear.

"I saw your mother's face," he said. "I saw you seven kids, (no. 8 came later), and although nothing was spoken, I was shown that it would be difficult, but I felt I had to go back, no matter what it cost me."

That cost proved immense: a shattered back that confined him to a Stryker frame with two years of intermittent hospitalization hovering between life and death, followed by permanent paralysis below the waist, and a lifetime dependence on Canadian crutches. Yet as he spoke of this sacrifice at the dinner table, there was no trace of regret in his voice, only the quiet certainty that love demanded nothing less.

As I looked at my Dad in an even more favorable light, the famous passage from Corinthians suddenly sprang into my mind:

"If I speak in the tongues of men and of angels, but have not love, I am only a resounding gong, or a clanging cymbal. If I have the gift of prophecy and can fathom all mysteries and all knowledge, and if I have a faith that can move mountains, but have not love, I am nothing."

My father embodied this passage. When offered heaven, he chose pain for love's sake. When given rest, he chose struggle to remain with those who needed him. This wasn't just parental duty, it was love in its purest, most sacred form.

He passed away in June 1996, while I was embroiled in the case of Dr. Deepak Chopra vs News Corp case. *Litigator 3*. Now, at 81, with decades of my own life experiences behind me, I recognize my father for what he truly was: a warrior of the highest order, a quiet hero whose greatest battles were fought not on foreign soil but in hospital rooms and on the unforgiving terrain of his own damaged body.

His love didn't end in death, and to this day it remains tangible, not as memory alone, but as a living presence that continues to guide and strengthen me, especially as I recall him telling the story of his NDE. It always takes me back to that dinner table listening in awe as he helped me glimpse through his eyes what lies beyond the veil of mortality; not oblivion, but continuation...a transformation of consciousness.

The parallels between Brinkley's experience and my father's were striking, the tunnel of light, the life review, the conscious choice to return. Yet while Brinkley returned with a mission to share his story with the world, my father returned quietly, his heroism known only to those who witnessed his daily struggle and the love that fueled it. Both men in their own ways offered profound testimony to the reality of consciousness beyond death and the power of love to transcend even the final threshold.

They were part of the 'Greatest Generation', those who seemed to embody morality, courage and real patriotism for a country that promised, and at that time could deliver the 'American Dream' to hard working citizens. Many of that generation were examples of selfless bravery that made them extraordinary individuals. They believed in God, family, and country. In their inner lives of Catholic faith, my parents were part of God's incredible, mystical, blessings of pure grace in my life and the lives of my siblings. They were so full of the happy, sad, sorrowful, joyful, traumatic experiences of life that they taught us children the qualities of loyalty, nobility, faith, love and hope.

I now realize that my Dad's NDE was a gift to all of us kids and my Mom for enabling him to come back, and come back he did, literally; years after his passing he returned to me in the same sort of way as the Spitfire pilot did to his son. He appeared to me one night when I was just drifting off to sleep, in a mystical, dreamlike way, to let me know he was 'good'. It was a completely lucid experience to me, and even today as I recall the event I feel a tingling in my spine. I'm sure millions of other humans have had similar experiences. I encourage you all to share your experiences and spread the widening awareness of continuing consciousness.

PROOF OF HEAVEN: DR. EBEN ALEXANDER'S JOURNEY

My Father's near death experience was not an isolated event. Many writers and even medical literature now contain literally thousands of studies and accounts of what are called NDEs. Neurological studies alone report detailed statistical evidence, albeit mostly subjective, of currently thousands of such incidents involving individuals who have 'died' and returned to subjectively report what happened to them. Most report that they went to what they describe as "heaven." A few say they experienced hell. My client, Fred, the victim of the defective, leaking endotracheal tube, after months in coma, reported "nightmares."

Dr. Eben Alexander is a highly experienced clinical and academic neurosurgeon with the highest medical credentials, including 'Hahvad' (Harvard) Medical School, and Mass General Hospital. He admittedly charged into a career as a neurosurgeon without being fully conscious of his choice; you see, he was raised in a family of neuro-doctors. For as long as he had known, he had accepted, along with his colleagues, the neurosurgical belief that NDEs were merely the result of a trick of the brain in its bio-chemical changes at death. This was exactly the attitude of Sisi's doctors. Next chapters.

Dr. Alexander was at the center of what he now calls a neuro-scientific community of "dogmatic believers" in "scientific materialism". That is, until he had an extremely nasty case of gram-negative bacterial meningitis that up-ended his dogmatic belief system with a spectacular and colorful life-altering experience of God and Heaven during a seven-day coma.

Generally, the neurosurgery conducted over 25 years by Dr. Alexander involved surgical intrusion into the eight lobes of the human brain, including the cerebral cortex. The cerebral cortex with four lobes is purportedly the area of the brain where man's most evolved thinking, reasoning, memory, intellectual, and consciousness capabilities reside. It is generally accepted among neuroscientists that the cerebral cortex is the largest, most dominant area of neural integration in the entire central nervous system of our species. Thus, many of them conclude that consciousness arises in the cerebral cortex, and dies along with it.

As a neurosurgeon, Dr. Alexander had been convinced throughout his career that the reality of brain death was axiomatic – no brain activity = death. Any subjective experiences by NDE reporters, purportedly coming back from death, only meant that the biochemical changes which actually enabled the brain and body to return from "death," explain their experiences.

As a litigator, I am trained to follow the evidence wherever it leads, even when it contradicts my initial assumptions. The evidence from multiple scientific disciplines now points in a direction that would have been unthinkable fifty years ago.

Meanwhile, near-death experience research has documented thousands of cases in which individuals report verifiable information they could not have obtained through normal sensory channels while clinically dead. Taken together, this body of evidence suggests a conclusion that many scientists are now willing to entertain: that consciousness is not produced by matter, but may be a fundamental feature of the universe itself. Science and spirituality, it seems, are not opposed but complementary—two different methods of investigating the same underlying reality.

My own perspective aligns with this convergence, shaped by personal experiences written in previous chapters of this book and by studying Paramahansa Yogananda's teachings, which include many examples of what the average person would call miracles, but that yogis would call natural occurrences. I agree with Dr. Alexander and Paramahansa Yogananda: there is no time and space in the force presence of God's love. Many people struggle to explain this 'force' yet they innately believe in it without needing words to define it.

History provides a useful lesson about the dangers of confusing authority with truth. The Roman Catholic Church, claiming infallibility, insisted for centuries that the Earth was the center of the universe. When Galileo presented telescopic evidence to the contrary, he was tried by the Inquisition and forced to recant. When Copernicus proposed a heliocentric model, his work was placed on the Index of Forbidden Books. The Church's error was not in its theology but in its epistemology, it confused institutional authority with empirical truth.

The irony is striking: while European religious authorities were suppressing scientific inquiry in the name of protecting divine revelation, yogis in India had been conducting their own form of empirical research for thousands of years. Through disciplined meditation and direct experiential investigation, they arrived at a conclusion that Western science is only now beginning to entertain: that consciousness is not a byproduct of matter but may be fundamental to reality itself. This teaching, known as Advaita Vedanta or non-dualism, asserts that all matter emerges from consciousness, not the reverse.

For centuries, Western science dismissed this as mystical speculation. But today, as quantum mechanics reveals the observer's role in collapsing wave functions and neuroscientists struggle to explain how subjective experience arises from objective neural processes, the question is no longer so easily dismissed. The debate over whether consciousness produces the brain or the brain produces consciousness has become one of the most contentious frontiers in modern science. The ancient yogis, it seems, were not mystics evading reality but empiricists exploring it from a different angle. Dr. Alexander, like virtually every neurosurgeon and neural scientist in the world, operated his clinical practice under a belief that turns out to be a non-scientific assumption: namely that consciousness arises from, is created by, and maintained in the cerebral cortex.

WHEN THE BRAIN DIES: SEVEN DAYS IN COMA

At the height of his medical career, in November 1980, Dr. Eben Alexander contracted E. coli cerebral meningitis, a condition with a staggering 98% mortality rate. This terminal infection plunged him into a deep coma lasting almost a full week, during which his brain activity ceased completely. All eight lobes were infested with E. coli, showing no discernible electrical or biochemical activity despite the most advanced brain function testing available. By every medical standard, he was effectively gone, as in dead.

His treating physicians and family, confronted with these grim realities, made the heart-wrenching decision to turn off the ventilator that had been sustaining him at a regular twelve breaths per minute. The medical consensus was clear; Dr. Alexander showed no signs of consciousness whatsoever. He was, in technical clinical terms, as dead as a door-nail. Then came the inexplicable. After his week-long coma with what medical science had measured to be a dead brain, Eben woke up and said 'Hi everybody, what's the fuss!' Well, not quite. Although his return to consciousness wasn't immediate and it took time for his brain to shed what he called "the murkiness of death by E. coli", his medical records unequivocally document both his catastrophic condition and his remarkable recovery.

More astonishing than his survival was his account of where he had been. Dr. Alexander claimed he had gone to "Heaven"...imagine trying to explain this to your relatives and loved ones...they would send you directly to the psychiatrist – Dannion Brinkley's fear, same with my dad. Luckily for Dr. Alexander, he was a respected neurosurgeon who had a track record of previously dismissing such experiences as mere hallucinations, so he was taken much more seriously, especially because he consistently maintained his new beliefs and bravely backed them up with many public appearances.

In his book *Proof of Heaven* and numerous YouTube podcasts, Dr. Alexander now acknowledges a higher level of conscious reality exists apart from the brain. He suggests that his experience when his brain ceased to function proved that consciousness doesn't necessarily end with physical death...which is a profound challenge to conventional neuroscience.

I have a hunch these NDE experiences represent a form of divine intervention that enables mankind to confront it's human arrogance of presuming to know better with science, and offers guidance, wisdom and revelation for our journey towards realizing the real self. Perhaps God permits such profound suffering and near-death experiences as a merciful wake-up call, especially for hard-core medical scientists like Dr. Alexander, compelling them to reconsider the limitations of their materialist worldview.

THE PARADOX OF CONSCIOUSNESS: SCIENCE MEETS THE INEXPLICABLE

Dr. Alexander's case illuminates a fundamental conundrum in the study of consciousness. While his account is necessarily subjective, it raises profound questions about the nature of scientific inquiry itself. Science relies on measurable, observable, and repeatable experiments to transform hypotheses into objective facts. Yet all scientific experimentation occurs within the consciousness of the scientists themselves, which is a reality that, paradoxically, cannot be objectively measured by the very methods science employs. An interesting and rigorously tested experiment proves that human interaction with matter adjusts reality. The double-slit experiment as it is known, shows that particles exhibit wave-like interference when not observed and particle-like behavior when observed. A popular quantum physics phrase illustrates this:

"When you are not looking, there are infinite possibilities and when you look there are finite possibilities".

Dr. Alexander's journey suggests that perhaps the most profound truths lie beyond the reach of our scientific instruments in realms that can only be accessed through direct experience, even if that experience comes at the threshold between life and death.

This paradox hasn't deterred researchers. Scientists at the University of Groningen and elsewhere are pioneering efforts to measure consciousness, publishing their work in peer-reviewed academic journals. Their extraordinary research, experiments, results, and conclusions represent the cutting edge of this field, yet they too must confront the fundamental question: Can consciousness, the very medium through which we perceive and interpret reality, ever be fully understood through the tools of material science? See for example:

"Consciousness in the Universe is Tuned by a Musical Master Code, Part 2: The Hard Problem in Consciousness Studies Revisited" by Dirk K F Meijer

"Phonon Guided Biology: Architecture of Life and Conscious Perception Are Mediated by Toroidal Coupling of Phonon, Photon and Electron Information Fluxes at Discrete Eigenfrequencies" by Dirk K F Meijer

"Quantum-Assisted Process of Disembody Under Near-Death Conditions: An Informational-Field Support Model" by Dr. Florin Gaiseanu

"Information: From Philosophic to Physics Concepts for Informational Modeling of Consciousness" by Dr. Florin Gaiseanu

Einstein is often quoted as saying "I want to see what God sees". That may be an irreconcilable conundrum, unless any of the above scientists seeking to measure consciousness become 'God'. Perhaps the closest we humanoids get to experiencing God, and seeing what he sees, is in studying the consciousness of an illumined Master such as a Paramahansa Yogananda who tells us about it in his writings like the *Autobiography Of A Yogi*, and shows us how to experience God in his extensive spiritual teachings including the ancient Himalayan technique of Kriya Yoga.

Likewise in the "Spiritual Regeneration Movement" of Maharishi who shows us how to transcend. Assuming such avatars (the manifestations of realized souls in bodily forms) and sages know God, the conundrum seems to be that unless we are operating on their level of consciousness, how are we to know? Fortunately, in the last several decades, there has been so much research into consciousness, particularly in the studies of those who have had Near Death Experiences, that we seem to be edging closer to realizing higher states within ourselves.

TO HEAVEN AND BACK: DR. MARY NEAL'S PROPHETIC VISION

Dr. Mary Neal, a spinal orthopedic surgeon and scientist like Dr. Alexander, in her book *To Heaven and Back*, describes how she died in a kayaking accident and went to Heaven, but then came back. To me, these two cases and their books stand out because they both involve highly trained neural scientists who had as complete an understanding of the human spine and cerebral cortex as modern medicine dogmatically embraces.

Dr. Neal's experience also involves a remarkably prophetic, but very painful and traumatic event. Other NDE'ers have also experienced and reported so called prophetic events taking place in the future. But Dr. Neal's experience of, and reporting of a future event stands out as one of the most extraordinary in any of the NDE literature that I have studied. She experienced the traumatic death of her 18-year-old son while she was 'dead' and in Heaven. When she came back, she documented her experience.

Tragically, her 18-year-old son, an Olympic level skier, was in training to increase the mass and strength of his legs, employing a form of roller blades on a back road in Maine. A car came by, struck, and killed him.

Sadly, another premature young adult death teaching us what? There is no death? If you understand that concept, and believe it to be true, it makes it far easier to deal with loved ones who have 'passed over'. Dr. Neal's experience has some extraordinary components of reality to it, similar to Dr. Alexander's. As a medical scientist and trained medical reporter with impeccable credentials, Dr. Neal, like all physicians, underwent rigorous training to document every diagnostic and treatment detail according to precise medical protocols, ensuring accuracy in patient care. This meticulous approach naturally extends to how she reports subjective experiences within her own consciousness, lending particular weight to her account of her own NDE.

Her experience finds a similar parallel in Dr. Alexander's journey. Both physicians were trained in advanced neurology, grounded in a deep understanding of neural systems yet paradoxically, their near-death experiences occurred beyond all physical, measurable, and scientifically accepted parameters, a contrast made all the more striking by their clinical training, which shines through as they recount their 'heavenly' experiences in their respective books.

These two distinguished medical professionals join thousands of other NDE'ers who report being in heaven...a place of pure and pristine beauty, where they existed free from their physical bodies, beyond all normal human experience. This consistency raises profound questions about our understanding of consciousness and reality.

Epilogue

THE UNIVERSAL ASPIRATION: WHY HUMANS SEEK HEAVEN

Throughout recorded millennia, billions of humans have aspired to go to heaven when they die. Could this universal desire be merely a fabrication? Has the human species collectively invented this concept merely to cope with death? Have we been brainwashed by cultural forces to pursue this aspiration? Have all the scriptures across multiple, varied, and historically documented religions simply constructed elaborate post-death realities to offer our species some form of hope or salvation?

If so, we must ask why we would do this? The persistence of these beliefs however, across cultures and throughout history, suggests something much deeper at work.

The NDE experiences reported by medical professionals like Dr. Neal and Dr. Alexander make profound sense when considered alongside statements such as "Time and space are linked in the presence of God" by sages like Yogananda. In his accounts of the "Kingdom of God Within,", there exists no time and space as we understand them, and consequently, no death as we conceive it. These NDE experiences, some of them which may sound wildly fanciful to some readers, match the stories that Yogis relate. Dr. Neal and Dr. Alexander report their experiences in a slightly different way; with the precision of medical training that describe realities beyond scientific measurement, and out of our earthly ability to understand. They thus invite us to consider that consciousness may transcend the physical limitations we have long assumed to be absolute.

In my dead priest experience in July, 1987, and my Unity experience, January, 1978, there was no death. There was no beginning and end. Sometimes, when I review my sins, it would be a comfort if there was an abrupt end so I didn't have to come back and repeat the lessons I didn't learn this time around. I am now convinced however, that I don't get off that easily and accept that that is the purpose and explanation for suffering and that we do go to heaven.

I now accept that the tragic death and suffering of Father Michael Griffin, whether or not it connects to me through reincarnation, is merely a fleeting moment in the span of eternity alongside the tens of thousands, perhaps millions, who have had near-death experiences, most of them never disclosed, like my father. They collectively offer evidence to help us understand why we humans suffer on our journey to being self realized.

THE ANCIENT HIGHWAY: CONSCIOUSNESS AND THE SPINE

For thousands of years, as recited in the ancient scriptures of India called the Vedas, and based on their own actual experience, the seers, maharishis and sages have proclaimed that consciousness exists apart from, yet is also a part of, the body, spine and brain; and consciousness itself is the creative force that manifests them. Perhaps most remarkably, these sacred teachings describe the spine not merely as a structural component of the body, but as a channel, like a highway through which creative energy flows. This energy originates in the body's lower energy centers and ascends through what is called the 'Sushumna', the main energy channel of the subtle body. The energy travels upward through the spine to the medulla oblongata at the base of the skull, continues through the cerebral cortex, and ultimately reaches the 'Christ center' or Ajna Chakra, located between the eyebrows. I kid you not, this is not metaphorical language but a description of an energetic process that practitioners have experienced for millennia.

When I sat in Mother Meera's living room, circa 1995, asking her if I could do a little Kriya in her presence, she agreed and looked down. I started. My spine began to explode with energy. I couldn't take it. I looked up after about a minute, Meera was staring at me, her eyes alive with streams of light. I then realized that I am far down on the scale of Self – Realization after 50 years of meditating.

My own exploration of this ancient science began with Transcendental Meditation (TM) in 1974 – excluding prior, unrealized lifetimes? Or the period 1939–41 when I may have met Yogananda, then wanted to be an F4U pilot, and got myself killed in the war in 1943??

The most extraordinary experience came in July 1987, during my TM practice, when my spine and "being" suddenly experienced what I can only describe as energy from a prior incarnation – Father Griffin. For skeptics, I acknowledge this might sound like a very odd, strange, and inexplicable experience...and indeed it was...but it was also profoundly real and transformative to me. The TM Sidhi's Program, specifically, Patanjali's "Flying Sutra," somewhat similar to Kriya practice, involves the transmission of energy up the spine through the crown chakra. In that two week course, I did experience the flow of spinal energy up the spine, but I never levitated or even hopped like some around me – spiritual slug.

During the early years, before the Sidhi's Program, I realize now that I was only unconsciously allowing this energy to move through my spine because I lacked the specific techniques to direct it consciously. After the Sidhi's Program, I consciously directed the flow of spinal energy. In the summer of 1988 when I began practicing Kriya Yoga through the teachings of Paramahansa Yogananda, which offered precise methods for channeling this energy, I dropped the TM Sidhi's Program and have stayed intermittently disciplined vs monkey mind in spinal energy awareness.

The meditation techniques SRF and the Sidhi's Program teach employ millennia-old practices centered on the human spine, designed to help practitioners experience elevated states of consciousness. The ultimate goal of these practices is the direct experiential knowledge that one exists apart from the physical body. And that deserves an exclamation point! This isn't philosophical speculation or religious belief, but direct experience accessible through disciplined practice of these ancient techniques.

Now even Dr. Alexander says meditation is the answer to awakening human consciousness and healing human suffering. Just so the parameters of his particular case are clear, we have a 25-year hard-core agnostic neurosurgeon being transformed into a purveyor of the OM sound and meditation to deal with life and reality. We are living in an exciting and transformational age!

THE SOUND OF OM: WHEN DEAD BRAINS HEAR THE DIVINE

For over 2600 years, Yogi 'Masters' have proclaimed that the sound of OM can be heard and realized in higher states of consciousness; and that the sound is not in the brain, nor is it even in the mind. Yogananda's published lesson series contain thorough, insightful, and detailed instructions on experiencing the sound of OM. Our hearing capacities normally function through the eighth cranial nerve. Remarkably, Dr. Alexander, whilst in a coma and his eighth cranial nerve turned to 'puss' by invading E Coli., heard the sound of OM resonating throughout his being. Eben vibrated in the higher realms with a totally dead brain.

Other scientists like Nikola Tesla predicted the ultimate scientific dead-ends involved in the enigma of quantum mechanics, seeking to refine matter into finer and finer levels of observable particles including atoms, electrons, photons and quarks. In 1905, Einstein's 'miracle year', he published papers on the particle theory of light, special relativity, and $E = mc^2$. This was the dawn of quantum mechanics in which science sought to explain the Universe and the existence of all matter through reductionist observation and measurement of particles.

Tesla thereafter observed:

> "The day science begins to study non-physical phenomena; it will make more progress in one decade than in all the previous centuries of its existence."

The CERN accelerator has proved him correct. After observing traces of what was deemed to be a particle, without quantifying the particle itself, the traces being called the Higgs Bosun, or, the 'God particle', CERN scientists observed that the most accelerated traces ended up in a "vacuum state".

Dr. Meijer's groundbreaking research into wave resonance in quantum entanglement (discussed in Chapter 9) has revealed something profoundly exciting; the existence of a field outside the brain that transmits information instantaneously. This field of consciousness, once the domain of mystics and philosophers, is now entering the realm of scientific inquiry through quantum physics. Over the past three decades, we've witnessed an unprecedented scientific investigation into consciousness. Researchers have meticulously documented and analyzed millions of near-death experience (NDE) reports, while simultaneously advancing our understanding of neurology, brain function, biochemistry, brain death, and neocortex 'layering'. This dual approach has dramatically accelerated our knowledge of consciousness itself, the very medium through which we observe and know ourselves, our planet and the universe around us.

ANCIENT WISDOM MEETS MODERN SCIENCE

What's most remarkable is how these cutting-edge scientific discoveries align with teachings that have existed for millennia. Paramahansa Yogananda and countless sages throughout history have consistently maintained that what we perceive as physical reality is merely a thought or dream of God, possessing no ultimate reality in higher and finer levels of consciousness.

This ancient wisdom was illustrated dramatically in Dr. Eben Alexander's experience. When bacterial meningitis effectively removed his brain function, he didn't cease to exist, instead he experienced non-physical phenomena that his scientific training had previously led him to dismiss as impossible. Upon his return, he began recommending meditation and acoustic sounds as practical ways to access these higher states of consciousness.

The coming together of modern science and ancient wisdom, producing similar conclusions through entirely different paths is extraordinary. While Dr. Alexander now advocates meditation and acoustic sounds based on his personal experience in higher realms, Paramahansa Yogananda and sages throughout the age's or Yuga's' (Cycles of 24,000 years, divided into four distinct periods; Satya, Treta, Kali and Dwapara) have consistently recommended meditation as the surest path to higher consciousness. They have always proclaimed OM to be the ultimate acoustic sound, the primordial vibration from which all creation emerges.

Although some medical facts in Dannion Brinkley's book have been challenged, the reported case histories and the more recent Drs'. Alexander and Neal books confirm the experiences I have had in my litigation and meditation experiences.

I know through these experiences that consciousness exists apart from the feeble workings of my mind and brain. In fact, the latter have generally just blocked my complete awareness of it...indeed a lot of meditation guidance goes into bypassing the mind as a distraction, or 'veil of Maya'.

So, should we ask ourselves: does life experience, with all its joys and sorrows, make up our consciousness? Or does our consciousness exist as a distinct and separate reality that, with the tools of prayer, meditation, and even faith, shape our life experiences toward healing and wholeness?

MULTI-INCARNATIONAL SOULS: THE GREATER REALITY

Mysteriously, we all possess an awareness, something in our consciousness, which informs us that we are more than just these bodies and brains. This awareness suggests an afterlife and that we experience life within the realm of spirit...we are 'multi-incarnational souls experiencing human life'. From towering figures like Paramahansa Yogananda, to Wil Smyly, and his daughter Sisi, (next chapters), and Drs. Alexander and Neal, they have all experienced consciousness as a reality greater than their thinking, their minds, and certainly their egos. Paramahansa Yogananda teaches us about this expanded consciousness and how to experience and live within it. I judge them all to be accurate, if necessarily subjective reporters.

The same can be said for Jesus Christ. I don't believe that two thousand years of reporting about his life, crucifixion, and resurrection as recited in the New Testament is an accident, a human-created fabrication, or even necessarily a mystery. Likely, millions of devoted Christians over two millennia have actually experienced a glimpse of his consciousness. Many Christian saints have described it in detail and they often match the information we know about the consciousness of sages of other true faiths. As recently as 2016, Sister Clare Crockett, a young Irish nun who grew up with the violence of Northern Ireland at her doorstep, experienced Christ on such a deep and mystical level that she left the material world at age 19, became a Catholic nun, and prayed fervently to be united with Him at the age of 33, the age of His crucifixion.

Her wish was granted. Sister Clare died in an earthquake at age 33 in Ecuador while serving the poorest of the poor. She diligently lived the Sermon on the Mount, and I cannot help but conclude that Christ rewarded her. That's what she herself said just before she died, foreshadowing her own passing.

There is no doubt, if you read the book about Clare, "Alone with Christ Alone," or view the documentary on her life, that she was one of those souls possessing a 'heroic consciousness' that transcends education, career path, life circumstances, or religious affiliation. She aspired to be an actress and became a nun! In many ways, given her life circumstances, Clare's life itself offers evidence that consciousness exists apart from the body, brain, and all the triumphs and sorrows of life.

Heroic consciousness is not limited to saints immersed in the teachings of their Church. Individuals like Marine Congressional Medal of Honor winner John Basilone who was a bit of a 'wild man', possessed it in spades. His biography, "I'm Staying with My Boys", reveals not only his penchant for the ladies but a heroic consciousness. All such individuals seem to have one thing in common when performing heroic deeds or living heroic lives; they rise above their egos and function in a higher consciousness. Basilone manifested this consciousness by risking his life again and again for his comrades with little regard for his own life, thus displaying an absence of ego.

The advances in scientific understanding of the near-death experience are rapidly gaining credence among medical doctors who regularly observe them in life-and-death situations. Dr. Pim van Lommel's book, *Consciousness Beyond Life: The Science of the Near-Death Experience*, is replete with his case studies and the reports of other scientists now specializing in this area of medicine. He focuses on how to scientifically define the experience, providing footnoted and documented support for his work on consciousness in the context of near-death experiences.

"On the basis of prospective studies of near-death experience, recent results from neurophysiological research, and concepts from quantum physics, I strongly believe that consciousness cannot be located in a particular time and place. This is known as non-locality. Complete and endless consciousness is everywhere in a dimension that is not tied to time or place, where past, present, and future all exist and are accessible at the same time. This endless consciousness is always in and around us. We have no theories to prove or measure non-local space and non-local consciousness in the material world. The brain and the body merely function as an interface or relay station to receive part of our total consciousness and part of our memories into our waking consciousness."

He continues:

> "There is also increasing evidence that consciousness has a direct effect on the function and anatomy of the brain and the body, with DNA likely to play an important role. Near-death experience prompted the concept of a non-local and endless consciousness, which allows us to understand a wide range of special states of consciousness, such as mystical and religious experiences, deathbed visions (end-of-life experiences), perimortem and postmortem experiences (non-local communication), heightened intuitive feelings (non-local information exchange), prognostic dreams, remote viewing (non-local perception), and the mind's influence on matter (non-local perturbation). Ultimately, we cannot avoid the conclusion that endless consciousness has always been and always will be, independently of the body. There is no beginning and there will never be an end to our consciousness. For this reason, we ought to seriously consider the possibility that death, like birth, may be a mere passing from one state of consciousness into another and that during life the body functions as an interface or place of resonance."

Dr. van Lommel's credentials are impeccable. He is a world-renowned cardiologist and medical expert on near-death experiences who worked as a clinical cardiologist at an eight-hundred-bed teaching hospital in the Netherlands for 25 years. There he began studying near-death experiences in patients who survived cardiac arrest. In addition to his groundbreaking study published in the distinguished British medical journal The Lancet, van Lommel has authored chapters in several books about near-death experiences and published many articles on the subject. Over the past several years, he has been lecturing throughout the world on near-death experiences and the relationship between consciousness and brain function.

In the final chapters of this book and subsequent books in the Litigator series, we will explore the profound connection between litigation and meditation, two seemingly opposite practices that defined my life's journey...and were indispensable to my success in the litigation arena and in maintaining my psychological balance amidst the powerfully seductive material dangers of success. Through the lens of quantum entanglement, we can examine how these disparate paths converge in the search for ultimate truth and self-realization.

As Paramahansa Yogananda teaches us: "Time and space are linked instantly in the presence of God."

This fundamental insight provides the framework for understanding my own extraordinary experiences, including the Irish priest encounter that has haunted and enlightened me for decades. The quantum entanglement of consciousness, where particles separated by vast distances instantaneously affect one another in ways that defy conventional physics, offers a scientific metaphor for spiritual truths that mystics have known for millennia. Just as entangled particles remain connected regardless of distance, our consciousness remains connected to higher dimensions of reality regardless of our physical circumstances.

CHAPTER 18

Smyly vs. The Nazis: Unfathomable Hell At 28,000 Feet

"Cannon to left of them, Cannon behind them
Volley'd and thunder'd; Storm'd at with shot and shell,
While horse and hero fell, They that had fought so well
Came thro' the jaws of Death, Back from the mouth of Hell,
All that was left of them, Left of six hundred."
Tennyson, "The Charge of the Light Brigade"

Sometimes the universe brings together two souls whose stories need to intertwine for some reason, regardless of age, background, or circumstance. Wil Smyly became one of my closest friends, golfing companions, and drinking buddies despite the twenty-one-year gap in our ages. Our lives became linked in ways that transcended ordinary friendship, bound together by litigation, tragedy, and a shared understanding of how evil can reach across decades to wound the innocent.

The case that brought us together, his seventeen-year-old daughter Sisi's tragic accident and subsequent year and a half coma would prove to be far more than a legal matter. Her life, like the lives of her mom and dad's, radiated goodness. It was similar to the short life of Karen in Chapter 15. As Wil and I became friends, the parental grief that besieged Wil when I first met him, gradually overtook my own professional experience and ability to deal with it. The suppressed horrors of World War II would resurface to meet contemporary tragedy, creating a convergence of consciousness that challenges the boundaries between history and metaphysics. Wil's story, Sisi's case, and my life are inextricably woven together with threads that stretch back to the bombing campaigns over Nazi Germany, forward through a drunk driver's wrong-way collision on Route 93 outside Boston Massachusetts, and into realms of consciousness that everyday life and litigation cannot adequately address.

When Wil and I first met in 1986, we each carried our own burdens of consciousness. His shaped by twenty-eight bombing missions over German cities, mine by years of meditation practice and the ongoing Scientology litigation that was like a war, tearing my family apart. As we worked together on Sisi's case, sharing late-night conversations over dinner and cocktails, our individual struggles merged into something larger; something that would in some mysterious process bridge the chasm between World War II trauma and parental grief.

Wil's consciousness was formed by observable history; his service as a B-17 pilot, his survival when so many of his comrades died, and his decades of suppressing memories too terrible to fully process. Our consciousness operates on levels beyond the merely historical, even from our ancestral DNA and prior incarnations, with quantum entanglement occurring at many levels, perhaps all. With Wil, I would also discover that trauma can echo across generations and conditions in ways that demand we investigate. On this point why would we assume that Quantum Entanglement would occur selectively? Is it not a constant? My experience with the dead Irish priest had shown me that awareness can transcend individual lifetimes, and that this one is on record only because of the circumstances that enabled me to experience that incident. Could we extrapolate from this that there are many more awaiting remembrance?

The litigation involving Sisi's tragedy became the vehicle through which Wil's long-buried war experiences would finally surface. The suppressed horrors of strategic bombing campaigns began to emerge like ghosts demanding reconciliation. What started as a wrongful death case evolved into a complex reckoning with the nature of evil, the reality of redemption, and the mysterious ways in which consciousness operates across time and space. The facts I must relate span forty years, from 1944-45 to 1985-88, and some events involve what can only be described as abominable human conduct. Yet within this darkness, something redemptive emerged, a demonstration of how divine grace can bridge the seemingly impossible gulf between the utter insanity of human cruelty and the divine mercy that can transform even our darkest experiences into sources of healing and understanding. Wil Smyly survived the cataclysmic events of WW II as a B-17 bomber pilot, only to suffer through the shockingly tragic, year and a half coma and death of his daughter, 'Sisi' Sandra Lee Smyly.

Although separated by four decades these events create a consciousness entangled story that forces us to re-examine what we think we know about causation, justice, and existence. The culmination of the litigation we interacted in resulted in some type of reclamation, even redemption, arising out of Sisi's loss to our observable senses, but was she even lost in the truest sense? My experiences of the dead priest and the Unity experience, suggest that her body may have died, but she did not.

Wil and I and his wife Ellie initially discussed all of the facts involving the legal aspects of the case, as well as the clinical aspects of Sisi's medical status in 1985. When I first met with them, Sisi lay in a coma from a hangman's fracture of the C2 vertebrae, suffered in an unspeakable car accident caused by a drunk driver going the wrong way on Rt 93, a limited access freeway coming out of Boston. The drunk had entered on an exit ramp driving south in the northbound lane when Sisi's car crested a hill and collided head on with the drunk about 10 PM.

The doctors tried to determine whether her condition indicated brain death or if she was in a persistent vegetative state, which is usually diagnosed by examining the brainstem, a diagnosis complicated by too many variables to explain here. At that time in the mid 1980's, few neurologists in the world recognized consciousness as a state beyond either brainstem death or a persistent vegetative state. Sisi's case may or may not bridge that scientific gap. God and his quantum mechanics may help. You, dear reader can decide.

By the time I met Wil and his family, the medical consensus was absolute. For over a year, his daughter Sisi had been on total life support; a ventilator to breathe for her, intravenous tubes to feed her, all under the care of the world's leading neurologists. Their diagnosis was brainstem death, the result of a catastrophic C2 fracture. In the mid-1980s, the neurological understanding of such conditions was still in its infancy, but the verdict was clear: Sisi was completely unresponsive to any external stimuli. The doctors had given up all hope of recovery and recommended terminating life support.

But Wil had not given up on his daughter. For reasons that defied medical logic, he believed Sisi was still present, and for the longest time he refused to let her go. Then, just before the machines were to be turned off, a remarkable event occurred, one we recorded on videotape: a single tear emerged from Sisi's eye. Medically, it was impossible. Neurologically, it shouldn't have happened. It was a silent testament that challenged the boundaries of everything we thought we knew about life, death, and the nature of consciousness itself.

As the family endured the ongoing life support, Wil and I became close friends and began to commiserate over Sisi's condition and the decisions that needed to be made both medically and in the litigation aspect. As our discussions progressed, we shared our experiences; Wil's WW II experiences, and my situation regarding the evils of Scientology, especially with regards my family.

Sisi was in a vegetative state, but Wil refused to accept that she was actually dead, believing that she would eventually regain her faculties. For me, I was in a semi-vegetative state from the trauma of the Scio wars which were then in their 7th year and as a result, Laima was severely ill with Rheumatoid Arthritis, and she and my children were seriously traumatized from unrelenting Nazi-type operations of Scio abuse...I'm not exaggerating. They sued me over 21 times, all frivolous, all designed to harrass and stop my litigation against them. All cases were dismissed in court.

In 1985-86, there seemed to be no hope for either of our situations. I told Wil I greatly admired him for serving our country in WW II fighting the Nazi's, and that Sisi's dire situation was beyond all human understanding. He said from his perspective the Church of Scientology sounded like the Nazis he had fought against. We both wondered about the risks we had each taken in opposing our respective enemies. I shared my 'engine out' emergency with my son and two friends in the plane, and although it was no comparison to his wartime experiences as a pilot, Wil understood the dangers of losing the engine in a single engine plane under inexplicable circumstances. The engine gauges were normal, so he thought my concerns were warranted. I also shared their more brazenly violent incident, when their Scio thug, an ex-cop, jumped out of the bushes and exposed a gun under his jacket saying "Do you know how easy this would be Mr. Flynn?". He thought that event was 'just a threat'. It seemed a bit more real for me I must say! The latter incident happened shortly after I had met Wil. (See *Litigator 2* for the full story).

From everything I had read about piloting a B17, It made my little Scio war seem insignificant. He had to sit in a glass cockpit flying directly into deadly 88mm exploding flak, not to mention the swarming squadrons of Nazi Messerschmitt 109 fighters trying to shoot him and his comrades down...then he would have to go back up the next day or a few days later, and repeat the exercise day after day, over and over again.

There were no spoils of war for Wil or our brave countrymen in either of the world wars, a stark departure from the traditions of combat that had defined human history for millennia. For the Roman legionary, victory meant a share of the captured treasure, land grants in conquered territories, and the right to parade defeated enemies through the streets of Rome... This ancient contract between the soldier and the state, that personal risk would be rewarded with personal gain was absent for the American G.I. in the trenches of France or the flak-filled skies over Germany. They fought and died for an idea: the preservation of a free citizenry and the defense of a nation... This makes their sacrifice and Wil's all the more profound, a testament to a generation that gave everything and asked for nothing in return.

We increasingly commiserated over dinner and cocktails, and more and more raw emotions began to flow. Wil's WW II horrors slowly surfaced with more details as he faced the inexplicable tragedy of his life; his beloved daughter was in a coma as the result of a drunk driver going the wrong way on Route 93 coming out of Boston. His sense of injustice almost overwhelmed him, and me.

A FRIENDSHIP FORGED IN GRIEF

My wife was suffering, and my family life was in shreds from the Scio wars, and as we got into it, Wil's real war tragedies against the Nazi's also ended up on our collective plates. He knew I was a WW II buff, also a pilot flying my own plane, and we speculated about flying an F4 Phantom jet over Hanoi vs piloting a WW II heavy B-17 bomber, dropping 3-5 tons of explosives on German cities amidst flak and fighters. Despite the age gap between us of just over 20 years, our friendship deepened to the point that we would play rounds of golf together and greatly enjoyed each others company.

Wil mostly remained quiet and evasive on specific questions of his service, but at some point he very quietly said that enduring 88 flak was far worse than the Nazi fighters. Ultimately that little comment opened a dark pandora's box of suppressed frustration, fear, anger and raw emotion. He and his crew could not fight back against the flak. They could against the fighters. At first in our discussions, the adventure of piloting a B-17 in his 28 missions over Nazi cities in service of our country came out as 'just doing his job'.

The night before this new opening up from Wil, when I asked him that difficult question, we had been preparing for the final day of the four-day Oyster Harbors Golf tournament in Massachusetts, and we were on a roll. Despite drinking the night before until 3 AM and arriving at our 7 AM tee time severely hungover, I paradoxically played the best round of my life and Wil wasn't far behind. Perhaps in that impaired state, our overthinking minds, usually the greatest opponent on the golf course, finally stepped aside. We were euphoric. It was probably due to this state that I was able to ask these probing questions, and for Wil to be able to answer them. Wil later framed the scorecard from that day, a small bright moment amid our shared exploration of life's deepest sorrows.

The distress from Sisi's condition was always on his plate and seemed to eclipse his war memories. At first it seemed to me that there was no correlation or comparison between the two, however, as our discussions deepened, the Sisi tragedy seemed to resurrect a depth of emotion that put him back in his war frame of mind, only this time in a battle with God. We shared that battle mostly in unspoken, veiled, and subliminal ways. With more cocktails one evening, more raw emotion erupted, but still he managed to suppress more detailed descriptions and reminiscences. Eventually, fragmented, partial discussions of the unspeakable horrors of strategic area bombing came forth like a resurrected ghost directly out of a grave of suppressed rage.

It seemed as if Wil had abandoned God, because he railed against the shocking reality of aerial combat from his experiences 40 years earlier which he had suppressed over and over again. It wasn't that Wil's faith and courage had left him, on the contrary, he seemed invincible. A new realization...a reclamation and redemption began to emerge in our commiserations.

He endured the worst horrors humans can experience. Human inhumanity manifesting in the insanity of war is one of the primary themes of this book. Wars are generally waged by the money changers, and ending them to save our species relies on us manifesting God's Grace with our ally Jesus Christ, and other true messengers from other faiths who convey the principles I know as the Sermon on the Mount teachings from the Christian Bible. I believe it's our only salvation.

THE HORRORS OF STRATEGIC AREA BOMBING

The infamous Nazi 88mm anti-aircraft flak, and ME 109's, 110's and Focke Wolfe 190 fighters were far more deadly to American bomber crews than the primitive cannons of the Crimean War described in the above quote by Tennyson. Indeed, both the fatality rate and combat horrors of WW II bomber crews were exponentially worse than a cavalry charge employing sabres and lances against the cannon batteries at Balaclava, in which about 110 of the 668 in the Light Brigade had died.

It is impossible to convey the "Unbelievable Courage of WW II Bomber Crews." This YouTube video is a must watch to get a feeling for this chapter. See link on our website Litigator.cloud

The bomber crews in the Eighth Air Force bombing of German cities had a 71% fatality rate; and the second highest fatality rate of all branches of all the military of all nations in all combat theatres in WW II, the first being German submariners who had an unbelievable 70-75% fatality rate. Of the over 400,000 American combat fatalities in WW II, 20 % were airmen.

The few details I dragged out of Wil relating to his unbelievable courage flying through the "jaws of death" in a B-17 over German cities, as I found out, was nothing compared to the shockingly tragic events he experienced that involved the car accident, coma and death of his daughter Sisi...and this led to a strange form of realization and redemption in the context of both experiences.

I could only conclude after Sisi's case, that there is no such thing as an accident in the ways of Spirit. As to legal causation, once again, like my burning hand experience in chapter 8, I found in Sisi's case that there is a definable level of causation on God's level, a quantum entangled level, not cognizable in litigation, that, like Einstein postulated, we can only call "spooky". Same with the dead Irish priest. When that experience happened in July, 1987, Wil and I were close friends. He was a client and trusted me, but he thought my description of the dead priest experience was "nuts". Maybe I am?

Initially, the incomprehensible circumstances of Sisi's coma and death, were far more mentally and emotionally devastating to Wil than piloting his B17 into the "jaws of death." But something mystical and inexplicable happened in Sisi's case. I will try to explain the inexplicable in the next chapter. God works in mysterious ways. First, Wil's WW II trauma.

Beyond the impact of my words and quotes, the horror of watching his comrades die in plummeting balls of fiery death five miles above the earth, "the mouth of hell," as he called it, knowing he was 71% likely to be next at any moment, injected in Wil Smyly 40 years of a suppressed, unrecognized, "Hell" inside himself. The dauntless courage that these valiant men needed in bombing Nazi cities often led to extreme psychological breakdown during and after the war. Not Wil. He fought off the fear, death and loss of comrades from enemy flak and fighters. As to residual guilt, I am not so sure? Stay tuned.

Many men buried the horror at the time only to have it resurface later as guilt, sometimes decades on, returning in recurring nightmares and the same trapped feeling of having to climb back into the air again and again. And there was another weight, more devastating than flak or fighters: a guilt that politicians, generals, and even bomber crews could not, or would not name. It was the mass killing of non-combatants; those civilians on the ground, directly beneath the B17's, praying that they would not be at the receiving end of the bombs.

In the post WW II media climate, the political and military leadership of the Allied Victors generally suppressed their own and the allied bomber crews guilt of incinerating between at least half a million to over one million German civilian men, women and children. The scale of it will never be known. There are no reliable statistics. Mostly, there were no bodies left to count. They were vaporized, incinerated, blown to pieces.

Modern warfare technology as of 1939–1945, specifically by strategic area bombing, advanced the ability of humans to indiscriminately kill both combatants and civilians, on a scale never seen in human history. Nothing like the WW II strategic area bombing, with each B-17 capable of carrying 10,000 pounds, (often reduced for fuel), of high explosive and incendiary bombs, had ever occurred. It inflicted the instantaneous mass murder of non-combatants, using explosive and incendiary bombs, ranging from 100 lb. bomb clusters to 4000 lb. 'Blockbusters' dropped on German and Tokyo city blocks resulting in a massive death toll, preventing any accurate measurement. Humans were literally burned or blown into an oblivion that rendered statistical record keeping impossible.

Intelligent, conscientious, dutiful and courageous pilots like Wil Smyly and their crews who delivered the deadly bomb loads, together with the Generals and politicians who ordered it all knew exactly what they were doing. Many had no appearance of a conscience, or apparent residual guilt, even from General Curtis Lemay, Churchill, Roosevelt and Stalin.

They specifically employed the strategic area bombing campaign to destroy civilian morale, not to destroy military targets.

The propaganda of the planners of American strategic bombing campaigns of both Germany and Japan fed an unbridled myth to the American media and citizenry throughout WW II that the sole targeting was military objectives. This was to circumvent the reality that vast populations of defenseless members of our species were the object of unprecedented mass murder. Our political and military leadership propagated the myth. Our bomber crews went along with it. Truth.

Wil was one of the best humans I have ever met. He was no saint, not a churchy or outwardly religious person, but I put him in a class of people of evolved consciousness like my own mother and father and my deceased wife. Wil named his plane Elegant El after his wife, Ellie. As part of the

American Bomber Command, Wil flew 28 missions, three more than the generally required 25 at that time. Wil repeatedly charged into the aerial bombardment of Nazi Germany. It was his duty...but it was the repetition, then the downtime afterwards, thinking about it, knowing you were going back up that caused many brave and strong men to break down, unable to go back up. Wil refused to talk about the 'downtime demons'. He didn't like to talk about the war, and I uncovered most of it only as part of our case research into his and his family's' damages.

Through a developing camaraderie, and increasingly over many drinks, he released pockets of raw emotion over Sisi. It assailed his mind and heart, his consciousness, and the core of his being on a level that nobody realised in the immediacy of flying through German fighter or flak. It caused Wil to ask all the why's we are left with in such acute moments of suffering. His wartime bombing of Nazi cities lasted for about eight months, the emotional residue continued until the conclusion of the litigation involving Sisi, which went on for three years.

THE NORDEN MYTH: PRECISION BOMBING AND THE REALITY OF WAR

Wil was part of the legendary U. S. Eighth Air Force's, 490 Bomb Group, 850 Squadron, day-light strategic bombing campaign over German cities and supposedly Nazi war-making factories in Berlin, Cologne, Hamburg, Hanover, Kassel, Merseburg, Schweinfurt, and Munster. Ultimately, his squadron participated in the mass incineration of Dresden.

This strategy had its foundation in what was euphemistically called "strategic area bombing." It was a euphemism by our political and military leadership given to the media to conceal civilian massacres.

The planners and experts would target specific military targets like the ball bearing factories at Schweinfurt, but the best the bomber crews could accomplish even with the Norden bomb-sight, was to drop tons of bombs in the area of the factories. These were generally located within or near the largest German cities. Statistically, on any given bombing raid involving hundreds of bombers, dropping hundreds of bombs, supposedly targeting war making factories, one or two bombs would strike within 1000 feet of a target with occasional direct hits.

The German civilian population was being exterminated on a level unlike any war in human history.

The accuracy of the Norden bomb sight was an unmitigated, propaganda myth. There were so many lies, cover-ups, schemes, and media fabrications about it during the war, that were all designed to convince our citizenry that it accurately targeted only Nazi war making factories. There is only one conclusion: our political and military leadership brazenly lied to the 'Greatest Generation' of young bomber crews, like 21-year-old Wil Smyly to send them into an unfathomable hell. They were mass murdering civilians in a strategic area bombing campaign to destroy civilian morale and covering it up with the myth of the Norden bombsight. See the youtube video: "The Biggest Lie of WW II? The myth of the Norden bombsight." Also on our website Litigator.cloud

Every time an American B-17 took off in that 25,000-foot campaign of terror for both pilots above and citizens below, they were bombarded with flak so thick "you could walk on it", and the risk of any particular crew member never coming back was about 20%. The ultimate fatality rate spread over 28 missions was 71%. Over 26,000 American bomber crew members died during the war; more even than marines killed in the Pacific theater. Arguably, daylight bombing involved the most hazardous exposure to German flak and fighters compared to the night missions of the RAF.

Central to the debate was the Churchill driven British Royal Air Force mission to destroy civilian morale by area bombing German cities at night, while American bombers were supposed to target military installations by day and determine effectiveness. Churchill used our Eighth Air Force to accomplish his objective. In truth, Churchill was a butcher both in WW I and in WW II.

Crime is generally more effective at night. Bombing at night relieved immediate and contemporaneous Brit visual knowledge, photography and consciousness of the mass murder of civilians. The photos generally came later during U.S. daytime missions. The photos and documents became instantly classified. Our government and military, along with the Brits, used a system of classifying documents, photos and communications to conceal war crimes in WW II that brazenly violated all of the rules of war adopted in the 1929 so called Geneva Convention.

When you start breaking natural law, the rotten apple analogy applies. In this case, after the war, in 1947, the American intelligence Service, the Office of Strategic Services, (OSS), became the Central Intelligence Agency, (CIA). The CIA was created by the National Security Act. The CIA was quickly taken over by Allen Dulles and his henchmen in 1952. In short, they were a group of ruthless criminals masquerading as patriots, operating for private clients like the Rockefellers, adopting and implementing an abominable system of classifying evidence of their horrendous and unspeakable crimes. It lead to the worst crime of all; Dulles, as head of the CIA orchestrated the murder of President Kennedy. (*Litigator 4*)

NAZI AIR DEFENSES

The Nazis possessed a relatively sophisticated air defense system with radar and accurate, omnipresent, "8.8 cm FLAK 41" anti-aircraft batteries, using mechanics and optics to pinpoint its exploding shells at the same height and location as advancing bombers. These were generally located around their cities and manufacturing facilities that were being targeted. Flying a B17 to avoid flak but stay in diamond formations with sometimes hundreds of planes in order to increase defensive 30 and 50 caliber machine gun fire against German fighters became a cat and mouse game of evading known flak batteries from mission to mission with route and altitude changes.

The 1943, early 1944 period, before the introduction of P51 fighter escorts that possessed long range fuel tanks, involved the worst losses in defending against swarming German fighters. The 8th Air Force suffered terrible losses in 1943 from the fighters. Added to this, the anti-aircraft flak batteries became more numerous and accurate. B17 aircraft production increased, and quantities of bombs dropped increased. Whilst the ratio of overall proportionate airplane losses decreased due to increased production, substantial losses of planes and crews remained and the terror and carnage to German cities and population increased.

In general, the bomber crews feared the flak more than the fighters because they couldn't fight back. In his book, "Half a Wing, Three Engines and a Prayer" the author, Brian O'Neill, describes the terror of a B17 bombing mission:

> "The sky was covered with quite a number of planes, and debris from planes that had exploded. It was really tough, close fighting. We were being hit from all sides. The slower German fighters were hitting us from the back with 20mm cannon shells and rockets. The Me-110s kept picking on this one plane off our right wing. They knocked all the fabric off its elevator and rudder, and eventually set it on fire, but apparently this didn't slow the plane down

> much, since they stayed with us another five to ten minutes. Then this German plane came back of us and under us, in a vertical bank that almost cut our wing off, and set the plane on fire again. It was mostly smoke, coming from the bomb bay, and then it flared up. We tried to move over to get out of the way of this plane, and shortly after I looked around and it was gone."

Every pilot and crew member of every American bomber knew when they took off they were flying into pure hell, the "Valley of Death." Wil reported to me that the psychological anticipation was often worse than the fear experienced during the flak itself. They might randomly escape swarming German fighters in their 3 level diamond formations, but never the flak. Wil lost his tail gunner, his plane was shot up, but he and the rest of his crew survived the war.

THE SURVIVOR'S BURDEN

It didn't end there...in the aftermath of WW II, B17 pilots grappled with the conscious awareness of what they had actually accomplished in their missions by dropping bombs on to German cities. Military historians delicately tried to deal with how they justified their strategic bombing campaigns.

Pilots that survived, like Wil Smyly, lived with it on a day-to-day basis after the war. Some, like Wil, possessed a consciousness of its consequences which matched their courage to do it. Wil was 21 years old when he bombed Nazi targets. Both the British and American bomber pilots knew why the Brits bombed at night and the Americans bombed during the day. Daylight bombing was considered more accurate but as we know the accuracy of the Norden sight was a myth. The RAF knew from experience that daylight bombing was much more dangerous, and the logic was, without what they thought was a precise bomb sight like the Americans had, why risk daytime bombing? The American media and public opinion would not tolerate indiscriminate mass murder of civilians, so the spin was that daylight bombing enabled accuracy with the Norden bombsight. Utter rubbish many might say.

The reason I provide such detailed accounts in this book is to examine consciousness on three levels. First, the consciousness of the war makers, the politicians and generals who planned and ordered mass civilian, aerial death in WW II, and trench warfare insanity in WW I. My dad was born in the latter. I was born in the former. Second, the residual consciousness, the unhealed trauma that men like my dad and Wil carried for decades after the war ended. Third. The vibrational cellular consciousness of war and violence in our species either collectively or individually passed from father to son, generation to generation. All my life I have dealt with the profound paradox between all of the purportedly "Christian" European nations, genociding each other, notwithstanding the essence of Christ's teaching in the Sermon on the Mount that I was taught in supposedly "Catholic" schools, age 7 to age 21.

YALTA: DRESDEN AND TOKYO: MASS MURDER

My quantum entangled thoughts, feelings and education on the above paradox came face to face with Wil's quantum entangled thoughts, feelings and actual combat experiences in Sisi's case. I now feel, there are no accidents in life. The February 4th to 11th 1945 Yalta Conference with Roosevelt's explicit approval, changed and exposed both American and British "strategic area bombing" policy when Churchill, Roosevelt and Stalin agreed to incinerate the City of Dresden and its swollen refugee populace, which had previously been considered a non-strategic target.

When I penetrated Wil's unwillingness to discuss those 40-year-old nightmares of the dead and dying civilians under his B-17, and the flak and fighter fears of him and his crew, it highlighted the pure courage required to perform his duty knowing that death was imminent. Surrounded by flak explosions and being attacked by fighters as they were, if they were not killed in that flight, there was always the additional psychological difficulty of getting back in the "left seat" of a massive weapon of death and destruction, the B-17, and going back up to face the same trauma yet again the next day or a few days later. It was a repetitive nightmare, psychological torture no less.

Just one well located flak shell in a B-17 filled with 6000 - 9600 lbs. of high explosive or incendiary bombs, would remove any trace of what was once a human being. Their wives and families would be left with that reality. Despite this, Wil said that watching his daughter in coma for years was far worse than his war time demons. He wondered if he was being punished for his service to our country in WW II. It was consciousness at work in conscience.

These were our fellow citizens just a few generations ago. I was born in August 1944 when Wil began bombing German cities. When I observe what is happening in our country now, I wonder how prior generations of our patriot-heroes who sacrificed so much would react to the modern political madness enveloping their country. Instead, I'm writing about it from my own journalistic perspective with the liberties that they fought for, with over 400,000 losing their lives. I'm grateful, that's why I write about it, so that we can all recognize the insanity of both wars, how they have enveloped our collective consciousness and how our collective consciousness can evolve – something I do believe in after 5 decades in the PIT.

THE B-17, A WEAPON OF STRATEGIC DEATH

B-17's dropped over 640,000 TONS of bombs in WW II on supposedly Nazi military targets. More than any other bomber. The crews that manned them likely did as much to win the war as the foot soldiers. The terror of being 25,000 feet in the air, in minus forty degree cold, wearing a bulky heated flight suit for eight plus intensely concentrated flying hours, all the while trying to remain in formation while "stormed at with shot and shell,". Many were blown to bits, crash landed or the lucky few bailed out on a flimsy parachute, sometimes only to get pitchforked by German farmers when they landed. Was there any difference to soldiers sheltering in a foxhole during a German artillery barrage? The reality is, they both caused the same result; terror and death, above and below.

For the pilots in particular, the physical, mental and emotional demands and stress of flying B17's was intense. The planes were loaded with 3 -5 tons of bombs, making the planes sluggish to fly. As the pilot, they were responsible for the survival of their 8-10 crew members for 8 plus hours, flying in tight formations, and especially whilst at the dropzone, confronted with furious bursts of flak. It was unforgettable, resulting in nightmarish, suppressed terror. Wil Smyly endured these gruelling missions, and survived afterwards by suppressing the accrued darkness. His consciousness on that subject resurrected itself in Sisi's case.

The same military and strategic motives existed as the cavalry in the bungled Charge of the Light Brigade at Balaclava where almost 120 men and 475 horses were killed. Kill the enemy, destroy his fortifications, and occupy his land. The means of destruction had changed; the B17's replaced horses; formations of them replaced cavalry units; 9600 pounds of bombs and thirteen 50 cal machine guns replaced sabers and lances. Additionally, civilians mostly replaced actual combatant targets.

DOWNTIME

Our pilots had an even more insidious and deadly obstacle than flak and fighters...it lurked in 'downtime'; thinking about doing it again. In my discussions with Wil, as the drinks flowed and the emotions released, a different component of human consciousness involved in WW II firebombing emerged. The victims could be in the thousands, or even tens of thousands of civilians that they had never met, had no personal feelings about, intended no harm toward, and wanted nothing from. They could just as easily be your close friends or a companion at a local pub. Being a human being assumes you will ponder your personal responsibility if involved in another's death; and then, with the added weight of conscience, being assigned the next mission and preparing to do it all over again... returning, if you survive...with an ever greater payload of guilt. In such circumstances, the mind can turn against itself.

At the time, they were 'just doing their job', or so they thought. However, 5, 10, 20, or 40 years later if one had any conscience, the demons emerged. Big problem. I have also watched it with my close friends after Vietnam, making me ask who and what caused that war – only to find out that it was our CIA, which I later litigated against.

I came to understand that the men with the greatest courage to do their duty, like Wil Smyly, were also the ones most haunted by what they had done and had more to deal with in later life. Heroism and conscience go hand in hand. The elevated consciousness that makes a man capable of extraordinary acts also makes him capable of realizing their weight. Truth is an unforgiving companion.

THE DRESDEN FIRESTORM: A DESCENT INTO HELL

Whilst the Eighth Air Force's daylight bombing campaign inflicted death and terror on German civilian populations the British nighttime bombing was even more indiscriminate. The infamous fire-bombing of Dresden, initially demanded by Churchill, and approved by Stalin and Roosevelt at the Yalta Conference, was carried out just days later on February 14th and 15th, 1945, when the war was essentially over. Germany surrendered just eight weeks later. Before ordering the bombing they knew the war would be over soon. The Russian army was only 70 miles from Dresden. It involved wanton carnage and mass murder on a scale no army had ever inflicted on civilian populations.

That fire-bombing created a human bonfire of between 135,000 and 200,000 men, women and children. Compare this to the total Japanese dead at Hiroshima and Nagasaki from the two atomic bombs resulting in an estimated 120,000 dead. The Dresden bombing however, revealed something equally chilling; that when deployed with enough technical sophistication the creation of a firestorm could achieve similar devastation without the splitting of atoms. It was well planned and well executed mass murder. There is no doubt that such a massive strategic air bombardment of Dresden, as the war ended, was at least approved in principle at Yalta by Roosevelt, unable to stand up to Churchill and the allies "top brass". Roosevelt died a few weeks later.

There were reports of civilians fleeing along the Elbe River allegedly being machine gunned by low flying British planes. It is the subject of debate but there is no reliable evidence. The bombing and strafing attacks throughout the war were well planned, executed, reported, debriefed and generally classified, so we will probably never find out the truth.

Churchill, Roosevelt and Stalin publicly side-stepped personal culpability. Stalin and his Generals knew that at the time of bombing Dresden, their armies, just 70 miles away, would take Dresden, a non-military objective, within days. The communists later used the Dresden massacre for propaganda, even though they were in on it. The UK and US responded that the Russians had requested the bombing.

There is no doubt that one of the collective decisions coming out of Yalta by the three of them was to firebomb Dresden to destroy civilian morale and hasten the end of the war. The strategic and tactical preparation for the bombing, in itself, proves the cold insanity of that decision making. Dresden, was followed in rapid order with the devastating firebombing of Tokyo, and the nuclear bombing of Hiroshima and Nagasaki.

Victor Gregg was a British POW being held in a building in the center of Dresden, awaiting execution for sabotage. He lived through the bombing. In his book *Dresden: A Survivor's Story, February 1945* he describes the waves of bombers incinerating the city. It is an indescribable and unforgettable recounting of a human horror story. I quote the following from his book beginning with the second wave of bombers to give you some concept of the madness and horror of it all:

"A lot of survivors from the burning ruins were now out in the open, spread along this low embankment with no shelter or cover of any kind. The inferno was growing fiercer and noisier by the minute, but even so, above the noise I could hear the pulsating throb of hundreds of heavy aircraft bearing down on us. There was no need for flares to lead these bombers to their target, the whole city had become a gigantic torch and must have been visible to the pilots from a hundred miles away. The people around me started to gather in small bunches as if to shield each other from the onslaught. Dresden had no defenses, no anti-aircraft guns, no searchlights, nothing. The planes were thousands of feet up but even so it was possible to make out their outlines reflected in the glow of the flames." Victor Gregg and Rick Stroud, *Dresden: A Survivor's Story, February 1945* (Kindle Single) (pp. 18-19). Bloomsbury Publishing. 2013. Kindle Edition.

The young men ordered to carry out the bombing, like 21-year-old Wil Smyly were barely out of their teens. Despite whatever heroics they displayed, their grasp of the situation was limited. Most never fully understood or confronted on any deeper level what they were truly doing at the time. The up-close and personal consequences of the bombs they dropped on civilians that Victor Gregg later described in horrific detail, were far from their consciousness until suppressed facts gradually emerged in the weeks, months, years, and sometimes decades after their missions ended.

That's why Gregg wrote his book...to force the world to face the sheer, almost unthinkable evil of the Dresden firebombing. He sets that darkness in stark relief against what we claim to believe: our Christian ideals. In this way he exposes the abyss between creed and conduct.

Tolstoy was reaching for the same moral reckoning in 1893 with *The Kingdom of God Is Within You*, a confrontation between institutional religion and inner truth. Christ, too, became the ultimate mirror, accepting crucifixion at the hands of the money changers to reveal that a higher kingdom is not a place we conquer, but a reality within us if we choose to awaken to it. But awakening has a cost. It demands the surrender of ego; of the materialist hunger lodged deep in our consciousness, and the willingness to let that old self die so something truer can live.

The U. S. leadership tried to sweep Dresden under the proverbial 'chaos of war' rug. It came up for me because of my representation of Wil. It emerged from his suppressed consciousness because of Sisi. There is unrelenting suffering until realization. There are no secrets, no suppression, and no guilt in God consciousness.

I was only six months old when 'we' incinerated the Dresden populace. Years after Dresden, when I was in high school, 1958-62, the horror of it began to emerge in more books, articles and publications worldwide. Some who chose to understand what really happened in Dresden, like me, were shocked, but only to the very limited degree that my inexperienced, unrealized, lower consciousness at that time absorbed. No more.

Gregg's book was not published until 2013, but I read several books about the bombing of Berlin, Dresden, Tokyo, Hiroshima and Nagasaki as a teenager. The correlations in that knowledge and consciousness only came together years later when I represented the Wil Smyly family.

Gregg's book provides an eyewitness account of what is described in many articles and books, which was more or less suppressed for many years following the war. It was definitely suppressed in Wil. The truth on this subject is no longer capable of being politically and governmentally massaged to deceive a democratic electorate. I have attempted to come to a conclusion from a higher level of meditative consciousness, but I'm not there yet. 'Look at what the Japanese did in the Rape of Nanking, the Nazis did with the ovens at Auschwitz, Buchenwald...and don't forget the London blitz. An eye for an eye said the world in February, 1944 and for years thereafter.

Gandhi's reply was: "An eye for an eye makes the whole world go blind"

THE 'KINGDOM OF GOD WITHIN'

It wouldn't surprise me if Christ recognized that our only hope as a species lay in the revolutionary type of teachings especially as contained in the Beatitudes from the Sermon on the Mount, and other true teachings. After all, ninety-nine percent of all species that have ever existed on Earth are now extinct, why should homo sapiens be any different? Extinction is both the history and likely destiny of our planet unless we raise our consciousness and embrace practices like meditation and follow the guidance of Beatitude type teachings to help us out of the mess we've created.

Our planet is infested with predators in the animal kingdom, and unfortunately our species is no different. Christ offered a pragmatic alternative; turn the other cheek. If someone wants your shirt, give them your coat too. As for his 'resist not evil' aphorism, it may be the only solution to get us out of our limbic brains and material consciousness. Most religions advocate non-violence in thought, word and deed, with some exceptions. For my own 'sins', at the end of the Scio wars, God's Grace presented me with an alternative to the aggressive occupation of litigation, but I balked at turning the other cheek and I didn't 'resist evil' when I was later confronted with it in my cases.

Gandhi's nonviolence and Tolstoy's support for Quakerism, non-violence, not resisting evil, and the extinction of national armaments and war making is likely the only salvation to prevent nuclear extinction. His remarkable 1893 book, *The Kingdom of God is Within You. Christianity Not as a Mystic Religion, but as a New Theory of Life*, should be read by every world leader contemplating violence of any kind.

Just four weeks after Dresden, on March 9-10, 1945, Roosevelt approved the Tokyo fire-bombing which created a firestorm that destroyed the entire city and burned up at least 120,000 men, women and children. The Dresden operation planners learned exactly how to firestorm Tokyo to maximize a human bonfire. When Roosevelt ordered it along with the approval of the Joint Chiefs of Staff, particularly Curtis Lemay, and General Marshall, they all had a full briefing on the aftermath of Dresden. They knew exactly what they were doing. Payback? Maybe Roosevelt's conscience got to him because he died a few weeks later on April 12, 1945.

I suppose he considered his options of possibly sacrificing tens of thousands of American soldiers in an invasion of Japan, and chose the Tokyo civilian massacre instead. A devil's choice. Not so with Dresden because the Allies were already in Germany and Soviet divisions were only 70 miles away. It was mass murder and Wil, as a patriotic airman serving his country had unwittingly been part of it.

Wil's story forced me to confront a difficult truth, that the consciousness required to survive war is not the same as the consciousness required to live in peace. To fly into a wall of flak requires a man to wall off a part of his own soul, to suppress the empathy and fear that would otherwise make such an act impossible. For forty years Wil kept those horrors behind a wall, but trauma doesn't fade; it waits. And in a strange, quantum-entangled way, the tragedy of his daughter's life would become the key to unlocking the prison of his own.

CHAPTER 19

Wil's Redemption: From Flak-Filled Skies to Divine Grace

"Forgiveness is the fragrance that the violet sheds on the heel that has crushed it." **Mark Twain**

The reality of Wil's life became clearer during the time we spent together, often with drinks that loosened the control he had over his suppressed emotions. The coma and death of Sisi caused such emotional upheaval in Wil that it made the Post Traumatic Stress Syndrome (PTSD) from repeated forays into the flak-filled skies over Germany almost like a meaningless dream. He repeatedly begged God to take him, not Sisi. When that didn't happen, some WW II demons of indescribable intensity resurrected within his consciousness and evolved to a level which then caused their release and perhaps his redemption. That is how I see it now. I offer his and Sisi's story as one of redemption in a field of consciousness beyond death where love is realized.

After Wil survived WW II, he then experienced the normal ups and downs of life on many levels, but few experiences bring greater suffering than watching your teenage daughter linger in a coma for 18 months as you and your family slowly lose hope, ultimately agreeing with doctors to turn off the ventilator, and enduring her death even though you feel that she was still 'present' in her coma, and perhaps even after life support was withdrawn.

I lived through this extraordinary story with Wil, all the while counting my blessings; nothing like this had happened to my kids. I have to admit it shook me up on many levels but left me with remarkable perspectives on life and death. His story teaches us that love, not the sentimental or superficial kind, but real love that endures through immense suffering, the kind exemplified by Christ carrying the cross—is the answer to life's hardships.

THE ANATOMY OF A TRAGEDY
THE SEQUENCE OF EVENTS

A drunk going the wrong way on a major freeway, Rt 93, north of Boston, just behind a rise in the road, which obscured the drunk's car and Sisi's car.

A broken seat belt in a new Dodge Daytona car sold by Wil, and operated by his daughter.

Sisi suffers from a fractured C2 vertebrae, a 'hangman's fracture', when all three of the other occupants wore seat belts and suffered no injury?

The Karen McCuish case all over again involving no other occupant injury?

A year and a half of persistent vegetative state coma culminating in a right eye tear captured on video tape as I whispered in Sisi's ear.

An experience by Wil and I flying home from Iacocca's office, Chairman of Chrysler Corporation in which his WW II experiences left him?

Wil owned a Dodge dealership in Malden Massachusetts. Although never college educated, his innate leadership abilities and business acumen earned him the trust of car industry higher ups after the war ended. He developed several automobile franchises into one of the most successful dealerships in Massachusetts.

The Smylys had four children of which Sandra or 'Sisi' was the baby. One terrible night in 1984, Sisi and three of her high school friends were driving north on Route 93 out of Boston at about 10 pm. They were in a Dodge Daytona, one of the dealer cars from Wil's dealership. The road they took, a major limited-access freeway intended for faster traffic, is one of the two main arteries in and out of Boston; the Mass Turnpike running east-west, and Route 93 running north-south.

Just a few miles from downtown Boston at about 10 PM, a drunk driver entered this same highway via an exit ramp, a ramp lit up with signs, warning he was going the wrong way. Undeterred, he barreled south in the northbound lanes of Route 93, occupying the middle lane. At that fateful moment, Sisi, heading north, crested a gentle rise that momentarily blocked her view ahead. At exactly the same instant, the drunk driver, with his headlights off, topped the hill from the opposite side. There was almost no time for braking. The two cars collided head-on.

Everyone in both vehicles, including Sisi and the drunk driver, wore seat belts. In a cruel twist, the seat belts did their job for everyone except Sisi. Hers snapped, and she was flung forward, head-first into the windshield. She sustained a catastrophic fracture of her C2 vertebra, the so-called 'hangman's fracture'. She had been transported from Mass General Hospital where

Dr. Eben Alexander later taught, (Coincidence or QE?), to a rehabilitation facility for this type of coma patient. Dr. Alexander was not involved in her treatment at that time but the collective views of the Mass General neurosurgeons that Sisi was brain dead with no consciousness, permeated the medical history, her records and the subsequent legal issues. Sisi was on 100% life support on a respirator with intravenous feeding.

Wil, Ellie, and their family were devastated beyond words. Amid this overwhelming grief, they, like Karen's parents earlier, desperately sought answers. "How could someone drive the wrong way on a major freeway? Was the driver so drunk he didn't realize, or was it an intentional act? Was it suicide? How could a small hill, at just that particular time and place, have blocked Sisi's view of the drunk driver in her lane on a four-lane highway? What was known about the drunk driver's history? Please, find out." These were hard and probably impossible questions to answer. How could such an improbable series of events, an almost unbelievable perfect storm of tragedy claim the life of their baby girl? Having heard of my reputation they wanted these questions and others answered by me. It was a tall order.

Could Sisi understand anything they said to her during almost non-stop 24/7 vigils that lasted over 18 months? Like Dr. Eben Alexander, who experienced a near death experience in his short weeklong coma, Sisi displayed no signs of consciousness notwithstanding the love being poured into her by her family, friends and relatives. The routine nurses' notes confirmed total and absolute "vegetative state" coma. The doctors universally said there was no hope, Sisi was dead, and only the ventilator with intravenous feeding was keeping her young heart and body in its then condition.

At first glance, given the circumstances, the cause of this tragedy was a drunk driver, nothing more. Blame him? Period. End of case?

We investigated the accident, visited Sisi, and spent time with Wil, often drinking together as raw emotion poured out over copious amounts of alcohol. It was during these moments as his love for Sisi collided with memories of strategic bombing, that Wil shared sorrows he had never voiced before. My persistent questions about the world wars, along with my own experience as a pilot, encouraged Wil to gradually reveal the tragedies he endured; the loss of comrades, the constant gnawing fear, never certain he would return each time he took flight in his bomber, named "Elegant El" after his wife.

Yet Wil recounted these wartime horrors only in the shadow of his grief for Sisi. For him, the fears and traumas of World War II seemed insignificant compared to witnessing his little girl's lifeless body. Again and again, I listened as he struggled to comprehend why God would allow him to survive Nazi flak and fighters, only to lose his daughter. Beneath his searching for meaning, there was a deep, suppressed rage. Together, as we tried to make sense of life, death, and God's role in Sisi's loss, we found no answers, only the comfort of shared sorrow.

The issue in the case became the failed and defective seat belt manufactured by X seat belt company installed in Dodge Daytonas, Wil's dealership car! Our investigators filmed and fully documented the failed seat belt, how and why it broke, and its defective design and manufacture. Wil was selling them. He believed in their 1980's absolute 'state of the art' safety engineering. To Wil and the family, these answers were at first met with blank stares and "so what, our little girl is gone, the drunk killed her".

In private moments, Wil's anger against the 'real' cause of Sisi's death, the drunk driver, emerged like a typhoon, but was that what really killed Sisi?

Our investigators and "accident reconstructionist" confirmed the facts of the accident, and the doctors expressed no hope as Sisi languished in full coma. Wil's hope turned to deep anger as his human mind failed to grasp what had caused this seismic devastation in his life. They were answers anyone would search for in times of tragedy, but his was fueled by the PTSD from his B17 mission. It had built up gradually but was now an emotional eruption of unconsolable magnitude. I have seen this type of behavior repeatedly over the years with cases and clients. In 1986–87 I told Wil repeatedly that sometimes there is no answer, at least on the human level...however I was wrong.

As a litigator my own mind also had to have rational answers. The drunk who was driving the wrong way was only part of the story. The instantaneous time and place on an interstate freeway coupled with the broken seat belt made ultimate issues of causation almost incomprehensible. Members of the family were reduced to accepting Sisi's tragedy as 'fate'. Wil would not accept it. He wanted to blame God.

My job was to blame Sisi's coma and death on the failed seat belt as a "superseding, intervening cause" to weigh against the drunk going the wrong way. Seat belts are designed to save lives in catastrophic collisions. The statistics were overwhelmingly in our favor that a properly designed and manufactured seat belt would have prevented Sisi's C2 fracture. Her seat belt broke at the stitching point with the buckle. It was documented. The seat belt of the right front passenger, manufactured by the same manufacturer did not break? But the right front passenger did not slam into the steering wheel or windshield.

THE LITIGATION ESCALATES

When I showed Wil the reports and fully explained how the seat belt failed and was defective in a car that his dealership routinely sold, his anger turned against Dodge and the Chrysler corporation. It soon knew no bounds. He terminated his highly successful Dodge franchise and sued Chrysler Corporation. Chrysler and its President, Lee Iacocca, hired Tom B, a well known defense attorney with a reputation in Boston's legal circles for being both fierce and nearly unbeatable. The litigation war commenced and Sisi languished in coma. Between visits to Sisi's rehab hospice and waging a litigation war which rapidly turned into a war of attrition with pleadings, discovery, depositions, motions and deepening emotional conflicts between the lawyers and clients on both sides, I became distraught over trying to make sense of it all while visiting Sisi and listening to Wil.

In my litigation practice, I was coming to grips with deeper questions in the aftermath of the settlement with the Scientology organization, and in the context of my TM practice: if there are really no accidents in life, but deeply connected cause and effect circumstances; and death is only a transition between lives; and we suffer as humans to realize that the earth plane is a school to elevate our consciousness to return to God, and perhaps not to reincarnate again in a world of violence, suffering and genocide, when you face death and coma in the trenches, what is reality? Does reality exist beyond our five senses? I realized I was in school and not passing my tests.

THE TEAR OF LIFE

As we were getting closer to trial, I decided to do a 'day in the life video' of Sisi in coma in the facility. Calling it a 'rehab' facility in this instance with no signs of consciousness for over two years was an oxymoron. Such a film is generally used in such cases to show the jury what a typical day in Sisi's so-called 'life' actually involved. And the Doctors were then recommending termination of all life support. Hope for Sisi was gone in the Smyly family.

In the period leading up to doing the film, I had visited Sisi many times with Wil, talked to her, whispered in her ears, told her stories, told her how much her family loved her, told her about my many meetings with her dad, his courage in the war, our friendship, and suggested that perhaps she should consider 'coming back'. Nothing. It was a similar scene to other cases I had been involved in.

Somehow, I got the repeated feeling from studying coma, talking to the docs, experiencing the psychic events of other cases I have reported, in my visits with Sisi, it seemed that she was listening attentively to me, taking it in, hearing me, feeling her dad's and mom's love. It felt like she was in a place in which a pervading environment of love enveloped her and all who visited.

It reached a point where I began to believe that Sisi was doing her 'duty', fulfilling a responsibility, completing a commitment of love in the depth of a silence we didn't understand. When I expressed my feelings on this subject to Wil, we ultimately agreed that Sisi was communicating back to us within a domain of love neither of us understood, but that she knew there was no need for her to respond. Only the silence of love could heal the tragedy. Were we just deceiving ourselves to compensate for the grief? One specific event confirmed our evolving belief that Sisi was still present.

This seemed to be confirmed the day we did the 'day in the life' film captured on camera! After filming for about three hours, talking to Sisi, explaining what we were doing, I went up and sat next to her head, and began quietly talking to her, gently stroking her forehead and the 'Christ center' just above the bridge of the nose, conveying that this would be one of our final meetings, if not the last because a decision was then being made to take her off life support. I explained that we all loved her, missed her, and that we would 'see' her again when we left the earth.

Prior to this, Sisi's eyes had never moved, and no tears or reaction of any type had ever occurred in 18 months. The routine nurses' notes confirmed total and absolute "vegetative state" coma. But as I talked to her, I knew she was listening to me! When I was nearly done talking, I said "Ok Sisi, we are leaving now, thank you for your time today and being my friend." As the words came out of my heart and mouth, a huge tear emerged from Sisi's right eye! It was caught on camera.

It occurred to me in that moment that I was witnessing an event that would forever alter my understanding of consciousness. It was now hovering in between science and mysticism. The medical equipment continued its mechanical rhythm, the ventilator pulsing up and down, monitors tracked her levels...but something beyond their ability to measure was occurring in that hospital room. Somehow, and I can't quite articulate why, I felt there was a connection being formed between this moment and events forty years earlier, when a young bomber pilot flew through flak-filled skies to bomb German cities. The litigator in me dismissed it as fanciful, a grief-induced delusion with no basis in evidence.

But the meditator knew better. The meditator recognized a deeper truth, a higher law of causation that no courtroom could ever admit: that the universe demands balance, and that the trauma of Wil's past and Sisi's present were not two separate stories, but a single, quantumly entangled event unfolding across forty years of time.

Shortly thereafter, Sisi was removed from life support.

After the film was copied on cassettes, and Sisi had passed, I called defense counsel, with whom I had developed a very conflicted relationship, and said I had something I wanted him to see. He said just send it and he would review it. I refused, saying I wanted to bring it personally and sit with him to review it. At first, he refused, then relented. Like others, when he watched the tape, his demeanor changed radically...grown men, professional litigators don't cry, right? Particularly a hard-core litigator like Tom B.

THE DETROIT REDEMPTION

A few weeks later, Wil, myself, and defense counsel flew to Detroit and walked into the sumptuous offices of Lee Iacocca, President of Chrysler Corporation, and met with him and one of his senior VP's. At first it seemed like a formal legal confrontation, but the energy transformed into something far more sublime as we all viewed Sisi's film. It didn't take long to observe the non-verbal reactions of those present; it was obvious that everyone in that room watching was being affected, and that an indefinable but palpable healing was in process. Hard to define but my intuition was instant and solid; "Sisi is here".

Even though I'm a hard-bitten litigator, not at all prone to emotions in the presence of clients and my opposition, I could feel her presence...it was all I could do to hold back some tears myself. I can't speak to what the others felt, but Iacocca was clearly moved. He became instantly interested in the case beyond a mere legal transaction; he inquired about Wil's wartime service, acknowledged how much he respected those who had served in actual combat, how flying a B 17, bombing German populations must have been difficult with on-going life-long trauma. He also explained, almost apologetically, how he had missed serving in WW II because of his physical disability.

The meeting turned into a mutual admiration expression between Wil and Iacocca; and a heart wrenching commiseration over the loss of Sisi.

Wil had a natural ability, like few I have ever met, to engender deep and pervading, real and raw emotions in people, whether friend or foe. Iacocca was visibly moved not only by Sisi's film, but even more so by the 'presence' of Wil Smyly. And to me, Sisi was clearly present in that room, gently looking after her Father, and easing what had at first seemed like difficult negotiations. Miraculously, after watching the video we resolved our differences and came to an amicable understanding which eventually led to a settlement.

On the flight home, I continued to feel the presence of Sisi Smyly. Without prompting, Wil also said he knew she was there and that somehow he felt he had been healed of both his WW II trauma and Sisi's loss. Later that month Wil confided in me that the healing had then spread to his wife and family.

I know Sisi was present in that meeting and on the flight home. Both Wil and I knew that God had intervened, and some form of redemption occurred. It was just as clear as the night I experienced the survival of Sandra and Lester. Sisi's consciousness was surrounding us on that plane. My consciousness knew it. Wil's consciousness knew it. I then knew that somehow, beyond my understanding, beyond all 'normal' human comprehension, God had commissioned beautiful Sisi Smyly to heal all the suppressed fears and guilt caused by her Father performing his duty to his country whilst dropping bombs on other humans.

I do not know how to further explain it. It just is. There are experiences words cannot convey, so I won't even try. It was not long after this that I experienced the dead Irish priest. 'Ok God, I admit that I'm a slow learner, but your ways are so subtle and unusual for the likes of us mere mortals. Gradually, inch by inch I am beginning to get the picture.'

The body may be on the lowest plane of existence. The concepts 'spirit' and 'soul' may do a grave injustice to the magnitude, the scope, the vastness and infinity of higher dimensions of life...dimensions of consciousness.

HISTORICAL UNDERSTANDING TO RAISE CONSCIOUSNESS

The facts in this chapter which are experienced and observed through multiple layers of mind and consciousness, I believe, establish the existence of a loving God energy...and on the flip side, Sisi's tragic coma and death, and WW II area bombing, appear to support an attempt by dark forces to exert control over our species.

Wil Smyly's WW II heroism and Sisi's tragedy appeared to be a connection that transcended ordinary causation. What we witnessed together revealed the devastating evils embedded in human consciousness when it is devoid of God consciousness. It also showed how divine mercy might redeem us in the suffering that ensues from the catastrophic realities that we create, experience, or suffer from when we eclipse the reality of God from our lives.

The quantum entanglement between Wil's war experiences and Sisi's tragedy operated on a level that our legal system could never address. If consciousness survives physical death, as my experience with the Irish priest suggested, then what happens to the consciousness and the pain of those who suffer unjustly? And the pain of those who inflict injustice? How is it resolved in the greater scheme of existence? Retrospectively, looking back, the answer came as we prepared for what would be the most difficult decision of Wil's life – letting Sisi go, which somehow on some level let 28 bombing missions go.

Obviously, Wil Smyly's heroism and the 'Greatest Generation' on our side did not create the evils of Nazism and the horrors of WW II. Those evils and horrors can be understood and explained on a causational level from examining the minds of evil men warring over money, power and property. There is observable logic in the historical record to show the generational damage that Monarchies, Fiefdoms and Caliphates arising out of medieval, feudal, 'Lord making', and aristocratic pomposities, reduced other humans to vassals, serfs, untouchables in caste systems, and worse, young soldiers doing the dirty, deadly war-work of the ruling classes in various cultures and empires right up to this precarious moment in our history. Smedley Butler's book, *War is a Racket* condenses the reality of war.

The choice seems to be ours. Getting swept up by the tribal collective is the problem for our best and bravest citizens because they are always being deceived by the propaganda, of the money changers. Their lies generally involve a manufactured threat plus some forms of patriotism, religious ideology, or any "ism" which seems to work every time, so it is understandable why so many people are ignorant of the forces controlling and herding them into ever new wars.

The so called 'Allied Strategic Area Bombing Campaign' of WW II constituted a collective evil in response to the collective evil of Nazism, resulting from the individual evil of Hitler, and the more concealed evil of First Lord of the Admiralty, Winston Churchill. They were in competition with each other beginning in WW I. Hitler, a commoner, was gassed in the German trenches while he was running messages. At the same time as his Lordship Churchill and his henchmen...aristocratic Generals like Field Marshall Douglas 'Butcher' Haig as he was known, were sending tens of thousands of serfs to gruesome deaths at Gallipoli, the Somme, and Passchendaele.

As I sat with Wil during our commiserating sessions, watching him struggle with memories of combat together with the fresh wound of his daughter's condition, I began to see that the transformation taking place in his consciousness was a reconciliation of past and present suffering, a form of redemption I had never witnessed before. The collective 'strategic area bombing campaign' that individual heroes like Wil directly participated in, dwarfed any mass murders like those at Amritsar, or Wounded Knee, by body count; but perhaps matched other atrocities like the Holocaust.

Why does it seem that the body count in human atrocities always seems to reflect some form of an Old Testament "eye for an eye" reaction, like Israel killing the men, women and children of Gaza, rather than a New Testament "resist not evil," "turn the other cheek," and if you want my shirt, you can have my coat too – humans seems bent on self-extinction. No one listens to or adheres to the Sermon on the Mount; but Christ seems to have the only solution to raise human consciousness beyond the limbic region of the brain.

I don't believe human evils are lost within the collective consciousness of the 'tribe' even 40 years later after a blood bath like the two world wars end. Wil and Sisi demonstrated to me at least, that such horrors survive in consciousness and are eventually resurrected to be expiated. The coma and death of Sisi that Wil experienced 40 years after his 28 missions to wipe out German cities because Roosevelt hooked up with Churchill to preserve the British Empire; and used 21-year-olds to do it, may, in truth, reflect some form of Grace. Impossible to reconcile? Horrific individual tragedy on top of the collective tragedies of war?

After 80 years on this planet, in the aftermath of the two world wars, I believe God's grace and mercy somehow prevails. I observed the suppressed suffering in Wil's consciousness become resurrected and redeemed. At 21 years old he never fully understood, let alone confronted the realities of a war to destroy "civilian morale," as Roosevelt, Churchill and Stalin agreed upon at Yalta before firebombing Dresden. He had just followed orders with patriotic, noble and courageous faith in his country.

But conscience and consciousness seems to automatically evolve in our species as we gain life experiences. Suffering seems to be how we return to God. Suffering seems to resurrect in us when we confront our past conduct regardless of how it is justified in the past.

Consciousness is simultaneously an individual and collective reality. The individual consciousness and 'energies' of a Father Michael Griffin for instance, responding to the evils that had been imposed on Ireland for centuries, were not destroyed by his death. Certainly, the Crown Forces intended to accomplish that goal by killing him and thousands of his comrades in the fight for their freedom. But the War for Independence in Ireland was won within 13 months of his death. The Irish and the British signed the Anglo-Irish Treaty on December 21, 1921.

The Irish Free State became a partially self-governing country on December 6, 1922, when it adopted its own Constitution. But Ireland was still labeled as a Dominion of the British Empire. In 1937, following a general election, the 1922 Constitution was repealed and Ireland adopted a new Constitution freeing itself from multiple British laws and making it a completely sovereign nation. However, to this day, Ireland is split between the six British held counties in Northern Ireland and the completely independent Republic of Ireland in the south.

As a result of the British division of Ireland, the violence, bloodshed, and sectarian conflict between the Protestant unionists and the Catholic nationalists known as "The Troubles," raged between 1968 and 1998. In that 30 year period, over 3,600 were killed and 50,000 injured.

Following Ireland's independence in 1937, on August 15, 1947, India suffered the same fate. It declared its independence, and became a sovereign, autonomous, nation but not before the British divided it into Hindu and Muslim states; India and Pakistan. Both Ireland and India emancipated themselves on the backs of patriots like Michael Collins, killed in 1922 in the Civil War; and Mahatma Gandhi, killed in 1948. In both cases, and similarly in the middle east, the British divided those nations creating ongoing conflict that lasts to this day.

The current Israeli atrocities against the Palestinians in Gaza are a direct result of British duplicity in WW I, taking money from the Rothschilds to keep the insanity in the trenches going, while lying to the Arabs to help the British to attack the Turks.

America's War for Independence from the British Empire began in April, 1775 at the Battles of Lexington and Concord. Independence was declared in July, 1776, but our Revolutionary War did not end until September, 1783. It took over seven years of violent conflict to emancipate ourselves from British tyranny and imperial colonization.

Less than 134 years later, between in April 1917, America entered WW I in the defense of the British Empire which had enveloped Europe in the utter insanity of trench warfare which it was losing. President Wilson had lied to the American voters who elected him proclaiming America would never enter the war! But he caved to the money changers and banking interests. He sent the Smedley Butlers to preserve their financial status. Our entry into that war resulted from the political gamesmanship of that era, the banking interests of the rich and powerful, like the Rothschilds, to insure that their loans were repaid, as exemplified by the creation of the Federal Reserve in 1913. 'The Fed' was created by the deep state money changers at the turn of the 20th century who were mostly controlled by Great Britain, and its central bank. They sucked America into WW I, mostly on false or contrived propaganda. It was all about money and power. A central bank was designed to insure loan repayment.

Irony of all ironies; America became engaged in a global war sacrificing our citizens, including the famous Fighting 69th Irish Regiment, in the defense of an evil Empire. During the same period, Ireland, and its citizenry were fighting for its independence, inspired by patriots like Michael Collins, (and Michael Griffin), while Irish regiments were being slaughtered at Passchendaele, the Somme and Gallipoli. All utter interconnected madness.

The insanity of the trenches in WW I represented collective consciousness quantum entangled with evil. As QE operates, WW I then led to WW II. Enter brave young souls like Wil Smyly being used by the money changers to fight their wars for global control and power. Nothing changes when it comes to human aggression for power fueled by greed.

Wil Smyly's individual consciousness was courageous enough in WW II to deal with the horrors of flak, fighters, and area bombing; and it was courageous enough in 1986 to terminate Sisi's life support, then meet her in their mutual consciousness of God's love. That is what happened, and I was privileged to experience it firsthand, so I pray that it's useful in bringing some added understanding of consciousness and human suffering. It has helped this poor journeyman.

THE SEARCH FOR A HIGHER LAW

I have wrestled with the incomprehensible circumstances involving all aspects of this case throughout the last 30 years of my litigation and meditation life. I am still at a loss. None of Sisi's case makes any sense. A wrong-way drunk ending the life of a beautiful young woman, and causing indescribable suffering when her seat belt breaks in a head on collision, while all others in the car are spared? Religious dogma and dictums provide no legitimate, rational, and acceptable explanation of, or emotional relief from the facts of Wil's, heroic, B 17 bomber life, and Sisi's case. His live fire combat experience flying into the jaws of death is tragic in itself. It seemed to be very cut and dried; good vs evil. God's love and grace vs. demonstrable evils and insanities. However, to me, in my causal-bound litigation mind, seeking to explain to juries and myself, for 50 years of how and why unspeakable wrongs, crimes, corruption, murder, violence, death and patterned insanities occur in our world, I was left stupefied...bereft of belief in a loving and almighty force after Wil Smyly explained in detail what he experienced.

The coma and death of his daughter Sisi Smyly, left me confused. Wil gave heroic service to all of us, and clearly had a noble state of consciousness, but as if that wasn't enough, he was in the midst of a family crisis that dwarfed his WW II experience. An interesting entanglement was my own personal crisis shaped by the Scientology wars...you could say against Satan himself. It's leader, L. Ron Hubbard, who personally stated he was Satan, was trying to destroy me with his maniacal operations implemented per his written policy of "Fair Game". It caused both of us to become angry and confused at our perceived 'Gods' for allowing such evil to even happen.

Against rational perceptions, this motivated us to keep searching for a God whose essence seemed unfathomable and unknowable. After the dead Irish priest, Sisi's case, and experiencing Wil's redemption, I found Yogananda, Kriya yoga, and Mother Meera.

These high consciousness individuals suggest that at a higher level of consciousness the inexplicable madness inherent in our limbic brains can become the tool that delivers us from our own suffering. The so called Christian nations including the Roman Church have historically participated in this madness whilst at the same time professing scriptures, dogmas, and beliefs against it. Has the Roman Church ever obeyed the Beatitudes of Christ? When it murdered and persecuted the Cathars, where was papal and Catholic fidelity to Christ? A hypocrisy beyond understanding. Their crimes are now becoming public knowledge and we can only hope it will lead to some form of redemption.

There were no such realizations between 1985 when I met Wil, and January, 1992, when I first met Meera. For Wil, the central question was why his beloved daughter had to endure 18 months of brainstem death and coma on life support, while having consciousness. Both of us became absorbed in an indistinct search for understanding. Why did Sisi's seat belt fail while she was driving one of Wil's Chrysler dealership cars? Why did she break her neck in a head-on collision with a drunk driver going the wrong way, cresting a hill, at that exact moment on a limited-access interstate? How could such terrible events coincide at a single instant in time and space to cause such unrelenting suffering? If time and space truly dissolve in the linkage of our consciousness to God, why did this tragedy happen at that unfathomable instant connecting Sisi to God? No matter how the events are measured, explained, or filtered through religious language, it simply made no sense.

In a collective analysis, did Wil's B 17 area bombing, particularly of Dresden, somehow connect to the tragedy of his daughter? Guilt can be an unrelenting companion constantly searching for meaning. The Roman Church taught me that this world is a 'veil of tears' and that we must 'pick up our crosses' just like Christ, in order to deal with the inexorable suffering of life in order to achieve salvation. But as I matured, I learned that the Roman Church has never truly followed the essence of Christ's teachings.

In the beginning of our meetings, Wil found his crosses between area bombing and Sisi were irreconcilable with any rational or redemptive explanation. I tried also, then Sisi left me with an unforgettable, and medically inexplicable experience. Still later, mystically, Sisi left Wil and his family with an experience that gave emotional comfort and a realization that could only be understood as God's Grace, love and compassion. There is no death and they will be reunited.

In the late 1980's, several years after Sisi's life support had been turned off, and she had 'left', I told Wil I didn't believe any of the Roman Church nonsense that I was brought up in. After experiencing eight years of Hubbard's satanic attacks, I started to question the reality of God, despite continued efforts to maintain a new faith I had found in observing my own consciousness. Similarly, Wil couldn't reconcile Catholic or Christian scripture with his wartime experiences and Sisi's accident. The Germans, like Wil, were Christians warring against the British and American Christians.

In my case, my enemies, the Scientologists were neither type of Christian. They were self-professed Satanists. It was even written in their Church policies ("OT VIII"). They even challenged Christ as a pederast, and God as an illusion. They did this based on their altar which was characterized as "making money, and make others make money." *Litigator 2 and 5.*

After Sisi's tragedy, Wil and to a lesser extent myself, were undergoing such a range of unresolved emotions that God seemed to both of us a questionable reality. However, these unrecognizable emotions, thoughts, and feelings trapped between guilt and remorse, began to create a new realization for both of us.

THE UNFATHOMABLE WEIGHT OF SUFFERING: A FATHER'S JOURNEY

In my mediocre level of spiritual awareness at that time, I had accepted Sisi's death as the ultimate reality. Subsequent events in her case, however, along with my own experiences such as the encounter with the dead priest, and the now widely reported near-death experiences (particularly that of neurosurgeon Dr. Eben Alexander, and my deepening meditation practice, have confirmed to me that we are not our bodies.

Paramahansa Yogananda and sages throughout millennia have affirmed this truth: The 'Kingdom of God' is indeed 'within us' with or without our physical forms. I don't make this assertion merely on faith. This book documents my direct experiences. Western science and medicine, grounded in materialism rather than spirituality, has never been able to fully explain so-called miracles. I don't fault their approach to healing, which definitely has it's benefits, however through Sisi's case and my own spiritual journey, I have glimpsed a far more expansive reality.

To dig deeper into the inexplicable mystery of the extraordinary circumstances involving Sisi Smyly, we need to understand Wil's consciousness. Admittedly, his consciousness in the mid 1980's as a father, 40 years after his consciousness in the mid 1940's, as a B 17 pilot, are separated by time and space.

But in reality, are they separated at all? Are time and space linked in the presence of God, where they do not exist, as Paramahansa Yogananda postulates; and as the physicists of quantum entanglement opine?

My dead priest experience would suggest that Yogananda and thousands of saints and sages are correct about no time and space in the presence of God. But that experience and its correlates have no place in American courtrooms. All such evidence would be excluded as a matter of law. The latter is where I have lived in my litigation career. Not so in my meditation career. The only rational answer to the above, in a normal state of consciousness is that there is no God. But the sages and saints say that "in the presence of God, there is no time and space." And no death. Personally, and after many years of trial and error, my litigation and meditation life experiences have provided me with an understanding for the Sisi case, and the world around me.

The experience with the dead priest occurred around the same time the Sisi Smyly case concluded in July 1987. It also occurred when I gave Laima our home and she moved to California. It was a period of immense suffering for me. The timing raises an interesting, if somewhat unsettling question; did these events converge because, in encounters like this, time and space don't operate the way we assume they do? Did the energy surrounding the Smyly case trigger my dormant unresolved past emotions, in both litigation, meditation and my personal life so that I could also heal and move on like Wil? It took me years to recover. This was not the last of such experiences, by any means. The next one I will share happened when I met Mother Meera in Germany.

REDEMPTION IN THE HEART OF THE WOUND

Fast forward to December, 1991, after several more cases, the Mahaldars called me to come have dinner at the Maharishi Ayurveda Health Center in Lancaster, MA, with some of his celebrity guests, including Mike Love of the Beach Boys who needed a lawyer. One of the wives in the dinner meeting had recovered from breast cancer after meeting Mother Meera, an Indian 'saint' living in Thalheim, Germany. I became immediately interested in seeing her because of Laima's rheumatoid arthritis, even though we were separated at that time.

I told my partners to investigate the Mike Love case. I jumped on a plane immediately after New Year, in January, 1992, flew to Frankfurt Germany, and drove the 50 or so kilometers to Thalheim, a small German village where Mother Meera lived, and offered free "Darshans" (an opportunity of seeing a holy person or image) from her home. She had turned her living room into "the Darshan Room" which accommodated about 120 individuals seated close together.

The "darshan" lasted about two hours with each person getting into a queue to kneel or sit in front of her for about a minute or less, have her touch your temples and look into your eyes. I intended to stay for the four days she set aside every weekend, Friday through Monday, then go skiing.

What I experienced in Mother Meera's presence, as has happened many times to me in my life, once again defied my rational understanding. The silent exchanges, her gaze, the atmosphere of the room, all contributed to an inner shift that I couldn't immediately articulate but could certainly feel.

Instead of departing after four days to go skiing as planned, I remained in Thalheim for three weeks, attending as many Darshans as possible. My ski equipment stayed packed away, unused. Whatever had drawn me to this small German village had proven far more compelling than I could have anticipated, transforming what was meant to be a brief spiritual detour into a significant turning point in my life.

During those three weeks with Mother Meera, a profound healing process began within me. Years of accumulated trauma from the Scientology battles, the relentless demands of litigation, my internal struggles with perceived 'sins', and the unresolved mystical elements of the Smyly case and others documented in this book, began to unwind in her silent presence.

The impact was so significant that I encouraged Laima to experience Mother Meera for herself. When she did, something remarkable occurred... her rheumatoid arthritis went into remission. This wasn't an isolated phenomenon. Over the next decade, as I returned for Darshan whenever possible, I met people from across the globe; Americans, British, Germans, and others, who shared their own extraordinary experiences of healing and transformation in Mother Meera's presence.

My connection to this spiritual work deepened over time. I became acquainted with her small staff and eventually represented her in minor legal matters in the United States. Each visit furthered my own healing journey, gradually restoring what years of legal battles and anguished spiritual questioning had worn away.

The setting itself contained layers of historical significance that seemed to amplify the healing work taking place there. Many visitors, myself included, stayed in a hotel in the town adjacent to Thalheim, a place with its own dark history. Before the war, Hitler had established what amounted to a death camp there for those deemed undesirable by Nazi standards; people with intellectual disabilities, those labeled as imbeciles, and others with extremely low IQs. While not a Holocaust concentration camp, the facility carried a distinct and troubling energy. When asked about why she was in Thalheim, Germany, Mother Meera said it was "the heart of the wound" but that the German people as a whole were good people. Her illuminated approach to healing was to not avoid darkness but to work directly at its source.

Several visitors reported experiencing a sacred healing process in this very town with its difficult past.

The physical landscape itself seemed to reflect this interplay between darkness and healing. The area surrounding Mother Meera's home in Thalheim, including the nearby medieval city of Limburg had remained largely untouched by Allied bombing during the war. Those unbombed, intact streets and buildings felt like quiet witnesses. reminders of what humanity can destroy, and what it can choose to preserve.

THE BRITISH JOURNALIST'S STORY

Generally, before and after Darshan, those attending would meet in the hotel bar to discuss their experiences with Mother. One Friday afternoon in 1995, before the scheduled 7 PM Darshan I met a mid-30's British journalist working for the London Times on assignment. He said he was there to investigate and write an article about the mysteries surrounding Mother Meera that were being rumored and discussed in the UK. He was a cynical, agnostic type, slightly aggressive, who laughingly wondered if mass hypnotism was involved.

We discussed Mother Meera's darshan. I asked him to let me know what he experienced. I also told him of my Irish roots and that I had an innate antipathy to British Empire Building. He was sufficiently open minded to appreciate my feelings, so I was more optimistic that his openness might help him to have a healing. After Darshan that same night we had a beer and he said he didn't feel or experience anything unusual, and didn't know what to make of it. I asked him if he went up for the actual Darshan interchange with Meera to have a 'reality check' so to speak. He said yes, but that he didn't experience anything. I asked if he was going to give it another try, and he said he would.

The next night at the Saturday Darshan, I saw him go up, receive Mother's darshan, and sort of stumble back to his chair. Afterwards, unlike the previous evening, he did not come down from his room for the post darshan discussion which the attendees generally did. I saw him the next morning. He related the following incident to me: "You wouldn't believe what happened last night. During the Darshan experience I was silently explaining the situation with my Father to Mother Meera. I felt a wave of forgiveness surround me, encourage me I think but I was a little resistant, then after the short experience I returned to my seat, but I was feeling light-headed and unsteady on my feet, a very strange experience. Afterwards I didn't feel like talking so went straight to my room without joining the others to chat. I was drifting off to sleep in my room, when suddenly, somewhere between sleeping, dreaming, and being wide awake, my deceased father appeared, saying to me: "I don't know where to go? Please help me." Inexplicably I replied by telling my father to come to Darshan with me the next night. I don't really know why I told him this, it just came out."

He shared with me that his father had been a war hero, a Spitfire pilot who had flown in the Battle of Britain against the Nazi blitz. Like many veterans, his father's story didn't end with victory parades. After the war, he struggled to adjust to civilian life, failed in his professional endeavors, and descended into alcoholism. The drinking led to violence and he brutalized his wife and children before eventually dying during a drunken binge. The war had never truly left him, it had merely transformed into addiction and rage. Understandably, the family had grown to hate their father.

Sensing a connection to my own experiences with consciousness beyond death, I shared my 'dead Irish priest' experience with him. I wanted to convey the possibility that the deceased might still interact with the living in meaningful ways. He looked at me skeptically, as though I might be unbalanced, but I sensed that some element of my story seemed to resonate with him nonetheless.

I also told him of my friendship with Wil and Wil's 28 missions over German cities; and asked him if his father had participated in any missions accompanying American or British bombers. He didn't know but speculated that his father had likely done so, and had mentioned the evil Nazis who deserved to have their cities bombed into oblivion along with the entire country. His father died in an alcoholic mixture of heroism and hatred involving his war experiences.

The following evening, after Darshan, the journalist joined me in the hotel bar. His demeanor had changed completely. Gone was the aggression, and now with visible emotion, he told me he had felt his father's 'presence' in the Darshan room both before, during, and after his time with Mother

Meera. In that sacred space, something remarkable had occurred, he had finally forgiven his father for everything done to their family. More surprisingly, he sensed some type of 'release' in his father's spirit as well, as though a burden carried beyond the grave had finally been set down. He said that "I could sense my father had been released, and was ever so thankful." He mentioned that he would write his article but would have to do so carefully as his editor would never let him write it the way it occurred, "He would think I had gone crazy" he said.

I couldn't help but think Father Michael Griffin might have been some use here. The quantum entanglement of consciousness connects us beyond the limitations of our individual minds, beyond time, beyond death itself. The journalist later sent me the article he wrote about Mother Meera. It was a positive piece, but one that never mentioned the profound personal transformation he had experienced. Perhaps for him the healings were too intimate to share publicly, or he thought nobody would believe his experience.

MY FATHER PAYS ME A VISIT

Years after my father died in June 1996 when I was litigating against News Corp, I experienced a similar phenomenon, my dad came to me in that state between sleeping and waking, a dreaming reality that felt as authentic as any physical encounter. Unlike the journalist's initially painful reconciliation, mine was a joyful meeting. My father told me everything was good where he was and that he loved me. I expressed the same to him. These experiences have clarified something important for me; later experiences of suffering in life often resurrect the raw emotions of earlier sufferings. Together, they teach us that our own pain can engender compassion for others who suffer. If that compassion fails to arise, only anger remains, as seen in the journalist's father, whose unprocessed war trauma transformed into alcoholism and abuse.

I believe consciousness works this way. On higher levels, it operates beyond time, space, and death. I witnessed this process in Wil's journey with Sisi. I observed it in the transformation of the angry son of the alcoholic Spitfire pilot, finding redemption in the presence of Mother Meera's consciousness. These are not isolated incidents but patterns that reveal deeper truths about our existence.

A Final Word to the Jury

What say you, the jury...poppycock or truth? Allow me to offer a civil law jury instruction for your deliberations. Under human civil law, you may consider the legal cause of Sisi's car accident to be the drunk driver going the wrong way on Route 93. Under our criminal law, you may consider the legal cause of the accident to be vehicular homicide...a violation of statutes prohibiting operation of an automobile while under the influence of alcohol. Under civil law, you may also consider the legal cause of Sisi's death to be a "superseding, intervening cause" specifically, the failure of her seat belt resulting from a defective product in either design or manufacture. And you may also consider the legal cause to be both the seat belt failure and vehicular homicide. If you find both factors contributed, you may apportion damages between the seat belt manufacturer and the drunk driver in whatever percentages you deem appropriate, or find them both fully liable.

Regarding Sisi's damages for "conscious pain and suffering" during her three years in a coma, you must determine if she was conscious during this period. This is where Sisi's case leaves the norm...she was not conscious according to the medical devices they used to detect consciousness, however she did have one physical display that 'shouldn't have occurred' according to medical monitors at the time.

Sisi's case never went to trial, so the foregoing jury instructions were never given. Sisi's case was settled between Wil, Lee Iacocca, and Sisi in an atmosphere of what I can only describe as 'commercial love'. And that, dear jurors, in this particular case, is not an oxymoron. Ultimately, Wil even reconciled something inside him about the drunk not being completely at fault and forgave him! Now, that was heroic. That was Wil...and he didn't do it for religious reasons. Maybe he felt his anger and rage would destroy him? But knowing Wil, he was bigger even than that.

Additionally, from the journalist's account, his father the Spitfire pilot received some form of redemptive healing through Mother Meera, and in Sisi's case, so did her father Wil. In both instances, healing transcended the boundaries of time, space, and even death itself.

In God's presence, these dimensions that we consider separate become unified. The quantum entanglement of consciousness reveals itself not as abstract theory but as lived reality that connects fathers and children, the living and the dead, past trauma and present healing in ways our conventional understanding struggles to comprehend, but our hearts somehow recognize.

Epilogue

There are moments in a litigator's career when the courtroom falls away and you realize you are standing on holy ground. Sisi Smyly's case was one of those moments for me. What began as a wrongful death lawsuit became a meditation on the nature of consciousness, the reality of divine grace, and the mysterious ways in which suffering can become a doorway to redemption. Wil Smyly's journey from the flak-filled skies over Nazi Germany to the quiet hospital room where his daughter lay in a coma is highly unusual...a story of quantum entanglement, of consciousness operating across time and space in ways that defy our legal categories and challenge our materialist assumptions. The impossible tear that rolled down Sisi's cheek was not just a physiological anomaly; it was a message from a realm beyond the reach of neurology, a testament to the enduring presence of love even in the face of death.

What I learned from Wil is that heroism is not confined to the battlefield. It is also found in the quiet act of forgiveness, in the willingness to let go of anger and blame, and in the courage to trust that there is a divine order operating beneath the chaos of our lives. Wil's forgiveness of the drunk driver who killed his daughter was not a religious gesture; it was an act of pure consciousness, a recognition that we are all participants in a reality far grander than our individual stories. The mystical experiences that followed; Mother Meera's silent healing, the British journalist's encounter with his deceased father, Laima's remission from rheumatoid arthritis, are not anomalies to be explained away. They are glimpses of the truth that consciousness is not bound by the body, that love transcends death, and that the universe is not indifferent to our suffering.

These experiences belong in this book not as digressions from the legal narrative, but as essential evidence of a deeper reality that the law cannot address but that every human heart recognizes. As I reflect on Wil's story, I am reminded of the paradox at the heart of my own life: I have spent decades arguing for justice in courtrooms governed by material causation, while simultaneously experiencing a reality where consciousness operates beyond time and space. Sisi's case taught me that these two worlds are not separate. They are two perspectives on the same mystery, two languages describing the same ineffable truth: that we are not alone, that love endures, and that even in the darkest valley, grace is at work.

Wil Smyly charged into the jaws of death over Nazi Germany and came back from the mouth of hell. But his greatest battle was not fought at 28,000 feet; it was fought in the quiet of his own heart, where he had to reconcile the guilt of area bombing with the unbearable grief of losing his daughter. In the end, he found redemption not through a legal verdict, but through the mystical realization that Sisi had never truly left, that her consciousness remained present in a realm beyond the reach of medical science.

This is the ultimate truth of Sisi's case: we are not the doers, but participants in a divine drama whose script we can only dimly perceive. And in that drama, every act of love, every moment of forgiveness, every impossible tear is a testament to the eternal presence of God's grace.

CHAPTER 20

Beyond Reasonable Doubt: The Case for Consciousness

"Not only is the Universe stranger than we think, it is stranger than we can think." **Werner Heisenberg**

THE CONVERGENCE OF LITIGATION AND MEDITATION

We have traveled a long road together. You have journeyed with me through the perils of the high-stakes courtrooms of America; and we have touched on man's inhumanity to man in the world wars, the Irish War of Independence; and the realities of self-reflection in meditation. You have witnessed how the mobsters, their murders, and their prosecutors work, the devastation of child death, the brutal murder of an Irish priest, the psychic realities of quantum entanglement, the insanity of wars and abortion, fraudsters, and the insidious evil of a destructive cult. You have stood beside me in the trenches of litigation, in the depths of personal crisis, and on the serene heights of meditative experiences. You have seen the evidence of a reality that transcends our five senses in the haunting visions of a psychic, the impossible tear of a comatose woman, and the scientifically documented accounts of those who have returned from the brink of death.

This book has been a testament to a life lived in two worlds: the world of evidence, logic, law, and the world of consciousness, spirit, and non-duality. For decades, I treated these as parallel paths. But as we have seen, they are not parallel at all. They are convergent. The same principles of truth, justice, and causality that govern a courtroom also govern the cosmos. The same search for evidence that drives a litigator also drives the spiritual seeker.

In this final chapter, we arrive at the destination to which this entire journey has been leading: the synthesis. Here, we will weave together the disparate threads of this life, the legal and the mystical, the scientific and the spiritual, the personal and the universal. We will examine how the insights of quantum physics mirror the ancient wisdom of the yogis, how the evidence for consciousness survival demands a new understanding of reality, and how my own half-century of experience as both a litigator and a meditator has led me to this unshakeable conclusion.

This is the verdict in the case I have been building for over fifty years and the question before us has always been the same: what is the nature of reality, and what is our place within it? Here, in this final chapter, I will present my answer, not based on faith alone, but as a conclusion compelled by the overwhelming weight of the evidence.

"By ascent of the consciousness through the subtle centers of life and spiritual awakening in the spine, the yogi learns the inner science of changing the consciousness of gross matter into the consciousness of its primordial principles."

Paramahansa Yogananda: "Lesson No. 9." (Copyright, 2019 Self-Realization Fellowship)

We will explore how the techniques of Kriya Yoga enable practitioners to channel energy through the spine to experience levels of consciousness that exist apart from the body, including my own experiences with this practice since 1988, including the remarkable moment in July 1987 when my "spine burst forth with the energy of a prior incarnation". This experience was so radically different to any I had encountered in my life, that newcomers and skeptics might describe it as a 'very odd, even eerie and certainly inexplicable experience'.

Nevertheless, through these explorations, we will come to understand how the seemingly separate paths of litigation and meditation ultimately converge in the quest for truth, justice, and self-realization. The courtroom and the meditation cushion, it turns out, may be two radically different doorways to the same destination: a consciousness that transcends the limitations of the physical world and connects us to the divine reality and truth that underlies all existence. Indeed, this explanation comes from my teacher, Paramahansa Yogananda, to whom I give attribution for leading me back to God...the primary theme of this book.

YOGANANDA'S QUANTUM CONSCIOUSNESS: THE DYING NAVAL CAPTAIN

Paramahansa Yogananda has reported in the *Autobiography of a Yogi*, and in his talks and tapes, a remarkable experience that somewhat resembles my own experience of being murdered as an Irish priest, but there are very significant differences. I didn't put 2 plus 2 together in connection with my Father Griffin experience until writing this book in the fall of 2022, and then researching the facts.

In Yogananda's example, during his meditation, he was transmuted, (for want of a better word), into the body of a dying naval Captain at the moment the captain was then being killed. As far as I have been able to determine, Paramahansa Yogananda's transcendental experience was contemporaneous with the Captain's death. Here is his excerpt:

"In 1915, shortly after I had entered the Swami Order, I witnessed a strange vision. Through it I came to understand the relativity of human consciousness, and clearly perceived the unity of the Eternal Light behind the painful dualities of maya. The vision descended on me as I sat one morning in my little attic room in Father's Garpar Road home. For months the First World War had been raging in Europe; I had been reflecting sadly on the vast toll of death. As I closed my eyes in meditation, my consciousness was suddenly transferred to the body of a captain in command of a battleship. The thunder of guns split the air as shots were exchanged between shore batteries and the ship's cannons. A huge shell hit the powder magazine and tore my ship asunder. I jumped into the water, together with the few sailors who had survived the explosion. Heart pounding, I reached the shore safely. But alas! a stray bullet ended its swift flight in my chest. I fell groaning to the ground. My whole body was paralyzed, yet I was aware of possessing it as one is conscious of a leg gone to sleep. "At last, the mysterious footstep of Death has caught up with me," I thought. With a final sigh, I was about to sink into unconsciousness when lo! I found myself seated in the lotus posture in my Garpar Road room. Hysterical tears poured forth as I joyfully stroked and pinched my regained possession: a body free from a bullet hole in the breast. I rocked to and fro, inhaling and exhaling to assure myself that I was alive. Amidst these self-gratulations, again I found my consciousness transferred to the captain's dead body by the gory shore. Utter confusion of mind came upon me. "Lord," I prayed, "am I dead or alive?" A dazzling play of light filled the whole horizon. A soft rumbling vibration formed itself into words: "What has life or death to do with light? In the image of My light, I have made you. The relativities of life and death belong to the cosmic dream. Behold your dreamless being! Awake, My child, awake!" Yogananda, Paramahansa. *Autobiography of a Yogi* (Self-Realization Fellowship) (pp. 305-306). Self-Realization Fellowship. Kindle Edition.

Paramahansa Yogananda's entire message to us is that we are "One with God." All we need to do is awaken to this reality and drop the ego, expand consciousness, and awaken to the self-realization of God within us. Even the physicist, Federico Faggin, (chapter 9) said he had an experience at age 49, of a "white light" enveloping him saying that he became "one" with the light and felt an intense love and a sense of unity with the universe. It was life-changing and led him to focus the rest of his career on the scientific study of consciousness.

Yogananda's experience while he was in his meditation room in Calcutta, occurred in 1915, contemporaneous with the British assault on Gallipoli, when British battleships were being sunk in the naval bombardment of Turkish shore batteries... another Churchillian disaster. In my case, the entanglement persisted across decades before completing the circuit, waiting for the right moment and presumably the right consciousness, prepared through years of meditation and spiritual practice.

My experience is similar to Yogananda's in that he was in the body of the dying naval captain at the actual time the captain was being shot and killed, and I was in the body of Father Griffin experiencing what he felt as he was being shot 67 years earlier! The Griffin death and Captain's death were both violent, killed by the enemy, and both occurred in approximately the same time frame, 1915–1920.

IMPERIAL VIOLENCE AND SPIRITUAL AWAKENING

The temporal proximity of these violent deaths cannot easily be dismissed as coincidence. Both men died as victims of British imperial policy. Since high school, I have harbored an indefinable angst towards the British, and specifically Winston Churchill, a privileged British aristocrat and 'First Lord of the Admiralty', a title that seemingly gave him the right to send young men to their deaths by the thousands. Now, I understand these feelings in the context of documented studies of the genocides committed during British Empire building. I suspect that my Irish friends, perhaps even relatives, were among those slaughtered in the Irish Regiments, 'The Dubliners' at Gallipoli for instance. He also organized the brutalities of the Black and Tans against the Irish.

These are not abstract historical grievances but visceral, personal connections that I now understand through the lens of quantum entanglement, and reincarnation. The documented horrors of British Empire building constitute the historical matrix within which these profound spiritual experiences occurred. The quantum physics theories of how the spin of electrons are altered by some instantaneous connection between them beyond time and space provide a scientific foundation for understanding how consciousness and thought energy might transcend conventional limitations of time and space. If quantum entanglement can link particles across vast distances instantaneously, why should we assume that our mysterious human consciousness operates under more restrictive laws?

WHEN CONSCIOUSNESS TRANSCENDS TIME AND SPACE

Yogananda's 1915 experience demonstrates that consciousness can indeed bridge any distance when conditions align. The traumatic nature of both deaths may have created the intense energetic conditions necessary for such quantum entanglement to occur. In Yogananda's case, the connection was immediate and contemporaneous. This is neither reincarnation in the traditional sense nor resurrection as understood by conventional Christianity. It is something more subtle and profound; a quantum-level connection in and between energy or consciousness that transcends death itself, linking souls across time through invisible threads of shared experience, shared trauma, and shared purpose. Modern physics teaches us that energy is infinitely transferrable, never created nor destroyed, only transformed from one state to another. In this light, what we call 'death' becomes a redundant medieval concept, a primitive misunderstanding of what is actually an energetic transformation. The consciousness that animated Father Griffin and the naval captain did not cease to exist; it simply shifted into a different energetic state, one that remained accessible through the quantum field that connects all consciousness across the apparent 'boundaries' of time and space.

Having practiced meditation for decades, I was trained to receive and understand this connection. In the stillness of deep meditation, traditional boundaries evaporate; between self and others, between past and present, between the living and the dead...everything becomes permeable. It is in this state that quantum entanglement of consciousness becomes not just possible but normal.

The convergence of my personal experience, Yogananda's parallel encounter, the historical context of British imperial violence, and the scientific framework of quantum mechanics creates a compelling case for the continuity of life beyond physical death.

This continuity operates through the elegant laws of quantum physics applied to consciousness itself. We are all entangled through invisible threads that the illusion of 'death' cannot sever. The violent deaths of the naval captain and Father Griffin created quantum disturbances that rippled across time, perhaps seeking resolution through a consciousness prepared to receive them.

In finding that resolution, in my case by experiencing the Unity that dissolves all boundaries, I have discovered not just the continuity of life, but the fundamental interconnectedness of all existence. This is the ultimate teaching, the final chapter in a journey that begins with anger and confusion but ends with understanding and peace. Through quantum entanglement, through the grace of Christ, God and guru, and through the transformative power of meditation, I have learned that death is not an ending but a transformation, a deeper connection to the eternal fabric of consciousness that binds us all.

FATHER GRIFFIN: A SOUL'S JOURNEY ACROSS TIME

Understanding the Griffin experience as reincarnation might mean that I am currently the reincarnated soul of Father Michael Griffin, living now in the physical form of Michael Flynn; and / or it might mean that I somehow received the energy of his death? Does the fact that my Grandmother was born 4 years before Griffin in the next village in Galway relevant to this metaphysical analysis? Do the vibrations she inherited when her family rebelled against the British in the Irish republican Brotherhood as she fled Ireland in 1899, a relevant factor – getting too remote for the rational mind? How about in a universal field of consciousness within her cellular connection to me?

In that Washington hotel room in July 1987, I was simultaneously the present consciousness of Michael Flynn and the eternal soul that had once inhabited Griffin's body. When I experienced 'his' death in November 1920 while energizing my spine through Patanjali's and Maharishi's resurrected Yoga Sutras in 1987, was the spinal energy surging in me actually awakening on a cellular consciousness level my own past-life death in an instantaneous experience across time and space? The Kriya Yoga teachings of Yogananda actually explain the spinal energies during Kriya as taking place in three energy columns in the physical spine, the Ida, Pingala and Sushumna, which arise from an "astral spine" containing the energies. The astral spine transcends the physical spine and the physical death of the body. My experience of the Father Griffin death was more "real" to me than any experience in my life, except the previous "Unity experience" I had in meditation!

The soul that I am, the consciousness that animates this current incarnation as Michael Flynn, never died in 1920. Griffin's physical body perished at the hands of the British soldiers, but the soul simply transitioned, eventually taking form again in this present lifetime. The 1987 experience was not a mystical connection to another being, but rather my own soul's memory surfacing through the spiritual practices that opened the deeper channels of consciousness. I believe that we are all in the same reincarnation boat – different times and places for all of us.

Reincarnational memory explains why the Griffin death felt so intensely personal and real. It's because it was my death, experienced by this same soul in a previous physical form. The sixty-seven years between Griffin's murder and my remembering it in 1987 represents the interval between that soul's death and its current incarnation's spiritual readiness to access those memories. The soul, under the right circumstances can bridge all apparent gaps in time and physical form. Apparently, as Yogananda teaches, the astral spine beyond death transmutes cellular consciousness in our physical spines.

If life is but a dream in the streams of God's Light...the most fundamental energy in the physical cosmos according to Einstein, Yogananda, Faggin, and countless mystics...then my purpose as a human is to awaken from this dream and enter God's presence where time and space are linked. The Griffin and Unity experiences are part of this cosmic dream. Beyond them lies Self-Realization, the recognition that God and the Self are one. As Jesus taught two thousand years ago, "The Kingdom of God is within us." I'm still in the process of awakening to this ultimate truth.

THE RESURRECTED CHRIST: YOGANANDA'S VISION AT ENCINITAS

There is more evidence from Paramahansa Yogananda which we might describe as either resurrection, reincarnation, recycling, near death experience, or even 'no death' depending on your approach to neuroscience, quantum physics, religion, Yoga and spirituality. Paramahansa Yogananda was visited on multiple occasions by Christ, as have innumerable saints and sages. In both the AY and the *Second Coming of Christ*, he writes of several experiences with the "formless Christ" and of one experience with an actual visitation of Christ in Christ's resurrected body as described here:

"It was in the Hermitage at Encinitas, California. I was sitting in my darkened room in meditation, praying deeply from my soul, when suddenly the blackness gave way to a celestial opal-blue effulgence. The entire room was like an opal flame. In that light the radiant form of the blessed Lord Jesus appeared. His face was divine. His appearance was of a young man in his twenties, with sparse beard and moustache; his long black hair, parted in the middle, had a golden light about it. His feet were not touching the floor. His eyes were the most beautiful, the most loving eyes I have ever seen. The whole universe I saw glistening in those eyes. They were infinitely changing, and with each transition of expression I intuitively understood the wisdom conveyed. In his glorious eyes I felt the power that upholds and commands the myriad worlds. As he gazed down at me, a Holy Grail appeared at his mouth. It descended to my lips and touched them; then went up again to Jesus. After a few moments of rapt silent communion, he said to me: "Thou dost drink of the same cup of which I drink." At that I bowed down. I was joyous beyond dreams to receive the testimony of his blessings, of his presence. Exactly the words that he said to me in this vision he also said to Thomas, which I never read before. His words meant that I was drinking of his wisdom through the Holy Grail of his perceptions which he has dropped in my consciousness, and he was pleased. He approved very dearly and blessed me for writing these interpretations. This I can say without pride, because the interpretation of Christ's words herein is not mine. It has been given to me. I am happy this book is coming through me; but I am not the author. It is Christ. I am only the vehicle through which it is explained."

Yogananda, Paramahansa. *The Second Coming of Christ: The Resurrection of the Christ Within You* (pp. 36-37). Self-Realization Fellowship. Kindle Edition. Printed edition at p. xxxii. (Italics supplied.)

The most fascinating part of this passage for me, the litigator, was not just the actual vision of the resurrected Christ appearing to Paramahansa Yogananda in his hermitage. What was also fascinating for me was "footnote 12" in the *Second Coming of Christ* which explains the Vision. It is reported as a Publisher's Note in *The Second Coming*, published in 2004, derived from a magazine article that Yogananda wrote in 1937 after he had the visitation from Christ! Note the dates.

The footnote reads:

> "Jesus' words are recorded in the noncanonical "Gospel of Thomas", (called and condemned as a "Gnostic" Gospel by the early Christians, circa 60-100) verse 13: "'Compare me to someone and tell me whom I am like.' "Simon Peter said to him, 'You are like a righteous angel.' "Matthew said to him, 'You are like a wise philosopher.' "Thomas said to him, 'Master, my mouth is wholly incapable of saying whom you are like.' "Jesus said, 'I am not your master. Because you have drunk, you have become intoxicated from the bubbling spring which I have measured out.'"

Elsewhere in the Gospel of Thomas (verse 108), Jesus declares: "He who will drink from my mouth will become like me. I myself shall become he, and the things that are hidden will be revealed to him." (Translation by Thomas O. Lambdin, in *The Nag Hammadi Library in English*, James M. Robinson, ed.; Harper San Francisco, 1990.)

Fragments of this Gospel were discovered in the late 1800s; but the complete Gospel, including the portion cited here, was not discovered until 1945. It was part of a collection of Coptic manuscripts from the second century, unearthed at Nag Hammadi in Egypt, and was not translated into English until 1955. (Paramahansa Yogananda left his body in 1952.) However, it was in 1937 that Paramahansaji made the above statement that the words spoken by Jesus to him conveyed the same message as Jesus' words to Thomas. (Publisher's Note)"

The Second Coming of Christ: The Resurrection of the Christ Within You. Self-Realization Fellowship. Kindle Edition. Printed edition at p. xxxii. (Italics Supplied).

DOCUMENTARY EVIDENCE: THE GOSPEL OF THOMAS AND YOGANANDA'S VISION

The Nag Hammadi codices, including the Gospel of Thomas, were discovered between 1945 and 1947 in the Egyptian desert near the town of Nag Hammadi. Verse 108 of the Gospel of Thomas, was not fully translated until 1955, and these translations did not become publicly available until the late 1960s or early 1970s.

The Gospel of Thomas is recognized by some biblical scholars as the oldest written, non-canonical gospel of Jesus, written either during his lifetime, or within a year or so after his crucifixion. It probably predates the Canonical Gospels. It was excluded from them by Emperor Constantine and the Bishops attending the Council of Nicea in 325 A.D., when Christianity became the religion of the Roman Empire. It is true that elements of what Paramahansa describes do appear to have at least some aspects in common with established Christian traditions, including the Last Supper narrative and the Catholic doctrine of the Eucharist, which involves the transmutation of bread and wine into the body and blood of Christ. The linguistic parallels between Yogananda's reported vision and this ancient text include the concept of drinking from the same cup that Christ's mouth touched, the theme of unity or becoming one with Christ, and references to hidden knowledge being revealed. The chronological sequence presents the following facts:

Gospel of Thomas was written approximately 30-70 A.D.
Yogananda's vision reported in 1937
Nag Hammadi discovery in 1945-1947
Yogananda's death: March 7, 1952
First complete translation of verse 108: 1955
Public availability of translations: Late 1960s-1970s

The timeline clearly shows that Yogananda did not have access to the Gospel of Thomas text through conventional means during his lifetime. There are undisputable linguistic similarities between Yogananda's 1937 account and verse 108 that remained undiscovered until 1945 and untranslated until the 1950s. Was it a strange coincidence that the mystical language and imagery are similar, or did Yogananda have access to states of consciousness that transcend the constraints of linear time and physical availability of texts?

I submit that the similarity of language between these two sources, separated by nearly two millennia, yet sharing remarkable similarity, provides documentary support for Yogananda's teachings which are replete with examples and ideas involving time and space.

In the Nag Hammadi quote Jesus says to his disciples. "He who will drink from my mouth will become like me" namely that, in a somewhat similar vein to Yogananda, his diciples will need to (drink from my mouth), ie listen to the teachings he tells them in order to progress. It is also interesting to note that Jesus and Paramhansa both attribute their wisdom to God as 'the Father'. Jesus says "I am not your Master", humbly implying that he is only passing on information. Paramhansa also told his devotees not to worship him, and even went so far as to say: "Anyone can become a Yogananda". I strongly recommend studying the SRF "Lessons."

FAITH BEYOND INTELLECT: THE MUSTARD SEED AND THE MOUNTAIN

The message was crystal clear; we can all achieve higher states of consciousness if we follow the teachings of 'the Father' that both Jesus and Paramahansa had learned. It goes even deeper with Jesus' parable of the mustard seed:

> "For truly I tell you, if you have faith the size of a mustard seed, you will say to this mountain, 'Move from here to there,' and it will move; and nothing will be impossible for you." (**Matthew 17:20-21**).

This ancient teaching reveals profound truth when we consider that modern physics increasingly recognizes consciousness as a fundamental force field in shaping reality. Faith, often dismissed by skeptics, may actually operate as a focused form of consciousness that influences the material world through principles that science is now beginning to understand. The Centurion's story of faith from the bible demonstrates this principle beautifully:

> "Lord, I do not deserve to have you come under my roof. But just say the word, and my servant will be healed" (**Matthew 8:5-13**).

He understood that healing could transcend physical distance, a concept that mirrors what physicists now call quantum entanglement, where particles remain mysteriously connected across time and space, much like the "spooky action at a distance" that Einstein found so troubling. Check out Edgar Cayce's "Readings " on treating patients; and their subsequent "healings" while in altered states of consciousness.

As early as the 1920s, Paramahansa Yogananda wrote in his lesson series:

> "Time and space are linked in the presence of God."

He was describing from spiritual experience what physicists like Einstein, Podolsky, and Rosen would later document in 1935, that quantum entanglement defies our normal understanding of space and time. When Yogananda as a young monk experienced himself simultaneously "dead on the battlefield" at Gallipoli in a ship captain's body, while at the same time sitting in meditation in his attic room on 4 Garpar Road Calcutta, he was demonstrating the same transcendence of normal physical limitations that scientists are now discovering in quantum physics. Likewise, and closer to home, the Sandra and Lester case where I smelled my hand burning one night at the very same time my clients house was burning down, leaving three dead children.

Current theories in physics increasingly suggest that time and space are illusions; observable properties of deeper processes rather than absolute realities. This aligns cleanly with Yogananda's direct experiences that describe physical reality as maya or the cosmic dream. When Yogananda later experienced the resurrected Christ in 1937 in Encinitas, it might be said that he was accessing a timeless dimension that quantum physics suggests underlies our apparent material world.

Think of how people have persisted in faith. Inventors like Edison maintaining belief through thousands of failed experiments, visionaries like the Wright brothers sustaining their dream of flight despite many failures and ridicule. Their faith operated like a quantum field, gradually influencing probability, creating opportunities and shifting reality toward their envisioned possibilities. Consciousness operates at levels where intention and material outcomes intersect and transcend rational belief supporting a higher form of faith, one that is greater than normal human intelligence routinely experienced in the cerebral cortex. Modern research on consciousness and healing, from the placebo effect to studies of focused intention increasingly supports what spiritual traditions have long taught; that consciousness, when properly focused through faith, can influence material reality in measurable ways. It's a compelling argument for faith being considered as a fundamental force rather than mere church dogma or psychological phenomenon.

For me, the meditating litigator, I know not whether I am a reincarnation of Father Michael Griffin or merely someone who stumbled across a ripple of energy from his traumatic death at the hands of British soldiers. The resentment I have held since childhood against the British could have been the force that attracted the event. Quantum understanding suggests both possibilities may be simultaneously true; consciousness exists as information that can be transmitted across time and space, whether through reincarnational continuity or energetic resonance with events that create persistent disturbances in the fabric of reality.

I'm now comfortable with knowing that it's all just a dream, not in the sense of unreality, but as Yogananda taught, recognizing physical existence as a cosmic dream within divine consciousness. This understanding acknowledges the profound power of faith to influence the dream's unfolding progress. Faith operates as the mechanism through which individual consciousness participates in the cosmic creative process, shaping reality through alignment with spiritual principles that both ancient wisdom and modern science are close to agreeing upon.

A century ago, the philosopher Rudolf Steiner identified a force he called Ahriman, an entity whose sole purpose is to imprison human consciousness entirely within material existence. Ahriman is the prince of solidification, the lord of absolute materialism, the voice that whispers constantly in our collective ear: 'You are only body, only brain, only a temporary arrangement of atoms destined for dissolution'. Every time we doubt the reality of our own soul, every time we reduce love to neurochemistry, every time we accept death as absolute annihilation, we align with this influence.

Steiner's diagnosis is chillingly relevant to the modern courtroom and our broader culture. According to Steiner, this force is highly intelligent, and does not attack our spirituality directly because that would create resistance. Instead, it makes the spiritual dimension irrelevant, unnecessary, embarrassing to intelligent people. It accomplishes this through the seduction of a purely materialistic science, the promise of total control through technology, and the elevation of measurable reality as the only legitimate reality. Under this influence, the universe becomes a clockwork mechanism without a clockmaker, and the human being loses its cosmic dignity, becoming merely another component in a soulless machine.

As a litigator who has spent fifty years navigating the battle between human truth and systemic deception, I recognize the fingerprints of this 'Ahrimanic force' everywhere: in the legal fictions that deny the sanctity of life, in the corporate greed that commodifies human suffering, and in the modern cultural narratives that mock any suggestion of meaning beyond material processes. Recognizing this force is a call to conscious awareness, it's the first step toward reclaiming our own consciousness from a matrix that has held it captive whilst we slept...and in many cases whilst we obsessively swipe through our social media.

MORE QUANTUM-ENTANGLED RESURRECTION

I have further testimonial evidence of these dreamlike aspects of reality, regardless of whether they are categorized as resurrection, reincarnation or visions. In addition to the resurrected Christ extending "a cup" from Christ's mouth to Paramahansa Yogananda's mouth to drink, and become one with Christ, Paramahansa Yogananda was also 'visited' by a resurrected Sri Yukteswar.

Shortly after Sri Yukteswar had died, left the body, passed, and been observed being buried as a dead body, he showed up in Paramahansa Yogananda's hotel room, of all places.

In the AY, Paramahansa Yogananda writes:

> "Sitting on my bed in the Bombay hotel at three o'clock in the afternoon of June 19, 1936, one week after the vision of Krishna, I was roused from my meditation by a beatific light. Before my open and astonished eyes, the whole room was transformed into a strange world, the sunlight transmuted into supernal splendor. Waves of rapture engulfed me as I beheld the flesh and blood form of Sri Yukteswar! "My son!" Master spoke tenderly, on his face an angel-bewitching smile. For the first time in my life, I did not kneel at his feet in greeting, but instantly advanced to gather him hungrily in my arms. Moment of moments! The anguish of past months I counted weightless against the torrential bliss now descending. "Master mine, beloved of my heart, why did you leave me?" I was incoherent in an excess of joy. "Why did you let me go to the Kumbha Mela? How bitterly have I blamed myself for leaving you!" "I did not want to interfere with your happy anticipation of seeing the pilgrimage spot where first I met Babaji. I left you only for a little while; am I not with you again?" "But is it you, Master, the same Lion of God? Are you wearing a body like the one I buried beneath the cruel Puri sands?" "Yes, my child, I am the same. This is a flesh and blood body. Though I see it as ethereal, to your sight it is physical. From cosmic atoms I created an entirely

> new body, exactly like that cosmic-dream physical body which you laid beneath the dream-sands at Puri in your dream-world. I am in truth resurrected — not on earth but on an astral planet."

Yogananda, Paramahansa. *Autobiography of a Yogi* (Self-Realization Fellowship) (pp. 456-457). Self-Realization Fellowship. Kindle Edition.

Here are some questions to ponder and vote on as literary jurors: Is Faith more powerful than intellect? Is there a force field all around us that can connect us to Christ, God...and even the saints? Are we indeed quantum entangled with God though this 'spooky' force field that defies the speed of light?

THE SERMON ON THE MOUNT: HUMAN SALVATION OR SURVIVAL OF OUR SPECIES

Tolstoy had many ideals in common with innumerable saints and sages, as well as many in opposition to worldly materialism, which built the empires that slaughtered billions of our species. Based on Christ's teachings in the Sermon on the Mount, Tolstoy opposed the Tsarist and British empires and their rapidly expanding pre-WW I armies. He also supported the greatest, most successful British Empire opponent, Mahatma Gandhi. Following Ahimsa (Non-violence) and Satyagraha (Truth), and the teachings of Christ, Gandhi got rid of the British without firing a shot. I wish my ancestors had been contemporaneously as smart.

In his 1893 book, *The Kingdom of God is Within You*, published the same year Paramahansa Yogananda was born, Tolstoy expounded that Christ's "Sermon on the Mount", the "Beatitudes", provided the prescription for the salvation of souls and the survival of our species. Gandhi and Tolstoy corresponded on the subject of nonviolence and Christ's teachings. Litigation involves intellectual violence and meditation involves spiritual peace. A real dilemma for me. Christ, Tolstoy and Gandhi all advocated non-violence in heart, mind, and soul.

Tolstoy considered Christ's central teaching to be:

> "resist not evil (with evil)" (**Matthew 5:39**)

Yogananda has an added nuance:

> "evil should be resisted only with its logically effective opposite: goodness or love." *Autobiography of a Yogi* (Self-Realization Fellowship) (p. 308). Kindle edition.

Through the teachings of Christ, Paramahansa Yogananda, Maharishi, and the many true saints I have studied for over fifty years, I have discovered a truth that applies equally to courtroom battles and spiritual warfare: the only solution to evil is to transcend it. Not to ignore it, not to appease it, but to rise above it into a consciousness where it cannot reach. This is the hardest lesson I have learned in a lifetime of litigation and meditation. It is easier said than done...far easier. But the implications of not doing this work, both for individuals and for our species as a whole, are catastrophic. We have seen those implications in every chapter of this book: in murdered priests and aborted children, in medical malpractice and cult manipulation, in wars fought by Christians against Christians. The path forward is not more argument, more litigation, more violence. It is transcendence. It is the consciousness of Christ. It is love. This is my final verdict, after fifty years of evidence. May we all have the courage to embrace it.

Epilogue

FROM CHILDHOOD FAITH TO COSMIC UNDERSTANDING

God works in very mysterious ways. As a kid I accepted our family's Catholic religion, its sacraments, masses, rosary and teachings, however my acceptance was with the consciousness of a child brought up in the trappings of my birth family. The connection I had to Christ was embedded in my consciousness through the Catholic Faith administered by hard working Roman Church priests. But that consciousness has not been fully realized or experienced in me as a mature adult.

However, there might be some integrating light at the end of that very long tunnel of my time on earth. As recounted in this book, my very Catholic consciousness increased in high school, became suspect in college, and disappeared in law school. Most of my adult life, I had no complete realization of how God and Christ had really worked in my life. Whereas I felt gratitude and grace for the blessings in my life, I did not have the deep connection to God and Christ described by Paramahansa Yogananda and the Masters, even though in his teachings and lessons Yogananda did teach us to 'open the heart' in meditation...to receive blessings.

During my years as a litigator and meditator, age 30 - 81, I felt a vague amorphous connection to Christ as a Guru in my Self Realization Fellowship meditation practices but I had more or less abandoned the Roman Church throughout those years. My mother had constantly prayed for me and my siblings throughout those same years knowing myself and several others in our family and circle of friends had abandoned the Catholic Faith. To my mom, her Faith in God, Christ and the Catholic Church was a living reality that sustained her. We knew that she was incessantly praying for our fallen souls, but we did not experience the power of her prayers sufficiently to return to the Church. While writing the Litigator series in 2023, four years after my mother's passing and as I was finishing this book, I decided to conduct a "consciousness experiment": I attended a Roman Catholic Mass and received Holy Communion. I approached it as an experiment because I had no faith in the Roman Church, had not followed its Sacraments or teachings, and regarded my meditation practices as superior to anything the Church could offer – the ego is a relentless deceiver.

For 55 years I had detested the corruption, wealth, and decadence of the Roman Church. I had little respect for its clerics, many of whom were child molesters, and homo predators engaged in perversions characteristic of devil worshipers. But I decided to see if the 'Eucharist', which the Catholic Faith had espoused for 2000 years as actually containing the body and blood of Christ in a metaphysical reality, would impact my consciousness. It did.

What happened I deem to be an enlightenment and 'realization' experience. Christs mercy and God's Grace opened my heart. After returning to my seat, I was transported into a love that rose up, enveloping my heart and permeating my whole being. I had not experienced that level of love since my youth, and then it was mystical and surreal. This experience was as real as my unity experience, (chapter 12), yet also infused with soul-awakening love. Words cannot describe its awakening realization in my heart and mind. It just is what it is, beyond language to describe, yet the Bible gives the best approximation words can achieve with this short sentence:

"The peace that surpasses understanding".

I began to repeat my experiment regularly, receiving the Eucharist for a period of weeks. Then one day, it hit me. After communion with Christ, I returned to my seat and had this overwhelming realization that my mother's prayers had saved my relationship with God and Christ. Her prayers, based on faith as we just discussed, manifested Christ's love itself and embodied their existential reality in me. I realized that being raised in the Catholic faith, together with her spiritual strength was a divine blessing, a grace of such profound magnitude, that it was restoring me into a level of reality beyond description. This was the realization I had been seeking through forty-eight years of meditation. Yet I must be precise about what this means.

This faith, this direct experience of Christ's love in the Eucharist is not a validation of the Roman Church's claim to exclusive salvation. It is, in fact, the opposite. What I discovered is that Christ consciousness is universal. It is not owned by any institution, controlled by any hierarchy, or limited to any particular interpretation of his teachings. My faith is in Christ himself, in the consciousness of love that he embodied and that every true saint has demonstrated, regardless of their religious affiliation. The Roman Church may be a vessel for this consciousness, but it is not the only vessel, nor does it have a monopoly on grace. The love I encountered belongs to all who seek it, wherever they may be.

Please don't misunderstand me. I believe that Christ's love and consciousness permeates everything on this planet. Historically, supposed Christians have been murdering, raping, pillaging and plundering other humans 'in the name of Christ' as Tolstoy writes, for over 2000 years. The warring nations in both World Wars killing each other were predominantly Christians. In my world view, Christ's consciousness represents the only salvation for our species, otherwise, World War III, as Paramahansa Yogananda predicted, may be the cataclysmic future of our species. When Christ gave the Sermon on the Mount, he was prophesying and teaching how our species could survive.

THE END AND THE BEGINNING

After all of life's highs and lows, the courtroom victories and defeats, the mystical visions and dark nights of the soul, the battles won and the losses endured...I stand before you today as a man at peace. Not because I have lived a perfect life, but because I have lived an examined one. When the time comes to look my Maker in the eye, I will not claim to have been without fault. But I will be able to say that I sought truth with everything I had, that I fought for justice when I could, and that I opened my heart to love when it was offered. That is all any of us can do. For you, dear reader, I offer not advice but a vision. It is the vision of the great Indian poet Rabindranath Tagore, who saw what our world could become if we chose consciousness over fear, truth over habit, and love over division:

WHERE THE MIND IS WITHOUT FEAR

Where the mind is without fear and the head is held high
Where knowledge is free
Where the world has not been broken up into fragments
By narrow domestic walls
Where words come out from the depth of truth
Where tireless striving stretches its arms towards perfection
Where the clear stream of reason has not lost its way
Into the dreary desert sand of dead habit
Where the mind is led forward by thee
Into ever-widening thought and action
Into that heaven of freedom, my Father, let my country awake."

Rabindranath Tagore

This is the world I have fought in for fifty years of litigation and meditation. This is the consciousness I encountered in the Eucharist, in my mother's prayers, in the teachings of Christ and Yogananda. It is not a fantasy. It is a possibility, one that depends on whether we choose to transcend our divisions or remain trapped within them.

If you have traveled with me through these pages and witnessed the evidence I have presented...if you have felt even a glimmer of the truth I have tried to convey, then you have options and know what must be done. The choice is yours. The time is now. May you find peace. May you find love. May you find the courage to awaken.

"In The Harvest Field Now Ripened

There's A Work For All To Do;
Hark! The Voice Of God Is Calling
To The Harvest Calling You.
Little Is Much When God Is In It!
Labour Not For Wealth Or Fame.
There's A Crown And You Can Win It,
If You Go In Jesus' Name.
In The Mad Rush Of The Broad Way,
In The Hurry And The Strife,
Tell Of Jesus' Love And Mercy,
Give To Them The Word Of Life.
Does The Place You're Called To Labour
Seem Too Small And Little Known?
It Is Great If God Is In It,
And He'll Not Forget His Own.
Are You Laid Aside From Service,
Body Worn From Toil And Care?
You Can Still Be In The Battle,
In The Sacred Place Of Prayer.
When The Conflict Here Is Ended
And Our Race On Earth Is Run,
He Will Say, If We Are Faithful,
"Welcome Home,
My Child Well Done!"

About the Author

Michael J. Flynn is a trial lawyer who spent more than fifty years in the trenches of the American courtroom, taking on difficult cases, confronting corruption, and fighting for truth where the cost of truth was often high. Over the course of a long legal career, he witnessed the power of the justice system at its best—and its failures at its worst.

Litigator is also the story of an inner journey. As the pressures of conflict, power, and disillusionment deepened, Michael increasingly turned towards meditation and higher states of consciousness, not as escape, but as a way to remain clear, grounded and whole in the midst of darkness. That search became a path of transformation: from outrage to insight, from battle to stillness, and from the outer struggle for justice to the inner experience of peace.

In this book, Michael brings together a lifetime in law with a profound spiritual inquiry into truth, consciousness, and the possibility of personal and societal renewal.

He lives in California. Visit LitigatorBook.com for book updates, read bonus material, watch videos and additional resources.

Join our mailing list and get a free chapter of Michael Flynn's next book Litigator 2, available fall 2026.

Made in the USA
Columbia, SC
06 July 2026

501e725e-33a7-4e3e-a69f-d976ce876ef0R01